COMIC CARDS AND THEIR PRICES

STUART WELLS III

Wallace-Homestead Book Company
Radnor, Pennsylvania

Published in Radnor, Pennsylvania 19089 by Wallace-Homestead,
a division of Chilton Book Company.

Designed by Stuart W. Wells III
This book was copyedited by Brian Kelly and Dean Sasso
Manufactured in the United States of America

Wallace-Homestead ISBN: 0-87069-727-7

1 2 3 4 5 6 7 8 9 3 2 1 0 9 8 7 6 5 4

#9

ACKNOWLEDGMENTS

The author expresses his special thanks to: George White, Top Dog Marketing; SkyBox International; Cardz Distribution, Inc.; Denis Kitchen, Kitchen Sink Press; James Rocknowski, Speed Racer Enterprises; Peter David; Rob Liefeld; Erik Larsen; Tim Toffoli, Mirage Publishing; Todd Johnson; Nelson DeCastro; J. Winston Fowlkes; Maureen Kelly, Majestic Entertainment; Chaz Fitzhugh, Upper Deck Company; Mark Heike, AC Comics; Reed Waller and Kate Worley; Nicola Banucci; Now Comics; Adam Sokol, Classic Games; Steve Stern, Zen Comics; Tom Mason, Malibu Comics; M. C. Chadwick, Harris Comics; Jim Whiting, FantaCo Publications; Robert Burden, Flaming Carrot Comics; Walter Rowan, Cornerstone Communications, Inc.; Don Chin, Entity Comics; Steve Zyskowski, Lightning Comics; Kevin Alsop, Krome Productions, Inc.; Dennis Malonee, Heroic Publishing Inc.; Maureen McTigue, DC Comics, Inc.; Sven Larsen, Marvel Comics.

CONTENTS

COLOR PLATES

DESCRIPTION

Comics trading cards are the '90s hottest collectibles. Superman! Spider-Man! X-Men! Aladdin! The Lion King! This book covers them all and every other comic and animation-related trading card produced in the United States from 1940 to June 1994. The book covers all the regular cards that are sold in packs or in boxed sets, individual cards that come bagged in comic books or magazines, and promotional cards given away at comics shows.

The cards' artists are identified wherever possible and checklists are given for virtually every set. All bonus, chase and other special cards are also listed, along with special promotional sheets containing one or more cards. The comments and descriptions give the reader all the inside information needed to collect and trade these cards.

This book also includes pictures of cards from almost every set to aid the reader in identifying the most collectible cards (although a few small sets would not reproduce well here).

The *Triton Price Guide to Comic Cards* includes all of the above, plus prices for every card and two hundred color photos!

INTRODUCTION: A SHORT HISTORY OF COMICS CARDS

Strange as it seems, the vast majority of comics trading cards were issued in the last seven years, and most of those were produced in the last four years.

Superman (Gum Inc., 1940); Batman (Topps, 1966)

However, the first comics trading card set was the *Superman* set produced by Gum, Inc. in 1940 (and reprinted in 1984). It featured comic book style images of Superman performing various super feats of strength such as flying or battling sharks or tanks, etc. The art was primitive by today's standards, but the cards showed the things Superman did in the early comic books, and his exploits were treated seriously. Except for the *Superman in the Jungle* test set in 1968, and a few comic book cover reprints, no other card set featured serious comic book art until 1987!

There weren't any other comics cards in the 1940s or 1950s. Finally, in 1966, Topps issued comics cards, but they were based on the *Superman* and *Batman* TV shows, not the comic books. The Topps Superman set from 1966 contained black and white photos from the classic TV show of the late 1950s and 1960s starring George Reeves as Superman and Noel Neill as Lois Lane. The five Batman card sets from this same year were based on the campy TV show, and even though three of the sets used comic book art, all of the cards reflected the humor of that incredibly popular show.

It took more than a decade for any comic book character to be taken seriously in the aftermath of the *Batman* TV show. Almost every superhero on a card was treated as a humorous, juvenile subject. The four most widely distributed superhero cards from 1966 to 1977 were *Marvel Superheroes* (Donruss, 1966); *Super Heroes Stickers* (Philly Gum, 1967); *Comic Book Heroes* (Topps, 1975) and *Marvel Super Heroes Stickers* (Topps, 1976). All were designed with pictures of the superheroes and funny sayings. In the 1940s Captain America was saving the world from Nazi tyranny but in 1976 he was worried that his pants would fall down! The only excep-tions were a few sets of bread stickers and cards from Sunbeam, Taystee and Wonder Bread.

There were a few serious representations of superheroes on trading cards during this period. Topps produced card sets from the *Incredible Hulk* TV show (1979), the three *Superman* movies (1978–1983), the *Supergirl* movie (1983) and from *Howard the Duck* (1986). However, all of these cards contained photos, not comics art. While these movies did much to erase the kid-vid image of the *Batman* TV show, the cards were really part of the many Topps movie and TV show cards from this era. The only attempt at comic art cards during this era was by FTCC in 1984. It reproduced a number of covers from the first issues of Marvel comic books on a cheap card stock.

Marvel Superhero Stickers (Topps 1976); Superman (Topps, 1978)

The current era in comics card collecting started in 1987, but hardly anybody recognized it at the time. Comic Images was the first company to sell serious superhero art cards in anything like the current form. This was before UV coating, fancy bonus cards and other glitz but their first card sets look remarkably modern. They started in 1987 with 90 *Marvel Universe* cards. This set pictured most of your favorite Marvel heroes and contains the first appearance of

Colossal Conflicts (Comic Images, 1987); Batman (Topps, 1989)

many on any kind of card. They followed with *Colossal Conflicts* (1987); and in 1988 with *Wolverine, Heroic Origins* and *The Punisher*. In 1989 they concentrated on artists cards with *Excalibur* (Alan Davis), *Arthur Adams*, *The Best of John Byrne*, *Todd McFarlane* and *Mike Zeck* (followed by others in 1990, including the first *Jim Lee* set). They helped set the stage for the 1990s but they were just a little bit early. What really changed the landscape was Tim Burton's Batman movie in 1989. In the first Superman movie we learned to believe that "a man can fly," but in the Batman movie we finally met a comic book hero who was an adult. The Topps cards from the movie were not a departure from their movie cards from the previous 20 years and were not influential. It was the movie that woke everybody up to the possibilities of an adult, serious superhero and it was the popularity of baseball cards that gave manufacturers the smell of money.

Comics card collecting finally took off in 1990. The trading card world changed forever with the *Marvel Universe I* cards from Impel. This was the first card set which combined fine comic art, good card design, quality production, bonus cards and marketing in just the right proportions. High quality production had actually been around for a couple of years in sports cards, but it was new to what was then considered the non-sport card market. *DC Cosmic Cards* followed in 1992, but they weren't quite as good and were not innovative and have not been highly sought. The follow-up *DC Cosmic Teams* in 1993 were slightly better, but still behind the times. The first *X-Men* set featuring all Jim Lee art was more exciting.

Comics card collecting went into orbit in late 1992 when *Marvel Masterpiece I* came out featuring wonderful painted art by Joe Jusko. The same month DC hit it big with *Doomsday: The Death of Superman* cards which captured the most important comics event in 30 years and had the first (and maybe still the best) Spectra cards. The last *Marvel Universe* cards, *X-Men II*, and the second *Marvel Masterpiece* series kept Marvel cards on top in 1993; while 1993 DC follow-ups *DC Bloodlines* and *The Return of Superman* were both quite successful.

Ghost Rider II (Comic Images, 1992); X-Men (Impel, 1992)

Comic Images continued to produce Marvel cards during this period, but they were taken from comic book pages rather than baseball card type portraits. Still, they issued *Spider-Man*, *Wolverine*, *Punisher* and *X-Men* sets, featuring art by Todd McFarlane and other important artists. The most innovative sets from Comic Images were the all-prism *Silver Surfer* set in 1992 and the all-chromium *Conan* set in late 1993.

So far, in 1994, we have seen several spectacular comics card sets. Fleer started with a bang with its *Ultra X-Men* cards and followed with the wonderful *Spider-Man* cards and the extra-thick (and extra-expensive) *Marvel Universe Inaugural Edition* cards. SkyBox produced the very original *Sandman* set, *Batman: The Saga of the Dark Knight* series and the first of the *SkyBox Master* series, the DC edition. Topps has just produced the *Comics Greatest World* set as this book was completed and it looks like they are determined not to be left behind. Dozens of new sets are scheduled for the second half of 1994 and 1995 and comics cards show no sign of cooling off as a collectible in the near future. On the contrary, they have become available everywhere, from comic shops to toy stores to sports card shows.

PROMO AND PROTOTYPE CARDS

Four card sheet of Marvel Universe I promo cards (Impel 1990)

Promotional and prototype cards are samples issued by card companies for the purpose of encouraging stores to buy their cards and magazines to give coverage to their cards. Stores are happy to get advance samples of cards because it gives them a better idea what the card set will look like when it is finally issued, and a magazine is happy to get cards in advance so it can tell you about new and forthcoming card sets and run photos of them. Many magazines also come bagged with promotional cards, which operate as an advertisement by the card company to the magazine buyer (and potential card buyer). *Previews*, the magazine put out by Diamond Comic Distributors, and *Advance Comics*, the magazine put out by Capital City Distribution, go to comic shops to get them to solicit orders for comics, cards and most of the other things you find in a comic shop. Those magazines frequently contain card samples and have consumer editions for customers interested in information on forthcoming comics and cards.

Card samples come in a variety of different forms. The company can simply send out actual packs of the cards. However, these cards are identical to the regular issue cards and thus are not worth much money. The fact that owners of card shops and magazine editors are often card collectors is certainly not lost on the card companies. In order to make the cards scarce and collectible, a card company must make them different from the regular cards. Therefore most samples are marked "prototype" or "sample" or are otherwise different in some way from the real cards. Sample copies are also designed to get the dealer's attention by being valuable. Any card dealer is delighted to get something for free which he then can sell to you. You pay an exorbitant price for these samples because they are scarce and you're a serious collector (an addict).

Sample cards can also come on sheets that contain several cards. This method is used because the sheet can easily be bound into a magazine. Loose cards can only be sent with a magazine or comic if both are enclosed in a poly bag, which is surprisingly expensive. You can keep the entire sheet or (gasp, horrors!) cut the cards (carefully) to put them in plastic card holders. Complete sheets are slightly more valuable and most stores now sell the sheets rather than cutting out the cards, even though it's easier to display and sell them as single cards.

This book lists **sample** cards along with the **bonus** cards which come in the regular packs, such as holograms, prism, and chromium cards and every other gimmick card (because they sell for a lot of money!). The card companies announce all their bonus cards (loudly) on the packs and in the promotional literature because it induces you to indulge your gambling nature by buying a pack in the hope of getting lucky. However, they don't announce their sample cards, so we have to find out about them ourselves.

In addition to samples provided to the trade and in magazines with national distribution, card companies and comics publishers often make up special samples for important trade shows. These are only available at the shows. However, no one can go to *every* show, so there are undoubtedly some cards we have missed.

Product samples have been given out for years, but special promotional cards are a 1990s phenomenon.

The October 1990 issue of Diamond *Previews* magazine contained a bound-in set of four sample cards of the first of Impel's *Marvel Universe* series. The cards are Sabretooth, Enchantress, Deathlok and Ghost Rider. The card backs are slightly different from the regular issue and can be easily identified by the diamond symbol in the center of the card. This symbol is used on a number of other samples in *Previews* magazine.

We also have three additional uncut *Marvel Universe I* prototypes with a diamond logo. They are listed on pages 64 and 65. These cards are identical to the cut promotional cards distributed in cello packs by the company (except for the diamond logo). There are slight differences from the final versions of the cards. There ought to be a fifth such uncut sheet, containing the final four prototype cards, but Impel (now SkyBox) can't tell us for sure whether or not it exists.

Incidentally, nine cards from this same set were also issued in the original nine Marvel Super Heroes action figures from Toy Biz. These cards have "Toy Biz" in red on the back. These are variant cards, not promos or prototypes, and they are hard to collect because only one comes with each toy.

Marvel Universe III promo cards with Diamond symbol

The DC comics set had a similar sheet of sample cards in the January 1992 issue of *Previews*. The cards were Wonder Woman (Modern Age), Lobo, Deathstroke the Terminator, and Superman (Modern Age). There were no logos on the back to help the collector distinguish the cards from the real thing, but the card number in the upper right hand corner is missing and there are other minor differences. The background color of these cards is the same medium gray that was used in the actual series. Impel also issued five regular sample cards: Wonder Woman, Deathstroke the Terminator, Superman, Flash and Green Lantern. The background color on these cards is a blue gray. The first two cards are otherwise identical to the *Previews* sheet and the last two are entirely different characters, but the Superman card has a different picture of Clark Kent on the back, with shorter hair. This card back is pictured on page 31. The *Previews* sample has the same picture that was used in the actual card series.

Four card sheet of DC Cosmic promo cards (Impel 1992)

The *Marvel Universe Series II* cards had a sample sheet in the April 1991 issue of *Previews* magazine. There were five cards on the sheet with the sixth space being used as a description. The cards were #1 Spider-Man, #45 Silver Surfer, #51 Cyclops, #57 Magneto, #124 Fantastic Four vs. Dr. Doom. All had a diamond logo on the back.

Marvel Universe Series III samples included a sheet of four cards which was bound into the March 1992 issue of *Previews* magazine. The cards of Human Torch, Silver Surfer, Spider-Man and Thanos form an integrated image and no cut lines are shown. The diamond symbol is on the back. There are also sample cards marked "prototype" of Invisible Woman, Captain America and Spider-Man which were sent out by Impel.

The first *Marvel Masterpieces* set had two different types of samples. Those marked "prototype" were sent out by the company and include Spider-Man, Hulk and Wolverine. There were also samples of Psylocke, Silver Surfer, Spider-Man and Captain America. These had a different back from the regular cards. These backs announce in red letters: "Coming in October 1992—Don't Miss It!"

Recently, every issue of *Previews* magazine has had some kind of sample cards inserted. Generally these have been sheets containing one or two sample cards and information about the forthcoming card set. However, nine-card sheets have become increasingly popular. These sheets have been bound in and perforated so that they can be removed and collected. This book lists these sheets and their current values. They make a very fine collectible, but you should put them in plastic holders to protect them.

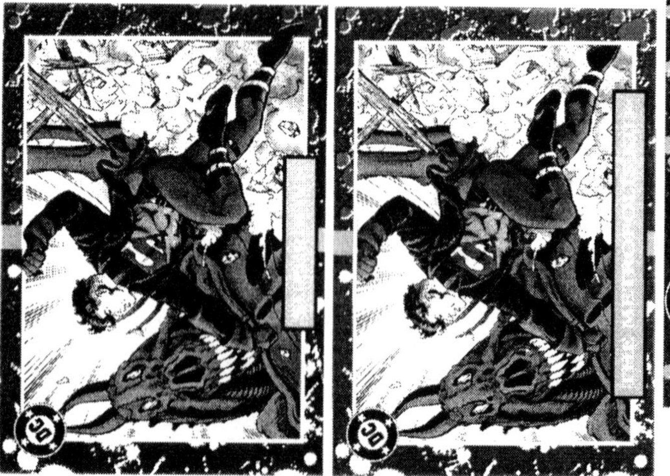

DC Bloodlines promo cards (fronts). The one on the left is titled "Superboy." The one on the right is titled "The Metropolis Kid."

Capital City Distribution also had samples in *Advance Comics*. For instance, they issued a Venom hologram promoting the *Marvel Universe III* cards and a Magneto hologram promoting the *X-Men* cards. They are easily distinguishable from the regular holograms because they say "Advance Comics" on the back. We have spent less time in this article discussing these cards because they are easier to distinguish, but they are generally more valuable than other promo or sample cards. In 1993 and 1994 each *Advance Comics* has contained one card from a special set of 12 Image comics cards not available anywhere else. These cards are in addition to the promo cards and promo sheets which are distributed widely.

Many card and comic magazines come bagged with promo or prototype cards. Sometimes the same promo cards are available from several sources and sometimes the magazine has an exclusive deal. *Wizard* magazine started this craze with its issue #11 and other magazines followed suit. Special magazine cards are listed under the name of the magazine, so look under *Hero Illustrated*, *Overstreet*, *Triton* and *Wizard* for checklists of these cards.

One of the most interesting groups of promo cards from 1993 was issued for *DC Bloodlines* cards. There are two separate sets of four promo cards which use the same images of the four "faux" Superman as the foil-embossed insert cards. The most common set of four is numbered P1 to P4 and promotes the card series. The less common four cards are unnumbered and say "Which, if any, is the real Man of Steel?" Check the backs to make sure which ones you have.

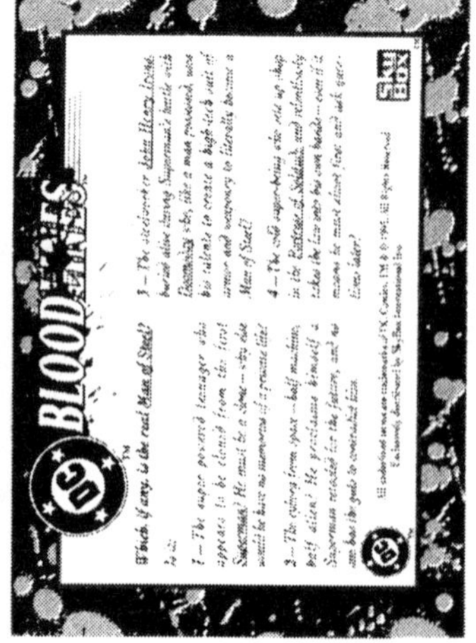

DC Bloodlines promo cards (backs). These are the backs of the same cards as in the previous illustration

The most highly sought promo or prototype cards from 1994 are the silver foil *Sandman* prototype cards which were sent out by SkyBox to magazines and dealers. There are seven of these cards, matching the seven gold foil insert cards in the set, but SkyBox only sent one to each person on its mailing list. These cards sold for $10 when they first came out, but as dealers realized how scarce they were, the price shot up to $35 to $40 each.

Promotional or prototype cards are now issued for just about every new set of cards and seemingly every major show. Collecting them can be challenging and fun. None of them are exceptionally expensive and many can be obtained for free at major comics and card shows.

HOW TO COLLECT TRADING CARDS

Successful Sets

The first wildly successful set of comic cards was *Marvel Universe I* from Impel (now SkyBox) in late 1990. That set created the current craze for comics cards and other fine sets appeared in 1991, but late 1992 brought the two biggest winners of all: *Doomsday: The Death of Superman* and *Marvel Masterpiece I*. While these three sets have shown the greatest value increases since their release, we have identified 14 other winners below. If you bought a box of any of these cards when they came out, you made money.

Doomsday & Marvel Masterpiece I cards from SkyBox

The Big Three

Doomsday: The Death of Superman (#1) . . SkyBox
Marvel Masterpiece I (#2) . . . . SkyBox
Marvel Universe I (#3) . . . . Impel (SkyBox)

Other winners (alphabetical order)

Comics Greatest World . . . . Topps
Conan (all chromium) . . . . Comic Images
Creator's Universe . . . . Dynamic
Marvel Universe, Inaugural Edition . . . . Fleer/Flair
Marvel Universe II . . . . Impel (SkyBox)
Return of Superman . . . . SkyBox
Sandman . . . . SkyBox
Silver Surfer (all-prism) . . . . Comic Images
SkyBox Master: DC Edition . . . . SkyBox
Spider-Man . . . . Marvel/Fleer
Unity . . . . Comic Images
Valiant Era . . . . Upper Deck
X-Men . . . . Fleer Ultra
X-Men I . . . . SkyBox (Impel)

Features of Successful Sets

Marvel Universe I featured portrait art work of your favorite superhero on high quality card stock which was coated front and back, plus the innovation of the six hologram bonus cards. *Marvel Universe II* had the same features, and just about every serious card set since then has been on quality stock and had bonus cards. *Marvel Masterpiece* had painted art rather than comic style art which is inked and colored. *Doomsday* had all the hype of the death of Superman plus four beautiful bonus cards.

Much of the collecting interest and therefore the price increases have centered on the bonus cards (or "insert" cards or "chase" cards) in these sets. But, you can have too much of a good thing. Most of the increases in bonus card values have been in sets with from six to ten bonus cards. Some highly limited special bonus cards, such as the X-Men II Wolverine 3-D hologram and the Marvel IV Spider-Man vs. Venom hologram, have proved quite valuable, However, many special bonus cards, which don't have any extra charisma beyond being rarer than level one bonus cards, are not worth much more money. For example, the *Tribe* prism cards come one in twelve packs and sell for $7.00, which is a typical price for this type of card. The *Tribe* thermofoil cards come just one in every 36 packs, but they sell for $11.00. The *Deathmate* bonus cards from Upper Deck show similar price patterns.

We think that card sets and bonus cards with these features have increased the most in the past, so you should look for these features in the future. Not every set will have all these features, but the more of them the better.

1. The cards should have portraits of comic book heroes rather than pictures taken from comic book pages or cover reproductions.
2. High quality card stock with color on both the front and back is a must. Scarce special stock, like chromium can also work as long as it doesn't overwhelm the card art.
3. Innovation. The first cards with a new gimmick usually retain their charisma even if later innovations surpass them. Just being different isn't enough. The cards must also be new and exciting.

4. There should be a restricted number of hot-looking bonus cards with a gimmick that enhances the art. Even bonus cards can become common if every dealer has lots of them. Also, bonus cards shouldn't be so scarce that the ordinary buyer has no chance of getting one. Two or three bonus cards to the box and ten or less over-all to collect is a good guideline.
5. Well-known, continuing, characters increase interest. One movie is not enough, unless the movie is a huge success and the cards are scarce.
6. Famous or hot new card artists also draw attention.

Condition

There is one hard and fast rule for all recent trading cards: If the card isn't in mint or near mint condition it is *worthless*. This is because there are lots of every card available in top condition so no one wants one in a lower grade. Older cards are another story. Bonus cards in less than top condition may not be worthless, but they are close to worthless.

Best Companies

The company with the best track record for price increases in recent years is **SkyBox**. Of the 17 card sets we just named, almost half are from SkyBox, including the three sets which increased the most—*Doomsday*, *Marvel Masterpiece I*, and *Marvel Universe I*. Many other SkyBox sets, such as *Marvel Masterpiece II* and the other *Marvel Universe* sets, have also been winners. The year 1994 may be the **year of DC cards**, with current sets such as *Sandman* and *Batman: Saga of the Dark Knight* doing well with several *SkyBox Master* series to follow. However, not all SkyBox sets have appreciated, or are likely to appreciate. You still must look at the subject matter and other factors like the general charisma of the set.

Many of SkyBox's best cards were Marvel cards, and SkyBox no longer produces Marvel cards. **Fleer**, recently acquired by Marvel, now has that privilege. Their first set, *Ultra X-Men,* was very successful and *Spider-Man* was hot as well. Their most recent set, *Marvel Universe, Inaugural Edition* looks like a winner as well despite or perhaps because of its high price, so make room for Fleer cards in your collection. However, don't forget the fundamental rule: Prices go up when **demand** exceeds **supply**. High demand **and** high supply does not result in price increases. Dealers are ordering a lot of Fleer's cards, so don't expect miracles, but don't miss out.

Topps has had great success recently with its *Jurassic Park Gold* cards and *Star Wars Galaxy* cards. Their *Comics Greatest World* series was just released and it looks like a winner. Topps is coming back strong with its own unique style. Keep your eye out for their next sets.

There are several other companies with excellent possibilities as well. They produce very fine cards and collectors are beginning to take more notice.

1. **Comic Images**: This is one of the most innovative companies in the field. Their all chromium sets (*Conan* and *Melting Pot*) have been winners with collectors and they started the craze for fantasy and science fiction cards with sets by Boris, Frazetta and Hildebrandt. Their most popular comic series to date are the all prism *Silver Surfer* set and the *Unity* set, whose six chromium bonus cards of Valiant rookies increased dramatically and still command high prices. Look for their early comics card sets from the 1980s to appreciate as their pioneering efforts become known.
2. **Cardz**: We really like the recent sets from this company including *Tom & Jerry* and *The Flintstones*. Its hard to judge whether these will go up in value, because the X-Men crowd may think they are too juvenile. However, a lot of adult collectors are very fond of these characters so the cards won't go down in value. Check out the *Hanna-Barbera* cards and buy them if you like them. Their most popular set to date with collectors has been the *Julie Bell* fantasy cards.
3. **Upper Deck**: This is a very strong company in the sports card field, but their impact on comics cards has been limited. Their four *Looney Tunes Comic Ball* sets were popular, but seem to have peaked. Their two 1993 sets, *Valiant Era* and *Deathmate*, were well done and fairly popular, but neither has shown dramatic price increases.
4. **Dynamic Entertainment**: *Creators Universe* was one of the best sets to appear recently and it has been quite popular with collectors. Their future plans are uncertain as of this writing, but watch them.
5. There are several other fine companies, such as **Friedlander** (FPG cards), which have created fantasy and science fiction cards of high quality, but have not yet tried to produce comics trading cards. Check them out if they expand into this field.

How to Get the Best Deals

Most card sets are hot when they first come out and they remain hot for few months at most. You can use this to your advantage in shopping for the best deal. Go to shows as well as comic shops and don't ignore the small shows or the sports and comics shows. There are good bargains there.

1. Many dealers, particularly those at larger shows, will break down several boxes of cards when they first come out so that they can be the first dealer to sell sets and bonus cards at the next show. They make their money on turnover more than high prices and on the bonus cards rather than the sets. That means that they want to sell the pieces of that $30 box as soon as possible and that you can often get a complete set of the regular cards for $10 or less when the going rate in a comic shop is $12.50 to $15.00. At most shows there are two or more dealers pursuing this strategy and you should naturally pick the cheapest.

Left: SkyBox Master Series: DC Edition (SkyBox)
Right: Comic Greatest World (Topps)

2. If you don't already have the promo card(s) for the set, look for them at the same time. Promo cards drop in price when the real card set appears. If the dealer has any left you can probably get him to sell you one with the set for no extra price. If there are three promos you can get them all for an extra $1, when a month ago, (and a month from now) they sold for $1 each.
3. The bonus cards can be bought from the same dealer at this time for a fairly reasonable price, because this dealer is trying to sell quickly. However, this is where the dealer's profit lies so you can't expect too much of a break. You should pick up the bonus cards *now* if you expect this to be one of the year's (not the month's) hottest sets and if you don't see these cards at every dealer's table.
4. Some of the sets with the most demand also have the greatest supply. If every dealer at the show has several boxes for sale, wait a month or so and then look for your bonus cards. By then, the dealer will have tried to sell off his stock at several shows and will have seen that everyone else has the same items for sale. Just shop for the best deal.
5. If you like the cards, but you don't think it will be one of the year's hottest, wait one to three months and then look for those bonus cards. Some dealer will be very eager to sell his remaining bonus cards by then. Go to some smaller shows, or to a sports card show. Just keep looking until you find the deal you want. You may not be able to buy all the bonus cards at once, but you'll find them.
6. If you missed getting the set cheaply when it first came out, look for a cheap unopened box from a dealer. You can put together a set or two and get some bonus cards from a box. The real problem is that you won't get all the bonus cards, but you will get some partial sets left over. It's hard to sell the partial sets, but maybe you have a friend or two who collects. They call them trading cards because that's how you are supposed to collect them!
7. So, you missed the world's hottest card set that doubled in value over-night? One place to look is at a local toy store or discount chain store. You had better be quick, but if they are selling the cards, they won't have raised the prices yet. Toy stores, drug stores, and particularly chain stores are not in tune with recent price trends. Some genius back at headquarters sets the prices solely on what the store paid for the products and he doesn't go to card shows. The flip side of this is that these stores won't get around to lowering their prices very quickly either. They may have packs for sale for $1.29 when every dealer has lowered his prices to two for $1.00. On the other hand, they may have some old packs for sale that the same genius has reduced to 29¢ when no dealer has any of these cards left. Most of these stores won't have a price on a full box, so you will just have to buy it priced as 36 packs.

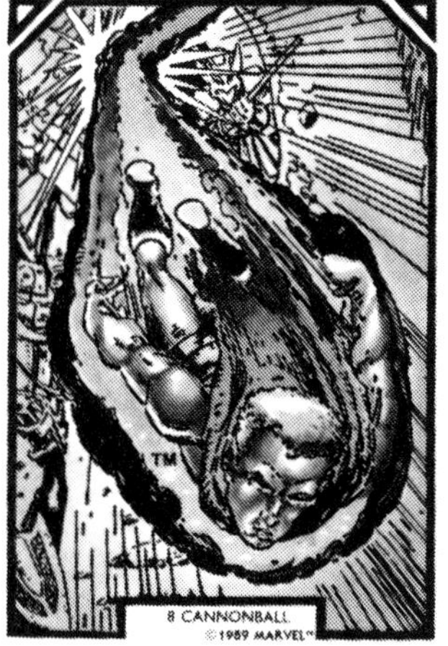

Arthur Adams © Marvel Entertainment Group, Inc.

ADAMS, ARTHUR

Comic Images (1989)

The card fronts depict various Marvel characters in portrait style drawings, plus the card caption and number. The backs form two puzzle pictures, one 4 x 5 and the other 5 x 5. The name of the set appears only on the checklist card. Art Adams began working for Marvel in 1985 and is co-creator of the character Longshot.

Set: 45 cards (AAd) 17.00

Box: 48 packs
Pack: 5 cards 1.50

CARD CHECKLIST

1 Checklist .35
2 Phoenix .35
3 Gateway .35
4 Reborn .35
5 Hands-On .35
6 Fantastic Four .35
7 Watcher .35
8 Cannonball .35
9 Magma .35
10 Cloak & Dagger .35
11 Surtur .35
12 Approach .35
13 Storm .35
14 Frightened .35
15 Polaris .35
16 Conflict .35
17 Starjammers .35
18 Beast .35
19 New Mutants .35
20 Firelord .35
21 Contemplating .35
22 Hold Him! .35
23 Rogue .35
24 Colossus .35
25 Phoenix II .35
26 Breakout .35
27 Gang-Way .35
28 Longshot .35
29 Sentinels .35
30 Get Back! .35
31 Unicorn .35
32 Silver Surfer .35
33 Magneto .35
34 Mojo .35
35 Wolverine .35
36 Galactus .35
37 Loki .35
38 Eric the Red .35
39 Illyana .35
40 Marvel Girl .35
41 Classic X-Men .35
42 Dominated .35
43 Logan .35
44 Odin .35
45 Warlock .35

ADVENTURES IN TOON WORLD

Upper Deck/Pyramid (1993)

Chuck Jones & Mort Drucker art

Each pack is a 9-card, 2 page story and packs are numbered to aid set assembly. The stories star Looney Tunes characters plus animated versions of sports stars Reggie Jackson, Michael Jordan, Wayne Gretzky and Joe Montana. The cards have story art and word balloons on both sides and are separately numbered both front and back as "Act x Scene x." Scene 1 contains the title. The cards aren't really designed for 9 pocket sheets, since they don't form super panels and are oriented sideways. The Hare-os cards are oriented upright and feature Bugs and a comic drawing of the sports figure. The card backs show the backside of the same drawing and are numbered. The holograms are not numbered or captioned and have blank white backs. I used the word balloons for titles below. Each pack comes with either a Hare-o or a hologram.

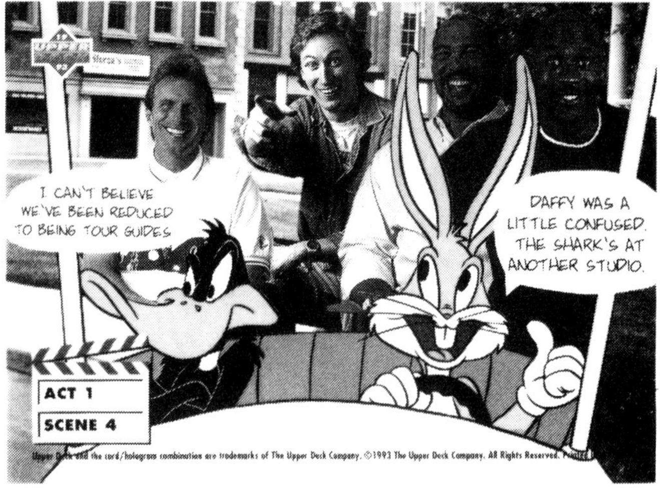

Adventures in Toon World © Warner Bros. Inc. & Upper Deck

Set: 90 cards, 5 holograms, 5 Hare-os 10.00

Bugs Bunny Hare-os cards (1:2)
BBH1 Joe Montana .50
BBH2 Wayne Gretzky .50
BBH3 Michael Jordan .50
BBH4 Reggie Jackson .50
BBH5 Bugs Bunny Hare-os (all 4) .50

Holograms, (1:2) Chuck Jones art
"What happened to mah gol-durned pistols?!?" .50
No words, Joe plays golf .50
"Beep! Beep!" .50
"Look at this. We can stretch!" .50
"This machine does have possibilities" .50

Pack: 9 cards, 1 bonus card 1.00

STORY CHECKLIST
(9 card stories in numbered packs.)

1 Tour de Duck .50
2 Cartoon World .50
3 Yosemite Blam! .50
4 Rocket Blade Runner .50
5 Reggie's Race Day .50
6 Looney Links .50
7 Sherwood Like to Sink This Putt .50
8 Puck Amuck .50
9 Looney Olympics .50
10 There's No Place Like Home .50

ADVENTURES OF AMETHYST WELLES

Karl Art (1994)

This promo card has full bleed art on a foil surface and was given away at a New York Comics show.

Comic Promo 2.00

Adventures of Amethyst Wells © Barry Kraus Prods. Akira © 1994, Cornerstone Communications, Inc. Akira art & logos © & ™ Akira Committee, 1987, Produced under license from Kodansha Ltd., All rights reserved.

AKIRA

Cornerstone (1994, Animated Movie)

Promo cards and the Akira preview set were given away at the 1994 distributor trade shows. The preview set of 10 cards came in a clear cello pack. The regular set was not out at press time.

Promo 1 1.00
Promo 2 1.00
Preview Set: 10 cards in cello pack 10.00
Sparkle promo 5.00
1 "The Power of Akira" .50
2 "Kaneda takes aim at Tetsuo" .50
3 "Follow-the-leader on Highway 26" .50
4 "An Akira module" .50

5 "Tetsuo engulfs the Colonel" ..... .50
6 "Streamline Pictures" .... .50
7 "Kaneda jumps for his life" ...... .50
8 "The military police locate Takashi" .... .50
9 "Kaori approaches Tetsuo's throne" .50

Aladdin (Panini) © The Walt Disney Company

ALADDIN
Panini (1993, Animated Movie)

Panini had the Canadian license for cards from this Disney animated movie. The cards have a purple border with white stars, both front and back. The backs contain the card title and text, plus a number in a magic lantern and a detail picture from the front. These cards use many of the same pictures as the SkyBox set listed below, but they are not related. This set has very attractive stickers, but the card art is not as good as the SkyBox set.

Set: 100 cards, 10 game cards, 10 stickers 18.00
Boxed Set: 20.00
Pack: 13 cards+ game card & sticker 1.50

CARD CHECKLIST

1 Arabian Nights .... .15
2 Invitation to the Adventure ...... .15
3 A Magic Scarab .... .15
4 Across the Desert .... .15
5 A Monstrous Head .... .15
6 The Cave of Wonders .... .15
7 In Agrabah .... .15
8 A Hungry Young Man .... .15
9 The Sultan's Men .... .15
10 A Hard Decision .... .15
11 A Majestic Prince .... .15
12 To the Rescue .... .15
13 Locked Out .... .15
14 Home Sweet Home .... .15
15 Aladdin's Wish .... .15
16 Palace Life .... .15
17 Free as a Bird .... .15
18 A Furtive Princess .... .15
19 The Blue Diamond .... .15
20 A Strange Transaction .... .15
21 In the Secret Lab .... .15
22 Jasmine Visits the Marketplace .. .15
23 An Angry Merchant .... .15
24 Aladdin Steps In .... .15
25 The Getaway .... .15
26 Something in Common .... .15
27 Taken by Surprise .... .15
28 "Do You Trust Me?" .... .15
29 Trapped! .... .15
30 A Princess Commands .... .15
31 An Angry Princess .... .15
32 A Sad Night .... .15
33 The Dungeon .... .15
34 A Foolish Notion .... .15
35 "Nothing But the Lamp" .... .15
36 The Treasure Chamber .... .15
37 A Magic Carpet .... .15
38 The Old Lamp .... .15
39 Catastrophe! .... .15
40 Wrath of the Tiger-God .... .15
41 Escape! .... .15
42 "Give Me the Lamp" .... .15
43 At Last! .... .15
44 Trapped in the Cave .... .15
45 Abu, the Thief .... .15
46 A Genie! .... .15
47 Three Wishes .... .15
48 A Few Quid Pro Quo .... .15
49 Limitations? .... .15
50 Free from the Cave .... .15
51 Itty Bitty Living Space .... .15
52 A Promise .... .15
53 The First Wish .... .15
54 From Rags to Robes .... .15
55 Abu, the Elephant .... .15
56 A Wicked Plot .... .15
57 The Plot in Action .... .15
58 A Royal Procession .... .15
59 Prince Ali Ababwa .... .15
60 A Problem for Jafar .... .15
61 The Sultan's Problems Solved? . .15
62 "How Dare You!" .... .15
63 Aladdin Alarmed .... .15
64 A Talk in the Garden .... .15
65 A Lonely Princess .... .15
66 Bee Yourself .... .15
67 A Magic Carpet Ride .... .15
68 A Whole New World .... .15
69 A Rooftop Under the Stars ..... .15
70 Good Night .... .15
71 A Kiss .... .15
72 Caught Again .... .15
73 Into the Sea .... .15
74 The Second Wish .... .15
75 A Husband for Jasmine .... .15
76 Aladdin Returns .... .15
77 A Sorcerer Exposed .... .15
78 The Sultan Recovers .... .15
79 The Happy Couple .... .15
80 A Dilemma .... .15
81 A Stolen Lamp .... .15
82 A New Master .... .15
83 A New Sultan .... .15
84 The Old Sultan .... .15
85 A Powerful Sorcerer .... .15
86 To the Ends of the Earth ...... .15
87 A Desperate Race .... .15
88 A Clever Princess .... .15
89 Reflection in a Crown .... .15
90 The Battle .... .15
91 The Snake .... .15
92 An Idea .... .15
93 Life in a Lamp .... .15
94 The Spell Ends .... .15
95 Goodbye, Princess .... .15
96 The Third Wish .... .15
97 The Sultan's Law .... .15
98 The Princess's Choice .... .15
99 A Farewell Hug .... .15
100 Goodbye, Goodbye .... .15

Color-in cards

1 Aladdin .... .10
2 Jasmine .... .10
3 Genie .... .10
4 Abu .... .10
5 Rajah .... .10
6 Jafar .... .10
7 Iago .... .10
8 Sultan .... .10
9 Jasmine .... .10
10 Aladdin .... .10

Gold Stickers, untitled

1 (Aladdin) .... .25
2 (Abu) .... .25
3 (Jasmine) .... .25
4 (Sultan) .... .25
5 (Jafar) .... .25

Aladdin (Panini) Gold Sticker
© The Walt Disney Company

6 (Genie) .... .25
7 (Iago) .... .25
8 (Rajah) .... .25
9 (cast) .... .25
10 (Abu) .... .25

Aladdin (SkyBox) © The Walt Disney Company

ALADDIN
SkyBox (1993, Animated Movie)

These cards are based on the Disney animated movie. The set features 10 character cards, 71 story cards, 7 activity cards and 2 checklists. The story card art is inside a gold border and comes directly from the movie. Artists are not credited. The card backs are predominately purple with white line drawings of magic lanterns. The card title and text are in black and the card number is in a gold magic lantern at the top. The backs also contain a small detail drawing of the front picture inside a circular pattern. The character cards are all gold, with a picture of the character both front and back. Character names are on the front and the back contains the card number. SkyBox had the U.S. license for movie cards and this set is not related to the Panini set covered above, even though many of the cards use identical art. Generally, the SkyBox version uses sharper art. The Spectra-Etch bonus cards are full-bleed foil enhanced pictures and the backs are numbered.

Set: 90 cards 14.00

Spectra-etch cards (1:30)
S1 of 3 Let's make some magic! . . . 8.00
S2 of 3 A friendship blossoms 9.00
S3 of 3 A presence felt... . . . . 8.00
Preview cards
S1 The Introduction 1.00
S2 Aladdin and Jasmine 1.00
Pack: 8 cards 1.00
Two different wrappers.

CARD CHECKLIST

1 Logo Card 20
Character Cards
2 Aladdin 20
3 Jasmine .20
4 Sultan 20
5 Jafar 20
6 Genie 20
7 Abu 20
8 Iago 20
9 Rajah 20
10 Magic Carpet 20
Story Cards
11 Let me tell you a tale... 20
12 The scarab's trail... 20
13 Only one may enter here... 20
14 Meanwhile, in the marketplace... . .20
15 Dreaming of a better life... 20
16 Jasmine must marry... 20
17 Jafar's hypnotic control... 20
18 "Who can enter the cave?" 20
19 Run-away princess 20
20 A pretty necklace... 20
21 A daring rescue... 20
22 New friends... 20
23 Trust me... 20
24 Jafar's orders... 20
25 Jasmine confronts Jafar 20
26 Heartbroken princess... 20
27 Meanwhile, in the palace dungeon... 20
28 Jafar makes an offer... 20
29 "Touch nothing but the lamp." 20
30 Treasures untold 20
31 A fine flying friend... 20
32 A dangerous climb 20
33 Abu and the Monkey Idol 20
34 The Temple of the Lamp 20
35 A forbidden jewel... 20
36 Scene of destruction 20
37 A frantic escape attempt... 20
38 "Give me the lamp!" 20
39 The Carpet saves Aladdin and Abu 20
40 A lamp in hand... 20
41 Poof! 20
42 Rub a lamp-look who pops out! . .20
43 Genie of the Lamp... 20
44 Wish fulfillment... 20
45 Can your friends do this? 20
46 Genie on the job! 20
47 A few rules for wishing... 20
48 Aladdin's first wish... 20
49 Jafar's newest plot... 20
50 Make way for Prince Ali Ababwa! .20
51 Mighty Prince Ali 20
52 Cheers for Prince Ali! 20
53 Aladdin arrives... 20
54 Bad first impression... 20
55 Aladdin acts himself... 20
56 Soaring hearts... 20
57 A romantic evening... 20
58 Into the sea... 20
59 The second wish... 20
60 Genie to the rescue... 20
61 Jafar's treachery exposed... 20
62 Broken promises... 20
63 Lamp-nabbed by a parrot! 20
64 A new Sultan! 20
65 Jafar's first wish is granted 20
66 Jafar's second wish... 20
67 At the ends of the earth... 20
68 Jasmine–a slave! 20
69 Jasmine plays for time 20
70 Time runs out for Jasmine 20
71 Aladdin battles Jafar 20
72 The serpent strikes... 20
73 Caught in evil's coils... 20
74 Jafar's third wish... 20
75 The end for Jafar... 20
76 Jafar's itty-bitty living space.. 20
77 Aladdin's third wish at last... 20
78 An ex-Genie says goodbye... 20
79 The Sultan's new law 20
80 Big group hug... 20
81 Happy endings...new beginnings . .20

Aladdin (SkyBox) Activity Card
© The Walt Disney Company

Activity Cards
82 Aladdin's Show and Tell 20
83 Abu and the Marketplace 20
84 Aladdin's Adventure! 20
85 Jasmine's Secret Wish 20
86 Jafar letter grid 20
87 Aladdin's true friends 20
88 Genie Says 20
89 Checklist One 20
90 Checklist two 20

ALIENS

Dark Horse (1993)

These two cards form a single side-by-side picture of your favorite Aliens with a red foil border. They came bagged in Hero Illustrated.

1 of 2 Aliens (Hero master-foil) 1.00
2 of 2 Aliens (Hero master-foil) 1.00

ALIENS

Dark Horse (1993)

Full bleed art, with comic checklist and a little text on the back. The cards each picture one of the characters from the series. Mark Nelson supplied the art, but we have supplied the names.

Aliens © Dark Horse Comics, Inc. & 20th Cent. Fox Film Corp.

Set: 5 Comic Book Checklist cards, in cello pack 5.50

1 Book One (Hicks) 1.00
2 Book Two (?) 1.00
3 Earth War (Ripley) 1.00
4 Genocide (Bishop?) 1.00
5 Hive (Mayakovsky?) 1.00

ALIENS/PREDATOR UNIVERSE

Topps/Dark Horse (1994)

This eagerly awaited set was not yet available at press time. The promo card has a fine painted alien by Dave Dorman.

Promo card, DvD art 1.00

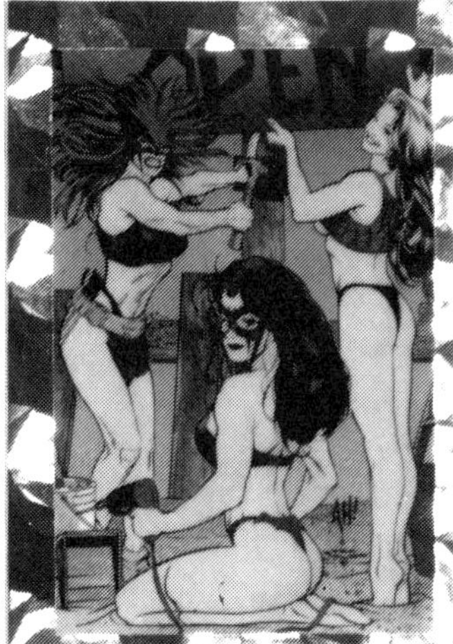
Walter Koenig & Swimsuit Special promos © Amazing Heroes Publishing

AMAZING HEROES PROMOS

Amazing Heroes (1993-4, Comics)

The cards have a silver prismatic border. The backs are white with printing in blue. They were issued to promote various comic book and card projects from Amazing Heroes.

Batbabe prism promo 1.50
Scavengers #1 prism promo sealed in plastic holder with gold stickers . . . 5.00
Scavengers #1 prism promo 1.50
Swimsuit Special prism promo (Mike Witherby) 1.50
Walter Koenig prism promo 1.50

AMUROL MINIATURE COMICS

Amurol Products (1981)

These miniature comics are 10 pages long and are trading card size. They came with bubble gum and a back flap which describes them as "Bubble Funnies" and contains the product code #22110 05070.

Set: 6 booklets 15.00

Amurol Miniature Comics © Marvel Entertainment Group, Inc.

- #1 Spider-Man ... 3.00
- #2 Hulk ... 2.50
- #3 Capt. America ... 2.50
- #4 Spider-Woman ... 2.00
- #5 Archie ... 2.00
- #6 Sabrina the Teen-Age Witch ... 2.00

Ania: Ebony Warrior © Eric Griffen

ANIA

Comic Images (1993)

Ania is the Association of Black Comic Book Publishers and a set of 90 cards was scheduled for November 1993 production. However, the set was cancelled after the special insert cards had been printed (along with others for other sets). These inserts are high quality cards, like others produced by Comic Images and have excellent artwork. All six cards were available from Ania at the 1993 Philadelphia ComicFest. A number of copies remain in their hands as of this writing and will probably be sold or given away at later shows. Get them if you can!

Chromium cards
- C1 Ebony Warrior (Eric Griffin) ... 5.00
- C2 Heru, Son of Ausar (Roger Barnes) ... 5.00
- C3 Turner (Eric Griffin) ... 5.00

Spectrascope cards
- S1 Zwanna, Son of Zulu (Nabile Hage) ... 5.00
- S2 Turner (Eric Griffin) ... 5.00
- S3 Purge (Roosevelt Pitt) ... 5.00
- Ebony Warrior promo card ... 2.50

ARCHIE COMIC CARDS

SkyBox (1992)

The cards have a comic book picture inside a colorful border that differs for each subset. The backs are white and have an additional drawing and text. The card title and number are at the top. The 000 and 62 "prototype" cards are actually promo cards since their backs contain promotional information about the card series. There are two different card 000's: one has the same front as prototype #8 and the other has the same front as prototype #37. All these cards were changed somewhat and re-numbered in the actual card set. Press releases and promo cards for the series state that there are six holograms, including the double image hologram, but only four regular holograms were issued, not five. The hologram exchange card has a border like a regular card and the SkyBox logo instead of a picture, plus information on how to exchange the card for the double image hologram of Archie, Betty and Veronica.

Archie hologram & prototype (backs) © Archie Comic Publications

Set: 120 cards ... 12.00

Holograms (Silver foil)
- H-1 America's Oldest Teenager ... 6.00
- H-2 Wet Kiss ... 6.00
- H-3 Easy Rider ... 6.00
- H-4 Jumpin' Jalopy ... 6.00
- Hologram exchange card ... 20.00
- B-1 The Eternal Triangle double image exchange hologram ... 10.00

"Prototype" cards
- 8 "A Handful" prototype ... 1.00
- 000 Promo version of #8 (Wizard) ... 1.00
- 37 "Sun Fun" prototype ... 1.00
- 000 Promo version of #37 (in Up 'n Coming) ... 2.00
- 62 Archie promo prototype ... 1.00
- Pack: 10 cards ... 1.00

Archie © Archie Comic Publications

CARD CHECKLIST

Archie
- 1 Jeepers, Peepers ... .10
- 2 Beach Peach ... .10
- 3 Tooth or Consequences ... .10
- 4 Dinner's on Me ... .10
- 5 Light House ... .10
- 6 Short Changed! ... .10
- 7 A Handful ... .10
- 8 Inner Tube Boob ... .10
- 9 Another Grand Slam ... .10

Veronica
- 10 Work Quirk ... .10
- 11 The Three S's ... .10
- 12 Flaming Fury ... .10
- 13 Shout It Out ... .10
- 14 Stylie Smile ... .10
- 15 Primping Up ... .10
- 16 Ocean View ... .10
- 17 Prom Queen ... .10
- 18 Ooh La La! ... .10

Reggie
- 19 Rude Dude ... .10
- 20 Mirror, Mirror ... .10
- 21 Drummer Bummer ... .10
- 22 Royal Pain ... .10
- 23 Prez ... .10
- 24 Hells on Wheels ... .10
- 25 Bubble Trouble ... .10
- 26 Out of Tune ... .10
- 27 Mail Chauvinist ... .10

Betty
- 28 Yummy, Yummy! ... .10
- 29 What a Catch ... .10
- 30 Jazz Pizazz ... .10
- 31 Scream Date ... .10
- 32 Snow a Go-Go ... .10
- 33 Liberty Belle ... .10
- 34 Betty's Trivia ... .10
- 35 Blonde Buddy ... .10
- 36 Sun Fun ... .10

Jughead
- 37 The Jughead Anthem ... .10
- 38 Ruff Competition ... .10
- 39 Food Frenzy ... .10
- 40 Lip Service ... .10
- 41 Pool Fool ... .10
- 42 Dong's Best Friend ... .10
- 43 Jughead's Diner ... .10
- 44 Cool Cat in the Hat ... .10

45 Chocklit Shoppe .10
Roughin' It
46 Camping with Archie .10
47 Three on a Hike .10
48 Camp Vamp .10
49 That Sinking Feeling .10
50 Not-So-Hot-Dog .10
51 What a Load! .10
52 Skunk Funk .10
53 Bear Scare! .10
54 All Tied Up! .10
The Gang
55 Dinin' Canine .10
56 Swing Fling .10
57 What's Up, Jug? .10
58 Photo Dodos .10
59 Burger Burner .10
60 Dance, Dance, Dance .10
61 Surfing Silliness .10
62 Hip-Hop .10
63 Piano Ham .10
Winter Sports
64 Snowboardin' Frenzy .10
65 Hot Dog – Cold Boy .10
66 Skate Fate .10
67 Hockey Schtick! .10
68 Ski Plea! .10
69 Dope on a Rope .10
70 Slope Dope .10
71 Rug Hug .10
72 Curvy Slopes Ahead .10
Amigos
73 True Blue .10
74 Boys Ahoy .10
75 Up, Up and Away! .10
76 Pig Gig .10
77 Cooking Something Up! .10
78 Picture Perfect .10
79 Beach Nuts .10
80 Ship of Fools .10
81 Mooseburger .10
Riverdale Diary
82 Blemish Dilemma .10
83 Double Vision .10
84 Fifties Nifties .10
85 3-Duh Movie .10
86 Limo-Ted Funds .10
87 Mess-Demeanor .10
88 Blast from the Past .10
89 Jean Scene .10
90 Money Plea .10
Earth to Archie, forms 3x3 card super-panel (Dan De Carlo art)
91 Use Alternate Forms of Transportation! .10
92 Stop Noise Pollution .10
93 Pick Up Trash .10
94 Don't Deface Nature with Graffiti! .10
95 Recycle .10
96 Stick to the Trails .10
97 Be Kind to Wildlife .10
98 Don't Pollute the Water .10
99 Enjoy Nature! .10
Riverdalians
100 Pop Tate .10
101 Mr. Weatherbee .10
102 Miss Beazly .10
103 Professor Flutesnoot .10
104 Miss Grundy .10
105 Big Ethel .10
106 Hot Dog .10
107 Fred & Mary Andrews .10
108 Moose .10
109 Coach Kleats .10
110 Mr. Lodge .10
111 Midge .10
112 Miss Haggly .10
113 Nancy .10
114 Dilton Doiley .10
115 Chuck Clayton .10
116 Smithers .10
117 Svenson .10
118 Sugar, Sugar .10
119 Checklist #1 .10
120 Checklist #2 .10

Arcomics promo cards © Terrance Henry, Ralph Lumley & Arcomics, Inc.

ARCOMICS

Promo #1 was given away to promote Arcomics Premiere #1. It employs a double image technology which was also used on the cover of the comic book. Promos #2 and #3 are also quite dazzling.

1 Renticular Animation promo 18.00
1A Promo card (part of #1) 1.00
1B Promo card (other part) 1.00
2 Aegis with Overstreet Sticker 1.00
without Overstreet sticker 2.00
3 Inspectre "Optigraphics" card 7.50

BATMAN

Batmen Series #1 © DC Comics, Inc.

BATMAN
Topps Series #1 (1966, TV)

These cards are color illustrations of the dynamic duo and their enemies in action. They're from the TV show era and the action seems appropriate, but it's not humorous (even though this Batman is definitely not the "Dark Knight" of the '90s). The fronts have a white border and a ***black bat logo*** *with the card title in white. The backs are orange with a drawing of Batman running on the right side plus card number and text. Most of the cards have an additional number, at the end of the text, indicating that the card is "No.x of 11 Batman vs. The Joker (or other villain) cards." The card text for these sections contains portions of a multi-part story featuring the named villain. The first two cards picture the dynamic duo and the last seven have them facing various dangers. As with many card sets from the '60s and '70s, the pack wrapper is scarce, especially in near mint condition.*

Set: 55 cards 200.00
Wrapper: 25.00

CARD CHECKLIST
1 The Batman 4.50
2 Robin-Boy Wonder 4.25
Batman vs. The Joker
3 The Bat Signal 4.00
4 Midnight Conference 4.00
5 Roof Top Vigil 4.00
6 Chloroform Victim 4.00
7 Grim Realization 4.00
8 Into the Batmobile 4.00
9 Face of the Joker 4.50
10 Crime Czar 4.00
11 Poison Pellet 4.00
12 Batman Strikes! 4.25
13 The Joker in Jail 4.50
Batman vs. The Penguin
14 Nightly Patrol 4.00
15 Batman In Action 4.25
16 The Penguin's Trap 4.50
17 Spikes of Death 4.00
18 Robin In Action 4.25
19 Fiery Encounter 4.00
20 Robin to the Rescue 4.25
21 Narrow Escape 4.00
22 Double Cross 4.00
23 Umbrella Duel 4.00
24 Penguin Captured 4.50
Batman vs. The Catwoman
25 The Cat Woman 4.25
26 Queen of Crime 4.00
27 Sinister Smile 4.00
28 "Let's Go!" 4.00
29 Robin is Kidnapped 4.25
30 Fighting Back 4.00
31 Threat of the Cat Woman 4.25
32 Bat-A-Rang Bulls-eye 4.00
33 The Enemies Clash 4.00
34 Deadly Claws 4.00
35 Cat Woman Defeated 4.25
Batman vs. The Riddler
36 The Riddler 4.50
37 A Trap for Batman 4.25
38 Robin Rescued 4.25
39 "To the Batcave" 4.00
40 Following the Clue 4.00
41 Time for a Rescue 4.00
42 Robin in Peril 4.25
43 The Bat-Gasmask 4.00
44 Flying Fists 4.00
45 Trap for the Riddler 4.50
46 The Bat-A-Rang 4.00
Batman vs. various dangers
47 Deadly Robot 4.00
48 Monstrous Illusion 4.00
49 Decoy 4.00
50 Beastly Encounter 4.00
51 Flaming Welcome 4.00
52 Winged Giant 4.00
53 Race Against Death 4.00
54 Whirlpool 4.00
55 Hidden Loot 4.00

Batman, 2nd Series © DC Comics, Inc.

Batman, 3rd Series © DC Comics, Inc.

BATMAN–2ND SERIES (Topps 1966)

The second series is often called the "A" series because the cards are numbered 1A to 44A. The caption is found in white lettering inside a **red bat logo** *on the front. The pictures are color paintings, similar to the first series. The backs have text, but no caption, and the bottom half is part of a puzzle. The card number is in a black circle and a secondary number relates to the puzzles. The puzzles are sequential, so we have identified them in the listing below.*

Set: 44 cards # w/A 160.00
Wrapper: 20.00

CARD CHECKLIST

Batman Puzzleback
1A The Ghostly Foe 4.00
2A Grappling a Gator 4.00
3A The Menacing Mummy 4.00
4A Target of the Trapper 4.00
5A Pendulum Peril 4.00
6A Facing the Ace 4.00
7A The Batline Lifeline 4.00
8A Tentacled Terror 4.00
9A Knighting a Thief 4.00
10A Cycling Crusader 4.00
Riddler Puzzleback
11A Landing a Big One 4.00
12A Boiling Bath 4.00
13A Out on a Limb 4.00
14A Danger in the Depths 4.00
15A Gotham Gallants 4.00
16A Portable Bat Signals 4.00
Catwoman Puzzleback
17A Link to Lincoln 4.00
18A Death Spins a Web 4.00
19A Leap for Life 4.00
20A Surfing Sleuths 4.00
21A Batman Wins a Prize 4.50
22A Death Skis the Slopes 4.00
Joker Puzzleback
23A Battling Nature's Fury 4.00
24A Tight Squeeze 4.00
25A In the Batlab 4.00
26A The Joker's Last Laugh 4.50
27A Striking Out the Cobra 4.00
28A Victorious Duo 4.00
Penguin Puzzleback
29A Danger from the 25th Century . 4.00
30A Undone by an Umbrella 4.00
31A Flying Foes 4.00
32A Captain Kidd's Caper 4.00
33A Dynamite in Robin's Nest 4.25
34A The Batman Baby Sitter 4.25
Robin Puzzleback
35A Crime Above the Harbor 4.00
36A Cliff Hangers 4.00
37A Watery Warfare 4.00
38A In the Path of Death 4.00
39A Stopping the Sub 4.00
40A Inferno of Flame 4.00
41A Duel of Death 4.00
42A Counterfeit Caped Crusader . . . 4.00
43A Menace in Fairyland 4.00
44A Batman on Broadway 4.50

BATMAN–3RD SERIES (Topps 1966)

The third series is often called the "B" series because the cards are numbered 1B to 44B. The caption is found in white lettering inside a **blue bat logo** *on the front. The pictures are color paintings, similar to the first and second series. There are two different versions of the backs for all cards. Version one is similar to series two: The backs have text and the caption and the bottom half is part of a puzzle. Unlike series two, the puzzles are not in sequence so they are not indicated in the listing. There are 10 card puzzles of Batman, and The Riddler and 6 card puzzles of Batman, Robin, The Dynamic Duo, and The Joker. Version two has the caption and text in white inside a blue bat design and no puzzle.*

Set: 44 cards # w/B 180.00
Wrapper: 20.00

CARD CHECKLIST

1B The Joker's Icy Jest 6.00
2B The Penguin Prevails 5.00
3B Hydro-foil Hotspot 4.50
4B Branded Boy Wonder 4.50
5B Caged by the Catwoman 4.50
6B Canape for a Cobra 4.50
7B The Grim Gladiator 4.50
8B Snaring the Sheik 4.50
9B Bashed on a Billboard 4.50
10B Amphibious Attackers 4.50
11B To Robin's Rescue 4.50
12B Renegade Roulette 4.50
13B Batman's Coffin 4.75
14B Neanderthal Nemesis 4.50
15B The Joker Wishes Robin Well . . 5.00
16B Penned by the Penguin 5.00
17B Prehistoric Peril 4.50
18B The Penguin's Prey 5.00
19B Cornered on a Cliff 4.50
20B Distorted Dynamic Duo 4.50
21B Toll of Torture 4.50
22B Routing the Riddler 5.00
23B The Joker's Juggernaut 5.50
24B Fangs of the Phantom 4.50
25B Dragged from Death's Door . . . 4.50
26B Jack Frost's Jinx 5.00
27B Pasting the Painter 4.50
28B Concrete Conquest 4.50
29B A Wretched Riddle 4.50
30B Jostled by the Joker 5.50
31B Batman Bucks Badman 4.50
32B Frozen by Frost 5.00
33B Gassed by a Geranium 4.50
34B A Fatal Joust 4.50
35B Holy Rodents 4.50
36B A Pressing Position 4.50
37B Riddler on the Roof 5.00
38B Beware the Bat-A-Rang 4.50
39B Caught in a Cavern 4.50
40B Batman Bails Out! 4.50
41B Aquatic Attack! 4.50
42B Inhospitable Hatter! 4.50
43B A Perilous Penny 4.50
44B Riddler Robs a Rainbow! 5.00

Batman Deluxe (reissue) © DC Comics, Inc.

BATMAN DELUXE
Topps (1989, TV)
(Reissue: 1966 Series #1, #2 & #3 cards)

These cards come in a box which says "Deluxe Reissue Edition" and originally sold for $19.95. The cards are reprints of the above three series on super glossy stock, from the original film negatives. The Series #3 cards are the puzzle back version. The top of the box reproduces the wrapper art and the back gives artist credits for the *series, something which was originally missing: pencils by Bob Powell and paintings by Norm Saunders. Each card is marked "1966 Deluxe Reissue Edition" so it's easy to tell these cards from the originals. This is a good way to collect the series, given the high price of the originals and the high quality of this set.*

Set: 143 cards, boxed 25.00

Batman (Riddler Back) © DC Comics, Inc.

BATMAN [RIDDLER BACKS]

Topps (1966, TV)

Riddler Backs, Real Photos

These cards feature color photos inside red photo mounts and a black border. The backs contain the caption and "The Riddler's Riddle" which gives these cards their common name. The Bat-decoder was used to obtain the answer to the riddle. The packs mention the Riddler's Riddle and say "Special."

Set: 38 cards, (photos) 210.00
Decoder 25.00
Wrapper 20.00

CARD CHECKLIST

1 Batman's Butler 6.00
2 Boy Wonder 5.25
3 Robin's Time Out 5.25
4 Rarin' to Go 5.00
5 A Lesson For Robin 5.25
6 Bookworm Batman 5.25
7 A Batly Gesture 5.00
8 The Caped Crusader 5.25
9 Batmobile Breakdown 5.00
10 Beaming Batman 5.25
11 Studious Crimefighter 5.00
12 The Clown Prince of Crime 5.00
13 A Dual Decision 5.00
14 Convention Caper 5.00
15 To the Bat-Foil 5.00
16 Hide-and-Go-Riddle 5.00
17 Cautious Caped Crusader 5.00
18 A Fearsome Foursome 5.00
19 A Purr-fect Plot 5.00
20 Attacked 5.00
21 United Underworld 5.00
22 Awesome Foursome 5.00
23 Boy Wonder's Batcart 5.25
24 A Desperate Leap 5.00
25 The Princess of Plunder's Prey . . 5.00
26 A Nefarious Note 5.00
27 De-clawed 5.00
28 Close Call 5.00
29 A Riddle for Robin 5.50
30 Dashing Dick Grayson 5.00
31 Bat on a Buoy 5.00
32 Whacking Robin Wings 5.25
33 Pudgy Penguin 5.50
34 Docking the Bat-Foil 5.00
35 A Dastardly Duo 5.00
36 A Catly Caper 5.00
37 Showdown on the Sea 5.00
38 Rescued by Robin 6.00

BATMAN [BAT LAFFS]

Topps (1966, TV)

"Bat Laffs, Real Photos"

These cards feature color photos of the cast, sets and vehicles from the TV show and many were posed specifically for this card set. Other photos were taken from the TV episodes. The cards have a "Bat Laffs" joke on the back and a piece of a puzzle picture. There are eight puzzles made up of either six or eight cards each. The cards are not captioned, so there is no checklist, but the puzzles are listed below:

Batman (Bat Laffs) © DC Comics, Inc.

Set: 55 cards (color) 165.00
Common card 3.50
Wrapper 20.00

Puzzle Checklist

Batman: #45, 53, 55, 43, 39, 54, 41, & 35.
Robin: #46, 38, 50, 42, 40, 48, 44, & 36.
Batman & Robin: #4, 12, 18, 21, 14, & 9.
Bruce Wayne: #28, 5, 25, 33, 30, & 23.
Commissioner Gordon & Batman: #57, 32, 22, 15, 26, & 2.
The Joker: #37, 49, 34, 51, 47 & 52.
Penguin: #29, 1, 3, 19, 24, 6, 10, 27 & 17.
The Riddler: 20, 16, 13, 11, 31 & 8.

Batman: The Animated Series © DC Comics, Inc.

BATMAN: THE ANIMATED SERIES

Topps (1993, Animated TV)

The "vinyl mini-cel" insert cards all have white backs. Most of them say "Collect all 6", but some are blank and none of them are numbered or captioned. We have provided the names of the characters depicted. The first 50 of the regular cards contain images of the heroes, villains, gadgets and vehicles from the animated TV series and the last 50 form 10 card episodes. The cards were distributed primarily to comic shops. The promo sheet is 5.3" x 7.8" of card stock, with a background picture of Batman's head and cape and a card front inset of Batman capturing a crook in the foreground. One prototype card shows Batman in action with flames in the background (found in Advance Comics #51*) and the other shows him battling Manbat. Both card backs have the same red and black picture of Poison Ivy with Batman tied up and identical wording, which also appears on the back of the promo sheet. None of these pictures appear in the actual card set, although the Manbat prototype is almost identical to card #57.*

Set: 100 cards 15.00

Vinyl Mini-cel (1:12)
(Batman) 9.00
(Robin) 7.00
(Joker & Batman) 8.00
(Penguin & Batman) 8.00
(Poison Ivy & Batman) 8.00
(Two-Face & Batman) 8.00
Batman Prototype card (Advance) . . 2.00
Prototype card on promo sheet 2.50
Prototype card w/Manbat 3.00
Pack: 10 cards 1.50

CARD CHECKLIST

1 Logo card 20
2 Batman 20
3 Robin 20
4 Bruce Wayne 20
5 Dick Grayson 20
6 Alfred 20
7 Commissioner Gordon 20
8 Batgirl 20
9 Harvey Dent 20
10 Officer Montoya 20
11 Detective Bullock 20
12 Summer Gleeson 20
13 Mayor Hamilton Hill 20
14 Selina Kyle 20
15 Gotham City 20
16 Wayne Manor 20
17 The Batcave 20
18 The Batcave 20
19 Arkham Asylum 20
20 Crime Alley 20
21 The Joker 20
22 The Penguin 20
23 The Riddler 20
24 Catwoman 20
25 Two-Face 20
26 Poison Ivy 20
27 Dr. Hugo Strange 20
28 Scarecrow 20
29 Rā's al Ghūl 20

Batman: The Animated Series
© DC Comics, Inc.

30 Talia 20
31 Man-Bat 20
32 Mr. Freeze 20
33 Clayface 20
34 Killer Croc 20
35 Mad Hatter 20
36 Harley Quinn 20
37 Rupert Thorne 20
38 The Ninja 20
39 Spider Conway 20
40 Joey the Snail 20
41 The Batmobile 20
42 The Batplane 20
43 The Batboat 20
44 The Batcycle 20
45 Gotham City Police Vehicles 20
46 The Batarang 20
47 Batman's Grappling Gun 20
48 Batman's Utility Belt 20
49 Batman's Homing Locator 20
50 Batman's Spray Gun & Goggles . .20

Episode: On Leather Wings

51 "When a nightwatchman..." 15
52 "Batman uses his unique..." 15
53 "Following the lead..." 15
54 "My wife tried to..." 15
55 "Batman confronts the ..." 15
56 "Batman snags the escaping..." . . .15
57 "Batman holds on tightly..." 15
58 "Batman's eyes widen..." 15
59 "Batman looks up..." 15
60 "Batman's scientific efforts..." 15

Episode: Nothing to Fear

61 "Night. A helicopter hovers..." 15
62 "The criminal known as..." 15
63 "In their hideout..." 15
64 "Batman fights the effects..." 15
65 "A huge zeppelin floats..." 15
66 "On top of the zeppelin..." 15
67 "Batman faces his fear..." 15

Batman: The Animated Series
© DC Comics, Inc.

68 "Scarecrow aims his dart gun..." . .15
69 "Batman grabs the bewildered..." .15
70 "At Gotham City..." 15

Episode: The Last Laugh

71 "It's April Fools' Day..." 15
72 "Stricken by The Joker's..." 15
73 "Merry mayhem overtakes..." 15
74 "Wearing a gas mask,..." 15
75 "Captain Clown,..." 15
76 "Rescued by the Batboat..." 15
77 "Captain Clown yanks..." 15
78 "Batman squares off..." 15
79 "The Joker sends..." 15
80 "The fleeing Joker..." 15

Episode: Pretty Poison

81 "It all began..." 15
82 "Harvey Dent and..." 15
83 "Batman brings the chopper..." . . .15
84 "Bruce finally shows..." 15
85 "Batman suspects that..." 15
86 "Batman is caught..." 15
87 "The monster flytrap holds..." 15
88 "Batman kicks out,..." 15
89 "The lights in the greenhouse..." . .15
90 "The greenhouse has become..." .15

Episode: Two-Face

91 "DA Harvey Dent..." 15
92 "As captured thugs..." 15
93 "'Handsome Harvey' Dent..." 15
94 "Bruce Wayne's mansion..." 15
95 "Hypnotized by his psychiatrist..." .15
96 "Harvey Dent receives..." 15
97 "When Thorne and his flunkies..." .15
98 "Look out, Harvey!" 15
99 "Days later at the hospital..." 15
100 "Grace sees Harvey Dent..." 15

Batman: The Animated Series Two © DC Comics, Inc.

BATMAN: THE ANIMATED SERIES TWO

Topps (1994, Animated TV)

These cards are a direct continuation of the previous series, with six more TV show episodes depicted in 10 card subsets. The last 30 cards cover the animated movie "Batman: Mask of the Phantasm." There are only four "vinyl mini-cels" this time and they are somewhat scarcer – two per box instead of three. They are numbered and captioned and have a pictorial back, making them more bonus cards from other manufacturers. The promo sheet is 5.3" x 7.8" of card stock with an insert card front of Batman walking toward you. The promo card pictures Catwoman and Batman in action. The "Mask of the Phantasm" movie opened Christmas day, 1993, but the cards did not appear until the end of January, which probably cost Topps some sales and reduced collector interest in the series.

Set: 90 cards 15.00

Vinyl Mini-Cels (1:18)
1 Batman 8.00
2 Batman Battles the Joker 8.00
3 Batman Faces the Phantasm 8.00
4 The Dark Knight of Gotham City . . 8.00
Promo card sheet 2.00
Catwoman/Batman promo card 2.00
Pack: 8 cards 1.25

CARD CHECKLIST

Episode: Two Face, part II

101 A raid is underway 15
102 Rupert Thorne's criminal 15
103 Batman is tormented 15
104 Two-Face and his men 15
105 Confronting Two-Face 15
106 Lost without his fiancee 15
107 Thorne's thugs 15
108 Two-Face tackles Rupert 15
109 As Two-Face is about to shoot . .15
110 His rage spent 15

The Cat and the Claw

111 On a moonlit night 15
112 Batman catches up 15
113 Soon, at Gotham Hills 15
114 It's a pleasure 15
115 Commissioner Gordon 15
116 Bruce Wayne arranges 15
117 Soon, in the headquarters 15
118 Red Claw orders her men 15
119 As Catwoman falls 15
120 Back at her apartment 15

The Cat and the Claw, Part II

121 Looking for information 15
122 Red Claw and her hoods 15
123 Red Claw threatens 15
124 Bruce Wayne takes Selina 15
125 Alfred discovers a hair 15
126 Catwoman sneaks into 15
127 As Batman and Catwoman 15
128 Since you wanted the plague . .15
129 As Red Claw's compound 15
130 Red Claw prepares to kick 15

Heart of Ice

131 In the midst of the hottest 15
132 A heavily armored truck 15
133 Inside a Gothcorp warehouse . .15
134 Since you ally yourself 15
135 Despite a bad cold 15
136 Outside the Gothcorp 15
137 Batman reaches street level . . .15
138 Mr. Freeze kicks the cap 15
139 Batman bursts onto the scene . .15
140 Batman smashes a thermos . . .15

Feet of Clay

141 As armed gunmen 15
142 With the sound of gunfire 15
143 The last of the hoods 15
144 Movie Star Matt Hagen 15
145 Scooping out the last 15
146 In the Batcave 15
147 Batman tracks down Bell 15
148 Carrying Bell and his car 15
149 Who was impersonating 15
150 Teddy Lupus finds his boss . . .15

Feet of Clay, Part II

151 Matt Hagen's assistant 15
152 As Matt Hagen recounts 15
153 As Daggett's goon 15
154 As Batman interrogates 15
155 The clay creature carries 15

156 The clay creature leaps 15
157 The clay creature creates 15
158 Clayface shoots a gigantic hand .15
159 Batman turns on screen 15
160 With Clayface's impersonations . .15

Mask of the Phantasm

161 The Story begins 15
162 Chuckie Sol pulls out his gun . . .15
163 As Bruce Wayne wines 15
164 Years of physical and mental . . .15
165 After beating an entire gang 15
166 In present day Gotham City 15
167 As Batman visits the graves 15
168 After catching a glimpse 15
169 Bruce and Andrea arrived 15
170 As Bruce Wayne 15
171 Seated comfortably in his study .15
172 Soon, Bruce Wayne 15
173 Investigating the murders 15
174 Ecstatic at the prospect 15
175 On the grounds 15
176 Andrea Beaumont returns 15
177 The Phantasm arrives 15
178 The Phantasm has barely 15
179 The Phantasm has escaped 15
180 At Wayne Manor 15
181 As Andrea Beaumont gets up . . .15
182 The Joker pays a call 15
183 Looking for clues 15
184 Andrea Beaumont 15
185 Not one for gallantry 15
186 The Joker has lured Andrea 15
187 Batman tells Andrea to leave . . .15
188 As they spiral downward 15
189 With the Gotham City 15
190 In the Batcave 15

Batman (Movie) © DC Comics, Inc.

BATMAN (MOVIE)

Topps-Series #1 (1989, Movie)

These cards contain color photos from the first Tim Burton Batman movie starring Michael Keaton, Kim Basinger and Jack Nicholson. This is one of the last of the old style Topps card series, with cheap cardboard materials, wax wrappers and a stick of bubble gum. The pictures are inside a white border and are captioned at the bottom. There is a batlogo in the lower left corner. The backs repeat the caption and have text telling the story of the movie. The stickers have a red border and the backs form a movie poster when assembled.

Set: 132 cards/22 stickers 25.00

Pack: 9 cards, 1 sticker 1.00
Two different wrappers, both with yellow backgrounds: One pictures Batman and the other has the Joker; both say "#1 Hit Movie!"
Cello Pack: 2.00
Two different cello wrappers.

CARD CHECKLIST

1 Introduction 20
2 Darknight Detective 20
3 Bruce Wayne 20
4 The Clown Prince of Crime 20
5 Jack Napier 20
6 Vicki Vale 20
7 Alexander Knox 20
8 Commissioner Gordon 20
9 Alfred the Butler 20
10 D.A. Harvey Dent 20
11 Crime Boss Carl Grissom 20
12 Alicia Hunt 20
13 Gotham City After Dark 20
14 Mugged!! 20
15 Rooftop Rendezvous 20
16 Night of the Bat 20
17 Nailed by the Dark Avenger 20
18 "Who..What Are You?!!" 20
19 Gotham City's Dark Knight 20
20 The New D.A. 20
21 Knox on the Job! 20
22 The Set-Up 20
23 Bruce in Wayne Manor 20
24 Meeting Their Host 20
25 View From the Batcave 20
26 The Axis Chemical Factory 20
27 Mysterious Manhunter 20
28 Batman's Weapon 20
29 Toxic Flood! 20
30 In the Batman's Clutches 20
31 Commissioner Gordon-Hostage! . .20
32 Holding Batman at Bay! 20
33 Hero and the Horror 20
34 Jack Loses His Grip! 20
35 Plunge Into Toxic Oblivion! 20
36 Rising Above It All 20
37 Spotted by Comm. Gordon! 20
38 Front Page Story! 20
39 Ghastly Revelation 20
40 Back From the Dead 20
41 No Deals, Grissom! 20
42 "Call Me...Joker!" 20
43 Grissom's Gruesome Demise 20
44 "Wait'll They Get a Load of Me!" . .20
45 "Hi Honey" 20
46 The New Crime Boss 20
47 Gotham City's Gang Lords 20
48 Joy-Buzzed to Death! 20
49 Evil of the Joker 20
50 Fried Alive! 20
51 "I'm in Charge Now!" 20
52 A Final Farewell 20
53 Lord of Wayne Manor 20
54 Outside City Hall 20
55 The Mime of Mayhem! 20
56 Funny Meeting You Here! 20
57 City Hall Massacre! 20
58 Outrageous Assault! 20
59 Who's the Wildest One of All? . . .20
60 The Joker's Lair 20
61 Vicki's Most Devoted Fan 20
62 "Keep up the Bat Work!" 20
63 Smylex Attack! 20
64 The Joker Conquers TV! 20
65 "Love That Joker!" 20
66 "Let's Go Shopping!" 20
67 At the Flugelheim 20
68 The Art of Crime 20
69 A Date With Vicki 20
70 You Light Up My Life 20
71 Alicia's New Look 20
72 "No! No! I'm Melting!!" 20
73 Crash!!! 20
74 The Rescue 20
75 Swing to Safety! 20
76 A Daring Escape! 20
77 The Batmobile 20
78 Fantastic Chase! 20
79 The Batmobile Tears Away! 20
80 Cocooned! 20
81 "Is It Halloween?" 20
82 "How Much Do You Weigh?" 20
83 Death-Defying Duo! 20
84 Hang On, Vicki! 20
85 Batman Overpowered 20
86 The Challenge 20
87 Urban Warriors 20
88 Slashing Assault! 20
89 Photographed by Vicki! 20
90 Friend...Or Mad Vigilante? 20
91 Within the Batcave 20
92 Vicki in a Jam! 20
93 The Joker is Wild! 20
94 Haunting Memory 20
95 Fate of the Wayne Family 20
96 Gearing Up For Danger 20
97 Knight Patrol! 20
98 Sabotage! 20
99 The Axis Fireball! 20
100 Escape From Flaming Death! . . .20
101 The Master of Disaster 20
102 Bicentennial Nightmare 20
103 Twisted Terrorists! 20
104 Flight of the Batwing 20
105 Batwing Cockpit 20
106 The Joker's Secret Weapon 20
107 Taking Aim at the Batwing! 20

Batman (Movie) © DC Comics, Inc.

108 Super-Sleek Craft! 20
109 Crash Dive! 20
110 Vicki to the Rescue! 20
111 The Joker Takes a Hostage 20
112 Batman Lives! 20
113 Grim Vendetta 20
114 In Danger's Domain 20
115 Watch Out Behind You...! 20
116 Assault on the Caped Fury 20
117 Desperate Struggle! 20
118 Grip of Death! 20
119 Perilous Plunge! 20
120 Batman in Action! 20
121 No Match For Batman! 20
122 Bruised But Not Beaten! 20
123 The Joker's Final Stand 20
124 Dance of Death 20
125 Vicki Imperiled! 20
126 The Titans Clash! 20
127 Batman vs. Madman 20
128 The Dark Knight Triumphs 20
129 The Joker–Over the Edge! 20
130 He Who Laughs Last 20
131 The Bat-Signal 20
132 The Guardian of Gotham City . . .20

Sticker

1 ("BATMAN") 35
2 (Bat Symbol) 35
3 (Bruce Wayne & Vicki Vail) 35
4 (Batman & Batmobile) 35
5 ("The JOKER") 35
6 (The Joker's Gang) 35
7 (Batman & The Joker) 35
8 (The Batmobile) 35
9 (Three Faces of the Joker) 35
10 (Joker's Costume) 35
11 (Batman standing) 35
12 (Batman mug shot) 35
13 (Bat Plane front view) 35
14 (Bat Plane top view) 35
15 (The Joker clowns) 35
16 (The Joker smiles) 35
17 (Batman stands by Batmobile) . . .35
18 (The Joker at the Beach) 35
19 (Batman) 35
20 (Batman head & shoulders) 35
21 (Joker face) 35
22 (Vicki Vail) 35

BATMAN (MOVIE) FACTORY SET

Topps also issued a factory boxed set, on glossy card stock, with 11 bonus cards, which sold for $29.95. You can find it for a little less these days. The "Bonus Cards" contain movie storyboard drawings, inside black borders.

Factory set: 132 cards, 22 stickers plus 11 bonus cards . . 25.00

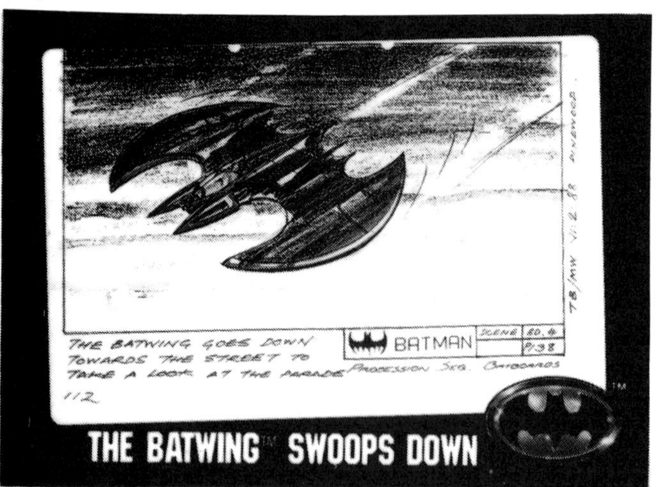

Batman (Movie) Factory Set, bonus card © DC Comics, Inc.

Bonus Cards
A Batman in Batwing Cockpit ..... .50
B The Batwing Swoops Down ..... .50
C Canyons of Gotham City .... .50
D Zeroing in on the Joker .... .50
E Setting the Missile Sights .... .50
F Hitting the Switch .... .50
G Firing Away! .... .50
H The Joker Avoids the Onslaught . .50
I The Dark Knight Reacts .... .50
J The Batwing Bounces .... .50
K Cathedral Directly Ahead! ...... .50

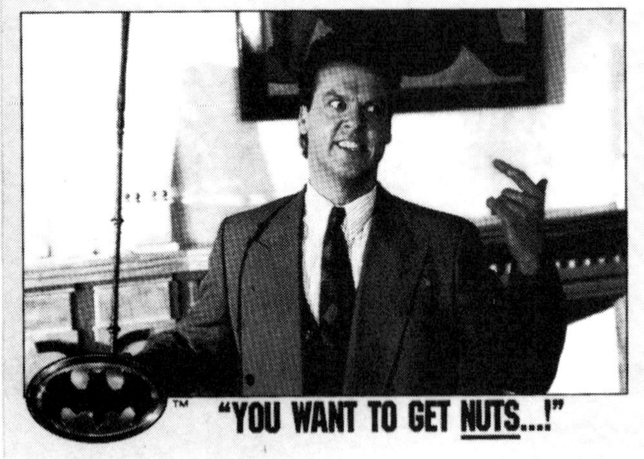

Batman (Movie) Series #2 © DC Comics, Inc.

BATMAN (MOVIE) SERIES #2 (Topps, 1989)

More of the above photos, with yellow borders. The stickers have puzzle backs, which form an orange bordered picture of Batman and a blue bordered picture of The Joker.

Set: 132 cards/22 Stickers 20.00

Pack: 9 cards, 1 sticker 0.75
Two different wrappers with red backgrounds, both say "All New 2nd Series"
Cello Pack: 19 cards, 1 sticker 2.00
Two different cello wrappers.

CARD CHECKLIST
133 Batman-The 2nd Series ...... .20
134 The Man and His Quarry ..... .20
135 Hand of Vengeance .... .20
136 Parked in the Batcave .... .20
137 Fistfuls of Funny Money! ..... .20
138 Onward, to His Fate... .... .20
139 Doppelganger .... .20
140 Time to Die, Grissom! .... .20
141 "Armadillo" Effect .... .20
142 The Last of Eckhardt .... .20
143 Leer of the Clown Prince ..... .20
144 "I've Got to Work Tonight" .... .20
145 Leap from the Belltower ...... .20
146 March of the Misfits .... .20
147 Meltingly Beautiful .... .20
148 You Know Who I Mean...! ..... .20
149 Power of the Batmobile ...... .20
150 Flugelheim Aftermath .... .20
151 Alley Bat .... .20
152 Aiming to Kill! .... .20
153 News of the Battle! .... .20
154 The Wayne Manor Party ...... .20
155 Of Mimes and Memories ..... .20
156 Danger in the Streets .... .20
157 The Oddest Couple .... .20
158 Knight and the Damsel .... .20
159 Hanging on for Life! .... .20
160 Murder...Just for Laughs ...... .20
161 Twisted Pitchman .... .20
162 'Copter Escape! .... .20
163 Instructions for Alfred .... .20
164 Gotham City Landscape ...... .20
165 Flugelheim Museum Interior ... .20
166 Elevated Subway Exterior ..... .20
167 Flugelheim Museum Exterior ... .20
168 Grissom's Office .... .20
169 Their Final Bow? .... .20
170 The Batmobile–Head On ..... .20
171 Dangling Devil .... .20
172 See Rotelli Roast .... .20
173 The Defeat of Batman .... .20
174 Sneaking Up Behind Jack... ... .20
175 Festival of Madness .... .20
176 Battered But Unbowed! ...... .20
177 Mission Accomplished! .... .20
178 Retreat Into Darkness .... .20
179 "You Want to Get Nuts...!" .... .20
180 The Master's Mimes .... .20
181 Knox Chats With Alfred ...... .20
182 Savage Sneak Attack! .... .20
183 Madness Wears a Smile ...... .20
184 The Batmobile Escapes! ...... .20
185 Jack and Alicia .... .20
186 Trick or Treat! .... .20
187 The Fiend Flies High! .... .20
188 His Card... .... .20
189 Silent But Deadly .... .20
190 The Phantom Avenger .... .20
191 A New Mad Plan! .... .20
192 Friends and Lovers .... .20
193 Fiery Finale .... .20
194 Another Man Down .... .20
195 The Batwing Soars! .... .20
196 The Joker (By Tim Burton) .... .20
197 Batman Costume Design ..... .20
198 The Joker Costume Design ... .20
199 Batman Design Concept ...... .20
200 Metal Walkway .... .20
201 Tugging the Line .... .20
202 The Hanging Hood .... .20
203 Over the Gantry .... .20
204 The Joker Knocked Backwards . .20
205 Danger Directly Ahead! ...... .20
206 Clearing the Trigger .... .20
207 Preparing for an Assault ...... .20
208 Cathedral Dead Ahead! ...... .20
209 Goons in Hot Pursuit! .... .20
210 Mysterious Millionaire .... .20
211 Alleys of Gotham City .... .20
212 The Villain Supreme! .... .20
213 Who Is Jack Napier? .... .20
214 The Joke's On Alicia .... .20
215 Weapon Against Evil .... .20
216 His Foul and Fiendish Grin .... .20
217 Armor Inspiration .... .20
218 Grotesque Reflections .... .20
219 A Gift For Vicki .... .20
220 The Night is His Again! .... .20
221 Kids Playing 'Batman' .... .20
222 Brains+Beauty=Vicki .... .20
223 Everyone Needs a Hobby! .... .20
224 Throttling a Punk .... .20
225 An Artist Most Bizarre .... .20
226 Batman's Public Service ...... .20
227 A Goon and His Tune .... .20
228 City of Light and Danger ...... .20
229 Heroic Escape! .... .20
230 How the Joker Lives .... .20
231 Batman in the Belfry .... .20
232 Classic First Issue .... .20
233 Directing Grissom's Murder .... .20
234 The Clown and the Clapboard . .20
235 The Director's Vision .... .20
236 Maniacal Murderer! .... .20
237 Knox Takes a Shot at Heroism . .20
238 What Tim Burton Wants... ..... .20

Batman (Movie) Series #2
© DC Comics, Inc.

239 Getting the Worst From Grissom .20
240 Directing Helicopter Escape ... .20
241 Special Advice For Batman .... .20
242 Directing Michael Keaton ..... .20
243 Flight of the Dark Avenger .... .20
244 Interviewed by Knox .... .20
245 Tim Burton, Filmmaker .... .20
246 Alicia–Exquisite! .... .20
247 Presenting the Batmobile! ..... .20
248 Relaxing With Key Players .... .20
249 Filming the Dance Macabre ... .20
250 Shooting the Rescue Scene ... .20
251 Dining at Wayne Manor ...... .20
252 Secret Life of Bruce Wayne ... .20
253 City Street Miniature .... .20
254 At the Nerve Center .... .20
255 Computerized SFX .... .20
256 Fantastic Miniature Set .... .20
257 Trail of the Mystery Man ...... .20
258 Directing Jack Nicholson ..... .20
259 Dance of the Deranged ...... .20
260 From Burton to Batman ...... .20
261 Batman's Revenge .... .20
262 Gruesome Grimace .... .20
263 Building of Gotham City ...... .20
264 The Killer Clown's in Town! ... .20

Sticker (Posterbacks)
23 (Joker & Batman) .... .25
24 Batman .... .25
25 The Joker .... .25
26 Batman .... .25
27 (Joker) .... .25
28 (Batman, full length) .... .25
29 (Joker, face) .... .25
30 (Batman, drawing) .... .25
31 (Joker, full length) .... .25
32 (Batman, full length, drawing) ... .25
33 (Joker, full length, drawing) ..... .25
34 (In Batcave) .... .25
35 (Batman) .... .25
36 (Bruce Wayne) .... .25
37 (Joker) .... .25
38 (Batman symbol logo) .... .25
39 (Batman, head & shoulders) .... .25
40 (Joker) .... .25
41 (Batman, hiding) .... .25
42 Puzzle D depicted on back ..... .25
43 Puzzle C depicted on back ..... .25
44 (Batmobile) .... .25

BATMAN (MOVIE) FACTORY SET

The glossy factory set for the second series comes boxed with 11 Weapons and Gadgets "Bonus Cards." It's scarcer than the first series factory set, so it has held its value.

Factory set: 132 cards, 22 stickers plus 11 bonus cards .. 30.00

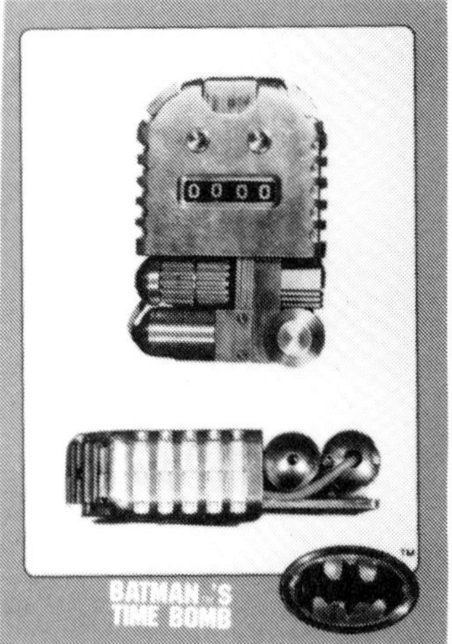

Batman (Movie) 2nd Series Factory Set bonus cards © DC Comics, Inc.

Bonus Cards
L Grappling Hook, Spring Action Reel .50
M Batarang (Folded and Unfolded) . .50
N Darkly Humorous Pistols 50
O Batman's Time Bomb 50
P Smoke Capsules 50
Q Handset & Tracer 50
R Batmobile Communicator 50
S Cocooned Batmobile (front & rear) .50
T Acid-Squirting Flower 50
U Batman's Gauntlet 50
V Utility Belt, Body Armor 50

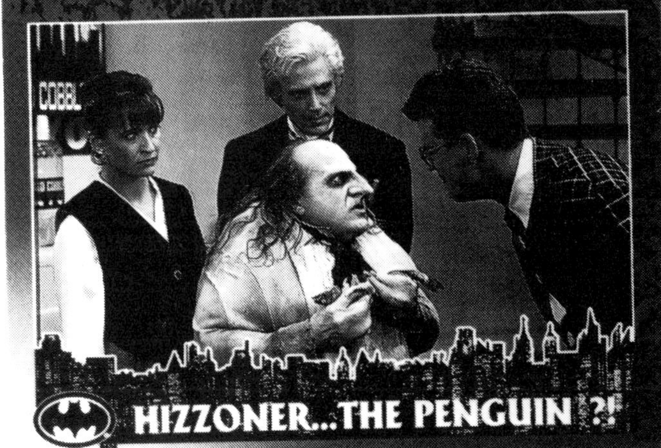

Batman Returns © DC Comics, Inc.

BATMAN RETURNS

Topps (1992, Movie)

These color photo cards are from the second Batman movie, starring Michael Keaton, Michele Pfeiffer and Danny DeVito. These are nice looking cards, and of slightly better quality than previous Topps cards, but not up to the competition. Basically, they mark the end of this type of cheap card stock. Topps tried its hand at gimmicks with this series by including a "Stadium Club" card in each pack. These are not the same cards as the "Stadium Club" set listed below, but they are of the same quality and most of them duplicate photos from that series, as we have noted. The white back promo card is from Advance Comics *#42 and the blue back card is from* Previews *magazine.*

Set: 88 cards +10 Stadium Club cards 15.00

Promo Cards
The Dark Knight Returns (blue back) 4.00
Roar of the Batmobile (white back) . 3.50
Pack: 8 cards & 1 Spec. card 1.00

CARD CHECKLIST
1 A Recipe For Success 15
2 The Dark Knight of Gotham City . . .15
3 Introducing the Penguin 15
4 Introducing Catwoman 15
5 Evil Prince of the City 15
6 Nightmare as a Child 15
7 Master of the Lower Depths 15
8 Peering Out of the Darkness 15
9 Addressing Gotham City 15
10 A Secretary Named Selina 15
11 Watching From Wayne Manor . . .15
12 "What In the Name Of...?!" 15
13 A Ghoulish Gift 15
14 A Giant Surprise Package 15
15 All Hell Breaks Loose 15

Batman Returns © DC Comics, Inc.

16 Roar of the Batmobile 15
17 Plowing Into Peril 15
18 Cycling Psychos 15
19 Terror in Gotham Square 15
20 Scene of the Crime 15
21 In the Clown's Clutches 15
22 "Let Her Go" 15
23 Human Flame Thrower 15
24 Counterattack! 15
25 The Fire Breather Aflame! 15
26 Icy Lair .15
27 Sultan of the Sewers 15
28 Unholy Alliance 15
29 Shreck's Way 15
30 Through a Window Harshly 15
31 Revived by Feline Friends 15
32 Birth of Catwoman 15
33 An Acrobatic Surprise 15
34 Gotham's Unlikely Hero 15
35 In Search of His Roots 15
36 The List of Oswald Cobblepot 15
37 Cemetery Pilgrimage 15
38 Destiny of the Cobblepots 15
39 Hizzoner...The Penguin?! 15
40 Feline on the Prowl 15
41 Night Watchers 15
42 "Meow" .15
43 Cat Challenges Bat 15
44 Sinful, Sinuous Catwoman 15
45 Only Eight Lives Left... 15
46 Burn, Baby, Burn!! 15
47 The Plan to Destroy Batman 15
48 Bruce and Selina Unmasked 15
49 Rescuing the Ice Princess 15
50 "What Do You Want" 15
51 Sabotaging the Batmobile 15
52 Innocent Victim 15
53 A Long Way Down... 15
54 Over the Edge 15
55 Wild Batmobile 15
56 Gordon Against Him 15
57 Flight of the Batmissile 15
58 Cop Car Catastrophe 15
59 A Penguin Scorned... 15
60 On the Campaign Trail 15
61 Oswald Outwitted! 15
62 Turning on the Crowd 15
63 Back to the Depths 15
64 The Max-Squerade 15
65 Bruce Wayne "In Costume" 15
66 Crashing the Party 15
67 The Penguin's Revenge 15
68 Fearsome Felon 15
69 "The Time is at Hand" 15
70 The Kiddie Express 15
71 Rallying His Troops 15
72 Penguins on the March 15
73 Missiles Away! 15
74 Invading Gotham City 15
75 Gliding Gladiator 15
76 Battered by Batman 15
77 The Dark Knight Triumphant 15
78 Batskiboat Attack! 15
79 Fury of the Penguin 15
80 When Titans Collide 15
81 The Penguin's Plunge 15
82 Vengeance Is Hers! 15
83 "Don't Interfere, Batman!" 15
84 Shreck's Final Stand 15
85 Lashing Out! 15
86 No Escape For Shreck 15
87 Destroying His Life Support 15
88 Farewell, Penguin! 15

Spec. Stadium Club Cards
A {See Stadium Club #75} 25
B {See Stadium Club #85} 25
C (Batmobile) 25
D {See Stadium Club #34} 25
E (Penguin commandos in formation) .25
F {See Stadium Club #76} 25
G {See Stadium Club #15} 25
H {See card #37} 25
I {See Stadium Club #12} 25
J {See card #55} 25

BATMAN RETURNS STADIUM CLUB

(Topps 1992)

Stadium Club cards have a silver batsymbol logo on the front and are printed on a glossy UV coated paper with a full bleed high quality photo front and a smaller full color back photo. This is Topps' first attempt to catch up the high quality cards which their competitors had been selling for a few years. All subsequent Topps cards used quality card stock and UV coating. There are no card titles and the text on the back of the cards usually has nothing to do with the picture on the front. Many of the cards have the same photos as the regular Batman Returns cards, and we have used the same titles. The other card titles are our own. The white back promo card is from Advance Comics *#42 and the blue back card is from* Previews *magazine.*

Set: 100 cards 30.00

Promo Cards
Batman (white back) 5.00
Batmobile (blue back) 4.00
Pack: 15 cards 2.00

CARD CHECKLIST
1 (Dark Knight of Gotham City) 25
2 {Introducing the Penguin} reversed .25
3 {Vengeance is Hers!} 25
4 (Michael Keaton) 25
5 (Michael Pfeiffer) 25
6 (Catwoman sits on Batman) 25
7 (Alfred the Butler) 25

Batman Returns Stadium Club © DC Comics, Inc.

8 (Commissioner Gordon) .25
9 {A Recipe For Success} .25
10 (Batman & Batskiboat) .25
11 {Human Flame Thrower} .25
12 {Cat Challenges Bat} .25
13 {Revived by Feline Friends} .25
14 {The Penguin's Plunge} .25
15 (Batman glares) .25
16 (Catwoman threatens) .25
17 {Penguins on the March} .25
18 (Penguin with bats) .25
19 {When Titans Collide} .25
20 (Bruce eyes a turban) .25
21 (In the batcave) .25
22 {On the Campaign Trail} .25
23 {A Penguin Scorned} .25
24 (Batman stands tall) .25
25 (Clown exhales flames) .25
26 (Attack of the circus troops) .25
27 (Penguin's flaming umbrella) .25
28 {"What Do You Want"} .25
29 {Wild Batmobile} .25
30 (Catwoman vamps Penguin) .25
31 (Penguin underground) .25
32 (Batmobile rotates) .25
33 {Burn, Baby, Burn!} .25
34 {"Meow"} .25
35 (Shreck and Catwoman) .25
36 (Penguin feeds his troops) .25
37 {Only Eight Lives Left...} .25
38 {Destiny of the Cobblepots} .25
39 (Lighting the tree) .25
40 (Batman looks left) .25
41 (The penguin's horde marches) .25
42 (Batman eyes Catwoman) .25
43 {Flight of the Batmissile} .25
44 (Penguin goes upstairs) .25
45 (Batman looks at you) .25
46 {Feline on the Prowl} .25
47 (Catwoman attacks!) .25
48 {Farewell, Penguin!} .25
49 (In the plaza) .25
50 {No Escape for Shreck} .25
51 {Missiles Away!} .25
52 {Plowing Into Peril} .25
53 {Fearsome Felon} .25
54 (Batman wired) .25
55 (Max Shreck) .25
56 (Catwoman laughs) .25
57 {Rallying His Troops} .25
58 (Catwoman & Batman) .25
59 (Batman appears) .25
60 (In front of Arcticworld) .25
61 (Oswald Cobblepot for Mayor) .25
62 {Night Watchers} .25
63 {Let Her Go} .25
64 {Crashing the Party} .25
65 {Gliding Gladiator} .25
66 (Batmobile) .25
67 (Batman fights for his life) .25
68 {Cycling Psychos} .25
69 {"The Time is at Hand"} .25
70 (Oswald can write!) .25
71 {The Dark Knight Triumphant} .25
72 {The List of Oswald Cobblepot} .25
73 {A Giant Surprise Package} .25
74 (Batmobile in action) .25
75 (Batman eyes you!) .25
76 {Fury of the Penguin} .25
77 {All Hell Breaks Loose} .25
78 (Penguin & his duckmobile) .25
79 (Batman rules the night) .25
80 {Battered by Batman} .25
81 {Roar of the Batmobile} .25
82 (The Dark Knight's head) .25
83 (Alfred the butler) .25
84 (Catwoman attacks Shreck) .25
85 (Penguin and his hat) .25
86 (Catwoman clawed, but sultry) .25
87 (Batman fights) .25
88 (Batman hides his face) .25
89 {Oswald Outwitted!} .25
90 (Batman poses) .25
91 (Alfred brings tea) .25
92 {Don't Interfere, Batman!} .25
93 {Introducing Catwoman} .25
94 {The Fire Breather Aflame!} .25
95 (Catwoman glares) .25
96 (Penguin plans to leap) .25
97 (Catwoman with whip & chair) .25
98 {Nightmare as a Child} .25
99 {Back to the Depths} .25
100 (Penguin & Catwoman) .25

BATMAN RETURNS MOVIE PHOTO STICKERS

Topps (1992, Movie)

This test set had yellow borders and a very limited release.

Set: 66 stickers 25.00

Batman Returns Movie Stickers & Zellers Collection © DC Comics, Inc.

BATMAN RETURNS

Zellers Collection (1992, Movie)

Zellers is a Canadian department/discount store which created this set as a promotion. Excess full sets were available in the U.S. through hobby and comic shops. The cards have English and French text on the back and are easily identified by the "Zellers Collection" and yellow right side stripe on the front. They are just a little taller than regular size, so they don't quite fit in a standard plastic card box.

Set: 24 cards 7.00

1 Batman arrives... .30
2 Batman and Catwoman... .30
3 Batman assesses the situation... .30
4 Batman! .30
5 Batman's uniform vault... .30
6 The Penguin! .30
7 The Penguin! .30
8 The Penguin! .30
9 Catwoman and The Penguin... .30
10 The Penguin frightens... .30
11 Catwoman in the Penguin's lair... .30
12 Catwoman confronting Batman... .30
13 Catwoman on the rooftops! .30
14 Catwoman in The Penguin's... .30
15 Members of the Red Triangle .30
16 Sculptures in Gotham Plaza! .30
17 A Gotham City... .30
18 The Penguin drives... .30
19 Red Triangle Circus Gang... .30
20 The Penguin's Commandos... .30
21 Commissioner Gordon! .30
22 The Organ Grinder... .30
23 The Batmobile in action... .30
24 The Batmobile! .30

Batman, Saga of the Dark Knight © DC Comics, Inc.

BATMAN: SAGA OF THE DARK KNIGHT

SkyBox (1994)

This is the first set of Batman cards ever taken from the comic books and the first time Batman has appeared on a SkyBox card. Topps produced all of the previous Batman cards and they were all taken from TV or the movies, except for the three Norm Saunders/Bob Powell painted card series from the 1966 TV show era. This new card series draws on the recent story lines from the Batman comic books from issues #400 to #500 and various mini-series and includes Bruce Wayne's early life, Batman's early career, the death of Robin, Bane crippling Batman and Azrael taking up the cowl. Some of the comic book covers are printed as small illustrations on the card backs. Most of the cards are full bleed comics art, but two sub-sets (Robin and Nemeses) plus the title card are painted, as are the five SpectraEtch "Portraits of the Batman" bonus cards. The SkyDisk Hologram is the only new bonus card technology and it is by far the most significant part of this card series. It has a plain white back similar to the special 3-D holograms in Marvel Universe IV and X-Men II, but it is scarcer and designed to be placed on a flat surface so as to project its image upwards rather than to be viewed straight on. Only 13,333 individually sealed and numbered 20-box cases were produced, which is less than the Marvel Universe and Marvel Masterpiece series from SkyBox, but still a lot of cards!

Set: 100 cards 17.50

SpectraEtch (1:18) "Portraits of the Batman" (all are untitled)
B1 Mark Chiarello 9.00
B2 (BSf) 10.00
B3 (DvD) 10.00
B4 (JBo) 10.00
B5 Phil Winslade 9.00
SD1 Skydisk Hologram (1:240) . . . 50.00
Promos
Promo: Batman & Georgia Dome, Superbowl XXVIII (50,000 made) . 2.00
Promo: Batman & Camden Yards Diamond show #11 (50,000 made) 2.00
Batman Promo (DvD) (Triton #4) . . . 2.00
Pack: 8 cards 1.25

CARD CHECKLIST

1 Saga of the Dark Knight (DvD) 25
Year One (Rich Burchett pencils & inks)
2 The Cave 20
3 The Permanent Nightmare 20
4 Training Abroad 20
5 Shamen .20
6 Crime Alley 20
7 The Omen 20

Batman, Saga of the Dark Knight © DC Comics, Inc.

8 Two Sides of the Same Coin 20
9 Face to Face 20
10 Falsely Accused 20
11 Feline Fatale 20
12 Finding a Friend 20
13 Birth of the Joker 20
14 First Impressions 20
15 Partners in Crime 20
16 Not...strong...enough... 20
17 The Power of Venom 20
18 Withdrawal 20
Robin (paintings)
19 Dick Grayson (DvD) 25
20 Robin Retires (DvD) 25
21 Nightwing (DvD) 25
22 Jason Todd (JBo) 25
23 Out of Line (JBo) 25
24 A Death in the Family (JBo) 25
25 Tim Drake (KB) 25
26 Uneasy Alliance (KB) 25
27 Severed Ties (KB) 25
Dynamic Duo (TG/SHa)
28 A Sacred Trust 20
29 Partners 20
30 Demon's Head 20
31 My Father's Killer 20
32 Equal Justice 20
33 The Cult 20
34 Proving Ground 20
35 Right of Passage 20
36 Seduction of the Gun 20
A Death in the Family (JAp/DG)
37 "That's It!..." 20
38 Freedom of Madness 20
39 The Search 20
40 Missile Deal 20
41 Reunion 20
42 Betrayal 20
43 Mourning Time 20
44 Ultimate Joke 20
45 Two-Minute Warning 20
Nemeses (paintings)
46 The Joker (BSf) 25
47 Catwoman (BSf) 25
48 Two-Face (BSf) 25
49 The Penguin (MMi) 25
50 Ra's Al Ghul (MMi) 25
51 The Scarecrow (MMi) 25
52 The Mudpack (MWg) 25
53 The Riddler & Poison Ivy (MWg) . .25
54 Killer Croc & Scarface (MWg) 25
A Lonely Dying Place (PJ/PrG)
55 Consumed By Guilt 20
56 "Am I Mad?" 20
57 Homecoming 20
58 Confrontation 20
59 Double Jeopardy 20
60 Reunited 20
61 Only a Boy 20
62 Never Again 20
63 Initiation 20
Sword of Azrael (BKi)
64 Inheritance 20
65 Lettah .20
66 Knight of St. Dumas 20
67 Hostage 20
68 Savior .20
69 Trial By Fire 20
Vengeance of Bane (EB/Geraldo Fernandez)
70 Birth 20
71 Transfusion 20
72 Hunt 20
Knightfall (GN/SHa)
73 Arkham Breakout 20
74 One Down... 20
75 Behemoth 20
76 Meet Mr. Zsasz 20
77 Tipping the Scale 20
78 Bloodlust 20
79 Inferno 20
80 The Vixen of Vines 20
81 Clueless 20
82 Fear Equals Rage 20
83 Face Me! 20
84 The Broken Bat 20
85 Accept the Cowl 20
86 Bad Blood 20
87 Anarchy/Law 20
88 Claws for Bane 20
89 The Vision 20
90 King of Gotham 20
Knightquest (JBa/SHa)
91 The Crusade 20
92 Back Off! 20
93 Charades 20
94 Prince of Fools 20
95 Corrosion 20
96 No Deals! 20
97 Off the Deep End 20
98 Dehumanized 20
99 KnightsEnd 20
100 Checklist 20

BATMAN HOLOGRAM

A lot of Batman hats and other products in 1991 or 1992 came with a hologram tag. It said "Batman" in white lettering all over the back and had a small hole at the top for the plastic "string" that attached it to the product and was difficult to break without a knife if you wanted to steal the hologram (but not the hat).

Official Licensed Product tag © 1991, 4" high 3.50

B

Beauty and the Beast © The Walt Disney Company

BEAUTY AND THE BEAST

Pro Set (1992, Animated Movie)

These cards are taken from the Disney movie and follow the story line. The card fronts are full bleed pictures. The backs contain the caption, text and number on a blue background with flowers on the left and a castle on the right. A small detail photo from the front is included in a mirror on the back. The magic mirror cards contain a "scratch and see" picture within a magic mirror design. All of the backs contain the same elegant picture of Beauty and the Beast. Even the wrappers are beautiful, one of the finest designs I've seen.

Set: 75 cards, 10 magic mirror cards, 10 color-in cards . . 15.00

Collector's Album 11.00
Pack: 8 cards, 2 activity 1.00

CARD CHECKLIST

1 Love's Magic Tale 15
2 The Selfish Prince 15
3 A Terrible Spell 15
4 An Enchanted Rose 15
5 A Peculiar Mademoiselle 15
6 Books and Big Dreams 15
7 A Braggart's Boast 15
8 Positively Primeval! 15
9 A Fine Invention 15
10 A Fond Farewell 15
11 Lost in the Woods 15
12 Hunted by Wolves! 15
13 A Narrow Escape! 15
14 An Odd Welcoming Committee . . .15
15 An Angry Host! 15

Beauty and the Beast © The Walt Disney Company

16 Wedding Bells for Belle? .15
17 Gaston Pops the Question .15
18 A Spurned Suitor .15
19 Belle's Dreams .15
20 Belle's Adventure Begins .15
21 Papa, Where Are You? .15
22 There's a Girl in the Castle! .15
23 Belle Finds Her Father .15
24 A Brave Bargain .15
25 Heartbroken Prisoner .15
26 Gaston's Boasts .15
27 A Cry for Help! .15
28 No Help in Sight .15
29 An Evil Plan .15
30 No Date for Dinner .15
31 Etiquette Lessons for the Beast .15
32 A Rough Beginning .15
33 A Hopeless Moment .15
34 A Midnight Snack .15
35 Entertainment a la Carte .15
36 The Show Goes On .15
37 Happy to Serve Again .15
38 The Grand Finale .15
39 A Strange Discovery .15
40 An Angry Meeting .15
41 Danger in the Forest .15
42 A Surprise Rescuer .15
43 A Moment of Trust .15
44 A Vicious Plot .15
45 A Precious Gift .15
46 A Tender Lesson in Manners .15
47 Something Different .15
48 New Feelings .15
49 Quiet, Happy Hours .15
50 A Big Night Ahead .15
51 A "Belle Mademoiselle" .15
52 A Handsome Beast .15
53 An Enchanted Dance .15
54 Song as Old as Rhyme .15
55 Bad News in the Mirror .15
56 A Family Reunion .15
57 A Little Stowaway .15
58 The Villains Strike! .15
59 The Beast is Revealed .15
60 Gaston Incites the Mob .15
61 Gaston's Prisoners .15
62 The Mob Attacks .15
63 Cogsworth in Command .15
64 Hot Water for the Invaders .15
65 Top-Drawer Maneuvers .15
66 A Victory Cheer .15
67 Gaston's Treachery .15
68 Chip Starts Chopping .15
69 A Beloved Face .15
70 End of a Villain .15
71 Words of Love .15
72 The Spell is Broken .15
73 Human Again! .15
74 Another Dance .15
75 And of Course... .15

Magic Mirror Cards

1 Beast .20
2 Belle .20
3 Lumiere .20
4 Cogsworth .20
5 Mrs. Potts .20
6 Chip .20
7 Feather Duster .20
8 Phillipe .20
9 Maurice .20
10 Gaston .20

Color-In Cards

1 Beast/Belle & Beast .10
2 Mrs. Potts/Chip .10
3 Lumiere/Feather Duster .10
4 Belle/Cogsworth .10
5 Belle/Beast .10
6 Belle/Lumiere .10
7 Footstool/Mrs.Potts & Chip .10
8 Cogsworth/Lumiere & Feather Duster .10
9 Beast/Belle & Beast .10
10 Belle/Armoire .10

BEAVIS & BUTT-HEAD
MTV (1994)

Promo clear cel (TV promo, not related to the Fleer set) .. 2.00

BEAVIS & BUTT-HEAD
Fleer (1994)

As the pack says, "Beavis and Butt-Head are not role models. They're not even human. They're cartoons. Some of the things they do would cause a real person to get hurt, expelled, arrested, possibly deported. To put it another way: Don't try this at home."

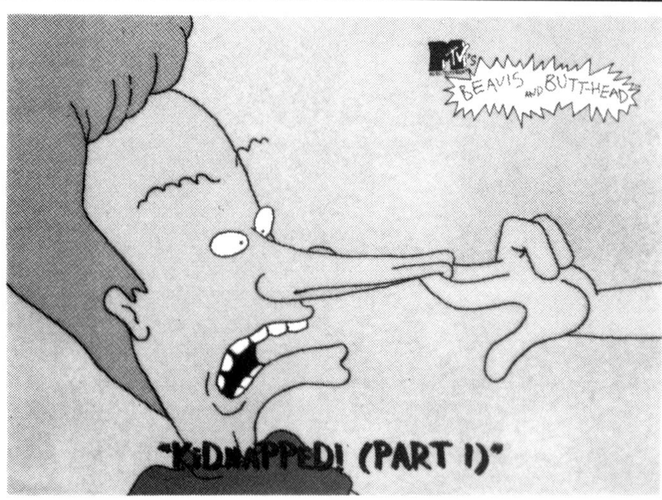

Beavis & Butt-Head © MTV Networks, a division of Viacom International Inc.

Well, a lot of collectors ignored this warning, bought the cards and tried them out at home. They liked the full bleed art, foil stamping and irreverant humor. The cards are numbered so that every card has "69" in the number. If you don't understand why this is supposed to be funny ask someone....or better yet, forget about it. When we got a box of the cards at the office, everyone tried the scratch and sniff cards to verify that they really did stink. All you have to do to prove that your intelligence exceeds ours is to take our word for it, but you won't because if you buy the cards your intelligence (and taste) are already questionable (like ours). The nine card promo sheet contains some "cards" that don't appear in the final set.

Set: 150 cards 20.00

Scratch & Sniff cards (1:4)

0690 "Buff 'N' Stuff" 3.00
0691 "Citizen Butt-Head (Part-1)" 3.00
0692 "Beavis and Butt-Head Clean House" 3.00
0693 Our Offices 3.00
0694 "Drive In II" 3.00
0695 Born to Hog Wild 3.00
0696 Chicks in Glasses are Cool 3.00
0697 Chemicals are Cool 3.00
0698 3.00
0699 "Friday Night" 3.00
Nine card promo sheet (in Advance Comics & Heroes World) 2.00
Pack: 10 cards 1.25

CARD CHEICKLIST

0069 "Beavis and Butt-Head Clean House" .20
0169 "Scared Straight" .20
0269 "Citizen Butt-Head (Part I)" .20
0369 "Tornado" .20
0469 "Naked Colony" .20
0569 "Kidnapped! (Part I)" .20
0669 "Kidnapped! (Part II)" .20
0769 "Citizen Butt-Head (Part II)" .20
0869 "Lotto" .20
0969 "Politically Correct" .20
1069 "Beavis and Butt-Head Meet God (Part I)" .20
1169 "Buff 'n' Stuff" .20
1269 "Eating Contest" .20
1369 "Drive-In" or "Beware of the Butt" .20
1469 "Incognito" .20
1569 "Beavis and Butt-Head Try Yogurt" .20
1669 "Friday Night" .20
1769 "Good Credit" .20
1869 "Home Improvement (Part I)" .20
1969 "Heroes" .20
2069 "Go Petitioning" .20
2169 "No Laughing (Part I)" .20
2269 "No Laughing (Part II)" .20
2369 "Balloon" .20
2469 "Customers Suck" .20
2569 "Couch Fishing" .20
2669 "Sugar Baby" .20
2769 "Way Down Mexico Way (Part I)" .20
2869 "Door to Door" .20
2969 "Way Down Mexico Way (Part II)" .20
3069 "Sideshow" .20
3169 "Be All You Can Be" .20
3269 "Burger World" .20
3369 "Stew" .20
3469 "Give Blood" .20
3569 "Science" .20
3669 "Drive In II" .20

Beavis & Butt-Head © MTV Networks, a division of Viacom International Inc.

3769 "Home Improvement II" 20
3869 "Haiku" 20
3969 "Bedpans and Broomsticks" . . .20
4069 "Sick" .20
4169 "The Trial" 20
4269 "Difficulty Urinating" 20
4369 "Ball Breakers" 20
4469 "Sperm Bank" 20
4569 "Canoe" 20
4669 "Closing Time" 20
4769 "Plate Frisbee" 20
4869 "Young, Gifted and Crude" 20
4969 "The Crush" 20
5069 "True Crime" 20
5169 "Foreign Exchange" 20
5269 "Wall of Youth" 20
5369 "Cow Tipping" 20
5469 "Most Wanted" 20
5569 "Comedians" 20

Beavis & Butt-Head © MTV Networks, a division of Viacom International Inc.

5669 "Beavis and Butt-Head Meet God (Part II)" 20
5769 "Washin' the Dog" 20
5869 "Badass Dudes" 20
5969 "Sporting Goods" 20
6069 "Car Wash" 20
6169 "The Butt-Head Experience" . . .20
6269 Peace and Love Suck 20
6369 Little Red Robin Hood 20
6469 Chicks in Glasses are Cool . . .20
6569 Love My Timber 20
6669 Rambutt 20
6769 Like, History Dudes 20
6869 Operation Desert Suck 20
6969 Prehistoric Times B.C. 20
7069 Yamahas 20
7169 Rushins 20
7269 Sometimes Art Doesn't Suck . . .20
7369 Trailer Ladies 20
7469 People Were Stupid In Olden Times 20
7569 Masturmony 20
7669 The Wizard of Ozzy 20
7769 Punks 20
7869 Andudes 20
7969 Farm Dudes 20
8069 Home Sweet Cave 20
8169 Fairos, huh huh 20
8269 Lolita and Tanqueray 20
8369 Stewart Stevenson 20
8469 Jail Guy 20
8569 President Uh, Clint 20
8669 Principal McVicker 20
8769 Mr. Buzzcut 20
8869 Todd .20
8969 Tanya the Gifted Teacher 20
9069 Mr. Van Driessen 20
9169 Cashier 20
9269 Stewart's Dad 20
9369 Daria Morgendorffer 20
9469 Gina .20
9569 Tom Anderson 20
9669 Stewart's Mom 20
9769 Todd's Gang 20
9869 The Grizzly 20

Beavis & Butt-Head © MTV Networks, a division of Viacom International Inc.

9969 Gorilla Dude 20
6901 Mistress Cora Anthrax 20
6902 Freak Chicks Rule 20
6903 This Rocks! 20
6904 Frogs get me, like, hot 20
6905 Senior Cinamons 20
6906 The End is Near, Beavis 20
6907 I'm, uh, Butt-Head 20
6908 I'm, like, Beavis 20
6909 Welcome to the Jungle 20
6910 Air Guitar 20
6911 Frog Baseball 20
6912 Thinking Doesn't Suck 20
6913 Male Man 20
6914 Our Offices 20
6915 Christmas 20
6916 Crapid 20
6917 Lepercans 20
6918 Jackyl Anthems 20
6919 Spanking the Turkey, heh heh .20
6920 Birthday 20
6921 Mary had a DAH DANT-DAH! . .20
6922 Pest Wishes 20
6923 Infence 20
6924 Beavis the Motorhead 20
6925 Chemicals are Cool 20
6926 Dolls Suck 20
6927 "You gonna buy that?" 20
6928 "Let's all get naked" 20
6929 "The 70s sucked" 20
6930 "At the Turbo Mall" 20
6931 "Welcome to prison" 20
6932 I Hate, Like, Homework or Something 20
6933 Beavis's Butt 20
6934 Chicks Like Us 20
6935 Born to Hog Wild 20
6936 Snot Bad 20
6937 Beavis Pumps Himself, huh huh .20
6938 Secret Cervix 20
6939 Gropies 20
6940 Hellocinations 20
6941 French Flies 20
6942 Mouse Burger 20
6943 Raw Incondiments 20
6944 Men at Work or Something 20
6945 Tattoos Rule 20
6946 Life Sucks 20
6947 Have a Nice Day 20
6948 Biker .20
6949 Shark 20
6950 Chick List 20

Bettlejuice © The Geffen Film Company

BEETLEJUICE

Dart (1990)

These cards are taken from the TV animated series, not the movie. The cards have color pictures inside a green border. Captions are on the front, inside a pink strip. The card backs repeat the caption and contain text and the card number. Stickers are not captioned, and are on white stock, with blank backs.

Set: 100 cards/20 stickers 20.00
Limited Collectors edition 100 cards/22 stickers 25.00
Pack: 5 cards, 1 sticker 0.80

CARD CHECKLIST

1 Logo/Header card 15
2 Lydia 15
3 Delia 15
4 Charles .15
5 Prudence ("Prune") 15
6 Bertha ("Burp") Goes Camping . . .15
7 Jacques Lalean 15
8 Ginger, Toe Tapping Fool 15
9 The Monster Across the Street . . .15
10 Claire Brewster, "Valley Girl" 15
11 Home Sweet Home 15
12 Panic at the Shocking Mall 15
13 I Get a Kick Out of Life! 15
14 Snack Time! 15
15 Now That's One Sharp Kid! 15
16 Gross-Out Meter Record! 15
17 Babysitting! 15
18 Starring Barf Bendman! 15
19 Lydia's Haunted House 15
20 Where'd They Go? 15
21 ...I'm an Old Cow Hand... 15
22 Bully's Back in Town! 15
23 "Where's the Sheriff?" 15
24 Chickenjuice on Boot Hill 15
25 I'm Really into Art! 15
26 MMMMM..., Lunch! 15
27 Double Deluxe Lung Tosser 15
28 "You Look Bad, Beetlejuice" 15
29 Double Trouble 15
30 Netherworld Beauties! 15
31 Slimy Beauty 15
32 "Shrimp Shells & Chicken Bones Please" 15
33 Who Invited You?! 15
34 The Best Part! 15
35 Beetlejuice Strikes Again 15
36 Buzzface 15
37 Dancing Fools 15
38 Where've I Smelt That?! 15
39 Door to the Netherworld 15
40 I Love a Buffet! 15
41 Spooky Sunset 15
42 Dead Letter Box 15
43 Nice Smile! 15
44 Beetlejuice's Ballad 15
45 Crab Grass Attack 15
46 Back Pack Surprise 15
47 Hedgehogs! 15
48 Nice Muscles! 15
49 Creepy Camping 15
50 Timber Wolves 15
51 Terrifying Sandworm 15
52 Bertha to the Rescue 15
53 The Rot Tub 15
54 Scummin' Through! 15
55 Goin' to Pieces! 15
56 Coffin Break 15
57 Scared My Pants Off! 15
58 The Thing in the Tub 15
59 Howdy Clare! 15

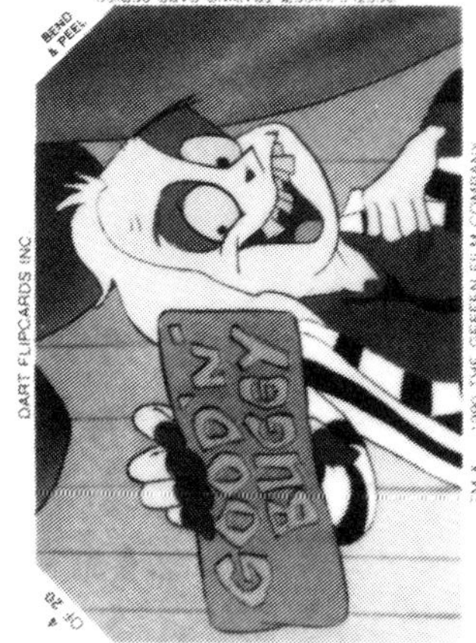

Bettlejuice sticker © The Geffen Film Company

60 Skeleton of the Year 15
61 Morning Breath 15
62 An Upset Stomach 15
63 Breakfast of Champion Ghouls . . .15
64 Howdy! 15
65 Need a Hand?! 15

66 Neighborhood Surprise 15
67 Toe Truck 15
68 Bug Attack 15
69 Netherworld Neighbors 15
70 It's Showtime! 15
71 Spare a Quarter? 15
72 Snakes Alive! 15
73 What's Cookin?! 15
74 Waiting Room Weirdos 15
75 Wake Up, Stinky 15
76 Pea Brain 15
77 Thanks for the Warning! 15
78 No Problem! 15
79 I Screamed My Head Off! 15
80 I'm a Monkey's Uncle! 15
81 All Snaked Up! 15
82 Twist My Arm, Lydia! 15
83 Armpit Musician 15
84 Netherworld Rock Stars 15
85 Egomaniac 15
86 Party Animal Arrives 15
87 Party Bats! 15
88 Punk-in-Pie 15
89 How 'bout that Punch?! 15
90 Tall, Dark & Hairy 15
91 Make My Day! 15
92 Snake! .15
93 Watch those Extra Toppings! 15
94 Loosen Up! 15
95 Cousin B.J. 15
96 B.J.'s Candy Bar 15
97 Foot Doctor 15
98 Garbageman 15
99 Proud Parents 15
100 Fill in the Skull checklist 15

Glow-in-the-Dark Stickers
1 through 22, untitled, each 20

The Best of Byrne © Marvel Entertainment Group, Inc.

THE BEST OF BYRNE
[JOHN BYRNE ART]
Comic Images (1989)

The cards have portrait style pictures on the front, inside a white border and black line frame, with the card title and number a the bottom. The card backs form a twenty card black and white puzzle of the Fantastic Four, and a twenty-five card black and white portrait puzzle of the X-Men. The cards came in clear cello packs, with a header card which contains the name of the series.

Set: 45 cards + header card 15.00
Box: 48 packs
Pack: 5 cards + header 1.50

CARD CHECKLIST

Header-Title card 50
1 Checklist .40
2 Captain America 40
3 Galactus 40
4 Guardian 40
5 Bruce Banner 40
6 Thing 40
7 Modok 40
8 I'm Home 40
9 Prince Namor 40
10 Lover's Spat 40
11 Baron Blood 40
12 Daredevil 40
13 Man-Thing 40
14 Lilandra 40
15 Sue Richards 40
16 Annihilus 40
17 Dazzler 40
18 The Watcher 40
19 Grey Gargoyle 40
20 Doc Samson 40
21 Wild Things 40
22 Union Jack 40
23 Doctor Doom 40
24 Spidey .40
25 Hulk 40
26 Doomed Love 40
27 Alpha Flight 40
28 Wolverine 40
29 Cyclops 40
30 Taking Flight 40
31 Beast .40
32 Living Monolith 40
33 Sauron 40
34 Beetle .40
35 Fantastic Four 40
36 Magneto 40
37 Take That 40
38 Human Torch 40
39 Colossus 40
40 Ka-Zar .40
41 Back from the War 40
42 Hitched 40
43 Hellfire Club 40
44 Snikt 40
45 Phoenix 40

BLACKBALL
SkyBox (1994)

These are promos for a card set which was not yet available at press time. Card art will be by Simon Bisley, Keith Giffen and Kevin O'Neill. The cards have an irregular brown border, with promo information on the back although they are labeled "prototype." The last two promos were distributed at comic shows and they are scarce as only 5,000 of each was made.

"Prototype" i.e. Promos
P0 Preying Mantis (from Hero #11)(SBs) 50
P00 Trenchermobile (KG) (from Cards Illustrated #5) 50
P01 Trencher (KG) 2.00
P02 John Pain (KON) 2.00

See also: TRENCHER

Blackball © Blackball

Black Web © Inks Comics

BLACK WEB
Inks Comics (1993)

These cards have full bleed art and say "Inks" on the front. The backs are white with black lettering. They were issued to promote Black Web comics and were give out at various comic shows. One variant batch is marked "West Coast National II."

Set: 5 Promo Cards 5.00
Set: for West Coast National II 6.00
1 Black Web 1.00
2 Widower 1.00
3 Black Web 1.00
4 Stinger 1.00
5 Black Web 1.00

Blood & Roses © Bob Hickey

Bloodshot © Voyager Communications, Inc.

BLOOD & ROSES
Arena Magazine (1993)/Sky Comics (1994)

The cards have a full bleed front and a white back with black text. The comic book promo card has a frame line. A set of 24 cards was scheduled for Spring 1994, but was not available at press time.

Comic promo card (Bobby Hickey) . . 2.00

Trading card set promo (Brad Gorby & Bob Hickey art) 2.00

BLOODSHOT

Voyager Communications/Valiant (1992)

The card has a chromium front and white back with text. It's a highly collectible promo for the comic book series.

Chromium cover replica of Bloodshot #1 art (BWS) 25.00

Bone © Jeff Smith

BONE

Comic Images (1994)

Fone Bone and his cousins Smiley and Phoney get out of Boneville (in a hurry) and manage to stay one step ahead of the Rat Creatures and the Hooded One in this set. The cards just became available at press time, so our prices are preliminary. Bone is drawn by Jeff Smith and has a lot of fans so we expect the set to be very popular. The cards have a full bleed front and a small inset drawing on the back along with the title and story information. The promo card from Comic Images looks the same, with promo information in black and white on the back. It looks like their other regular promo cards. However, the promo cards from Cards Illustrated are titled on the front and have a colorful back and don't look like other cards from Comic Images, or the "Bone" promo card. You had to buy three copies of the magazine to get nine of the cards. There are supposed to be 10 cards and we haven't actually seen #6, but it's on the checklist. We think it exists and that you had to buy a fourth copy of the same issue to find it.

Set: 90 cards 12.50

Chromium cards, 6 diff., untitled (3:box) each 7.50
Cartoon Covers subset cards (3:case), Three cards, each 15.00
Original Sketch cards (100 made) NYD
Medallion card (2:case) 20.00
Promo card (Jeff Smith) 1.00
Four card promo sheet (D-15 to D-18) (from *Previews* magazine) 1.50
Set: 7 cards + 3 standups from (*Cards Illustrated*) 5.00
1 Lucius 50
2 The Red Dragon 50
3 Thorn 50
4 Rat Creatures 50
5 Gran'Ma Ben 50
6 The Hooded One 50
7 Bone Checklist 50
C-1 Fone Cutout 50
C-2 Phoney Cutout 50
C-3 Siley Cutout 50

Pack: 10 cards 1.00

CARD CHECKLIST

1 Run Out Of Boneville 10
2 Fone Bone 10
3 Phoney Bone 10
4 Smiley Bone 10
5 Locusts! 10
6 Falling... 10
7 Separated! 10
8 Is It The One We Seek? 10
9 Who You Callin' Boy? 10
10 On The Dragon's Stair 10
11 The Valley 10
12 The Bug Brothers 10
13 Stupid, Stupid Rat Creatures 10
14 Winter Comes Quick In These Parts! 10
15 Miz 'Possum And Her Family 10
16 Adventures In Babysitting 10
17 They're Baaack! 10
18 The Chase 10
19 Foom! .10
20 Down At The Hot Springs 10
21 Thorn 10
22 Boneville? What's Boneville? 10
23 In Gran'ma Ben's House 10
24 Moby Dick 10
25 I'll Say It Again...Slower 10
26 Can You Milk 'Em? 10
27 Off To A Good Start 10
28 The Gilchy Feelin' 10
29 Phoney Bone Slips Off 10
30 Kingdok 10
31 The High Council 10
32 The Hooded One 10
33 Fone Bone Must Die 10
34 Thorn's Dream 10
35 Gran'ma Has A Plan 10
36 Okay, Kids...Run! 10
37 Fleeing In The Dark 10
38 Surrounded! 10
39 A Stranger In Town 10
40 Reunited 10
41 Lucius Down 10
42 The Rat Creatures Close In 10
43 Saved! .10
44 He Did It! 10
45 A Wild Ride 10
46 Disaster 10
47 Gran'ma Ben Is Alive! 10
48 An Uncomfortable Meeting 10
49 The Dragon Takes His Leave 10
50 Off To The Races! 10
51 Unfinished Business 10
52 Danger In The Trees 10
53 Family Reunion 10
54 The Spring Fair 10
55 The Honey Seller 10
56 Honey .10
57 Don't Look Down! 10
58 It Only Takes One! 10
59 Victory! 10
60 Phoney's Bettin' Booth 10
61 A Hot Tip 10
62 Cousin Against Cousin 10
63 The Mystery Cow 10
64 Thorn's Secret 10
65 Can't Sleep 10
66 High Noon 10
67 Dumped! 10
68 Kidnapped! 10
69 Mad Cow 10
70 Smiley Goes Wild 10
71 The Great Cow Race 10
72 Remember The Plan! 10
73 The Set Up 10
74 Backfire! 10
75 Change Of Plans 10

Bone (Cards Illustrated promo) © Jeff Smith

76 They're Off! 10
77 The Rat Race 10
78 Oh, My! 10
79 Gran'ma Ben Wants A Look 10
80 Out Of The Frying Pan 10
81 A Late Entry 10
82 Uh, Oh! 10
83 AAAH! .10
84 The Crowd Panics! 10
85 In The Straight-A-Way 10
86 Gran'ma Takes The Lead! 10
87 And The Winner Is... 10
88 Hot Diggity Dog! 10
89 The Gang's All Here! 10
90 Checklist 10

C

Cain © & ™ David Quinn & Hannibal King; Reprinted with permission of the publisher, Harris Comics (Card design by Craig Winkelman)

CAIN

Harris Comics (1993)

(Hanibal King and Matt Banning art)

The card from Wizard *magazine had a cut-out, which you placed over the card from Cain comic #1 to read clues and form an image.*

1 Decriptor Card (in Wizard) 1.00
2 Frenzy (in Cain #1) 1.00

Captain America [50th Anniversary] © Marvel Entertainment Group, Inc.

CAPTAIN AMERICA [50TH ANNIVERSARY]

Comic Images (1990)

The fronts of the first ten cards reprint the covers of the first ten Captain America comics and the remaining cards have art from the listed titles. The cards are not actually numbered, although they appear to be because they contain the **comic book** *number. This is misleading as a buyer could easily think that there are several hundred cards in the set. The card numbers only appear on the checklist. The backs of cards #1 to #25 form a black and white puzzle picture of the cover of* Captain America Annual #8 *and the backs of cards #26 to #45 form another black and white puzzle picture of the Captain.*

Set: 45 cards 12.00

Pack: (clear cello package) 1.00

CARD CHECKLIST

1 Captain America #1 20
2 Captain America #2 20
3 Captain America #3 20
4 Captain America #4 20
5 Captain America #5 20
6 Captain America #6 20
7 Captain America #7 20
8 Captain America #8 20
9 Captain America #9 20
10 Captain America #10 20
11 Tales of Suspense #59 20
12 Tales of Suspense #80 20
13 Tales of Suspense #98 20
14 Captain America #100 20
15 Captain America #103 20
16 Captain America #110 20
17 Captain America #111 20
18 Captain America #132 20
19 Captain America #176 20
20 Cap.America King Size Annual #1 .20
21 Captain America #182 20
22 Captain America #200 20
23 Captain America #212 20
24 Captain America #224 20
25 Captain America #241 20

Puzzle two, cards 26 through 45

26 Captain America #242 20
27 Captain America #248 20
28 Captain America #254 20
29 Captain America #255 20
30 Captain America #261 20
31 Captain America #266 20
32 Captain America #273 20
33 Captain America #275 20
34 Captain America #279 20
35 Captain America Annual #8 20
36 Captain America #280 20
37 Captain America #281 20
38 Captain America #284 20
39 Captain America #286 20
40 Captain America #287 20
41 Captain America #300 20
42 Captain America #321 20
43 Captain America #333 20
44 Captain America #337 20
45 Checklist 20

CAPTAIN CANUCK

Semple Comics (1993)

The card has a red border in front and a blue-green border in back. It was issued to promote Captain Canuck Reborn comics.

Captain Canuck promo card (Richard Comely?) 2.50

CHROMIUM COLLECTOR

We just call this Mr. Chromium because he looks like a superhero, is bursting through a wall or something and has a big "C" on his chest. Actually the card seems to be promoting the use of chromium in comic covers and cards.

(Mr. Chromium) "Chromium Collector promo card" 5.00

Captain Canuck © Semple Comics

Mr. Chromium © Maus

CHROMIUM MAN, THE

Triumphant Comics (1993)

Comic book promo with a black and white back.

Promo (AKu)(Advance Comics #56) 1.00

CLANDESTINE

Marvel UK (1994)

Full bleed front. Black back with text and faces.

The ClanDestine promo (AD) 1.00

Colossal Conflicts © Marvel Entertainment Group, Inc.

COLOSSAL CONFLICTS

{Marvel Cards, Series 2}

Comic Images (1987)

The card fronts portray a famous battle between the named Marvel villain and a famous hero. The backs repeat the title, give the card number and contain text about the character and the battle. The words "Series 2" on the back refer to Comic Images' Marvel cards, not to a prior issue of Colossal Conflicts. Series 1 was Marvel Universe, Comic Images 1987 (not the Impel cards). This set, and others from the late 1980s by Comic Images, had many of the elements that typify the current style of comics trading cards and thus they are an important precursor of today's cards. Also, this was the first appearance on a card, for many of the villains portrayed in this set. In addition, the set is quite scarce. We recommend that you buy this set if you can find it.

Set: 90 cards 24.00
Pack: 4 cards + sticker 2.00

CARD CHECKLIST

1 Abomination 25
2 Absorbing Man 25
3 Annihilus .25
4 Arcade 25
5 Attuma 25
6 Baron Blood 25
7 Baron Zemo 25
8 Beyonder 25
9 Blob 25
10 Brotherhood of Evil Mutants 25
11 Bullseye 25
12 Cobra 25
13 Collector 25
14 Constrictor 25
15 Deathlok 25
16 Death-Stalker 25
17 Destroyer 25
18 Doc Samson 25
19 Doctor Doom 25
20 Doctor Octopus 25
21 Dormammu 25
22 Dragon Man 25
23 Electro .25
24 Freedom Force 25
25 Green Goblin 25
26 Grey Gargoyle 25
27 Grim Reaper 25
28 Hela 25
29 Hellfire Club 25
30 Hellions .25
31 Hitler 25
32 Hobgoblin 25
33 Hydra 25
34 Juggernaut 25
35 Kang 25
36 Kingpin .25
37 Klaw 25
38 Kraven (the Hunter) 25
39 Kurse 25
40 The Leader 25
41 Lizard 25
42 Loki 25
43 Magneto 25
44 Magus 25
45 Man-Ape 25
46 Mandarin 25
47 Mandrill .25
48 Marauders 25
49 Maximus 25
50 Mephisto 25
51 Modok 25
52 Mojo 25
53 Mole Man 25
54 Living Monolith 25
55 Morgan Le Fey 25
56 Mr. Hyde 25
57 Mysterio 25
58 Nightmare 25
59 Nitro 25
60 Owl 25
61 Paladin .25
62 Phoenix .25
63 Pluto 25
64 Puppet Master 25
65 Red Skull 25
66 Rhino 25
67 Ringmaster 25
68 Sandman 25
69 Scarecrow 25
70 Scorpion 25
71 Sentinels 25
72 Serpent .25
73 Shuma-Gorath 25
74 Silver Samurai 25
75 Stilt-Man 25
76 Stranger 25
77 Surtur 25
78 Taskmaster 25
79 Thanos .25
80 Titanic Three 25
81 Ultron 25
82 Umar 25
83 Unicorn .25
84 Viper 25
85 Vulture .25
86 Wolverine 25
87 Wrecking Crew 25
88 Yellow Claw 25
89 Zzzax 25
90 Checklist 25

Comic Ball (I) © Upper Deck/Warner Bros. Inc.

[LOONEY TUNES] COMIC BALL

Upper Deck (1990)

These are high quality cards featuring Bugs Bunny, the Road Runner and Wile E. Coyote and the other Looney Tunes characters playing baseball, all with ***Chuck Jones*** *art. It proved to be a popular series and three sequels followed. The cards are numbered front and back in groups of nine in the following pattern:*

F - B	*F - B*	*F - B*
1 (16)	*2 (17)*	*3 (18)*
4 (13)	*5 (14)*	*6 (15)*
7 (10)	*8 (11)*	*9 (12)*

This allows them to be placed in albums to form a story. However it does make the numbering complex, and confusing, since there are twice as many numbers as cards. In addition, some stories start on the back! The holograms have plain white backs and are not numbered or captioned. The first six and #8 (as listed below) are center close-ups of the cards with the same number. You could also buy 99 of the cards in each of three blister packs, with albums to hold them, and three of the holograms. This was the best way to get the set, as the albums were reasonably priced and you did not receive extra, unwanted cards. The cards have no titles so we have listed the stories, but not the individual cards.

Set: 297 cards 25.00

Holograms
(H1) Bugs Bunny 2.50
(H2) Daffy Duck 2.50
(H3) Road Runner 2.50
(H4) Wile E. Coyote 2.50
(H5) Sylvester 2.50
(H6) Porky Pig 2.50
(H7) Speedy Gonzalez (sliding) 2.50
(H8) Yosemite Sam 2.50
(H9) Elmer Fudd (catching) 2.50
Promo Set: 9 cards + 1 hologram . . 8.00
Pack: 12 cards 1.00
Yellow Album + 1st 99 cards & 3 holograms 12.00

CARD CHECKLIST

Looney Tunes All Stars
1 Bugs Bunny 25
2 Daffy Duck 25
3 Road Runner 25
4 Wile E. Coyote 25
5 Sylvester 25
6 Porky Pig 25
7 Tweety .25
8 Yosemite Sam 25
9 Tasmanian Devil 25
Remaining 288 common cards, each .10

They form the following storylines:
Porky Pig & Charlie Dog (#19 thru #99)
Magnetic Field . . . . . . (#100 thru #153)
Swide, Swide . . . . (#154 thru #166)
Acme Battle . . . . (#167 thru #197)
Checklist . . . . (#198)
Red Album + 2nd 99 cards & 3 holograms 12.00
Father Knows Worst . . . . . (#199-#234)
Evening Ralph,Evening Sam(#235-#259)
Hold the Mustard . . . . (#260-#278)
Trick Baseballs . . . . (#279-#305)
Calamity Jane . . . . (#306-#333)
Rabbit Season . . . . (#334-#357)
Mighty Angelo . . . . (#358-#395)
Checklist . . . . (#396)
Green Album + 3rd 99 cards & 3 holograms 12.00
Hopalong Casualty . . . . . . (#397-#424)
Which Pitch is Witch . . . . . (#425-#464)
The Diamond and the Gruff (#465-#494)
Squeeze Play . . . . (#495-#545)
Baseball According to Daffy(#546-#565)
Curve Ball . . . . (#566-#593)
Checklist . . . . (#594)

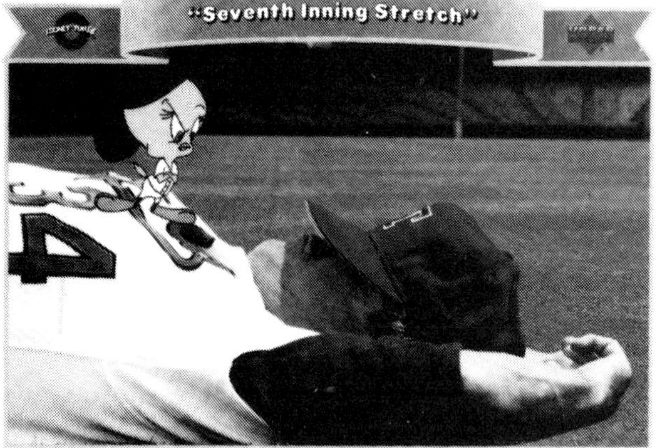

Comic Ball II © Upper Deck/Warner Bros. Inc.

COMIC BALL II

Upper Deck (1991, Comic + Photo)

(Art by the Dover Boys)

The second version of Comic Ball features baseball players and your favorite Looney Tunes characters. The story lines mostly involve the comic characters, with players appearing on selected cards. One reason for this was that Upper Deck used existing photos and drew the stories around the players, which limited the possibilities. Each story starts off with a card containing everybody, real or comic, and all these cards have the same illustration, only the story title differs. The backs of the cards contain the card number and form 3 x 3 puzzle pictures. Fortunately the cards only have one number each, unlike the numbering system of series one (which Upper Deck admitted was a mistake). The holograms have a plain white paper back and are not numbered or captioned. The images are drawn from the seventh inning stretch cards, as indicated below. Two albums were also sold, each designed to hold 99 of the cards.

Set: 198 cards 18.00

Holograms (1:9)
Set: 9 holograms 35.00
Reggie & Taz (#93) 4.50
Reggie & Speedy (#96) 4.50
Nolan & Sylvester (#97) 4.50
Nolan, Reggie, Wile E. Coyote & Road Runner (#98) 4.50
Reggie & Daffy 4.50
(H6) 4.50
(H7) 4.50
(H8) 4.50
(H9) 4.50
Promo cards: 4 diff., for "The National" 7/15/91, each 1.50
Album #1 . . . . . 4.00
Album #2 . . . . . 4.00
Pack: 1.25
Common cards, no player, each 10

SET 1 CHECKLIST

Favorite Interplanetary Pastime
Starring Marvin & Daffy (#1 to #18)
4 w/Nolan Ryan 25
Road Games (#19 to #36)
Starring Wile E. Coyote
36 w/Nolan Ryan 25
Couch Potato Baseball (#37 to #54)
Starring Elmer Fudd & Bugs Bunny
44 w/Nolan Ryan 25
Monster Flyball (#55 to #72)
Starring Bugs Bunny & Clyde
65 & 67 w/Reggie Jackson 25
Batting Twoubles (#73 to #90)
Starring Sylvester & Tweety
74, 79, 85 & 90 w/Reggie Jackson . .25

Seventh Inning Stretch
91 w/Nolan Ryan 30
92 w/Reggie Jackson 30
93 w/Reggie Jackson 30
94 w/Nolan Ryan 30
95 w/Nolan Ryan 30
96 w/Reggie Jackson 30
97 w/Nolan Ryan 30
98 w/Ryan & Jackson 30
99 Checklist 10

SET 2 CHECKLIST

Burger Ball (#100 to #117)
Starring Bugs & Yosemite Sam
109 & 117 w/Reggie Jackson 25
Chicken Wing Ding (#118 to #135)
Starring Foghorn Leghorn & Son
Patch of Greens (#136 to #153)
Starring Bugs & Yosemite Sam
149 & 150 w/Nolan Ryan 25
Baseball Appreciation (#154 to #171)
Starring Tweety & Sylvester
Get Your Souvenirs (#172 to #188)
Starring Elmer Fudd & Daffy
188 w/Reggie Jackson 25
Seventh Inning Stretch
190 w/Nolan Ryan 30
191 w/Reggie Jackson 30
192 w/Nolan Ryan 30
193 w/Reggie Jackson 30
194 w/Nolan Ryan 30
195 w/Reggie Jackson 30
196 w/Reggie Jackson 30
197 w/Reggie Jackson 30
198 Checklist 10

Comic Ball 3 © Upper Deck/Warner Bros. Inc.

LOONEY TUNES COMIC BALL 3

Upper Deck (1992, Comic + Photo)

Starring: Ken Griffey, Sr., Ken Griffey, Jr., & Jim Abbott

This set is a lot like the previous version. The baseball players interact more with the cartoon characters, and are more a part of the story lines. The first card in each story contains small pictures of each of the three ball players, and each of these cards has the same front, except for the story title. The backs of the story cards form 3 x 3 card super-panel backgrounds with text and questions. The holograms are drawn from the Seventh Inning Stretch cards, as indicated. Eleven-page albums to hold the cards were again produced.

Set: 198 cards 16.50

Holograms
Abbott & Taz (#97) 3.50
Griffey & Bear (#96) 3.50
Griffey & Bugs (#91) 3.50
Abbott & Tweety (#94) 3.50
(H5) 3.50
(H6) 3.50
(H7) 3.50
(H8) 3.50
(H9) 3.50
Set: 9 Holograms 25.00
Collector's Album #1 . . . . . 4.00
Collector's Album #2 . . . . . 4.00
Pack: 12 cards 1.25
Common cards, no player, each 10

SERIES 1 CHECKLIST

Batting Odor (#1 to #18)
6, 9, 11 & 16 w/Ken Griffey Jr. 20
Mechanical Mayhem (#19 to #36)
22, 23, 32, 34 & 35 w/Jim Abbott 20
Batty Practice (#37 to #54)
43, 44, 46 & 53 w/Jim Abbott 20
49 thru 52 w/Ken Griffey Jr. 20
To Teach His Own (#55 to #72)
58,59,60,62,65,67 & 72 w/Jim Abbott .20
Pacific Northwest Heights (#73 to #90)
76 w/Ken Griffey Sr. & Jr. 20
88 thru 90 w/Ken Griffey Jr. 20
Seventh Inning Stretch
91 w/Ken Griffey Jr. 25
92 w/Ken Griffey Jr. 25
93 w/Ken Griffey Jr. 25
94 w/Jim Abbott 25
95 w/Jim Abbott 25
96 w/Ken Griffey 25
97 w/Jim Abbott 25
98 w/Chuck Jones 35
99 Checklist 10

Set 2
Eye on Ball (#100 to #117)
107,108,110,111,113 & 116 w/Jim Abbott 20
Big Game Break Down (#118 to #135)
126 w/Jim Abbott, Ken Griffey Sr&Jr .20
127, 131 & 134 w/Jim Abbott & Ken Griffey Jr. 20
129 w/Jim Abbott 20
The Winning Scheme (#136 to #153)
137, 139, 148 & 153 w/Ken Griffey Sr. .20
Every Duck Has His Day (#154 to #171)
155, 156, 166, 167, 168 & 171 w/Jim Abbott 20
Base in the Hole (#172 to #189)
174, 175, 184, 186 & 189 w/Ken Griffey Sr. 20
Seventh Inning Stretch
190 w/Ken Griffey Jr. 25
191 w/Jim Abbott 25
192 w/Ken Griffey Jr. 25
193 w/Jim Abbott 25
194 w/Ken Griffey Jr. 25
195 w/Jim Abbott 25
196 w/Ken Griffey Jr. 25
197 w/Ken Griffey Jr. 25
198 Checklist 10

Comic Ball 4 © Upper Deck/Warner Bros. Inc.

LOONEY TUNES COMIC BALL 4

Upper Deck (1992)

Starring: Dan Marino, Lawrence Taylor, Jerry Rice & Thurman Thomas

If you find a winning formula, keep using it. This time it's football! The card fronts picture the players, both real and comic in various football situations. The backs of most cards form 3 x 3 super panel background paintings, with text on top. The holograms

THE EARLY YEARS (1940–86)

Superman, Gum Inc. (1940) © DC Comics Inc.

Superman, Topps (1966) © DC Comics Inc.

Batman, Topps Series #1 (1966) © DC Comics Inc.

Batman, Topps Series #2 (1966) © DC Comics Inc.

Batman, Topps Series #3 (1966) © DC Comics Inc.

Batman (Bat Laffs), Topps (1966) © DC Comics Inc.

Marvel Superheroes, Donruss (1966) © Marvel Entertainment Group

Super Hero Stickers, Philadelphia Gum (1967) © Marvel Entertainment Group

Comic Cover Stickers, Topps (1970) © DC Comics Inc.

DC/National Periodical/Warner Bros, Wonder Bread/Hostess (1974) © DC Comics Inc.

Comic Book Heroes, Topps (1975) © Marvel Entertainment Group

Marvel Super Heroes Stickers, Topps (1976) © Marvel Entertainment Group

DC Super Heroes Stickers, Taystee/Sunbeam (1978) © DC Comics Inc.

Superman The Movie, Topps (1978) © DC Comics Inc.

Superman The Movie, Series 2, Topps (1978) © DC Comics Inc.

Incredible Hulk, Topps (1979) © Marvel Entertainment Group & Universal City Studios, Inc.

Superman II, Topps (1981) © DC Comics Inc.

Superman II (Sticker), Topps (1981) © DC Comics Inc.

Supergirl, Topps (1983) © DC Comics Inc.

Superman III, Topps (1983) © DC Comics Inc.

Marvel Superheroes First Issue Covers, FTCC (1984) © Marvel Entertainment Group

Masters Of The Universe (Sticker), Topps (1984) © Mattel, Inc.

Howard The Duck, Topps (1986) © Marvel Entertainment Group

Robotech The Macross Saga, Fantasy Trade Cards (1986) © Harmony Gold USA Inc./Tatsunoko Prod. Co. Ltd.

DC Comics Strip Cards, DC Comics (1987) © DC Comics Inc.

THE FIRST COMIC IMAGES SETS (1987–1991)

Marvel Universe, Comic Images (1987) © Marvel Entertainment Group, Inc.

Colossal Conflicts, Comic Images (1987) © Marvel Entertainment Group, Inc.

Wolverine, Comic Images (1988) © Marvel Entertainment Group, Inc.

The Punisher, Comic Images (1988) © Marvel Entertainment Group, Inc.

Flaming Carrot, Comic Images (1988) © Bob Burden

[The Savage Sword of] Conan The Barbarian, Comic Images (1988) © Conan Properties

Heroic Origins, Comic Images (1988) © Marvel Entertainment Group, Inc.

Todd McFarlane Cards, Comic Images (1989) © Marvel Entertainment Group, Inc.

Mike Zeck Cards, Comic Images (1989) © Marvel Entertainment Group, Inc.

The Best of (John) Byrne, Comic Images (1989) © Marvel Entertainment Group, Inc.

Arthur Adams, Comic Images (1989) © Marvel Entertainment Group, Inc.

Excalibur, Comic Images (1989) © Marvel Entertainment Group, Inc.

Uncanny X-Men Covers I, Comic Images (1990) © Marvel Entertainment Group, Inc.

Spider-Man Team-up, Comic Images (1990) © Marvel Entertainment Group, Inc.

Captain America 50th Anniv., Comic Images (1990) © Marvel Entertainment Group, Inc.

Jim Lee, Comic Images (1990) © Marvel Entertainment Group, Inc.

Todd McFarlane II, Comic Images (1990) © Marvel Entertainment Group, Inc.

Ghost Rider, Comic Images (1990) © Marvel Entertainment Group, Inc.

Uncanny X-Men Covers II, Comic Images (1990) © Marvel Entertainment Group, Inc.

Wolverine: From Then 'til Now, Comic Images (1991) © Marvel Entertainment Group, Inc.

Jim Lee II, Comic Images (1991) © Marvel Entertainment Group, Inc.

The Incredible Hulk, Comic Images (1991) © Marvel Entertainment Group, Inc.

X-Force, Comic Images (1991) © Marvel Entertainment Group, Inc.

Marvel 1st Covers Series II, Comic Images (1991) © Marvel Entertainment Group, Inc.

X-Men, Comic Images (1991) © Marvel Entertainment Group, Inc.

DC COMICS CARDS (1989–1994)

Batman (Movie), Topps-Series #1 (1989) © DC Comics Inc.

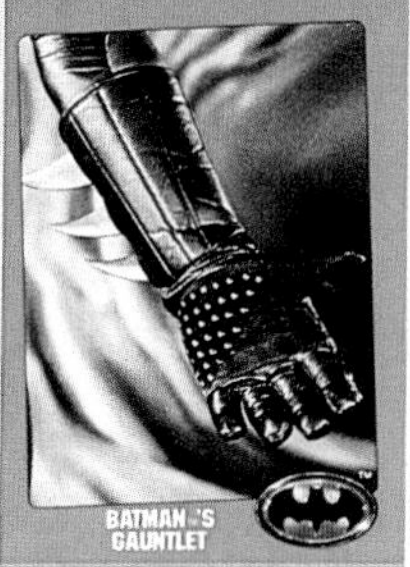

Batman Movie Deluxe, Topps (1989) © DC Comics Inc.

Batman Returns, Topps (1992) © DC Comics Inc.

Batman Returns, Topps Stadium Club (1992) © DC Comics Inc.

Batman Returns Stickers, Topps (1992) © DC Comics Inc.

Batman: The Animated Series © Topps (1993) © DC Comics Inc.

Batman: The Animated Series Two © Topps (1993) © DC Comics Inc.

Batman/Superbowl promo card, Skybox (1994) © DC Comics Inc.

Batman: Saga of the Dark Knight, SkyBox (1994) © DC Comics Inc.

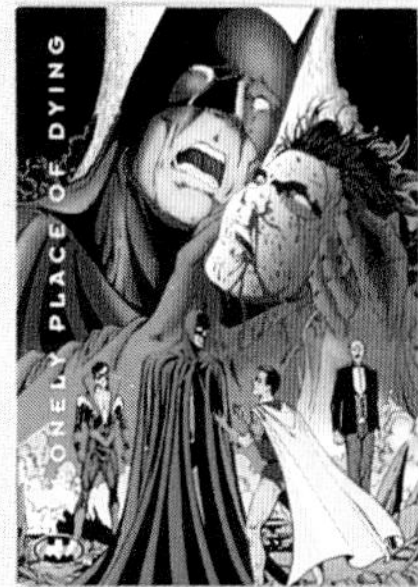

Batman: Saga of the Dark Knight, SkyBox (1994) © DC Comics Inc.

DC Cosmic Cards, Impel (1992) © DC Comics Inc.

Doomsday: The Death of Superman, Skybox (1992) © DC Comics Inc.

DC Cosmic Teams, Skybox (1993) © DC Comics Inc.

DC Bloodlines promo card, Skybox (1993) © DC Comics Inc.

DC Bloodlines, Skybox (1993) © DC Comics Inc.

Return of Superman, Skybox (1993) © DC Comics Inc.

Return of Superman (Factory Set), Skybox, (1993) © DC Comics Inc.

Superman promo card, Wizard magazine © DC Comics Inc.

DC Stars, Skybox (1994) © DC Comics Inc.

Skybox Master: DC Edition, Skybox (1994) © DC Comics Inc.

DC Cosmic Teams, Skybox (1993) © DC Comics Inc.

Batman: The Animated Series © Topps (1993) © DC Comics Inc.

DC Bloodlines, Skybox (1993) © DC Comics Inc.

DC Stars, Skybox (1994) © DC Comics Inc.

Skybox Master: DC Edition, Skybox (1994) © DC Comics Inc.

MARVEL COMICS CARDS (1990–1994)

Marvel Universe Series I, Impel (1990) © Marvel Entertainment Group, Inc.

Marvel Universe Series II, Impel (1991) © Marvel Entertainment Group, Inc.

X-Force (comic promo), Impel (1991) © Marvel Entertainment Group, Inc.

Trading Card Treats, Impel (1991) © Marvel Entertainment Group, Inc.

(The Uncanny) X-Men, Impel (1992) © Marvel Entertainment Group, Inc.

Marvel Universe Series III, Impel (1992) © Marvel Entertainment Group, Inc.

Ghost Rider II, Comic Images (1992) © Marvel Entertainment Group, Inc.

The Punisher, War Journal Entry, Comic Images (1992) © Marvel Entertainment Group, Inc.

Spider-Man The Todd McFarlane Era, Comic Images (1992) © Marvel Entertainment Group, Inc.

Spider-Man II 30th Anniversary, Comic Images (1992) © Marvel Entertainment Group, Inc.

Wolverine: From Then Till Now II, Comic Images (1992) © Marvel Entertainment Group, Inc.

X-Cutioner's Song, Skybox (1992) © Marvel Entertainment Group, Inc.

Marvel Checklist (Bi-Weekly), Marvel (1992) © Marvel Entertainment Group, Inc.

1992 Marvel Masterpieces, Skybox (1992) © Marvel Entertainment Group, Inc.

1992 Marvel Masterpieces Spectra Etch, Skybox (1992) © Marvel Entertainment Group, Inc.

Marvel Checklist Cards, Marvel (1993) © Marvel Entertainment Group, Inc.

Marvel 1993 Annuals, Marvel Comics (1993) © Marvel Entertainment Group, Inc.

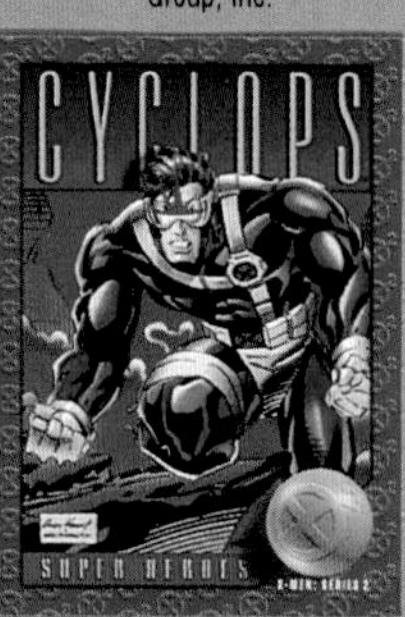

X-Men Series II, Skybox (1993) © Marvel Entertainment Group, Inc.

Marvel Universe IV, Skybox (1993) © Marvel Entertainment Group, Inc.

1993 Marvel Masterpieces, Skybox (1993) © Marvel Entertainment Group, Inc.

Gene Cards, Marvel UK (1993) © Marvel Comics UK, Inc.

Ultra X-Men, Fleer (1994) © Marvel Entertainment Group, Inc.

Amazing Spider-Man, Marvel/Fleer (1994) © Marvel Entertainment Group, Inc.

Amazing Spider-Man Gold Web, Marvel/Fleer (1994) © Marvel Entertainment Group, Inc.

Marvel Universe, Inaugural Edition, Fleer Flair (1994) © Marvel Entertainment Group, Inc.

OTHER COMICS CARDS (1992–1994)

Shadow Hawk, Comic Images (1992) © Jim Valentino

Unity, Comic Images (1992) © Voyager Communications, Inc.

The Savage Dragon, Comic Images (1992) © Erik Larsen

Youngblood, Comic Images (1992) © Rob Liefeld

Sachs & Violens, Comic Images (1993) © To Be Continued…& George Perez

Melting Pot, Comic Images (1993) © Kevin Eastman

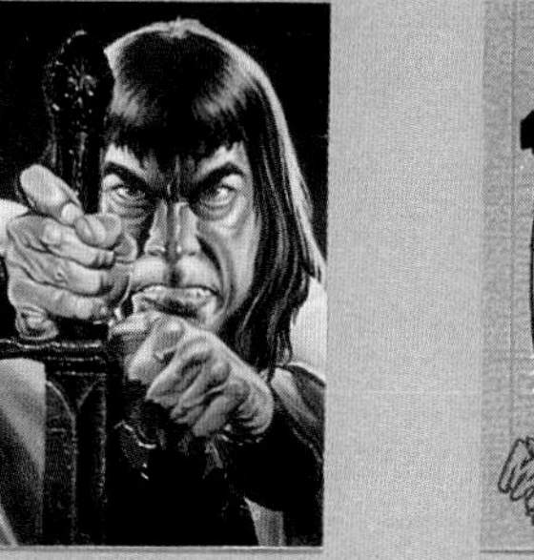

Conan (Chromium), Comic Images (1993) © Conan Properties, Inc.

Maxx, The, Topps (1993) © Sam Kieth

Plasm Zero Issue, The River Group (1993) © EEP, L.P. & The River Group, Inc.

Tribe: The Intro, Press Pass © Larry Stroman & Todd Johnson

Milestone: The Dakota Universe, Skybox (1993) © Milestone Media, Inc.

Legacy #0, Majestic Entertainment (1993) © Majestic Entertainment Inc.

WildC.A.T.S, Topps (1993) © Aegis Entertainment, Inc.

Dark Dominion Zero, River Group (1993) © EEP & The River Group, Inc.

Comics Future Stars '93, Majestic Entertainment (1993) © Majestic Entertainment, Inc. & Dan Lawlis

Ultraverse, Skybox (1993) © Malibu Comics Entertainment

Valiant Era I, Upper Deck (1993) © Voyager Communications, Inc.

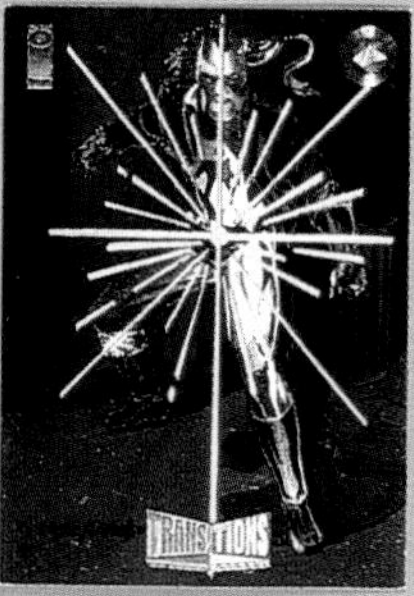

Deathmate (Transition), Upper Deck (1993) © Image & Voyager Communications, Inc.

Tek World (bonus card), Cardz (1993) © William Shatner Enterprises

Creators Universe, Dynamic Entertainment (1993) © Dynamic Entertainment Inc. & Art Thibert

Evil Ernie, Krome Productions (1993) © Krome Productions

Images of Shadowhawk, Image (1994) © Jim Valentino

Ultraverse II: Origins, Skybox (1994) © Malibu Comics Entertainment

Valiant Era II, Upper Deck (1994) © Voyager Communications, Inc.

Comics Greatest World, Dark Horse (1994) © Dark Horse Comics, Inc.

ANIMATION CARDS (1990–1994)

Disney Collector Cards, Impel (1991) © The Walt Disney Company

Disney Collector Cards II, Skybox (1993) © The Walt Disney Company

Minnie 'n Me, Impel (1991) © The Walt Disney Company

Minnie 'n Me II, Just For Fun, Impel (1992) © The Walt Disney Company

Beetlejuice, Dart (1990) © The Geffen Company

Fievel Goes West, Impel (1991) © Universal City Studios & Amblin Entertainment

The Little Mermaid (Stand-Up), Pro Set (1991) © The Walt Disney Company

Beauty And The Beast, Pro Set (1992) © The Walt Disney Company

Snow White And The Seven Dwarfs, Skybox (1993) © The Walt Disney Company

Aladdin, Skybox (1993) © The Walt Disney Company

Ferngully, The Last Rainforest, Dart Flipcards (1992) © FAI Films Pty, Ltd.

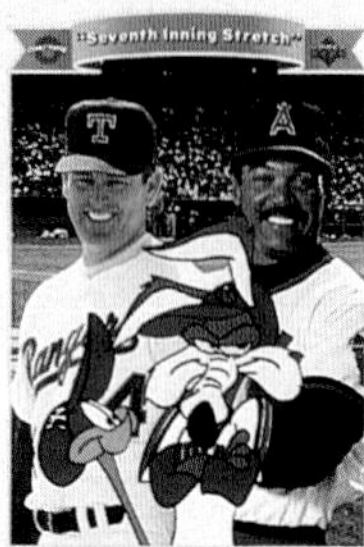

Comic Ball II, Upper Deck (1991) © Upper Deck/Warner Bros, Inc.

Comic Ball 3, Upper Deck (1992) © Upper Deck/Warner Bros, Inc.

Comic Ball 4, Upper Deck (1992) © Upper Deck/Warner Bros, Inc.

Flinstones, Cardz (1993) © Hanna-Barbera Productions, Inc.

Flintstones/NFL, Cardz (1993) © Hanna-Barbera Productions, Inc.

Return of the Flintstones, Cardz (1994) © Hanna-Barbera Productions, Inc.

Hanna-Barbera Classics, Cardz (1994) © Hanna-Barbera Productions, Inc.

Tom & Jerry, Cardz (1993) © Turner Entertainment Co.

Tiny Toon Adventures (Sticker), Topps (1991) © Warner Bros, Inc.

Tiny Toon Adventures (promo), Cardz (1994) © Warner Bros, Inc.

Simpsons (Sticker), Topps (1990) © Twentieth Century Fox

Simpsons, The, Skybox (1993) © Bongo Comics

Teenage Mutant Ninja Turtles-Cartoon, Topps (1990) © Mirage Studios, USA

Speed Racer (Gold), Prime Time (1993) © Speed Racer Enterprises, Inc. (All rights reserved)

COMIC BOOK PROMO CARDS (1992–1994)

Aliens/Predator Universe, Topps/Dark Horse (1993) © Dark Horse Comics, Inc.

Batbabe, Amazing Heroes (1993) © Amazing Heroes Publishing

Black Web, Inks Comics (1993) © Inks Comics

Comics Greatest Trading Cards, Topps/Dark Horse (1993) © Dark Horse Comics, Inc.

Dagger Force (Scorpion Corps), Dagger Comics (1993) © Dagger Comics

Daredevil foil card, Triton Magazine (1993), © Marvel Entertainment Group, Inc.

Deathmate Prelude, Continuity Comics (1993) © Continuity Comics Inc.

Dracula, Vlad the Impaler, Topps (1993) © Columbia Pictures

FaniMation, Upper Deck (1993) © Upper Deck Company

Hell Shock, Triton Magazine (1994) © Jae Lee

Jurassic Park, Topps (1993) © Universal City Studios, Inc. & Amblin Entertainment, Inc.

Kirbychrome, Topps (1993) © Jack Kirby

Mr. T & T-Force, Now Comics (1993) © Now Entertainment Corporation

Phantom Force, Image (1993) © Jack Kirby/Mike Thibedeaux/Richard French

Reiki Warriors, Heroic Publishing (1993) © Daerick Gross

Riot Gear, Advance Comics (1993) © Triumphant Comics

Satan's Six, Topps (1993) © Jack Kirby

Secret City Saga, Topps (1993) © Jack Kirby

Solitaire, Malibu Comics (1993) © Malibu Comics Entertainment, Inc.

Ultraverse (Rune), Hero Illustrated Magazine (1993) © Malibu Comics Entertainment, Inc.

Valiant, Chaos Effect checklist, Valiant Comics (1994), © Voyager Communications, Inc.

Xone Force, Mall Comics (1993) © Mall Comics

Youngblood, Advance Comics (1994) © Rob Liefeld

Youngblood, Inside Comics (1992) © Rob Liefeld & Marvel Entertainment Group, Inc.

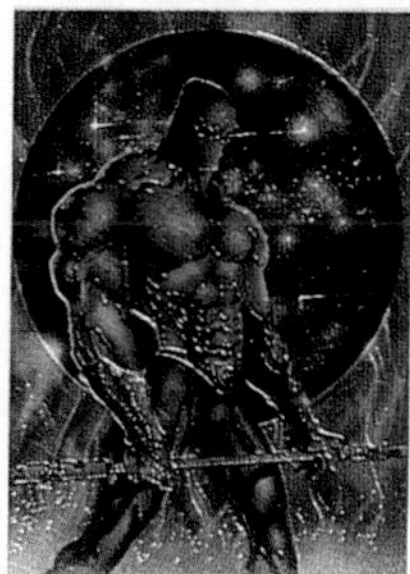
Zen Intergalactic Ninja, Maxx Cards (1993) © Zen Comics Inc.

COMICS CARDS HEROINES (1975–1994)

Comic Book Heroes, Topps (1975) © Marvel Entertainment Group, Inc.

Superman The Movie, Series 2, Topps (1978) © DC Comics Inc.

Batman (Movie), Topps-Series #1 (1989) © DC Comics Inc.

DC Cosmic Cards, Impel (1992) © DC Comics Inc.

Batman Returns, Topps Stadium Club (1992) © DC Comics Inc.

Marvel Universe Series I, Impel (1990) © Marvel Entertainment Group, Inc.

Marvel Universe Series II, Impel (1991) © Marvel Entertainment Group, Inc.

Marvel Universe Series III, Impel (1992) © Marvel Entertainment Group, Inc.

(The Uncanny) X-Men, Impel (1992) © Marvel Entertainment Group, Inc.

X-Men Series II, Skybox (1993) © Marvel Entertainment Group, Inc.

1992 Marvel Masterpieces, Skybox (1992) © Marvel Entertainment Group, Inc.

Ultra X-Men, Fleer (1994) © Marvel Entertainment Group, Inc.

Marvel Universe, Inaugural Edition, Fleer Flair (1994) © Marvel Entertainment Group, Inc.

Creators Universe, Dynamic Entertainment (1993) © Dynamic Entertainment Inc. & Walter Simonson

Ultraverse II: Origins (Insert) Skybox (1994) © Malibu Comics Entertainment

Sachs & Violens, Comic Images (1993) © To Be Continued…& George Perez

Spider-Man II 30th Anniversary, Comic Images (1992) © Marvel Entertainment Group, Inc.

Ultraverse, Skybox (1993) © Malibu Comics Entertainment

Ultraverse II: Origins, Skybox (1994) © Malibu Comics Entertainment

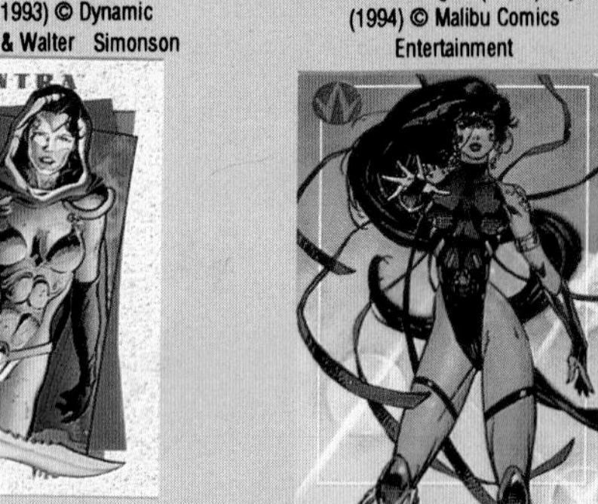

WildC.A.T.S, Topps (1993) © Aegis Entertainment, Inc.

Evil Ernie, Krome Productions (1993) © Krome Productions

Maxx, The, Topps (1993) © Sam Kieth

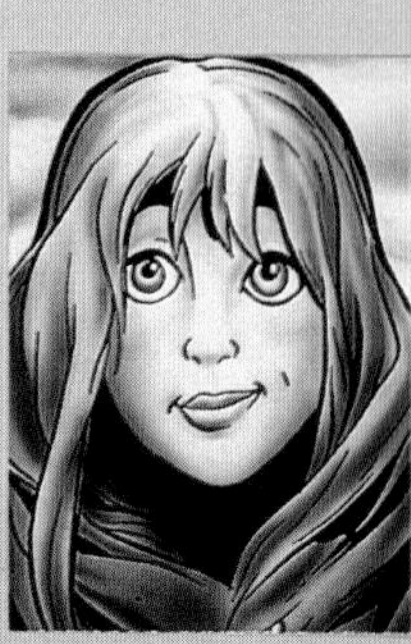

Bone, Comic Images (1994) © Jeff Smith

Legacy #0, Majestic Entertainment (1993) © Majestic Entertainment, Inc.

Deathmate, Upper Deck (1993) © Image and Voyager Communications, Inc.

are taken from the Half Time cards, as indicated.

Set: 198 cards 15.00

Holograms (unnumbered)
Marino, Wile E. Coyote & Elmer (91) 3.50
Marino & Bugs (92) 3.50
Rice & Daffy (93) 3.50
Taylor & Daffy (98) 3.50
Thomas & Wile E. Coyote (97) 3.50
Taylor & Daffy (98) 3.50
(H7) 3.50
(H8) 3.50
(H9) 3.50
Set: 9 Holograms 22.50
Pack: 12 cards 1.00
Common cards, no player, each 10

CARD CHECKLIST

Pop Goes The Martian (#1 to #18)
10 All four players 20
11 Taylor & Marino 20
15 Marino 20
Hang Time (#19 to #36)
24 & 25 Taylor 20
27 & 31 Marino 20
36 Taylor & Marino 20
Run & Shout (#37 to #54)
44, 46, 47, 48, 51 & 52 Thomas 20
49 Taylor .20
50 Taylor & Thomas 20
I Get a Kick Out of You (#55 to #72)
57 & 58 Rice 20
60 & 72 Rice & Marino 20
Zee Smell of Victory (#73 to #90)
74 Thomas & Taylor 20
82, 85, 86 Thomas 20
Half Time
91 Bugs & Dan Marino 20
92 Bugs & Dan Marino 20
93 Daffy and Jerry Rice 20
94 Tasmanian Devil & Jerry Rice 20
95 20
96 w/Thurman Thomas 20
97 Wyle E. Coyote & Thurman Thomas .20
98 w/Lawrence Taylor 20
99 Series 4, Set 1 checklist 20
Crowd Control (#100 to #117)
109, 112, 113 Thomas 20
110, 111, 116, 117 Thomas & Taylor .20
Repeat Defender (#118 to #135)
120, 125, 126, 127, 131 Taylor 20
Hoppin' Half Time (#136 to #153)
137, 142, 147, 149, 151 Rice & Marino.20
153 Marino 20
Martian Touchdown (#154 to #171)
155 & 159 Taylor 20
169, 170, 171 Marino & Taylor 20
Gut-Check Time (#172 to #189)
174 Marino 20
175, 177, 180 Thomas, Rice & Marino .20
176, 178 Rice & Marino 20
179 Marino & Thomas 20
Half Time
190 w/Thurman Thomas 20
191 Daffy & Thurman Thomas 20
192 Bugs & Jerry Rice 20
193 Bugs & Jerry Rice 20
194 w/Dan Marino 20
195 Marvin & Dan Marino 20
196 Taz & Lawrence Taylor 20
197 w/Marino & Taylor 20
198 Series 4, set 2 checklist 20

COMIC BOOK FOLDEES

Topps (1966)

The gimmick here is that you can refold the card pieces various ways to form "9 funny pictures" such as a Superman top with a dress on the bottom. Only one picture on each card is a DC comic book superhero, the rest are famous people or stock pictures. This set comes in two different sizes, the larger of which has only forty-three cards (missing #44), which sell for $1.00 more per foldee.

Set: 44 folding "cards" 150.00
Set: 43 larger folding "cards" 190.00

[Larger foldees are $1.00 more]
1 inc. Flash 3.50
2 inc. Jimmy Olsen 3.00
3 inc. Superhero 3.00
4 inc. Kid Flash 3.00
5 inc. Green Arrow 4.00
6 inc. Riddler 3.00
7 inc. Old Flash 3.00
8 inc. Green Lantern 3.50
9 inc. Atom 3.00
10 inc. Green Lantern 3.50
11 inc. Krypto 3.00
12 inc. Wanda 3.00
13 inc. Supergirl 3.25
14 inc. Mischievous Imp 3.00
15 inc. Martian Man Hunter 3.25
16 inc. Saturn Girl 3.00
17 inc. Batman 4.00
18 inc. Penguin 4.00
19 inc. Gold the Metalman 3.00
20 inc. Alfred the Butler 3.00
21 inc. Joker 4.00
22 inc. Hawkgirl 3.00
23 inc. Supergirl 3.00
24 inc. Bat Mobile 3.00
25 inc. Crusading Editor 3.00
26 inc. Superman 4.00
27 inc. Green Arrow 3.50
28 inc. Bizarro 3.00
29 inc. Penguin 4.00
30 inc. Robin 3.25
31 inc. Robin 3.25
32 inc. Hawkman 3.25
33 inc. Wonder Woman 3.25
34 inc. Riddler 3.50
35 inc. Luthor 3.00
36 inc. Stretching Hero 3.00
37 inc. Metamorpho 3.00
38 inc. Plastic Man 3.00
39 inc. Comic Book Reporter 3.00
40 inc. Aquaman 3.25
41 inc. Flash 3.50
42 inc. Spectre 3.50
43 inc. Catwoman 3.25
44 inc. Superman w/Kryptonite 4.00

COMIC BOOK HEROES

STICKERS/Brown or White Backs

Topps (1975)

Comic Book Heroes © Marvel Entertainment Group, Inc.

These are die-cut stickers picturing Marvel characters with a humorous word balloon. There are two varieties, one with a thin brown paper backing and one with a white paper backing. The brown paper stickers have one star before the Topps copyright and the white paper stickers have two stars. Both variations sell for the same prices. Each pack came with one of nine puzzle checklist cards, which combine to form the cover of Fantastic Four #100. *The checklist that comes with the brown back stickers is grey and not as nice as the one that came with the white back stickers. The series name doesn't appear on the stickers, which are quite similar to Marvel Super Heroes Stickers, issued the next year, but these can be identified by the 1975 Topps and 1974 Marvel copyrights.*

Set: 40 stickers & 9 puzzle/ checklist cards 100.00

Pack: 4 cards + 1 puzzle 10.00

CARD CHECKLIST
Black Widow "I'm Natasha fly me to Miami!" (GK) 3.00
Captain America-1 "I'm a Yankee Doodle Dandy!" (JK) 4.00
Captain America-2 "Look, Ma, no cavities!" (JR) 4.00
Captain Marvel "Fly the friendly skies of United!" (JSn) 3.00
Conan "Trick or Treat?!" 2.75
Daredevil "Badness makes me see RED!"(JK) 2.50
Dracula-1 "Sure doesn't taste like tomato juice!" (NA) 2.50
Dracula-2 "Flying drives me bats!" . . 2.50
Dr. Doom "I'm dressed to kill!" (copy of GC) 2.50
Dr. Octopus "I'm just a well-armed crook!" 2.50
Dr. Strange "Darn those house calls!" 2.50
The Falcon "You bet your bird!" (JR) 2.50
Frankenstein's Monster "Maybe it's my breath!" (MP) 2.50
Ghost Rider "Peter Fonda LOOK OUT!" 11.00
Hawkeye "Annie Oakley I ain't!" 2.50
Hulk-1 "Who stole my Right Guard?" (HT) 4.00
Hulk-2 "Green power!" (JR) 4.00
Human Torch-1 "Tan...Don't burn!" (JR) 2.75
Human Torch-2 "When you're hot, you're hot!" 2.75
Iron Fist "Kung Fooey!"(GK/JR) 3.00
Iron Man "Fight rust!"(JK) 3.50
Ka-Zar "Be kind to animals... OR ELSE!"(JR) 2.50
Kull "These pants don't fit!" (RA) . . . 2.50
The Living Mummy "Which hand has the M&M's?" 2.50
Luke Cage "I was a 98 lb. Weakling!" 2.50
Man-Thing "I dropped the soap in the shower!" 4.00
Medusa "Darn that cheap hairspray!" 2.50
Morbius "Which way to the blood bank?" 2.50
Mr. Fantastic "I'm the long arm of the law!" 4.00
Shang-Li, Kung Fu "All aspirin is not alike!" (JSn) 2.50
The Son of Satan "The Devil made me do it!" 2.50
Spider-Man-1 "Who'd you expect?... Little Miss Muffett?" 6.00
Spider-Man-2 "You drive me up a wall!" 6.00
Submariner "Don't pollute my waters" (JR) 2.50
The Thing-1 "It's clobberin' time!" (JK) 2.50
The Thing-2 "I'm going to pieces" (JK) 2.50
Thor-1 "Support your local Thunder-god!" (JB) 2.75
Thor-2 "Who said blondes have more fun?" 2.75
Valkyrie "Support Women's Lib!" (JB/TP) 2.50
Werewolf "Only my hairdresser knows for sure!" 2.50
Puzzle/Checklist Cards (Fantastic Four)
1 thru 9 . . . . 12.00

See also: Marvel Super Heroes Stickers

Comic Cover Stickers © DC Comics, Inc.

COMIC COVER STICKERS

Topps (1970)

All of the pictures used for this set are comic book covers. The single stickers picture just one cover and have a white back with black text telling you to "Fold corner on dotted line." The four-on-ones contain four cover pictures and are peeled on the front, between the stickers, so that they can be removed individually. The back is white with no text. The set is not numbered.

Set: 44 stickers 200.00

SINGLE STICKERS

Batman 5.00
Detective Comics 4.50
Enemy Ace 4.00
Falling in Love 4.00
Flash 4.50
Girls' Love 4.00
Green Lantern 4.50
Superman 4.50
Teen Titans 4.50
Tales of The Unexpected 4.50
Wonder Woman 4.00
Young Love (Lisa St. Claire) 4.00
Young Love (20 Miles to Heartbreak) 4.00
Young Romance (Have a Fling With...) 4.00
Young Romance (Two Different Worlds) 4.00

FOUR-ON-ONES

Batman; Aquaman; Falling in Love; Hellcats 4.50
Batman; Enemy Ace; Teen Titans; Girls' Love 4.50
Batman; G.I. Combat; Girls' Romances; The Witching Hour . . . 4.50
Batman; Sgt. Rock; Girls' Romances; Debbi 4.50
Batman & Robin; Adam Strange; Young Love; Action Comics 4.50
Batman & Robin; Young Love; Adam Strange; Adventure Comics 4.50
Binky; Batman; Falling in Love; Young Romance 4.50
Binky's Buddies; Girls' Romances; Batman; Superman 4.75
Enemy Ace; Wonder Woman; Binky; Batman 4.50
Girls' Love; Detective; Tomahawk; Teen Titans 4.50
Girls' Love; The House of Secrets; Batman; Jimmy Olsen 4.50
Girls' Romances; The House of Mystery; Challengers of the Unknown; Batman & Batgirl 4.50
Girls' Romances; The Phantom Stranger; Batman and Batgirl; Action Comics 4.50
Girls' Romances; Wonder Woman; Aquaman; The Phantom Stranger . 5.00
Green Lantern; Batman and Robin; Beyond the Unknown; Girls' Romances 4.50
Jimmy Olsen; Adam Strange; Jason's Quest; Young Love 4.00
Lois Lane; Debbi; Witching Hour Young Romance 4.00
Lois Lane; Scooter; Falling in Love The Witching Hour 4.00
Sgt. Rock; Batman and Batgirl; Girls' Romances; Action Comics . 4.50
Teen Titans; Scooter; Tomahawk; Adventure Comics 4.50
The House of Secrets; Beyond the Unknown; Girls' Love; Batman and Batgirl 4.50
The House of Secrets; Tomahawk; Superboy; Girl's Love 4.00
The Unexpected; Falling in Love; Batman; Binky 4.50
The Witching Hour; Binky's Buddies; World's Finest; Wonder Woman . . 4.50
The World's Finest; Scooter; Young Love; The Phantom Stranger 4.00
Young Love; Adventure; Tomahawk; Batman and Batgirl 4.50
Young Love; Superman; Binky; The House of Secrets 4.50
Young Romance; Superman; Binky; The House of Secrets 4.50
Young Romance; Superman; The Unexpected; Challengers of the Unknown 4.50

Comics Future Stars © Majestic Ent., Inc. & L: David Ammerman; R: Dan Lawlis

COMICS FUTURE STARS '93

Majestic Entertainment (1993)

This set consists of cards by hot young comic artists who drew portraits of their own characters. Since no artist gets more than four cards, there is a lot of variation in style and subject matter. This book uses artist's initials to identify the best known artists (based on information in Comics Values Monthly*), but only a couple of these artists are on the list. That's what "future stars" means! The cards feature full bleed portrait art and the backs contain the character name, artist name, and the card number in a green strip. There is also text concerning the artist and character plus a photo in an orange center, all surrounded by a black border. The last three cards have no art.*

***Card #98** is scarce because it was packed only one per box and could be sent in for the MVP bonus card, but it's too late for that now! Look for it anyway if you buy a hand assembled set or find individual cards for sale. There are a lot of other bonus cards with this set, and one or two of each type are in each box. If that isn't enough to look for, each box also contains one or two Legacy #0 black and white preview cards. Prototypes P1 thru P3 have text in a white box and no artist photo. P1 uses the same art as the HP4 and the other two are the same as cards #72 and #73. The three promo cards have the same art as the Hot Picks cards of the same name. According to Majestic Entertainment, only 10,000 of each prototype and promo card were made, which makes them fairly scarce (almost as scarce as the bonus cards).*

Set: 100 cards 12.00
Set: 99 cards [omitting #98] 11.00

Litho Foil "Hot Picks" (1:27)
HP1 Treason (SAP) 7.00
HP2 Turbulence (Frank Gomez) . . . 7.00
HP3 Watchdog (DoC) 7.00
HP4 Bullitt (KJa) 7.00
HP5 Ironhorse (PhH) 7.00
HP6 Dr. Raven (Lionel Talaro) 7.00
HP7 The Point Man (Randy Clark) 7.00
HP8 Gai-Jin (DvA) 7.00
Star Players (1:27)
SP 1 Pixie (DIB) 5.00
SP 2 Shallot-Head: Man of Shame (Rick Geary) 5.00
SP 3 Drako (VMk) 5.00
SP 4 Jarod (E. Silas Smith) 5.00
SP 5 Annie Ammo (Richard Case) 5.00
MVP card (Mail-in)
MVP Snake (DLw) 15.00
also: MVP Snake, autographed, (1:case)

Hot Pick Promo cards
P1 Turbulence (Frank Gomez) 2.50
P2 Treason (SAP) 2.50
P3 Gai-Jin (DvA) 2.50
Prototype cards
P1 Bullitt (KJa) 2.00
P2 Arsenault (Les White) 2.00
P3 Razer (Nick Napolitano) 2.00
Pack: 9 cards 1.25

CARD CHECKLIST

1 Optica (DLw) 10
2 Legacy (DLw) 10
3 Hydro (Brian McGovern) 10
4 Hackisack (Rachel Ketchum) 10
5 Epiphany 10
6 The Blue Demons (John Christian Estes) 10
7 Free-Lancer (SAP) 10
8 The Posse (Paul Lee) 10
9 Chrome (Scott Jackson) 10
10 Lynch (Wayne Losey) 10

Comics Future Stars © Larry Welch & Majestic Entertainment, Inc.

11 Gabriel (Lionel Talaro) 10
12 Dr. Ptolemy (John Clapp) 10
13 Tau (Sandra Chang) 10
14 Kunoichi (LyW) 10
15 Stealth Microchip Monkeys (Mike Lemos) 10
16 Potato Man (Steve Carr/ Deryl Skelton) 10
17 Lunatech (JmP) 10
18 Glory (Lea Hernandez) 10
19 Cademous Zark (DLw) 10
20 Wonder (Greg Simanson) 10
21 Styx (John Stanisci) 10
22 Mr. Fist (RCa) 10
23 Twilight (David Antoine Williams) .10
24 Weathertamer (David Antoine Williams) 10
25 Triphammer (Mike Jones) 10
26 Passion Assassin (Mike Jones) . . .10
27 Animus (SnW) 10
28 Spectrum 1 (David Antoine Williams) 10
29 Spectrum 2 (David Antoine Williams) 10
30 Flashpoint (Jim Higgins) 10
31 Versus (Mark Miraglia) 10
32 Dominoe (CrB) 10
33 Vagabond (Rodney Gates) 10
34 Virtue (Ngiha Lam) 10
35 Kasey Venus (Jeff Parker) 10
36 Rankar Vuul (Doug Heinlein) 10
37 Quinn Zybane (Doug Heinlein) . . .10
38 Night Justice (Jonathan Daryl Rash) 10

Comics Future Stars © Tom Simonton & Majestic Entertainment, Inc.

39 Rebecca Harlocke(Craig Gilmore) .10
40 Codename: Jericho (Rick Forgus) .10
41 Big Guns (PhH) 10
42 Threshold (Stephen B. Jones) . . .10
43 Gridlock (Stephen B. Jones) 10
44 Echo (S. David Lee) 10
45 Sebastian Sok (Justin Norman) . . .10
46 Squire (Ken Hooper) 10
47 Pharisee (Ken Hooper) 10
48 Pyromaniac (Scott Tolson) 10
49 The Rider (Christopher Schenck) .10
50 The Twist (Christopher Schenck) .10
51 Razor (Tom Simonton) 10
52 Texoma Red (Tom Simonton) 10
53 Valcanic Man (Nathan Simonton) .10
54 The Cure (Bill Marimon) 10
55 Eliminator (Pav Kovacic) 10
56 Lady Zero (Andrew Pepoy) 10
57 Feral (Ken Meyer Jr.) 10
58 Gutter (Woj) 10
59 Silencer (Kyle Hotz) 10
60 Phantasm (Kyle Hotz) 10
61 Dragon Head (Dale Berry) 10
62 War Trip (Mike Mayhew) 10
63 August (Scott Rosema) 10

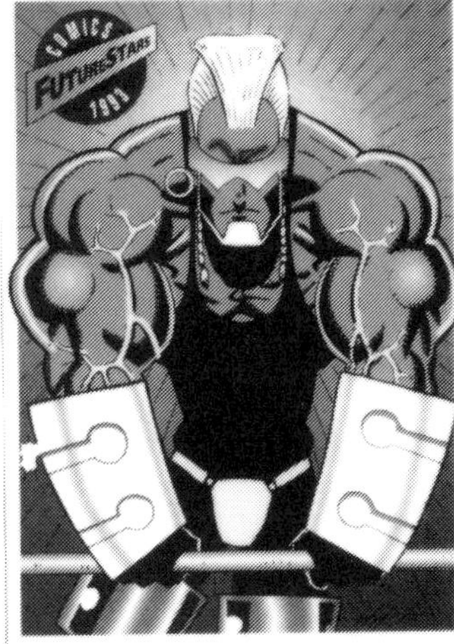

Comics Future Stars © Les White & Majestic Entertainment, Inc.

64 Hurlent (Russell Miller) 10
65 Clodia (Scott Pentzer) 10
66 Prince Fergus (Dennis Cramer) . .10
67 Maelstrom & Seizure (TyD) 10
68 Mortis (Warren Martineck) 10
69 Lynx (Andy Price) 10
70 Nanoman (Jeremie Johnson) 10
71 Kickstart (JAl) 10
72 Arsenault (Les White) 10
73 Razer (Nick Napolitano) 10
74 Death Grip (JiC) 10
75 Danger-Boy (KJa) 10
76 Man-X (DvA) 10
77 Tonk (PhH) 10
78 Notch 56 & Rotterdam (Frank Gomez) 10
79 Riktus & Fraktal (Eric Vincent) . . .10
80 Kallus (BVa) 10
81 Ruffnek (J. B. Bonivert) 10
82 Dellego (Dan Schaffer) 10
83 Volt (Al Bigley) 10
84 The Astomatic Man (Batton Lash) .10
85 Radius (Ellis Goodson) 10
86 Alpha Nova (Andrew Smith) 10
87 Jurney (Dan Schaffer) 10
88 Matrix (Randy Clark) 10
89 Stage (C. Michael Patrick) 10
90 Kabuki (David Mack) 10
91 Death Mark (Frank Turner) 10
92 The Talon (BHr) 10
93 Crimson Steel (Chuck Von Schaaf) 10
94 Thunder God (John Statema) 10
95 Zora (Brian Michael Bendis) 10
96 Tempest 7 (Roger Robinson) 10
97 Foxglove (Robert Chang) 10
98 MVP Prize Redemption (1:36) . . 1.00
99 Ballot Submission 10
100 Checklist 10

COMICS FUTURE STARS 2
Majestic Entertainment (1993)

The three promo cards are numbered to follow the similar cards from series 1, described above. Only 10,000 of each were produced. The set itself was scheduled for the end of 1993, but is currently on indefinite hold.

Hot Picks promo cards
P4 The Black Yeti (Martin Egeland) . 2.50
P5 Cetan (Fred Von Tobel) 2.50
P6 Graffiti (TBd) 2.50

Comics Future Stars 2 © Martin Egeland & Majestic Entertainment, Inc. Comics' Greatest World © Dark Horse Comics Inc.

COMICS' GREATEST WORLD
Dark Horse/Topps (1993)

These promo cards were given out in 1993 and 1994 at comic book shows to promote both the comic and the card series.

Barb Wire promo 1.50
Division 13 promo 1.50
Rebel promo (JOy) 1.50
X promo ("FM") 1.50

Comics' Greatest World © Dark Horse Comics, Inc.

COMICS' GREATEST WORLD
Topps (1994)

This card set is taken from the Dark Horse comic book universe which was introduced in the summer of 1993. The cards contain full bleed art on the front with a full color back, sometimes with text, sometimes without text, but always with artist credits. It's an excellent representation of the characters from this popular comic book series. The series appeared at the end of June 1994 in some locations, but not until mid-July in New England. This is the last card set to make it into this book, and therefore our prices are very preliminary. We had an early report that it is hard to make a set out of a box, but the box we bought (and the one Topps sent us) each produced a complete set. Much of the set consists of four card subsets of the major characters, with art by Randy Green and two other artists plus a sketch by Chris Warner. This is quite effective, as these characters haven't appeared on prior card sets.

Set: 100 cards 15.00

VortexMatrix (1:18)
M1 X 7.50
M2 Ghost 7.50
M3 Monster 7.50
M4 Barb Wire 7.50
M5 Machine 7.50
M6 Vortex 7.50
VortexMatrix promo, 2 diff., each . . . 5.00
Monster Matrix card, 1 per box, same numbers as VortexMatrix, each . . . 5.00
One card promo sheet (Previews November 1993) 1.00
Promo Card (Advance) 1.00
Pack: 8 cards 1.25

CARD CHECKLIST

Arcadia
1 Arcadia 15
2 X (CW/TBd) 15
3 X (RG) 15
4 X (Frank Miller) 15
5 X (CW) 15
6 Pit Bulls (JoP) 15
7 Pit Bulls (RG) 15

Comics' Greatest World
© Dark Horse Comics, Inc.

8 Pit Bulls (Bob McLeod) 15
9 Pit Bulls (CW) 15
10 Ghost (AH) 15
11 Ghost (RG) 15
12 Ghost (DvD) 15
13 Ghost (AH) 15
14 Monster (Darek Thompson) 15
15 Monster (RG) 15
16 Monster (Doug Mahnke) 15
17 Monster (CW) 15

Golden City
18 Golden City logo 15
19 Rebel (T.Hamilton/G.Martin) 15
20 Rebel (RG) 15
21 Rebel (JOy) 15
22 Rebel (CW) 15
23 Mecha (C.Woj/J.Lowe) 15
24 Mecha (RG) 15
25 Mecha (D.Johnson/K.Story) 15
26 Mecha (CW) 15
27 Titan (BS) 15
28 Titan (RG) 15
29 Titan (WS) 15
30 Titan (CW) 15
31 Catalyst (D.Willis/B.Garvey) 15
32 Catalyst (RG) 15
33 Catalyst (GP) 15
34 Catalyst (CW) 15

Steel Harbor
35 Steel Harbor logo 15
36 Barb Wire (PG) 15
37 Barb Wire (RG) 15
38 Barb Wire (DvD) 15
39 Barb Wire (CW) 15
40 The Machine (Ted Naifeh) 15
41 The Machine (RG) 15
42 The Machine (Mike Mignola) 15
43 The Machine (CW) 15
44 Wolfgang (CW/TBd) 15
45 Wolfgang (RG) 15
46 Wolfgang (CW) 15
47 Wolfgang Hunter (CW) 15
48 Motorhead (Vince Giaranno) 15

Comics' Greatest World
© Dark Horse Comics, Inc.

49 Motorhead (RG) 15
50 Motorhead (Vince Giaranno) 15
51 Motorhead (CW) 15

The Vortex
52 The Vortex logo 15
53 Division 13 (Doug Mahnke) 15
54 Division 13 (RG) 15
55 Division 13 (Doug Mahnke) 15
56 Division 13 Wrath (Doug Mahnke) .15
57 Hero Zero (Eric Skandower) 15
58 Hero Zero (RG) 15
59 Hero Zero (AAd) 15
60 Hero Zero (RG) 15
61 King Tiger (Paul Chadwick) 15
62 King Tiger (RG) 15
63 King Tiger (Geof Darrow) 15
64 King Tiger (Paul Chadwick) 15
65 Vortex (Bob McLeod) 15
66 Vortex (RG) 15
67 Vortex (Frank Miller) 15
68 Vortex (CW) 15
69 Gamble (Doug Mahnke) 15
70 Grenade (T.Hamilton/G.Martin) . . .15
71 Deathcard (CW) 15
72 Destroyers (D.Willis/B.Garvey) . . .15
73 New Series: X (CW) 15
74 New Series: Out of the Vortex(CW).15
75 New Series: Barb Wire (CW) 15
76 New Series: Catalyst (CW) 15
77 Puzzle A (part 1) 15
78 Puzzle A (part 2) 15
79 Puzzle A (part 3) 15
80 Puzzle B (part 1) 15
81 Puzzle B (part 1) The Vortex 15
82 Puzzle B (part 1) Arcadia 15
83 Puzzle B (part 1) Steel Harbor . . .15

Prologue
84 Part 1: Spaceship Arrives (LW) . . .15
85 Part 2: Builds Machine (LW) 15
86 Part 3: Explosion (LW) 15
87 Part 4: The Vortex (LW) 15

Featured Players
88 Seekers (CW) 15
89 Superswat (CW) 15
90 Catalyst: Warmaker (CW) 15
91 Catalyst: Ruby (CW) 15
92 Madison (CW) 15
93 Wolf Gang: Burner (CW) 15
94 Wolf Gang: Bomber (CW) 15
95 Wolf Gang: Cutter (CW) 15
96 Wolf Gang: Breaker (CW) 15
97 X (TBd) .15
98 The Machine (CW) 15
99 Mace Blitzkreig (CW) 15
100 Checklist 15

(THE SAVAGE SWORD OF) CONAN THE BARBARIAN

Comic Images (1988)

These cards reproduce color covers from The Savage Sword of Conan *black and white comic magazine and the backs form a puzzle. There are no card numbers on the cards themselves, just issue numbers. The card numbers are only on the checklist card. The backs form a black and white puzzle picture of Conan.*

Set: 50 cards 18.00

Pack: 5 cards, cello 1.50

CARD CHECKLIST

1 Checklist 35
2 Issue #3 35
3 Issue #16 35
4 Issue #18 35
5 Issue #21 35
6 Issue #23 35
7 Issue #24 35
8 Issue #25 35
9 Issue #27 35
10 Issue #28 35
11 Issue #31 35
12 Issue #32 35
13 Issue #39 35
14 Issue #40 35
15 Issue #42 35
16 Issue #43 35
17 Issue #44 35
18 Issue #47 35
19 Issue #52 35
20 Issue #54 35
21 Issue #55 35
22 Issue #57 35
23 Issue #59 35
24 Issue #60 35
25 Issue #62 35
26 Issue #64 35
27 Issue #66 35
28 Issue #67 35
29 Issue #74 35
30 Issue #79 35
31 Issue #81 35
32 Issue #82 35
33 Issue #86 35
34 Issue #88 35
35 Issue #89 35
36 Issue #90 35
37 Issue #91 35
38 Issue #92 35
39 Issue #93 35
40 Issue #98 35
41 Issue #114 35
42 Issue #117 35
43 Issue #120 35
44 Issue #121 35

Conan the Barbarian
© Conan Properties, Inc.

45 Issue #126 35
46 Issue #129 35
47 Issue #132 35
48 Issue #142 35
49 Issue #143 35
50 Issue #148 35

CONAN

Comic Images (1993)

This is a marvelous collection of Conan cover art work, enhanced by the all chromium card stock. Most of the covers are from the Savage Sword *comic book and almost all of the great Conan artists are present. Comic Images noticed that 100 cards could be fit on the expensive chromium sheets, but they only had 90 pieces of art and 90 card backs. They changed the background color on 10 of the cards and used them again to make a 100 card set, not the 90*

Conan © Conan Properties, Inc.

card set originally advertised. They should have made different card numbers for the variations, but they didn't, so there is no way to distinguish two variations of the same picture except by color. Some of these variations were very close to the original, so it can be hard to tell when you have a complete set. Not only that, they mixed the cards so that it is very hard to complete a set from a single box of cards. All these factors contribute to making a beautiful, expensive and frustrating card set! The card backs contain the card number, title, text, artist credits and a small black and white drawing of Conan. Six different background colors were used: red, purple, green, dark green, blue, and black, all with a stone textured look. The chromium promo card, by Joe Jusko, has the same art as card #89. It has a white back with black printing. It is not hard to find, but still commands a hefty price. Comic Images also experimented with 200 sheets of holochrome card stock and mixed in the resulting 20,000 cards – about one per box. (See also Melting Pot*, listed below, which came out the same month.) Holochrome cards break up reflected light into component colors, like a rainbow. These cards are hard to find, although we know one fanatic Conan collector who has about 70 different ones already on his quest to obtain a full set. We don't recommend that you try.*

Set: 90 Chromium cards (+10 variant cards 37, 44, 51, 58, 62, 64, 65, 67, 69, 82) 30.00

Prism Cards (1:18)
P1 The Valley of Howling Shadows (JJu) 10.00
P2 Daughter of the God King (JCh) . 9.00
P3 Conan the Conqueror (BV) 10.00
P4 The Treasure of Tranicos(EN) . . 9.00
P5 The Star of Khorala (BLr) 9.00
P6 The Iron Lions of the Kharamun (BSz) 9.00
Chromium promo card (JJu) 7.50
Holochrome variant, each 10.00
Pack: 7 cards 2.00

CARD CHECKLIST
1 Savage Sword #114 (Steve Hickman) .35
2 Road of Kings (Les Edwards) 35
3 Savage Sword #136 (Doug Beekman) 35
4 Savage Sword #126 (Doug Beekman) 35
5 Savage Sword #111 (Steve Hickman) 35
6 Savage Sword future (JuB) 45
7 Conan the Liberator (Les Edwards) .35
8 Savage Sword #212 (JuB) 45
9 Savage Sword #43 (BLr) 35
10 Savage Sword #42 (BLr) 35
11 Savage Sword #27 (BLr) 35
12 Savage Sword #82 (BLr) 35
13 Savage Sword #94 (VM) 35
14 Savage Sword #87 (John Pound) .35
15 Savage Sword #26 (JSn) 35
16 Savage Sword #67 (Romas Kukalis) .35
17 Savage Sword #11 (Ken Barr) . . .35
18 Savage Sword #13 (Richard Hescox) 35
19 Savage Tales #3 (Pablo Marcos) .35
20 Savage Sword #6 (AN & Magsino) .35
21 Savage Sword #49 (NR) 35
22 Savage Sword #52 (NR) 35
23 Conan Saga #2 (BWS) 50
24 Savage Sword #56 (NR) 35
25 Savage Sword #26 (JCh) 35
26 Savage Sword #84 (JCh) 35
27 Savage Sword #1 (BV) 45
28 Savage Sword #88 (Steve Hickman) 35
29 Savage Sword #9 (BV) 45
30 Savage Sword #12 (BV) 45
31 Savage Sword #15 (BV) 45
32 Savage Sword #7 (BV) 45
33 Savage Sword #35 (ECh) 35
34 Savage Sword #34 (ECh) 35
35 Savage Sword #29 (ECh) 35
36 Savage Sword #53 (EN) 35
37 Savage Sword #81 (JCh) blue . . .35
37 Savage Sword #81 (JCh) gray . . .35
38 Savage Sword #73 (JCh) 35
39 Savage Sword #79 (JCh) 35
40 Savage Sword #71 (JCh) 35
41 Savage Sword #50 (NR) 35
42 Savage Sword #48 (NR) 35
43 Savage Sword #45 (NR) 35
44 Savage Sword #57 (NR) red 35
44 Savage Sword #57 (NR) yellow . .35
45 Savage Sword #54 (EN) 35
46 Savage Sword #51 (EN) 35
47 Savage Sword #36 (EN) 35
48 Savage Sword #110 (EN) 35
49 Savage Sword #129 (Doug Beekman) 35
50 Savage Sword #14 (EN) 35
51 Savage Sword #39 (EN) brown . . .35
51 Savage Sword #39 (EN) light 35
52 Savage Sword #55 (EN) 35
53 Savage Sword #127(Peter Manko) .35
54 Savage Sword #83 (Jeff Easley) . .35
55 Savage Sword #105 (MGo) 35
56 Savage Sword #97 (Gaetano Liberatore) 35
57 Savage Sword #30 (FB) 35
58 Savage Sword #18 (DA) green . . .35
58 Savage Sword #18 (DA) purple . .35
59 Savage Sword #59 (Clyde Caldwell) 35
60 Savage Sword #19 (Ken Morris) . .35
61 Savage Sword #91 (MK) 35
62 Savage Sword #93 (MK) purple . .35
62 Savage Sword #93 (MK) silver . . .35
63 Savage Sword #31 (HC) 35
64 Savage Sword #22 (VM) red 35
64 Savage Sword #22 (VM) gray 35
65 Conan the Unconquered (Les Edwards) blue 35
65 Conan the Unconquered (Les Edwards) light 35
66 Savage Sword #147 (BLr) 35
67 Savage Sword #147 (JJu) light . . .45
67 Savage Sword #147 (JJu) blue . . .45
68 Savage Sword #131 (JJu) 45
69 Savage Sword #159 (JJu) blue . . .45
69 Savage Sword #159 (JJu) black . .45
70 Conan Saga #3 (BWS) 50
71 Savage Sword #132 (JJu) 45
72 Savage Sword #28 (EN) 35
73 Savage Sword #144 (JJu) 45
74 Savage Sword #154 (JJu) 45
75 Savage Sword #156 (JJu) 45
76 Savage Sword #113 (EN) 35
77 Conan the Barbarian movie (Casaro) 35
78 Savage Sword #125 (Thomas Kidd) 35
79 Savage Sword #157 (Dorian Vallejo) 35
80 Savage Sword #119 (ECh) 35
81 Savage Sword #140 (JJu) 45
82 Savage Sword #139 (JJu) red . . .45
82 Savage Sword #139 (JJu) blue . . .45
83 Savage Sword #123 (Ernie Chan) .35
84 Savage Sword #134 (JJu) 45
85 Savage Sword #122 (Ernie Chan) .35
86 Conan paperback cover (JuB) . . .45
87 Conan Paperback cover #2 (JuB) .45
88 Savage Sword #96 (JJu) 45
89 Savage Sword #108 (JJu) 45
90 Checklist 35

CONAN II

Comic Images (1994)

This second all chromium Conan set is scheduled for release in mid 1994, but was not available at press time. It will probably be as popular as the first series. Chromium card stock seems to be just the right enhancement for this kind of art.

Promo card, chromium (EN) 3.50
Two card chromium promo sheet (D-19 & D-20)(in Previews, June 1994) . 3.50

Conan II © Conan Properties, Inc.

Madman © Mike Allred

CREATOR'S PORTFOLIO

Wizard (1993-4)

These promo cards came bagged in the comic shop versions of Wizard *magazine. The backs are blue, with the series title, card number and text in white, plus some art and a photo of the artist. This is a continuing series, which is attractive and well designed.*

1 Mike Allred's Madman promo 1.00
2 Nelson's Mordare promo 1.00
3 Matt Wagner's Grendel promo . . . 1.00
4 Jeff Smith's Bone 1.00

Three card promo strip © Dynamic Entertainment, Inc. & Adam, Andy & Joe Kubert

Strangehands © Barry Windsor Smith

CREATORS UNIVERSE, THE

Dynamic Entertainment (1993)

This card series appeared in December 1993 (one month late). It was advertised as "100 New Original Characters From The Minds Of The Comic Megagods" and proved to be a very attractive set of cards which sold quickly. The checklists are scarce and are not numbered as part of the 100 card series. The Family Fusion Titanium cards, by the Kuberts, are the same art as the three card promo strip. The cards contain full-bleed art, with a character name in gold. The backs repeat the card name and contain the number, some text and an inset view of the head of the character. There is also a small picture of the whole character. Most of the card backs are laid out in "landscape" style and have a background painting of the sky and the earth with grid lines. All in all, a very nice set. This is one of the ten sets you ***must own*** *to be a legitimate comics cards collector. According to the company, promos X1 and X2 were given away at a show and sent to dealers. We have only ever seen one of them for sale, so we suspect that they are quite scarce compared to the other promo cards.*

Set: 100 cards 17.50
Checklists (1:18) CL1-CL5, each 5.00

Super Dimension Bonus Cards (1:6)
SD1 Intrepid (DvJ) 10.00
SD2 Enemy (MZ/StG) 10.00
SD3 U.S. Marshals (CHm) 10.00
SD4 Power & Glory (HC) 10.00
Family Fusion Titanium cards (1:6)
FF1 Syvil (NKu) 10.00

The Creators Universe © Dynamic Entertainment, Inc. & Brandon Peterson

FF2 Tartar (JKu) 10.00
FF3 Sgt. Major Acre (AKu) 10.00
Serigraph Card
SG1 Hellshock redemption card (JaL) (1:Case) 25.00
22Kt Gold Signature Card, each . . 25.00
Promo cards
Three card promo strip: Syvil, Tartar & Sgt. Major Acre (NKu,JKu,AKu) . . 5.00
Stronghold promo (BPe) 2.00
Redline promo (AKu) 2.00
The Silencer promo (SR) 1.50
Warhorse promo (JJu) 2.00
P1 Pheros prototype (BS) 2.00
P2 Sgt. Major Acre proto (AKu) 2.00
P3 Blitzkrieg prototype (HNg) 2.00
Four card promo/proto sheet, 8"x8½" 5.00
The four card promo/proto sheet contains Warhorse and P1 through P3 and some side-bar text advertising the cards. The Redline, Stronghold, and The Silencer cards have the same promo backs as Warhorse, but the backs of these three cards are upside down relative to the front.
X1 Bron (BWS) 15.00
X2 Strangehands (BWS) 15.00
Note: X1 & X2 contain different images of these characters from the regular cards.
Pack: 6 cards 1.50

CARD CHECKLIST
1 All American Girl (AH) 25
2 American Flagg (HC) 35
3 Ano-Tok (MPn) 25
4 Aquan (DJu) 25
5 Arc (BPe) 25
6 Ava (FM) 25
7 Beta (DvJ) 25
8 Blast (JD) 25
9 Bloodsidhe (JBg) 25
10 Bloodwyche (JMd) 25
11 Body Bags (JPn) 25
12 Body Blades (Jordan Raskin/ Ray Weisfeld) 25
13 Brave (CHm) 25
14 Breed (JSn) 25
15 Bron (BWS) 35
16 Bulldog (DaR) 25
17 Bunker (BPe) 25
18 Chayne (DJu) 25
19 Dr. Kiln (DIB) 25
20 Dr. Nob (KN) 25
21 Daybreak & Nightfall (RyL) 25
22 Deuce (DJu) 25
23 Dichotomy (JJ) 25
24 Dragun (DPs) 25
25 Dwight (FM) 25
26 Dyce (BPe) 25
27 Edge (GK/StG) 25
28 Electron (MMy) 25
29 Fluffy (JQ) 35
30 Force (JMd) 25
31 Foward Motion (JP/Dan Didio) . . .25
32 Full Otto (DvJ) 25
33 Hadron (Joe DeVito) 25
34 Hellfyre (Dan Fraga) 25
35 Heretic (JoP) 25
36 Invertigo (AH) 25
37 Io (Joe DeVito) 25
38 Johnny Redcap (JBg) 25
39 Khalif (John Czop) 25
40 Kid Death (JQ) 35
41 Knighthawk (NA) 25
42 Krane (DPs) 25
43 Lady Channel Cat (John Estes) . .25
44 Laserheart (JD) 25
45 Luana Sikes (Steve Woron) 35
46 Maxim (HNg) 25
47 Merope (E.Silas Smith) 25
48 Mine Field (DaR) 25
49 Monad (BPe) 25
50 Monkey Man & O'Brien (AAd) 25
51 Necroteck (JP/Dan Didio) 25
52 Nightfire (ATi) 25
53 Nightmaere (Joe Linsner/ Joe Monks) 25
54 Obsidean Stone (Joe Linsner) . . .25
55 Rojas (WS) 25
56 Oniko & Gorildozer (AAd) 25
57 Pastor Prime (CHm) 25
58 Penumbra (Andy Smith) 25
59 Phaedra (WS) 25
60 Pheros (BS) 25
61 Procrustean (JJ) 25
62 Queen Sikora (MPn) 25
63 Red Death (TMd) 25
64 Red Tide (John Estes) 25
65 Redline (AKu) 35
66 Sgt. Major Acre (AKu) 35
67 Savage (GK) 25
68 Seige (Jordan Raskin/ Ray Weisfeld) 25
69 Sensi & Huge (MPa) 25
70 Sera (AKu) 35
71 Shellcase (John Estes) 25
72 Sifu Hara (TMd) 25
73 Singularity (KIS) 25
74 Slyce (BPe) 25
75 Solo (Bill Marimon) 25
76 Squire (Ken Hooper) 25
77 Starfish (DIB) 25
78 Starwing (ATi) 25
79 Strangehands (BWS) 35
80 Syvil & Co. (NKu) 35
81 Terra Firma Irma (KN) 25
82 Terradax (MPa) 25
83 The Moth (SR) 25
84 The Righteous (HNg) 25
85 The Silencer (SR) 25
86 The Veteran (LW) 25
87 Thrashur (BS) 25
88 "Trash Can" Mann Joe (HNg) 25
89 Turbine (NKu) 35
90 Uplink (KIS) 25
91 Voortexx (AKu) 35
92 Warhorse (JJu) 35
93 Weezul (MPa) 25
94 Werewolf Alpha (DIB) 25
95 Widow-Maker (JJ) 25
96 Woe/Min (MPa) 25
97 Wolfhound (BS) 25
98 Wraithchild (HNg) 25
99 Wreckage (LW) 25
100 Wryscher (Greg Williams) 25

Franklin Crunch 'N' Munch © Marvel Entertainment Group, Inc.

CRUNCH 'n' MUNCH

(Franklin, 1993)

(Neal Adams/Continuity Assoc. art)

These cards came in specially marked boxes of Franklin Crunch 'n' Munch Butter Toffee Popcorn. They were extensively advertised in Marvel comics. The second edition cards came out in April 1994, also in marked boxes. The boxes, with card and popcorn sold for about $1.00 for the 5 ounce size and about $2.00 for the 10 ounce size. If you weren't a big popcorn eater you bought the smaller package and still got the card!

1st Edition (1993)

Card	Price
Storm	2.00
Wolverine	2.00
Hulk	2.00
Spider-Man	3.00
Cage	3.00
Superheroes	2.00

2nd Edition (1994)

Card	Price
Cable (TR)	2.00
Cyclops (TR)	2.00
Gambit (TR)	2.00
Spider-Man (TR)	2.00
Wolverine	2.00
Jean Grey	2.00

[H.P. LOVECRAFT'S] CTHULHU

Millennium Comics (1993)

The cards were bound into comics in three card strips, which consisted of two cards and a Millennium logo card.

Card	Price
1	.50
2	.50
3 Hastur (Joe Phillips/Deirdre DeLay)	.50
4 Mi-Go (Joe Phillips/Deirdre DeLay)	.50
5 Yig Father of Serpents (Deirdre DeLay)	.50
6 Quachil Uttaus (Deirdre DeLay)	.50

Cthulhu © Millennium Comics

Cyber Force © Top Cow Productions, Inc.

CYBER FORCE/STRYKE FORCE

Hero/Cards Illustrated (1994)

This series was promoted with cards in both Hero *and* Cards Illustrated. *The three cards in Hero came in three different issues, but you had to buy two copies of each to get both the blue border and the red bordered versions. They are foil cards and form a triptych image. The 10 card series has a marble border and a light colored back with text in black and a cute inset picture in the lower right corner. The cards came bagged in* Cards Illustrated #5, *three per copy. That meant that you had to buy more than three copies of the issue to find all the cards. The three copies we bought were missing card #9, so we haven't seen it, but it's on the checklist.*

"Master Foil" cards (Hero)

Card	Price
Set: 3 promo cards (MS/BPe)	
blue borders	4.00
red borders	4.00

Cards Illustrated set

Card	Price
#1 Major Stryker (BPe)	.50
#2 Cyblade	.50
#3 Velocity	.50
#4 Ripclaw (MS)	.50
#5 Ballistic	.50
#6 Tempest (BPe)	.50
#7 Black Anvil	.50
#8 Kill Razor	.50
#9 Weapon Zero	.50
#10 Mark Silvestri (photo)	1.00

D

DAGGERFORCE

Dagger Comics (1993)

This is a promo for an 85 card set which should have been out at press time, but we haven't seen it. Too bad, because this is a nice looking promo, with a dark outer border and a blue back with white printing. There's no date, but it was available at shows in 1993.

Card	Price
Scorpion Corps, Tork "prototype" promo	1.00

DARK, THE

Continum Comics (1993)

These are comic book promos from Joseph Naftali and Continum Comics *which were given away at comics shows in 1993 and 1994. The backs of all three are black and white and contain the same information about the hero. The fronts all say "The Dark" and have different images, which we have identified by background color, since they are not numbered or titled. Our copies are autographed and we believe a great many such exist, so don't pay a lot extra for an autographed version.*

Card	Price
Yellow & Red promo (Todd Lidstone & GP)	1.00
Green promo (BS)	1.00
Black promo (MBr & DPs)	1.00

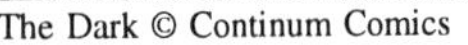
The Dark © Continum Comics

Dark Dominion Zero © TRG & EEP, L.P.

DARK DOMINION ZERO

River Group (1993)

Jim Shooter, creator

The fronts and backs of the first 117 cards form a 26 page comic book when put in 9 pocket sleeves. None have captions, but they are

Dark Dominion Zero © TRG & EEP, L.P.

numbered on the front lower right hand corner and say "Dark Dominion" while the back has a "Defiant" logo. The remaining 33 cards contain character pictures on the fronts and biographical information on the back and are captioned with the character's nickname (front) and true name (back). The level one bonus cards form a 9 card superpanel. The Steampit promo came in a group of 3 River Group promos along with a Plasm promo and a Good Guys promo. The art for these cards is by Steve Ditko and Steve Leialoha.

Set: 150 cards 15.00

Bonus Cards, Level One (1:18)
1 of 9 Bo Peep's Boudoir 6.00
2 of 9 Central Park 6.00
3 of 9 Michael's Apartment 6.00
4 of 9 The Bowels 6.00
5 of 9 The Growth 6.00
6 of 9 The Steampit 6.00
7 of 9 Chasm's Penthouse 6.00
8 of 9 The Atrium 6.00
9 of 9 The Shanty (from Album) . . . 7.00
Bonus Cards, Level Two (1:72) (SD)
1 of 4 Michael and Charlemagne . . . 9.00
2 of 4 Michael and Wardancer 9.00
3 of 4 Michael and Glory 9.00
4 of 4 Michael and Lorca (tin set) . 12.00
Quantum View Lens 2.50
Album, with ashcan comic, Quantum View lens for bonus cards 20.00
Michael Alexander promo card 1.00
Four card promo sheet, San Diego con 4.00
Four card promo sheet, Comicfest '93 . . . . 3.50
Four card promo sheet, Diamond Distribution 3.00
2 of 3 Steampit promo card 5.00
Two card, one panel promo sheet . . 1.50
Six image blank back promo 2.50
Notes: 6 different wrappers; also includes
Plasm Level 2 #4 Bonus card (1:360)
Orig. SD art, 10 made (1:216,000)
Pack: 9 cards 1.00

CARD CHECKLIST
1 thru 117, not listed, each 10
118 Glimmer/Michael Alexander 20
119 Hamster/Thea Hamston 20
120 Hootch/Bill Hamston 20
121 Peaches/Substratum superheroine 20
122 Hustle/Shahood Dinwiddie 20
123 Lurk/Substratum Arch-Demon . .20
124 Calamari/Giuseppe Lercio 20
125 Scat/Substratum scoundrel 20
126 Shylock/Melanie Yee 20
127 Skunk/Samuel Monsour 20
128 Skinner/Allen Miller 20
129 Skewer/Skip Ceyrolles 20
130 Oink/Arnold Luncher 20
131 Oak/Substratum strongman 20
132 Mercy/Mercedes Kieselbach 20
133 Leper/Robert Jolley 20
134 Dusk/Real name unknown 20
135 Galahad/Substratum Superhero .20
136 Elephant/Real name unknown . . .20
137 Diesel/Substratum Rogue 20
138 Savage/Eleanor McDonald 20
139 Torment/Substratum Arch-Demon 20
140 Oak/Substratum Arch-Demon . . .20
141 Moray/Substratum Slimefiend . . .20
142 Bottom/Substratum Arch-Demon .20
143 Ludwig/Ludwig Von Knickelbein .20
144 Clunk/Clarence Wazenegger 20
145 Butter/Charlotte Mudge 20
146 Mule/Real name unknown 20
147 Muriel/Muriel Powers 20
148 Bo Peep/Bo Pepperman 20
149 Boil/Joseph Kettle 20
150 Chasm/Charles Mal 20

DARK HORSE [BATMAN VERSUS PREDATOR]

Dark Horse/DC Comics (1991)

*The cards have a silver border (except at the bottom) and depict Batman fighting a Predator, by various artists. Short comments about **other** artists are on the back.*

Set: 16? cards 20.00

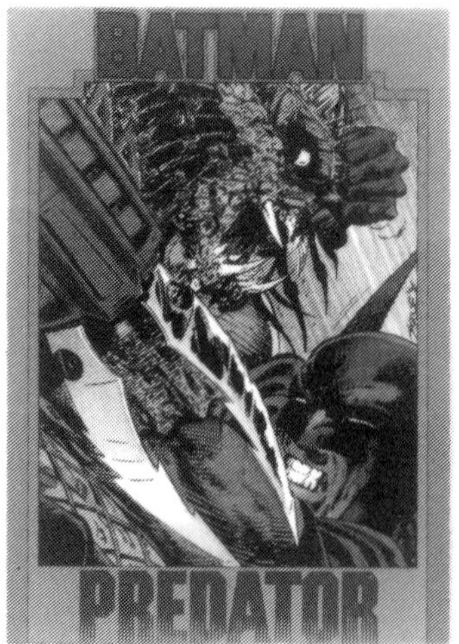

© DC Comics/Dark Horse Comics, Inc.

© Dark Horse Comics, Inc.

DARK HORSE: MAGNA MONTH

Dark Horse (1993)

Full bleed fronts, with titles; grey back with checklist information. The cards came bagged with Advance Comics #51.

1 Outlanders comic promo 50
2 Venus Wars II comic promo (Johnson) 50

DC COMICS

DC Bloodlines © DC Comics, Inc.

DC BLOODLINES

SkyBox (1993)

*Cards 1 through 54 feature pictures of top DC Superheroes (and new characters) centered around the invading parasites from the 1993 DC comic book annuals. The card backs form a 6 x 9 card color puzzle picture which shows one ugly creature about to devour the whole earth! Cards 73 to 79 have front and back pictures of these parasites, while cards 55 to 73 feature new characters introduced in these annuals, with text and a mug shot picture on the back. The foil embossed bonus cards and the promo cards feature the four beings claiming to be the one true Superman. The scarcest card is the Superman Redemption card, which is blue, with a red and yellow Superman "S" logo. You could send this card in to exchange it for a card of the One True Superman. The promo cards and the foil-embossed cards both have the same art as their namesake regular cards, which is economical (for DC and SkyBox anyway). All five of the **un-numbered** promo cards have the same backs, with text in a yellow box with a green border which asks*

Which, if any, is the real Man of Steel? *Four of them have the same art (depicting one of the "faux" Supermen) as the foil-embossed cards of the same name, but they are not foil-embossed. The fifth promo card contains four small portraits of these same characters. The four* ***numbered*** *promo cards have the same "faux" Supermen, and contain promo information about the card set, rather than the characters. They have a number on the back in the upper right-hand corner and are more common than the un-numbered cards.*

Set: 81 cards 11.00

Foil-Embossed Cards (1:18)
S1 The Man of Steel (JBg/DJa) . . . 15.00
S2 The Man of Tomorrow(DJu/BBr) 15.00
S3 The Last Son of Krypton (JG) . . 15.00
S4 Superboy (TG/KK) 15.00
S5 Redemption Card (1:72) 15.00

Superman mail-in © DC Comics, Inc.

The One True Superman(KGa/JG) 35.00
Promo cards
Four images (in *Adventures of Supermen* comic #500) 4.00
The Man of Steel (JBg/DJa) 3.00
P1 The Man of Steel (JBg/DJa) 2.00
The Man of Tomorrow (DJu/BBr) . . . 3.00
P2 The Man of Tomorrow (DJu/BBr) 2.00
The Last Son of Krypton (JG) 3.00
P3 The Last Son of Krypton (JG) . . . 2.00
The Metropolis Kid (TG/KK) 3.00
P4 Superboy (TG/KK) 2.00
Pack: 8 cards 1.50

CARD CHECKLIST

Action Cards *Backs form large parasite puzzle with art by Christian Alamy.*
1 Deadly Genesis! 10
2 Lobo Out For Blood! 10
3 Lobo and Layla–Bad to the Bone! . .10
4 The Demonseed's Arrival! 10
5 The Man of Steel! (JBg/DJa) 10
6 Battle on the Edge! 10
7 Glonth's Abattoir! 10
8 Flash & Argus–Race to Action! 10
9 Linked in Blood! 10
10 Blood Magic! 10
11 Assault on the Innocent! 10
12 Titans Clash! 10
13 Gemir's Primal Hunger! 10
14 The Man of Tomorrow! (DJu/BBr) 10
15 To Save Her Soul! 10
16 Lissik's Blood Passion! 10
17 Green Lantern & Nightblade! 10
18 Nightblade's Retribution! 10
19 Lionheart–Battleground Zero! 10
20 Cry for Blood! 10
21 Knights and Warriors! 10
22 Loose Cannon Rages! 10
23 The Last Son of Krypton! (JG) . . .10
24 Against Cannon Fire! 10
25 Storm of Blood and Anger! 10
26 Valor in a Jamm! 10
27 Jamm Jams! 10
28 Lust's Deadly Arrow! 10
29 The Hook & Green Arrow! 10
30 Lissik is Hooked! 10
31 The Ray Unleashed! 10
32 Plague of the Terrorsmith! 10
33 Amazon Fury! 10
34 In Blood's Rapture! (TG/KK) 10
35 Superboy! (TG/KK) 10
36 Sparx Fly! 10
37 The Sky Rains Blood! (JD/RM) . . .10
38 Mongrel's Frenzy! (JD/RM) 10
39 Hawkman Versus Mongrel! (JD/RM) 10
40 Lock and Load! 10
41 The Heat of Gunfire! 10
42 Deathstroke & Gunfire 10
43 Devils Face Off! 10
44 The Rage King! 10
45 Prism's Light! 10
46 Slay the Beast! 10
47 Hitman Versus the Demon! 10
48 Demon's Ire! 10
49 Experience Chimera! 10
50 Warriors United! 10
51 A New Horror is Born! 10
52 Pax Brings the War Home! 10
53 Parasites From the Stars! 10
54 Death World! 10
New Blood
55 Layla .10
56 Edge .10
57 Argus .10
58 Anima 10
59 Myriad (DL) 10
60 Nightblade 10
61 Lionheart 10
62 Loose Cannon 10
63 Jamm (JoP) 10
64 The Hook (JBa) 10
65 Terrorsmith 10
66 Sparx (TG/KK) 10
67 Mongrel (JD/RM) 10
68 Gunfire 10
69 Prism .10
70 Hitman 10
71 Chimera (PJ) 10
72 Pax 10
Parasites
73 Pritor (AAd) 10
74 Angon (AAd) 10
75 Lissik (AAd) 10
76 Glonth (AAd) 10
77 Gemir (AAd) 10
78 Venev (AAd) 10
79 Slood (AAd) 10
80 Checklist A 10
81 Checklist B 10

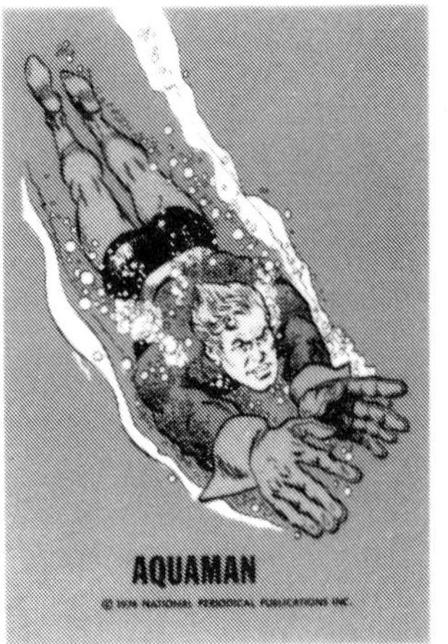

DC & Warner Bros. cards © National Periodical Publications, Inc. & Warner Bros. Inc.

DC/NATIONAL PERIODICAL/ WARNER BROS. CARDS

Wonder Bread/Hostess (1974)

These cards have either DC comic book heroes, or Warner Bros. Looney Tunes characters on the front, with a four panel black and white comic book type back. There is no series title or card number, but the DC heroes are portrayed seriously.

Set: 30 cards 125.00

Aquaman 4.50
Batman 5.50
Cat Woman 6.00
Clark Kent 5.00
Lois Lane 5.00
Robin 4.50
Superman 5.50
The Joker 4.50
The Penguin 4.50
The Riddler 4.50
Wonder Woman 4.50
Warner Bros., with comic back
Beaky Buzzard 2.50
Bugs Bunny 4.00
Cool Cat 2.50
Daffy Duck 4.00
Elmer Fudd 4.00
Foghorn Leghorn 3.50
Henery Hawk 2.50
Honey Bunny 2.50
Merlin The Magic Mouse 3.50
Pepe Le Pew 4.00
Petunia Pig 2.50
Porky Pig 2.50
Road Runner 4.50
Speedy Gonzales 3.50
Sylvester 4.00
Tasmanian Devil 4.50
Tweety 3.50
Wile E. Coyote 4.50
Yosemite Sam 3.50

DC Strip Cards I © DC Comics, Inc.

DC COMICS STRIP CARDS I

DC Comics (1987)

These cards came on 8 card strips which were used as backing and hanging boards for overprint comics sold in three comic packs. In addition to the cards, each board had a strip picturing Superman,

Batman and Wonder Woman with a hole for hanging. Two different versions are known, one mentioning Batman on the back and one mentioning Superman. The cards are somewhat primitive by today's standards, but the characters are treated seriously and represent the first card appearances for many of the characters. Since the cards had to be hand cut along the dotted lines, there is no such thing as a mint set.

Set: 48 cards, cut out 20.00

8 card strips, 6 diff., each 5.00

Great Heroes

1 Superman 50
2 Batman 50
3 Aquaman 50
4 Green Lantern 50
5 Green Arrow 50
6 Firestorm 50
7 Dr. Fate 50
8 Hawkman 50
9 Hawkwoman 50
10 Cyborg 50
11 Nightwing 50
12 Wonder Girl 50
13 Raven 50
14 Starfire 50
15 The Changeling 50
16 Jericho 50
17 Martian Manhunter 50
18 Mister Miracle 50
19 Flash 50

Great Villains

20 Mr. Freeze 50
21 Tyr .50
22 Penguin 50
23 The Joker 50
24 The Riddler 50
25 The Catwoman 50

Great Heroes

26 The Man of Steel #1 50

Great Moments in Comics (Covers)

27 Action Comics #1 50
28 Justice League of America #31 . . .50
29 Justice League of America #21 . . .50
30 Action Comics #252 50
31 Action Comics #340 50
32 Superman #1 50
33 Superman #199 50
34 Detective Comics #27 50
35 Detective Comics #38 50
36 Detective Comics #359 50
37 Batman #1 50
38 Crisis #1 50
39 Captain Atom #1 50
40 The New Teen Titans 50
41 Infinity, Inc. #1 50
42 Showcase #4 50
43 Adventure #307 50

Great Villains

44 The Terminator 50
45 Two-Face 50
46 The Trickster 50
47 The Key 50
48 Eclipso 50

DC Strip Cards II © DC Comics, Inc.

DC COMICS STRIP CARDS II

DC Comics (1989)

This second, higher number series of comic book hanger cards is dated 1989, but DC did not use up its supply of some of this series until 1993 and we have seen some in toy stores right up to press time. However, we have only seen the cards named below, so the others may have been used up earlier.

Set: 72? cards 30.00

8 card strips, 9 diff., each 2.50
49 25
50 Justice League Europe 25
51 Mr. Mxyzptlk 25
52 Superman 25
53 25
54 25
55 Starman 25
56 25
57 25
58 Black Hand 25
59 Ocean Master 25
60 Black Lightning 25
61 25
62 25
63 Wonder Woman 25
64 25
65 25
66 The Phantom Stranger 25
67 Blackhawk 25
68 Hawkman 25
69 25
70 25
71 Amazo 25
72 Superman 25
73 25
74 Black Manta 25
75 Brave and the Bold 25
76 El Diablo 25
77 25
78 25
79 25
80 Kobra 25
81 25
82 Man-Bat 25
83 Poison Ivy 25
84 Blue Beetle 25
85 25
86 The Question 25
87 25
88 Flash .25
89 25
90 Atom & Hawkman 25
91 Black Canary 25
92 Ra's Al Ghul 25
93 25
94 Batman 25
95 25
96 The Atom 25
97 25
98 Halo .25
99 Batgirl 25
100 25
101 25
102 The Warlord 25
103 25
104 Green Lantern 25
105 25
106 The New Teen Titans 25
107 Krypton 25
108 25
109 25
110 Zatanna 25
111 25
112 Flash 25
113 Geo-Force 25
114 Animal Man 25
115 Metallo 25
116 25
117 25
118 Robotman 25
119 25
120 Ambush Bug 25

DC Cosmic Cards © DC Comics, Inc.

DC COSMIC CARDS

"Inaugural Edition"

Impel (1992)

This was Impel's attempt to do for DC characters what it had done for Marvel in the first two Marvel Universe cards. The set was popular, at first, but holograms were not a new gimmick anymore and the basic card design was okay, but not inspired. If the set had come out a year earlier it would have been much more popular, but it's still a fine set of cards. The fronts have a grey border and the DC logo along with the card title. The backs have the same border with text in a cream colored box, detail pictures and a trivia question. The cards say "DC Comics" and are only called "DC Cosmic Cards" on the wrapper. There are ten holograms, which resemble the regular card design. The backs list all the holograms and are not individually numbered. They have a color picture of Superman, but with different background colors. The five promo cards have a blue-grey border (rather than the grey border of the final version) and there are other slight variations as well, such as the "mug-shot" of Clark Kent on the back of the Superman promo card versus the smiling wavy-haired Clark on the regular card. The borders on the promo sheet are grey and they are otherwise just like the regular cards. The primary way to distinguish the promo cards and cards cut from the promo sheet from the regular cards is the absence of the card number in white in the upper right-hand corner. There was an error in the production of card #44 (Deathstroke) which was explained to us in a letter from SkyBox as follows: "For mysterious production reasons never uncovered, a small amount of these cards did not have a Q&A; the black box in which this copy belonged was simply black. It was very strange. The copy on the completed cards reads: 'By what name is Wilson's son Joe better known? Jericho, formerly of the New Titans.*' My official story for this error card was that Deathstroke broke into our production facility and removed the plate because he did not want to remind his wife, from whom he was estranged, about their son, who was formerly of the* New Titans *because Deathstroke killed him."*

Set: 180 cards 17.50

DC Hologram Hall of Fame (WS art) (1:9)
DCH1 Clark Kent & Lois Lane 9.00
DCH2 Darkseid 6.00
DCH3 Deathstroke the Terminator . . 7.00
DCH4 Flash 6.00
DCH5 Green Lantern 6.00
DCH6 Hawkman 6.00
DCH7 Lobo 8.00
DCH8 Superman 10.00
DCH9 Wonder Woman 6.00
DCH10 Waverider 6.00
Promo sheet: Modern Age Wonder Woman, Lobo, Deathstroke the Terminator & Modern Age Superman 7.50
Cards cut from sheet, each 1.50
Promo Set, 5 cards in cello pack . . 12.50
Modern Age Flash (#6) 2.00
Modern Age Green Lantern (#9) . . 2.00
Modern Age Superman (#18) 3.00
Modern Age Wonder Woman (#21) 2.00
Deathstroke the Terminator (#44) . 2.00
Pack: 12 cards 1.00
Four different wrappers

Superman promo (back)
© DC Comics, Inc.

CARD CHECKLIST

Hero Heritage
1 Golden Age Blue Beetle (PCu/KK) .15
2 Silver Age Blue Beetle (PCu/RbC) .15
3 Modern Age Blue Beetle (DJu/BBr) .15
4 Golden Age Flash (JKu) 20
5 Silver Age Flash (Cl/MA) 20
6 Modern Age Flash (GrL/JMz) 20
7 Golden Age Green Lantern (MnN/MA) 20
8 Silver Age Green Lantern (GK) 20
9 Modern Age Green Lantern (MBr/JMz) 20
10 Golden Age Hawkman (JKu) 20
11 Silver Age Hawkman (MA) 20
12 Modern Age Hawkman (GN) 20
13 Golden Age Shazam! (KS/GN) . . .15
14 Silver Age Shazam! (KS/GN) 15
15 Modern Age Shazam! (GN) 15
16 Golden Age Superman (SR/JOy) .20
17 Silver Age Superman (CS/MA/JOy) .20
18 Modern Age Superman (JOy) 20
19 Golden Age Wonder Woman (TrR) .15
20 Silver Age Wonder Woman (JD) . .15
21 Modern Age Wonder Woman(JIT) .15

Villain Heritage
22 Golden Age Cheetah (TrR) 15
23 Silver Age Cheetah (PCu/KK) 15
24 Modern Age Cheetah (PCu/RbC) .15
25 Golden Age Luthor (PCu/RbC) . . .20
26 Silver Age Luthor (CS/MA) 20
27 Modern Age Luthor (JBg/DJa) . . .20
28 Golden Age Mr. Mxyztplk (SvS) . .15
29 Silver Age Mr. Mxyztplk (JO&SvS) .15
30 Modern Age Mr. Mxyztplk (HwP/JO & SvS) .15

Earth's Mightiest Heroes
31 Animal Man (TMd) 20
32 Aqualad (K.Hooper/SL) 15
33 Aquaman (K.Hooper/TS) 15
34 Black Condor (G.Guler/DG) 15
35 Black Lightning (TVE/B.Smith) . . .15
36 Blackhawk (R.Burchett) 15
37 Blue Devil (PCu/RbC) 15
38 Booster Gold (DJu/BBr) 15
39 Bronze Tiger (RE/DvC) 15
40 Changeling (TG/AV) 15
41 The Creeper (GN) 15
42 Crimson Fox (G.Guler/KK) 15
43 Cyborg (TG/AV) 15
44 Deathstroke, the Terminator (StE/B.Smith) 25
44(A) Deathstroke, error card 4.00
45 Dr. Light (BS/R.Elliott) 15
46 Dove (G.Guler/DG) 15
47 Elongated Man (BS/R.Elliott) 15
48 Fire (G.Guler/DG) 15
49 Firehawk (TMd) 15
50 Firestorm (TMd) 15
51 Gangbuster (JBg/DJa) 15
52 Geo-Force (JAp/RbC) 15
53 The Guardian (JBg/DJa) 15
54 Guy Gardner (JSon/B.Smith) 15
55 Hawk (G.Guler/KK) 15
56 Hawkwoman (GN) 15
57 Hourman (Napolitano/NKu) 15
58 Ice (G.Guler/KK) 15
59 Jade (TG/AV) 15
60 John Stewart (JSon/B.Smith) 15
61 Katana (JD) 15
62 Metamorpho (BS/R.Elliott) 15
63 Mr. Bones (TVE/CR) 15
64 Nightshade (PCu/RbC) 15
65 Nightwing (TG/AV) 20
66 Nightwind (TVE/Napolitano) 20
67 Nuklon (SwM) 15
68 Pantha (TG/AV) 15
69 Peacemaker (BS/R.Elliott) 15
70 Phantom Lady (DG) 15
71 Power Girl (JO/DG) 15
72 Ragman (George Pratt) 20
73 Raven (TG/AV) 15
74 Rocket Red (TTn) 15
75 Speedy (TG/AV) 15
76 Troia (TG/AV) 15
77 Vixen (LMc/M.Clark) 20
78 Wildcat (PCu/RbC) 15

Earth's Mightiest Villains
79 Amazo (KM/DvC) 15
80 Big Sir (Cl/DvC) 15
81 Black Manta 15
82 Blockbuster (PCu/RbC) 15
83 Bolt (PCu/RbC) 15
84 Brainiac (JBg/DJa) 20
85 Captain Boomerang (LMc/Clark) . .15
86 Chemo (SwM) 15
87 Chronos (GK) 30
88 Copperhead (G.Guler/KK) 15
89 Count Vertigo (TVE/KK) 15
90 Deadline (TL/SHa) 15
91 Deadshot (LMc/M.Clark) 15
92 Dr. Light (Mike Clark) 15
93 Dr. Polaris (GK) 30
94 Eclipso (TVE/DvC) 15
95 Goldface (GK) 30
96 Gorilla Grodd (Cl/R.McCarthy) . . .15
97 Houngan (TG/AV) 15
98 Jerico (TG/AV) 15
99 Kestrel (G.Guler/KK) 15
100 Monarch (DJu/DG) 15
101 Ocean Master 15
102 Parasite (JBg/DJa) 15
103 Phobia (TG/AV) 15
104 Plasmus (TG/AV) 15
105 Psycho-Pirate (NKu) 15
106 Shadow Thief (GN) 15
107 Silver Swan (JIT) 15
108 Sonar (GK) 30
109 Toyman (JO) 15
110 Vandal Savage 15
111 Warp (TG/AV) 15

Heroes From Beyond
112 Adam Strange (Cl/DG) 15
113 Arisia (JSon/DvC) 15
114 Big Barda (KM/DvC) 15
115 Black Racer (RHo) 15
116 Fastbak (RHo) 15
117 G'Nort (JSon/SvS) 15
118 Kilowog (JSon/SvS) 15
119 Lightray (RHo) 15
120 Lobo (SBs) 60
121 Martian Manhunter(KM/DvC) 15
122 Metron (RHo) 15
123 Mr. Miracle (KM/KK) 15
124 Orion (RHo) 15
125 Starfire (TG/AV) 15

Villains From Beyond
126 Ares (PCu/RbC) 15
127 Blackfire (TG/AV) 15
128 Darkseid (RHo) 20
129 Desaad (RHo) 15
130 Despero (TVE/R.McCarthy) 15
131 Glorious Godfrey (RHo) 15
132 Granny Goodness (RHo) 15
133 Kalibak (RHo) 15
134 Kanjar Ro (GN) 15
135 Manga Khan (TTn) 15
136 Maxima (DJu/BBr) 15
137 Mr. Nebula (TTn) 15
138 Sinestro (PCu) 15

DC Cosmic Cards © DC Comics, Inc.

139 Starro (KM/DvC) 15
140 Steppenwolf (RHo) 15
141 Yuga Khan (RHo) 15

Great Battles
142 Crisis on Earths One and Two (card A) (PCu/DvC) 15
143 Crisis on Earths One and Two (card B) (PCu/DvC) 15
144 Crisis on Earths One and Two (card C) (PCu/DvC) 15
145 Crisis on Infinite Earths (card A) (PCu/RbC) 15
146 Crisis on Infinite Earths (card B) (PCu/RbC) 15
147 Crisis on Infinite Earths (card C) (PCu/RbC) 15
148 Legends (A) (PCu/KK) 15
149 Legends (B) (PCu/KK) 15
150 Legends (C) (PCu/KK) 15
151 Millennium (A) (JSon) 15
152 Millennium (B) (JSon) 15
153 Millennium (C) (JSon) 15
154 Invasion! (A) (BS/BBr) 15
155 Invasion! (B) (BS/BBr) 15
156 Invasion! (C) (BS/BBr) 15
157 Cosmic Odyssey (A) (PCu) 15
158 Cosmic Odyssey (B) (PCu) 15
159 Cosmic Odyssey (C) (PCu) 15
160 The Great Darkness Saga (card A) (KG/AG) 15
161 The Great Darkness Saga (card B) (KG/AG) 15
162 The Great Darkness Saga (card C) (KG/AG) 15
163 Armageddon 2001 (A) (DJu/ATi) .20
164 Armageddon 2001 (B) (DJu/ATi) .20
165 Armageddon 2001 (C) (DJu/ATi) .20
166 War of the Gods (A) (PCu/RT) . .15
167 War of the Gods (B) (PCu/RT) . .15
168 War of the Gods (C) (PCu/RT) . .15

Classic Covers
169 Action Comics #1 (JoS) 15
170 All-American Comics #16 15
171 All Star Comics #3 (EHi) 15
172 The Brave and the Bold #34 (JKu) 15
173 New Gods #1 (JK) 15
174 Sensation Comics #1 (JK) 15
175 Showcase #22 (GK) 15
176 Showcase #34 (GK/MA) 15
177 Superman #1 (JoS) 15
178 Wonder Woman #1 15
179 Checklist A 15
180 Checklist B 15

DC Cosmic Teams triptych cards © DC Comics, Inc.

DC COSMIC TEAMS

SkyBox (1993)

This card series includes the first portrait cards of Death and of Doomsday (who was, of course, featured earlier in ***Doomsday: The Death of Superman*** *card release), and there's also a nice Lobo card. The cards have blue borders and an inner frame of colors which varies by team. The backs are yellow/orange and have text, number and a small picture titled "DC Flashback!" for all of the cards except the team triptychs. The triptych cards naturally fit together side by side and the backs have an identification guide for the characters on the front (instead of the picture). The cards all say "DC" but "Cosmic Teams" is only mentioned on the wrapper. The holograms do say "DC Cosmic Teams" and feature full bleed images. The backs list all six holograms, but are individually numbered as well, and each one has a different border color. By the time this set came out bonus holograms were a very old sales gimmick and SkyBox itself had produced much better bonus cards for the highly popular Doomsday: The Death of Superman series the previous fall.*

The three card prototype set was distributed widely. The Deathstroke prototype is less common. They are just like the real cards, except the SkyBox logo is at the top, instead of the bottom, and they say "Prototype" in white over the text. The four promo cards have white backs and all have the same text.

The ***Hologram Hall of Fame*** *cards feature art by Jon Bogdanove, Kim DeMulder, Jan Duursema, Scott Eaton, Tom Mandrake, Jerry Ordway and Val Semelks.*

Set: 150 cards 17.50

Hologram Hall of Fame
DCH11 Captain Marvel (JOy) 5.00
DCH12 Hawkman 5.00
DCH13 Lobo 6.00
DCH14 The Spectre 6.00
DCH15 Superman 7.00
DCH16 Swamp Thing 5.00
Promo & Prototype cards
Proto cards #34-#36, Foes of Superman triptych set (TG/DHz) 3.00
Proto card #60 (TG/AV) 2.00
P1 Apparition promo 2.50
0 Deathstroke promo card (1993 NY Comic Show) 2.00
00 Dragonmage promo (Wizard #19) 2.00
000 Catspaw promo (in CBG Price Guide) 2.00
0000 Computo promo card (in Legionnaires comic #1) 2.00
Pack: 8 cards 1.25

CARD CHECKLIST
Team Triptychs
1 Justice League America 10
2 } pencils by Dan Jurgens 10
3 } and inks by Rick Burchett 10
4 Justice League International 10
5 } pencils by Ron Randall 10
6 } and inks by Randy Elliott 10
7 Justice Society of America 10
8 } by Joe Kubert 10
9 } alone .10
10 New Titans 10
11 } pencils by Tom Grummett 10
12 } and inks by Alvey 10
13 Team Titans 10
14 } pencils by Phil Jimenez 10
15 } and inks by Ray McCarthy 10
16 L.E.G.I.O.N. 10
17 } pencils by Barry Kitson 10
18 } and inks by Robin Smith 10
19 Legionnaires 10
20 } pencils by Chris Sprouse 10
21 } and inks by Karl Storey 10
22 Green Lantern Corps 10
23 } pencils by M.D. Bright 10
24 } and inks by Romeo Tanghal 10
25 Worlds of Magic 10
26 } pencils by Chris Bachalo 10
27 } and inks by Rick Bryant 10
28 Foes of the Justice League 10
29 } pencils by Travis Charest 10
30 } and inks by Ray McCarthy 10
31 Society of Sin 10
32 } pencils by Kerry Gammill 10
33 } and inks by Will Blyberg 10
34 Foes of Superman 10
35 } pencils by Tom Grummett 10
36 } and inks by Doug Hazlewood . . .10
Justice League America
pencils: Dan Jurgens/ inks: Rick Burchett
37 Superman 15
38 Blue Beetle 10
39 Booster Gold 10
40 Fire 10
41 Ice 10
42 Guy Gardner 10
43 Bloodwynd 10
Justice League International
pencils: Ron Randall/ inks: Randy Elliott
44 Green Lantern 10
45 Flash .10
46 Metamorpho 10
47 Crimson Fix 10
48 Dr. Light 10
49 Elongated Man 10
50 Power Girl 10
Justice Society of America
pencils: Mike Parobeck/ inks: Mike Machlan
51 Golden Age Flash 10
52 Golden Age Green Lantern 10
53 Golden Age Hawkman 10
54 Golden Age Dr. Mid-Nite 10
55 Golden Age Atom 10
56 Golden Age Hourman 10
57 Golden Age Starman 10
58 Golden Age Wildcat 10
New Titans
pencils: Tom Grummett/ inks: Al Vey
59 Nightwing 10
60 Deathstroke 10
61 Cyborg 10
62 Pantha 10
63 Phantasm 10
64 Wildebeest 10
Team Titans *pencils: Phil Jimenez/*
65 Mirage (inks: Al Vey) 10
66 Killowat (inks: Al Vey) 10
67 Nightrider (inks: Al Vey) 10
68 Redwing (inks: Ray McCarthy) . . .10
69 Terra (inks: Ray McCarthy) 10
70 Battalion (inks: Ray McCarthy) . . .10
71 Troia (inks: Al Vey) 10
L.E.G.I.O.N.
pencils: Barry Kitson/ inks: Robin Smith
72 Vril Dox 10
73 Phase .10
74 Garryn Bek 10
75 Strata .10
76 Stealth 10
77 Lady Quark 10
78 Garv 10
79 Telepath 10
80 Lobo 10
81 Captain Comet 10

DC Cosmic Teams © DC Comics Inc.

Legionnaires *pencils: Chris Spouse or Jason Pearson/ inks: Karl Story*
82 Cosmic Boy (Spouse/Story) 10
83 Saturn Girl (Spouse/Story) 10
84 Live Wire (Spouse/Story) 10
85 Apparition (AH) 10
86 Triad (Ty Templeton) 10
87 Chameleon (Spouse/Story) 10
88 Invisible Kid (Pearson/Story) 10
89 Leviathan (Pearson/Story) 10
90 Shrinking Violet (AH) 10
91 Inferno (Spouse/Story) 10
92 Andromeda (AH) 10
93 Brainiac 5 (Pearson/Story) 10
94 Ultra Boy (Spouse/Story) 10
95 Matter-Eater Lad (Ty Templeton) .10
96 Alchemist (Pearson/Story) 10
97 Gossamer (AH) 10
98 Ferro (Spouse/Story) 10
99 Computo (Ty Templeton) 10
100 Dragonmage (Pearson/Story) . . .10
101 Catspay (Pearson/Story) 10
102 Kid Quantum (Pearson/Story) . . .10
Green Lantern Corps
pencils M.D. Bright/ inks: Romeo Tanghal
103 John Stewart (Cully Hamner) . . .10
104 AA and Amanita 10
105 Boodikka 10
106 Brik 10
107 Chaselon 10
108 Kreon 10
109 Larvox 10
110 Tomar-Tu 10
111 G'nort (JSon) 10
Worlds of Magic
112 Amethyst (JIT) 10
113 Deadman (KJo) 10
114 Death (CBa) 25
115 The Demon (VS) 10
116 Zatanna (EM) 10

DC Cosmic Cards © DC Comics Inc.

117 Madame Xanadu (MK) 10
118 Phantom Stranger (JAp) 10
119 Sandman (JIT) 10
120 Anton Arcane (SEa/KDM) 10

Foes of the Justice League

121 Weapons Master (DJu/ Rick Burchett) 10
122 Starbreaker (DC) 10
123 Deconstructo (Randall/Elliott) . . .10
124 Despero (BS) 10
125 Starro (BS) 10

Society of Sin

pencils: Tom Grummett/ inks: Al Vey

126 Houngan 10
127 Phobia 10
128 Plasmus 10
129 Warp .10
130 Trinity 10

Foes of Superman

131 Luthor II (JG/DRo) 25
132 Mxyzptlk (JBg/DJa) 25
133 Brainiac (TG/DHz) 25
134 Doomsday (JBg/DJa) 25
135 Parasite (TG/DHz) 25
136 Cerberus (JBg/DJa) 25
137 Silver Banshee (KGa/DHz) 25
138 Blaze (BBr) 25
139 Lord Satanus (BBr) 25
140 Mr. Z (TG/DHz) 25

The New Breed

141 Agent Liberty (DJu/Burchett) 10
142 Darkstar (Charest/McCarthy) 10
143 Eclipso (BS) 10
144 Heckler (KG) 10
145 Thunderbolt (Collins/Marzan) . . .10
146 The Ray (JQ/ANi) 10
147 Timber Wolf (Phillips/Gordon) . . .10
148 Valor (Bright/Gordon) 10
149 Checklist A 10
150 Checklist B 10

DC Master Series © DC Comics, Inc.

DC MASTER CARDS

Skybox (1994)

This is the first of the SkyBox Master series cards, and we expect them all to be highly collectible like this set. It came out just as we were completing the book, so our price information is preliminary. The cards feature full bleed painted art, with the name foil stamped on the front. The back has a small, false-color insert painting. The series name (which is actually "SkyBox Master Series: DC Comics Edition") is only given on the copyright line on the card, but the SkyBox Master Cards logo identifies the cards. We have listed the cards under "DC" where most people will expect to find them.

Set: 90 cards 25.00

Foil Cards (1:18)

F1 Wonder Woman(Cathleen Thole) 10.00
F2 Aquaman (DFg) 10.00
F3 Green Arrow (Doug Gregory) . . 10.00
F4 Hawkman (Nick Choles) 10.00

Double-sided Spectra-Etch (1:36)

DS1 Gr.Lantern/H.Jordan(J.Devito) 15.00
DS2 Batman/The Joker (SBs) 15.00
DS3 Superman/Doomsday(Fleming) 15.00
DS4 Flash/Reverse Flash (BV) . . . 15.00
DS5 Lobo/Lobo (BSz) 15.00
Skydisk exchange card (1:240) . . . 60.00
SD2 Superman **SkyDisk** 75.00

Promo cards

P1 Doomsday promo (Triton) 2.00
C1 Doomsday (Capital City show) . . 5.00
H1 Doomsday (Heroes World show) 5.00
D1 Doomsday (Diamond show) 5.00
N1 Aquaman (Non-Sport Update) . . 2.00
Ci1 Maxima (Cards Illustrated) 2.00
Pack: 6 cards 1.50

CARD CHECKLIST

1 Superman (John Estes) 25
2 Supergirl (John Estes) 25
3 Superboy (John Estes) 25
4 Steel (John Estes) 25
5 Cyborg (John Estes) 25
6 Lex Luthor II (John Estes) 25
7 The Eradicator (John Estes) 25
8 Mongul (John Estes) 25
9 Doomsday (John Estes) 25
10 Glorith & Mordru (Nel) 25
11 Valor (Juda Tverski) 25
12 Emerald Dragon (Nel) 25
13 Live Wire (Juda Tverski) 25
14 Saturn Girl (Juda Tverski) 25
15 Cosmic Boy (Juda Tverski) 25
16 Virus & Pulse (Nel) 25
17 Andromeda (Nel) 25
18 Polestar (Nel) 25
19 Vril Dox (Thom Ang) 25
20 Captain Atom (JuB) 25
21 Mirage (Paul Lee) 25
22 Martian Manhunter (Bruce Jensen) .25
23 Nightwing (Bruce Jensen) 25
24 Geo-Force (Bruce Jensen) 25
25 Battalion (LuH) 25
26 Arsenal (LuH) 25
27 Ferrin Colos (LuH) 25
28 Batman (DvD) 25
29 Robin (DvD) 25
30 Azrael-Batman (DvD) 25
31 Bane (DvD) 25
32 Oracle (DvD) 25
33 The Joker (DvD) 25
34 Ra's Al Ghul (DvD) 25
35 Catwoman (DvD) 25
36 Two-Face (DvD) 25
37 Monarch (JHi) 25
38 Vandal Savage (JHi) 25
39 Raven (JHi) 25
40 Poison Ivy (JHi) 25
41 Black Adam (JHi) 25
42 Darkseid (JHi) 25
43 Brimstone (JHi) 25
44 Doctor Polaris (JHi) 25
45 Blaze (JHi) 25
46 Green Lantern (TyH) 25
47 Alan Scott (TyH) 25
48 Guy Gardner: Warrior (TyH) 25
49 Sinestro (TyH) 25
50 Hal Jordan (Evil) (TyH) 25
51 Guardians of the Universe (TyH) . .25
52 Impulse (Hector Gomez) 25
53 The Flash (Hector Gomez) 25
54 Max Mercury (Hector Gomez) 25
55 The Spectre (TMd) 25
56 The Demon (TnS) 25
57 Phantom Stranger (SHp) 25
58 Deadman (KW) 25
59 Eclipso (DFg) 25
60 Dr. Fate (JMu) 25
61 Orion (Dave Devries) 25
62 Lobo (Dave Devries) 25
63 Deathstroke (Dave Devries) 25
64 Green Arrow (RyL) 25
65 Gypsy (Hector Gomez) 25
66 Changeling (RyL) 25
67 Crimson Fox (Hector Gomez) 25
68 Metamorpho (RyL) 25
69 Maxima (Hector Gomez) 25
70 Aquaman (Hector Gomez) 25
71 Huntress (Hector Gomez) 25
72 The Atom (Hector Gomez) 25
73 Damage (JoP) 25
74 Anima (JoP) 25
75 Argus (JoP) 25
76 Triumph (JoP) 25
77 Technocrat & Wylde (JoP) 25
78 The Ray (JoP) 25
79 Starman (JoP) 25
80 Gunfire (JoP) 25
81 Faust (JoP) 25
82 Hawkman (JBo) 25
83 Hawkwoman (JBo) 25
84 The Guardian (SR) 25
85 Wonder Woman (JBo) 25
86 Blue Beetle & Booster Gold(Thole) .25
87 Black Canary (JBo) 25
88 Power Girl (JBo) 25
89 Shazam (SR) 25
90 Checklist 25

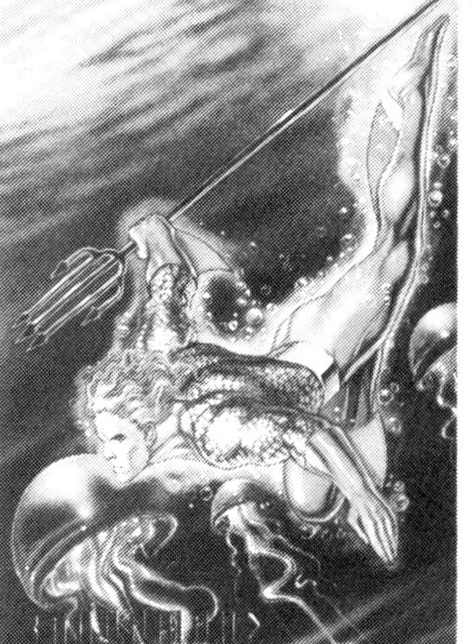

DC Master Cards & DC Stars © DC Comics, Inc.

DC STARS

SkyBox (1994)

These packs were available at Wal-Mart stores only. The cards have a light yellow and white border and a blue back, with character name and set title both front and back. They are of slightly lower quality that other SkyBox cards and consist of previously published, but still attractive, artwork. The cards were designed by SkyBox to lure children, who might not know about comics card collecting, into this hobby with a check-out line impulse purchase. Production is not limited, so these cards will be printed until everybody who wants one has one. That will keep the investment value of the cards down, unless it turns out to be possible to tell first printings from later printings.

Set: 45 cards + 9 puzzle cards 7.50

Foil-enhanced cards (1:18) 10.00
Box: 100 packs
Foil Bonus cards (1:18)
F1 Superman 9.00
F2 Batman 9.00
F3 Wonder Woman 9.00
F4 Green Lantern 9.00
Pack: 5 cards + puzzle card 1.00

CARD CHECKLIST

Superman
1 Superman (DJu/Burchett) 15
2 Ma & Pa Kent (JBg/DJa) 15
3 Lois Lane (JBg/DJa) 15
Foes of Superman
4 Doomsday (JBg/DJa) 25
5 Mr. Mxyzptlk (JBg/DJa) 15
6 Lex Luthor (JBg/DJa) 15
Batman
7 Batman 15
8 Robin (TL/Bob Smith) 15
9 Alfred (EiS) 15
Foes of Batman
10 The Joker (BB) 20
11 Catwoman (BSf) 25
12 Penguin (JAp) 15
Justice League
13 Guy Gardner (JSon/Bob Smith) . .15
14 Bloodwynd (DJu/Burchett) 15
15 Blue Beetle (DJu/BBr) 15
16 Flash (RoR/R.Elliott) 15
17 Wonder Woman (J.Thompson) . . .15
18 Booster Gold (DJu/BBr) 15
19 Fire 15
20 Ice (Greg Gutter/KK) 15
21 Metamorpho (BS/R.Elliott) 15
22 Elongated Man (BS/R.Elliott) 15
23 Aquaman (Hooper/Sutton) 15
24 Martian Manhunter(KM/DvC) 15
Power Players
25 Hourman 15
26 John Stewart 15
27 Black Condor (Greg Guler/DG) . . .15
28 Black Lightning (TVE/Smith) 15
29 The Creeper (Graham Nolan) 15
30 Deathstroke (StE/Bob Smith) 20
31 Geo-Force (JAp/RbC) 15
32 Guardian (JBg/DJa) 15
33 Nightwing (TG/AV) 15
34 Pantha (TG/AV) 15
35 Peacemaker (BS/R.Elliott) 15
36 Hawkman (Graham Nolan) 15
37 Shazam! 15
38 Lobo (SBs) 25
39 Orion 15
Super Villains
40 Deadshot (McDonnell/Clark) 15
41 Monarch (DJu/DG) 15
42 Ocean Master 15
43 Phobia (TG/AV) 15
44 Vandal Savage (GrL/DvC) 15
45 Checklist 15
Puzzle Cards (form 3x3 super panel)
P1 Batman 20
P2 Flash 20
P3 Hawkman 20
P4 Robin 20
P5 Superman 20
P6 Wonder Woman 20
P7 Shazam! 20
P8 Aquaman 20
P9 Green Lantern 20

DC Super Heroes Stickers © DC Comics, Inc.

DC SUPER HEROES STICKERS

Taystee/Sunbeam (1978)

The stickers are 2¼" x 3" and came with either the Taystee or the Sunbeam brand names. The fronts have a colorful action drawing of a DC Super Hero and the backs are a thin brown paper designed to be peeled away from the sticker. The backs have the sticker number, character name and several lines of text. There is no name for the series on any of the stickers, but there is a folder (containing a checklist and pictures of the stickers) titled "Super Heroes Fun Book" so we have chosen the name above to list them with other DC products.

Set: 30 stickers 125.00

1 Superman 5.00
2 The Man of Steel 5.00
3 Clark Kent 5.00
4 Lois Lane 5.00
5 Leaving Krypton 5.00
6 Jimmy Olsen 5.00
7 Jor-El and Lara 5.00
8 Jonathan and Martha Kent 5.00
9 Superman and Lois Lane 5.00
10 Superman and Supergirl 5.00
11 Wonder Woman 5.00
12 Batman and Robin 5.00
13 Batgirl 5.00
14 The Riddler 5.00
15 The Joker 5.00
16 Batman 5.00
17 Good vs. Evil 5.00
18 The Penguin 5.00
19 More Powerful Than
  a Locomotive 5.00
20 Perry White 5.00
21 Krypto 5.00
22 Aquaman 5.00
23 Lex Luthor 5.00
24 Flash 5.00
25 Green Arrow 5.00
26 Hawkman 5.00
27 Plastic Man 5.00
28 Super Heroes 5.00
29 The Villains 5.00
30 Green Lantern 5.00

Deathmate © Image and Voyager Communications, Inc.

DEATHMATE

Upper Deck/Pyramid (1993)

The atlas cards each have a detail picture from one of the cards in the series, with red arrows which mark the location of the action on a puzzle map of North America, Europe and North-west Africa which is formed by the cards. The backs of the cards have a puzzle background, but primarily contain text describing the story line. The next 99 cards feature "the best of Deathmate prologue, yellow and blue." The cards have full bleed art with number, title and text on the backs in a shield design on a marbled background, with a black border. The story is broken up into five parts, each marked with a different inset photo on the card backs. The Two Ericas runs from #10 to #17 and A Shot in Time runs from #18 to #23. Deathmate Prologue runs from #24 to #35; Deathmate Yellow runs from #36 to #72; and Deathmate Blue runs from #73 to #108. There are three levels of bonus cards. The Transitions cards all have a lightburst on the front, over the picture. They don't say "Deathmate" anywhere, but the backs look like the regular cards. The Players of Deathmate are depicted on the top of a silver holographic under-picture. The two Lithograms join together to form a single image with the characters on each side and a skull in the middle. The Topps promo card advertises a trading card cross-over series which doesn't seem to have been produced. It is quite different from the Upper Deck cards and promos.

Set: 110 cards 15.00

Transitions Cards (1:12)
T1 Sting (MLe) 5.00
T2 Soft Core (MLe/Autio) 5.00
T3 Archer (MLe/Autio) 5.00
T4 Perp (MLe/Bolinger) 5.00
T5 Ax (MLe/JP) 5.00
T6 Shadowman (MLe/JP) 5.00
T7 Master Darque (MLe/Autio) 5.00
T8 Sandria Darque (MLe/Autio) 5.00
Players of Deathmate (1:18) (all MLe)
P1 A love to end all time (/Autio) . . . 7.00
P2 Darque Night (/Autio) 7.00
P3 Fists of Steel (/Autio) 7.00
P4 Crossed Blades (/Ryder) 7.00
P5 Raw Power (/Autio) 7.00
P6 Geomancer's Strike Team 7.00

Lithogram (1:90)
D1 Casualties: Magnus 20.00
D2 Casualties: Battlestone 20.00
Promo card (MLe,BL) Upper Deck . . 3.00

Deathmate (Topps Promo) © Image and Voyager Communications, Inc.

Promo card (JLe,SW) Topps 3.00
Oversize promo card, Upper Deck . . 2.50
Pack: 8 cards 1.50

CARD CHECKLIST

1 Atlas: Estonia 10
2 Atlas: Rome, Italy 10
3 Atlas: New Orleans, Louisiana 10
4 Atlas: Battlezone, New York City . .10
5 Atlas: New York, New York 10
6 Atlas: Washington, D.C. 10
7 Atlas: Alberta, Canada 10
8 Atlas: Albuquerque, New Mexico . .10
9 Atlas: Phoenix, Arizona 10
10 The Two Ericas 10
11 The Black Hole 10
12 The Accidental Killer 10
13 Prophet of the Sun God 10
14 Erica Attacks 10
15 Into the Breach 10
16 Prophet Strikes 10
17 Into the Void 10
18 A Shot in Time 10
19 Grifter Waits 10
20 Shadowman 10
21 Archer Takes Aim 10
22 Grifter Intervenes 10
23 A Fallen Shadow 10
24 Deathmate Prologue 10
25 Gayle Discovered 10
26 A Welcome Release 10
27 Emptiness 10
28 Purged of Pain 10
29 Through Time and Space 10
30 The Meeting 10
31 Empathy 10
32 Feelings Reborn 10
33 The Kiss to End All Time 10
34 Union 10
35 The End of the Beginning 10
36 Deathmate Yellow 10
37 The Brothers 10
38 Underground Rumble 10
39 The Geomancer's Maze 10
40 Dissolution 10
41 Where to Now? 10
42 When in the World? 10
43 Unexpected Encounter 10
44 The Search 10
45 Zealot of the H.A.R.D. C.A.T.S. . .10
46 Chamber of Darque 10
47 Ninjak's Assignment 10
48 First Blood 10
49 Face-Off 10
50 Ninjak Falls 10
51 The Trap 10
52 Ninjak Reports 10
53 H.A.R.D. C.A.T.S. 10
54 To the Rescue 10
55 Back to Back 10
56 Betrayed 10
57 Softcore 10
58 Brain Pop 10
59 Flatline .10
60 Spartan Strives 10
61 Enter Big Boy 10
62 Inside Out 10
63 Not to Be 10
64 Hold the Line 10
65 Revenge 10
66 Darque Bayou 10
67 Evasive Maneuvers 10
68 Timing is Everything 10
69 Down, But Not Out 10

Deathmate © Image and Voyager Communications, Inc.

70 Right Back At Ya 10
71 I Am The Night 10
72 Grifter's Plea 10
73 Deathmate Blue 10
74 Battlezone 10
75 The Challenge 10
76 Under the Gun 10
77 Battlestone Acts 10
78 Once is Not Enough 10
79 Bad Idea 10
80 Down for the Count 10
81 Beginning of the End 10
82 Spoiled Shot 10
83 Magnetic Personality 10
84 The One Who Knows 10
85 Strike Team 10
86 Aerial Assault 10
87 The Target 10
88 Ask it Nice 10
89 Explosive Entrance 10
90 Egg-Brigade 10
91 Frozen .10
92 Fire and Ice 10
93 Harada's Lieutenant 10
94 Harbinger Duel 10
95 Wrapping Things Up 10
96 Sting Falls 10
97 Disarmed 10
98 Powerhouses 10
99 Nerve Center 10
100 Harada Knows 10
101 Enter Solar 10
102 On Harada's Mission 10
103 Supreme Effort 10
104 With a Little Help 10
105 Eclipsed 10
106 Eclipse Totaled 10
107 Darqueness Falls 10
108 Uneasy Allies 10
109 Checklist 10
110 Checklist 10

DEATHWATCH 2000: PRELUDE

Continuity Comics (1993)

The first 13 of these cards came in issues #1 through #3 of Armor; Hybrids; Megalith; Ms. Mystic; Earth 4; *and* Cyber-Rad *comics from Continuity, which appeared beginning in April 1993 and continued over that summer. The comics contained a cross-over series called "Deathwatch 2000: Prelude." The first 11 cards were randomly distributed and hidden inside the cover of the comic, so it is hard to complete a set just by buying the comics. Cards numbered 12 and 13 are scarce, as these are foil chase cards from these same comics. The rest of the cards appeared in later issues of these comics, but in those books you can see which card you are getting. None of the cards have any indication of the name of the card series, which is taken from the promo sheet.*

Set: 29 cards 75.00

Four card promo sheet, 7½"x7¼" (Previews, February 1993) 5.00
1 Ms. Mystic (AH) 3.00
2 Armor (KN) 3.00
3 Silver Streak 3.00
4 Crazyman (NA/BB) 3.00
5 Megalith 3.00
6 CyberRad (RiB) 3.00
7 Fyre 3.00
8 Watr 3.00
9 Urth 3.00
10 Ayre 3.00
11 Samuree 3.00
12 Valeria She-Bat (NA) (1:25 comics) 15.00
13 Shaman (1:50 comics) 25.00
14 Horror 75
15 Highperion 75
16 Spanng Ting 75
17 Shealth .75
18 Gymcrack 75
19 Cyclone .75
20 Mite 75
21 Devilspawn 75
22 She Bat II (NA) 75
23 FireBat .50
24 Hellheart 50
25 Hellfire .50
26 Void 50
27 Rem 50
28 Leper 50
29 Dragon .50

DEATHWATCH 2000

Classic Games (1993)

Neal Adams art

If you like Neal Adams art, you'll like Deathwatch 2000, but you'd better be able to put up with a lot of purple! The backs are a bright purple, with an inset photo, title, number and text. The fronts have a purple border and the card title (as well as the packs) are also purple. The first six hybrid cards are part clear with an overprinted image like an animation cel. When the cards are put together, the purple(!) backgrounds spell Hybrids. The superhero cards are primarily valuable because of cross-demand from sports cards collectors.

Set: 100 cards 15.00

Deathwatch 2000 © Classic Games & Neal Adams

Superhero cards (NA)
SS1 Shaquille O'Neal 35.00
SS2 Manon Rheaume 25.00
SS3 Ken Griffey, Jr. 20.00
Hybrid cards (NA)
HC1 Highperion 12.00
HC2 Shealth 12.00
HC3 Cyclone 12.00
HC4 Mite 12.00
HC5 Gymcrack 12.00
HC6 Horror 12.00
HC7 Spanng Ting 12.00
Jacquarundi (NA autograph card) . 50.00
Promo cards
PR1 Desperate Rescue 1.50
PR2 Escape from Death-Jaws 1.50
PR3 Inches From Death 1.50
PR4 Lith Kasti 1.50
PR5 Valeria the She-Bat 2.00
Variation promos, foil stamped
"May 2-5, 1993 Capital" each 5.00
Four card promo sheet, 8¼"x7¾" . . 5.00
Numbered five card promo sheet, inc.
3 super-heroes, 40,000 made . . . 25.00
Pack, 8 cards . . . .

CARD CHECKLIST

1 Deathwatch 2000 Begins 15
2 Hybrid Power Versus
Elemental Evil 15
3 A Startling Transformation Horror . .15
4 Armor's Own Weapons
Could Kill Him 15
5 Devilspawn's Fateful Discovery 15
6 Urth Faces The Wrath
of "The Dragon" 15
7 Cyberrad Faces His Creator/Father .15
8 Megalith Faces a Steroid Monster . .15
9 Highperion Fights Devilspawn 15
10 Energy Vampire Strikes 15
11 The Horror Revealed 15
12 Fyre-Fight 15
13 Megalith Rescued By
Security Team 15
14 Void and Armor Clash Amidst
Incendiary Havoc 15
15 Ancient Lost God
Saves Werebreds 15
16 Shaman Restores
Cyberrad's Flesh 15
17 Shaman's Attack 15
18 Hellheart's Last Hope 15
19 Rem's Wicked Web 15
20 Void and Leper Take Aim 15
21 Mite Defies Devilspawn's Words . .15
22 Hellheart Absorbs
Nuclear Detonation 15
23 Armor Alone 15
24 Devilspawn's Ally 15
25 Megalith's White-Hot Rage 15
26 Horror Left Alone 15
27 Lith Kasti's Victory 15
28 Fiiiiiir's Revenge 15
29 Escape From Death-Jaws 15
30 Hovering Death 15
31 Desperate Rescue 15
32 Inches From Death 15
33 Hostage 15
34 Lith Kasti 15
35 Megalith's Flight 15
36 Horror's Narrow Escape 15
37 Hybrid's Fateful Decision 15
38 Devilspawn Faces Mite's Wrath . .15
39 Cyberrad's First Battle 15
40 First Strike 15
41 Stunning Underworld Beauty 15
42 Monstrous Rescue 15
43 Fyre's Pain 15

Deathwatch 2000 © Classic Games & Neal Adams

44 "Are You Scared?!" 15
45 True Form 15
46 Dinosaur Terror 15
47 Desperate Warning 15
48 Crushing Blow 15
49 Painful Realization 15
50 Out of Body Experience 15
51 Ms. Mystic Captured 15
52 Truncheon's Introduction 15
53 Concrete Missile 15
54 The Mutant Winds 15
55 The Dragon's Laughter 15
56 Spanng Ting Joins Ms. Mystic . . .15
57 She-Bat's Curiousity 15
58 Truncheon's Fervor 15
59 Mystic's Search 15
60 A Cyclone of Power 15
61 Ms. Mystic's Sympathy 15
62 Caught In-Between Seconds 15
63 A Prisoner of Metal 15
64 Mystic Versus Insect 15
65 Preemptive Measures 15
66 By Megalith Impaled 15
67 Talons of Death 15
68 Mystic's Mutated Savior 15
69 Stop That Madman 15
70 Morph's Deadly Gaze 15
71 Ms. Mystic's Fall 15
72 Into the Caverns 15
73 Prepare For Fear 15
74 Urth Collides With Ursssss 15
75 Rem's Wicked Trick Fails 15
76 Gravity Battering Ram 15

Deathwatch: 2000 © Classic Games & Neal Adams

77 Earth 4 Attacks Their
Dopplegangers 15
78 Mite Bounces Into the Fray 15
79 Evil Elementals 15
80 Dinosaur Rampage 15
81 "I'm Comin' Ta Get Ya" 15
82 Mental Link-Up 15
83 Ayre's Thunderstorm 15
84 Hellfire's Burning Evil 15
85 Cyberrad's Future 15
86 Hellheart's Revenge 15
87 Megalith Explodes Towards
The Final Battle 15
88 Cyclone's Wrath 15
89 Mite On The Rampage 15
90 Gymcrack Destroys The
Evil Elementals 15
91 Shaman's Nightmare 15
92 No Escape 15
93 Horror's Fury 15
94 Hellbenders Attack 15
95 She-Bat's Justice 15
96 Cyberrad's Resistance 15
97 Payback Time 15
98 Mistaken Identity 15
99 Checklist 1 15
100 Checklist 2 15

Jumbo Pack Prism cards
(NA)

These are full bleed prism cards, with purple backs just like the regular cards.

Set: 20 prism cards 40.00

CARD CHECKLIST

BC1 Highperion Faces Extinction! . . 2.50
BC2 Silver Streak's Horror! 2.50
BC3 Dinosaur Military 2.50
BC4 Mite Debugged! 2.50
BC5 Spanng Ting's
Incendiary Rockets! 2.50
BC6 Armor Faces The
Elusive Dragon 2.50
BC7 Armor Attacks! 2.50
BC8 The Central Core! 2.50
BC9 Dinosaur Military Police! 2.50
BC10 Snapshot! 2.50
BC11 The Phantasm of Gymcrack . . 2.50
BC12 Dragon's Rage! 2.50
BC13 Armor's Foolish Rage! 2.50
BC14 CFC Island Nightmare! 2.50
BC15 Devilspawn Recruits
a Monster! 2.50
BC16 And Here We Have 2.50
BC17 A Brother's Fate Revealed! . . 2.50
BC18 Armor's Kamikaze Assault . . . 2.50
BC19 Dinosaur Citadel 2.50
BC20 First Blood! 2.50

Defective Comics © Active Marketing International, Inc. & Mark Voger

DEFECTIVE COMICS

Active Marketing (1993)

Mark Voger art

These are parodies of famous comics covers. The cards have a multi-colored border and the back contains parody text, along with

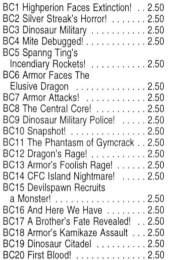

the card number and a detail picture from the front. A lot of the cards are hilarious and it's a fun idea for a set of cards.

Set: 50 cards, boxed 10.00
Set: 50 cards, hand assembled 7.50

Silver Foil Cards (1:1)
Set: #SF1-#SF50 . . . . . . 30.00
Card 50
Gold Foil Card (1:10)
Each 5.00
Autographed Card (1:400)
Original Sketch card (1:4320)
Promo Cards
P1 Sprain #1 . . . . . . 1.50
P2 Defective Comics #27 . . . . 1.50
P3 Unfazing Fantasy #15 . . . . 1.50
Pack: 7 cards, 1 foil card 1.00

CARD CHECKLIST
1 Lamest Funnies #1 20
2 Drip Drop Comics #1 20
3 Hyper-Action #1 20
4 Defective Comics #27 20
5 Marvy Comics #1 20
6 Rash Comics #1 20
7 Wimp Comics #2 20
8 All-Bore Comics #3 20
9 Sappy American #1 20
10 All-Losers Comics #1 20
11 Marvy Misery Comics #20 20
12 Blunder Woman #1 20
13 Battyman #47 20
14 Scent of Beer #12 20
15 Bad #1 20
16 No-Dimension Comics #1 20
17 Grime Suspensgories #22 20
18 Schmoface #4 20
19 Mis-Adventure #247 20
20 Schmoface #20 20
21 The Lame and the Old #28 20
22 Spastic Four #1 20
23 Schmoface #37 20
24 Inedible Hunk #1 20
25 Unfazing Fantasy #15 20
26 Unfazing Spider-Sam #1 20
27 Tales to Suspect #39 20
28 ?-Men #1 20
29 Offenders #4 20
30 The Lame and the Old #57 20
31 Lois Lame #70 20
32 Schmoface #75 20
33 Blunder Woman #178 20
34 Trampirella #1 20
35 X-Farce #1 20
36 Evil Mikey #1 20
37 Barswinger #1 20
38 Bumb-Blood #1 20
39 So-Lame #10 20
40 Spain #1 20
41 Shallowman #2 20
42 Infernal Borer #1 20
43 ChildC.A.T.S. #1 20
44 Bagnus: Bonut Biter #4 20
45 Psycho Force #1 20
46 Rye #0 20
47 Pigg #1 20
48 Buttshot #1 20
49 B-O Stenchowwar #14 20
50 Stuporman #75 20

Defiant Universe © TRG & EEP, L.P.

DEFIANT UNIVERSE

River Group (1994)

These are promos for a card set that isn't out at press time. Too bad, because the cards are very attractive. They have full bleed art with a little foil stamping and an attractive color back with inset photo and white text. We like these character portrait cards from Defiant's comics and we hope ***The River Group*** *leaves the comic book panels (see* ***Plasm****) in the comic books where they belong.*

Promo cards
1/3 Skipper (Warriors of Plasm) 2.00
2/3 Billy Ballistic (WarDancer) 2.00
3/3 Ngu (Charlemagne) 2.00

DIMENSION X

Karl Art (1994)

A foil promo card which was given away at Comics shows.

Comic promo (Roy Krenkel art) 2.00

Disney Collector Cards © The Walt Disney Company

DISNEY COLLECTOR CARDS

Impel 1991

The first 99 cards of this set are organized into 11 full color "Favorite Stories" from Disney animated short subjects, which are retold using both the front and back of the cards. The cards are designed to be put in nine pocket pages for viewing the story, with the numbers on the reverse, running up and down. That way the story is in order when looked at sideways, which is the orientation of the card pictures. The next 72 cards are "Family Portraits" which are designed to look like photographs in an album. In the last part of the set your favorite characters take a "World Tour." The series name is not mentioned on the cards.

Set: 210 cards 25.00

World Tour hologram 25.00
Fantasia hologram 35.00
Pack: 15 cards (black wrapper) 1.25

CARD CHECKLIST
Favorite Stories
#1-#9 **Brave Little Tailor**, set 1.00
#10-#18 **Bone Trouble**, set 1.00
#19-#27 **Clock Cleaners**, set 1.00
#28-#36 **Thru the Mirror**, set 1.00
#37-#45 **Orphan's Benefit**, set 1.00
#46-#54 **Pluto's Judgement Day**,set 1.00
#55-#63 **Symphony Hour**, set 1.00
#64-#72 **Lonesome Ghosts**, set . . . 1.00
#73-#81 **The Mad Doctor**, set 1.00
#82-#90 **Donald's Crime**, set 1.00
#91-#99 **The Art of Skiing**, set 1.00

Family Portraits
Bio's
100 Mickey's Bio 25
101 Minnie's Bio 25
102 Goofy's Bio 25
103 Pluto's Bio 25
104 Donald's Bio 25
105 Daisy's Bio 25
106 Mickey's Bio 25
107 Donald's Bio 25
108 Goofy's Bio 25
Cartoons
109 Brave Little Tailor (1938) 10
110 Magician Mickey (1937) 10
111 Sorcerer's Apprentice (1940) . . .10
112 The Nifty Nineties (1941) 10
113 Brave Little Tailor (1938) 10
114 Hawaiian Holiday (1937) 10
115 Society Dog Show (1939) 10
116 Mickey's Kangaroo (1935) 10
117 Pluto's Quin-Puplets (1937) 10
118 Sea Scouts (1939) 10
119 Fire Chief (1940) 10
120 Modern Inventions (1937) 10
121 Don Donald (1937) 10
122 Donald's Diary (1954) 10
123 Mr. Duck Steps Out (1940) 10

Disney Collector Cards © The Walt Disney Company

124 Hawaiian Holiday (1937) 10
125 Clock Cleaners (1937) 10
126 The Olympic Champ (1942) 10
127 'I Only Have Eyes For You' 10
128 Lonesome Ghosts (1937) 10
129 Goofy and Wilbur (1939) 10
130 Brave Little Tailor (1938) 10
131 Old MacDonald Duck (1941) 10
132 Hawaiian Holiday (1937) 10
133 'The Princess of Polka Dots' 10
134 Pluto, Junior (1942) 10
135 Boat Builders (1938) 10
Trivia Questions
136 Mickey's Fire Brigade (1935) . . .10

137 The Olympic Champ (1942) 10
138 Truant Officer Donald (1941) . . .10
139 Mr. Duck Steps Out (1940) 10
140 Pluto's Quin-Puplets (1937) 10
141 Self Control (1938) 10
142 The Nifty Nineties (1941) 10
143 Society Dog Show (1939) 10
144 Donald's Better Self (1938) 10
145 Hawaiian Holiday (1937) 10
146 The Art of Skiing (1941) 10
147 The Sleepwalker (1942) 10
148 Mickey's Amateurs (1937) 10
149 Don Donald (1937) 10
150 Donald's Golf Game (1938) 10
151 Beach Picnic (1939) 10
152 How to Swim (1942) 10
153 Donald's Ostrich (1937) 10

Sunday Comic Strips

154 Sunday Comic Strip (1935) 10
155 Sunday Comic Strip (1935) 10
156 Sunday Comic Strip (1939) 10
157 Daily Comic Strip (1940) 10
158 Sunday Comic Strip (1941) 10
159 Sunday Comic Strip (1936) 10
160 Sunday Comic Strip (1940) 10
161 Sunday Comic Strip (1939) 10
162 Sunday Comic Strip (1940) 10
163 Sunday Comic Strip (1937) 10
164 Sunday Comic Strip (1937) 10
165 Sunday Comic Strip (1934) 10
166 Sunday Comic Strip (1939) 10
167 Sunday Comic Strip (1936) 10
168 Sunday Comic Strip (1936) 10
169 Sunday Comic Strip (1939) 10
170 Sunday Comic Strip (1940) 10
171 Sunday Comic Strip (1940) 10

World Tour Postcards

172 Mickey's World Tour-
1001 Hellos! 10
173 Seeing Red 10
174 Wrestling, Japanese Style 10
175 Safari Surprise 10
176 A Camel Built for Two 10
177 The 'Goofy Express' 10
178 Donald's Calypso Beat! 10
179 Ooh La La, Can They Can-Can! .10
180 Donald Goes for the Gold 10

World Tour Fun Guides

181 Donald the Gondolier 10
182 Mickey's Crash Course in Greek .10
183 A Moscow Chorus Line 10
184 Mickey Scores Again! 10
185 Pluto's Tail of India 10
186 Ancient Egyptian Comic Strips . .10
187 Have Bagpipes, Will Travel 10
188 G'Day, Mate! 10
189 Daisy the Diva 10
190 Paris Originals 10
191 Luau Ladies 10
192 Samurai Duck 10
193 Hanging Around the Alps
with Goofy 10
194 The Sombrero Stomp 10
195 Mickey in Russia 10
196 Mickey's Passport 10
197 Goofy's Alpine Antics 10
198 Flight 110 10
199 Pasta a la Pluto 10
200 Goofy Guards the Guard 10
201 Gold Medal Googy 10
202 Miki Tiki 10
203 Mickey's Dutch Dilemma 10
204 Time on His Hands 10
205 Flamenco Fun! 10
206 Chiquita Minnie 10
207 Mickey's Oom-Pah Band 10

Checklists

208 Checklist – Favorite Stories 25
209 Checklist – Family Portraits 25
210 Checklist – World Tour 25

Disney Collector Cards II © The Walt Disney Company

DISNEY COLLECTOR CARDS, SERIES II

SkyBox (1992)

*The first 99 cards of this set are exactly the same as the first series, except for new stories (and except that the first story takes 18 cards instead of the usual nine). Cards 100 to 171 are called Family Portraits again. They contain movie poster reproductions and scenes, with information about the film on the back. The last six are "How to draw..." cards. The final group of cards are called "Get Goofy" and they picture Goofy on the front with text on the back. There are three nine-card subsets: "**Famous Goof Ups**, with fractured history;" "How To" with Goofy's personalities and careers; and "Wild Cards," with puzzles and optical illusions.*

These 27 cards have pictures on the back that create an animated "flip book" when fanned in sequence. The series name doesn't appear on the cards; if they are mixed together, the best way to tell them apart from series I is by the SkyBox logo on the back. Series I has an Impel logo. There are also two cards which are not numbered and thus not part of the card series. One contains a story picture on one side and describes the "Favorite Story" cards on the other (incorrectly saying that there are 100 such cards, instead of 99). The other describes the "Get Goofy" cards on the back and has a picture like one on the front.

Set: 200 cards 20.00

Holograms, double sided

Mickey and the Beanstalk 20.00
title unknown 20.00
Get Goofy promo card 1.00
Favorite Stories promo card 1.00
Pack: 12 cards 1.00

CARD CHECKLIST

Favorite Stories

#1-#18 **Mickey & the Beanstalk**, set 2.00
#19-#27 **Goofy and Wilbur**, set . . . 1.00
#28-#36 **Lend a Paw**, set 1.00
#37-#45 **The Mail Pilot**, set 1.00
#46-#54 **Mickey's Trailer**,set 1.00
#55-#63 **Mr. Duck Steps Out**, set . . 1.00
#64-#72 **The Nifty Nineties**, set . . . 1.00
#73-#81 **Society Dog Show**, set . . . 1.00
#82-#90 **Moose Hunters**, set 1.00
#91-#99 **How to be a Sailor**, set . . . 1.00

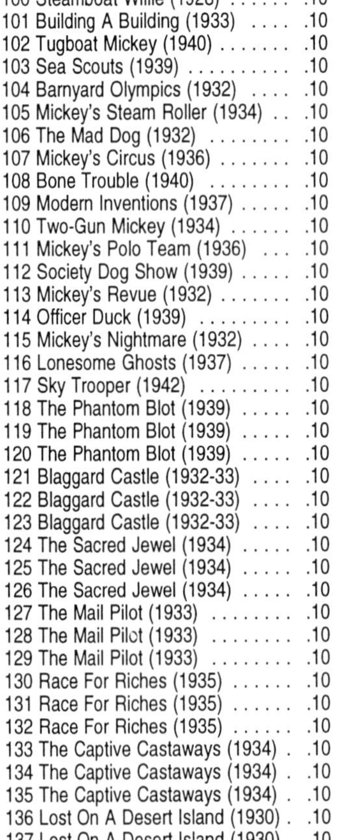

Family Portraits

100 Steamboat Willie (1928) 10
101 Building A Building (1933) 10
102 Tugboat Mickey (1940) 10
103 Sea Scouts (1939) 10
104 Barnyard Olympics (1932) 10
105 Mickey's Steam Roller (1934) . . .10
106 The Mad Dog (1932) 10
107 Mickey's Circus (1936) 10
108 Bone Trouble (1940) 10
109 Modern Inventions (1937) 10
110 Two-Gun Mickey (1934) 10
111 Mickey's Polo Team (1936) 10
112 Society Dog Show (1939) 10
113 Mickey's Revue (1932) 10
114 Officer Duck (1939) 10
115 Mickey's Nightmare (1932) 10
116 Lonesome Ghosts (1937) 10
117 Sky Trooper (1942) 10
118 The Phantom Blot (1939) 10
119 The Phantom Blot (1939) 10
120 The Phantom Blot (1939) 10
121 Blaggard Castle (1932-33) 10
122 Blaggard Castle (1932-33) 10
123 Blaggard Castle (1932-33) 10
124 The Sacred Jewel (1934) 10
125 The Sacred Jewel (1934) 10
126 The Sacred Jewel (1934) 10
127 The Mail Pilot (1933) 10
128 The Mail Pilot (1933) 10
129 The Mail Pilot (1933) 10
130 Race For Riches (1935) 10
131 Race For Riches (1935) 10
132 Race For Riches (1935) 10
133 The Captive Castaways (1934) . .10
134 The Captive Castaways (1934) . .10
135 The Captive Castaways (1934) . .10
136 Lost On A Desert Island (1930) . .10
137 Lost On A Desert Island (1930) . .10
138 Lost On A Desert Island (1930) . .10
139 Mickey and Tanglefoot (1933) . . .10

Disney Collector Cards II
© The Walt Disney Company

140 Mickey and Tanglefoot (1933) . . .10
141 Mickey and Tanglefoot (1933) . . .10
142 Bobo the Elephant (1934) 10
143 Bobo the Elephant (1934) 10
144 Bobo the Elephant (1934) 10
145 Steamboat Willie (1928) 10
146 The Band Concert (1935) 10
147 Mickey's Circus (1936) 10
148 Thru The Mirror (1936) 10
149 The Pointer (1939) 10
150 Mickey's Birthday Party (1942) . .10
151 Plane Crazy (1928) 10
152 Mickey's Rival (1936) 10
153 Brave Little Tailor (1938) 10
154 The Wise Little Hen (1934) 10
155 Good Scouts (1938) 10
156 Self Control (1938) 10
157 Don Donald (1937) 10
158 Cured Duck (1945) 10
159 Donald's Diary (1954) 10
160 Mickey's Revue (1932) 10
161 Lonesome Ghosts (1937) 10
162 How To Swim (1942) 10
163 On Ice (1935) 10
164 The Pointer (1939) 10
165 Lend a Paw (1941) 10
166 How to Draw Mickey 10
167 How to Draw Minnie 10
168 How to Draw Goofy 10
169 How to Draw Donald 10
170 How to Draw Daisy 10
171 How to Draw Pluto 10

Get Goofy(untitled)

172 to 198, each 10
199 Checklist 10
200 Checklist 10

DOCTOR CHAOS

Triumphant Comics (1993)

Comic book promo with a black and white back.

Promo card (Advance comics) 1.50

Doomsday: The Death of Superman © DC Comics, Inc.

DOOMSDAY: THE DEATH OF SUPERMAN

SkyBox (1992)

These cards tell the story of the death of Superman, the biggest comics event of the decade. They follow the comic book story line from the emergence of Doomsday, to the fight of the century, to Lois weeping at Superman's grave. Everyone bought the cards when they first came out and they shot up in value. The fronts have a picture inside a black and grey border, with the card title in red along the side. The card art is by the same four teams of artists that drew the four Superman titles in which this story line appeared. The card backs are grey, with the same border, plus text and card number. The backs of cards C1 to C9 form a 3 x 3 card poster of Superman's funeral. The Spectra cards have a full bleed picture, with a Superman "S" symbol on the back. The puzzle cards fit together to form a foil stamped "S" symbol, with blood dripping and Superman's tombstone on the back. There is no indication of the card series on any of the bonus cards. This is one of the ten sets you ***must own*** *to be a legitimate comics cards collector.*

Set: 100 cards (1-90,C1-C9,CL01) 60.00

Spectra Cards "A Memorial Tribute"
S1 (TG/DHz) 18.00
S2 (JBg/DJa) 18.00
S3 (DJu/BBr) 17.00
S4 (JG/DRo) 17.00
Foil-Stamped puzzle cards
F1 (Tomb stone, top) 14.00
F2 (Tomb stone, bottom) 14.00
Prototypes
0 Superman's Tombstone with red inner border 2.50
00 Superman's Tombstone with yellow inner border (in Superman #75) . . 5.00
000 Bleeding "S" shield with silver inner border (in Wizard #17) 2.50
Pack: 8 cards 4.00

CARD CHECKLIST

1 Behold, the Hero! (JBg/DJa) 50
2 Who Lurks Below? (JBg/DJa) 50
3 Escape! (JBg/DJa) 50
4 Freedom! (DJu/Burchett) 50
5 Call Him "Doomsday" (JBg/DJa) . . .60
6 Civilization's Scourge! (JBg/DJa) . .50
7 Highway Holocaust! (JG/DRo) 50
8 Forty-ton Showdown! (DJu) 50
9 Laughter by Firelight! (JBg/DJa) . . .50
10 Guy Gardner Steps In! (DJu) 50
11 One Hero Down! (DJu) 50
12 The Ice Maiden Cometh! (DJu/BBr) 50
13 Iced! (DJu/BBr) 50
14 Justice League America! (DJu) . . .50
15 The Man of Steel (DJu/BBr) 50
16 Superman Stands Tall! (DJu/BBr) .50
17 Low Blow! (DJu/BBr) 50
18 The Gathering of Power! (DJu/BBr) 50
19 The League Attacks! (DJu/BBr) . . .50
20 The Face of Evil! (DJu/BBr) 50
21 Doomsday Strikes Back! (DJu/BBr) 50
22 Heroes' End? (TG/DHz) 50
23 The Agony of Defeat! (TG/DHz) . .50
24 The Lone Hero! (DJu/BBr) 50
25 Frontal Attack! (TG/DHz) 50
26 Fists of Thunder...(TG/DHz) 50
27 ...Fists of Justice! (TG/DHz) 50
28 Innocent Bystanders! (DJu/BBr) . .50
29 to 42: Tom Grummett/Doug Hazlewood
29 Team Work! 50
30 Guided Missiles! 50
31 Superman to the Rescue! 50
32 Missile Attack! 50
33 Scratch One Cruiser! 50
34 Footfall! 50
35 Walls Asunder! 50
36 The Heat of Battle! 50
37 Iron Grip! 50
38 Enter: Maxima! 50
39 Now Strikes Maxima! 50
40 Sucker-punched! 50
41 Power Dive! 50
42 Blow-up! 50
43 to 50: Jackson Guice/Dennis Rodier art
43 The Guardian Steps In! 50
44 Desperate Situation! 50
45 Contact! 50
46 One on One! (TG/DHz) 50
47 Metropolis–60 Miles! (ATi) 50
48 Connections Made! 50
49 The Fourth Estate 50
50 The Power of Doomsday! 50

Doomsday: The Death of Superman © DC Comics, Inc.

51 to 70: Jon Bogdanove/Dennis Janke art
51 City Limits! 50
52 The Gauntlet is Thrown! 50
53 Monster at Large! 50
54 From the Ashes! 50
55 Trouble Down Below! 50
56 Sky High! 50
57 Underworld Havoc! 50
58 A Family's Fear! 50
59 Into the Stratosphere! 50
60 First Blood! 50
61 And Now–Supergirl! 50
62 Uncommon Allies! 50
63 Laser on Target! 50
64 Never Give Up! 50
65 The Living Shield! 50
66 Barrage! 50
67 Turpin on the Fly! 50
68 Helping Hand! 50
69 In Battle Rejoined! 50
70 Face to Face! 50
71 to 90: Dan Jurgens/Brett Breeding art
71 Man vs. Monster! 60
72 As a World Watches! 60
73 Doomsday Triumphant? 60
74 Midair Collision! 60
75 Air Rescue! 60
76 Last Kiss! 60
77 Out for Blood! 60
78 This is War! 60
79 Final Battleground! 60
80 Superman Strikes Back! 60
81 Heat Vision! 60
82 Desperate Moments! 60
83 Takedown! 60
84 The Final Round! 60
85 Do or Die! 60
86 Killing Blows! 60
87 Last Words! 60
88 Tears for the Fallen 60
89 Death of a Hero! 1.00
90 Rest in Peace 60
Funeral for a Friend *(Backs form poster; card fronts are untitled comic cover)*
C1 (Friends weep) 75
C2 (Jimmy Olsen's Photo) 75
C3 (Supergirl lifts car) 75
C4 (Monument revealed) 75
C5 (The torn cape) 75
C6 (Superman's Statue) 75
C7 (Supergirl) 75
C8 (Pa Kent collapses) 75
C9 (Superman flies away) 75
CL01 Checklist 1.00

DRACULA AND VLAD THE IMPALER

Topps (1993)

These cards were bagged with the first four issues of the comic book adaptation of Bram Stoker's Dracula. *There is also a series of cards from the Francis Ford Coppola-directed movie, but these cards have the Topps Comics logo in white on the back. The first card of each four card group features a movie photo, and the others have comic book or cover art. The backs have movie photos, numbers and text. The* Advance Comics *promo uses the same art as card 14 and has a white back, with black text and red logos. There is a similar movie promo card. Topps also produced nine cards which were bagged with the first three issues of* Dracula: Vlad the Impaler *comics. The cards are not captioned or numbered, and the backs form a 3 x 3 card super-panel of Dracula.*

Set: 16 Dracula cards (Topps Comic) 9.00
Set: 9 Vlad the Impaler cards (Topps Comic) 6.00

Promo sheet, movie & comic card . . 2.00
Promo card (Advance comics #46) . 2.50
Cards are not captioned
1 Movie photo of Vlad in his chapel . .50
2 Cover art for issue #2 (MMi) 50
3 Three Brides (John Nyberg) 50
4 Von Helsing portrait (Mark Chiarello) 50
5 Movie photo of the Brides 50
6 Cover art for issue #3 (MMi) 50
7 Werewolf (John Nyberg) 50
8 Old Dracula (Mark Chiarello) 50
9 Movie photo of Old Dracula 50
10 Cover art for issue #4 (MMi) 50
11 Bat Dracula (John Nyberg) 50
12 Portrait of Dracula (Mark Chiarello) 50
13 Movie photo of Von Helsing 50
14 Cover art for issue #1 (MMi) 50
15 Lucy/crucifix (John Nyberg) 50
16 Young prince Dracula (Mark Chiarello) 50
Vlad the Impaler
(1) thru (9), each 50

E

EPOCH
SAGA OF THE AGES
Karl Art (1994)

This promo card has full bleed art on a foil surface and was given out at a New York show in early 1994.

Comic Promo (Esteban Maroto) 2.00

Eudaemon & Mordare © Manta Comics, Inc.

THE EUDAEMON, FUTURE VISIONS
Press Pass (1994)

This card set was originally scheduled for early 1994, but had not appeared at press time. The promos are highly collectible anyway. As you can see above, the cards from Comic Book Collector and Card Collector's Price Guide form a single picture. This isn't obvious when you look at the cards individually, since their background colors seem so different.

Two card promo strip 2.00
Three card promo sheet 3.00
Mordare promo (Comic Book Collector) (Nelson) 2.50
The Eudaemon promo (Card Collector's Price Guide) (Nelson) 1.50
P.P.2 Eudaemon promo (Wizard) . . 1.00

Evil Ernie © Krome Productions, Inc.

EVIL ERNIE
Krome Productions (1993)
(Brian Pulido story/Steve Hughes art)

Evil Ernie is an "undead teenage psychotic with the supernatural ability to reanimate and control the dead" and he looks like it too. Lady Death gives the orders, but at least she looks good even with dead white skin. The cards have borders of purple, orange or red with a reddish back which has the card number in a skull, the series title and a Chaos! Comics logo. The cards don't have titles, so we have invented the names/descriptions used below. The chromium chase cards have a silver border, with backs like the regular cards. Promo cards #1 (of 2) and #2 (of 2) have the same art as cards 1 and 85, but in full bleed and on chromium stock, with reddish backs. They actually promote the boxed ***Evil Ernie chromium*** *card set which consists of 55 cards from this set plus a new card by Jim Balent (which we haven't seen yet). Promo #1 was given away at trade shows with Lady Death promo #1. She's going to have her own card series so her promos are listed under "L." The Arena magazine promo is for the comic book, not the card set. It has a white back with black text and doesn't resemble the cards from the series. Neither does the silver foil promo card, but we didn't want to take up a whole set entry just to describe these two cards.*

Set: 100 cards 12.50

Chromium cards (1:18)
1 (Evil Ernie) 8.00
2 (Lady Death) 8.00
3 (Smiley) 8.00
4 (Lady Death) 8.00
5 (Evil Ernie) 8.00
Autographed card (1:200)
Promo card, chromium (Steven Hughes) black & white back 3.50
Chromium Promo card #1 (of 2) . . . 2.50
Chromium Promo card #2 (of 2) . . . 2.50
Comic Book promo cards
Comic book promo card (Arena) . . . 1.00
Silver comic book promo card, B&W (McKenna) blank back 1.00
Pack: 8 cards 1.25

CARD CHECKLIST

1 Evil Ernie (w/RgM) 10
2 Lady Death (w/RgM) 10
3 Smiley 10
4 Dr. Price 10
5 Mary Young 10
6 Ernest Fairchild (child) 10
7 Ernie Fairchild (teenage) 10
8 Evil Ernie 10
9 Ramsey 10
10 Crush (w/RgM) 10
11 Cremator (w/RgM) 10
12 thru 24, Story Cards, each 10
25 Lady Death 10
26 Evil Ernie 10
27 Evil Ernie 10
28 Evil Ernie & Lady Death 10
29 Lady Death 10
30 Dr. Price 10
31 Ghoul .10
32 Evil Ernie 10
33 Evil Ernie 10
34 Evil Ernie 10
35 Evil Ernie 10
36 Evil Ernie 10
37 Lady Death 10
38 Lady Death 10
39 Evil Ernie 10
40 Evil Ernie #1 cover (Eric Mache) . .10
41 Evil Ernie #2 cover (Eric Mache) . .10
42 Evil Ernie #3 cover 10
43 Evil Ernie Special #1 cover 10
44 Evil Ernie graphic novel cover 10
45 cover by Joe Quesada & Jimmy Palmiotti 25
46 cover by Chris Bachalo 10
47 Conquest of Washington D.C. 10
48 The Resurrection, final cover 10
49 Evil Ernie #0 cover (GCa) 10
50 Evil Ernie 10
51 Lady Death (JBa) 25
52 Lady Death (GP) 25
53 Erniebo (Joel Thomas) 10
54 Evil Ernie 10
55 Evil Ernie & Lady Death 10
56 Evil Ernie & Lady Death 10
57 Lady Death "Arrival" 10
58 Evil Ernie 10
59 Lady Death 10
60 Evil Ernie 10
61 Evil Ernie 10
62 Evil Ernie (Roman Morales) 10
63 Lady Death (Roman Morales) 10
64 Evil Ernie (Paul Pelletier) 10
65 Lady Death (Mark Morales) 10
66 Evil Ernie (Jason Jensen) 10
67 Lady Death (Kevin Taylor) 10
68 Evil Ernie 10
69 Evil Ernie "Kill" 10
70 Evil Ernie 10
71 Evil Ernie 10
72 Evil Ernie 10
73 Lady Death 10
74 Evil Ernie 10
75 Evil Ernie 10
76 Evil Ernie 10
77 Evil Ernie 10
78 Evil Ernie 10
79 Evil Ernie 10
80 Evil Ernie 10
81 Evil Ernie 10
82 Evil Ernie 10
83 Lady Death 10
84 Evil Ernie 10
85 Lady Death 10
86 Evil Ernie 10
87 Evil Ernie 10
88 Lady Death 10
89 Evil Ernie 10
90 Lady Death 10
91 Evil Ernie 10
92 Evil Ernie 10
93 Killzone comic promo 10
94 Lynch Mob comic promo 10
95 The Crawler comic promo 10
96 Lady Death/Mike Holliman 10
97 Evil Ernie/Jason Jensen 10
98 Steve Hughes (photo) 10
99 Brian Pulido (photo) 10
100 Checklist 10

Excalibur © Marvel Entertainment Group, Inc.

Extreme Caricatures © Extreme Studios

EXCALIBUR

Comic Images (1989)

The card fronts depict various Marvel characters in dramatic, portrait style drawings, plus the card caption and number. The backs form a 5 x 5 card black and white puzzle picture of the Excalibur team and logo by Alan Davis and another 4 x 5 card puzzle picture of the team.

Set: 45 cards + header card (AD) 15.00

Box: 48 packs
Pack: 5 cards, + header, cello pack . 1.50

CARD CHECKLIST

1 Checklist .... .40
2 Goblin Princess .... .40
3 Daydreaming .... .40
4 Trouble .... .40
5 Widget .... .40
6 Excalibur .... .40
7 Psychic Attack .... .40
8 Gate Crasher .... .40
9 Whoops .... .40
10 Captain Britain .... .40
11 Lockheed .... .40
12 Meggan .... .40
13 Concern .... .40
14 Ready .... .40
15 Stalking .... .40
16 One Kiss .... .40
17 Take That! .... .40
18 Warlord .... .40
19 Surrounded .... .40
20 Free-e-e .... .40
21 Britains .... .40
22 Changeling .... .40
23 Agony .... .40
24 Scatterbrain .... .40
25 Angry .... .40
26 Ghouls .... .40
27 Phoenix .... .40
28 Shadowcat .... .40
29 Warwolves .... .40
30 'Til Death .... .40
31 Exploding .... .40
32 Restrained .... .40
33 Crazy Gang .... .40
34 Nightcrawler .... .40
35 Arcade .... .40
36 Sobering .... .40
37 Saturnyne .... .40
38 Nightmare .... .40
39 Juggernaut .... .40
40 King Arthur .... .40
41 Stop! .... .40
42 Slashed .... .40
43 Tea Party .... .40
44 Bodybag .... .40
45 Enough! .... .40

EXTREME

Extreme Studios (1993)

Extreme Studios was distributing these cards at the 1993 Philadelphia ComicFest and the San Diego Comics Con. We have 13 of them, and the company says that there are 15 cards in all, but could only give us one more name. The cards are caricatures of the artists at Extreme and make them look like LA street gang toughs rather than rich young artists. We like them a lot. The pictures have brown borders and the backs have white text on a brown background. All the caricatures are by Marlo Alguiza, and 5,000 of each were printed.

Set: 15? Caricatures of Extreme Studios Personnel. 9.00

Dan Fraga .... .50
Richard Horie .... .50
Jason Irwin .... .50
Chuck Jones .... .50
Andre Khromov .... .50
Rob Liefeld .... .50
Danny Miki .... .50
Marat Mychaels .... .50
Dan Panosian .... .50
Norm Rapmund .... .50
Ron Rife .... .50
Eric Stephenson .... .50
Byron Talman .... .50
Art Thibert .... .50

Extreme cards © Extreme Studios

EXTREME

Cards Illustrated (1994)

Three of these ten cards came in each copy of issue #3 of Cards Illustrated, *so you had to buy three copies and look for the tenth card at a card show to get them all. They feature full bleed art, which repeats on the back as a faint background painting, overprinted with black text. The card name is on the back in a red strip and the number is in a yellow box.*

1 Cybrid (CNn/Alquiza) .... .50
2 Cybrid (Winn/Sibal) .... .50
3 Metaforce (JMs/NRd) .... .50
4 Code 9 (CYp/NRd) .... .50
5 Law 'N' Order (MMy) .... .50
6 L.A.N.C.E.R.S. (RHe/DaM) ...... .50
7 Black Flag (Dan Fraga) .... .50
8 Risk (Jones/NRd) .... .50
9 Checklist .... .50
10 Black & White (ATi) .... .50

F

FAMOUS COMIC BOOK CREATORS

Eclipse (1992, photos)

These cards feature a color photo of the comic artist, writer or editor inside a white border. The backs are a light yellow, with card number, name, credits and a small black and white drawing. Many of the true greats in comicdom are included.

Set: 110 Cards 16.00

WILL EISNER
Writer, Artist, Painter, Letterer, Editor, Publisher

Famous Comic Book Creators © Eclipse

Silver-autographed blue back cards:
Chuck Dixon 7.00
Tom Lyle 7.00
Two card promo sheet 1.00
Pack: 12 cards 1.00

CARD CHECKLIST
1 Will Eisner 15
2 Wally Wood 15
3 Gary Kwapisz 15
4 Walt Kelly 15
5 Keno Don Rosa 15
6 Mark Gruenwald 15
7 Norm Breyfogle 15
8 Jim Shooter 15
9 Steve Rude 15
10 Bob McLeod 15
11 John Buscema 15
12 Dan Brereton 15
13 Rick Geary 15
14 Jim Starlin 15
15 Joe Simon 15
16 John Romita, Sr. 15
17 Kate Worley 15
18 Reed Waller 15
19 Howard Cruse 15
20 Eddie Campbell 15
21 Martin Nodell 15
22 Larry Marder 15
23 Doug Moench 15
24 Dick Ayers 15
25 Michael T. Gilbert 15
26 Bob Burden 15
27 Brent Anderson 15
28 Murphy Anderson 15
29 Mike Baron 15
30 Kurt Schaffenberger 15
31 Curt Swan 15
32 Neil Gaiman 15
33 Marv Wolfman 15
34 Len Wein 15
35 George Perez 15
36 Sergio Aragones 15
37 Bob Kane 15
38 Al Williamson 15
39 David Boswell 15
40 Jim Engel 15
41 Matt Wagner 15
42 Gerard Jones 15
43 Erik Larsen 15
44 Steve Leialoha 15
45 Trina Robbins 15
46 Scott McCloud 15
47 Wm. Messner-Loebs 15
48 Carl Potts 15
49 Moebius 15
50 Bill Sienkiewicz 15
51 Stan Sakai 15
52 Wayne Vansant 15
53 Julius Schwartz 15
54 Larry Hama 15
55 Steve Englehart 15
56 Sam Glanzman 15
57 Todd McFarlane 15
58 Charles Vess 15
59 Timothy Truman 15
60 Paul Chadwick 15
61 Mark Verheiden 15
62 Ken Steacy 15
63 Tom Lyle 15
64 Bryan Talbot 15
65 Mike Barr 15
66 Frank Springer 15
67 Timothy Bradstreet 15
68 Ron Frenz 15
69 Klaus Janson 15
70 Al Gordon 15
71 Ann Nocenti 15
72 Tom Yeates 15
73 Marie Severin 15
74 Marc Hempel 15
75 Roy Thomas 15
76 Paul Mavrides 15
77 Don McGregor 15
78 Joe Staton 15
79 Fred Kida 15
80 Gray Morrow 15
81 Mark Wheatley 15
82 Mike Ploog 15
83 Marc Silvestri 15
84 Mark Nelson 15
85 Mark Evanier 15
86 Paul Gulacy 15
87 Sam Kieth 15
88 Mark Schultz 15
89 Ken Macklin 15
90 Lela Dowling 15
91 Beau Smith 15
92 Bill Reinhold 15
93 Gilbert Shelton 15
94 Dan Spiegel 15
95 Bill Finger 15
96 Bill Everett 15
97 Reed Crandall 15
98 Wayne Boring 15
99 Milton Caniff 15
100 Jack Kirby 15
101 Chuck Dixon 15
102 Clive Barker 15
103 John Bolton 15
104 George Herriman 15
105 Harvey Pekar 15
106 David Wenzel 15
107 Sal Buscema 15
108 Lou Fine 15
109 P. Craig Russell 15
110 Checklist 15

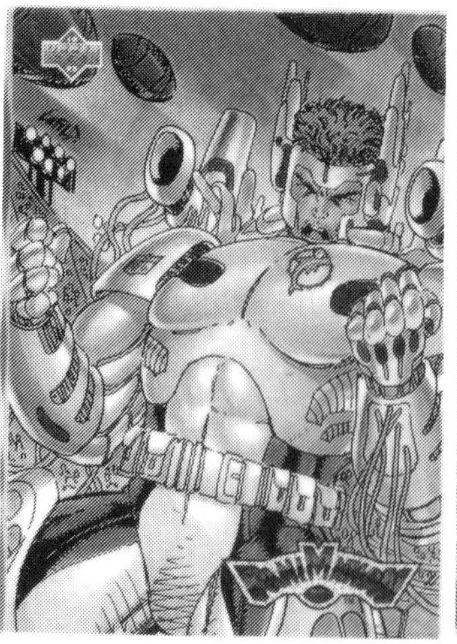

Fanimation © Upper Deck Company

FANIMATION

Upper Deck (1992, 1993)

These cards were distributed as sports cards, but they are by several of the best comic book artists and done in a comic book style, making the sports hero look like a superhero.

Football (1992)
Set: 10 cards 50.00
F1 Jim Kelly (JLe) 5.00
F2 Dan Marino (RLd) 7.00
F3 Lawrence Taylor (RLd) 4.00
F4 Deion Sanders (RLd) 5.00
F5 Troy Aikman (JLe) 10.00
F6 Junior Seau (JLe) 5.00
F7 Mike Singletary (RLd) 4.00
F8 Eric Dickerson (JLe) 5.00
F9 Jerry Rice (RLd) 8.00
F10 Kelly/Marino checklist (JLe) . . . 5.00

Basketball (1993)
Promo sheet (JLe & RLd) 7.50
Set: 5 cards 6.00
506 Agent 23 (JLe) 1.75
507 Birdman (JLe) 1.50
508 The Mailman (MS) 1.00
509 The Warrior (MS) 1.00
510 Birdman & Agent 23 (JLe) 1.50

Fem Force (I) © AC Comics

FEM FORCE

AC Comics (1992)

The FemForce is a band of super-powered females who protect us against paranormal threats. They appear in Femforce, Good Girl Art Quarterly *and* Fem-Force Up Close. *The cards contain their color pictures inside a white border. The backs are white with text about the character. The first printing of Set 1 was distributed only through Capital City Distribution and came with a blue wrapper, while the more common second printing had a green wrapper, with a different picture. There is a slight variation in card #5 between the two printings. In the first printing this card has a white background and in the second printing it has a pink background.*

Set: 14 cards & blue wrapper 15.00

Set: 2nd printing, green wrapper 9.95
Set: 2nd printing, signed & numbered, orange wrapper, 1000 made 15.00

Card	Price
Ms. Victory sticker (Femforce Up-close #6) untitled	.50
1 Ms. Victory	.80
2 Nightveil	.80
3 She-Cat (also in Fem Force Up Close comic #4)	.80
4 New Ms. Victory	.80
5 Tara	.80
6 Stardust	.80
7 Synn. Girl from LSD	.80
8 Rad	.80
9 Dragonfly	.80
10 Colt	.80
11 The Blue Bulleteer	.80
12 Buckaroo Betty	.80
13 Yankee Girl	.80
14 Jet Girl	.80

Fem Force II & III © AC Comics

FEM FORCE II: FRIENDS OF FEMFORCE

AC Comics (1993)

A continuation of the above set, numbered to follow.

Set: 14 cards & purple wrapper 9.95
Set: 2nd printing, signed & numbered, green wrapper ... 15.00

Card	Price
15 Garganta (double size)	1.00
16 Dragonfly	.75
17 She-Cat	.75
18 Tara	.75
19 Miss Victory	.75
20 Miss Masque	.75
21 Rio Rita	.75
22 Rayda	.75
23 Rocketman	.75
24 Paragon	.75
25 Catman & Kitten	.75
26 The Avenger	.75
27 Reddevil	.75
28 Black Venus	.75

FEM FORCE III: FEM FORCE FOES

AC Comics (1993)

The third set, similar to the above two.

Set: 14 cards & yellow wrapper 9.95
Set: 15 cards & red wrapper, Diamond Stores exclusive, with special 15th card #43 No-Nose Nanette card 11.00

Card	Price
29 Rip-Jaw	.75
30 Madam Boa	.75
31 Black Shroud	.75
32 Capricorn	.75
33 Black Commando	.75
34 Alizarin Crimson	.75
35 Darkfire	.75
36 Stella Stargaze	.75
37 Garganta	.75
38 Lady Luger	.75
39 Singapore Sal	.75
40 Victorad	.75
41 Fem Paragon	.75
42 Umbra	.75

AC Comics Promo Pack © AC Comics

[FEM FORCE] AC COMICS PROMO PACK

AC Comics (1993)

These cards were distributed individually as promo cards for various AC Comics in 1992 and 1993. They look like the FemForce cards described above and they were available as a set through the FemForce Fan Club ("The Secret Society of Synn") in late 1993. In addition, they mostly promote FemForce comics, all of which is why they are listed here, instead of under "A."

Set: 8 cards with wrapper 10.00

Card	Price
43 No Nose Nanette	1.50
Wildside	1.00
Sentinels of Justice	1.00
Paragon, Dark Apocalypse	1.00
Nightveil (Femforce #57)	1.00
Reddevil vs. Claw	1.00
Rayda (photo) (Femforce #63)	1.00
Sky Gal (Sky Gal #1)	1.00

FernGully, The Last Rainforest © FAI Films Pty, Ltd.

FERNGULLY, THE LAST RAINFOREST

Dart Flipcards (1992, Animated Movie)

Crysta is a 15 year old forest fairy and Zak is a 17 year old city kid working for a logging company one summer. Crysta eventually saves the forest with her magic and Zak returns to tell the humans to stop chopping it down. You can tell that this is a kid's fantasy because in real life greed almost always wins! The card fronts have pictures from the movie inside a white border. The backs are uncoated and have the caption, number and text on a green forest background. The CBG promo card is just a card from the set with "CBG PRICE GUIDE Promo" stamped in blue ink.

Set: 100 cards 15.00
Boxed Limited Factory Set, numbered (3000 made) 16.00

Promo Card 1.00
CBG Promo Card 1.00
Pack: 8 cards 1.00

CARD CHECKLIST

Propaganda cards
1 Title/Think Globally, Act Locally . . .15
2 Collision Course 15
3 Lungs of the Earth 15
4 A New Day 15
5 The Forest Song 15
6 Life is a Magic Thing 15
7 Magical Creatures 15

Character Cards
8 Crysta 15
9 Zak 15
10 Pips 15
11 Batty Koda 15
12 Magi Lune 15
13 The Beetle Boys 15
14 Stump .15
15 Twig 15
16 Knotty .15
17 Bark 15

The story begins
18 Symphony of Noise 15
19 Sky's the Limit 15
20 Above the Canopy 15
21 Warning on the Horizon 15
22 Look Out, Below! 15
23 Spread the News 15
24 Rock and Ock 15
25 Endless Sky 15
26 The Web of Life 15
27 The Balance of Nature 15
28 The Spirit of Destruction 15
29 The Powers of Nature 15
30 Music to her Ears 15
31 Batty Koda Arrives 15
32 Dazed and Confused 15
33 Flying Free 15
34 Human Tales 15
35 Battered and Bruised 15
36 Batty Raps 15
37 Erratic Logic 15
38 Last Place in the World 15
39 X Marks the Spot 15
40 At the Controls 15
41 Ants Don't Wear Shoes 15
42 Bat Dreams 15
43 Who's the Monster? 15
44 Leaf It to Zak 15
45 Dinner Time! 15
46 I'm Gonna Eat Ya 15
47 Welcome to the Food Chain 15
48 He's Got Good Taste 15
49 Never Eat Your Friends 15
50 I.O.U. 15
51 New Friends 15
52 All Ears 15
53 Welcome to FernGully 15
54 Fools Rush In 15
55 Looks can be Deceiving! 15
56 There Goes the Neighborhood! . . .15
57 Machine or Monster? 15
58 Partners in Grime 15
59 Crysta's Missing 15
60 Amazing Discovery 15
61 Givers of Life 15
62 Stumped Again! 15
63 Hair-Raising Experience 15
64 The Sound of Music 15
65 Catch the Beat 15
66 Rock On! 15
67 FernGully Wild Life 15
68 Tense Times 15
69 Making A Splash 15
70 Fairy Tag 15
71 Breath of Death 15
72 Guilty! 15
73 Crysta's Pain 15
74 Guardians of the Forest 15
75 The Seed of Life 15
76 Magi's Power 15
77 Frozen By Fear 15
78 FernGully Besieged 15
79 Clouds of Poison 15
80 No Escape 15
81 Bat Rescue 15
82 Inside The Monster 15
83 Never Forget 15
84 Beetle Boys Bid Goodbye 15
85 The Seed of Creation 15
86 Fairy Magic 15
87 The Forest Floor 15
88 Water Life 15
89 Giants of the Forest 15
90 Crysta's Power 15

Coloring Cards (black & white)
91 Crysta/Crysta 15
92 Ock & Rock/Zak 15
93 Hang A Fang/Batty Koda 15
94 Pips/Pips 15
95 Magi Lune/Magi Lune 15
96 Twig/Stump 15
97 Knotty/Bark 15
98 Ash/Snake 15
99 Ock & Rock/The Goanna 15
100 Checklist 15

FIEVEL GOES WEST (AN AMERICAN TAIL)

Impel (1991, Animated Movie)

The art is from the animated movie and follows the adventures of an immigrant mouse family as they settle in the west. It was a kid's movie and it's a kid's card series, but with the high quality card production that made Impel's cards famous. The first 14 cards are portraits of the main characters and the next 11 describe the relationship between pairs of characters. The story starts with card #26 and runs to card #102. These cards have a picture inside a rough wood frame and white border. The backs have text and a small close-up photo. Cards #103 to #134 tell "An American Tail" of how the Mousekewitz clan left Russia and came to America. The pictures are framed to look like they are in a photo album. The rest of the cards describe the process of making an animated film and give advice to the youthful card reader. The holograms are taken from the western part of the storyline. Artists are not credited.

Fievel Goes West © Universal City Studios, Inc. & Amblin Entertainment, Inc.

Set: 150 cards 15.00

Collector's album 20.00

Holograms:
H-1 Rolling Tuna Tin 4.00
H-2 Shooting the Rapids 4.00
H-3 Hawk Attack! 4.00
H-4 The Paw Fight 4.00
H-5 Fievel Gets His Badge 4.00
Pack: 12 cards 1.00

CARD CHECKLIST

Portraits
1 Fievel Mousekewitz 10
2 Tanya Mousekewitz 10
3 Papa Mousekewitz 10
4 Mama Mousekewitz 10
5 Yasha Mousekewitz 10
6 Cat R. Waul 10
7 T. R. Chula 10
8 Wylie Burp 10
9 Tiger 10
10 Miss Kitty 10
11 "One-Eye" 10
12 Earless Poultroon 10
13 "Frenchy" 10
14 Geronimouse 10

Pairs
15 Fievel & Tiger 10
16 Fievel & Tanya 10
17 Fievel & Wylie Burp 10
18 Mama & Papa 10
19 The Architect & Cat R. Waul 10
20 Cat R. Waul & Chula 10
21 Miss Kitty & Tiger 10
22 Tanya & Miss Kitty 10
23 Mousekewitz Family 10
24 The Waul Gang 10
25 The Wylie Bunch 10

Story
26 New York, 1885 10
27 Hester Street 10
28 Tanya Sings for Supper 10
29 Reading About Wylie 10
30 Fievel's Fantasy 10
31 "Filly the Kid" 10
32 Miss Kitty & Tiger 10
33 Miss Kitty's Farewell 10
34 Mousekewitzes at Dinner 10
35 Alarm! 10
36 Cat Attack! 10
37 Mice on the Run 10
38 Escape Devices 10
39 Tiger's Aborted Rescue 10
40 Fievel Faces "One-Eye" 10
41 Fievel is Cornered 10
42 Papa to the Rescue 10
43 Rolling Tuna Tin 10
44 Escaping from "One-Eye" 10
45 Shooting the Rapids 10
46 Hustler Mouse 10
47 The Crowd Goes Crazy 10
48 Fievel's Note 10
49 Grand Central Station 10
50 Fievel Says Goodbye 10
51 Tiger Dodging Dogs 10
52 The Dog Pound 10
53 Tiger Leaps On The Train 10
54 Tiger in the River 10
55 Tiger on Stage 10
56 Fievel Explores the Train 10
57 Fievel Entangled 10
58 Playing Poker 10
59 "Mouseburgers!" 10
60 "What Do We Have Here?" 10
61 Mouse Overboard 10
62 Green River 10
63 Cats Are Nice in the West 10
64 The Raging Sun 10
65 Tiger & Fievel's Mirage 10
66 Indian Village 10
67 The Indian Chief 10
68 Hawk Dive-Bombs Fievel 10
69 Fievel & Scorpions 10
70 The Hawk Gets Fievel 10
71 The Indian God 10
72 Fievel's Rescue? 10
73 Fievel Un-eaten 10
74 Talkin' Tumbleweed 10
75 Home at Last 10
76 Saloon Raising 10
77 Blueprints 10
78 The Giant Mousetrap 10
79 Catching the Spy 10
80 A Talent Discovered 10
81 Tanya Transformed 10
82 Tanya's Debut 10
83 Fievel & The Dawg 10
84 We Need You! 10
85 Desperado Gulch 10
86 Practice Makes Purr-fect 10
87 Bark School 10
88 Lazy Eye 10
89 Dog Practice 10
90 Heroes Are Born 10
91 Ruff & Ready 10
92 Town Square 10
93 Mousetrap in Disguise 10
94 Just in Time! 10
95 The Paw Fight 10
96 Showdown 10

97 Tanya's Warning .10
98 Tiger the Hero .10
99 Cat-a-pult .10
100 Prairie Dog Hill .10
101 Fievel Gets His Badge .10
102 Sunset .10

An American Tail

103 Happy in Russia .10
104 Hanukkah Gifts .10
105 Papa's Stories .10
106 Cossack Attack .10
107 Leaving Russia .10
108 The Boat Trip .10
109 The Storm at Sea .10
110 Overboard .10
111 Floating in a Bottle .10
112 Immigration .10
113 Henri the Pidgeon .10
114 Showing Fievel America .10
115 Warren T. Rat & Digit .10
116 Putting Fievel to Work .10
117 Tony Toponi .10
118 Looking for Papa .10
119 Lost in America .10
120 Reunion with Tony .10
121 The Mayor .10
122 Thinking of Tanya .10
123 The Town Meeting .10
124 Fievel's Idea .10
125 The Museum .10
126 Papa? .10
127 Trapped .10
128 A Sensitive Cat .10
129 The Chase .10
130 Giant Mouse of Minsk .10
131 Soaking Cats .10
132 Family Reunion .10
133 Flying with Henri .10
134 Statue of Liberty .10

Fievel Goes West

135 The Story & The Screenplay .10
136 Story Sketches & Early Visuals .10
137 Character Development .10
138 The Characters Come to Life! .10
139 Backgrounds & Scene Painting .10
140 Animation Drawings .10
141 Coloring, Ink & Paint .10
142 Painting & Finishing Cels .10
143 Final Assembly & Filming .10
144 Play It Safe! .10
145 Making Friends .10
146 Fun Adventures .10
147 Family of Friends .10
148 Movie Poster .10
149 Checklist 1 .10
150 Checklist 2 .10

FLAMING CARROT

Comic Images (1988)

This set contains art by Bob Burden from his comic book of the same name. We couldn't find a set anywhere; even Comic Images didn't have any samples, but Bob was kind enough to send us some in time to make the color page which shows all the early Comic Images sets and for the black and white picture below.

Set: 40 cards 15.00

Pack: 5 cards, cello pack 1.50

CARD CHECKLIST

1 Header card & checklist .35
2 Home Run King .35
3 Mr. Death .35

Flaming Carrot © Bob Burden

4 Most Dangerous Man Alive! .35
5 The Panic .35
6 Carrots In Nose .35
7 Bowling For Love .35
8 The Goo Man .35
9 Get Those Ghosts .35
10 Toilet Plunger .35
11 To The Rescue .35
12 What Is It? .35
13 Six-Gun Justice .35
14 Numismatist Extraodinaire .35
15 The Zooomy Car! .35
16 Ride'em Cowboy! .35
17 Bombs Away .35
18 The Green Eye .35
19 Blazing Bullets .35
20 No Rest For The Evil .35
21 Mystery In The Woods .35
22 Narrow Escape .35
23 Sponge Boy .35
24 Calling Flaming Carrot .35
25 Man of Mystery .35
26 The Deadliest Game .35
27 Bikini Teens .35
28 Pogo .35
29 Dead Dog .35
30 Voo Doo Men .35
31 Hitler's Feet .35
32 Demon Creature .35
33 Blowing Bubbles .35
34 The Artless Dodger .35
35 Why Dr. Why? .35
36 Most Happy Fellow .35
37 The Blazing Carrot .35
38 Let Them Laugh .35
39 Buzzard Men .35
40 Stink Bomb .35

FLINTSTONES

Cardz (1993, Animated & Comic)

These are full bleed pictures from the TV shows, with card title, number and text on the back. The backs also contain a small inset picture in a Bedrock TV set. The first 50 cards cover TV episodes,

Flintstones © Cardz Distribution, Inc. & Hanna-Barbera Productions, Inc.

and the pictures are not as sharp as the later pictures. Cards 51 thru 65 cover the engagement and wedding of Pebbles and Bamm-Bamm. The fronts say "I Yabba-Dabba Do!" in a heart design and the backs have a floral design with pictures of the lucky twosome. Cards 65 to 80 have a different design on the back and cards 81 to 90 have a blue background with a close-up from the comics. The remaining character cards have a supplementary character picture on the back.

Set: 100 cards+10 coloring 14.00

Holograms

H1 "Sports" 6.00
H2 "Friends" (Bamm-Bamm & Pebbles) 6.00
H3 "Family" 6.00

Tekchrome

T1 "The Flintstones" 10.00

Prototype cards

The Flintstone Flyer 1.00
Dating 1.00
(Title unknown) 1.00
Pack: 8 cards 1.00

Four different wrappers featuring Fred, Barney, Dino, & Pebbles & Bamm Bamm.

CARD CHECKLIST

Episodes

1 The Flintstone Flyer .10
2 The Swimming Pool .10
3 Hollyrock Here I Come .10
4 The Snorkasaurus Story .10
5 The Hot Piano .10
6 Love Letters on the Rocks .10
7 In the Dough .10
8 Fred Flintstone Before and After .10
9 The Soft Touchables .10
10 The Masquerade Ball .10
11 The X-Ray Story .10
12 The Entertainer .10
13 Fred Strikes Out .10
14 Trouble-In-Law .10
15 Latin Lover .10
16 Dino Goes Hollyrock .10
17 The Bowling Ballet .10
18 The Buffalo Convention .10
19 Baby Barney .10
20 Nothing But the Tooth .10
21 Foxy Grandma .10
22 The Blessed Event .10
23 Ventriloquist Barney .10
24 The Big Move .10
25 The Birthday Party .10
26 Ann-Margrock Presents .10
27 Little Bamm-Bamm .10
28 Dino Disappears .10
29 Fred's Monkey Shines .10
30 Ten Little Flintstones .10
31 Ladies Night at the Lodge .10
32 Son of Rockzilla .10
33 Bachelor Daze .10
34 Operation Switchover .10
35 Hop Happy .10
36 Itty Bitty Fred .10
37 A Haunted House is Not a Home .10
38 The Gruesomes .10
39 The Indianrockolis 500 .10
40 Adobe Dick .10
41 Sheriff for a Day .10
42 No Biz Like Show Biz .10
43 Return of Stoney Curtis .10
44 Samantha .10
45 The Great Gazoo .10
46 Rip Van Flintstone .10
47 The Masquerade Party .10
48 Curtain Call at Bedrock .10
49 Dripper .10
50 The Story of Rocky's Raiders .10

The Wedding

51 Dating .10
52 The Engagement .10
53 The Announcement .10
54 Preparations .10
55 The Proud Parents .10
56 Ready to March .10
57 Down the Aisle .10
58 Dino as Ring Bearer .10
59 Giving Pebbles Away .10
60 The Ceremony .10
61 The Kiss .10
62 Throwing Bouquet .10
63 Feeding Cake .10
64 The Reception .10
65 Mr. and Mrs. Rubble .10

The various TV shows and specials

66 The Flintstones .10
67 The Pebbles and Bamm-Bamm Show .10
68 The Flintstone Comedy Hour .10
69 The New Fred and Barney Show .10
70 The Flintstone Comedy Show .10
71 The Flintstone Kids .10

& Frankenstone .10
74 The Flintstones: Fred's Final Fling .10
75 The Flintstones: Wind-Up Wilma .10
76 The Flintstones: Jogging Fever .10
77 The Flintstones Little Big League .10
78 The Man Called Flintstone .10
79 The Jetsons Meet the Flintstones .10
80 I Yabba-Dabba Do! .10

Comic Book Covers

81 World's Fair Comic cover .10
82 Gold Key Comic #36 cover .10
83 Dell Giant Comic #1 cover .10
84 Gold Key Comic #11 cover .10
85 Gold Key Comic #16 cover .10
86 Gold Key Comic #24 cover .10
87 Gold Key Comic #34 cover .10
88 Gold Key Comic #1 cover .10
89 Gold Key Comic #12 cover .10
90 Gold Key Comic #30 cover .10

Meet the Flintstone characters

91 Fred Flintstone .10
92 Wilma Flintstone .10
93 Pebbles .10
94 Dino .10
95 Barney Rubble .10
96 Betty Rubble .10
97 Bamm-Bamm .10
98 Hoppy .10
99 Mr. Slate .10
100 The Great Gazoo .10

Coloring Cards

A1 Baby Buggy .10
A2 Phonograph .10
A3 A Traffic Light .10
A4 Garbage Disposal .10
A5 Mixer .10
A6 Snoots .10
A7 Schneider .10
A8 Chipsie .10
A9 Doosey .10
A10 Kitty .10

Flintstones/NFL © Cardz Distribution, Inc. & Hanna-Barbera Productions, Inc.

FLINTSTONES/NFL
Cardz (1993)

These cards show Fred, Barney and Dino in football poses. They are wearing the uniforms (more or less) of the named team and the picture is inside a white border. The card backs are numbered and contain football information. There are 16 "Stone Age Signals" cards which show Fred, in referee's shirt, giving the signal in front of a blue background and an explanation of the signal on the back. His pants are not up to the NFL standard dress code. There are also 10 color-in cards with trivia questions on the back. The holograms are full bleed images on the front and don't say "Flintstones/NFL" anywhere, but do have football information on the back, so they should not be confused with those from the previous series. The prototype cards are marked as such in the upper right corner, next to the card number, but don't correspond to the final versions of the cards.

Set: 100 cards + 10 coloring cards 14.00

Holograms

H1 A Decade of Super Bowl champs 6.00
H2 The 1993 NFC Pro Bowl line up 6.00
H3 The 1993 AFC Pro Bowl line up 6.00

Tekchrome

T1 Cowboys, Super Bowl Champs 9.00

Prototype cards

1 Miami (team leaders) 1.00
2 San Francisco (record) 1.00
3 Buffalo (team) 1.00
4 Dallas (record) 1.00
5 Philadelphia (team leaders) 1.00
6 San Diego (season story) 1.00

Pack: 8 cards 1.00

CARD CHECKLIST

1993 Draft Picks

1 Atlanta .10
2 Buffalo .10
3 Chicago .10
4 Cincinnati .10
5 Cleveland .10
6 Dallas .10
7 Denver .10
8 Detroit .10
9 Green Bay .10
10 Houston .10
11 Indianapolis .10
12 Kansas City .10
13 LA Raiders .10
14 LA Rams .10
15 Miami .10
16 Minnesota .10
17 New England .10
18 New Orleans .10
19 NY Giants .10
20 NY Jets .10
21 Philadelphia .10
22 Phoenix .10
23 Pittsburgh .10
24 San Diego .10
25 San Francisco .10
26 Seattle .10
27 Tampa Bay .10
28 Washington .10

1993 Schedules

29 Atlanta .10
30 Buffalo .10
31 Chicago .10
32 Cincinnati .10
33 Cleveland .10
34 Dallas .10
35 Denver .10
36 Detroit .10
37 Green Bay .10
38 Houston .10
39 Indianapolis .10
40 Kansas City .10
41 LA Raiders .10
42 LA Rams .10
43 Miami .10
44 Minnesota .10
45 New England .10
46 New Orleans .10
47 NY Giants .10
48 NY Jets .10
49 Philadelphia .10
50 Phoenix .10
51 Pittsburgh .10
52 San Diego .10
53 San Francisco .10
54 Seattle .10
55 Tampa Bay .10
56 Washington .10

Team Stats

57 Atlanta .10
58 Buffalo .10
59 Chicago .10
60 Cincinnati .10
61 Cleveland .10
62 Dallas .10
63 Denver .10
64 Detroit .10
65 Green Bay .10
66 Houston .10
67 Indianapolis .10
68 Kansas City .10
69 LA Raiders .10
70 LA Rams .10
71 Miami .10
72 Minnesota .10
73 New England .10
74 New Orleans .10
75 NY Giants .10
76 NY Jets .10
77 Philadelphia .10
78 Phoenix .10
79 Pittsburgh .10
80 San Diego .10
81 San Francisco .10
82 Seattle .10
83 Tampa Bay .10
84 Washington .10

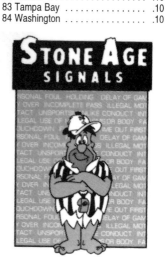

Flintstones/NFL © Cardz Distribution, Inc. & Hanna-Barbera Productions, Inc.

Stone Age Signals

85 Touchdown or Successful Field Goal .10
86 Time Out .10
87 First Down .10
88 Personal Foul .10
89 Delay of Game .10
90 Offsides or Encroachment .10
91 Holding .10
92 Illegal Motion .10
93 Unsportsmanlike Conduct .10
94 Blocking below the Waist .10
95 Intentional Grounding of a Pass .10
96 Illegal Contact .10
97 False Start .10
98 Illegal Use of the Hands, Arms, or Body .10
99 Interference .10
100 Incomplete Pass .10

Coloring Cards

101 NFL Football Facts (I) .10
102 NFL Football Facts (II) .10
103 NFL Football Facts (III) .10
104 A Team Scramble .10
105 Lost in the Pocket .10
106 The NFL Position Condition .10
107 AFC Match Game .10
108 NFC Match Game .10
109 A-Mazing .10
110 It's a Mad Scramble .10

RETURN OF THE FLINTSTONES
Cardz (1994, Animated TV)

This is the third Flintstones Cardz set from or based on the animated characters and it's as good as the first two. This listing is from a preliminary checklist furnished by Cardz.

Set: 60 cards 10.00

Tekchrome cards

T1 Meet the Flintstones 7.50
T2 Yabba Dabba Do! 7.50
T3 Modern Stone Age Family 7.50

Pack: 8 cards 1.00

CARD CHECKLIST

The Good Scout (Episode #26)

1 Fred Joins the Scouts .15
2 Fire! .15
3 Exhausted From a Long Day .15
4 Water Fall! .15
5 "In the News" .15
6 A Pooped Troop .15
7 A Note of Gratitude .15

The Rock Quarry Story (Episode #34)

8 News About Town .15

9 Accidental Meeting .15
10 New Buddies .15
11 Gus Schultz .15
12 "It's Me Rock" .15
13 "It's Really Rock!" .15
14 In Hot Water .15
The Impractical Joker (Episode #49)
15 You've Gone Too Far Fred .15
16 Sudsy Wudsy Money .15
17 Just the Scoop .15
18 A Real Money Maker .15
19 Shop 'Til He Drops .15
20 Held Up .15
21 Surprise! .15
Cinderellastone (Episode #20)
22 Not Invited .15
23 A Bedtime Story .15
24 Fred's Fairy Godmother .15
25 Charmed, I'm Sure .15
26 The Clock Struck 12 .15
27 Fred, Wake Up! .15
28 A Promotion? .15
The Hatrocks & The Gruesomes (#133)
29 Telegram! .15
30 Armed And Ready! .15
31 The Takeover .15
32 A Dining Experience .15
33 TV Time .15
34 Gruesome Neighbors .15
35 Bug Off! .15
The Gravelberry Pie King (Episode #140)
36 Fired Freddy .15
37 A Pie of a Deal .15
38 The Gravelberry Pie King .15
39 Pie in the Sky .15
40 But We Had a Deal .15
41 Sale! Sale! Sale! .15
42 The Gravelberry Pie Queen .15
Hollyrock-a-bye-baby
43 Good News...Baby Due! .15
44 Snack Time .15
45 A Shower for Baby .15
46 Getting Ready .15
47 It's a Boy! Its a Girl! .15
48 Koochie Koo .15
49 A Family Portrait .15
Flintstones Friends
50 Checklist .15
51 Fred .15
52 Wilma .15
53 Pebbles .15
54 Dino .15
55 Barney .15
56 Betty .15
57 Bamm Bamm .15
58 Hoppy .15
59 Gazoo .15
60 Mrs. Slaghoople .15

FOODANG
Continum Comics (1994)

Promo card 1.00

Foodang © Continum Comics

Gene Cards © Marvel Comics UK, Inc.

G

GENE CARDS
Marvel UK (1993)

These cards came bagged with comic books and are portraits of the characters from this Marvel UK series. The cards have full bleed art and a close-up picture on the back with text and card number.

From Gun Runner #1
1 Gun Runner .25
2 Smith .25
3 Heavy Duty .25
4 Lure .25
From Gene Dogs #1
5 Pacer & Cat .25
6 Tyr .25
7 Kestrel .25
8 Howitzer .25
From Genetix #1
9 Base .25
10 Vesper .25
11 Shift & Ridge .25
12 Stinger .25
From Deathmetal Vs. Genetix #1
13 Shift .25
14 Death Metal .25
From Deathmetal Vs. Genetix #2
15 Ridge (KHd) .25
16 Krista Marwan (KHd) .25

Ghost Rider © Marvel Entertainment Group, Inc.

GHOST RIDER
Comic Images (1990)

The card fronts depict various Marvel characters in dramatic, portrait style drawings, plus the card caption and number. The backs form a 5 x 9 black and white puzzle drawing of the Ghost Rider #1 *comic book cover.*

Set: 45 cards + header card 12.00
Pack: 5? cards + header card 1.25

CARD CHECKLIST
1 Ghost Rider .25
2 Blaze .25
3 The Spirit .25
4 Gas Cap .25
5 Transformation .25
6 Rescue .25
7 Hostage .25
8 Payback .25
9 Upholding .25
10 Police .25
11 Blockade? .25
12 Up The Wall .25
13 Workout .25
14 The Bike .25
15 Wheelie .25
16 Gangs .25
17 Up Above .25
18 Gotcha .25
19 Blackout .25
20 Rage .25
21 Canisters .25
22 Deathwatch .25
23 Scarred .25
24 Kingpin .25
25 Mr. Hyde .25
26 Punks .25
27 Supernatural .25
28 Knock-Knock .25
29 Vigilantes .25
30 Talk! .25
31 AAKGG! .25
32 Dan .25
33 Stacy .25
34 Punisher .25
35 Whoa! .25
36 Punched .25
37 Flag Smasher .25
38 Surrounded .25
39 Two Skulls .25
40 Scarecrow .25
41 Insane .25
42 Justice .25
43 Roasted .25
44 X-Factor .25
45 Checklist .25

GHOST RIDER II
Comic Images (1992)

The card fronts have a comic book close-up picture in a black border. The backs contain the card number, title and text. The glow-in-the-dark cards have a slightly sandy feel and are numbered G1 to G10, but otherwise resemble the regular cards. Most of the art is by Mark Texeira.

Set: 80 cards/10 glow-in-dark 13.00
Ghost Rider promo card 3.50
Pack: 10 cards 1.25

CARD CHECKLIST
1 Blood Signs .15
2 Zodiak .15
3 Possesses .15
4 Asleep .15
5 Zarathos .15
6 Dr. Strange .15
7 Captured .15
8 Snowblind .15
9 Johnny Blaze .15
10 The Original .15
11 Old Times .15
12 Control .15
13 Freedom .15
14 Confrontation .15
15 Hellfire .15
16 Shot! .15
17 Wounded .15
18 No Escape .15
19 Stop It! .15
20 Scarred .15
21 Exhausted .15
22 Team-up .15
23 Hobgoblin .15

Ghost Rider II © Marvel Entertainment Group, Inc.

24 Spider-Man .15
25 Fire Power .15
26 Styge .15
27 Bare Bones .15
28 In Between .15
29 Suicide .15
30 Mephisto .15
31 Death .15
32 Punishment .15
33 Penance Stare .15
34 Ninjas .15
35 Buried .15
36 Deathwatch .15
37 Hag and Troll .15
38 Final Conflict .15
39 You Will Die .15
40 Revenge .15
41 Dan's Death .15
42 Nightmare .15
43 New Orleans .15
44 Frenzy .15
45 Wolverine .15
46 Cable .15
47 Hearts of Darkness .15
48 Blackheart .15
49 Sleepwalker .15
50 Deathlock .15
51 Moon Knight .15
52 Daredevil .15
53 Fear .15
54 Fantastic Four? .15
55 Four of Us .15
56 The Midnight Sons .15
57 Lilith's Motive .15
58 Lilith .15
59 Morbius .15
60 Duo .15
61 Nightstalkers .15
62 Mistaken I.D. .15
63 Darkhold .15
64 Spirits of Vengeance .15
65 Partners .15
66 Teacher .15
67 Vendetta .15
68 First Mission .15
69 Demon? .15
70 Transformation .15
71 Emblem .15
72 The Chain .15
73 Powers and Abilities .15
74 Pain .15
75 Taking A Human Life .15
76 First Series .15
77 The Start .15
78 The Champions .15
79 Restarted .15
80 Checklist .15

Glow in the Dark

G1 Illuminating .25
G2 Vigilantes .25
G3 My Arsenal .25
G4 Power Source .25
G5 Wolverine .25
G6 The Flames .25
G7 Punisher .25
G8 Hot Air .25
G9 Cable .25
G10 Grin and Bear It .25

G.I. JOE FILES

Comic Images (1987)

This is a very early card set from Comic Images which we have mentioned here primarily for completeness. It's not really a comics card set; the cards depict characters from the toy line. The characters are presented as portraits inside a thick black frame, with white outer border. The name is on the front, inside its own black frame and some text and the card number is on the back.

Set: 55 cards . . . 15.00

GOOD GUYS GENESIS, THE

The River Group (1993)

The Good Guys promo came in a group of 3 River Group promos along with a Plasm promo and a Steampit promo. Several of the card sets announced by The River Group were delayed in early 1994 and this one was not released at press time. We don't know if it will ever come out.

Two card promo sheet .3.50
3 of 3 Mr. Fingerman promo .5.00

G.I. Joe Files © Hasbro, Inc.

Good Guys Genesis © TRG & EEP, L.P.

GREEN HORNET COMICS

Now Comics (1992-3)

These cards came bagged with Green Hornet comics. 1H celebrates Green Hornet's third anniversary with Now Comics and 4H celebrates the fourth anniversary. We can't reproduce holograms in this book, so there are no pictures of these cards above.

1 Green Hornet (JSo) (from Sting of the Green Hornet #1) 1.00
1H Green Hornet promo Hologram card (from Tales of the Green Hornet Annual #1) 7.50
2H Green Hornet promo Hologravure card (from Green Hornet #22) 2.50
3H Green Hornet promo Hologravure card (from Green Hornet #23) 2.50
4H Green Hornet Promo Hologravure card (from Green Hornet #27 & Green Hornet Anniversary Special) 2.00
Feel The Sting promo (James Martin) 1.50

H

HANNA-BARBERA CLASSICS

Cardz (1994, Animation)

This set chronicles the many wonderful animated TV shows from Hanna-Barbera over the years. Yogi Bear, The Flintstones and The Jetsons are part of our cartoon cultural heritage and we hope that more of these card sets follow. The cards are made from the original animation cels and the art is crisp (which is the way it should be.)

Set: 60 cards . . . 10.00

Tekchrome cards

T1 The Ruff & Reddy Show 8.00
T2 William Hanna 7.00
T3 Joseph Barbera 7.00

Promo cards

P1 Yogi Bear: Ice Box Raider 2.00
P2 The Jetsons:The Coming of Astro 2.00
P3 Scooby-Doo: Scooby-Doo, Finds A Clue 2.00
Pack: 8 cards + Curad bandage .90

CARD CHECKLIST

Through the Years

1 The Huckleberry Hound Show .15
2 The Quick Draw McGraw Show .15
3 Top Cat .15
4 Wally Gator .15
5 Magilla Gorilla .15
6 Ricochet Rabbit .15
7 Atom Ant .15
8 Precious Pupp .15
9 The Secret Squirrel Show .15
10 Squiddly Diddly .15
11 Space Ghost .15
12 The Impossibles .15
13 Shazzan .15
14 The Banana Splits Adventure Hour .15
15 The Arabian Knights .15

Hanna-Barbera Classics
© Hanna-Barbera Productions, Inc.

Hanna-Barbera Classics © Hanna-Barbera Productions, Inc.

16 Dastardly & Muttley in Their Flying Machines .15
17 The Perils of Penelope Pitstop .15
18 The Funky Phantom .15
19 Butch Cassidy and the Sundance Kids .15
20 Speed Buggy .15
21 Hong Kong Phooey .15
22 Captain Caveman and the Teen Angels .15
23 The Biskitts .15
24 Galtar and the Golden Lance .15
25 The Pirates of Dark Water .15

Yogi Bear Subset

26 The Yogi Bear Show–Title Card .15
27 "Yogi Bear's Big Break" .15
28 "Slumber Party Smarty" .15
29 "Spy Guy" .15
30 "Ice Box Raider" .15

The Flintstones Subset

31 The Flintstones–Title Card .15
32 "Kleptomaniac Pebbles" .15
33 "The Bedrock Hillbillies" .15
34 "Pebbles Birthday Party" .15
35 "Surfin' Fred" .15

The Jetsons Subset

36 The Jetsons–Title Card .15
37 "A Date with Jet Screamer" .15
38 "The Coming of Astro" .15
39 "The Flying Suit" .15
40 "Miss Solar System" .15

Jonny Quest Subset

41 The Adventures of Jonny Quest–Title Card .15
42 "Mystery of the Lizardmen" .15
43 "Turu the Terrible" .15
44 "Quetong Missile Mystery" .15
45 "Monsters in the Monastery" .15

Scooby Doo Subset

46 Scooby Doo, Where are You?–Title Card .15
47 "What a Night for a Knight" .15
48 "A Clue for Scooby Doo" .15
49 "A Gaggle of Galloping Ghosts" .15
50 "Jeepers, It's the Creeper!" .15

Magic Activity Cards

51 Shaggy's Magic String .15
52 George's Appearing Coin .15
53 Yogi's Magic Salt .15
54 Fred & Barneys' Magic Puzzle .15
55 Where Did He Go? .15
56 Judy's Magic for Your Eyes .15
57 Scooby's Haunted Napkin .15
58 Cindy's Appearing Coins .15
59 Checklist .15
60 Checklist .15

WANT A CHANCE AT AN ULTRA RARE METALLIC COVER VERSION OF SACHS & VIOLENS #1?!!

Sure you do! It's easy! It's fun! Here's what to do.

There are four different trivia questions scattered on the 23 Heavy Hitters cards bound into the various Heavy Hitters titles on sale from September thru December of 1993.

Send in the correct answers to all four questions and your entry will go into a random drawing for one of 100 copies of the special metalic cover version of **Sachs & Violens** #1 we're setting aside for this contest.

Enter as often as you like but mail each entry separately. You can only win once no matter how many times you enter.

On a 8.5" X 11" piece of paper, write the numbers one through four. After each number, write the answer to the corresponding question.

The odds of winning will be determined by how many correct entries we receive. All entries must be postmarked by 3-31-94 and received by 4-10-94. No purchase necessary. You must be 17 years old or older to enter. Send your entries to:

Heavy Hitters Trivia Contest
Marvel/Epic Comics
387 Park Avenue South
New York, NY 10016

This contest is sponsored by Marvel Entertainment Group, Inc. Employees of Marvel Entertainment Group, Inc. are not eligible and entries are void where prohibited by law. Entries will not be returned and will become property of Marvel Entertainment Group, Inc. which assumes no responsibility for lost, mutilated or misdirected entries.

All taxes (federal, state, and local, if any) will be the responsibility of the winners. No cash equivalent or substitute prizes will be offered. The prizes will be offered in the name of the prize winners and are not transferable. Got it?

Winners will be notified by mail no later than 6-15-94. If you want a list of winners, send a self addressed stamped envelope to the address above. Add 'ATTENTION: Winners List Request' to the bottom of the envelope. Requests for winners list must be received by 6-15-94. Allow six weeks for delivery of winners list.

QUESTION # 2 of 4

Heavy Hitters © Marvel Entertainment Group, Inc.

HEAVY HITTERS

Epic Comics (Marvel 1993)

These are strip cards which were stapled into the center of Marvel Epic "Heavy Hitters" comics. The card side of the strip has a silver border with picture in the center, title at the top and series name at the bottom. The number is on the back along with the credits and a space for an autograph. The other side of the strip is slightly larger, with promo information and a contest. The cards say that they come in comics "on sale from September through December" (1993) but many of the comics appeared in 1994 and the final ones didn't come out until July!

Set: 23 cards 25.00

1 Sachs & Violens (GP) (from Sachs & Violens #1) 1.00
2 Terrarists (John Erasmus) (from Terrarists #1) 1.00
3 Spyke (Conal U'Det) (BR) (from Heavy Hitters Annual #1) 1.00
4 Alien Legion: Lawdog vs. Grimrod (HNg) (from Lawdog vs Grimrod #1) 1.00
5 Monkey King, Pigsy & Sandy (from Dragon Lines: Tao #1) 1.00
6 Alien Legion (HNg) (from Alien Legion:Binary Deep) 1.00
7 War Man (Juan Zanotto) (from War Man #1) 1.00
8 Law Dog (Law Dog & Lina) (FH) (from Law Dog #7) 1.00
9 Brats Bizarre (Duke Mighten) (from Brats Bizarre #1) 1.00
10 Dragon Lines: Monkey King (RLm) (from Sachs & Violens #2) 1.00
11 Tor (JKu) (from Terrarists #2) 1.00
12 Spyke (Spyke Jones) (BR) (from Dragon Lines: Tao #2) 1.00
13 Midnight Men (HC) (from Law Dog #8) 1.00
14 Law Dog (FH) (from War Man #2) 1.00
15 Feud (Mark Nelson) (from Brats Bizarre #2) 1.00
16 Offcasts (MV)(from Terrarists #3) 1.00
17 Midnight Men (HC) (from Sachs & Violens #3) 1.00
18 Sachs & Violens (GP) (from Law Dog #9) 1.00
19 Untamed (Neil Hansen) (from Brats Bizarre #3) 1.00
20 Terrarists (John Erasmus) (from Sachs & Violens #4) 1.00
21 Sachs & Violens (GP) (from Terrarists #4) 1.00
22 The Trouble With Girls (BBI) (from Law Dog #10) 1.00
23 Checklist (from Brats Bizarre #4) 1.00

HERO ILLUSTRATED

Hero Illustrated (1994)

Three of these cards were available in each copy of Hero Special Edition, The Year in Review *which came out in January 1994. You had to buy three copies to get all nine cards! The cards have cover reproductions from* Hero Illustrated *magazine for 1993.*

H-1 Prototype cover (BCh) .75
H-2 Issue Two cover (DvD) .50
H-3 Issue Three cover (MS/BPe) .50
H-4 Issue Four cover (KJo) .50
H-5 Issue Five cover (K.Alstaetter) .50
H-6 Issue Six cover (Alex Ross) .50
H-7 Issue Seven cover (JLe) .50
H-8 Prototype cover (NBy) .75
s-1 Batman special (KJo) .50

Super Villains

From Hero Illustrated Special Edition. You had to buy 3 copies to get all three cards!

1 Lort Pumpkin 1.00
2 Unleash 1.00
3 Violator 1.00

Scratch Off's

Harbinger cover .50
Venom .50

HERO TEAM-UP

Cards Illustrated (1994)

These are comic book promos rather than card set promos which came bagged with Cards Illustrated *starting in June 1994 and continuing in later issues.*

from June 1994 issue

1 Eclipse (Brad Gorby) .50
2 Legend (AAd) .50
3 Image (JV/Don Simpson) .50

from July 1994 issue

4 Sam & Max (Steve Purcell) .50
5 Axis Comics (JiC/LSn) .50
6 Slave Labor (Evan Dorkin) .50

HEROIC ORIGINS

Comic Images (1988)

This is the fourth set of Marvel cards from Comic Images and is subtitled "Series IV, Marvel Universe Continued" on the back. The previous three series were Marvel Universe, Colossal Conflicts and Wolverine. The characters are presented as portraits, with information on their origins and a question on the card backs. The cards are on a high quality white card stock. This would be an excellent set to buy, if you find one for sale. Don't be surprised if the price has gone up, based partially on the influence of this book.

Set: 90 cards 30.00

Box: 48 packs
Pack: 5 cards, cello pack 2.00

CARD CHECKLIST

1 Alpha Flight .40
2 Avengers .40
3 Battlestar .40
4 Beast .40
5 Black Knight .40

Heroic Origins © Marvel Entertainment Group, Inc.

6 Black Panther .40
7 Box .40
8 Cannonball .40
9 The Captain .40
10 Captain America .40
11 Captain Britain .40
12 Captain Marvel .40
13 Cloak .40
14 Colossus .40
15 Counterweight .40
16 Crystal .40
17 Cyclops .40
18 Dagger .40
19 Daredevil .40
20 Dazzler .40
21 Death .40
22 Destroyer .40
23 Dr. Druid .40
24 Dr. Pym .40
25 Dr. Strange .40
26 Elektra .40
27 Excaliber .40
28 Falcon .40
29 Fantastic Four .40
30 Forge .40
31 Galactus .40
32 Goblyn .40
33 Havok .40
34 Hawkeye .40
35 Hulk .40
36 Human Torch .40
37 Iceman .40
38 Invisible Girl .40
39 Iron Man .40
40 Kingpin .40
41 Longshot .40
42 Madelyn(e) Pryor .40
43 Magik .40
44 Magneto .40
45 Marvel Girl .40
46 Mary Jane Parker .40
47 Meggan .40
48 Mirage .40
49 Mr. Fantastic .40
50 Ms. Marvel .40
51 Mockingbird .40
52 Molecula .40
53 Moon Knight .40
54 New Mutants .40
55 Nightcrawler .40
56 Nomad .40
57 Nova .40
58 Phoenix II .40
59 Power Pack .40
60 Professor X .40
61 Psylocke .40
62 Punisher .40
63 Purple Girl .40
64 Rogue .40
65 Sasquatch .40
66 Scarlet Witch .40
67 Shadowcat .40
68 She-Hulk .40
69 Silver Surfer .40
70 Spider-Man .40
71 Starstreak .40
72 Storm .40
73 Sub-Mariner .40
74 Sunspot .40
75 Tattletale .40
76 Thing .40
77 Thor .40
78 Tigra .40
79 Vindicator .40
80 Vision .40
81 Warlock .40
82 Wasp .40
83 Watcher .40
84 West Coast Avengers .40
85 Wolfsbane .40
86 Wolverine .40
87 Wonder Man .40
88 X-Factor .40
89 X-Men .40
90 Checklist .50

HEROIC PUBLISHING PROMO CARDS

Heroic Publishing (1993)

A letter from the publisher states that all three of these cards, together with the eight Reiki Warriors cards and the two Mr. Fixitt cards, listed elsewhere, were printed on the same 15 card sheet, with the Arena Magazine *Flare card printed 3-up. 5,000 sheets were printed, but only 4,500 were cut so 4,500 copies of each card exist (13,500 of the* Arena Magazine *Flare card.) There are also 500 uncut sheets in existence, and some of them may show up in the collectors market.*

C 01 Chrissie Claus 1.00
L 01 Flare 1.00
L 01 Flare (Arena magazine) .50
Uncut 15 card sheets . Not Determined

Flare © Heroic Publishing; Howard the Duck (sticker) © Marvel Comics Group

HOWARD THE DUCK

Topps (1986)

These cards are taken from the movie, which was adapted from the comics. They are similar to other Topps movie cards from the '70s and '80s. Before the movie came out, the comics were quite popular, but the movie was disappointing, which started the comic books on a downward slide. Actually, the movie isn't that bad, but it was not up to expectations. The cards have movie photos on the front inside a red border. The card number is also on the front, inside the movie logo picture of Howard's bill, smoking a cigar and breaking out of an egg. The backs contain text, series title and a drawing of Howard in a business suit. There are two kinds of puzzle back stickers: half have film sprocket holes on top and bottom borders and the other half have color backgrounds.

Set: 77 cards/22 stickers 12.00
Pack: 9 cards, 1 sticker 1.25

CARD CHECKLIST

1 Howard the Duck (Title Card) .15
2 Introducing Howard! .15
3 Beverly Switzler .15
4 Phil Blumburtt .15
5 Dr. Jenning .15
6 Howard on Duck World .15
7 Duck-O-Vision: The Game Show .15
8 Duck-O-Vision: Crazy Webby .15
9 Duck-O-Vision: Teen Bandstand .15
10 Duck-O-Vision: Medical Program .15
11 Duck-O-Vision: Public Affairs .15
12 Duck-O-Vision: Football Commercial .15
13 Duck-O-Vision: Count Duckula .15
14 Landing on Earth (Plop) .15
15 Motorcycle Maniacs! .15
16 Cherry Bomb's Best Lady .15
17 Bev in a Jam! .15
18 No More Mr. Nice Duck! .15
19 Little Duck Lost .15
20 Weird...But Cute! .15
21 Special Delivery! .15
22 A Feathered Phenomenon! .15
23 At the Dynatechnics Lab .15
24 'Ascent of Duck' .15
25 Waddling Off in a Huff .15
26 Bug Off, Blumburtt! .15
27 Humans..Phooey! .15
28 So Long, Ducky! .15
29 How a Duck Can Make a Buck .15
30 Howard in Hot Water .15
31 Howie & Bev...Together Again! .15
32 A Scientist Possessed! .15
33 Jenning's Mad Lab .15
34 A Fowl Shakedown! .15
35 Beverly's Packin'! .15
36 Master of Quack Fu .15
37 The Thing within Jenning .15
38 Diner Dilemma .15
39 Bottoms Up! .15
40 Eggs? You're Kidding! .15
41 Duck vs. Truckers .15
42 Stop That Duck! .15
43 Doctor of Doom! .15
44 Ketchup Catastrophe! .15
45 Howard the Swinger! .15
46 Destroying a Duck .15
47 He's Not on the Menu! .15
48 Dr. Destructo! .15
49 Earth Vs. the Flying Cleavers .15
50 Howard Gets a Lift! .15
51 The Dark Overlord .15
52 Everything's Ducky! .15
53 'Help Us, Howard!" .15
54 Hell On the Highway .15
55 Hit Me with Your Best Shots .15
56 The Immunity Syndrome .15
57 Facing the Fiend .15
58 Howard to the Rescue! .15
59 How About Plan 'B'? .15
60 The Switzler Sacrifice .15
61 The Girl Has Problems .15
62 Diabolical Dynamo! .15
63 'He's Unstoppable!' .15
64 Zapped! .15
65 Howard's Last Chance .15
66 Howard, The Hero! .15
67 Overloaded Overlord .15

68 Duck, You Sucker! 15
69 Spectroscopic Disaster 15
70 One Last Chance! 15
71 Ka-Blooey! 15
72 Quack to Me, Howard! 15
73 Lord Love a Duck! 15
74 Cleveland Triumphant! 15
75 I Want My H-TV! 15
76 A Comic Classic! 15
77 Checklist 15
Stickers, uncaptioned.
1 thru 22, each 30

I

(Image Cards) Newmen © Rob Liefeld

IMAGE COMICS CARDS

Listed below are several groups of cards whose only common element is that they are based on Image comics and bear the Image logo. They don't have any series titles, so we have listed them here. They are all really promo cards and highly collectible, but generally available since the magazines and comics they came in have high circulations.

From Darker Image #1 (1993)
Bloodwulf (RLd) 1.50
The Maxx (SK) 1.50
Deathblow (JLe) 1.50

Brigade © Rob Liefeld

From Advance Comics #52 (1993)
Deathblow (JLe) 1.50
Brigade (RLd) 1.50
Advance Comics #56-#67 (1993-4)
#1 Code Name:Strike Force (BPe) . . 1.50
#2 Shadowhawk (JV/E.Vincent) 1.00
#3 Vanguard (EL/Gary Carlson) 1.00
#4 The Kindred (BBh) 1.00

Bloodwulf © Rob Liefeld

#5 Freak Force (Vic Bridges/KIS) . . . 1.00
#6 The Maxx (SK) 1.00
#7 . . . . 1.00
#8 Extreme Prejudice (RLd??) 1.00
#9 Newmen (Eric Stephensen & Jeff Matsuda) 1.00
#10 Team 7 (JLe) 1.00
#11 Youngblood (RLd) 1.00
#12 Doom's IV (MPa/DaM) 1.00
From Wizard #31 & Kingred #1
Promo card pair, right side 1.00
left side 2.00

INCREDIBLE HULK COMIC COVERS

Drakes Cakes (1978)

Set: 24 comic book cover cards 90.00

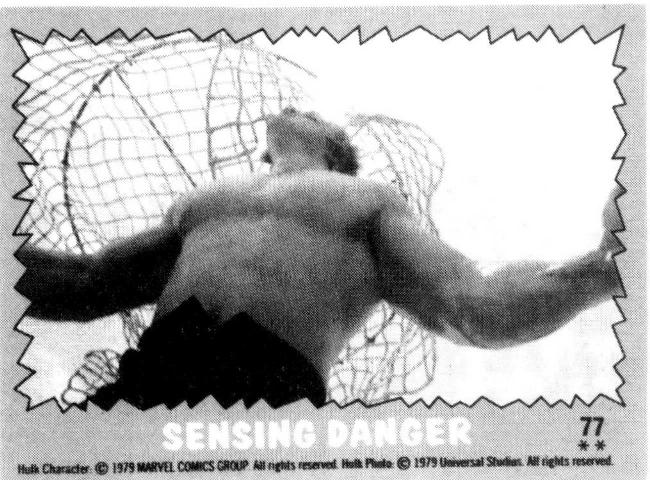

The Incredible Hulk © Marvel Entertainment Group, Inc. & Universal City Studios, Inc.

INCREDIBLE HULK

Topps (1979, TV)

These are color photos from the TV series inside a (what else?) green border. The caption and number are on the front of the cards. Ten of the backs have "TV Facts." The rest form four poster puzzles (two 15-card and two 20-card pictures) plus 8 puzzle preview cards. The cheap grey cardboard stock makes the puzzle pictures on the back unattractive and hard to see. The stickers have plain white backs and no captions, but the pictures are all taken from the cards, so we have used the corresponding card caption.

Set: 88 cards/22 stickers 20.00
Pack: 7 cards, 1 sticker 1.25

CARD CHECKLIST
1 No power to Save Her! 20
2 Experiment: Perilous! 20
3 Unearthly Seizure 20
4 Birth of the Beast Man 20
5 This Man..This Monster! 20
6 Friend..or Fiend? 20
7 The Hand of Fear 20
8 The Creature's Plan 20
9 Power of the Brute 20
10 To Rescue a Child 20
11 The Make-Shift Bridge 20
12 The Creature..Shot! 20
13 Fury of the Hulk 20
14 The Charging Terror 20
15 The Monster Strikes! 20
16 In the Clutches of Horror! 20
17 The Incredible Man Monster 20
18 Prehistoric Mutant 20
19 Portrait of a Monster 20
20 Horror in the Woods 20
21 Stirrings within the Beast 20
22 The Pawn of Destiny 20
23 Monstrous Reflection 20
24 Metamorphosis 20
25 Inside the Hyperbaric Chamber . . .20
26 Engine of Destruction 20
27 No Walls Can Hold Him! 20
28 The Creature is Loose! 20
29 Living Nightmare 20
30 The Abomination 20
31 Modified Hulk Make-Up 20
32 Back from Beyond 20
33 Ferrigno in Character 20
34 Filming the Episode 'Married' 20
35 The Flame and the Fury 20
36 The Inferno 20
37 Death of Dr. Marks 20
38 The Hulk Strikes Back! 20
39 Nightmare at the Ranch 20
40 Has the Hulk Met His Match? 20
41 Battle of the Behemoths 20
42 Monster in the Mansion 20
43 No Escape from the Brute 20
44 A Titan in Times Square 20
45 Manhattan Mayhem 20
46 The Beast Bursts Through 20
47 The 747 Affair 20
48 Stranger at the Door 20
49 Face of Fear 20
50 The Dark Journey Back 20
51 Bringing in a 747 20
52 'No! It Can't Happen Now!' 20
53 Caught in Mid-Transformation 20
54 Banner's Titanic Struggle! 20
55 Suppressing the Demon within Him 20
56 Creature in the Pilot's Seat 20
57 Monster at the Controls 20
58 Panic in the Cockpit 20
59 The Life-Saving Thrust 20
60 Greetings from Our Captain! 20
61 Racing Through the Airliner 20
62 Stan Lee's Creation..the Hulk 20
63 Creature on the Runway! 20
64 Nobody Fences in the Hulk! 20
65 David Banner Confronts..Himself! .20
66 Hope Through Hypnotherapy 20
67 A Man Possessed 20
68 The Raging Spirit 20
69 The Humanoid Appears 20
70 Tower of Strength 20
71 No Longer Human 20
72 The Captive Creature 20
73 The Tranquilizing Gas 20

74 The Two Faces of Dr. Banner 20
75 Nothing Can Stop the Hulk! 20
76 Netting the Hulk 20
77 Sensing Danger 20
78 The Capture 20
79 David Banner's Wedding Day 20
80 The Recurring Dream 20
81 The Force Inside Banner 20
82 Demon With a Soul 20
83 The Mindless Primitive 20
84 Mightiest Creature on Earth 20
85 The Monster Within Us All! 20
86 Being of Fantastic Proportions . . .20
87 Victim of Gamma Radiation 20
88 The Eyes of David Banner 20

Stickers, captions from similar card.

1 {Modified Hulk Make-Up} 35
2 {Metamorphosis} 35
3 {Hope Through Hypnotherapy} 35
4 {The Hulk Strikes Back!} 35
5 {The Monster within Us All} 35
6 {Manhattan Mayhem} 35
7 {Portrait of a Monster} 35
8 {Mightiest Creature on Earth} 35
9 {Suppressing the Demon within Him} 35
10 {The Monster Strikes!} 35
11 {This Man..This Monster!} 35
12 {The Creature..Shot!} 35
13 {Racing Through the Airline} 35
14 {The Incredible Man Monster} 35
15 {Friend..or Fiend?} 35
16 {Ferrigno in Character} 35
17 {In the Clutches of Horror!} 35
18 {A Titan in Times Square} 35
19 {Has the Hulk Met His Match?} . . .35
20 {The Pawn of Destiny} 35
21 {Experiment: Perilous!} 35
22 {The Mindless Primitive} 35

The Incredible Hulk © Marvel Entertainment Group, Inc.

THE INCREDIBLE HULK

Comic Images (1991)

(Dale Keown art)

The card fronts are character close-ups of the Hulk and friends inside a white border and black frame design. The card number and caption appear on the front and are repeated on the back, with some text. The text tells the story of the grey Hulk, and then the green Hulk, as these two incarnations battle for control of Bruce Banner's mind (until the three personalities merge to form the powerful, emotional and smart Hulk). Naturally, he kicks a lot of butt along the way!

Set: 90 cards 15.00
Pack: 10 cards 60

CARD CHECKLIST

1 Transformation 15
2 I'm Grey! .15
3 Wolverine 15
4 Poisoned .15
5 What's Wrong 15
6 The Leader 15
7 Madman .15
8 Too Weak 15
9 Phil 15
10 Antidote 15
11 Freedom Force 15
12 Discovered 15
13 Abused? 15
14 Mystique 15
15 Pyro 15
16 Commando 15
17 Blob 15
18 Defenders 15
19 New York 15
20 Unknown 15
21 Inside 15
22 Argue 15
23 Grabbed 15
24 Darkness 15
25 Dark Hulk 15
26 Take-Over 15
27 Namor 15
28 Dr. Strange 15
29 Revived .15
30 Betty 15
31 Speeding 15
32 He's Back 15
33 ...And Green 15
34 Shocked 15
35 Rejoined 15
36 I Get It! .15
37 No-o-o! .15
38 Skinned .15
39 Doc Samson 15
40 Tank You 15
41 Come On 15
42 Mouthful 15
43 Not You! 15
44 Rick Jones 15
45 The Thing? 15
46 Now Listen 15
47 Thugs 15
48 To Sleep 15
49 Rick's Past 15
50 Tortured 15
51 Super Skrull 15
52 On Board 15
53 Skrull 15
54 Locked Up 15
55 Stretch .15
56 Fight On 15
57 On Fire .15
58 Captain? 15
59 Invisible 15
60 Marlo 15
61 Conflict .15
62 Going Home 15
63 Prometheus 15
64 Agamemnon 15
65 Help Me! 15
66 Stay Back 15
67 Battle 15
68 Put Me Down 15
69 In the Middle 15
70 Stop It 15
71 Who's Inside? 15
72 Monster .15
73 Let's Go 15
74 Escape .15
75 Murder .15
76 Mom 15
77 Graveyard 15
78 You Did It 15
79 Father 15
80 Resolved 15
81 New Hulk 15
82 Barkeep 15
83 Ajax 15
84 Ulysses .15
85 Atalanta 15
86 Hector 15
87 Achilles .15
88 Rebound 15
89 Oh Yeah! 15
90 checklist 15

J

JASON GOES TO HELL

Topps Comics (1993)

This card set is from the Topps comics, but it contains photos from the movies. If you don't know who Jason is you won't be collecting the cards (hint: He wears a hockey goalie mask and uses a large knife on teenagers).

Set: 9 cards, photos (Issues #1-#3) 4.50
Comic promo card 1.00

Jurassic Park (comics) © Universal City Studios, Inc. & Amblin Entertainment, Inc.

JURASSIC PARK

Topps (1993, Comics)

These cards came bagged with the Jurassic Park *comic books (or other Topps Comics books) and have the Topps Comics logo on the back. This distinguishes these cards from the two series of movie adaption cards which are not covered in this book. (The toy blister pack cards aren't covered either.) There should be nine cards in the comic set, ten if you count card #0, but they don't work out quite right. There's no number 3; #2 looks like the other 7 cards, but should have been numbered "2 of 9"; and the card that is numbered "2 of 9" doesn't look like the other cards because it has movie photos! We have also listed the four trading card promos, three of which have dinosaur art, rather than movie photos.*

Trading card promos:
(T-Rex) (AAd) . . . 1.00
(Triceratops) (JeJ) . . . 1.00
(Jeep on head) (Nel) . . . 1.00
Top Secret, photo . . . 1.00
Comics promos:
Comics promo, Movie Logo card . . . 1.00
Park Entrance photo, comics promo, (In Ray Bradbury comic #1) . . . 1.00
2 of 9 Raptors on the Prowl, photo . .50
Comic book series:
0 Velociraptor (John Van Fleet) (In Ray Bradbury comic #3) 50
1 of 9 Walter Simonson's Brachiosaurus 50
2 (JP #2 promo) 50
4 of 9 Raptor (WS) 50
5 of 9 (JP #1 promo) 50
6 of 9 (JP #3 promo) 50
7 of 9 Spitter (WS) 50
8 of 9 T-Rex (WS) 50
9 of 9 (JP #4 promo) 50
Hologram Stickers, 4 diff., same as Movie cards (from JP #4), each . . 3.50

Jurassic Park (comic) © Universal City Studios, Inc. & Amblin Entertainment, Inc.

JURASSIC PARK: RAPTOR
From Raptor Comic Book (1993-4)
William Stout art

Three of these cards came bagged in each of the two issues of this mini-series.

1 Velociraptor 50
2 Gallimimus 50
3 Triceratops 50
4 Brachiosaurs 50
5 Pteranodons 50
6 Procompsognathus 50

JUSTICE LEAGUE OF AMERICA
Fleer (1970)

These aren't trading cards, but they are listed in most price guides and collected as if they were. They came with gum, inside a wrapper, either yellow or white, which is worth more than the tattoos themselves.

Set: 17 Tattoos . . . 25.00

Atom . . . 3.00
Batman, 4 diff., each . . . 2.00
Flash, 2 diff., each . . . 2.00
Green Arrow, 2 diff., each . . . 2.00
Green Lantern . . . 2.00
Hawkman . . . 2.00
Martian Manhunter . . . 3.00
Superman, 4 diff., each . . . 2.00
Wonder Woman . . . 2.00

K

KILLZONE
Cardz (1994)

These are from a forthcoming comic/novel published by Galaxi Novels. The character names aren't listed on the cards.

Promo Cards
P1 . . . 1.00
P2 . . . 1.00

KIRBYCHROME
Topps (1993)

These cards have foil enhanced portrait art on a pebbled surface. The backs are purple, with text in a blue box and a close-up of the character in full color. They came bagged with the initial issues of Topps comics of the same name, which were collectively called "Kirbyverse" after comics legend Jack Kirby, who created them. They are interesting looking cards, but we couldn't get them to reproduce in black and white, so we can't give you a picture here. The first three characters also appear in Jack Kirby's Secret City Saga *which also came bagged with trading cards (see below).*

Set: 4 cards, Jack Kirby art in Topps comic books . . . 6.00

1 Captain Glory . . . 1.50
2 Night Glider . . . 1.50
3 Bombast . . . 1.50
4 Satan's Six . . . 1.50

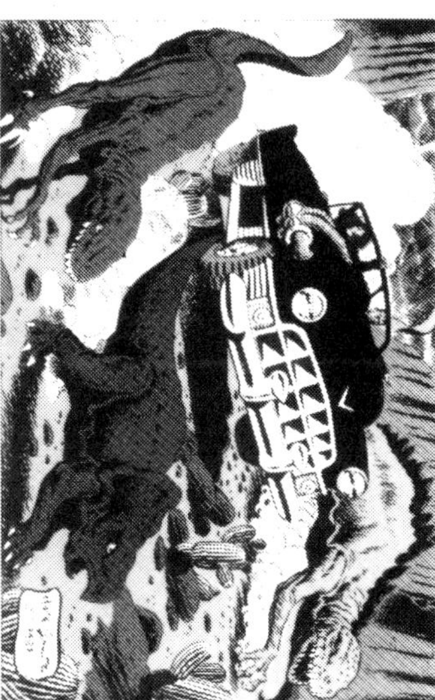

(Kitchen Sink) Outer Space Spirit © Will Eisner; Cadillacs & Dinosaurs © Mark Schultz

KITCHEN SINK CARDS
Kitchen Sink (1988-9)

These are two-color, oversized cards that were issued individually to persons who purchased items from Kitchen Sink catalogs. One card was sent each week for 36 weeks to celebrate Kitchen Sink's 20th anniversary. The cards are mostly comics related, so we have listed the set.

Set: 36 cards, oversized . . . 50.00

1 The Spirit (WE) . . . 7.50
2 Li'l Abner (Al Capp) . . . 5.00
3 Megaton Man (Donald Simpson) . . 3.00
4 Xenozoic Tales (Mark Schultz) . . . 2.00
5 Death Rattle (Peter Poplaski) . . . 1.00
6 Blab! (Charles Burns) . . . 1.00
7 Twist (Drew Friedman) . . . 1.00
8 Steve Rude Sketchbook . . . 1.00
9 Kings in Disguise (Dan Burr) . . . 1.00
10 Howard Cruse . . . 1.00
11 Male Call (Milton Caniff) . . . 1.00
12 Melody (Jaques Boivin) . . . 1.00
13 Mr. Natural (R. Crumb) . . . 1.00
14 Harvey Kurtzman . . . 1.00
15 Flash Gordon (Alex Raymond) . . 2.00
16 The Outer Space Spirit (WE) . . . 2.00
17 Goodman Beaver (Will Elder) . . . 1.00
18 Omaha, The Cat Dancer (Reed Waller) . . . 1.00
19 City People Notebook (WE) . . . 2.00
20 Snarf (Rand Holmes) . . . 1.50
21 Steve Canyon (Milton Caniff) . . . 1.50
22 Cadillacs and Dinosaurs (Mark Schultz) . . . 2.00
23 Denizens of Deep City (Doug Potter) . . . 1.50
24 Li'l Abner (Al Capp) . . . 2.50
25 A Life Force (WE) . . . 2.50
26 Nard 'N Pat (Jay Lynch) . . . 1.50
27 Nancy (Ernie Bushmiller) . . . 1.50
28 Home Grown Funnies (R.Crumb) 1.50
29 Sleazy Scandals of the Silver Screen (Art Spiegelman) . . . 1.50
30 Flash Gordon (Austin Briggs) . . . 1.50
31 Harvey Kurtzman's Jungle Book . 1.50
32 The Oddly Compelling art of Denis Kitchen . . . 1.50
33 The Secret of San Saba (Jaxon) . 1.50
34 Omaha, The Cat Dancer (Reed Waller) . . . 2.50
35 Charles Burns' Big Baby: Curse of the Mole Men . . . 1.50
36 Kitchen Sink Press 20th Anniv. . . 2.50

L

LADY DEATH

Lady Death is drawn by Steve Hughes and comes from the same

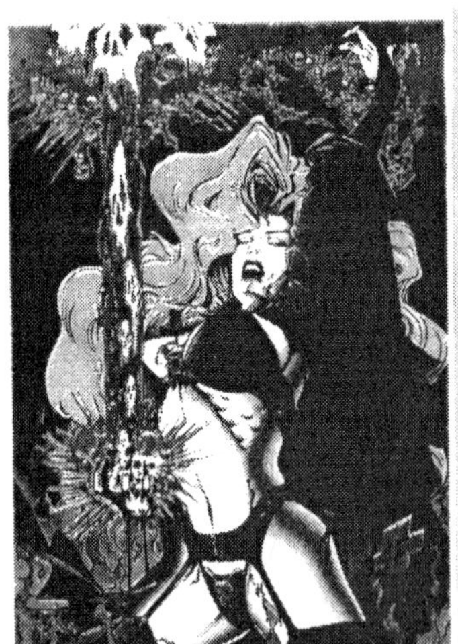

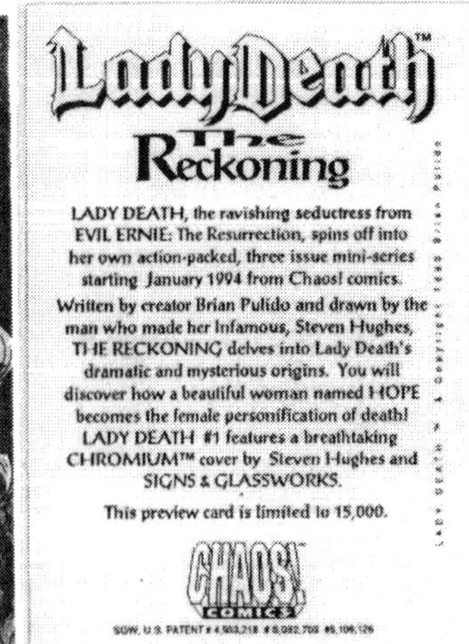

Lady Death © Brian Pulido

*Chaos comics as **Evil Ernie**. She now has her own comic and is scheduled to get her own card series from Krome Productions.*

Lady Death, The Reckoning chromium comic preview (15,000 made) . . . 10.00
Lady Death #1 chromium promo . . . 3.00

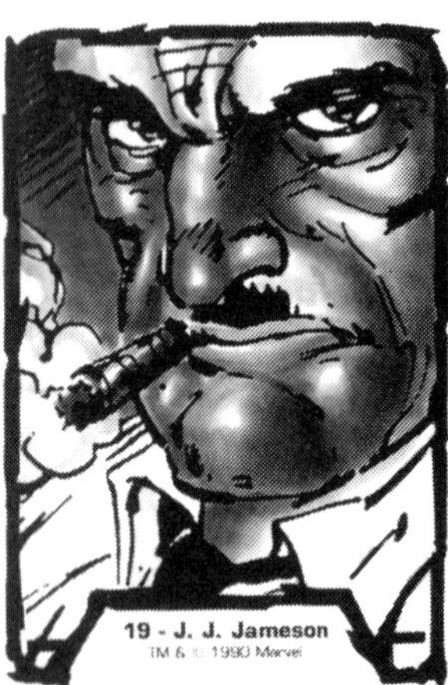

Jim Lee cards © Marvel Entertainment Group, Inc.

LEE, JIM

Comic Images (1990)

The card fronts depict various Marvel characters in dramatic, portrait style drawings, plus the card caption and number. The backs form a 5 x 9 black and white puzzle drawing of Wolverine and the Punisher. The header card is thin, with a black back.

Set: 45 cards + header card 14.00
Pack: 5 cards + header, cello pack . 2.00

CARD CHECKLIST

1 Surprise! 30
2 Beast 30
3 Two against... 30
4 Dreamqueen 30
5 Puck 30
6 Blast Off! 30
7 Purple Man 30
8 Sub-Mariner 30
9 Double Take! 30
10 To the death! 30
11 African Saga 30
12 Gator fight 30
13 Survival 30
14 Shot! 30
15 Black Widow 30
16 Bushwacker 30
17 Stay back! 30
18 Teamwork 30
19 J. J. Jameson 30
20 Vacation 30
21 Jet ski 30
22 Aloha! 30
23 Armory 30
24 Mandarin 30
25 Here I am! 30
26 Lady Mandarin 30
27 Meditation 30
28 Banshee 30
29 Jean Grey 30
30 Animal Rage 30
31 It's my turn! 30
32 Night stalker 30
33 Youth 30
34 Logan & Reed 30
35 Hulk 30
36 Blackheart 30
37 Ghost Rider 30
38 Harriers 30
39 Trio 30
40 Quasar 30
41 Wild Child 30
42 Caught 30
43 Vindicator 30
44 Fight back! 30
45 Checklist 30

Jim Lee cards II © Marvel Entertainment Group, Inc.

LEE, JIM II

Comic Images (1991)

The card fronts depict various Marvel characters in dramatic, portrait style drawings, plus the card caption and number. The first nine cards depict Punisher and a number of others picture Wolverine. The backs form a 5 x 9 black and white puzzle drawing of Wolverine. The header card is thin, with a black back.

Set 45 cards + header card 13.00
Pack: 5 cards + header, cello pack . 2.00

CARD CHECKLIST

1 Punisher 30
2 Survivalist 30
3 Hang On! 30
4 Camo 30
5 Biker 30
6 The Blade 30
7 Armory II 30
8 The Past 30
9 Rules... 30
10 Microchip 30
11 Dr. Doom 30
12 Moonknight 30
13 Kingpin 30
14 Hercules 30
15 Bushwacker 30
16 Black Panther 30
17 Heroes 30
18 Magik 30
19 Nightcat 30
20 Brother Voodoo 30
21 Black Widow 30
22 Speedball 30
23 Captain America 30
24 Wolverine 30
25 Struggle 30
26 Rage 30
27 I'm Ready 30
28 Three of Us 30
29 Deathstrike 30
30 Lian 30
31 Hounds 30
32 Orphan Maker 30
33 Magneto 30
34 Four of Us 30
35 Beast 30
36 Havok 30
37 Hodge 30
38 X-Tinction 30
39 Psylocke 30
40 Duel 30
41 Cable 30
42 Savage Land 30
43 Storm 30
44 Glory Days 30
45 Checklist 30

LEGACY #0

Majestic Entertainment (1993)

Dan Lawlis/Stan Woch art

The first 126 cards are designed to be placed in a binder so that they can form 3 x 3 comic style pages. They are numbered on the front, but there are no titles. The last nine of these cards complete the story on their fronts and the backs form a superpanel of Punch, Hurt, Kill, (Kill is the main villain of the comic). Cards 127 to 135 form an attractive nine-card superpanel image of Protector, the main hero. This art was used on the front cover of Legacy #1. *Art for these two pieces was also used for the two San Diego Comicon limited edition prints. The advertising for this card set promised 10 character cards, 7 information cards and a 9-card comic-in-progress subset, in addition to the story cards. It turned out differently, but probably better. The next 5 cards picture other major characters and the next 4 picture the principal creators. There are only 5 cards showing a comic in the process of being drawn and prepared for printing. The last card is a mail-in bonus card. Of course, if you mail it in, you don't have a complete set of the cards! The nine-card promo set has the same art as the first "page" of the cards, but the numbers are absent and the "Legacy" logo is always in the lower left corner. The promo backs are all the same, except for the card number. The nine black and white promo cards also have the same art as the first "page" of cards. They were packed with* Comics Future Stars #1, *one or two per box. The packs for this set contain similar cards for S.T.A.T. #0, packed two per box.*

Set: 150 cards 19.00

Dyna Etch foil (1:18)
D1 The Protector 6.00
D2 Triphammer 6.00
D3 Cademous Zark 6.00
D4 Dark Bob 6.00
D5 Dumbstruck 6.00
D6 Bodycount 6.00
D7 Legacy 6.00
D8 Iron Will 6.00
D9 Punch-Hurt-Kill-Kill 6.00

Promo Cards
Set: 9 cards, B&W with same pictures as first nine cards 10.00
Set: 9 cards, color, from first nine cards with promo backs 10.00
Limited Edition Prints, San Diego Comicon:
Punch-Hurt-Kill-Kill (5,000 made) . 7.00
Legacy #1 cover (5,000 made) . . . 7.00
Limited Edition Print, Chicago Comicon:
Three Villains (5,000 made) 5.00
(Binder, 2 different, silver or gold)
Pack: 9 cards 1.00

CARD CHECKLIST

Story cards. They form 3x3 comic book pages, with art both front and back.
1 thru 117, each 10
Last page of story, backs form superpanel of Punch, Hurt, Kill, Kill
118 to 126, each 20
Protector superpanel. *Card backs all have the same text on a purple background with a black border.*
127 to 135, each 20
Card backs have text on a blue background with black strips at the top and bottom.

Characters
136 Howard 20
137 Grill .20
138 Fire Flight 20
139 Venture Island 20
140 Caroline Rand 20

Creators *Color photos;*
141 Fred Schiller, *Script* 10
142 Dan Lawlis, *Pencils* 10
143 Stan Woch, *Inks* 10
144 Paul Mounts, *Color Art* 10

A Comic in Progress *Card backs have text on a green background with a black border.*
145 Script & Pencils 10
146 Letters & Inks 10
147 Production 10
148 Colors 10
149 Post Production/Checklist 10
150 Majestic logo, Bonus card 1.00

Legacy #0 © Majestic Entertainment

LION KING, THE

SkyBox (1994)

This set of cards, based on the June 1994 animated movie from Disney, came out just before press time. That means that the price information given below is preliminary and will probably have changed by the time you read this. The cards follow the story line of the movie and have excellent, clear, crisp reproduction of the movie art. In case you didn't know, the good young lion (Simba) and his animal side-kicks win over the evil lion (Scar) and his gang of Hyenas. The pop-up cards have a pull-tab at the top, which you shouldn't pull too often, or you will ruin the value of the cards. We know you're going to do it anyway, but don't say we didn't warn you! The promo cards are untitled, but all three have drawings of lions (naturally). There is also a premium set of cards in the taller, Sandman, size which is available by now, but was not out at press time. Those cards are foil stamped with the series title.

Set: 90 cards 15.00

Lenticular Holograms (1:180)
L1 "I Never Get to Go Anywhere!" . 50.00
L2 Future King of the Jungle 50.00

Foil-Embossed Characters (1:12)
F1 Simba 5.00
F2 Mufasa 5.00
F3 Nala 5.00
F4 Scar 5.00
F5 Rafiki 5.00
F6 Zazu 5.00
F7 Pumbaa 5.00
F8 Timon 5.00
F9 Shenzi, Banzai and Ed 5.00

Pop-Up cards (1:24)
P1 Simba–I Just Can't Wait to be King! 9.00
P2 Rafiki–Circle of Life 9.00
P3 Mufasa–Remember Who You Are 9.00
P4 Banzai–Who You Callin' Oopid-Stay? 9.00
P5 Scar–The Evil Uncle 9.00

Promo cards
SB1 . . . . 1.00
S1 . . . . 1.00
T1 (from Collect!, July 1994) 1.00
Pack: 8 cards 1.25

CARD CHECKLIST

01 A tale of courage, adventure and humor 15
02 Animals and birds stir 15
03 The animals wait 15
04 The ceremony is about to begin . .15
05 Rafiki lifts Simba for all to see . . .15
06 "Don't turn your back on me!" 15
07 Everything the light touches is our kingdom 15
08 The forbidden elephant graveyard .15
09 Eager for adventure 15
10 "I just can't wait to be king." 15
11 The getaway 15
12 A spectacular zebra salute 15
13 A brightly-colored pyramid 15
14 Toward the elephant graveyard . . .15
15 A spooky sight to behold 15
16 "I laugh in the face of danger." . . .15
17 A trio of vicious, wise-cracking hyenas .15
18 "Did we order this dinner to go?" . .15
19 Trapped! 15
20 A mighty roar erupts 15
21 "Dad, I'm...I'm sorry." 15
22 The kings will always be there to guide you." 15
23 Scar sings of his plan 15
24 A surprise to die for 15
25 Simba runs for his life 15
26 Mufasa plunges into the gorge . . .15
27 "Hold on!" 15
28 Mufasa catches Simba 15
29 Mufasa disappears 15
30 Mufasa fears for his life 15
31 "Long live the king." 15
32 "Noooooooo!" 15

The Lion King (pop-up card)
© The Walt Disney Company

33 Simba runs away 15
34 Escape from the hyenas 15
35 Pin cushions and cactus butts . . .15
36 Scar assumes the throne 15
37 Buzzards fly overhead 15
38 "Jeez, its a lion!" 15
39 Hakuna Matata 15
40 A jungle paradise 15
41 Fresh out of zebra 15
42 The fine art of eating bugs 15
43 The great kings of the past 15
44 It is time 15
45 Run for your life 15
46 It's Nala! 15
47 "You wouldn't understand." 15
48 "You said you'd always be there..." .15
49 An odd little voice sings 15
50 "I know your father." 15
51 "He lives in you." 15
52 "Remember who you are." 15
53 Simba marches toward his destiny .15

The Lion King © The Walt Disney Company

54 Forced to hunt for food 15
55 There is no food 15
56 Simba is revealed 15
57 "I'm a little surprised to see you–alive." 15
58 Either step down as king or fight . .15
59 "It was an accident." 15
60 A blast of fury 15
61 A large roar grows 15
62 "Eeeee-yaaaaa!" 15
63 To a pack of hungry hyenas below .15
64 Simba takes his place in the Circle of Life 15
65 A new lion king is born 15

Character cards

66 Simba .15
67 Mufasa 15
68 Sarabi .15
69 Nala 15
70 Scar 15
71 Zazu 15
72 Rafiki .15
73 Timon .15
74 Pumbaa 15
75 Hyenas 15

The circle of life

76 Birth 15
77 Childhood 15
78 Loss 15
79 Young Simba 15
80 Romance 15
81 Adulthood 15
82 Rebirth 15

Animal Humor

83 Man, are you ugleeeee! 15
84 Dangling at the bottom of the food chain. 15
85 Who you callin' oopid-stay? 15
86 Sit down before you hurt yourself. .15
87 Mooooooooove it! 15
88 Home is where your rump rests. . .15
89 Checklist A 15
90 Checklist B 15

The Little Mermaid © The Walt Disney Company

LITTLE MERMAID, THE

Pro Set (1991, Animated Movie)

These cards follow the storyline of the popular Disney animated movie. The fronts contain full bleed art from the movie. The backs contain the text, card number and detail picture from the front, on either an undersea or floating-in-the-water background. The cards are untitled, so the first line of the story is used below. The promo card shows Ariel plus some of her fishy friends. It's actually prettier than the regular cards in the series.

Set: 90 cards + 15 stand-ups + 15 color-ins + 7 Static Stick 'ems 10.00
Factory set, in box, with 6 character sponges 12.50

Promo Card 3.00
Little Mermaid collector's album . . . 11.00
Pack: 8 cards, 2 activity cards 75

CARD CHECKLIST

Story Cards

1 Once a mermaid princess 10
2 King Triton, ruler 10
3 We are the daughters of Triton 10
4 Sebastian, the King's 10
5 Miles away from the concert hall . . .10
6 We really shouldn't be doing 10
7 Have you ever seen anything 10
8 Ariel and Flounder swim 10

The Little Mermaid promo card © The Walt Disney Company

9 Swimming to the surface 10
10 Furious because Ariel has 10
11 Sebastian follows Ariel 10
12 I just don't see how a world 10
13 I've got gadgets and gizmos 10
14 Ariel gazes longingly at a painting .10
15 Sebastian is too shocked 10
16 Just then, the hull of a ship 10
17 Fireworks blossom 10
18 Sebastian follows Ariel 10
19 On board is the most handsome . .10
20 It is Prince Eric, himself 10
21 He's very handsome 10
22 Eric's advisor, Grimsby, ...10
23 As if responding to Eric's 10
24 Fire races 10
25 The statue plummets past 10
26 Safe ashore, Ariel gazes 10
27 Ariel's sisters are amazed 10
28 King Triton is puzzled 10
29 Meanwhile, in a Sea Garden 10
30 Sebastian is beside himself! 10
31 Sebastian tries talking sense 10
32 Ariel gets into the rhythm 10
33 Even the seaweed is swinging! . . .10
34 Everyone on the ocean floor 10
35 The ocean floor is really 10
36 Even Ariel can't resist 10
37 While Sebastian sings, ...10
38 Sebastian winds up for a grand . .10
39 Inside her treasure grotto 10
40 Meanwhile, a seahorse 10
41 Sebastian quakes in his shell 10
42 In a volcanic rage, Triton 10
43 As father and daughter argue 10
44 Ariel collapses sobbing 10
45 Unknown to Triton and Ariel 10
46 As Ariel sobs, ...10
47 As Ariel approaches Ursula's 10
48 Ariel hesitates before she 10
49 Ursula pretends to offer Ariel 10
50 Take a gulp and take a breath . . .10
51 Ursula bends over her 10
52 The mists form glowing hands . . .10
53 Ursula's spell takes effect 10
54 Soaked and covered in seaweed .10
55 As Ariel happily regards her 10
56 Max leads Eric to Ariel 10
57 At the palace, Ariel is taken 10
58 Meanwhile, Sebastian, who 10
59 As Ariel enters the dining room . . .10
60 Meanwhile Sebastian isn't 10
61 Leaping from the pot 10
62 Ariel spends a blissful day 10
63 Time is passing 10
64 At last, Sebastian 10
65 The setting is perfect 10
66 Ariel smiles shyly as Eric 10
67 Suddenly the boat tips over 10
68 That was a close one 10
69 With Ariel's beautiful voice 10
70 As evening falls on Ariel's 10
71 Scuttle races to warn Ariel 10
72 Back on shore, Ariel's friends 10
73 Ariel reaches the ship and 10
74 But it is too late! 10
75 Ursula grabs Ariel and drags 10
76 Ursula begins to turn 10
77 Showing Triton the contract 10
78 Solemnly, Triton bargains 10
79 Laughing hideously, Ursula 10
80 Eric dives into the water 10
81 Eric surfaces and swims 10
82 Frantically, Eric clambers 10
83 Beneath the sea, Ursula's 10
84 While Eric lies unconscious 10
85 Ariel is unaware that her father . . .10
86 Knowing it means he is giving . . .10
87 Once again, wedding bells ring . . .10
88 Even the happiest moments 10
89 Ariel turns to her father 10
90 As the merfold wave farewell 10

Stand-up Cards (untitled)

#1 through #15, each 15

Color-in Cards

1 Ariel & Flounder/Flounder 15
2 Ariel/Under the Sea 15
3 Ursula/Flotsam & Jetsam 15
4 Max/Grimsby 15
5 Sebastian/Chef Louie & Sebastian .15
6 Under the Sea/Ariel & Flounder . . .15
7 Eric & Ariel/Eric & Ariel 15
8 Ariel & Eric/Eric 15
9 Scuttle/Ariel & Flounder 15
10 Under the Sea/Ariel 15
11 Ariel/Under the Sea 15
12 Ariel & Flounder/Flounder 15
13 Scuttle/Ariel & Flounder 15
14 Ariel & Flounder/Under the Sea . .15
15 King Triton/Ariel 15

Static Stick 'Ems (not titled)

Ursula 50
Ariel as mermaid 50
Ariel as girl 50
Sebastian .50
Flounder .50
Scuttle 50
Eric 50

M

Todd McFarlane (I) © Marvel Entertainment Group, Inc.

McFARLANE, TODD

Comic Images (1989)

The fronts are portrait style pictures of various Marvel characters by Todd McFarlane and contain the caption and card number. The backs form two black and white pictures; cards #1 to #20 form a 4 x 5 card puzzle picture of Spider-Man and cards #21 to #45 form a 5 x 5 card puzzle picture of The Hulk.

Set: 45 cards + header card 20.00

Box: 48 packs
Pack: 5 cards + header, cello pack . 1.75

CARD CHECKLIST

Puzzle one, cards 1 through 20

1 Friends 50
2 Jump For Joy 50
3 Venom 50
4 Snikt 50
5 Oh, Yeah 50
6 Savage 50
7 The Leader 50
8 Spidey 50
9 X-Factor 50
10 Price of Fame 50
11 Chance 50
12 Thing 50
13 The Prowler 50
14 Don't Cry 50
15 Lizard 50
16 Who, Me? 50
17 Taskmaster 50
18 Busted 50
19 Silver Sable 50
20 Sandman 50

Puzzle two, cards 21 through 45

21 Out of the Fire... 50
22 Green Goblin 50
23 Hobgoblin 50
24 The Black Fox 50
25 There's No Key?! 50
26 Ho Ho Ho 50
27 Hey, Tiger 50
28 Aargh 50
29 The Chameleon 50
30 Killer Shrike 50
31 Peter 50
32 Mary Jane 50
33 Jolly Jonah 50
34 Styx & Stone 50
35 Smile 50
36 Wolverine 50
37 Mysterio 50
38 Down and Out 50
39 Humbug 50
40 Black Cat 50
41 Next 50
42 Hydro-Man 50
43 Buddies 50
44 Web Swinging 50
45 Checklist 75

McFARLANE, TODD II

Comic Images (1990)

The fronts are portrait style pictures of various Marvel characters by Todd McFarlane and contain the caption and card number. Most of the cards are viewed landscape style, i.e. sideways. The backs form one black and white 9 x 5 card picture of Spider-Man vs. The Hulk.

Set: 45 cards + header card 17.50

Pack: 5 cards + header, cello pack . 1.50

CARD CHECKLIST

1 Spider-Man 45
2 Sandman 45
3 Silver Sable 45
4 The Prowler 45
5 Black Cat 45
6 Chameleon 45
7 Bugged! 45
8 Caesar 45
9 I've missed you! 45
10 Shrike 45
11 Goblins 45
12 Lizard 45
13 ...like a fly! 45
14 Hydro Man 45
15 Venom 45
16 Black out! 45
17 Scorpion 45
18 Trio 45
19 No Anchovies! 45
20 Paladin 45
21 Doctor Octopus 45
22 Mary Jane 45
23 Captain America 45
24 Sabretooth 45
25 Red Skull 45
26 Hulk 45
27 Up above 45
28 Let's talk 45
29 In orbit 45
30 Caught 45
31 Iceman 45
32 Thermatronic Man 45
33 Classic X-Men 45
34 Juggernaut 45
35 The Beast 45
36 X-Men 45
37 Quasar 45
38 Back again 45
39 Spider-Man #1 45

Todd McFarlane II
© Marvel Entertainment Group, Inc.

40 Spider-Man #2 45
41 Spider-Man #3 45
42 Spider-Man #4 45
43 Spider-Man #5 45
44 Web-slinger 45
45 Checklist 50

Magnus Robot Fighter © Western Publishing Co., Inc. & Voyager Communications, Inc.

MAGNUS ROBOT FIGHTER

Valiant (1991)

These cards were a promotion for the Magnus Robot Fighter *comic book series. The card stock is slightly thinner than standard. The card fronts are full color, with a thin white border and the backs are white with text in black and a small drawing plus the card number. A set of the eight coupons could be redeemed for a copy of* Magnus Robot Fighter *#0 comic book plus the* Magnus Robot Fighter *trading card #0 by Barry Windsor-Smith.*

Set: 24 cards (#2 through #25) 6.00

Uncut sheet, with coupons 10.00
Coupons *(in* Magnus Robot Fighter *#1-#8)*
1 thru 8, each 25
Redemption card (BWS) 25.00

CARD CHECKLIST

2 Battle-Rob (MS) 25
3 Bunda the Great (BH) 25
4 Danae and Her Neo-Animals (SL) . .25
5 Doctor Lazlo Noel (BBI) 25
6 Elzy (JRu) 25
7 Giant-Rob From Planet X (RL) 25
8 H-8 (JKu) 25
9 Leeja Clane and Senator Zeramiah Clane (Alan Weiss) 25
10 Magnus (Moe) 25
11 Malev-6 (AH) 25
12 Mekman (Jose' Delbo) 25
13 Mogul Badur (Mike Harris) 25
14 Nadmot (AKu) 25
15 1-A (PCu/BL) 25
16 The Outsiders (KN) 25
17 Pert Doner and Friends (TA) 25
18 Rai (ANi) 25
19 Slagger (MGo) 25
20 T-1 (DHv) 25
21 Talpa (SD) 25
22 Tekla (BL) 25
23 V'Ril Trent (SDr) 25
24 Xyrkol (NKu) 25
25 Zypex and the Mini-Robs (PG) . . .25

MARVEL

MARVEL ADVERTISEMENT CARDS NEW SERIES PREMIERE

In early 1989 Marvel advertised six new comic book series with these 2¼" x 3¾" cards. There is a question on each card back which fans answered in order to be eligible to win original John Byrne artwork.

Jan. The Sensational She-Hulk 1.50
Mar. Moon Knight 1.50
Mar. What If 1.50
Apr. Nth Man 1.50
May Shield 1.50
June Quasar 1.50

Marvel Autograph Cards © Marvel Entertainment Group, Inc.

MARVEL AUTOGRAPH CARDS

"Live & In Person"

Meet your favorite live & in person (and in costume) superhero at your local comic shop and get his autograph on a special trading card! All the shop has to do is rent Spider-Man for the day.

Spider-Man card (1992) 3.00
Marvel Universe card (1992) 3.00

Marvel Autograph Cards © Marvel Entertainment Group, Inc.

MARVEL AUTOGRAPH CARDS–EDITORS

These cards depict editors, etc. at Marvel Comics. We only have two of them, but they have high numbers so there must be a lot of other cards somewhere. The cards are worth more autographed.

15 Marc McLaurin 50
32 Kelly Corvese 50

Marvel Checklist Cards © Marvel Entertainment Group, Inc.

MARVEL CHECKLIST CARDS

From time to time Marvel prints checklist cards for its annuals or cross-over series and distributes them to comic shops as give-away promotions. The fronts contain nice art and the backs have a checklist of the comics you will (theoretically) be eager to buy so that you don't miss any exciting developments in the series. The third group of cards doesn't form a series. It's just the only place we can conveniently group these checklists. There may be others.

MARVEL ANNUALS CARDS (1992)

Annuals 1: Shattershot (GCa) 2.00
Annuals 2: Return of the Defenders . 1.50
Annuals 3: The System Bytes 1.50
Annuals 4: Assault on Armor City . . 1.50
Annuals 5: The Hero Killers 1.50
Annuals 6: Citizen Kang 1.50

MARVEL BI-WEEKLIES CARDS (1992)

1 The Punisher 1.50
2 The Silver Surfer 1.50
3 Captain America 1.50
4 Wolverine 1.50
5 Avengers 1.50
6 Excalibur 1.50
7 The Mighty Thor 1.50
8 Spider-Man 1.50

OTHER CHECKLIST CARDS

Blood and Thunder (1993) 1.25
Bloodties (1993) 1.25
Infinity Crusade (Capitol)(RLm) 1.50
The Infinity War (1992)(RLm) 2.50
Marvel 1990 Annuals, Family Reunion 3.00
Siege of Darkness checklist 1.50
Siege of Darkness 3 card redemption strips:
Strange, Morbius & Zarathos 2.00
Centurious,Dr.Strange,Vengeance 2.00
Spider-Man, Maximum Carnage . . . 1.50
0 Magneto 5 comic receipt card 1.25

Marvel Checklist Cards © Marvel Entertainment Group, Inc.

MARVEL COMICS

Sugar-Free Bubble Gum Wrappers
Topps (1978)

These bubble gum wrappers have three panels of humorous color comic art and a Dr. Strange "fortune" on the insides. They aren't trading cards, but are usually listed in the same price guides.

Set: 34 gum wrappers 50.00

1 Sub-Mariner 2.00
2 Doctor Strange 2.00
3 The Incredible Hulk 2.25
4 Silver Surfer 2.50
5 The Incredible Hulk 2.00
6 The Incredible Hulk 2.00
7 Iron Man 2.00
8 Sub-Mariner 2.00
9 The Fantastic Four 2.25
10 The Amazing Spider-Man 2.00
11 The Amazing Spider-Man 2.50
12 The Incredible Hulk 2.00
13 The Fantastic Four 2.00
14 Iron Man 2.00
15 The Mighty Thor 2.00
16 The Incredible Hulk 2.00
17 The Incredible Hulk 2.00
18 Iron Man 2.00
19 Iron Man 2.00
20 The Fantastic Four 2.00
21 The Incredible Hulk 2.00
22 Captain America 2.00
23 Iron Man 2.00
24 The Incredible Hulk 2.00
25 Iron Man 2.00
26 Sub-Mariner 2.00
27 The Incredible Hulk 2.00
28 Sub-Mariner 2.00
29 The Incredible Hulk 2.00
30 The Incredible Hulk 2.00
31 The Incredible Hulk 2.00
32 The Amazing Spider-Man 2.00
33 The Fantastic Four 2.00
34 The Thing 2.00

Marvel Sugar Free Bubble Gum © Marvel Entertainment Group, Inc.

MARVEL COMICS
Bubble Gum Wrappers
Topps (1979)

These bubble gum wrappers have a three panel color comic on an inside sheet. It's the same comic with the same Dr. Strange Fortunes as the set above, except for #30, which was misnumbered as another #20, and #34, which was not used.

Set: 33 wrappers 30.00

1 Sub-Mariner 1.00
2 Doctor Strange 1.00
3 The Incredible Hulk 1.00
4 Silver Surfer 1.00
5 The Incredible Hulk 1.00
6 The Incredible Hulk 1.00
7 Iron Man 1.00
8 The Thing 1.00
9 The Fantastic Four 1.00
10 The Amazing Spider-Man 1.00
11 The Amazing Spider-Man 1.00
12 The Incredible Hulk 1.00
13 The Fantastic Four 1.00
14 Iron Man 1.00
15 The Mighty Thor 1.00
16 The Incredible Hulk 1.00
17 The Incredible Hulk 1.00
18 Iron Man 1.00
19 Sub-Mariner 1.00
20 The Fantastic Four 1.00
21 The Incredible Hulk 1.00
22 Captain America 1.00
23 Iron Man 1.00
24 The Incredible Hulk 1.00
25 Iron Man 1.00
26 Sub-Mariner 1.00
27 The Incredible Hulk 1.00
28 Sub-Mariner 1.00
29 The Incredible Hulk 1.00
20(A) The Incredible Hulk 1.00
31 The Incredible Hulk 1.00
32 The Amazing Spider-Man 1.00
33 The Thing 1.00

MARVEL COMICS SUPER HEROES
RUB-A-TATTOO
Donruss (1980)

We don't think that these tattoos are cards, but they are generally listed in the same price guides. They came with bubble gum.

Tattoos, 44? diff., each 1.00
Pack: 1 Tattoo+instruct card+gum .. 2.00

Marvel 1st Covers, Series II © Marvel Entertainment Group, Inc.

MARVEL 1st COVERS TRADING CARDS SERIES II
Comic Images (1991, Covers)

The fronts of these cards reprint the cover of a first issue comic book. The back has a black and white design, the series name, card title and number. Backs contain information on the creative team and a "Contents Capsule" description of the story of the comic depicted on the front. The "Series II" refers to ***Marvel Superheroes First Issue Covers*** *by FTCC (listed below), issued in 1984, not any series of cards by Comic Images. The cards omit the "Marvel" from the series name; it's only on the packs.*

Set: 100 cards 15.00

Pack: 10 cards 1.50

CARD CHECKLIST

Green wrapper, no art

1 Beware! .... .20
2 Giant Size Chillers featuring The Curse of Dracula .... .20
3 Peter Parker, The Spectacular Spider-Man (SB) .... .20
4 The Human Fly (LE) .... .20
5 Marvel No-Prize Book (MGo) .... .20
6 Marvel Super Hero Contest of Champions .... .20
7 Hercules (BL) .... .20
8 Wolverine (Lim. Series) (FM) .... .25
9 Vision and the Scarlet Witch (Lim. Series) .... .20
10 The Uncanny X-Men at the State Fair of Texas (JR2) .... .20
11 Marvel Age (WS & BLr) .... .20
12 Obnoxio the Clown vs. The X-Men .... .20
13 The Saga of Crystar – Crystal Warrior .... .20
14 Hawkeye .... .20
15 Cloak and Dagger (Lim. Series) (RL & TA) .... .20
16 Marvel Tailes starring Peter Porker .... .20
17 The Falcon .... .20
18 Magik (JB & TP) .... .20
19 The Jack of Hearts .... .20
20 The X-Men and the Micronauts (JG & BWi) .... .20
21 Secret Wars (MZ) .... .20
22 Power Pack (JBr & BWi) ...... .20
23 West Coast Avengers (BH & BBr) .20
24 Machine Man (Lim. Series) (BWS) .... .25
25 Web of Spider-Man (CV) ...... .20
26 Moon Knight (CW) .... .20
27 Cloak and Dagger (RL & TA) ... .20
28 Secret Wars II (JBy & TA) ..... .20
29 The Life of Captain Marvel (JSn) .20
30 Longshot (AAd) .... .20
31 Squadron Supreme (BH & JRu) . .20
32 Vision and the Scarlet Witch .... .20
33 Nightcrawler (DC) .... .20
34 Marvel Saga (RF & BL) .... .20
35 X-Men and Alpha Flight (PS & BWi) .... .20
36 The Punisher (mini-series)(MZ) .. .20
37 X-Factor .... .20
38 Classic X-Men (AAd) .... .20
39 Strikeforce: Morituri .... .20
40 The 'Nam (MGo) .... .20
41 The Comet Man (BSz) .... .20
42 Fallen Angels (KGa & TP) ..... .20
43 Strange Tales (BBl) .... .20
44 X-Men vs. The Avengers (MS) .. .20
45 Silver Surfer (MR & JRu) ...... .20
46 The Punisher (KJ) .... .20
47 Solo Avengers starring Hawkeye and Mockingbird (MBr & JRu) .... .20
48 Marvel Comics presents Wolverine (WS) .... .20
49 Spellbound (CP) .... .20
50 Nick Fury vs. S.H.I.E.L.D.(JSo) .. .20
51 Black Panther (DCw) .... .20
52 What The ?! (JBg & AM) ...... .20
53 Wolfpack (TKa) .... .20
54 Excalibur (AD & PNe) .... .20
55 X-Terminators (JBg) .... .20
56 Saga of the Sub-Mariner (RB) .. .20
57 The Punisher War Journal (CP & SW) .... .20
58 Wolverine (JB) .... .20
59 Semper Fi' (JSe) .... .20
60 Fred Hembeck Destroys the Marvel Universe .... .20
61 What If? (KP) .... .20
62 Solarman (MZ) .... .20

63 Damage Control (EC) .20
64 The Sensational She-Hulk (JBy) .20
65 Marc Spector-Moon Knight .20
66 Nth Man-The Ultimate Ninja (RoW & BMc) .20
67 Nick Fury Agent of Shield (BH) .20
68 Power Pachyderms .20
69 The Wolverine Saga (RLd & TA) .25
70 Quasar (PR) .20
71 Shadowmasters (JLe & FC) .20
72 The War (TMo) .20
73 Damage Control (Lim. Series) (EC) .20
74 Open Space .20
75 The Punisher: No Escape (JJu) .25
76 The Thanos Quest (JSn) .20
77 X-Men Spotlight on Starjammers (DC) .20
78 Namor, The Sub-Mariner (JBy) .20
79 The Saga of the Original Human Torch (RB & DBi) .20
80 Ghost Rider (JS) .20
81 Marvel Super-Heroes Spring Special (JLe) .25
82 Black Knight (RB & TD) .20
83 Guardians of the Galaxy (JV) .20
84 Deathlok (JJu) .25
85 The New Warriors .20
86 The Punisher Armory (JLe) .25
87 Spider-Man (TM) .30
88 Fool Killer (TD) .20
89 Nomad (Fry & McKenna) .20
90 Black Panther, Panther's Prey (DT) .20
91 Punisher P.O.V. .20
92 Darkhawk (MM) .20
93 Nightcat (JJu) .25
94 Sweet Sixteen (B.Slate) .20
95 Deadly Foes of Spider-Man (AM) .20
96 Damage Control Vol III (KB) .20
97 Sleepwalker (BBl) .20
98 Deathlok (DCw) .20
99 The Infinity Gauntlet (GP) .25
100 Checklist .20

1992 Marvel Masterpieces © Marvel Entertainment Group, Inc.

1992 MARVEL MASTERPIECES

SkyBox (1992, Superhero art)

It's hard to believe that SkyBox could top its own hot selling Marvel Universe and X-Men cards (which had revolutionized the industry and created comics cards as a whole new category) but they did! In the fall of 1992 SkyBox released the first Marvel Masterpiece set and it took the card market by storm. It featured painted portraits of all the Marvel superheros by ***Joe Jusko****. All previous sets had used comic style drawn and colored art. As if that wasn't enough, it also had really neat bonus cards which used a refractive engraving process to enhance details of the characters. The cards have full bleed art and the backs have a reproduction of the first comic cover appearance of the character, along with descriptive text. The Wolverine, Spider-Man and Hulk promo cards were distributed widely and the same art was used for three prototype cards, which were also distributed widely. However, the Captain America, Silver Surfer and Psylocke promo cards are much harder to find. All these cards use the same art as the regular series cards. Production was limited to 17,500 numbered cases (which is a lot), but prices rose quickly anyway. This promise of limited production did not prevent SkyBox from issuing a large number of complete tin boxed sets with all the Spectra Etch cards plus 5 completely new cards one year later! These came out with a retail price of about $60.00 (when a set of the cards plus all the bonus cards was selling for over $150.00). Buyer demand was so strong that the tin set shot up to about $95.00 within a few weeks and the original sets and bonus cards only dropped a little. This is one of the ten sets you* ***must own*** *to claim to collect comics cards. It's cheaper to buy the set than to buy individual cards.*

Set: 100 cards 60.00

Spectra Etch bonus cards (JJu)
1-D Thing vs. Hulk 15.00
2-D Silver Surfer vs.Thanos 17.00
3-D Wolverine vs.Sabretooth 20.00
4-D Spider-Man vs.Venom 19.00
5-D Captain America vs. Red Skull 15.00

Prototype & Promo cards
Captain America promo (Scoreboard) 4.50
Hulk, promo (in Marvel Age #118) 3.50
Hulk, prototype 3.50
Psylocke, promo (in Wizard #13) 4.00
Silver Surfer promo (in CBG) 4.50
Spider-Man, promo (Previews) 3.50
Spider-Man, prototype 3.50
Wolverine, promo (Up 'n Coming) 3.50
Wolverine, prototype 3.50
Tin set, 100 cards + 5 bonus cards (released Fall, 1993) 95.00

Bonus cards from Tin set:
LM-1 Scarlet Witch 3.00
LM-2 Feral 3.00
LM-3 Deathbird 3.00
LM-4 Typhoid Mary 3.00
LM-5 Jubilee 3.00
Pack, 6 cards 4.50
Two different wrappers: Spider-Man & Wolverine

CARD CHECKLIST

1 Blob 1.25
2 Blaze .50
3 Black Widow .50
4 Black Panther .50
5 Black Cat .50
6 Bishop 1.25
7 Beast 1.25
8 Archangel 1.00
9 Apocalypse 1.00
10 Adam Warlock .50
11 Darkhawk 1.00
12 Daredevil .55
13 Cyclops 1.00
14 Colossus 1.00
15 Captain Britain .50
16 Captain America 1.00
17 Cage .50
18 Cable 1.50
19 Bullseye .50
20 Dazzler .50
21 Enchantress .50
22 Elektra .75
23 Electro .50
24 Dr. Strange 1.00
25 Dr. Octopus .50
26 Dr. Doom .90
27 Dormammu .50
28 Deathlok .50
29 Gambit 1.50
30 Galactus .75
31 Human Torch .75
32 Hulk 1.25
33 Hobgoblin .60
34 Hawkeye .60
35 Havok 1.00
36 Green Goblin .75
37 Ghost Rider .95
38 Iron Man 1.10
39 Invisible Woman .75
40 Iceman 1.00
41 Lizard .50
42 Leader .60
43 Kingpin .60
44 Kang .50
45 Juggernaut .95
46 Jean Grey 1.25
47 Mandarin .50
48 Major Victory .45
49 Magneto 1.25
50 Loki .60
51 Moon Knight .65
52 Mole Man .50
53 Mojo .75
54 Mephisto .50
55 Meggan .50
56 Namorita .50
57 Namor 1.10
58 Mr. Sinister .60
59 Mr. Fantastic .70
60 Morbius .55
61 Nightmare .50
62 Nightcrawler 1.10
63 Night Thrasher .75
64 Nick Fury 1.25

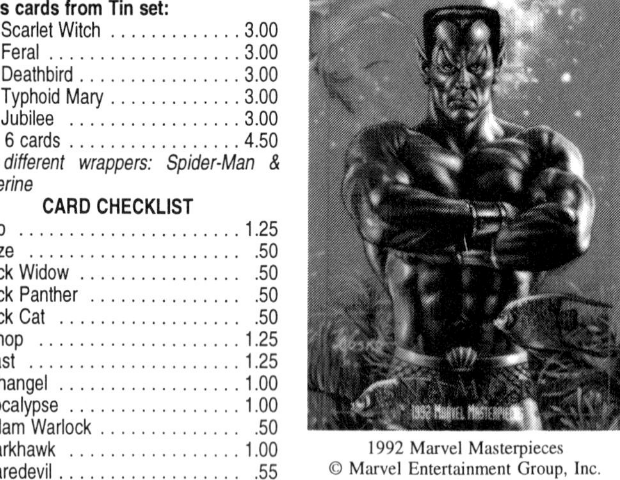

1992 Marvel Masterpieces © Marvel Entertainment Group, Inc.

65 Psylocke 1.50
66 Professor X 1.25
67 Phoenix 1.25
68 Nova .60
69 Northstar .50
70 Nomad .70
71 Quicksilver .65
72 Quasar .50
73 Punisher .90
74 Shatterstar 1.25
75 Shadowcat .90
76 Sauron .50
77 Sandman .50
78 Sabretooth 1.75
79 Rogue 1.50
80 Red Skull .75
81 Silver Sable .50
82 She-Hulk .55
83 Thanos .55
84 Super Skrull .50
85 Strong Guy 1.00
86 Storm 1.10
87 Spider-Man 1.35
88 Speedball .60
89 Sleepwalker .50
90 Silver Surfer 1.25
91 Thing .80
92 Thor 1.20
93 Wonder Man .50
94 Wolverine 1.50
95 White Queen .90
96 Weapon Omega .50
97 Venom 1.75
98 Ultron .50
99 Tombstone .50
100 Checklist .75

1993 Marvel Masterpieces © Marvel Entertainment Group, Inc.

1993 MARVEL MASTERPIECES
"FINAL EDITION"
SkyBox (1993, Superhero art)

Collectors waited eagerly for these cards because of the great popularity of the first Masterpiece cards and the fact that this was SkyBox's last set of Marvel cards. (Marvel now owned Fleer and intended to produce its own cards, so it did not renew SkyBox's license.) SkyBox wanted to "finish with a bang" and they did. The cards again feature painted, full-bleed art, this time by several different artists. There are 16 cards by Joe Jusko, several by Bill Sienkiewicz, Brian Stelfreeze and other Marvel artists and a couple each by George Perez, Julie Bell, Mike Kaluta & Jim Steranko. This year all the cards are foil stamped, in colors, at the top with "1993 Marvel Masterpieses" and at the bottom with the character's name. The backs have a detail picture which blends into a background for the text. The set includes 45 characters which didn't appear in the first set. The eight Spectra cards are done in etched foil and designed to look like the regular cards. The backs have close-up paintings and text over an "X-Men 2099" logo design. They aren't quite as spectacular as the first series, but they are still very nice cards. SkyBox produced 17,500 twenty-box cases, which is a lot, so these cards won't be scarce for quite a while, but they are highly collectible anyway.

Set: 90 cards 30.00

X-Men 2099 Spectra Cards (BLr)
(1:9) (RLm/AKu orig. on back)
S1 Meanstreak 10.00
S2 Cerebra 10.00
S3 Krystalin 10.00
S4 Metalhead 10.00
S5 Serpentina 10.00
S6 Bloodhawk 10.00
S7 Skullfire 10.00
S8 Xi'an 10.00
She-Hulk prototype card (JJu) 4.00
Hulk 2099 promo card (DvD) 3.50
Daredevil promo card (TnS) 5.00
Pack: 6 cards 1.50

CARD CHECKLIST

1 Hulk (BSz) 35
2 Human Torch (JSo) 30
3 Thor (LuH) 30
4 Iron Man (JuB) 30
5 Spider-Man (MK) 40
6 Wolverine (BSz) 45
7 Cyclops (JoP) 35
8 Doctor Strange (MK) 30
9 Namor (JSo) 30
10 Storm (MK) 35
11 Silver Surfer (JuB) 35
12 Vision (JJu) 35
13 Ghost Rider (BSz) 35
14 Thing (GP) 35
15 Captain America (JSo) 35
16 Archangel (JoP) 35
17 Beast (GP) 35
18 Cable (DIB) 40
19 Carnage (JJu) 45
20 Hulk 2099 (DvD) 30
21 Doctor Doom (GF) 30
22 Daredevil (TnS) 40
23 Iron Fist (JJu) 30
24 Psylocke (JuB) 35
25 Morbius (BSf) 30
26 Punisher (MZ/Phil Zimelman) 35
27 Rogue (BSf) 35
28 Sabretooth (BSz) 50
29 Forge (JJu) 35
30 She-Hulk (JJu) 30
31 Gambit (JoP) 45
32 U.S.Agent (FrS) 30
33 Spider-Woman (TnS) 30
34 Stryfe (JJu) 35
35 Thanos (RyL) 35
36 Blade (TP) 30
37 Adam Warlock (RyL) 30
38 Colossus (JuB) 30
39 Magneto (JP) 35
40 Vulture (BSz) 35
41 Spider-Man 2099 (JJu) 35
42 Punisher 2099 (JJu) 30
43 Doom 2099 (JJu) 30
44 Ravage 2099 (JJu) 30
45 Venom (DvD) 45
46 Domino (JJu) 35
47 Annihilus (GF) 30
48 Rhino (BBl) 30
49 Puma (JoP) 30
50 Cannonball (JJu) 35
51 Polaris (DLw) 35
52 Longshot (JoP) 35
53 Cyber (JJu) 35
54 Omega Red (BBl) 35
55 Deadpool (JJu) 40
56 Kingpin (JR) 30
57 Bishop (BSf) 40
58 Absorbing Man (DvD) 30
59 Darkhawk (KSy) 30
60 Mystique (BSf) 35
61 Abomination (JoP) 30
62 Wasp (John Estes) 30
63 Scorpion (BBl) 30
64 Captain Britain (?) 30
65 Black Knight (TP) 30
66 Sasquatch (BSf) 30
67 Black Widow (JCh) 30
68 Typhoid Mary (BBl) 30
69 War Machine (JJu) 35
70 Hawkeye (RyL) 30
71 Deathlok (DIB) 30
72 Nightcrawler (KW) 35
73 Thunderstrike (JJu) 30
74 Vengeance (TnS) 30
75 Jean Grey (CP) 35
76 Shatterstar (LuH) 35
77 Beta Ray Bill (JoP) 30
78 Night Thrasher (BBl) 30
79 Red Skull (MZ/Phil Zimelman) . . .30

1993 Marvel Masterpieces
© Marvel Entertainment Group, Inc.

80 Lilith (KW) 30
81 Falcon (KW) 30
82 Hercules (RyL) 30
83 Nova (RyL) 30
84 Havok (JoP) 35
85 Phoenix (LuH) 35
86 Crystal (BBl) 30
87 Drax (LuH) 30
88 Terrax (GF) 30
89 Vulture 2099 (KW) 30
90 Checklist 35

Marvel 1993 Annuals © Marvel Entertainment Group, Inc.

MARVEL 1993 ANNUALS
Marvel Comics (1993)

These cards were bagged with each of the 27 Marvel comics annuals released from March to August of 1993. The checklist card was given away to stores and contains a list of the annual comics, not the cards. Each card is clearly marked "1993 Annuals" at the top and has a picture of the new hero, villain or team which first appeared in the particular annual that included the card. In sports terms, each card is a "Rookie." The character name is at the bottom in large block letters and is repeated on the back. The backs also contain a closeup picture and details about the character, plus a card number. The cards have a uniform design, but the background colors differ, with the same color being used for three to six cards and then switching to a new one. All the colors could be described as "metallic pastels."

Set: 27 cards + checklist 20.00
1 Annex (TL) 1.00
2 Bantam (RLm pencils) 1.00
3 Darkling 1.00
4 Blood Wraith 1.00
5 Cadre 1.00
6 Charon (BWi inks) 1.00
7 X-Cutioner (JP/JB) 1.00
8 Wildstreak 1.00
9 Kyllian (GI) 1.00
10 Dreamkiller 1.00
11 Hitmaker (Gordon Purcel) 1.00
12 The Assassin 1.00
13 Lazarus (KJa/BVa) 1.00
14 Devourer 1.00
15 The Flame (TGb) 1.00
16 Face Thief (TMo) 1.00
17 Phalanx 1.00
18 The Irish Wolfhound (KWe) 1.00
19 Khaos (ChM/DPs) 1.00
20 Nocturne 1.00
21 Raptor 1.00
22 Night Terror (Cordovic/ Campenella) 1.00
23 Legacy (RL/TA) 1.00
24 Empyrean (Wiesenfeld/Turner) . . 1.00
25 Eradikator 6 . . . . 1.00
26 Tracer (John Herbert) 1.00
27 X-Treme 1.00
1993 Annuals Checklist card (JR/JR2/NKu collage) 0.50

Marvel Superheroes © Marvel Entertainment Group, Inc.

MARVEL SUPERHEROES
Donruss (1966)

These cards are divided into 11 card subsets, with comic style drawings of the six superheroes listed below. Most of the cards have humouous captions, except for 14 which encourage you to write your own. The backs of the cards form a large puzzle poster of all the superheroes. The series name appears only on the box and wrapper, but the cards are easily identified by the "Collect All 66 Cards" caption on the front.

Set: 66 cards 150.00

Captain America #s 1-11
1 I Love These Class Parties! 2.00
2 But Lady The Subscription Only Costs $3.98 . . . . 2.00
3 Blank Caption (Write Your Own) . . 2.00
4 You're Going to Love our Steam Room! 2.00
5 I Told You to Keep Those Pigeons Out of my Yard. 2.00
6 These Class Parties Give Me a Headache! 2.00
7 Blank Caption (Write Your Own) . . 2.00
8 You and Your Fire Sales! 2.00
9 Don't Go to Pieces Over the Crab Grass! 2.00
10 Blank Caption (Write Your Own) . 2.00
11 I Got It for 362 Books of Stamps! 2.00

Iron Man #s 12-22
12 "Get the Lead Out!" 2.00
13 I Hate These Toy Kits! 2.00
14 Do You Have Iron Deficiency Anemia? 2.00
15 Blank Caption (Write Your Own) . 2.00
16 To Get Your Atom Smasher Send In 5 Box Tops and $1,000.000 . . . 2.00
17 And You Said Add a Little More Lighter Fluid 2.00
18 Blank Caption (Write Your Own) . 2.00
19 Please, I'd Rather Do It Myself . . 2.00
20 Blank Caption (Write Your Own) . 2.00
21 That Chick Really Puts Me in Orbit! 2.00
22 When Did You First Notice Those Stomach Pains 2.00

Daredevil #s 23-33
23 But Halloween Is Next Week! . . . 2.50
24 Let Hurts Put You in the Drivers' Seat! 2.50
25 Blank Caption (Write Your Own) . 2.50
26 I'm Sorry I'm Tied-Up This Evening! 2.50
27 With These Trading Stamps.. You Can Get Anything! 2.50
28 He Still Thinks He's in the Circus! 2.50
29 Wait 'till I Turn the Antenna! 2.50
30 Blank Caption (Write Your Own) . 2.50
31 I Didn't Know You Had a Game Room! 2.50
32 How's This for a Finish? 2.50
33 Blank Caption (Write Your Own) . 2.50

Spider-Man #'s 34-44
34 Next Time I'll Fly the Kite! 2.75
35 Next Time You Change the Tire! . 2.75
36 Blank Caption (Write Your Own) . 2.75
37 Just What I Needed, a Bug Bomb! 2.75
38 What'ya Mean 50 cents Extra for Gift Wrapping! 2.75
39 I Made a Before and After Commercial 2.75
40 This Fly Paper Is Rough on the Hair! 2.75
41 Just Fixing a Little! 2.75
42 I Meant..Hang Up the Phone! . . . 2.75
43 Those Kids & Those Build-It-Yourself A-Bomb Kits! 2.75
44 Blank Caption (Write Your Own) . 2.75

Hulk #s 45-55
45 Blank Caption (Write Your Own) . 2.25
46 These P.T.A. Meetings Drive Me Crazy! 2.25
47 OK, So You're the Green Giant! . 2.25
48 When I Was a 82lb. Weakling . . . 2.25
49 Come on Out and Play 2.25
50 But, I wanted an A-Bomb for Christmas! 2.25
51 Let's Go Swimming Buddy! 2.25
52 From Now on Take Your Coffee Breaks with the Rest of the Guests 2.25
53 This Will Really Curl Your Hair! . . 2.25
54 Watch That First Step! 2.25
55 I Don't Believe I've Met You Guys 2.25

Thor #s 56-66
56 She's Always Hiding the Soap! . . 2.00
57 I'd Rather Fight...But I Don't Smoke 2.00
58 The Peasants Are Always Throwing Rocks 2.00
59 I Don't Care If You Do Have "We Tried harder Buttons!" 2.00
60 Just, Who Does Your Hair? 2.00
61 I Get 8 Shaves from Each Blade Koo-coo! 2.00
62 I Think the Trouble Is in the Fuel Pump! 2.00
63 So, I Don't Want Any Scout Cookies! 2.00
64 We Try Harder...We're Only No. Two 2.00
65 Blank Caption (Write Your Own) . 2.00
66 Blank Caption (Write Your Own) . 2.00

Marvel Superheroes First Issue Covers © Marvel Entertainment Group, Inc.

MARVEL SUPERHEROES
First Issue Covers
FTCC (1984)

The fronts are color reproductions of the covers of issue #1 of the comics listed, inside a thin white border. The backs are uncoated and contain the card number in a circle in the upper left corner, the comic title and a synopsis of the story.

Set: 60 cards, hand assembled 22.50
Set: 60 cards in factory box 25.00
Pack: 5 cards 2.00

CARD CHECKLIST
1 The Fantastic Four 1.00
2 The Amazing Spider-Man 75
3 Sgt. Fury and his Howling Commandos 50
4 The Avengers 50
5 The X-Men 1.00
6 Daredevil .75
7 Ghost Rider 1.25
8 Not Brand Echh 35
9 The Incredible Hulk 75
10 Captain Marvel 85
11 Nick Fury, Agent of S.H.I.E.L.D 50
12 Dr. Strange 50
13 The Silver Surfer 1.35
14 Tales of Asgard 35
15 Kazar the Savage 35
16 Fear 35
17 Marvel Spotlight on Captain Marvel 50
18 Marvel Feature: The Defenders . .35
19 Marvel Team-Up: Spider-Man and the Human Torch 35
20 Marvel Premier: The Power of Warlock 35
21 The Tomb of Dracula 35
22 Red Wolf 35
23 Combat Kelly and the Deadly Dozen 35
24 Luke Cage, Hero for Hire 50
25 The Defenders 50
26 The Cat .35
27 Shanna the She-Devil 50
28 Crypt of Shadows 35
29 The Monster of Frankenstein 35
30 The Man-Thing 50
31 Marvel Two-In-One: The Thing and Man-Thing 35

32 Night Rider 50
33 Giant Size X-Men 1.25
34 The Champions 50
35 The Inhumans 50
36 Marvel Chillers: Modred the Mystic 35
37 Iron Fist 50
38 Howard the Duck 50
39 The Power of Warlock 35
40 Black Goliath 50
41 The Man Called Nova 50
42 Peter Parker, The Spectacular Spider-Man 35
43 Ms. Marvel 35
44 The Spider-Woman 35
45 Machine Man 35
46 Devil Dinosaur 35
47 The Savage She-Hulk 35
48 Moon Knight 35
49 Dazzler 35
50 Marvel Spotlight on ...Red Wolf . . .35
51 Marvel Fanfare 35
52 The New Mutants 35
53 The Thing 35
54 Alpha Flight 35
55 Iron Man and Sub-Mariner 35
56 Chamber of Darkness 35
57 Astonishing Tales: Ka-Zar and Dr. Doom 35
58 The Inhumans and the Black Widow 35
59 Werewolf by Night 35
60 checklist 35

Marvel Super Heroes Stickers © Marvel Entertainment Group, Inc.

MARVEL SUPER HEROES STICKERS (White Backs)

Topps (1976)

These stickers are similar in design to "Comic Book Heroes" issued the previous year, but can be distinguished by the 1976 Topps and Marvel copyrights. They have a die-cut sticker, picturing the named superhero plus a humorous word balloon, all on a white back. It took over 10 years after these cards for trading cards to treat these characters seriously, starting with Marvel Universe cards from Comic Images, listed next. There are nine checklist cards with puzzle backs that form a picture of the cover of Conan the Barbarian #1 *comic. The interesting part of this set is the six caption variations, as noted in the checklist, for Conan, Hercules, Loki, Luke Cage, The Hulk and Volstagg.*

Set: 40 stickers (plus 6 caption variations) + 9 puzzle cards125.00

Wrappers: 3 diff., each 4.00
Blade "I'm a real cut-up!" (GC/TP) 2.00
Black Goliath "Bowling sure is fun!" (GT/ViC) 2.00
Bucky "How'd you like a knuckle sandwich?" (JK/FrG) 2.00
Captain America "I've got to stand this way or my pants fall down!" (JK/JR) 3.00
Conan "Shall we dance?" (GK/ECh) 2.00
Conan "Hold The Pickle..Or Else!" . . 2.50
Cyclops "I'm a sight for sore eyes!" (DC) 2.00
Daredevil "See no evil!" (GK) 3.00
Deathlok "I'm the **seven** million dollar man!" 7.50
Dracula "So this is how you do the hustle!" (CI/TP) 2.00
Dr. Doom "Anyone out there have a can opener!" (JB/JSt) 3.50
Dr. Strange "Did anyone see a flying sorcerer?" (FB) 2.50
Galactus "No, I'm not the Mad Hatter!" (JB/JSt) 2.00
Goliath "Wanna hear a **tall** story?" (DC) 2.00
Hercules "Like my nail polish?" 2.00
Hercules "Look, I Have A Hang-Nail!" (GK/JR) 2.00
Howard the Duck "I'm going quackers!" (FB) 2.00
Ice Man "I'll never eat another frozen dinner!" (GK) 2.00
Invisible Girl "I use vanishing cream!" (JR) 2.00
Iron Man "Quick-anyone have an oilcan?" (JR) 3.00
Kid Colt "I am not **kidding** around!" . 2.00
Killraven "I'll teach you to make fun of my hair-do!" (CR) 2.00
Loki "Who says I'm bull-headed?" . . 2.00
Loki "What An Awful Case of Ear-Wax!" (JB/SB) 2.50
Luke Cage "Like my denture work?" 2.00
Luke Cage "Two All Beef Patties Please!" (JR) 2.50
Peter Parker "Peter Parker picked a peck of pickled peppers!" 6.00
Red Skull "What makes you think I'm angry?" (JK/FrG) 2.00
Red Sonja "My sword gives six extra shaves!" (JB) 2.00
Sgt. Fury "War makes me fighting mad!" (JK/DAy) 2.00
Silver Surfer You'll take a shine to me!" 6.50
Son of Satan "Waiter, bring me a clean fork!" (JR) 2.00
Spider-Man "Insects scare me silly!" (JR) 4.00
Thor "Don't make me thor!" (JB) . . . 2.50
Tigra "Cat food for dinner again?" (JR) 2.00
The Angel "I'm heading south for the winter!" (GK) 2.00
The Hulk "Can't Anyone Make Cuffs Right?" (JR) 4.00
The Hulk "Help cure athlete's feet!" (JR) 3.00
The Human Torch "Who called me a hot-head?" (JB) 2.00
The Punisher "Oh boy! I Win the Kewpie doll!" 18.50
The Thing "Who said I'm a falling rock zone?" (JK/JSt) 2.00
The Vision "Who stole my yo-yo?" (JB/George Klein) 2.00
The Watcher "Hiya kids! Hiya! Hiya! Hiya!" (JK) 2.00
Volstagg "Fat is beautiful!" 2.00
Volstagg "I Was A 980 Pound Weakling!" (JK/ViC) 2.50
Warlock "Stop me if you heard this before..." (JSn) 3.50

Puzzle/Checklist Cards

Picture: Conan the Barbarian #1 cover

1 thru 9 (BWS) 10.00

Card variation: Either one or two stars before copyright notice.

See also: ***Comic Book Heroes***

Marvel Universe (Comic Images) © Marvel Entertainment Group, Inc.

MARVEL UNIVERSE

Comic Images (1987)

*The card fronts are color portraits of the listed Marvel characters and groups. The title is in a strip at the bottom and the character's group affiliation is indicated in a diagonal stripe. The backs contain the card number, name and text concerning the character. Each of the cards says "Series 1" which refers to the fact that this is the first series of Marvel cards by Comic Images. (Colossal Conflicts was Series 2, Wolverine was Series 3 and Heroic Origins was Series 4, although Wolverine doesn't state this.) The significance of these sets is that they treated comic book heroes as serious characters, not the dumb characters with silly sayings which appeared on the Topps sticker sets from the previous decade. Most of these cards contain the first appearance of the character on a card. Consequently, this is one of the 10 most important comic card sets and one you **should own** to be a legitimate comics cards collector. These cards are very hard to find (as are the other early Comic Images sets) and their prices may shoot up soon!*

Set: 90 cards 60.00

Pack: 4 cards + sticker 3.00

CARD CHECKLIST

1 X-Factor 75
2 Marvel Girl 75
3 Cyclops .75
4 Beast 75
5 Angel 75
6 Iceman .75
7 X-Men .75
8 Magneto 75
9 Nightcrawler 75
10 Wolverine 75
11 Storm .75
12 Colossus 75
13 Rogue .75
14 Phoenix 75
15 Phoenix II 75
16 Longshot 75

17 Lockheed .75
18 Shadowcat .75
19 Power Pack .75
20 Warriors Three .75
21 New Mutant .75
22 Karma .75
23 Wolfsbane .75
24 Mirage .75
25 Sunspot .75
26 Cannonball .75
27 Magma .75
28 Magik .75
29 Warlock .75
30 Cypher .75
31 Avengers .75
32 Wasp .75
33 Captain America .75
34 Hercules .75
35 Black Knight .75
36 Captain Marvel .75
37 Sub-Mariner .75
38 West Coast Avengers .75
39 Iron Man .75
40 Hawkeye .75
41 Wonder Man .75
42 Tigra .75
43 Mockingbird .75
44 Alpha Flight .75
45 Aurora .75
46 Northstar .75
47 Snowbird .75
48 Puck .75
49 Box .75
50 Vindicator .75
51 Jefferies .75
52 Fantastic Four .75
53 Mister Fantastic .75
54 Invisible Woman .75
55 Human Torch .75
56 She-Hulk .75
57 Thing .75
58 Spider-Man .75
59 Quicksilver .75
60 Jack of Hearts .75
61 Nomad .75
62 Watchers .75
63 Thor .75
64 Havok .75
65 Professor X .75
66 Spider-Man (Black costume) .75
67 Silver Surfer .75
68 Punisher .75
69 Power Man .75
70 Scarlet Witch .75
71 Galactus .75
72 Nova .75
73 Moon Knight .75
74 Callisto .75
75 Henry Pym .75
76 Hulk .75
77 Iron Man .75
78 Nick Fury .75
79 Forge .75
80 Falcon .75
81 Elektra .75
82 Doctor Strange .75
83 Daredevil .75
84 Cloak .75
85 Dagger .75
86 Doc Samson .75
87 Black Panther .75
88 Vision .75
89 Black Widow .75
90 Checklist 1.00

Marvel Universe (I) © Marvel Entertainment Group, Inc.

MARVEL UNIVERSE (SERIES I)

Impel (1990)

The whole comics world changed when these cards were issued! This is the first card set which combined fine comic art, good card design, quality production, bonus cards and marketing in just the right proportions. Others had tried, particularly Comic Images starting three years earlier, with the set listed above. These cards have comic character portraits with a black frame and white border. The art is clean and powerful and each character is treated as a serious subject. The card backs repeat the name, and add biographical information and text, plus a small head picture. The holograms were also incredibly popular, as no other sets had valuable chase cards. Now, they all do! The newer bonus cards are better, but these were the first! This is one of the ten sets you ***must own*** *to be a legitimate comics cards collector.*

Marvel Universe Uncut Diamond Promo © Marvel Entertainment Group, Inc.

Please note that the cards do not say Marvel Universe anywhere; that name is only on the packs. The holograms have a white border and the backs of all five are the same, listing the number and title of all 5 cards without indicating which one you have. There is a title within the holographic image so identification is not a problem.

Set: 162 cards 45.00
Tin box set (4,000 made) 200.00

Holograms

MH1 Cosmic Spider-Man (SB/JSt) 15.00
MH2 Magneto (TMo) 18.00
MH3 Silver Surfer (TMo) 17.00
MH4 Wolverine (JLe/TMo) 21.00
MH5 Spider-Man vs. Green Goblin (MBa/JRu) 17.00

Promo Cards

Diamond Promo packs, 5 cards in cello pack (rare) 30.00

Promo/Sample cards for this series were issued in randomly collated five-card cello-wrapped packs. Almost all of these were opened and so they are extremely rare (we have not seen one for sale). However, a cello wrapper is not worth much in itself and so it does not command a high premium over the individual card values. There are 20 sample cards in all. There are only small differences in the back text copy between these cards and the final versions and a few other differences, such as "The Hulk" and "The Thing" became just "Hulk" and "Thing" on the fronts of the regular cards. The same name change appeared on card #87, where they battle, and this card, plus #89, #125 & #136 were renumbered to #88, #90, #126 and #137. The one distinguishing feature that applies to all these promo cards is the line ***"Produced & distributed*** *by Impel Marketing, Inc." above the Marvel copyright information on the back of the card at the bottom. The regular issue cards say* ***"Exclusively distributed*** *by Impel Marketing Inc." and this line is below the Marvel copyright information. Please note that these same early versions of the cards were used for the Diamond Previews uncut sheets described below.*

3 The Hulk 5.00
6 The Thing 5.00
8 Cyclops 5.00
29 Spider-Man 6.00
32 Silver Surfer 6.00
39 She-Hulk 5.00
57 Sabretooth 7.50
60 Doctor Doom 5.00
62 Enchantress 5.00
63 Magneto 6.00
78 Mephisto 5.00
82 Ghost Rider 7.50

83 Deathlok 7.50
87 The Thing vs. The Hulk 5.00
89 Fantastic Four vs. Doctor Doom . 5.00
96 Silver Surfer vs. Mephisto 5.00
100 X-Men vs. Magneto 5.00
125 Amazing Fantasy #15 (Most Valuable Comics) 5.00
136 Fantastic Four 5.00
139 X-Men 5.00

Diamond Previews uncut sheets:
(Sabretooth, Enchantress, Deathlok, Ghost Rider); 25.00
(She-Hulk, Cyclops, The Hulk, Silver Surfer) 25.00
(Spider-Man, The Thing Mephisto, Doctor Doom) 25.00
(X-Men vs. Magneto, Fantastic Four vs. Doctor Doom, Silver Surfer vs. Mephisto, The Thing vs. The Hulk)25.00
(Magneto, Amazing Fantasy #15, Fantastic Four, X-Men)* 25.00
* *(SkyBox is not able to confirm whether or not this fifth uncut sheet exists.)*
Diamond Previews, cut, each 5.00
Diamond Previews cards can be identified by the grey diamond symbol overprinted on the card backs.
Pack: 12 cards 4.00
Three different wrappers

CARD CHECKLIST

Super Heroes
1 Captain America (TMo) 30
2 Spider-Man (black suit)(RF/JRu) . . .25
3 Hulk (green) (TMo) 20
4 Daredevil (MBa/TMo) 20
5 Nick Fury (TMo) 20
6 Thing (TMo) 20
7 Professor X (SB/JSt) 50
8 Cyclops (TMo) 25
9 Marvel Girl (MBa/TMo) 25
10 Wolverine (JLe/TMo) 1.15
11 Phoenix (MBa/JRu) 25
12 Power Man (MBa/TMo) 20
13 Dazzler (TMo) 20
14 Dagger (MBa/TMo) 20
15 Quasar (PR/JRu) 25
16 Sub-Mariner (TMo) 25
17 Hulk (Gray) (AAd) 75

Marvel Universe (Series I)
© Marvel Entertainment Group, Inc.

18 Thor (TMo) 35
19 Mister Fantastic (TMo) 25
20 Black Panther (PR/JRu) 50
21 Archangel (MBa/TMo) 50
22 Iceman (TMo) 35
23 Wolverine (yellow costume) (JLe/TMo) 1.10
24 Storm (MM) 25
25 Shadowcat (AAd) 50
26 Moon Knight (PR/MM) 35
27 Lockheed (MBa/TMo) 25
28 Aunt May (RF/JRu) 25
29 Spider-Man (original) (TMo) 75
30 Cosmic Spider-Man (SB/JSt) . . . 1.25
31 Captain America's Motorcycle (PR/JRu) 80
32 Silver Surfer (TMo) 95
33 Human Torch (TMo) 20
34 Doctor Strange (TMo) 20
35 Havok (MBa/TMo) 25
36 Colossus (MM) 50
37 Wolverine (Patch) (JLe/TMo) 75
38 Nightcrawler (TMo) 20
39 She-Hulk (TMo) 20
40 Captain Britain (MBa/TMo) 20
41 Rogue (MM) 50
42 Iron Man (PR/JRu) 50
43 Invisible Woman (RF/JRu) 20
44 Punisher's Battle Van (MBa/TMo) .40
45 Longshot (AAd) 35
46 The Beast (MM) 25
47 Punisher (TMo) 75
48 Storm (Punk costume) (JLe/TMo) .45
49 Elektra (MBa/TMo) 25
50 Cloak (MBa/TMo) 20
51 The Wasp 20

Super-Villains
52 Kingpin (RF/JRu) 25
53 Baron Zemo (PR/JRu) 20
54 Loki (RF/JRu) 50
55 Juggernaut (TMo) 50
56 Nightmare (AAd) 20
57 Sabretooth (TMo) 1.50
58 Electro (RF/JRu) 20
59 Doctor Octopus (RF/JRu) 20
60 Doctor Doom (TMo) 25
61 Ultron (PR/MM) 25
62 Enchantress (TMo) 20
63 Magneto (TMo) 75

Marvel Universe (Series I)
© Marvel Entertainment Group, Inc.

64 Bullseye (MBa/TMo) 35
65 Mr. Sinister (MBa/TMo) 85
66 Sandman (RF/JRu) 20
67 Lizard (MBa/TMo) 25
68 Mole Man (TMo) 20
69 Dormammu (AAd) 20
70 The Leader (SB/JSt) 20
71 The Blob (AAd) 60
72 Black Cat (RF/JRu) 20
73 Venom (MBa/TMo) 75
74 Green Goblin (RF/JRu) 55
75 Galactus (RF/JRu) 35
76 Mandarin (PR/JRu) 35
77 High Evolutionary (RF/JRu) 25
78 Mephisto (TMo) 20
79 Thanos (PR/JRu) 1.25
80 Apocalypse (AAd) 95
81 Red Skull (PR/JRu) 50

Rookies
82 Ghost Rider (TMo) 1.25
83 Deathlok (TMo) 1.20
84 Guardians of the Galaxy (MBa/BMc) 75
85 New Warriors (MBa/BMc) 95
86 Nomad (MBa/BMc) 50
87 Foolkiller (MBa/TMo) 55

Famous Battles
88 Thing vs. Hulk (TMo) 35
89 Fantastic Four vs. Galactus (RF/JS3) 35
90 Fantastic Four vs. Dr. Doom (TMo) 35
91 Thor vs. Surtur (RF/JS3) 35
92 Spider-Man vs. Kraven (SB/JSt) . .35
93 Spider-Man vs. Dr. Octopus (RF/JS3) 35
94 Daredevil vs. Bullseye (MBa/BMc) .35
95 Daredevil vs. Kingpin (MBa/BMc) .35
96 Silver Surfer vs. Mephisto (TMo) . .35
97 Capt.America vs.Red Skull (AAd) .50
98 Dark Phoenix Saga (MBa/JS3) . . .35
99 X-Men vs. Avengers (MBa/JS3) . .35
100 X-Men vs. Magneto (TMo) 35
101 Fantastic Four vs. X-Men (MBa/JS3) 35
102 Fall of the Mutants (MBa/JS3) . . .60
103 Evolutionary War (PR/MM) 35
104 Atlantis Attacks (PR/MM) 35
105 Acts of Vengeance (PR/MM) 35
106 Spider-Man vs. Venom (MBa/BMc) 35

Marvel Universe (Series I)
© Marvel Entertainment Group, Inc.

107 Nick Fury vs. Hydra (MBa/JS3) . .35
108 Armor Wars I (PR/MM) 35
109 Daredevil vs. Wolverine (MBa/JRu) 1.25
110 Daredevil vs. Punisher (MBa/JRu) 30
111 Spider-Man vs. Green Goblin (MBa/JRu) 35
112 Spider-Man vs. Hobgoblin (SB/JSt) 35
113 The Hulk vs. Wolverine (SB/JSt) .35
114 The Hulk vs. Spider-Man (AAd) . .50
115 Capt. America vs. Wolverine (MBa/BMc) 50
116 Silver Surfer vs. Thanos (MBa/JRu) 90
117 X-Factor vs. Apocalypse (MBa/JRu) 35
118 X-Men vs. Freedom Force (MBa/JS3) 35
119 Wolverine vs. Sabretooth (MBa/JRu) 95
120 X-Men in the Savage Land (MBa/JS3) 35
121 Iron Man vs. Titanium Man (MBa/JS3) 35
122 Thor vs. Loki (RF/JS3) 35
123 First Kree-Skrull War (PR/MM) . .35

Most Valuable Comics
124 Fantastic Four #1 25
125 X-Men #1 25
126 Amazing Fantasy #15 25
127 Punisher Vol. 2 #1 25
128 Journey Into Mystery #83 25
129 Amazing Spider-Man #129 25
130 Avengers #1 25
131 Amazing Spider-Man #1 25
132 Giant-Size X-Men #1 25
133 Wolverine Limited Series #1 . . .25
134 Incredible Hulk #181 25
135 Tales of Suspense #39 25
136 Avengers #4 25

Team Pictures
137 Fantastic Four (TMo) 35
138 Avengers (PR/MM) 35
139 X-Men (current)(MBa/JS3) 35
140 X-Men (Team of Annual #9)(TMo) 35
141 Cloak and Dagger (SB/JSt) 35
142 New Mutants (SB/JSt) 35
143 X-Factor (MBa/JS3) 35
144 Excalibur (MBa/JS3) 35
145 Brotherhood of Evil Mutants (MBa/JS3) 35
146 Sinister Six (MBa/JS3) 35
147 Hellfire Club (MBa/JS3) 35
148 Alpha Flight (MBa/JS3) 35

Spider-Man Presents
149 Spider-Man (JR) 25
150 Doctor Doom (JR) 25
151 Doctor Octopus (JR) 25
152 The Hulk (JR) 25
153 Silver Surfer (JR) 25
154 Thor (JR) 25
155 Punisher (JR) 25
156 Magneto (JR) 25
157 Captain America (JR) 25
158 Doctor Strange (JR) 25
159 Iron Man (JR) 25
160 Wolverine (JR) 25
161 Stan Lee (Arnie Sawyer) 1.35
162 Checklist 75

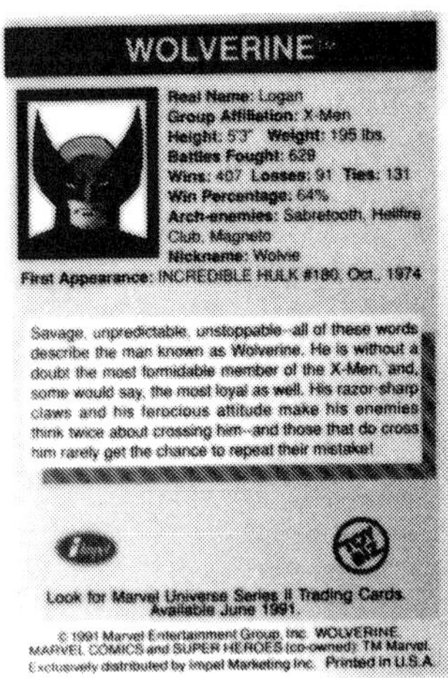

Marvel Universe, Toy Biz Variant
© Marvel Entertainment Group, Inc.

Toy Biz variants, unnumbered
These cards are identical to the regular cards in the series, except for the red "Toy Biz" logo in a red circle with yellow background, on the card backs (see above). They came in the blister packs for

the first editions of X-Men action figures (Toy Biz, 1991) of the same name. Later toys in that series used X-Men cards and the cards did not match the toy.
Apocalypse (AAd, card #80) 2.00
Archangel (MBa/TMo, card #21) . . . 1.50
Colossus (MM, card #36) 2.00
Cyclops (TMo, card #8) 1.50
Juggernaut (TMo, card #55) 2.00
Magneto (TMo, card #63) 1.50
Nightcrawler (TMo, card #38) 1.50
Storm (MM, card #24) 1.00
Wolverine (JLe/TMo, card #10) 2.00

Marvel Universe II © Marvel Entertainment Group, Inc.

MARVEL UNIVERSE SERIES II

Impel (1991)

This was the follow-up to the blockbuster first series. Collectors were looking for the cards this time and the set sold out in just six weeks. The card design was at least as good as series one. Super Heroes cards have a cream colored border, with the card title in a bottom band. The backs were grey with text and card number. The Super-Villains cards have a grey border, Arch-Enemies have a light purple border, Weapons cards have very light blue border and the rest use light green. The holograms are full bleed and are designed to look similar to the regular cards. At least this year the backs of each hologram have different numbers and different text.

As with the previous set, there is nothing on the cards which says "Marvel Universe"; only the packs use that name. The cards say "Marvel 1991" on the fronts.

Set: 162 cards 25.00

Holograms
H-1 Spider-Man (AAd) 13.00
H-2 Hulk (AAd) 13.00
H-3 Punisher (LW) 14.00
H-4 Dr. Doom (AAd) 12.00
H-5 Fantastic Four vs. the Mole Men (AAd) 12.00
Marvel Collector's set in tin box, with all 5 holograms (7,500 made) . . 100.00

Promo Cards
Diamond Pre-cut Set (Dealer) 14.50
1 Spider-Man (EL) 3.00
45 Silver Surfer (PR/TA) 3.00
51 Cyclops (RLm/JS3) 3.00
57 Magneto (RLm/JS3) 3.00
124 Fantastic Four vs. Doctor Doom 3.00
Diamond Previews uncut insert sheet (Spider-Man, Silver Surfer, Cyclops, Magneto, Fantastic Four vs. Dr. Doom & promo info) 17.50
Diamond Inserts, cut, each 2.50
Collector's Album 20.00
Pack 2.50

CARD CHECKLIST

Super Heroes
1 Spider-Man (EL) 25
2 Daredevil (JR2/AW) 15
3 Thing (EL) 15
4 Marvel Girl (AAd) 15
5 Phoenix (SLi) 15
6 Sub-Mariner (PR/TA) 15
7 Mister Fantastic (PR/TA) 15
8 Iceman (LW) 20
9 Shadowcat (RLm/JS3) 15
10 Human Torch (PR/TA) 15
11 Nightcrawler (PR/TA) 15
12 Captain Britain (PR/TA) 35
13 Iron Man (AAd) 45
14 Punisher (EL) 45
15 Cable (TMo) 1.00
16 Deathlok (AAd) 50
17 Gambit (JLe/TA) 50
18 Psylocke (RLm/JS3) 25
19 Vision (PR/TA) 15
20 Hawkeye (PR/TA) 15
21 Silver Sable (RF/JS3) 15
22 Night Thrasher (MBa/JSt) 60
23 Puck (MBa/JSt) 15
24 Union Jack (MBa/MM) 45
25 Quicksilver (PR/TA) 15
26 Scarlet Witch (PR/TA) 15
27 Havok (JLe/TA) 20
28 Iron Fist (MBa/MM) 15
29 Adam Warlock (AAd) 65
30 Wonder Man (PR/TA) 25
31 Sasquatch (EL) 25
32 Firestar (AAd) 15
33 Death's Head (AAd) 20
34 Speedball (AAd) 20
35 USAgent (PR/TA) 15
36 Banshee (LW) 20
37 Meggan (AAd) 25
38 Jubilee (MM) 35
39 Ghost Rider (AAd) 75
40 Beast (EL) 25
41 Invisible Woman (PR/TA) 20
42 Rogue (AAd) 55
43 She-Hulk (AAd) 55
44 Doctor Strange (AAd) 15
45 Silver Surfer (PR/TA) 45
46 Storm (AAd) 25
47 Archangel (MBa/JS3) 20
48 Thor (RF/JS3) 25
49 Quasar (PR/TA) 15
50 Wolverine (AAd) 75
51 Cyclops (RLm/JS3) 20
52 Nick Fury (BBl) 15
53 Hulk (AAd) 25
54 Captain America (AAd) 25

Marvel Universe II
© Marvel Entertainment Group, Inc.

Super-Villains
55 Kingpin (EL) 15
56 Sabretooth (JLe/TA) 30
57 Magneto (RLm/JS3) 55
58 Venom (LW) 75
59 Galactus (AAd) 60
60 Mandarin (LW) 45
61 Chameleon (LW) 45
62 Super Skrull (RLm/JS3) 35
63 Grim Reaper (PR/TA) 25
64 Mojo (MM) 15
65 Fin Fang Foom (AAd) 25
66 Jigsaw (MBa/MM) 15
67 Tombstone (LW) 15
68 Ulik (AAd) 40
69 Baron Strucker (MBa/MM) 15
70 Mysterio (SLi) 15
71 Sauron (AAd) 15
72 Annihilus (AAd) 25
73 Rhino (EL) 15
74 Absorbing Man (AAd) 15
75 Doctor Octopus (EL) 15
76 Baron Mordo (MM) 15
77 Saracen (MBa/MM) 15
78 Nebula (PR/TA) 15
79 Puma (LW) 15
80 Deathwatch (MBa/JSt) 15
81 Kang (MM) 15
82 Blackout (MBa/MM) 15
83 Calypso (BBl) 40
84 Ultron (AAd) 35
85 Thanos (AAd) 80
86 Hobgoblin (EL) 20
87 Lizard (EL) 15
88 Doctor Doom (AAd) 15
89 Loki (RF/JS3) 15
90 Red Skull (RLm/JS3) 15

Arch-Enemies
91 Spider-Man vs. Venom (MBa/JSt) .25
92 Fantastic Four vs. Skrulls (RLm/JS3) 15
93 Wolverine vs. Sabretooth (MBa/JS3) 25
94 Silver Surfer vs. Galactus (RLm/JS3) 25
95 Daredevil vs. Elektra (AAd) 30
96 Avengers vs. Kang (SLi) 15
97 Human Torch vs. Sub-Mariner (MBa/JSt) 20
98 Spider-Man vs. Hobgoblin (MM) . .25
99 Capt. America vs. Baron Zemo (AAd) 15
100 Punisher vs. Jigsaw (MBa/JSt) . .35
101 X-Factor vs. Apocalypse (RLm/JS3) 30
102 Punisher vs. Kingpin (MBa/JSt) . .20
103 Thing vs. Hulk (AAd) 35
104 Daredevil vs. Bullseye 25
105 Spider-Man vs. Dr. Octopus (EL) .15
106 X-Men vs. Sentinels (MBa/JS3) . .15
107 Fantastic Four vs. Galactus(SLi) .25
108 Wolverine vs. Hulk (EL) 25
109 Ghost Rider vs. Deathwatch (MBa/MM) 30
110 Dr. Strange vs. Baron Mordo (LW) 15
111 Nick Fury vs. Baron Strucker (SLi) 15
112 Spider-Man vs. Lizard (SLi) 15
113 Silver Surfer vs. Thanos (RLm/JS3) 45
114 Avengers vs. Ultron (MBa/MM) . .15
115 Capt. America vs. Red Skull (RLm/JS3) 15
116 Daredevil vs. Punisher (LW) 40
117 X-Men vs. Marauders (SLi) 40
118 Iron Man vs. Mandarin (JR2/AW) .40
119 Hulk vs. Leader (LW) 15
120 Thor vs. Loki (AAd) 40
121 Spider-Man vs. J. Jonah Jameson (JR) 15
122 Thor vs. Ulik (AAd) 15
123 Silver Surfer vs. Mephisto (RLm) .20
124 Fantastic Four vs. Dr. Doom (RLm/JS3) 15
125 X-Men vs. Magneto (LW) 30
126 Daredevil vs. Kingpin (JR2/AW) .20

Marvel Universe II
© Marvel Entertainment Group, Inc.

Weapons
127 Captain America's Shield (RLm/JS3) 15
128 Thor's Hammer (RF/JS3) 25

129 Daredevil's Billy Club (JR2/AW) .25
130 Ultimate Nullifer (RLm/JS3) .... .15
131 Spider-Man's Web-Shooters (JR) .... .15
132 Punisher's Arsenal (LW) .... .25
133 Iron Man's Armor (JR2/AW) ... .15
134 Infinity Gauntlet (RLm/JS3) .... .85
135 Quasar's Quantum Bands (MM) .40
136 Dr. Octopus's Arms (JR) .... .15
137 Mandarin's Rings (MBa/JS3) ... .25
138 Wolverine's Claws (JLe/TA) ... .35

Legends

139 Captain Marvel (MBa/MM) .... .25
140 Bucky (MBa/MM) .... .25
141 Green Goblin (JR) .... .25
142 Original Ghost Rider (Bob Budiansky/TA) .... .40
143 Kraven (SLi) .... .25
144 Dark Phoenix (BBI) .... .30

Rookies

145 Darkhawk (MM) .... .90
146 Sleepwalker (BBi) .... .50
147 Rage (PR/TA) .... .55
148 X-Force (TMo) 2.00
149 New Fantastic Four (AAd) .... .80

Teams

150 Fantastic Four (AAd) .... .25
151 Avengers (PR/TA) .... .15
152 Avengers West Coast (PR/TA) . .15
153 X-Men (MBa/MM) .... .75
154 X-Factor (MBa/JS3) .... .50
155 Excalibur (MBa/MM) .... .25
156 New Warriors (MBa/JSt) ...... .50
157 Masters of Evil (MBa/MM) .... .15
158 Marauders (MBa/MM) .... .75

Power Ratings

159 Strength/Speed .... .25
160 Agility/Stamina .... .25
161 Durability/Intelligence .... .25
162 Checklist .... .50

Marvel Universe III © Marvel Entertainment Group, Inc.

MARVEL UNIVERSE SERIES III

Impel (1992)

The basic design for 1992 was a galactic background with a window to the real world, through which the character "flies." The backs have purple stripes, top and bottom, with text in the center, plus a close-up picture. The background color for the center varies from card to card and the holograms are in different colors. The tin boxed set contains one extra card, but it's just a "Power Ratings" card with no art. It does have all five holograms, and all 200 cards in a nice looking tin-litho box.

Set: 200 cards 20.00
Tin box set (10,000 made) 60.00

Holograms

H-1 Hulk (SK) 9.00
H-2 Thing (WS) 7.00
H-3 Wolverine (KJa/BVa) 10.00
H-4 Venom (RLm) 9.00
H-5 Ghost Rider (LW) 10.00

Prototype Promo Cards:

Venom (Advance Comics #40 promo hologram) 8.00
1 Spider-Man (MBa/LMa) 3.00
34 Invisible Woman (PR/TA) 2.50
37 Captain America (RLm/TA) 2.50
Set: 3 cards in clear cello pack 9.00
These three cards have "prototype" printed on the back over the card text. They were distributed at shows in clear cello packs.
Diamond Previews March 1992 uncut insert sheet (Human Torch, Silver Surfer, Spider-Man, Thanos) ... 10.00
Diamond Inserts, cut, each 2.00

Mini Press 4 card sheet 3.00
Pack: 12 cards 1.50
Four different wrappers

CARD CHECKLIST

Super Heroes

1 Spider-Man (EL) .... .25
2 Quasar (GCa/Harry Candelario) .. .10
3 Sleepwalker (BBI) .... .10
4 Gambit (LW) .... .30
5 Cannonball (RLm/TA) .... .10
6 Beast (JS) .... .10
7 Quicksilver (RLm/AM) .... .10
8 Weapon Omega (TMo) .... .20
9 Dr. Strange (SK) .... .10
10 Major Victory (JV) .... .10
11 Phoenix (KM) .... .10
12 Black Widow (LW) .... .10
13 Hulk (KJa/JP) .... .15
14 Sunfire (JJ/TA) .... .10
15 Silver Surfer (RLm/TA) .... .15

Marvel Universe III Diamond promos © Marvel Entertainment Group, Inc.

16 She-Hulk (MS) .... .10
17 Captain Britain (JS) .... .10
18 Cage (DT) .... .10
19 Domino (BBI) .... .15
20 Daredevil (LW) .... .20
21 Morbius (RoW) .... .10
22 Nightcrawler (SK) .... .15
23 Black Panther (DT) .... .10
24 Ant-Man (PR/TA) .... .10
25 Ghost Rider (MT) .... .15
26 Darkhawk (MM) .... .10
27 Iceman (LW) .... .10
28 Punisher (JR2) .... .20
29 Wolfsbane (RLm) .... .10
30 Storm (LW) .... .10
31 Wonder Man (JJ/TA) .... .10
32 Moon Knight (DT) .... .10
33 Mr. Fantastic (PR/TA) .... .10
34 Invisible Woman (PR/TA) ...... .10
35 Shadowcat (MM) .... .10
36 Warlock (RLm/TA) .... .15
37 Captain America (RLm/TA) ..... .10
38 Wolverine (MS) .... .25
39 Namor (EL) .... .10
40 Nick Fury (LW) .... .10
41 Professor X (Karl Alstaetter/JLe) . .15
42 Shatterstar (RLm/TA) .... .10
43 Multiple Man (RLm/AM) .... .10
44 Blaze (MT) .... .10
45 Deathlok (DCw) .... .10
46 Colossus (Michael Bair) .... .15
47 Meggan (JS) .... .10
48 Thor (RF) .... .10
49 Namorita (KM/TA) .... .10
50 Cable (MT) .... .25
51 Psylocke (PR/TA) .... .20
52 Warpath (MT) .... .10
53 Nomad (S.C.Hawbaker) .... .10
54 Polaris (RLm/TA) .... .10
55 Charlie-27 (JV) .... .10
56 Thing (PR/TA) .... .10
57 Longshot (RLm/TA) .... .10
58 Human Torch (PR/TA) .... .10
59 Night Thrasher (AS/BVa) ...... .10
60 Siryn (AS/BVa) .... .10
61 Nova (EL) .... .10
62 Iron Man (PR/TA) .... .10
63 Archangel (MS/Harry Candelario) .20
64 Rogue (MS) .... .20
65 Silver Sable (RF) .... .10
66 Jean Grey (MS/Harry Candelario) .15
67 Feral (KM/TA) .... .10
68 Cyclops (LW) .... .15
69 Starhawk (JV) .... .10
70 Havok (JMd/Harry Candelario) .. .15

Team-Ups

71 Spider-Man & Human Torch (SB) .10
72 Spider-Man & Ghost Rider (JS) . .10
73 Spider-Man & Punisher (JR2) ... .10
74 Spider-Man & Wolverine (JR2) .. .10
75 Wolverine & Captain America (LW) .... .10
76 Wolverine & Hulk (KM/TA) ..... .10
77 Wolverine & Cable (TMo) ...... .10
78 Dr. Doom & Magneto (PR/TA) .. .10
79 Ghost Rider & Blaze (MT) ..... .10
80 Captain America & Nomad (RLm/TA) .... .10
81 Spider-Man & Darkhawk (AS/Kieth Williams) .... .10
82 Human Torch & Iceman (PR/TA) .10
83 Captain America & USAgent (RLm/TA) .... .10
84 Wolverine & Daredevil (LW) .... .10
85 Vision & Scarlet Witch (BBI) .... .10
86 Punisher & Deathlok (MM) ..... .10
87 Thor Corps (RF/JSt) .... .10
88 Wolverine/Punisher & Ghost Rider (Mike Harris) .... .10
89 Wonder Man & Beast (JJ/TA) ... .10
90 Ghost Rider & Daredevil (MT) ... .10
91 Wolverine & Havok (WS) ...... .10
92 Punisher & Daredevil (JR2) .... .10
93 Daredevil & Black Widow (LW) .. .10
94 Punisher & Captain America (Mike Harris) .... .10
95 Spider-Man & Sleepwalker (BBI) . .10
96 Power Man & Iron Fist (DT) .... .10
97 Spider-Man & Daredevil (Mike Harris) .... .10
98 Hulk & Thing (PR/TA) .... .10
99 Red Skull & Baron Zemo (RLm/TA).10
100 Juggernaut & Black Tom Cassidy (PR/TA) .... .10

Super-Villains

101 Abomination (KJa/JP) .... .10
102 Zodiak (MT) .... .10
103 Apocalypse (WS) .... .10
104 Sphinx (AS/BVa) .... .10
105 Destroyer (RF) .... .10
106 Red Skull (RLm/TA) .... .10
107 Puppet Master (PR/TA) .... .10
108 Venom (EL) .... .30
109 Diablo (TMo) .... .10
110 The Rose (AS/BVa) .... .10
111 Dr. Doom (PR/TA) .... .15
112 Magneto (KJa/BVa) .... .20
113 Necrom (DCw) .... .10
114 Green Goblin (SB) .... .15
115 Dracula (RoW) .... .10
116 Sauron (MT) .... .15
117 Cyber (SK) .... .15
118 Mephisto (RF) .... .10
119 Mad Thinker (PR/TA) .... .10

Marvel Universe III
© Marvel Entertainment Group, Inc.

120 Carnage (RLm/TA) .... .25
121 Hobgoblin (AS/TA) .... .15
122 Gideon (RCa) .... .10
123 White Queen (Mike Harris) .... .15
124 Omega Red (JJ/TA) .... .15
125 Maelstrom (GCa/Harry Candelario) .... .10
126 Thanos (RLm/TA) .... .15
127 Zarrko (RF) .... .10
128 Magus (RLm/TA) .... .10
129 Sabretooth (MS) .... .30
130 Kingpin (LW) .... .10
131 Silvermane (AS/BVa) .... .10
132 Cardiac (EL) .... .10
133 Blackheart (BBI) .... .10
134 Terrax (JJ/TA) .... .10
135 Mr. Sinister (WS) .... .15
136 Slug (RLm/TA) .... .10
137 Hate Monger (MM) .... .10
138 Crossbones (RLm/TA) .... .10
139 Shiva (MS) .... .10
140 Blackout (MT) .... .10

Rookies
141 Pantheon (KJa/JP) .... .10
142 Slapstick (James Fry) .... .10
143 Cerise (DCw) .... .10
144 Darkhold Redeemers (RCa) ... .10
145 Strong Guy (RLm) .... .10
146 Bishop (Karl Alstaetter/JLe) ... .25
147 Silhouette (BBI) .... .10
148 Kylun (DCw) .... .10
149 Talon (JV) .... .10

Cosmic Beings
150 Collector (MT) .... .10
151 Galactus (TMo) .... .10
152 Watcher (PR/TA) .... .10
153 Living Tribunal (PR/TA) ...... .10
154 Ego (PR/TA) .... .10
155 Eternity (PT/TA) .... .10
156 Celestials (RF) .... .10
157 Death (PR/TA) .... .10
158 Stranger (PR/TA) .... .10
159 In-Betweener (RLm/TA) ...... .10
160 Epoch (GCa/Harry Candelario) . .10

Origins
161 Hulk (SB) .... .10
162 Spider-Man (AS/BVa) .... .10
163 Silver Surfer (RLm) .... .10
164 Wolverine (TMo) .... .10
165 Iron Man (JR) .... .10
166 Captain America (JR) .... .10
167 Ghost Rider (TM) .... .10
168 Daredevil (JR) .... .10
169 Fantastic Four (PR/TA) .... .10
170 Thor (RF) .... .10

Teams
171 Avengers (SEp) .... .15
172 X-Force (Karl Alstaetter/JLe) ... .20
173 X-Factor (RLm/AM) .... .15
174 New Warriors (PR/TA) .... .15
175 Alpha Flight (TMo) .... .15
176 Avengers West Coast (TMo) ... .15
177 Nightstalkers (MT) .... .10
178 Guardians of the Galaxy (JV) .. .20
179 X-Men Gold (KJa/BVa) .... .25
180 Excalibur (TMo) .... .15
181 Fantastic Four (PR/TA) .... .15
182 X-Men Blue (JKa/BVa) .... .25
183 Serpent Society (RLm/JP) .... .10

Wars
184 X-tinction Agenda (KJa/BVa) ... .10
185 Evolutionary War (KJa/BVa) ... .10
186 Operation Galactic Storm (SEp) .10
187 Secret Wars (SEp) .... .10
188 Inferno (KJa/JP) .... .10
189 Infinity Gauntlet (RLm/JP) ..... .10
190 Kree/Skrull War (RLm/JP) ..... .15
191 Atlantis Attacks (RLm/JP) ..... .10

Milestones
192 I Married a Skrull (PR/TA) .... .10
193 Days of Future Past (BBI) ..... .15
194 All Hulks Unite (KJa/BVa) ..... .10
195 Dark Phoenix Saga (BBI) ...... .10
196 The Coming of Galactus (SEp) . .10
197 Death of Gwen Stacy (JR) .... .15
198 Fall of the Kingpin (LW) ...... .10
199 Wedding of Spider-Man (PR/TA) .10
200 Checklist .... .10

MARVEL UNIVERSE SERIES IV

SkyBox (1993)

This set is actually named Marvel Universe or Marvel 1993, but is refered to as Marvel Universe IV by everybody. The first 135 cards form super-panels when assembled in standard 9-pocket pages, but each card contains the named character, so it's really the background that is shared. We have included names for the super-panels from a preliminary checklist for the series. The backs are multi-colored and contain a large close-up picture, with power ratings, but little text. The unsolved mysteries don't look like the other cards. They have a question mark on the front, with the picture and the title and the backs have a small picture and text in a white box with a question mark background. The backs of the famous battles cards have angry faces of the contestants on the right and left with text describing the battle in the middle. This is a nice looking set of cards, but not as nice as Marvel Masterpieces, so it suffered by comparison. The really hot card was the 3-D hologram, which is scarce. It has a black back, so all the information is on the front, in the hologram. It's a lot like the X-Men Series II 3-D hologram but has a better picture. The Marvel 2099 foil cards form a super-panel, but their distinctive red foil background has just a light line drawing, so there's nothing more to see by putting the cards together. Every collector we know stores bonus cards in individual card holders anyway, not in 9-pocket card pages. The Silver Sable promo card has a yellow back with a red line frame.

Marvel Universe IV © Marvel Entertainment Group, Inc.

Set: 180 cards 20.00

Marvel 2099 Foil Cards (1:10) (RL/AW)
1 Doom 2099 .... 6.00
2 Vulture 2099 .... 6.00
3 Ravage 2099 .... 6.00
4 Fearmaster 6.00
5 Spider-Man 2099 .... 7.00
6 Punisher 2099 .... 7.00
7 Specialist 6.00
8 Dethstryk 6.00
9 Tiger Wylde 6.00

Hologram (1:180)
H-IV Spider-Man vs. Venom (BBI) . 75.00

Promo Cards
0 Deathlok Promo Card (CBG) 4.50
Silver Sable Promo 3.50
Pack: 10 cards 1.25
Four different wrappers

CARD CHECKLIST

Tech Knights (SBt)
1 Hulk .... .15
2 Moon Knight .... .10
3 Siege .... .10
4 Deadzone .... .10
5 Wild Pack .... .10
6 Silver Sable .... .10
7 Doc Samson .... .10
8 Deathlok .... .10
9 Moses Magnum .... .10

Galactic Gladiators (RLm/Tom Christopher)
10 Warlock .... .15
11 Silver Surfer .... .15
12 Quasar .... .10
13 Starhawk .... .10
14 Galactus .... .10
15 Goddess .... .10
16 Thanos .... .15
17 Morg .... .10
18 Drax .... .10

New Warriors (DaR/LMa)
19 Nova .... .10
20 Firestar .... .10
21 Cardinal .... .10
22 Namorita .... .10
23 Speedball .... .10
24 Turbo .... .10
25 Rage .... .10
26 Night Thrasher .... .10
27 Darkhawk .... .10

Mutant Mania (JMd/MFm)
28 Deadpool .... .20
29 Cannonball .... .15
30 Slayback .... .10
31 Sabretooth .... .20
32 Shatterstar .... .15
33 Apocalypse .... .15
34 Mr. Sinister .... .15
35 Cable .... .20
36 Stryfe .... .20

Multi-National Mutants (BPe/DPs)
37 Guardian .... .10
38 Micromax .... .10
39 Wildheart .... .10
40 Captain Britain .... .10
41 Phoenix .... .10
42 Nightcrawler .... .15
43 Havok .... .15
44 Psylocke .... .15
45 Strong Guy .... .15

Beings From Beyond (SLi)
46 Dr. Strange .... .10
47 Dormammu .... .10
48 Beta Ray Bill .... .10
49 Loki .... .10
50 Cobweb .... .10
51 Blackheart .... .10
52 Sleepwalker .... .10
53 Thor .... .10
54 Hellstorm .... .15

Web of Spider-Man (RLm/TA)
55 Venom .... .20
56 Demogoblin .... .10
57 Carnage .... .20
58 Hobgoblin .... .15
59 Spider-Man .... .20
60 Cardiac .... .10
61 Rhino .... .10
62 Shock .... .10
63 Daredevil .... .20

West Coast Warriors (JJ/SDR)

64 Scarlet Witch .10
65 Spider-Woman .10
66 Splice .10
67 Iron Man .10
68 Wonder Man .10
69 War Machine .15
70 Namor .10
71 Tiger Shark .10
72 U.S.Agent .10
Fantastic Four plus five (MM)
73 Mr. Fantastic .15
74 Invisible Woman .15
75 Human Torch .15
76 Lyja .10
77 Occulus .10
78 Molecule Man .10
79 Doctor Doom .10
80 Thing .15
81 Klaw .10
Urban Guerrillas (LW)
82 She-Hulk .10
83 Punisher .10
84 Falcon .10
85 Hardcore .10
86 Nomad .10
87 Terror, Inc. .10
88 Iron Fist .15
89 Cage .10
90 Scarecrow .10

Marvel Universe IV
© Marvel Entertainment Group

Avengers Assembled (RF & TP)
91 Black Knight .10
92 Crystal .10
93 Sersi .10
94 Thunderstrike .15
95 Captain America .10
96 Hercules .10
97 Bloodaxe .10
98 Red Skull .10
99 Proctor .10
Midnight Sons (Michael Bair)
100 Deathwatch .10
101 Lilith .10
102 Heart Attack .10
103 Blaze .10
104 Basilisk .10
105 Ghost Rider .15
106 Darkhold Redeemers .10
107 Morbius .10
108 Nightstalkers .10
X-Men (ATi)
109 Storm .15
110 Archangel .15
111 Beast .15
112 Rogue .15
113 Magneto .15
114 Gambit .15
115 Cyclops .15
116 Wolverine .20
117 Bishop .20
Alien Races (TMo)
118 Ovoids .10
119 Brood .10
120 Titans .10
121 Badoon .10
122 Asgardians .10
123 Skrulls .10
124 Shi'ar .10
125 Kree .10
126 Rigellians .10
Britain's Best (LSh/ALa)
127 Black Aze .10
128 Techno-Wizards .10
129 Motormouth .10
130 Bloodseed .10
131 Dark Angel .10
132 Wild Thing .10
133 Die-Cut .10
134 Death's Head II .10
135 Death Metal .10
Unsolved Mysteries
136 The Origin of Wolverine (GP) .25
137 The Origin of Cable (GP) .25
138 The Face of Darkhawk (Ian Akin) .10
139 The Origin of Ghost Rider (PB/Bruce Patterson) .10
140 The Fate of the X-Men (KJa/BVa) .15
141 The Face of Doctor Doom (PB/Bruce Patterson) .10
142 The Sixth Member of the Infinity Watch (ANi/AV) .10
143 The Secret of Spider-Man's Parents (AS/JRu) .15
144 The Origin of Nightcrawler (KJa/BVa) .10
Famous Battles
145 Spider-Man vs Carnage(AS/JRu) .15
146 Cable vs. Stryfe (PB/Bruce Patterson) .15
147 Ghost Rider vs. Lilith (GI/JP) .10
148 Silver Surfer vs. Morg (PO/Mark McKenna) .10
149 Wolverine vs. Sabretooth (JKa/BVa) .20
150 Thor vs. Loki (GP) .25
151 War Machine (PB/Bruce Patterson) .15
152 Spider-Man vs. Venom (AS/JRu) .20
153 Punisher vs. Thorn (GI/JP) .10
154 X-Cutioner's Song (KJa/BVa) .10
155 Spider-Man vs. Sinister Six (AS/JRu) .10
156 Infinity War (KJa/BVa) .10
157 Spirits of Venom (AS/JRu) .20
158 Hulk vs. Leader (KJa/BVa) .10
159 Ghost Rider vs. Blackout (PB/Bruce Patterson) .10
160 Dr. Strange vs. Dormammu (GI/JP) .10
161 Wolverine vs. Cyber (KJa/BVa) .10
162 Captain America vs. Crossbones (PO/Mark McKenna) .10
163 Punisher vs. Jigsaw (ANi/AV) .10
164 Wolverine vs. Venom (KJa/BVa) .10
165 Spider-Man vs. Juggernaut (AS/JRu) .10
166 Darkhawk vs. Evil Hawk (PB/Bruce Patterson) .10
167 X-Force vs. Brotherhood of Evil Mutants (ANi/AV) .10
168 Daredevil vs. Typhoid Mary (GI/JP) .10
169 Spider-Man vs. Kingpin(AS/JRu) .10
170 Thor vs. Bloodaxe (GI/JP) .10
171 Warlock vs. Man-Beast (PO/Mark McKenna) .10
172 Ghost Rider vs. Blaze (PB/Bruce Patterson) .10
173 Hulk vs. Hulk (KJa/BVa) .10
174 Fantastic Four vs. Secret Defenders (JKa/BVa) .10
175 Spider-Man vs. Cardiac(AS/JRu) .10
176 Punisher vs. Ghost Rider (ANi/AV) .10
177 Wolverine vs. Omega Red (KJa/BVa) .10
178 Cable vs. Deadpool (ANi/AV) .10
179 Hulk vs. X-Factor (KJa/BVa) .10
180 Checklist .10

Marvel Universe Inaugural Edition (Flair '94) © Marvel Entertainment Group, Inc.

MARVEL UNIVERSE INAUGURAL EDITION

Fleer/Flair (1994)

These cards feature a six color printing process and super high quality throughout. The original artwork is computer colorized and the card names and Flair logo are gold foil stamped on 24-point laminated paperboard. Each pack comes in a gold foil box. There is a numbering error: no card number 6 exists. It should have been Iron Man, which was numbered "8" as was the real card number 8 – Vulture vs. Spider-Man. In addition, cards #135 to #149 are not numbered at all, except on the checklist. There are only 24 "packs" in a box and you can't make a full set from one box; we came up missing about 15 cards. You will have a lot of nice duplicates to trade with your friend – that's why they call them "trading cards!" ***Please note*** *that this set came out just as this book was being completed and thus the prices given below are very preliminary and will undoubtedly change by the time you read this. We expect the cards in the set to have individual prices which vary widely from card to card. Still, this is one of the sets you* ***must own*** *to be a legitimate comics card collector.*

Set: 150 cards 75.00
Nine card promo sheet (Advance or Previews) 1.00
Three/Four card promo sheet 5.00
The promo sheet has the series logo plus the card art for Bone Claws, Phoenix & Maximum Carnage on the front. The back has the card art for Body Slide, Spider-Man 2099, Thunderstrike & The New Ghost Rider. There are two slightly different variants: on one the "Ships June 1994" is printed on the card and on the other this text is on a paste-on sticker.
Powerblast (1:2)
1 Cable 7.00
2 Cyclops 7.00
3 Iron Man 7.00
4 Magneto 7.00
5 Phoenix 7.00
6 Storm 7.00
7 Venom 7.00
8 Wolverine 7.00
9 Ghost Rider 7.00
10 Punisher 7.00
11 Captain America 7.00
12 Gambit 7.00
13 Thor 7.00
14 Silver Surfer 7.00
15 Spider-Man 7.00
16 Deadpool 7.00
17 Invisible Woman 7.00
18 Dr. Doom 7.00
Pack: 10 cards in Box 5.00
Four different boxes. Cello wrapped outside and inside.

CARD CHECKLIST
1 The Thing .50
2 The Incredible Hulk .50
3 With Great Power .50
4 God of Thunder .50
5 Spider-Man .50
(6) not used, was to be:
8 Iron Man .50
7 Hulk vs. Thing .50
8 Vulture vs. Spider-Man .50
9 Dr. Octopus .50
10 Xavier .50
11 Avengers .50
12 Dr. Strange .50
13 Quicksilver .50
14 Man Without Fear .50

Marvel Universe Inaugural Edition (Flair '94) © Marvel Entertainment Group, Inc.

15 Scorpion vs. Spider-Man 50
16 Captain America 50
17 Daredevil vs. Sub-Mariner 50
18 Invisible Woman 50
19 Sentinels 50
20 The Coming of Galactus 50
21 Power Cosmic 50
22 Spider-Man vs. Green Goblin 50
23 Rhino vs. Spider-Man 50
24 Mary Jane 50
25 Dr. Doom 50
26 Warlock 50
27 Behold the Vision 50
28 Mephisto 50
29 Morbius 50
30 The Original Ghost Rider 50
31 Thanos 50
32 Death of Gwen Stacy 50
33 The Punisher 50
34 Wolverine vs. Hulk 50
35 The Scarlet Witch 50
36 Invaders 50
37 The Black Cat 50
38 White Queen 50
39 She-Hulk 50
40 Moon Knight 50
41 Days of Future Past 50
42 Elektra 50
43 Death of Elektra 50
44 Hobgoblin 50
45 Northstar 50
46 Beat Ray Bill 50
47 The Trial of Mr. Fantastic 50
48 The Black Costume 50
49 Puma vs. Spidey 50
50 Silver Sable Inc. 50
51 Iceman 50
52 Apocalypse Now 50
53 Deadly Enemies 50
54 Nightcrawler 50
55 Creation of Archangel 50
56 Mr. Sinister 50
57 The Wedding 50
58 Jubilee 50
59 Armor Wars 50
60 Tombstone 50
61 Venom 50
62 Typhoid Mary 50
63 Mr. Fix-it 50
64 Speedball 50
65 Cap. vs. Cap 50
66 Quasar 50
67 Cosmic Spider-Man 50
68 Nomad 50
69 Thanos 50
70 Bodyslide 50
71 Ghost Rider 50
72 Creation of Deathlok 50
73 The New Nova 50
74 Cable vs. Wolverine 50
75 Gambit 50
76 X-tinction Agenda 50
77 The New Hulk 50
78 Deadpool 50
79 Shatterstar 50
80 X-Force 50
81 Johnny Blaze 50
82 Child of the Future 50
83 X-Factor 50
84 Blue & Gold 50
85 Bishop .50
86 Omega Red vs. Wolverine 50
87 Punisher vs. The Mob 50
88 Carnage 50
89 Cage 50
90 War Machine 50
91 Death of Mariko 50
92 Spider-Slayers 50
93 Nightstalkers 50
94 Spider-Man 2099 50
95 Hulk Leads the Pantheon 50
96 Stryfe .50
97 Mirror Images 50
98 Wonder Man 50
99 Doom 2099 50

Marvel Universe (Flair '94)
© Marvel Entertainment Group, Inc.

100 Lethal Protector 50
101 Punisher 2099 50
102 Green Goblin 50
103 Alternate Visions 50
104 Maximum Carnage 50
105 Namor 50
106 Random 50
107 Psylocke 50
108 Psi-Lord 50
109 Thunderstrike 50
110 Infinity Crusade 50
111 Hulk 2099 50
112 Cable Returns 50
113 The Death of Illyana 50
114 Gambit & Rogue 50
115 Vengeance 50
116 Daredevil 50
117 The New Ravage 50
118 Wolverine Defeated 50
119 Bone Claws 50
120 Magneto Returns 50
121 Xavier vs. Magneto 50
122 Colossus Defects 50
123 Exodus 50
124 Bloodhawk 50
125 Zarathos 50
126 Final Conflict 50
127 Centurios 50
128 The Thor Corps. 50
129 Sabretooth Surrenders 50
130 Venom: The Madness 50
131 Strange 50
132 Suicide Run 50
133 Legacy 50
134 Justice 50

Maximum Carnage

(135) Carnage 50
(136) Venom 50
(137) Spider-Demon 50
(138) Shriek 50
(139) Spider-Man 50
(140) Venom Lives 50

Mutant Genesis

(141) Cyclops 50
(142) Jean Grey 50
(143) Bishop 50
(144) Warpath 50
(145) Rogue 50
(146) Domino 50
(147) Boom Boom 50
(148) Wolverine 50
(149) Havok 50
150 Checklist 5.00

Masters of the Universe © Mattel, Inc.

MASTERS OF THE UNIVERSE

Topps (1984)

These cards have comic style pictures, with word balloons, which tells a story titled "Like Father, Like Daughter" about Teela, Man-At-Arms and He-Man in a spectacular battle against Trap Jaw's Serpentoids and, naturally, Skeletor. You will not be surprised to find out that 1) they win, 2) Skeletor vows revenge, and 3) Teela doesn't figure out that He-Man is Prince Adam. The cards have a red border and are on Topps cardboard stock. The backs have the storyline on a scroll design with a blue border. There are 21 stickers (front peel) with a picture on a white background and puzzle backs. They form a 3 x 3 card picture and a 5 x 2 card picture. The first two stickers have the preview pictures. Masters of the Universe was primarily a toy line, and the cards have Mattel's copyright. There was also a comic book series, an animated series and a live action movie. Card sets based on the toy line and the movie are omitted.

Set: 88 cards, 21 stickers 12.00

Pack: 10 cards, 1 sticker 1.00
Four different wrappers

CARD CHECKLIST

1 Welcome to Eternia! 12
2 Like Father, Like Daughter! 12
3 Within These Walls of Evil... 12
4 Monstrous Alliance! 12
5 Plan of Skeletor 12
6 Duo For Destruction! 12
7 Home of the Brave 12
8 A New Invention! 12
9 Gripe of Teela 12
10 The Adventure Begins! 12
11 Commanding the Mystic Forces! . .12
12 Metamorphosis! 12
13 Trusted Ally! 12
14 Enter...Battle Cat! 12
15 The Road to Castle Grayskull! . . .12

16 Summoned to the Castle! .12
17 Keeper of the Castle! .12
18 The Plan of Skeletor Revealed! .12
19 Three Against Eternia! .12
20 Final Words of Warning! .12
21 Fixing the Laser Lasso .12
22 No Adventure for Teela? .12
23 He-Man is Coming! .12
24 The Monster-Maker! .12
25 Monarch of Menace! .12
26 A Friend in Need! .12
27 The Lasso Test .12
28 Experiment: Successful! .12
29 Poor Orko! .12
30 Dangerous Decision! .12
31 Orko...Free at Last! .12
32 Approaching the Fortress .12
33 Two Determined Heroes! .12
34 Attack from the Sky! .12
35 Reeling from the Attack .12
36 Device of Doom! .12
37 The Assault Continues! .12
38 The Plan to Capture Man-at-arms! .12
39 Power of the Bolts .12
40 Master of Evil Creatures! .12
41 Man-at-arms ...Helpless! .12
42 Beast Man Triumphant! .12
43 Disarmed! .12
44 And Now... Defeat He-Man! .12
45 Machine Madness! .12
46 Nearer to Danger...! .12
47 Metallic Monster! .12
48 The Man and the Challenge! .12
49 A Crushing Defeat? .12
50 Man Against Monster! .12
51 He-Man Wins the First Round! .12
52 Smashed Serpentoid! .12
53 No Turning Back! .12
54 The Evil Ones .12
55 Monsters on the March! .12
56 He-Man Strikes Back! .12
57 The Titans Clash! .12
58 Sneak Attack! .12
59 Strength of He-Man .12
60 Surrounded! .12
61 Teela to the Rescue! .12
62 Moment of Triumph! .12
63 Power of the Lasso .12
64 Snagged! .12
65 In the Right Hands! .12
66 Defeat of the Serpentoids .12
67 Storming the Fortress .12
68 Mighty Weapon of Teela .12
69 Bested by our Heroes! .12
70 Moment of Truth .12
71 We're Not Through Yet! .12
72 Outfoxed by Teela! .12
73 A Cool Reception! .12
74 Destroying the Machine of Trap Jaw .12
75 To Rescue a Warrior! .12
76 Last Minute Rescue! .12
77 Deadly Device .12
78 Bravery Wins the Day! .12
79 Our Friends Re-united! .12
80 Until Next Time?–?! .12
81 Warning of Skeletor .12
82 Courage: A Family Tradition! .12
83 Plight of Orko .12
84 Look Who's Here! .12
85 A Royal Put-Down! .12
86 If Only Teela Knew...! .12
87 Teela Continues .12
88 Checklist .12

Action Stickers

1 thru 10 untitled, each .12
11 Guardians of Eternia .12
12 Skeletor .12
13 Teela .12
14 Man-At-Arms .12
15 Man-E-Faces .12
16 Skeletor & Panthor .12
17 Sorceress .12
18 Ram-Man .12
19 He-Man & Battle Cat .12
20 Teela .12
21 Evil-Lyn .12

MAXIMUM FORCE

SkyBox (1993)

Promo card for a card set which was originally scheduled for December 1993. It had not appeared as of June 1994.

Blitz Prototype Card (SBs) 3.00

The Maxx © Sam Keith

THE MAXX

Topps (1994)

These cards by Sam Kieth star The Maxx, "an avenger who is even more brutal than the criminals he fights," and Julie Winters, a student who becomes "a feral blond goddess." They move back and forth between the primative Outback (Pangaea) and the City battling evil foes. The Maxx is a huge purple killing machine, but Julie Winters is cute and the cards chronicle their exploits. The first four etched foil cards are in the packs. The sixth one was distributed as a promo card and there is no fifth one that we know of. None have titles. All have the same back, except for the number.

Set: 90 cards (SK) 12.50

Etched Foil (1:18)

1 (Julie Winters) 7.00
2 (Queen of the Leopard Women) 7.00
3 (The Maxx) 7.00
4 (The Maxx & The ISZ) 7.00
5 not produced
6 untitled promo of The Maxx 2.00
Promo Card 1.50
See also Image Cards for comics promos
Promo sheet w/card (Previews August 1993) 2.00
Pack: 8 cards 1.00

CARD CHECKLIST

1 Header card .15
2 The Seedbringer .15
3 The Maxx: Tortured Hero of the Streets .15
4 Julie Winters: Freelance Social Worker .15
5 Julie Winters: Queen of the Leopard Women .15
6 The ISZ: Playful, Terrible Guardians of the Plains .15
7 The Maxx: Master of Two Worlds .15
8 Mr. Gone: Nearly a Sorcerer .15
9 Mr. Gone and His City .15
10 The Walking Mountains .15
11 The Primitive Maxx .15
12 A Guardian Keeps Watch .15
13 Julie Winters' Primitive Dreams .15
14 An Ancient Prophesy Fulfilled! .15
15 The Volcano .15
16 Primitive World–Primitive Woman .15
17 The Great White Hare .15
18 The Glowing Ghost-Spirit .15
19 A Dark ISZ .15
20 Confusion Rules! .15
21 The ISZ: Nature's Joyful Destroyer .15
22 The Mad Prophet .15
23 The Mocking Leer of the Dark ISZ .15
24 Intelligent Life .15
25 The Dexter-Balsco Building .15
26 Underground Terror .15
27 A Deadly Sense of Fashion .15
28 Mr. Gone: A Villain who Thinks He's a Hero .15
29 The Dexter-Balsco Building .15
30 A Mask of Rage! .15
31 Leaping Into Eternity .15
32 The Volcano Erupts! .15
33 The Great Northern Crabbit .15
34 A Battle to the Death! .15
35 The Lair of the Queen of the Leopard Women .15
36 A Vision of the Jungle Queen .15
37 A Cat For the Jungle Queen .15
38 Mr. Gone's Hideout .15
39 Maxx's Side of Town .15
40 Mr. Gone: Philosopher .15
41 Maxx at Home .15
42 The Maxx: Hero or Tragic Clown? .15
43 Julie Winters Chats with Sgt. Ocono .15
44 Glorie and Tommy .15
45 Maxx the Avenger .15
46 Mr. Gone Does His Trick .15
47 Cape Fear .15
48 ISZ and Fallen Hero .15
49 A Difficult Friendship .15
50 The Smile of a Human Shark .15
51 The Maxx: Sudden Warrior on the Plains of the Mind .15
52 Muggers at Work .15
53 A Cardboard Haven .15
54 Lord of the Veldt .15
55 A Dream of Julie .15
56 J'Gmaknl–He Who Screams .15
57 Julie: Wild and Free .15
58 Last Hope in the Urban Nightmare .15
59 The City Lockup: Home to the Dispossessed .15
60 Scuffle-Time! .15
61 Pounding Drumbeats .15
62 The Maxx vs. Mr. Gone .15
63 Claws of Justice .15
64 The Shining Nightmare .15
65 Prisoner of Obsession .15
66 The Maxx: A Stranger with a Hidden Face .15
67 The Struggle for Life and Sanity .15
68 The Tortured Hero of Rodin Street .15
69 The Pleasure Platform .15
70 The Scream of the Air Luger .15
71 The Ripe Scent of Death .15
72 Alien Enemies .15
73 Refrigerator Ambush .15
74 Battle Royal .15
75 Battle Royal .15
76 A Wraith of Terror .15
77 Madness and Conflict .15
78 The Bathroom of the Cows .15
79 Brains Against Bulk .15
80 Mind Games of a Killer .15
81 Julie Winters: Creator or Victim? .15
82 More Trouble For the Maxx .15
83 A Battle Against One's Nature .15
84 .15
85 Sudden Death in a Savage Wilderness .15
86 Maxx and Julie .15
87 Hero and Villain: The Classic Confrontation .15
88 Julie Winters: Volunteer for the Victimized .15
89 The Maxx: Jungle Lord .15
90 Credits .15

MEGATON

Entity Comics (1993)

Full bleed color front, grey Christmas tree ornament on back, no title, captioned as listed, bagged with Megaton *#1 comic.*

"Merry Christmas from Gary Carlson and Kelly Jones" 1.00

Black background with color art, white text on back.

"Megaton is Back! Christmas Special #1" (Bill Maus) 1.00

Melting Pot © Kevin Eastman

MELTING POT

Comic Images (1993)

Both this set and the similar Conan set appeared in the fall of 1993. Finding room for 100 cards on the expensive chromium card stock sheets, Comic Images produced 100 cards instead of the 90 cards that were advertised for the set. Since only 90 pieces of art were conveniently available, 10 cards' images were duplicated with different background colors. No distinction was made in the card number or text on the card backs, so it is difficult to know which variation one already owns, and which variation one needs to complete the set. We have identified the variations below, using imaginative color names which were supplied by Comic Images. To add to the confusion, some of the cards were printed on holochrome stock which Comic Images was testing at the time for use as bonus insert cards in other sets. To identify a holochrome card, look at the light reflected off the surface of the card and see if it is broken into its component colors, as in a rainbow. Presence of this prismatic effect identifies it as a holochrome card. We believe that 2,500 sheets of this stock were used.

Set: 90 cards + 10 variant cards, all chromium 25.00
Variant cards: 23, 25, 28, 50, 52, 59, 69, 73, 74 & 82

Prism cards (1:12)
P1 Eastman 7.50
P2 Talbot 8.00
P3 Bisley 10.00
P4 In the Beginning 7.50
P5 Inspiration 7.50
P6 The Melting Pot 7.50
Prism Promo Card (Advance Comics #58) (SBs) 2.00
Chromium Promo card (SBs) 5.00
Cards on Holochrome stock, each . . 5.00
Pack: 7 cards 1.50
Note: many packs have only 6 cards!

CARD CHECKLIST
1 Three Wise Men 25
2 Holyland Imperial Guard 25
3 Zarrah 25
4 Odin and Zeek 25
5 The Chosen Ones 25
6 On Top of the Battle Beast! 25
7 Clamhead & Smiley 25
8 Spanky's Gang 25
9 The Gorr .25
10 Scouts 25
11 Rakk Mon 25
12 In the Beginning 25
13 Bad Ass .25
14 The Big Dump 25
15 A Rude Awakening 25
16 The New World 25
17 Elimination 25
18 Tyler's Obsession 25
19 The Beginning of the End 25
20 Invincible Lord Tyler 25
21 Fighter Trouble in Space 25
22 Crash Landing on Unknown World 25
23 The First Attack (cian) 25
23 The First Attack (gold) 25
24 Death Strikes Twice 25
25 Lethal, Huge and Hungry (flaxen) .25
25 Lethal, Huge and Hungry (plum) . .25
26 Unseen Assassins 25
27 Lifeless Eyes 25
28 Jokk and Tookaa (purple) 25
28 Jokk and Tookaa (yellow) 25
29 Arrival in Juudas 25
30 The Gorr Fights 25
31 Spikes Tearing Flesh 25
32 One by One They Die 25
33 Jokk and Tookaa Lose Their Coin .25
34 Clamhead Attacks 25
35 Zeek Protects His Master 25
36 Odin Says No More Blood 25
37 Smiley's Soiled Departure 25
38 Zeek and Odin Head for High Ground 25
39 Traveling Tales of the Past 25
40 Evil Masses at Shantarr 25
41 Lord Tyler and Grinner 25
42 The Master Returns 25
43 The Bat Feeds 25
44 Entrance to the Master's Tent 25
45 The Ambassador's Pleas are Voiced 25
46 Lord Tyler Passes Judgment 25
47 Grinner's Appetizer 25
48 The Executioner 25
49 Judgment is Passed 25
50 Orders for Destruction (aqua) 25
50 Orders for Destruction (peach, golf ball texture) 25
51 The Ceremonies Before Battle . . .25
52 Stumbling Upon Horror (pistachio) .25
52 Stumbling Upon Horror (rust) 25
53 Remembrance 25
54 Zarrah the Carrier 25
55 Grinner Senses the Decay 25
56 Help Me, Kill Me 25
57 Grinner's Only Fear 25
58 The Night Before Continues 25
59 The Scent of Battle (blood) 25
59 The Scent of Battle (blue) 25
60 Dawn Attack 25
61 Through the Eyes of a Demon . . .25
62 Caught off Guard 25
63 At Shantarr's Gates 25
64 A Valiant Stand 25
65 Gate Buster 25
66 Shantarr Falls 25
67 Lord Tyler at the Palace Gates . . .25
68 Grinner at his Side 25
69 Charging Through Destruction (pindot blue, golf ball texture) 25
69 Charging Through Destruction (lavender) 25
70 Never Had a Chance 25
71 Into the Inner Chambers 25
72 The End is Near 25
73 Praying for Forgiveness (mint) . . .25
73 Praying for Forgiveness (goldenrod) 25
74 The Council of Shantarr Dies (flesh) 25
74 The Council of Shantarr Dies (orchid) 25
75 Tyler's View of the Aftermath 25
76 No Survivors, No Prisoners 25
77 Death Brings Excitement 25
78 Bring me a Woman of this Place . .25
79 Zarrah Gives Herself 25
80 The War Lord is Pleased 25
81 While the Destruction Rages... . . .25
82 Passion Abounds (chartreuse) . . .25
82 Passion Abounds (violet) 25
83 Content with Their Victories 25
84 Zarrah's Found Her Mate 25
85 Tyler Loves No One 25
86 We Must Part Forever 25
87 No, Don't Send Me Away 25
88 Cold as Ice 25
89 Lord Tyler, Beginning of the End . .25
90 Checklist 25

Milestone: The Dakota Universe © Milestone Media, Inc.

MILESTONE: THE DAKOTA UNIVERSE

SkyBox (1993)

Milestone comics features African-American characters created by artists of various cultures and are distributed by DC Comics. These cards feature color art work inside a distinctive "West African mudcloth pattern" border design. The backs repeat the title and include the card number and text. Cards #64 to #81 are caricatures of the artists and others at Milestone Studios. Promo cards M1 thru M7 (and the two basketball player cards from the Diamond Distribution show) all contain the same backs as each other. The four prototype cards are clearly marked "Prototype" on the back. The two foil cards are embossed and have full-bleed art. The backs have no text or title, other than copyright information, but contain a large Milestone logo "M" in a black circle.

Set: 100 cards 14.00

Foil-Embossed Cards: (1:36 packs)
M1 Hardware 14.00
M2 Static 14.00

Promo Cards (DCw)
M1 Hardware (in Hardware #1) 1.00
M2 Blood Syndicate (in Blood Syndicate #1) 1.00
M3 Icon & Rocket (in Icon #1) 1.00
M4 Static (in Static #1) 1.00
M5 Hardware vs. Alva (in CBC and in Card Collector's Price Guide) . . 1.00
M6 Boogieman (in CBG Price Guide) 1.00

M7 Holocaust (in Wizard #22) 1.00

Prototype Cards (DCw)

19 Icon & Rocket 1.00
20 Hardware 1.00
21 Static 1.00
23 Blood Syndicate 1.00

Milestone: The Dakota Universe
© Milestone Media, Inc.

Diamond Distribution Show promos

The Admiral (David Robinson) 15.00
Magic (Johnson) 15.00
Pack: 8 cards 1.00

CARD CHECKLIST

Icon, The Origin Mural

1 Icon I .10
2 Icon II .10
3 Icon III .10
4 Icon IV .10
5 Icon V .10
6 Icon VI .10
7 Icon VII .10
8 Icon VIII .10
9 Icon IX .10

Blood Syndicate, The Origin Mural

10 Blood Syndicate I .10
11 Blood Syndicate II .10
12 Blood Syndicate IV .10
13 Blood Syndicate V .10
14 Blood Syndicate VI .10
15 Blood Syndicate VII .10
16 Blood Syndicate VIII .10
17 Blood Syndicate IX .10
18 Blood Syndicate IX .10

Warriors

19 Icon and Rocket .10
20 Hardware .10
21 Static .10
22 Rocket .10
23 The Blood Syndicate .10
24 Icon .10
25 Reprise .10
26 Technique .10
27 Deathwish .10
28 Hotstreak .10
29 Tarmack .10
30 Virus .10
31 Payback .10
32 Holocaust .10
33 Mistress Mercy .10
34 Diva .10
35 Edwin Alva .10
36 Creator .10
37 Tempto .10
38 Systematic .10
39 Top Dog .10

The Next Wave

40 Mechanic .10
41 Twilight .10
42 Professor Night .10
43 Plus .10
44 Iron Butterfly .10
45 Jigsaw .10
46 Sideshow .10
47 Donner .10
48 Blitzen .10
49 Dharma .10
50 Highwayman .10
51 Queen-9 .10
52 Xombi .10
53 Lysistrata Jones .10
54 Buck Wild, Mercenary Man .10

Milestones

55 Tech-9 vs. Holocaust .10
56 Static vs. Hotstreak .10
57 Icon & Rocket: First Flight .10
58 Icon Meets Hardware .10
59 Hardware vs. Alva .10
60 Death of Tech-9 .10
61 The Big Bang .10
62 Icon vs. Blood Syndicate .10
63 Rocket & Static .10

Supporting Cast

64 Frieda Goren (JP) .10
65 Larry Wade .10
66 Jean Hawkins .10
67 Barraki Young .10
68 Jeong Lee & Ann Kim .10
69 Decon Stuart .10
70 Estelle Jackson .10
71 Miriam & Baby Augustus .10

Creators

72 Robert L. Washington III .10
73 Noelle Giddings .10
74 Dwayne McDuffie .10
75 Ivan Velez, Jr. .10
76 John-Paul Leon .10
77 Steve Mitchell .10
78 Mike Gustovich .10
79 M.D. Bright .10
80 Denys Cowan .10
81 Jimmy Palmiotti .10

Blood Syndicate

82 Tech-9 .10
83 Third Rail .10
84 Brickhouse .10
85 Wise Son .10
86 Boogieman .10
87 Flashback .10
88 Fade .10
89 Masquerade .10
90 DMZ .10
91 Dogg .10
92 Aquamaria .10
93 Kwai .10

Secret Lives

94 Augustus Freeman (Icon) .10
95 Virgil Hawkins (Static) .10
96 Curtis Metcalf (Hardware) .10
97 Raquel Ervin (Rocket) .10
98 Wilt Johnson (Deathwish) .10
99 Checklist A .10
100 Checklist B .10

MINNIE 'N' ME

Impel (1991)

This set is designed to sell to young girls and has a lot of hearts and pink which little girls like. It also has the adorable Disney art that all generations love. The card fronts have a white border and a dotted stripe at the top with the series logo. The backs have a similar design, with text and a small picture. The packs are pink too. Disney doesn't give credit to its artists. The fronts of the first nine cards form a super-panel, except they all have borders so the effect is largely lost. There is also a poster mail-in order form card, which isn't really part of the set, but does contain art. It's worth the same as the regular cards. Card sets for young girls are a fine idea, but card collecting is largely a male hobby, so don't expect a lot of price increase on this set.

Minnie 'n' Me © The Walt Disney Company

Set: 160 cards 15.00

Pack: 12 cards .75
Minnie 'N Me collector's album 15.00

CARD CHECKLIST

1 Minnie .10
2 Daisy .10
3 Minnie's Pet .10
4 Daisy's Pet .10
5 Clarabelle .10
6 Heather .10
7 Patti .10
8 T.J. .10
9 Lilly .10

Heartfelt Moments...

10 Birthday Party .10
11 Open Presents .10
12 Make a Wish .10
13 Tea Party .10
14 Slumber Party .10
15 Vacations .10
16 Mother's Day .10
17 Father's Day .10
18 Trick or Treat .10
19 Easter Egg Hunt .10
20 Valentine's Day .10
21 Visiting Grandma .10
22 Pets .10
23 Pet Show .10
24 My Favorite Pet .10
25 New Sister .10
26 Helping Hand .10
27 Welcome to the Neighborhood .10

Havin' Fun

28 Cooking .10
29 Dressing Up .10
30 Playing with Friends .10
31 Hopscotch .10
32 Paper Dolls .10
33 Dancing .10
34 Jumping Rope .10
35 Jump Rope Song .10
36 Jumping Rope with Minnie's Pet .10
37 On the Phone .10
38 Dominoes .10
39 Hide and Seek .10
40 Play House .10
41 Watching T.V. .10
42 Drawing .10
43 Dolls .10
44 Painting .10
45 Jigsaw Puzzle .10
46 Collecting Stamps .10
47 Music .10
48 Tennis .10
49 Softball .10
50 Swimming .10
51 Sleds .10
52 Snowmen .10
53 Playing in the Leaves .10
54 Sandcastles .10
55 Collecting Seashells .10
56 Camp .10
57 Climbing Trees .10
58 Pillow Fight .10
59 Butterflies .10
60 Bikes .10
61 Swings .10
62 Seesaw .10
63 Jungle Gym .10
64 Rain Puddles .10
65 Picking Flowers .10
66 Cartwheels .10
67 Somersaults .10
68 Kickball .10
69 Playing Store .10
70 Jacks .10
71 Marbles .10
72 Checkers .10
73 Hand Games .10
74 Picking Apples .10
75 Hula Hoop .10
76 Newspaper Hats .10
77 Clubhouse .10
78 Treehouse .10
79 Skipping .10
80 Playing Leap Frog .10
81 Leap Frog Fun .10
82 Feeding Pigeons .10
83 Sailing Boats .10
84 Handshadows .10
85 Dollhouse .10

86 Kites .10
87 Tag .10
88 Picnic .10
89 Ice Skating .10
90 Catching Snowflakes .10

School Days

91 Arts and Crafts .10
92 Gym .10
93 School Bus .10
94 Apple for the Teacher .10
95 Writing .10
96 Arithmetic .10
97 School Plays .10
98 Music Class .10
99 Storytime .10
100 Telling Time .10
101 Lunch .10
102 Recess .10
103 Reading .10
104 Making New Friends .10
105 Show and Tell .10
106 First Day at School .10
107 Ballet .10
108 My Locker .10

Fun Trips

109 Off to the Zoo .10
110 Zoo Animals .10
111 At the Zoo .10
112 Circus .10
113 Feeding the Elephants .10
114 Under the Big Top .10
115 Farm .10
116 In the Barn .10
117 Barnyard Animals .10
118 Hayride .10
119 Movies .10
120 Shopping for Clothes .10
121 Amusement Park .10
122 Water Slide .10
123 Bumper Cars .10
124 County Fair .10
125 Toy Store .10
126 Camp .10
127 Ice Cream Parlor .10
128 Puppet Show .10
129 Magic Show .10
130 Beach .10
131 Fun in the Surf .10
132 Swimming Hole .10
133 Pet Store .10
134 Restaurant .10
135 Candy Store .10
136 Aquarium .10
137 Boardwalk .10
138 Country .10
139 Planetarium .10
140 Fireworks Display .10
141 Bar-B-Que .10
142 Park .10
143 Summer in the Park .10
144 Lunch in the Park .10

Busy Days

145 Stretching .10
146 Jumping Jacks .10
147 Exercise Class .10
148 Receive a Letter .10
149 Write a Letter .10
150 Mailing a Letter .10
151 Bathing Pets .10
152 Waking Up .10
153 Pick a Dress .10
154 Getting Dressed .10
155 Bubble Bath .10
156 Setting the Table .10
157 Help Clean .10
158 Gardening .10
159 Checklist #1 .10
160 Checklist #2 .10
Poster mail-in order form card .15

Best friends?

Minnie 'n' Me 2 Just for Fun © The Walt Disney Company

MINNIE 'N ME 2 JUST FOR FUN

SkyBox (1993)

Basically, these cards look just like the previous set and are also designed to sell to young girls. If you ever mix the cards up, the best way to tell the two series apart is that this one has the "SkyBox" logo. There are two holograms, which are double sided and pink.

Set: 150 cards 15.00

Holograms, double sided
(Merry-go-round) 9.00
Surprise 9.00
Pack: 12 cards 1.00

CARD CHECKLIST

Holiday Crafts

1 Trim the Tree .10
2 Twinkle, Twinkle .10
3 Hot Cider .10
4 Party Plans .10
5 Pop-Up-Card .10
6 Gift Bag .10
7 Friendship .10
8 Lollipop Surprise .10
9 Happy Hearts .10
10 Summer Picnic .10
11 Orange Sparkler .10
12 Frozen Treat .10
13 Masquerade .10
14 Princess Hat .10
15 Magic Wand .10
16 Special Thanks .10
17 Hat Place Cards .10
18 Napkin Rings .10

Slumber Party

19 Party Planning .10
20 Funtime Invitation .10
21 Crunch "n" Chew Treats .10
22 Chocolate Sippers' Delight .10
23 Yummy Minnie Melts .10
24 Puppet "Pops" .10
25 Make a Puppet Stage .10
26 Tutti Frutti Guessing Game .10
27 Packing Puzzler .10

Play Time

28 Playing Baseball .10
29 Pet Tricks .10
30 Flyin' Pretty .10
31 Circle Shapes .10
32 Playing Cards .10
33 Sailing Boats .10
34 Snack Recipe .10
35 Telling Time .10
36 Making Jewelry .10
37 Leaf Rubbings .10
38 We Love Ice Cream .10
39 Pressed Flowers .10
40 Ice Cube Trick .10
41 Decorated Vase .10
42 Tee Shirt Autograph Party .10
43 Bubbles Galore .10
44 Homemade Clay .10
45 Enchanted Lands .10

Dear Diary

46 Favorite Subjects .10
47 After Homework .10
48 Ice Skating .10
49 The Class Trip .10
50 Getting Better .10
51 Best Friends? .10
52 Thunderstorm .10
53 Winning .10
54 Sharing with Friends .10

Vacation

55 Packing the Car .10
56 Buried Treasure Word Search .10
57 Seashell Hatband .10
58 What's in the Beach Bag? .10
59 Seashore Riddle .10
60 Row Your Boat Word Search .10
61 Ready, Set, Camp! .10
62 I Can Canoe, Can You! or Canoe Guess Who? .10
63 Lost 'n' Found Name Search .10
64 Hidden Forest Friends .10
65 Red Hot Chili Dogs .10
66 Outdoor Treasures Wreath .10
67 Country Living .10
68 Country Cobbler .10
69 Patchwork Pleasures .10
70 One for All, and All for Pie! .10
71 Riddle Dee Dee Daisy .10
72 Farmyard Sounds Service .10
73 City Park .10
74 Shopping Surprises .10
75 Sea Scramble .10
76 Sherbet Delight .10
77 Hidden Bows .10
78 Swimming Magic .10
79 Finders' Peepers .10
80 Pack 'em Up Puzzler .10
81 Travelling Poem .10

Patch of Green

82 Soda Bottle Feeder .10
83 Planting .10
84 Making Recycling Fun .10
85 Bird Treats .10
86 Travel Snacks .10
87 Kitchen Plants .10
88 Animal Facts .10
89 Animal Clues .10
90 Animal Tracks .10

Silly Riddles

91 After School .10
92 Talking Flowers .10
93 Favorite Hearts .10
94 High Jumps .10
95 Busy Day .10
96 Letters .10
97 Picturegram .10
98 Getting Wet .10
99 How Do We Share? .10

Silly Rhymes...

100 Hats .10
101 Travel .10
102 Pets .10
103 Games .10
104 Baking .10
105 Cooking .10
106 Walking .10
107 Spring .10
108 Friends .10

Silly Fill-Ins

109 Close Call .10
110 Ice Cream Treats .10
111 A Green Thumb .10
112 Movies .10
113 Strike Up the Band .10
114 Daydreaming .10
115 Hook, Line and Sinker .10
116 At the Theater .10
117 Thinking of You! .10

Nine Little Wishes

118 Prima Ballerina Minnie .10
119 Movie Star Minnie .10
120 Sea Diver Minnie .10
121 Forest Ranger Minnie .10
122 Dog Trainer Minnie .10
123 Mail Carrier Minnie .10
124 Marathon Minnie .10
125 Famous Writer Minnie .10
126 Just Herself Minnie .10

Travels with Minnie

127 The Mighty Mississippi .10
128 Niagara Falls .10
129 Rockefeller Center .10
130 The Lincoln Memorial .10
131 The Grand Canyon .10
132 Yosemite National Park .10
133 Alaskan Glaciers .10
134 Hawaii's Volcanoes & Beaches .10
135 No Place Like Home .10

Daisy's Brown Bear

136 Where is Teddy? .10
137 A Pocket Surprise! .10
138 A Tale of a Teddy Bear .10
139 Tea for Teddy .10
140 A Tune for Teddy? .10
141 Play Ball, Teddy .10
142 Hats Off for Teddy .10
143 A Trunk for Teddy .10
144 Hugs for Teddy! .10

Coloring Cards

145 Paint Party .10
146 Up, Up and Away! .10
147 Ice Cream Towers .10
148 Flower Gardens .10
149 Checklist .10
150 Checklist .10

Mirage/Next Xenotech characters © Michael Dooney

Mr. Fixitt © Heroic Publishing

Mr. T and the T-Force © Now Comics

MIRAGE/NEXT CHARACTERS

Mirage/Next (1993)

These card present characters from three Mirage/Next comics series: Xenotech *by Michael Dooney,* Bioneers, *by A. C. Farley and* Stupid Heroes, *by Peter Laird. The card fronts have a picture in a brown marbled frame and the backs have text in white on a black and grey surface. Pairs of the cards were stapled into the first three issues each of* Xenotech; Bioneers; *and* Stupid Heroes *comic books, Cards 19 and 20 were in* Stupid Heroes Haelstrom *comic and the others were in other comics which we would reveal if we knew. The cards were also handed out at trade shows, after being hand cut and enclosed in a brown paper band that said "Secret." That's where we got ours, but the dog chewed them so we had to beg for an uncut sheet from Next comics.*

Set: 24 cards in "Secret" band 12.00

1 Starker Helm (Xenotech) 50
2 Haywire (Xenotech) 50
3 Dr. Janus Kowalski (Bioneers) 50
4 Cypher Kray (Bioneers) 50
5 Araknon (Stupid Heroes) 50
6 Cinder (Stupid Heroes) 50
7 Gunner (Xenotech) 50
8 Chunk (Xenotech) 50
9 Fearless (Fe) (Bioneers) 50
10 Firebrand (Fi) (Bioneers) 50
11 Mister (Stupid Heroes) 50
12 Scott Poundstone (Stupid Heroes) .50
13 Medusa (Xenotech) 50
14 Pulse (Xenotech) 50
15 Carmilla O'Reilly (Bioneers) 50
16 Garth Felis (Bioneers) 50
17 SWAC Trooper (Stupid Heroes) . .50
18 Dementia Dominus (Stupid Heroes).50
19 Forward Alert (Fo) (Bioneers) 50
20 Mad Morris (Stupid Heroes) 50
21 Harper Bizarre (Xenotech) 50
22 Xenotech (Xenotech) 50
23 Fumigator (Fum) (Bioneers) 50
24 Alana Richardson (Stupid Heroes) .50

MR. FIXITT

Heroic Publishing (1993)

Only 4,500 of each of these cards were printed. The card backs state that these cards are "x in a series of 7" but the other five have not yet appeared. The publisher's name does not appear on the cards.

#1 Mr. Fixitt 1.00
#2 Veeza 1.00

MR. T AND THE T-FORCE

Now Comics (1993)

These cards come bagged with Mr. T and the T-Force *comics. Some have drawings and some have photos. The series was still ongoing at press time, so more will exist by the time you read this.*

Mr. T and the T-Force "Summer 1993" comic promo (NA) 2.50
June 17, 1993 "T-Day" 50
2 Mr. T and the T-Force (NA) embossed foil logo 2.50
3 Mr. T photo 75
4 Mr. T and the T-Force (NA) 75
5 Mr. T photo 1.00
6 Mr. T (NA) (issue #3) 75
7 Mr. T photo 50
8 Mr. T (NBy) 75
9 . . . .
10. Mr. T (NBy) (from issue #5) 75
I Met Mr.T at Comicfest '93 50
Call Mr. T.! (same photo as #5) 50

N

NEXT MEN

Dark Horse Comics (1992)

The cards came in pairs, one with a picture in a circle, brown and grey background design, and upright text on the back; and the other with the picture in a larger rectangular "N" frame, interlocking N background design, and text on the back printed sideways.

Set: 12 cards, mail in from Next Men comics #1-#6 (JBy) 12.00

CARD CHECKLIST

Bethany & Jasmine promo (from Arena #11) 1.00
1 Nathan 1.00
2 Scanner 1.00
3 Bethany 1.00
4 Hardbody 1.00
5 Jack 1.00
6 Brawn 1.00
7 Jasmine 1.00
8 Bounce 1.00
9 Danny 1.00
10 Sprint 1.00
11 Jillian 1.00
12 Squatter 1.00

Next Men © John Byrne

NINJA HIGH SCHOOL

Antarctic Press (1994)

This is a promo for a card set which was not available at press time. The art is by Robert DeJesus.

#2 Small Bodied Asrial prism prototype (from Small Bodied #2) 1.00

NINJAK

Valiant (1993)

This promo card for Ninjak *comic book #1 has a yellow gold border and a black and white back.*

Ninjak chromium promo (JQ & JP) 6.00

Now Comic Cards © Now Comics

The Price Keeper promo © Overstreet

NOW COMIC CARDS

Now Comics (1993)

Now comics gave away promos for these comic books in 1993.

Married with Children
(Bundy Checklist) 1.00
Promo card (cast photo) 50
Neon Knight (Temporary
Insanity) promo card 1.50
Supercops comic promo 2.00
Syphons promo card 1.50

O

Omaha, The Cat Dancer © Reed Waller & Kate Worley

OMAHA, THE CAT DANCER

Kitchen Sink (1993)

This is an adult oriented funny animal series. Omaha is a nude dancing cat living in Mipple city (Minneapolis) and the comics on which these cards are based was begun as a satire on local blue laws. The comic has been going on ever since and the cards picture many of its regular characters and tell one of Omaha's stories. These cards are 2.7" x 3.7", which is slightly larger than standard size. They have color art on the front, with a white border and text on an otherwise white background.

Set: 36 cards boxed (Reed Waller)+ 3 Cherry promo cards 14.00

1 Mipple City 40
2 Omaha 40
3 Chuck Katt 40
4 Charlie's Underground 40
5 Shelly Hine 40
6 Pet Magazine 40
7 Pong 40
8 De Roc .40
9 Joanne .40
10 Jerry 40
11 De Roc & Associates 40
12 Charlie 40
13 Kitty Corner 40
14 Huddle 40

Perg © Lightning Comics

Plasm promo (Overstreet) © TRG & EEP, L.P.

15 Rob 40
16 Maria .40
17 Althea .40
18 The Herd 40
19 Squeek 40
20 Bonner 40
21 "A" Block 40
22 Shelley's Heartthrobs 40
23 "Wildcat": The Video 40
24 The Photos 40
25 Lopez .40
26 Joanne II 40
27 Grover & Tray 40
28 San Francisco 40
29 Mr. Pip's 40
30 Mrs. Beeks 40
31 Jack 40
32 Cee Cee 40
33 Davey .40
34 Chuck II 40
35 Omaha II 40
36 Waller & Worley 40

OVERSTREET/CBM

Overstreet (1993)

These promo cards (called GiveAwayGimmicks) came bagged with issues of Overstreet's Comic Book Monthly. *Card #1 came with issue #2. Cards #3 & #4 came with issue #4 and cards #5 through #7 came with issues of the same number. The card backs are white with "Overstreet" written along the side (except for #4 where the Overstreet info is on a sticker).*

0 The Price Keeper 2.00
1 Spawn, purple letters (TM) 2.50
1 Spawn, blue letters (TM) 2.50
2 not found; exists?
3 Plasm Promo card (DL) 1.00
4 Red Rage, White Whirl
Baton Blue promo (ARC comics) . 1.00
5 Aegis (ARC comics #2) 1.00
6 Xenya (Hildebrandt) 1.50
7 Radioactive Man & Bartman 1.00

P

PERG

Lightning Comics (1993)

This is a comic book promo reproducing the cover of Perg #1 *with art by Kerschl and Anderson.*

#1 cover repro promo card (from Bloodfire #5 comic) 50

PHANTOM FORCE

(Image 1993)

Each of the five cards comes from the Phantom Force #1 *comic, so you have to buy 5 copies to get all of them.*

1 Sensei 1.00
2 Gin Seng 1.00
3 Professor Kublak 1.00
4 Apocalypse 1.00
5 Probe 1.00

PLASM

Zero Issue Trading Cards

River Group (1993)

The first 117 cards of this set are designed to be placed in the binder so that the fronts and backs form a 26 page comic book. Those cards are not titled or captioned, but they are numbered on

Plasm Zero Issue © TRG & EEP, L.P.

the back. They have a charcoal border with light grey "crack" lines. The rest of the cards have portraits of the characters inside an irregular green line frame and charcoal outer border. The character's name is at the top and the back has some text plus a small outline view of the character. Plasm is an organic society, and so there's a lot of dark leaf green on the packs and cards.

Not enough of the binders were printed originally, which accounts for their high price. The first edition binder can be distinguished from the second edition by the larger size of the cover picture. The Lorca promo came in a group of 3 River Group promos along with a Dark Dominion promo and a Good Guys promo. The level two raised foil (i.e. embossed) bonus cards came with the cases and were not in the packs. The 10 card promo packs were given away at trade shows, with different cards at each show. Both have a header card, marked with the name of the show's sponsor, and a nine card page from the series, marked "promo" and numbered "x/10." The Heroes World pack has the pages 7 and 8 from the series, and the header card pictures Lord Leviathan (card #130). The Diamond pack has the pages 5 and 6 and the header card pictures Lorca (card #118).

Set: 150 cards 20.00

Bonus Cards
1 Ironhead 10.00
2 Glory 10.00
3 Lightpath (DL) 10.00
4 The Great Grimmax (DL) 10.00
5 Hooky & Clipper 10.00
6 Killer 10.00
7 Nudge 10.00
8 Shooter 10.00
9 Oob (from binder) (DL) 18.00
Level 2 Bonus cards
1 Lorca & His Enemy 15.00
2 Lorca & His Lust-Mate 15.00
3 Lorca & His Lover 15.00
4 Heroes From Earth 15.00
Raised Foil Level 2 cards, ea. . . 25.00
1 of 3 Lorca promo (5,000 made) . . 5.00
Promo sheet 6½" x 9" 4.00
Promo-10 cards, cello pack
for Diamond Comics 8.00
for Heroes World 10.00
See also Overstreet Gimmick #3
Uncut sheet of 33 Plasm characters
(5,000 offered) 20.00
ComiCollector, w/16 page Splatterball
comic + bonus foil card 20.00
Album Binder, 1st printing 40.00
Album Binder, 2nd printing 15.00
Pack: 9 cards 1.50
There are six different wrappers, with images taken from cards 118, 122, 130, Level 1 bonus cards 7 & 8 and one other.

CARD CHECKLIST
1 to 117, no captions, each 10
Character cards
118 Lorca 20
119 Strafelord Maxilla 20
120 Laygen .20
121 Tibiarrum 20
122 Sueraceen 20
123 Trample-Zoms 20
124 Lord Thoraxolic 20
125 Grind-Zoms 20
126 Hortch .20
127 Lifescourge 20
128 Sky Czar Keel 20
129 Pleasure-Zoms 20
130 Lord Leviathan 20
131 Ulnareah 20
132 Phlogia 20
133 Body Barges 20
134 Zom-Mothers 20
135 Aeriaks 20
136 Grafters 20
137 Sludge Slaves 20
138 Chattelwagons 20
139 Covertrons 20
140 Flaktrons 20
141 Lichtor .20
142 Splicers 20
143 Cranialius 20
144 Abdoratchet 20
145 Slaughtermaster Gnash 20
146 Torpedrons 20
147 Mongrel Rude 20
148 Fleshthreshers 20
149 Armamentor Pharynx 20
150 Purgist Skullurk 20
Warriors of Plasm special tin set 40.00
*The tin set includes all 150 cards in an attractively embossed tin litho box that is too big for the card set. 25,000 were made and it also contains a raised foil level two bonus card #4 & four **Org of Plasm** cards*
1 of 4 Arhq Tsolmec 2.50
2 of 4 Zahnree Phla 2.50
3 of 4 The Council of Wizards 2.50
4 of 4 The Feathered Serpent 2.50
Warriors of Plasm 5"x7"
promo sheet 4.00
Premium set in different oversized box
inc. Audio comic (5,555 made) . 175.00

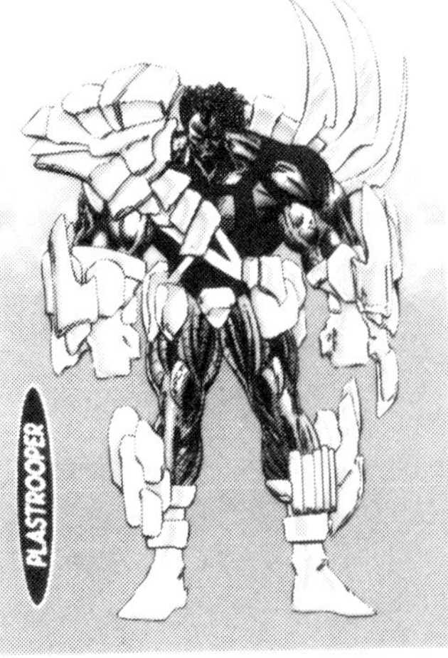

Plasmer © Marvel Comics UK, Inc.

PLASMER

Marvel U.K. (1993)

These comic book promos came with Plasmer *comic book #1.*

Plasmer (LSh/JBn/Cam Smith) 50
Plasmonster (LSh/JBn/Cam Smith) . .50
Plastrooper (LSh/JBn/Cam Smith) . . .50
Mrs. Mullarkey (EP/JBn/Cam Smith) .50

POST CEREAL STICKERS

Post (1979)

4 Sets (Superman, Batman, Wonder Woman, others): 10.00

Predator vs. Magnus Robot Fighter © Dark Horse Comics

PREDATOR VS. MAGNUS ROBOT FIGHTER

Dark Horse/Valiant (1992)

Lee Weeks & Chris Chalenor art

Cards 3 and 4 were bagged in Wizard *magazine and are easy to find. Cards 1 and 2 should have appeared somewhere and we have samples of the art work, but haven't located the cards yet.*

1 Predators 3.00
2 Magnus Robot Fighter 3.00
3 Promo card (Wizard #16) 2.00
4 Promo card (Wizard #16) 2.00

PROPELLER MAN

Dark Horse (1993)

Two card sheet (in Propeller Man #2 comic) 2.50

The Punisher (The Whole Tough Tale) © Marvel Entertainment Group, Inc.

THE PUNISHER, THE WHOLE TOUGH TALE

Comic Images (1988)

The card fronts are comic book style images inside a brickwork border, except for the five listed covers from The Punisher *limited series comics. The card backs contain the caption and the card number inside a Punisher logo skull together with some story line text from the series.*

Set: 50 cards 17.50

Pack: 5? cards, cello pack 2.00

CARD CHECKLIST

1 Logo/Checklist 40
2 Circle of Blood (Cover #1) 40
3 The Files .40
4 Attacked .40
5 Jigsaw 40
6 Prepare to Escape 40
7 Saved 40
8 Prison Break 40
9 Plan Two .40
10 The Offer 40
11 Forced Revenge 40
12 Back to the War (Cover #2) 40
13 Get Kingpin 40
14 The Trap 40
15 Boom! 40
16 Rescued 40
17 Alaric 40
18 Set Up .40
19 Ambushed 40
20 Face to Face 40
21 Angela's Secret 40
22 Slaughterday (Cover #3) 40
23 Santiago 40
24 The New Driver 40
25 Don't Snivel 40
26 You're Not Mob 40
27 Lookalike 40
28 One Down 40
29 Hello Marcus 40
30 Angela?! 40
31 Not you, Too! 40
32 Final Solution (Cover #4) 40
33 Surprise Visit 40
34 Dead Aide 40
35 Packing it in 40
36 Drive On 40
37 Jigsaw or Punisher? 40
38 Showdown 40
39 Come with Me 40
40 Down the Hatch 40
41 In the Chamber 40
42 Final Solution II (Cover #5) 40
43 Strategy Time 40
44 Vapor Lock 40
45 Breakout 40
46 Strike Back 40
47 Off Guard 40
48 Do it, Or else! 40
49 Enough Tony 40
50 Do Nothing 40

THE PUNISHER, WAR JOURNAL ENTRY (GUTS & GUNPOWDER)

Comic Images (1992)

The packs use the "Guts & Gunpowder" sub-title, while the cards use "War Journal Entry." The card fronts are full bleed comic book close-ups and the backs contain the card number, title and text plus a black and white drawing. Both promo cards use the same picture and say "Not For Sale" on the back. The prism bonus

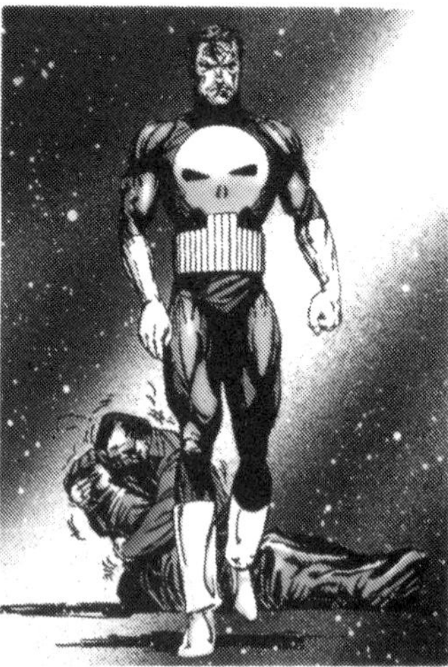

The Punisher, War Journal Entry © Marvel Entertainment Group, Inc.

cards are on a reflective polygon stock. The "prizm" promo card is on a different reflective surface, similar to the stock used for many vending machine stickers.

Set: 90 cards 12.00

Prizm promo card (KJ) 5.00
Promo card (KJ) 2.50

Prism Cards

1 Defense Mechanism 9.00
2 Popularity 9.00
3 Deathwish 9.00

Scratch & Sniff

1 Preparation 7.50
2 Stunts 7.50
3 The Actor 7.50

Pack: 10 cards 1.00

CARD CHECKLIST

1 Creating 15
2 First Appearance 15
3 Spider-Man 15
4 Bugged .15
5 Similar Pasts 15
6 Training 15
7 Soldier .15
8 The Catalyst 15
9 AWOL 15
10 Rage 15
11 Retribution 15
12 Punisher 15
13 Journal 15
14 Justice 15
15 Mornings 15
16 Preparation 15
17 Weapons 15
18 Arsenal 15
19 Maggia 15
20 Says Who? 15
21 Punishment 15
22 Mercy .15
23 Daredevil 15
24 Hornhead 15
25 Anti-hero 15
26 Indepth 15
27 Prison 15
28 Defense 15
29 Crime .15
30 Captain America 15
31 Kingpin 15
32 Fisk 15
33 Jigsaw 15
34 Microchip 15
35 Microchip, Jr. 15
36 A Father's Loss 15
37 The Board 15
38 Aides .15
39 To Die For 15
40 Sniper 15
41 Illusions (sic) 15
42 Ghost Rider 15
43 Vigilantes 15
44 Darkhawk 15
45 Wolverine 15
46 Africa 15
47 Bushwacker 15
48 Triple Threat 15
49 Van 15
50 Transport 15
51 Aloha! 15
52 Not Ready 15
53 Concealment 15
54 Inspirations 15
55 Group of One 15
56 Submerged 15
57 Practice 15
58 Shadowmasters 15
59 Kevlar 15
60 Disguises 15
61 Reflection 15
62 Doctor Doom 15
63 Deathlok 15
64 Moonknight 15
65 Dead Man's Hand 15
66 Blood & Glory 15
67 Hulk .15
68 Mr. Fixit 15
69 Reality 15
70 Undressed 15
71 Uzi 15
72 Colt .45 15
73 War Zone 15
74 Johnny Tower 15
75 User .15
76 Shotgun 15
77 Double-Crossed 15
78 Discovered 15
79 Countdown 15
80 Open Fire 15
81 Shark Island 15
82 Toxic 15
83 Cleaning 15
84 Fun .15
85 Favorite Gun 15
86 Hostages 15
87 Love 15
88 Black Widow 15
89 2099 15
90 Checklist 15

Q

Q-UNIT

Harris Comics (1993)

The first card came from Wizard *#24, the second from* Q-Unit *comics #1 and the third from* Q-Unit *#2.*

Layered Reality Cybercard Ver. 1.1 . 1.00
Layered Reality Cybercard Ver. 1.2 . 1.00
Layered Reality Cybercard Ver. 1.3 NYR

R

Ralph Snart Adventures © Now Entertainment Corporation

RALPH SNART ADVENTURES

Now Comics (1993)

Mark Hansen art

The cards have a white border and say "Ralph Snart Adventures" in a strip down the right side. The backs contain the card number, text and say "5th Anniversary Superset" on a white background. Cards 2 thru 15 are from Ralph Snart Adventures. *Card #24 is from* Ralph Snart #3

1 25
2 Ralph's stay in hell 20
3 Man has always considered... 20
4 Mr. Lizard knocks evil... 20
5 Cover: Vol. 2, No. 1 20
6 Cover: Vol. 2, No. 2 20
7 Cover: Vol. 2, No. 3 20
8 Cover: Vol. 2, No. 4 20
9 Cover: Vol. 2, No. 5 20
10 Cover: Vol. 2, No. 6 20
11 Cover: Vol. 2, No. 7 20
12 Cover: Vol. 2, No. 9 20

Now Comics (1993)

13 Cover: Vol. 3, No. 1 20
14 Cover: Vol. 3, No. 2 20
15 Cover: Vol. 3, No. 3 20
16 Cover: Vol. 3, No. 4 20
17 Cover: Vol. 3, No. 5 20
18 Cover: Vol. 3, No. 6 20
19 Cover: Vol. 3, No. 7 20
20 Cover: Vol. 3, No. 8 20
21 Cover: Vol. 3, No. 9 25
22 Cover: Vol. 3, No. 10 20
23 Cover: Vol. 3, No. 11 25
24 Cover: Vol. 3, No. 12 25
25 Cover: Vol. 3, No. 13 25
26 Cover: Vol. 3, No. 14 25

RAY BRADBURY COMICS

Topps (1993)

These are promo cards which came with issues of Ray Bradbury comics. There are no cards corresponding to numbers 8, 9 and 10 in the first five issues of the comic book. However comics #1 & #3 each also contained a Jurassic Park promo card and comic #4 also contained two promo cards for Mars Attacks.

Promo: Ray Bradbury (front = #4) . . 1.50
(1) Promo: A Sound of Thunder (in comic #1) (AW) 1.50
(2) Promo: Special Horror Issue (in comic #1) 1.50
3 Touched with Fire (T.Boonthanakit) (in comic #2) 50
4 Ray Bradbury (in comic #2) 50
5 Comic #3 promo (in comic #2) 50
6 Lost (Al) Williamson art (in #3) 50
7 Besides a Dinosaur (W.Stout) (in comic #3) 50
(8?) Jurassic Park promo 50
(9?) Mars Attacks promo 50

Ray Bradbury Comics © Byron Preiss Visual Communications, Inc.

(10?) Mars Attacks promo 50
11 Bradbury's Martians (JMu) (in comic #4) 50
12 The April Witch (JMu) (in comic #5) 50
13 The Homecoming (T.Boonthanakit) (in comic #5) 50
14 Bradbury Comics #6 (KJo) (in comic #5) 50

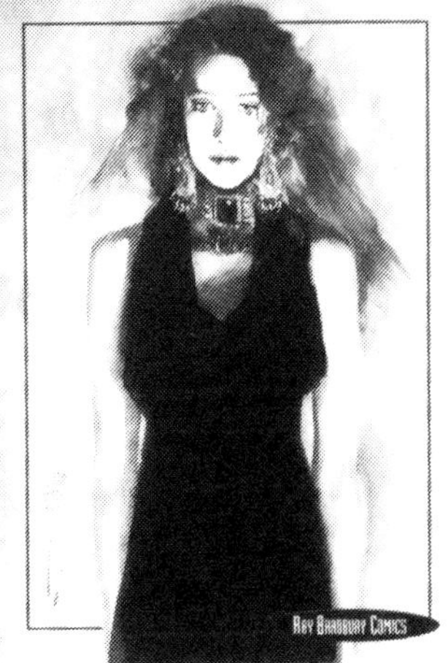

Ray Bradbury Comics © Byron Preiss Visual Com., Inc.; Reiki Warriors © Daerick Gross

REIKI WARRIORS

Heroic Publishing (1993)

(Daerick Gross art)

Only 4,500 copies of each card were printed. The cards came bagged with comic books, but we're not sure which ones.

#R 00 Reiki Warriors 50
#R 01 Murcielaga She Bat 50
#R 02 Mr. No 50
#R 03 Soliloquy Jones 50
#R 04 Rhesus 50
#R 05 Squamus 50
#R 06 Ethereal Black 50
#R 07 Sifu 50

REN & STIMPY SHOW

Topps (1993)

This is a really weird set of cards and stickers. The cards and the stickers have the same pictures, but are numbered differently. However, cards and stickers of the same number have the same puzzle back. There are three different types of prismatic card stock for each card: circles, splotches, and scribbles, with a fourth type for the stickers. I got one pack with three different versions of the same card! (We have also seen one sticker back with a card front, which we hope is just an error.) All of the cards and stickers have picture puzzle backs (except for the first four stickers, which are pictures of the completed puzzles). There are 2 puzzles, using 15 puzzle backs each and 2 puzzles using 8 puzzle backs each. Both

Ren & Stimpy © Nickelodeon

cards and stickers are captioned on the front and numbered on the back. Stickers have an additional copyright notice on the front and a small number in one corner, where it says "Peel." Since there are four times as many cards as stickers, sets of each are sold separately. However, one could argue that a true set consists of all three versions of each card plus the stickers, for a total of 200 items! If that's not enough, there are four "Cheesy Chase Cards" which are like old style Topps entertainment cards: cheap cardboard stock, without coating, foil or any other enhancement. We're so "cheesy" ourselves that we used one of them for our illustration. (Actually, the prismatic card stock made all our pictures turn out lousy in black and white.)

Set: 50 prismatic cards, mixed 9.00
Set: 50 prismatic cards, same 10.00
Set: 50 stickers 30.00

Cheesy Chase Cards
4 diff., each 4.00

Ren & Stimpy © Nickelodeon

TV show promo card 1.50
This isn't related to the series, and seems to be a promo for the TV series. Naturally, it makes a good picture, so we used it. It doesn't look like the cards in the series at all, but its a neat collectible anyway.
Pack: 4 cards, 1 sticker 1.00

CARD CHECKLIST
1 Big Baby Scam! 20
2 Robin Hoek and Maid Moron 20
3 Button Me, Ren 20
4 ? 20
5 I Wuv U Guys! 20
6 Sob Stinky! Sob 20
7 'Ten Hutt!! 20
8 The Loyal Order of Stupids 20
9 Wrestlemaniacs 20
10 The Money's Mine I'm the Cat! . . .20
11 Ren Hoek Esq. 20
12 The Good! The Bad and the Stupid! 20
13 The Joy of Nature! 20
14 Happy Happy! Peel Peel! 20
15 Royal Canadian Kilted Yaksmen . .20
16 Hold Everything! 20
17 You Eeediot! 20
18 "You Bloated Sack of Proto-Plasm!" 20
19 "See You Next Time Folks!" 20
20 Happy Happy! Joy Joy! Stinky Wizzleteats #1 Hit! 20
21 "The World According to Marlin Hoek" 20
22 Don't Make Me Use This!! 20
23 This Card Ain't Big Enough For Both of Us! 20
24 "No Sir, I Don't Like It" 20
25 "Tag, You're It!" 20
26 The Ren & Stimpy Show 20
27 Stressed? Who's Stressed, Man?! .20
28 Yee-Ooww!! 20
29 "It's Party Time!" 20
30 Roadkill Ren Hoek 20
31 Nurse Stimpy to the Rescue! 20
32 Get Ready for Yak Shaving Day . .20
33 Oh My Beloved Ice Cream Bar! . .20
34 You Filthy Swine! 20
35 You Sick Little Monkey 20
36 Reporting for Duty 20
37 Happy! Happy! Joy! Joy! 20
38 Leave Everything to Me 20
39 Oh Joy!! 20
40 It Has the Smell of Fresh Bison . .20
41 Fire Dogs 20
42 Welcome to "Untamed World" 20
43 The Muddy Mudskipper Show 20
44 Space Madness 20
45 Aaaaah! 20
46 Come on and Get Your Log! 20
47 The Beautiful Shiny Button 20
48 New! LOG for Girls 20
49 My Country Reeks of Trees... 20
50 Who Cut the Cheese, Man?! 20

Stickers
1 Aaaaah! 50
2 Space Madness 50
3 The Muddy Mudskipper Show 50
4 Welcome to "Untamed World" 50
5 Fire Dogs 50
6 It Has the Smell of Fresh Bison! . .50
7 Oh Joy!! 50
8 Happy! Happy! Joy! Joy! 50
9 Leave Everything to Me 50
10 Reporting for Duty 50
11 You Sick Little Monkey 50
12 You Filthy Swine! 50
13 Oh My Beloved Ice Cream Bar! . .50
14 Get Ready For Yak Shaving Day .50
15 Nurse Stimpy to the Rescue! 50
16 Roadkill Ren Hoek 50
17 "Its Party Time!" 50
18 Yee-Ooww!! 50
19 Stressed? Who's Stressed, Man?! .50
20 The Ren & Stimpy Show 50
21 "The World According to Marlin Hoek" 50
22 Don't Make Me Use This!! 50
23 This Card Ain't Big Enough for Both of Us! 50
24 "No Sir, I Don't Like It" 50
25 "Tag, You're It!" 50
26 Happy Happy! Joy Joy! 50
27 "See You Next Time Folks!" 50
28 You Bloated Sack of Protoplasm!" .50
29 You Eeediot! 50
30 Hold Everything! 50
31 Royal Canadian Kilted Yaksmen . .50
32 Happy Happy! Peel Peel! 50
33 The JOY of Nature! 50
34 The Good! The Bad and the Stupid! 50
35 Ren Hoek Esq. 50
36 The Money's Mine I'm the Cat! . .50
37 Wrestlemaniacs 50
38 The Loyal Order of Stupids 50
39 'Ten Hutt!! 50
40 Sob Stinky! Sob 50
41 I Wuv U Guys! 50
42 ? 50
43 Button Me, Ren 50
44 Robin Hoek and Maid Moron 50
45 Big Baby Scam! 50
46 Come on and get your LOG! 50
47 The Beautiful Shiny Button! 50
48 New LOG for Girls 50
49 My Country Reeks of Trees 50
50 Who Cut the Cheese, Man?! 50

Return of Superman © DC Comics, Inc.

RETURN OF SUPERMAN

SkyBox (1993)

These cards tell the story of the battle between the four pretenders who claim to be Superman, and the return of the real one (you just can't keep a profitable superhero dead). The card fronts are bordered with grey Superman "S" symbols and an inner frame line which varies in color from card to card. The backs repeat the "S" design in light colors and contain the card title, text and number. Card artists are credited for a change. The bonus cards are very attractive. They have a common background, the Superman "S" symbol in gold foil, and form a 5" x 7" puzzle when pieced together. The factory set has one extra card numbered SP1, titled "Earth's Greatest Hero." It shows the one and only true Superman and the four pretenders. The card looks like a regular series card with a back like the bonus cards. There is also a new header card which has the same art as the binder and the wrapper. The binder is double sided, with a picture from Doomsday, The Death of Superman on the other side.

Set: 100 cards 25.00

Foil Enhanced Bonus Cards (1:36)
SP1of4 Superman-The Man of Steel! (JBg/DJa) 15.00
SP2of4 Superman in Action! (JG/DRo) 15.00
SP3of4 The Adventures of Superman! (TG/DHz) 15.00
SP4of4 Superman! (DJu/BBr) 18.00
0 Promo card (DJu/BBr) 4.00
Complete factory set, with all bonus cards and inc. two special cards + double-sided binder (35,000 made) 80.00
Pack: 8 cards 1.50

CARD CHECKLIST
1 Reign of the Supermen! (DJu/BBr) .25
2 The Last Son of Krypton! (JG) 25
3 The Man of Steel! (JBg/DJa) 25
4 The Man of Tomorrow!(DJu/BBr) . .25
5 Superboy! (TG/DHz) 25
6 Living Energy! (KGa/JG) 25
7 Evil's Enemy! (JG/DRo) 25
8 Serving Justice! (JG/Dro) 25
9 Superman is Back! (DJu/BBr) 25
10 Lois Demands Proof!(DJu/BBr) . . .25
11 Chained Fury! (DJu/BBr) 25
12 Doomsday Lives! (DJu/BBr) 25
13 Armored Protector! (JBg/DJa) 25
14 Hammer Power! (JBg/DJa) 25
15 Steel Heart! (uncredited) 25
16 Steel Savior! (JBg/DJa) 25
17 Brash Style! (TG/DHz) 25
18 Stopped Cold! (TG/DHz) 25
19 Don't Call Me Superboy!(TG/DHz) .25
20 Pumped! (TG/DHz) 25
21 Shocking Discovery! (TG/DHz) . . .25

Return of Superman © DC Comics, Inc.

22 Hunter of the Night! (JG/DRo) 25
23 Heroic Challenge! (KGa/JG) 25
24 America's Guardian! (DJu/BBr) . . .25
25 Seal of Approval! (DJu/BBr) 25
26 Prince of the City! (TG/DHz) 25
27 Supergirl! (JG/DRo) 25
28 Boy Meets Girl! (TG/DHz) 25
29 Tracking the Truth! (JBg/DJa) 25
30 Rescue in the Skies! (JBg/DJa) . .25
31 Easy Targets! (JBg/DJa) 25
32 My Way or the Highway! (TG/KK) .25
33 Harsh Lecture! (JBg/DJa) 25
34 Let the Hammer Strike! (JBg/DJa) .25
35 Showoff! (JBg/DJa) 25
36 Lightning-Quick Attack! (JBg/DJa) .25
37 Standoff! (TG/DHz) 25
38 Silent Observation! (KGa/JG) 25
39 Angry Eyes! (JG/DRo) 25
40 Unstoppable War Suit! (JG/DRo) .25
41 Battleground Metropolis!(JBg/DJa) .25
42 Hero Vs. Hero! (JBg/DJa) 25
43 Righteous Rage! (JBg/DJa) 25
44 Disgraced in Defeat! (JBg/DJa) . . .25
45 Crisis Awaits! (JBg/DJa) 25
46 Surrounded by Death! (DJu/BBr) . .25
47 Ambushed! (DJu/BBr) 25
48 Simultaneous Attacks! (DJu/BBr) .25
49 A City Annihilated! (DJu/BBr) 25
50 From the Ashes! (JBg/DJa) 25
51 Bow to the Conqueror! (DJu/BBr) .25
52 Taking the Blame! (KGa/JG) 25
53 Murder without Mercy! (TG/DHz) . .25
54 Mayhem in the Skies! (TG/DHz) . .25
55 Evil's Victory! (TG/DHz) 25
56 Escape! (JBg/DJa) 25
57 Grim Determination! (JBg/DJa) . . .25
58 Superman? (JBg/DJa) 25
59 Lois is Convinced! (DJu/BBr) 25
60 Charging to War! (DJu/BBr) 25
61 Anticipating War! (DJu/BBr) 25
62 Schemes of Evil! (DJu/BBr) 25
63 At the Battlefront! (DJu/BBr) 25
64 Identity Revealed! (JG/DRo) 25
65 Taking Command! (DJu/BBr) 25
66 The Battle Begins! (TG/DHz) 25
67 Riding Hard! (TG/DHz) 25
68 Against the Odds! (KGa/JG) 25
69 Naked Assault! (JBg/DJa) 25
70 Resistance! (TG/DHz) 25
71 Armed and Dangerous! (JBg/DJa) .25
72 Blasting Away! (TG/DHz) 25
73 Into the Breach! (TG/DHz) 25
74 Punch-Out! (JG/DRo) 25
75 Fire Power! (JG/DRo) 25
76 To the Core! (JG/DRo) 25
77 Trouble Approaches! (JBg/DJa) . .25
78 Mongul's Death Grip! (JBg/DJa) . .25
79 Surprise Savior! (DJu/BBr) 25
80 Target Superman! (DJu/BBr) 25
81 Standing Tall! (DJu/BBr) 25
82 To the Rescue! (JG/DRo) 25
83 Surprise Ally! (DJu/BBr) 25
84 Eradicator Defeated! (JG/DRo) . . .25
85 Eradicator Victorious! (DJu/BBr) . .25
86 Fury Unleashed! (DJu/BBr) 25
87 Final Charge! (DJu/BBr) 25
88 Fists of Vengeance! (DJu/BBr) . . .25
89 Deadly Kryptonite! (DJu/BBr) 25
90 Noble Sacrifice! (DJu/BBr) 25
91 Full Power! (DJu/BBr) 25
92 Doomsday for the Cyborg! (DJu/BBr) 25
93 A Hero Restored! (DJu/BBr) 25
94 On to Metropolis! (DJu/BBr) 25
95 Haunted! (DJu/BBr) 25
96 Metropolis! (TG/DHz) 25
97 And Now–Clark Kent! (KGa/JG) . .25
98 The Daily Planet! (TG/DHz) 25
99 Lois and Clark! (TG/DHz) 25
100 Checklist 25

RIOT GEAR

Triumphant Comics (1993)

Comic book promo card (Advance Comics #57) 1.50

ROBIN II

From Robin II comics, DC (1991)

These holograms were bagged with Robin II *comic books in 1991, which makes these some of the earliest such promo cards. They are nice holograms, but we can't reproduce them in black and white.*

#1 Robin (DG) 4.00
#2 Batman 5.00
#3 The Joker (DG) 4.00
#4 (Bat Signal) 3.00

Robotech: The Macross Saga © Harmony Gold U.S.A., Inc./Tatsunoko Prod. Co. Ltd.

ROBOTECH

THE MACROSS SAGA

Fantasy Trade Cards (1986)

Robotech is the episodic story of cartoon teenagers who fight evil space aliens, robots and other hazards, all to save earth. These cards are taken from the cartoon and its art is reproduced inside a white border. The backs are dirty black with light blue and white lettering. Compare these cards with Speed Racer cards to see how far the quality of cards has risen in just a few years.

Set: 60 cards 12.50

1 Episode 1: Boobytrap 20
2 Rick Hunter 20
3 Lynn Minmei 20
4 Lisa Hayes 20
5 Khyron .20
6 Claudia Grant 20
7 Captain Gloval 20
8 Breetai .20
9 Episode 1 Continued 20
10 Episode 1 Continued 20
11 Episode 1 Continued 20
12 Episode 2: Countdown 20
13 Episode 2 Continued 20
14 Episode 3: Spacefold 20
15 Episode 4: The Long Wait 20
16 Episode 5: Transformation 20
17 Episode 6: Blitzkrieg 20
18 Episode 7: Bye Bye Mars 20
19 Episode 7 Continued 20
20 Episode 8: Sweet Sixteen 20
21 Episode 8 Continued 20
22 Episode 9: Miss Macross 20
23 Episode 10: Blind Game 20
24 Episode 11: First Contact 20
25 Episode 12: The Big Escape 20
26 Episode 13: Blue Wind 20
27 Episode 13 Continued 20
28 Episode 14: Gloval's Report 20
29 Episode 15: Homecoming 20
30 Episode 15 Continued 20
31 Episode 16: Battle Cry 20
32 Episode 17: Phantasm 20
33 Episode 18: Farewell Big Brother .20
34 Episode 18 Continued 20
35 Episode 19: Bursting Point 20
36 Episode 19 Continued 20
37 Episode 20: Paradise Lost 20
38 Episode 20 Continued 20
39 Episode 21: A New Dawn 20
40 Episode 22: Battle Hymn 20
41 Episode 23: Reckless 20
42 Episode 24: Showdown 20
43 Episode 25: Wedding Bells 20
44 Episode 25 Continued 20
45 Episode 25 Continued 20
46 Episode 26: The Messenger 20
47 Episode 26 Continued 20
48 Episode 27: Force of Arm 20
49 Episode 28: Reconstruction Blues .20
50 Episode 29: Robotech Masters . .20
51 Episode 30: Vive Miriya 20
52 Episode 31: Khyron's Revenge . .20
53 Episode 31 Continued 20
54 Episode 32: Broken Heart 20
55 Episode 33: Rainy Night 20
56 Episode 34: Private Times 20
57 Episode 35: Season's Greetings .20
58 Episode 36: To The Stars 20
59 Episode 36 Continued 20
60 Episode 36 Continued 20

ROBOTECH: GENESIS

Eternity Comics (1992)

Set: 10.00

Two card promo sheet 1.00
1 Genesis .50
2 Union 50

S

Sachs & Violens © To be continued... Inc. & George Perez

SACHS & VIOLENS

Comic Images (1993)

Juanita Jean "J.J." Sachs is a model and Ernie "Violens" Schultz is a photographer. One of Juanita's friends gets murdered and she wants vengeance, but the Axecutioner is powerful. Can Ernie save her? Well if he can't, they'll have to change the name of the series. These cards are from the comic book of the same name drawn by George Perez and written by Peter David. It's for an older audience than the usual superhero comics. The cards follow the same pattern as others from Comic Images, with full bleed art and a pink back with story text and a black and white drawing. While the subject matter is mature, there is no nudity. There are six prism cards and the picture from P1 was used for the series promo card and the pictures from P2 and P6 were used for the promo cards for Triton magazine.

Set: 90 cards 9.00

Prism Cards (1:16) (GP)
P1 Nice Lei 8.00
P2 Sachs 7.00
P3 ... & Violens 7.00
P4 Significant Assets 7.00
P5 Lotsaballs 7.00
P6 Just The Way You Are 7.00
Sachs promo card (GP)(Triton) 2.00
Violens promo card (GP)(Triton) . . . 2.00
Promo card (GP) 2.50
Pack: 10 cards 1.00

CARD CHECKLIST
1 The Moment 10
2 Wendy 10
3 Undress For Success 10
4 Going Down 10
5 The Moment Lost 10
6 The Artiste 10
7 Taking Direction 10
8 Head Hunters 10
9 The Unkindest Cut 10
10 Work With Me 10
11 Juanita Jean 10
12 Miss Fire 10
13 Bag Lady 10
14 Nuts 10
15 Crackhead 10
16 Is That Clock Right? 10
17 Ernie 10
18 Lucky Guess 10
19 A Nice Lei 10
20 Shutterbug 10
21 Hawaiian Eye 10
22 Working Late 10
23 Overexposed 10
24 Bert The Agent 10
25 Seeing What Develops 10
26 Bert & Ernie 10
27 Making A Point 10
28 When A Body Meets A Body... 10
29 Alas, Poor Wendy... 10
30 Mac Attack 10
31 Ball Breaker 10
32 Leather Lady 10
33 Model Career 10
34 Head Line 10
35 Sister Act 10
36 Getting The Axe 10
37 Head Trip 10
38 The Cutting Edge 10
39 Severance pay 10
40 Kelso 10
41 Just The Facts 10
42 Cop Out 10
43 Voice From Beyond 10
44 Call To Arms 10
45 Happier Times 10
46 Lamb To The Slaughter 10
47 Armed To The Teeth 10
48 Rock And Roll 10
49 Poor Reception 10
50 J.J. Out Of Patience 10
51 Tied Up Right Now 10
52 First Impression 10
53 Unwilling Subject 10
54 Busting His Chops 10
55 Eye To Eye 10
56 Shooting Off Your Mouth 10
57 One Of The Boys 10
58 In The Lion's Den 10
59 Unsafe Sachs 10
60 Photo Finish 10
61 Nailed 10
62 Lost In The Forest 10
63 Fighting Mad 10
64 Whipped Into A Frenzy 10
65 Say "Jeeeez!" 10
66 Recess 10
67 Losing Face 10
68 Beating A Retreat 10
69 Shutter Bugged 10
70 Floored 10
71 Second Wave 10
72 Knuckling Under 10
73 Down, But Not Out 10
74 Face To Mask 10
75 Moment Of Truth 10
76 First Strike 10
77 Boot To The Head 10
78 Axecutioner's Song 10
79 Prolonging The Agony 10
80 Weak Link 10
81 Final Moves 10
82 Out Of Luck? 10
83 Death From Above 10

Sachs & Violens © To be continued... Inc. & George Perez

84 Blaze Of Glory 10
85 Violens In Earnest 10
86 Axed 10
87 Violens Begets Violence 10
88 Sachs & The Single Girl 10
89 Safe Sachs 10
90 Checklist 10

Sandman © DC Comics, Inc.

SANDMAN

SkyBox (1994)

The set contains the first 50 comic book covers of the Sandman *plus 39 original cards created for the set and a checklist. The cards are 1" taller than normal and quite different looking than the "normal" comics cards. This fact, plus the popularity of the comic book series, makes this a highly collectible card set. The original wholesale price on boxes was quite high, and with only six cards per pack, the set is more expensive than normal. The* Sandman *comic book is in the DC Vertigo line which means that it is for an older audience than the usual comic book and features characters created by Neil Gaiman, Sam Kieth and Mike Dringenberg. All card art for the first 50 cards is by Dave McKeon. The art is difficult to describe, but each of these cards has a black/purple bottom strip which says "Sandman" and the name of the cover subset given below. The next 39 cards are portraits of characters from the comic books and have black/purple border stripes both top and bottom, with the name of the character at the bottom. The actual portrait would have fit in a standard 3½" tall card. Text, title and card number are on the back with an additional small picture by different artists. These 39 cards are by different artists, and the checklist card actually credits them (as does our checklist below) which is quite uncommon. The Endless Gallery cards contain portraits of the listed characters inside a gold foil border. The backs are dark green with text and number, but not additional art. This is one of the ten sets you* ***must own*** *to be a legitimate comics cards collector. The cards were originally scheduled for fall 1993, but were held back until February 1994. During the interim, SkyBox sent out silver foil versions of the seven Endless Gallery cards as promotions. No more than 2,000 sets were produced. Generally, they sent just one card to each person on their promotional freebee list, so sets of the silver foil cards are a lot harder to assemble than those of the regular gold foil bonus cards.*

Set: 90 cards, all 4½" tall 40.00

Endless Gallery Cards, Gold Foil (1:18)
I Dream (DMc) 17.00
II Destiny (KW) 17.00
III Desire (JMu) 20.00
IV Despair (George Pratt) 17.00
V Delirium (JIT) 17.00
VI Destruction (GF) 17.00
VII Death (BSz) 20.00
3-D Stereo Hologram Bonus Card (1:180)
a Morpheus (DMc) 75.00

Sandman foil card © DC Comics, Inc.

Silver Foil border prototype cards
I Dream (DMc) 35.00
II Destiny (KW) 35.00
III Desire (JMu) 40.00
IV Despair (George Pratt) 35.00
V Delirium (JIT) 35.00
VI Destruction (GF) 35.00
VII Death (BSz) 40.00
S1 Doll's House promo 4.00
Three card promo packs, 3 diff.
from *Cards Illustrated*, each 1.50
CI-1 Abel (KN) 50
CI-2 Matthew the Raven (MZi) 50
CI-3 The Doll's House (DMc) 50
CI-4 Guardians of the Gate (GyA) . . .50
CI-5 Season of Mist (DMc) 50
CI-6 Dream Country (DMc) 50
CI-7 Azazel & Choronzon (VcL) 50
CI-8 Dream Country (DMc) 50
CI-9 Master of Dreams (DMc) 50
Four card promo sheet (4,444 made) 5.00
Six card uncut sheet 5.00
Album, with pictoral cover &
large promo sheet 20.00
Pack: 6 cards 2.50

CARD CHECKLIST

Cover Art Cards (Dave McKean)
Master of Dreams/Preludes & Nocturnes
1 Sleep of the Just 50
2 Imperfect Hosts 50
3 Dream a Little Dream 50
4 A Hope in Hell 50
5 Passengers 50
6 24 Hours 50
7 Sound and Fury 50
8 The Sound of Her Wings 50
The Doll's House
9 Tales in the Sand 50
10 The Doll's House 50
11 Moving In 50
12 Playing House 50
13 Men of Good Fortune 50
14 Collectors 50
15 Into the Night 50
16 Lost Hearts 50
Dream Country
17 Calliope 50
18 A Dream of a Thousand Cats 50
19 A Midsummer Night's Dream 50
20 Facade 50
Season of Mists
21 Season of Mists, Prologue 50
22 Season of Mists, Chaper One 50
23 Season of Mists, Chaper Two 50
24 Season of Mists, Chaper Three . .50
25 Season of Mists, Chapter Four . . .50
26 Season of Mists, Chapter Five . . .50
27 Season of Mists, Chapter Six 50
28 Season of Mists, Epilogue 50
Distant Mirrors/Fables & Reflections
29 Thermidor 50
30 August 50
31 Three Septembers and a January .50
A Game of You
32 Slaughter on Fifth Ave. 50
33 Lullabies of Broadway 50
34 Bad Moon Rising 50
35 Beginning to See the Light 50
36 Over the Sea to Sky 50
37 I Woke Up and One of Us
Was Crying 50
Convergences
38 The Hunt 50
39 Soft Places 50
40 The Parliament of Books 50
Brief Lives
41 Brief Lives, Chapter One 50
42 Brief Lives, Chaper Two 50
43 Brief Lives, Chaper Three 50
44 Brief Lives, Chapter Four 50
45 Brief Lives, Chapter Five 50
46 Brief Lives, Chapter Six 50
47 Brief Lives, Chapter Seven 50
48 Brief Lives, Chapter Eight 50
49 Brief Lives, Chapter Nine 50
Distant Mirrors/Fables & Reflections
50 Ramadan 50
Dwellers in The Dreaming
51 Cain (SA) 50
52 Abel (KN) 50
53 Lucien The Librarian (JO) 50
54 Eve (MK) 50
55 Fiddler's Green (CR) 50
56 The Corinthian (DGb) 50
57 Mervyn Pumpkinhead (JIT) 50
58 Brute & Glob (MJ) 50
59 Nuala (JoP) 50
60 Matthew the Raven (MZi) 50
61 Guardians of the Gate (GyA) 50
Other Realms
62 The Three Witches (MZi) 50
63 Cluracan (SAP) 50
64 Ishtar (MiA) 50
65 Duma & Remiel (MBu) 50
66 Lucifer & Mazikeen (PBd) 50
67 Mad Hettie (DFg) 50
68 Thessaly (CDo) 50
69 Azazel & Choronzon (VcL) 50
70 Puck, Loki & the Cuckoo (CV) . . .50
Dreamers of Earth
71 Alex & Roderick Burgess (BT) . . .50
72 Emperor Norton (DCw) 50
73 The Wise Old Siamese (JWk) . . .50
74 John Dee (GyD) 50
75 Richard Madoc (DFg) 50
76 Rose Walker (GID) 50
77 Unity Kincaid (Craig Hamilton) . . .50
78 Barbie (MW) 50
79 Lyta Hall & Daniel (MaH) 50
80 Hazel & Foxglove (PBd) 50
81 Hector Hall & Garrett
Sanford (JTo) 50
82 Wanda (CDo) 50
83 Lady Johanna Constantine (SnW) .50
84 William Shakespeare (CV) 50
85 Rowland & Paine (MWg) 50
Intimates
86 Calliope (MZi) 50
87 Nada (MJ) 50
88 Hob Gadling (MZi) 50
89 Orpheus (BT) 50
90 Checklist 50

Satan's Six © Jack Kirby

SATAN'S SIX

Topps (1993)

Promo cards bagged with Topps Satan's Six comics. There should have been a card #5, but we haven't found it yet.

1 Frightful (JK?) 50
2 Hard Luck Harrigan 50
3 (no caption) (John Cleary) 50
from Satan's Six #3
4 Dezira (BSf) 50
(5) may not exist
6 Satan's Six (John Cleary) 50
from Satan's Six #4
7 Doctor Mordius 50
8 Kuga 50
9 Brian Bluedragon (JK) 50

THE SAVAGE DRAGON

Comic Images (1992)

These are full-bleed comic book close-up pictures with text, card number and caption on a green card back. Card text for the first 21 cards discusses the artist and the character. The rest of the cards usually discuss the storyline depicted on the front, with notes about the character. The prism bonus cards are on a reflective polygon stock. The "prizm" promo card is on a different surface, and has a white back with black text and "Not for sale" in red. All the cards are by ***Erik Larsen****, creator of the Savage Dragon.*

Set: 90 cards 11.00

Prizm promo card 5.00
Promo card 2.50
Prisms (1:12)
P1 First Print 10.00
P2 First Work 10.00
P3 Features 10.00

Savage Dragon © Erik Larsen

P4 Team 10.00
P5 Image 10.00
P6 Crossovers 10.00
Pack: 10 cards 1.00

CARD CHECKLIST

1 Bullseye .... .10
2 Graphic Fantasy .... .10
3 Megaton .... .10
4 Secret Identity .... .10
5 Powers .... .10
6 Transportation .... .10
7 Style .... .10
8 Oakland, CA .... .10
9 Control .... .10

Cards 10 thru 18 form a 3x3 super-panel with a black border, signed on card 16.

10 Variety .... .10
11 Goal .... .10
12 Introduced .... .10
13 Construction .... .10
14 Partners .... .10
15 Well Crafted .... .10
16 Flexibility .... .10
17 Co-existence .... .10
18 Crossovers .... .10
19 Bedrock .... .10
20 Dragon .... .10
21 Crime Buster .... .10
22 Cutthroat .... .10
23 Glowbug .... .10
24 Reality .... .10
25 Finished? .... .10
26 Standoff .... .10
27 Defiant .... .10
28 No Funny Stuff .... .10
29 It's My Job .... .10
30 Found .... .10
31 Q & A .... .10
32 A Fallen Hero .... .10
33 Personality .... .10
34 Name Calling .... .10
35 Frank Darling .... .10
36 Impression .... .10
37 Mildred Darling .... .10
38 Trouble .... .10
39 Freaks .... .10
40 No Thanks .... .10
41 Threats .... .10
42 Explosion! .... .10
43 News Flash .... .10
44 I'm Ready .... .10
45 On Call .... .10
46 I'm Here .... .10
47 Loaded .... .10
48 Up, Up & Away .... .10
49 Uninvited .... .10
50 Offense .... .10
51 Hot Shots .... .10
52 Wounded .... .10
53 Help! .... .10
54 Star .... .10
55 Media Vow .... .10
56 Evil Lurks .... .10
57 Status Quo .... .10
58 The Search .... .10
59 The Arachnid .... .10
60 Spun .... .10
61 Response .... .10
62 Disarmed .... .10
63 Electrocution .... .10
64 Marksman .... .10
65 I Don't Know .... .10
66 Cyborg .... .10
67 Debbie Harris .... .10
68 More Hostages! .... .10
69 Bad Guys .... .10
70 The Vicious Circle .... .10
71 Hellrazor .... .10
72 Here...Catch! .... .10
73 Advice .... .10
74 Shielded .... .10
75 Relations .... .10
76 Sliced .... .10
77 Down, But Far From... .... .10
78 Road Trips .... .10
79 He Returns .... .10
80 Guilty .... .10
81 Revenge .... .10
82 Mortified .... .10
83 One, Two, Punch .... .10
84 Good Bye .... .10
85 Freeze! .... .10
86 Last Strike .... .10
87 Blood .... .10
88 Critical .... .10
89 The End? .... .10
90 Checklist .... .10

SCAVENGERS

Amazing Heroes/Triumphant (1993)

Comic promo card 5.00

Secret City Saga © Jack Kirby

SECRET CITY SAGA

Topps Comics (1993)

Comic book promo cards bagged with Secret City Saga *comics from Topps.*

1 Captain Glory (Ted Boonthanakit) .. .50
2 Night Glider (Ted Boonthanakit) .. .50
3 Bombast (Ted Boonthanakit) .... .50

from Secret City Saga #2

4 Cal Cutta (JK/BSz) .... .50
5 General Ordiz (JK/BSz) .... .50
6 Dreena (JK & JBy) .... .50

from Secret City Saga #3??

7 President Clinton (AT) .... .50
8 Vice-President Gore (AT) .... .50
9 Doctor Roag (JBy) .... .50

from Secret City Saga #4??

10 Bombast (JV) .... .50
(11) may not exist
12 Members (SD/AAd) .... .50

Secret Origin minibooks © DC Comics, Inc.

SECRET ORIGIN STORIES

MINIBOOKS

Leaf (1981)

These are mini-comic books, but they are only a little bigger than cards, so they are usually listed with the cards in price guides.

Set: 8 Minibooks 15.00

Aquaman 1.50
Batman 2.00
Green Lantern 1.50
Hawkman 1.50
Justice League of America 1.50
Superman 2.00
The Flash 1.75
Wonder Woman 1.50

The Shadow © Advance Magazine Publishers Inc.

SHADOW, THE

Topps (1994)

Topps issued this set of cards in June 1994 for the live-action movie starring Alec Baldwin. However, only the first 70 cards are from the movie. The last 20 cards, plus the 10 Shadow Legends cards plus the Topps Finest Shadow chase cards are all from the comic book series (from Dark Horse comics, not Topps) or inspired by the original pulp magazines and contain painted art. We have listed these cards below, because they fit the theme of this book and (unfairly) ignored the very fine live action movie cards, which don't fit this theme.

Set: 90 cards + 10 Shadow Legends cards 15.00

Promo card 1.00
Topps Finest/Deluxe Gold foil cards (1:18)
S1 to S?, not titled, each 7.50
Pack: 8 cards 1.25

Card Checklist

1 thru 70, movie photo cards, not listed, each .... .15

Comic Book images

71 Michael Wm. Kaluta [A] .... .15
72 Michael Wm. Kaluta [B] .... .15
73 Michael Wm. Kaluta [C] .... .15
74 John Bolton .... .15
75 Michael Wm. Kaluta [D] .... .15
76 Geof Darrow .... .15
77 Michael Wm. Kaluta [E] .... .15
78 Gary Gianni [A] .... .15
79 Tim Bradstreet .... .15
80 Howard Chaykin .... .15
81 Mark Chiarello .... .15
82 Gary Gianni [B] .... .15
83 Bo Hampton .... .15
84 Ray Lago .... .15
85 Jon J. Muth .... .15
86 George Pratt .... .15
87 John H. Snyder III .... .15
88 John Van Fleet .... .15
89 Matt Wagner .... .15
90 Kent Williams .... .15

The Shadow Legend (Steranko)

L1 Who is the Shadow? .... .15
L2 Birth of the Shadow .... .15
L3 The Shadow of Radio .... .15
L4 Voices of the Shadow .... .15
L5 Creator of the Shadow .... .15
L6 The Shadow in Comic Books ... .15
L7 The Lovely Margo Lane .... .15
L8 The Shadow in Hollywood ..... .15
L9 The Shadow Motion Picture .... .15
L10 Illustrator Steranko .... .15

SHADOWHAWK

Comic Images (1992)

The card fronts are full bleed pictures that resemble close-ups of comic pages. The backs have the caption and card number plus some text in a blue border. Jim Valentino did the art.

Set: 90 Cards 11.00

Promo card 4.00

Prism Cards

P1 Coworkers 10.00
P2 Responsibilities 10.00
P3 Image Month 10.00
P4 Creation 10.00
P5 Self-Employed 10.00
P6 Conclusion 10.00
Pack: 10 cards 1.00

CARD CHECKLIST

1 Shadowhawk .... .10
2 Antihero .... .10
3 First Time .... .10
4 Prelude .... .10
5 Like A Fox .... .10
6 Punishment .... .10
7 Secret Identity .... .10
8 Mysterious .... .10
9 Nonverbal .... .10
10 Choices .... .10
11 Valentino .... .10
12 The Beginning .... .10

Shadowhawk © Jim Valentino

13 Costume .... .10
14 The Bait .... .10
15 Defense .... .10
16 Penalty .... .10
17 Genre (1st card of double) ..... .10
18 Respect (2nd card of double) ... .10
19 Sentenced .... .10
20 Attributes .... .10
21 Slippery .... .10
22 Image .... .10
23 Arson .... .10
24 Flame-Maker .... .10
25 Deception .... .10
26 Larceny .... .10
27 Suspect .... .10
28 The 'Hood .... .10
29 Hoodlums .... .10
30 Make My Day .... .10
31 Kevlar .... .10
32 Artist's Rights (1st card of double) .10
33 Benefit (2nd card of double) .... .10
34 Secrecy .... .10
35 Media .... .10
36 Vendetta .... .10
37 Ownership .... .10
38 Shuriken .... .10
39 Escape .... .10
40 Rieves .... .10
41 Duty .... .10
42 Confide .... .10
43 A Sure Thing .... .10
44 Murder .... .10
45 Vengeance .... .10
46 Change .... .10
47 Creation (1st card of double) ... .10
48 Interaction (2nd card of double) . .10
49 Criminals .... .10
50 Old Acquaintances .... .10
51 Conflicts .... .10
52 Fire Fighting .... .10
53 Two Sides .... .10
54 Comics .... .10
55 Suspicion .... .10
56 Christina .... .10
57 Limited Series .... .10
58 Youth .... .10
59 Spawn .... .10
60 Guest Star .... .10
61 Alike .... .10
62 In the Shadows .... .10
63 Guessing .... .10
64 Motive .... .10
65 Attack .... .10
66 Try Again .... .10
67 POW! .... .10
68 Hero .... .10
69 Toasted .... .10
70 Explosion .... .10
71 The News .... .10
72 Blackjak .... .10
73 Hospitalized .... .10
74 Revenge .... .10
75 Hojo .... .10
76 Liquifier .... .10
77 New Alliance .... .10
78 Sons .... .10
79 Team-Ups .... .10
80 The Law .... .10
81 The Future .... .10
82 Editors .... .10
83 Urban Storm .... .10
84 L.A. Riots .... .10
85 Violence .... .10
86 The Others (1st card of double) . .10
87 Evolution (2nd card of double) .. .10
88 Basic .... .10
89 Identification .... .10
90 Checklist .... .10

IMAGES OF SHADOWHAWK

Image (1994, Comic)

All of the cards except the comic book covers have full bleed art, with titles on the front of the card in a silver foil strip near the bottom which is a very attractive design even though the collector may have to let the light reflect off the silver to read the title. All the cards are bordered with a thin frame line indicating that they are to be placed in 3 x 3 pages, but except as noted, they do not form super-panels with a common background. We couldn't make a full set from a box of these cards, which irritates collectors and accounts for the relatively high price of a full set. We got the four expected bonus cards from the box, but only three different ones, also an irritation. The first 36 cards have images of ShadowHawk

Images of Shadowhawk © Jim Valentino

(thus the series name) drawn by the indicated artists. They all have a blue background with a picture of the Empire State building. Cards #37 to #54 have a blue background with a lengthwise cityscape picture. Card #37 shows the first appearance of ShadowHawk from card #89 in the Youngblood card set. The others show covers of various comic books and have a black border. Cards #55 through #72 have red backs. Cards #64 through #72 form a super-panel (inked by Chance Wolf with background by Brad Foster). Cards #62 through #64 form a three card strip. Cards #73 through #81 have a blue background with a picture of the Statue of Liberty and form another super-panel inked by Chance Wolf and Woz. The backs of the last 18 cards (not counting the checklist, of course) form two 3 x 3 full bleed posters. The first is a ShadowHawk II picture and the other is the same illustration used on the Cards Illustrated promo cards. Card numbers for these 18 cards appear in the silver foil front title strips. Cards #82 and #83 form a double image and cards #96 and #97 show ShadowHawk unmasked.

Set: 100 cards 20.00

Holofoil cards (1:9) (JV)
SP1 ShadowHawk 7.50
SP2 Foursquare 7.50
SP3 The Others 7.50
SP4 The Pact 7.50
SP5 The Regulators 7.50
SP6 U.S. Male 7.50
SP7 Rayn 7.50
Superchase card (1:12 boxes)
0: ShadowBart ..... NYD
Promo cards
Three card promo packs, 3 diff., from *Cards Illustrated*, each 1.00
Promo Sheet (Advance comics) 1.50
Promo sheet (Previews) 1.50
Three card promo packs, 3 diff. from *Cards Illustrated*, each 1.00
The nine cards form a superpanel with art by Giffen, Valentino and Wolf. They are numbered on the back but not captioned. The fronts are the same as the back poster formed by cards #91 to #99.
Pack: 1.25

CARD CHECKLIST

1 Introduction ..... .20
2 Keith Giffen ..... .20
3 Mark Texeira ..... .20
4 Jerry Ordway ..... .20
5 Jae Lee ..... .20
6 McDaniel/Banning ..... .20
7 Larry Stroman ..... .20
8 George Perez ..... .20
9 Nelson ..... .20
10 Murray/Ivy ..... .20
11 Mike Allred ..... .20
12 Dale Keown ..... .20
13 Javier Saltares ..... .20
14 McDaniel/Lopez ..... .20
15 Don Simpson ..... .20
16 Rick Veitch ..... .20
17 Dave Gibbons ..... .20
18 Sam Kieth ..... .20
19 Jordan Raskin ..... .20
20 Jerome K. Moore ..... .20
21 Chris Wozniak ..... .20
22 Tom King ..... .20
23 Malcolm Davis ..... .20
24 Kevin Maguire ..... .20
25 Dan Jurgens ..... .20
26 Larry Marder ..... .20
27 Marat/Miki ..... .20
28 Valentino/McFarlane ..... .20
29 Brad W. Foster ..... .20
30 Chance Wolf ..... .20
31 Randy Queen ..... .20
32 Valentino/Queen ..... .20
33 Eric Vincent ..... .20
34 Bill Sienkiewicz ..... .20
35 Rob Liefeld ..... .20
36 Valentino/Wolf ..... .20
Comic Book Covers (JV unless noted)
37 First Appearance ..... .20
38 Youngblood #2 (RLd) ..... .20
39 Ashcan #1 ..... .20
40 ShadowHawk #1 ..... .20
41 ShadowHawk #2 ..... .20
42 ShadowHawk #3 ..... .20
43 ShadowHawk #4 (JV & EL) ..... .20
44 ShadowHawk II #1 ..... .20
45 ShadowHawk II #2 (JV/CWf) ..... .20
46 ShadowHawk II #3 (JV/CWf) ..... .20
47 Inside Image #7 (KG) ..... .20
48 Inside Image #9 ..... .20
49 ShadowHawk II #3B ..... .20
50 ShadowHawk III #1 (JV/CWf) ..... .20
51 ShadowHawk III #2 ..... .20
52 ShadowHawk III #3C (JV/CWf) ..... .20
53 ShadowHawk III #3 ..... .20
54 ShadowHawk III #4 (JV/CWf) ..... .20
Other Characters (JV unless noted)
55 Carlton Sum (JV/CWf) ..... .20
56 Hojo ..... .20
57 Christina Ried ..... .20
58 Lt. Lou Jacks ..... .20
59 Capt. Frakes ..... .20
60 Jamie Anthonette ..... .20
61 Trencher (KG) ..... .20
62 J. P. Slaughter (JV) ..... .20
63 Savage Dragon (EL) ..... .20
64 Vendetta ..... .20
65 Blackjack ..... .20
66 Cold Blood (MT) ..... .20
67 HardEdge ..... .20
68 Vortex ..... .20
69 Hawk's Shadow ..... .20
70 Arson ..... .20
71 Dedline (CWf) ..... .20
72 Liquifier (Aaron Valentino) ..... .20
73 Klone ..... .20
74 Racket ..... .20
75 Rebound ..... .20
76 Blacklight ..... .20
77 Kontact ..... .20
78 Guardd ..... .20
79 Handgunn ..... .20
80 Slam! ..... .20
81 Cutlass ..... .20
82 Jump down ..... .20
83 Jump down II ..... .20
84 Nightmare ..... .20
85 Laura's Page ..... .20
86 On the ledge ..... .20
87 Revelation ..... .20
88 Hawk Moon ..... .20
89 Alley ..... .20
90 Anguish ..... .20
91 Roof running ..... .20
92 Alert ..... .20
93 Missed! ..... .20
94 Silhouette ..... .20
95 Battle ..... .20
96 Paul ..... .20
97 The Mask ..... .20
98 No Hero ..... .20
99 Contemplation ..... .20
100 Check list ..... .20

Silver Star © Jack Kirby

SILVER STAR

Topps Comics (1993)

The cards came with Silver Star *comics #1 thru #3? (#1 had 3 cards). The cards are not numbered or captioned, but they form a nine-card superpanel. We hope so anyway, since we have only seen the first three cards.*

Set: 9 puzzle piece cards (Rich & Rick Butler), each ..... .50

SILVER SURFER

Comic Images (1992)

The Silver Surfer card set is similar to others issued during 1992 by Comic Images: full bleed front close-up of comic book page, with text, caption and number on the back. However, there is one major difference–the cards are all printed on "Galaxy" prism card stock. The prismatic effect is circular, rather than triangular and makes a very attractive card, which enhances the picture. There were no bonus insert cards with this set. The prism promo card is on regular polygon prism stock. It can also be found with 1" of extra card stock on the left, which was used to bind the card into Advance Comics *#47. This is the first known set of all prism*

Silver Surfer © Marvel Entertainment Group, Inc.

cards and one of the ten sets you ***must own*** *to be a legitimate comics cards collector.*

Set: 72 Prism cards 40.00
Prism Promo Card (RL) 5.00
Pack: 7 cards 4.00

CARD CHECKLIST

1 First Issue (Comic cover) 50
2 Galactus 50
3 Zenn-La 50
4 The Herald 50
5 Cosmic Energy 50
6 Silver Surfer 50
7 Morals .50
8 In the Beginning 50
9 The Watcher 50
10 Fantastic Four 50
11 Betrayed 50
12 Confined 50
13 Presence 50
14 Dr. Doom 50
15 Mephisto 50
16 Home .50
17 Demon 50
18 Nova 50
19 Unchangeable 50
20 The Hulk 50
21 Doctor Strange 50
22 Sub-Mariner 50
23 Life Energies 50
24 Firelord 50
25 The Stranger 50
26 Inhumans 50
27 Celestrials 50
28 Eternity 50
29 Infinity 50
30 Hyperspace 50
31 In-Betweener 50
32 The Living Tribunal 50
33 Jack of Hearts 50
34 Mentor 50
35 Starfox 50
36 Thor 50
37 Humans 50
38 Captain Marvel 50
39 Thanos 50
40 Death .50
41 Destroyer 50
42 Judgment 50
43 Deathwish 50
44 Infinity Gauntlet 50
45 Genocide 50
46 Drax 50
47 Partners 50
48 Soul Gem 50
49 Inmates 50
50 Escape 50
51 Lord of Evil 50
52 Control 50
53 Infinity Watch 50
54 Philosopher 50
55 Peace .50
56 Mantis 50
57 Champion 50
58 Ego 50
59 Quasar 50
60 Skrulls 50
61 Super Skrull 50
62 Guilt 50
63 Inner Self 50
64 Darkside 50
65 Two Halves 50
66 Infinity War 50
67 Another 50
68 Morg 50
69 Casualty 50
70 Heralds 50
71 Resurrection 50
72 Checklist 50

SIMPSONS, THE

Topps (1990, TV)

(Matt Groening art)

These are old style Topps entertainment cards on grey stock. If you like the humor of the show, you will like these cards. The fronts have a TV set with the top button containing the card number and a picture on the screen with a word balloon. There is no caption, so we have used the word balloons as individual card titles. Forty card backs contain puzzle pieces and four more show the completed puzzle. The remaining 44 cards contain trivia questions about the TV show named "Bart's Bafflers," "Marge's Mindbenders," "Maggie's Mutterings," Lisa's Lowdown," or "Homer's Homeroom." The 22 stickers are also grey, but on better stock than the cards, with the characters in various poses. Sticker backs show Bart at the blackboard, being punished by writing different statements for each sticker.

The Simpsons (card & sticker) © 20th Century Fox

Set: 88 cards, 22 stickers 8.00
Pack: 8 cards, 1 sticker 1.00

CARD CHECKLIST

1 "Don't Forget Your Lunches!" 10
2 "Suck!" .10
3 "I'm Lisa Simpson..." 10
4 "I'm Bart Seemp-Seau,.." 10
5 "No More Television..." 10
6 "I Have an Announcement..." 10
7 "Marge–You're My Wife, But..." 10
8 "Calm Down, Boy!..." 10
9 "Comics Are For Kids, Boy!" 10
10 "time For Our Favorite..." 10
11 "The Family That Mombos Together, Stays Together" 10
12 "Bart!!" "Uh, Oh..." 10
13 "Are We at Weenie Barn yet?" . . .10
14 "We're The Grown-Ups..." 10
15 "Help! I'm A Fully Developed..." . .10
16 "Suck! Suck!" 10
17 "Now Get in There and Clean Up That Mess!" 10
18 "Come Back Her, You Little Smartass!" 10
19 "Tolstoy Schmolstoy!" 10
20 "I'm No Supervising Technican..." .10
21 "All Right!..." 10
22 "Ha! Ha! Ha! Ha!" 10
23 "Suck! Suck! Suck!" 10
24 "Homework is Society's Way..." . . .10
25 "No Reststops for the Next 16 Hours!" 10
26 "Zee Brave Undair..." 10
27 "Look Homer, Clean as a Whistle!" 10
28 "We Can Never Let Him Down.." . .10
29 "Don't Bug Me.I'm Studying, Man!" .10
30 "And Don't Come Out..." 10
31 "Maggie? Lisa? You In There?" . . .10
32 "Should I Turn On the TV?..." 10
33 "Don't Have a Cow, Man!" 10
34 "Bart! Get Back Here!!!" 10
35 "Anybody Seen Maggie?!" 10
36 "Marge, Let's Run Away From Home." 10
37 "She's Such an Adorable Infant!..." .10
38 "It's The Bart Simpson Show..." . .10
39 "Quiet! Genius at Work, Man!" . . .10
40 "Shut Up Back There,..." 10
41 "Bart! Did You Eat.." 10
42 "What'll It Be Tonight..." 10
43 "Suck! Suck! Suck!" 10
44 "March Your Butts Straight..." 10
45 "Happy Father's Day, Dad..." 10
46 "Stand Back, Comrades!..." 10
47 "There's Nothing More..." 10
48 "Right On, Dude!" 10
49 "Who Do You Think..." 10
50 "This Looks Like the Work..." 10
51 "You Said 'Left'" "I Said 'Right'" . .10
52 "It's Quiet..." 10
53 "Kids Out There in T.V. Land..." . .10
54 "There's Only So Much..." 10

The Simpsons © 20th Century Fox

55 "It's Amazing How Much..." 10
56 "Aaauuughhh!" 10
57 "Who Ate My Cookies?!!!" 10
58 "Back Off Homer...." 10
59 "I Said, Knock It Off!!" 10
60 "Don't Blame Us, Dad!..." 10
61 "Go To Bed!..." 10
62 "There's Only One Cookie Left!" . .10
63 "I Didn't Do It..." 10
64 "Gangway Man!" 10
65 "Which One of You Ate My Last Donut!" 10
66 "Bart?" "Uh Oh Gotta Hide." 10
67 "Last One to the Breakfast..." 10
68 "God Help Me." 10

69 "Bart, You're Such a Dimwit!" 10
70 "I'm Bart Simpson,..." 10
71 "Your Father's Chasing..." 10
72 "Bbaarrtttt!" 10
73 "I Can't Wait to See..." 10
74 "Why You Little...!!!" 10
75 "For the Last Time, ..." 10
76 "I Think It's Time to Go..." 10
77 "Let's Take Turns Yelling.." 10
78 "Marge! Where's the Personals..." .10
79 "We Have No Idea Who Made This Mess" 10
80 "This is the Life, Man!" 10
81 "Me, Bartunga!" "Me, Leesumba!" .10
82 "Unga, Bunga, Yunga, Ho!" 10
83 "There Is Justice in the World, Maggie" 10
84 "Suck, Suck, Suck,..." 10
85 "Uh, Oh..." 10
86 "Another Day of Parental Oppression" 10
87 "Aye, Carumba!" 10
88 "Apple Polisher!" 10

Stickers
1 Bartman, Avenger of Evil 25
2 "Underachiever" 25
3 "Peace, Man." 25
4 Bart Simpson 25
5 Maggie Simpson 25
6 Marge Simpson 25
7 Homer Simpson 25
8 The Simpsons 25
9 All-American Dad 25
10 (Family portrait) 25
11 "I'm Bart Simpson..." 25
12 "War is Hell, Man." 25
13 "There Was a Little Accident.." . . .25
14 "Go For It, Dude!!" 25
15 "No Way, Man!" 25
16 "Cowabunga, Man!" 25
17 "I'm Going to Tell Mom and Dad" .25
18 The All-American Family 25
19 Queen of the Blues 25
20 Suck Suck Suck 25
21 "Fun Has a Name and its..." 25
22 "That's My Boy!" 25

The Simpsons © Bongo Comics

SIMPSONS, THE
SkyBox (1994, Comics)

If you like the Simpsons you'll love this exotic card set with all its strange types of cards. The basic set consists of 40 character cards, numbered S1 to S40 (or #1-40). There are also 30 Itchy and Scratchy cards numbered I1 to I30 (or #41-70). The backs of these cards contain a "Flip-o-matic" picture which creates an animated cartoon of the cat and the rat (Itchy and Scratchy) clobbering each other with a mallet and a club. The ten Radioactive Man cards and the ten tattoos seem to be part of the regular set rather than bonus chase cards, although we often find them for sale as separate sub-sets, with a slightly higher price.

There are plenty of bonus cards. Easiest to find are the wiggle cards, which have two images which can be seen at slightly different viewing angles. The backs form a super-panel poster for the Simpson's cards, with all the characters, and advises you to "Collect 'em or else." There are two groups of three animation cel cards which consist of a background and two pictures on clear cel stock which combine to form a scene. There are also four "Genuine Bart Simpson Glow-in-the-Dark Happy Cards." The cel cards and the glow cards are neither numbered nor titled, which is somewhat confusing because numbers and titles are listed in the checklist on the back of card R10. The promo cel card(s) form a two-part scene of the Simpson family sitting on Homer and watching TV. The cel overlay, if sold separately, could be confused with a cel bonus card. The promo cel has four Simpsons in a row and "C1" on the back. The bonus cel overlays are unnumbered.

Set: 90 cards (Characters, Itchy & Scratchy, Radioactive Man, tattoos) 15.00

Autographed Matt Groening card (1:??)
Glow-in-the Dark (1:36)
(G1) Eyeballs (5 Simpsons) 12.50
(G2) Shock! (Cat & Mouse) 12.50
(G3) Smilin' Joe ("Nuclear Power") 12.50
(G4) TV ("The Simpsons") 12.50
Animation Cel cards (1:18)
(C1) Barber Shop background 8.50
(C2) Barber Shop chair 7.50
(C3) Barber Shop Cat's head 7.50
(C4) TV background 8.50
(C5) 17 characters watching TV . . . 8.50
(C6) Maggie & TV Set 7.50
Wiggle Cards (1:4)(Backs form poster)
W1 (Maggie) 3.00
W2 Itchy & Scratchy Anvil 3.00
W3 Greetings From The Containment Dome! 3.00
W4 Itchy & Scratchy Chase 3.00
W5 (Barney Belch) 3.00
W6 (Itchy & Scratchy Fan) 3.00
W7 (Radioactive Man & Dr. Crab) . . 3.00
W8 (Homer Strangles Bart) 3.00
W9 Bartman 3.00
Promo cards
Four Card promo sheet with P1 thru P4 promos 2.50
18 Otto the Busdriver promo 1.00
P3 Itchy & Scratchy promo 1.00
B1 & C1 two part cel promo card . . . 7.50
Pack: 8 cards + tattoo 1.25

CARD CHECKLIST

Tattoo cards (1:1)
1 Born to Chop 25
2 Burns Lizard 25
3 Flamethrower Itchy 25
4 Bart Fink 25
5 Mermaid Edna 25
6 Skull 25
7 Devil & Cat 25
8 Radioactive Man 25
9 Scratchy in Flames 25
10 Love/Hate 25

The Simpsons © Bongo Comics

Radioactive Man
R1 Fallout Boy 25
R2 Dr. Crab 25
R3 Radioactive Man 25
R4 Lava Man 25
R5 Radioactive Boy and Glowy, The Radioactive Dog 25
R6 "The 2 Loves of Radioactive Ape!" 25

The Simpsons © Bongo Comics

R7 "By My Sidekick Betrayed!" 25
R8 "Radioactive Man's UnSecret Identity!" 25
R9 "Radioactive Man...Public Enemy #1!" 25
R10 "To Betroth a Foe" (& Checklist) .25
Character Cards (#1-#40)
S1 Homer J. Simpson 10
S2 Marge Simpson 10
S3 Bart Simpson 10
S4 Lisa Simpson 10
S5 Maggie Simpson 10
S6 Clancy Wiggum 10
S7 Kent Brockman 10
S8 Lenny .10
S9 Sideshow Bob 10
S10 Apu Nahasapeemapetilon 10
S11 Tattoo Annie 10
S12 Edna Krabappel 10
S13 Dewey Largo 10
S14 Janey Powell 10
S15 Nelson Muntz 10
S16 Jimbo Jones 10
S17 Bumblebee Man 10
S18 Milhouse Van Houten 10
S19 Sideshow Mel 10
S20 Krusty the Clown 10
S21 Lurleen Lumpkin 10
S22 Groundskeeper Willie 10
S23 Rabbi Hyman Krustofski 10
S24 Princess Kashmir 10
S25 Jasper 10
S26 Patty & Selma Bouvier 10
S27 Abraham "Grampa" Simpson . . .10
S28 Smilin' Joe Fission 10
S29 Capital City Goofball 10
S30 Snowball II 10
S31 Bill & Marty 10
S32 Capt. Lance Murdock 10
S33 Horatio McCallister 10
S34 Blinky the 3-Eyed Fish 10
S35 Ms. Botz 10
S36 Troy McClure 10
S37 Dr. Nick Riviera 10
S38 Barney Gumble 10
S39 McBain 10
S40 Character Checklist 10
Itchy & Scratchy (#41-#70)
I1 Bone Appetit 10
I2 Strike Three, You're Dead 10
I3 Pleased to Beat You 10
I4 Gentlemen Prefer Bombs 10

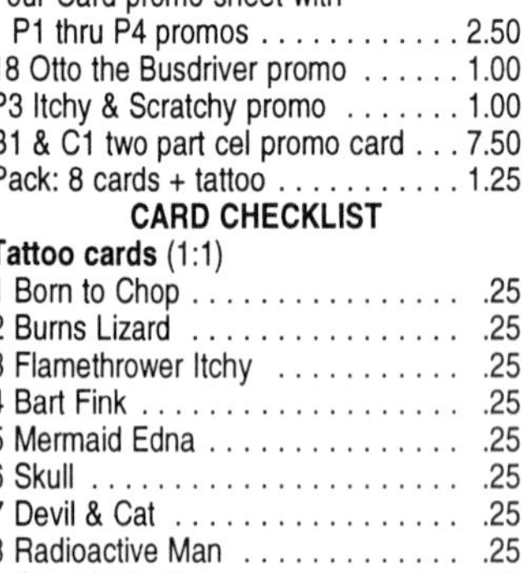

The Simpsons © Bongo Comics

I5 Itchy & Scratchy On Ice .10
I6 Crocodile Doomdee .10
I7 A Farewell to Arms and Legs .10
I8 Tee-House of the August Kaboom .10
I9 Desperately Shrieking Scratchy .10
I10 Bongo Comics #1 cover .10
I11 Third Down, Dead to Go .10
I12 Gun with the Wind .10
I13 Little Dead Corvette .10
I14 Between-Meal Smacks .10
I15 1982 Buzz Spokespersons .10
I16 It's a Wonderful Knife .10
I17 Dead and Butter .10
I18 On the Road Again .10
I19 Some Like It Very, Very Hot .10
I20 The Dead Scratchy Society .10
I21 I'd Like to Propose a Toasting .10
I22 Flesh as a Daisy .10
I23 Out of the Frying Pan, Into the Grave .10
I24 Itchy Blandings Builds His Scream House .10
I25 Porch Pals .10
I26 Candlelight and Whine .10
I27 It Ain't the Heat, It's the Fatality .10
I28 Up, Up and Oy Vay .10
I29 Itchy & Scratchy & Roger Meyers .10
I30 This Here Checklist .10

SKYBOX MASTER SERIES CREATORS EDITION

SkyBox (1994)

These promos look great! Look for all the various "SkyBox Master" series as they come out. They should be very hot!

P01 Dr. Phobic (Brom) 1.00
P02 Kromo (JuB) 1.00
P03 Shook (JuB) 1.00

See Also: DC, Ultraverse & Youngblood

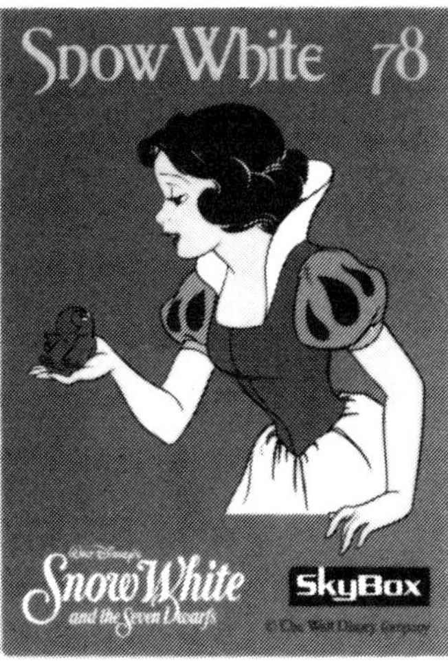

Snow White © The Walt Disney Company

SNOW WHITE

and the Seven Dwarfs

SkyBox (1993, Animated Movie)

The fronts of this set feature full bleed pictures from the classic Disney animated film of the same name. The backs have a red textured background with an additional color picture in a mirror and the card title and number plus the story text. The cards are beautiful on their own and the movie is worth seeing "by children of all ages." Cards 61 to 72 reproduce movie posters from various years; cards 73 to 77 show some production drawings; and cards 78 to 88 have double sided cel art of the main characters on a metallic blue-green background, which is completely unlike the other cards.

Set: 90 cards 15.00

Spectra Cards (1:18)
SP1 The Magic Mirror 8.00
SP2 Marching home 8.00
SP3 Diamond eyes 8.00

Snow White © The Walt Disney Company

SP4 Happily ever after 8.00
Pack: 8 cards 1.00

CARD CHECKLIST
1 Once upon a time... .15
2 A servant in the castle .15
3 "The Fairest one of all." .15
4 Snow White's wish .15
5 Love song .15
6 Love bird .15
7 The jealous Queen .15
8 "Bring back her heart." .15
9 "Come on, won't you smile for me?" .15
10 The Huntsman's shadow .15
11 "Run, run away child!" .15
12 Flight through the forest .15
13 Frightened and alone .15
14 "Do you know where I can stay?" .15
15 "Just like a doll's house." .15
16 "I like it here." .15
17 No one home .15
18 "Seven little chairs." .15
19 "Seven untidy little children." .15
20 Maybe they're orphans .15
21 "I'll use the broom." .15
22 The cottage is clean in no time .15
23 "What funny names." .15
24 The Seven Dwarfs .15
25 Jewels of many colors .15
26 Diamond eyes .15
27 Marching home .15
28 "There's trouble brewin'." .15
29 "There's dirty work afoot!" .15
30 "It's a monster." .15
31 "She's mighty purty." .15
32 "Hooray! She stays!" .15
33 Wash up for supper .15
34 "Cat got your tongue?" .15
35 Bubbles galore! .15
36 "I've been tricked!" .15
37 "Begin thy magic spell." .15
38 The transformation begins .15
39 The poison apple .15
40 The underground cavern .15
41 A silly song .15
42 Tall enough to dance with Snow White .15
43 Snow White tells a story .15
44 Bedtime .15
45 Off to work .15
46 "All alone, my pet?" .15
47 The animals sense danger .15
48 A warning .15
49 Running out of time .15
50 A magic wishing apple .15
51 The Witch flees .15
52 Too late .15
53 The rocky slope .15
54 Trapped! .15
55 "Look out!" .15
56 To her death below .15
57 Only love's first kiss .15
58 The Prince appears .15
59 Snow White awakens .15
60 And they live happily ever after... .15

Theatrical Releases
61 1937 A .15
62 1937 B .15
63 1944 .15
64 1952 .15
65 1958 .15
66 1967 A .15
67 1967 B .15
68 1975 .15
69 1983 .15
70 1987 .15
71 1993 Children's Poster .15
72 1993 Adult Poster .15

The Making of Snow White
73 Background Storytelling Settings .15
74 "The seven little men." .15
75 Creating Character .15
76 Soup's on! .15
77 A Bed for Snow White .15

Character Cards
78 Snow White .25
79 The Prince .25
80 The Evil Queen .25
81 The Wicked Witch .25
82 Doc .25
83 Grumpy .25
84 Happy .25
85 Sleepy .25
86 Sneezy .25
87 Bashful .25
88 Dopey .25
89 Checklist A .15
90 Checklist B .15

SOLITAIRE

Malibu Comics (1993)

The Solitaire Ace (Ultraverse) promo cards come from Solitaire *comic #1, which comes bagged in black so you can't tell which card you are getting. There is also have a Joker card, which is a a promo for the comic books.*

Aces

Spades 1.00
Hearts 1.00
Diamonds 1.00
Clubs 1.00
Solitaire Joker 2.00

Solitaire © Malibu Comics

Space Bananas © Karl Art

SPACE BANANAS

Karl Art (1993)

Comic book promo card with silver foil surface which was given away at comic and trade shows.

Comic promo 2.00

Speed Racer © Speed Racer Enterprises, Inc. All rights reserved

SPEED RACER

Prime Time (1993, comic)

Speed Racer is a cartoon series and a comic book (and a very attractive card series as well). Along the way to becoming the world's greatest race car driver, Speed has many adventures behind the wheel of his futuristic Mach 5 race car. When he gets in too much trouble, Racer X is always there to lend a hand. Can he save the world? Will he find true love with Trixie? Just who is Racer X anyway? You won't get all the answers in these cards, but you will meet the characters. The cards have a blue border, with a white line frame. The backs have a green border and text in a red framed box over a roadway background. The gold foil cards have a gold line frame and the "Speed Racer" logo in gold, plus they say "gold," just to leave no doubt in your mind that you have the gold foil card rather than the regular card (which is otherwise the same). You get one in every pack. The chromium cards have a full bleed front with a back that looks like the regular cards.

Set: 55 cards 7.50
Set: Gold foil 25.00
Gold foil cards, each 50

Chromium Cards

C1 Ready for Adventure 5.00
C2 Fully Loaded 5.00
C3 Wet & Wild 5.00
C4 Big Brother is Watching 5.00
C5 Belly of the Beast 5.00
C6 Classic Speed 5.00
Pack: 7 cards + gold foil card 1.00

CARD CHECKLIST

Episodes

1 The Great Plan 10
2 Challenge of the Masked Racer . . .10
3 The Secret Engine 10
4 Race Against the Mammoth Car . . .10
5 The Most Dangerous Race 10
6 Race for Revenge 10
7 The Desperate Desert Race 10
8 The Fire Race 10
9 Girl Daredevil 10
10 The Fastest Car on Earth 10
11 Mach 5 vs. Mach 5 10
12 The Royal Racer 10
13 The Car Hater 10
14 Race Against Time 10
15 The Snake Track 10
16 The Man on the Lam 10
17 Gang of Assassins 10
18 The Race for Life 10
19 The Supersonic Car 10
20 Crash in the Jungle 10
21 The Terrifying Gambler 10
22 The Secret Invaders 10
23 The Man Behind the Mask 10
24 The Car Destroyer 10
25 The Desperate Racer 10
26 The Dangerous Witness 10
27 Race the Laser Tank 10
28 The Great Car Wrestling Match . .10
29 Motorcycle Apaches 10
30 Car with a Brain 10
31 Junk Car Grand Prix 10
32 The Car in the Sky 10
33 The Trick Race 10
34 Race Around the World 10

Winner's Circle

35 Speed Racer 10
36 Racer X 10
37 Pops Racer 10
38 Trixie 10
39 Sparky .10
40 Spridle and Chim Chim 10
41 Mom 10
42 Inspector Detector 10

Speed Racer © Prime Time Productions & Speed Racer Enterprises

Mean Machines

43 Mach 5 10
44 Racer X's #9 10
45 Mammoth Car 10
46 GRX 10
47 Supersonic Car 10
48 Mallenge 10
49 Car Acrobatic Team Cars 10

Rogues' Gallery

50 Captain Terror 10
51 Cruncher Block 10
52 Ace Ducey 10
53 Tongue Blaggard 10
54 Mark Meglaton 10
55 Checklist 10

Speed Racer © 1994 Speed Racer Enterprises, Inc. All Rights Reserved

SPEED RACER

Now Comics (1993)

These Speed Racer cards are from the Now comic book and don't look like the animation cards listed above. They are nice, though.

Speed Racer Classic comic promo . 2.00
Speed Racer #1 promo (Hero)(KSy) 2.00
New Adventures of Speed Racer comic promo 2.00

Promo cards from *Speed Racer Featuring Ninja High School* #1 & #2

P1 Speed Racer card/comic promo . 1.50
P2 Classic Speed Racer promo 1.50

SPIDER-MAN

Spider-Man, Todd McFarlane Era © Marvel Entertainment Group, Inc.

SPIDER-MAN The Todd McFarlane Era

Comic Images (1992)

The card fronts are full bleed, comic close-up pictures of Spider-Man. All contain the richly detailed Todd McFarlane art that has proved to be very popular. The card backs contain the number, caption and one or two sentences of text inside a blue border. The text contains several short episodes in Spidey's career, together with some general facts. Each card back also contains a small black and white drawing. The promo card has the same picture as card #66, with a black and white back which says "Not for sale."

Set: 90 cards 15.00

Promo card 1.50

Prism Cards

P-1 Thirty Years 15.00
P-2 Dynamic 15.00
P-3 Number One 15.00
P-4 Impact 15.00
P-5 Image 15.00
P-6 Red & Blue 15.00
Pack: 10 cards 1.75

CARD CHECKLIST

1 The Beginning .... .15
2 Uptown .... .15
3 Arachknight .... .15
4 Arise .... .15
5 Married Life .... .15
6 The Lizard .... .15
7 Friendly, Neighborhood.. .... .15
8 Connors .... .15
9 A Spider .... .15
10 Spider-Sense .... .15
11 Attacked .... .15
12 Poison .... .15
13 Fatality .... .15
14 Alone .... .15
15 Resurrection .... .15
16 The Hunter .... .15
17 Rooftop .... .15
18 Trashed .... .15
19 Dazed .... .15
20 The Past .... .15
21 Drugged .... .15
22 Kraven .... .15
23 The Witch .... .15
24 Once Again .... .15
25 Explosion .... .15
26 Crawling Out .... .15
27 Voodoo .... .15
28 Last Time .... .15
29 Death .... .15
30 Home .... .15
31 Another Time .... .15
32 Dark Days .... .15
33 Hobgoblin .... .15
34 Heading Out .... .15
35 Tuning In .... .15
36 Ghost Rider .... .15
37 The Kid .... .15
38 Team-up .... .15
39 Busting In .... .15
40 Spirit of Vengeance .... .15
41 Ready .... .15
42 Fire Creature .... .15
43 Stop This .... .15
44 Perceptions .... .15
45 Folklore .... .15
46 Hanging Out .... .15
47 J.J. Jameson .... .15
48 Murder .... .15
49 Wolverine .... .15
50 The Mystery .... .15
51 Got'cha .... .15
52 The Hunter .... .15
53 The Myth .... .15
54 Investigation .... .15
55 Shot .... .15
56 Into The Woods .... .15
57 Wounded .... .15
58 Wendito .... .15
59 Primal .... .15
60 Time To Go .... .15
61 Crime Fighters .... .15
62 Evidence .... .15
63 Parker .... .15
64 Hurt .... .15
65 The Bullet .... .15
66 Pondering .... .15
67 Together .... .15
68 Stay Here .... .15
69 Masked .... .15
70 Trapped .... .15
71 Set-up .... .15
72 Sub-City .... .15
73 Keever .... .15
74 Web-Swinger .... .15
75 Black Costume .... .15
76 Morbius .... .15
77 Spotted .... .15
78 Vampire .... .15
79 Down Under .... .15
80 Too Many .... .15
81 Male Bonding .... .15
82 Mouthful .... .15
83 Bad Ones .... .15
84 I'm Gone .... .15
85 X-Force .... .15
86 Juggernaut .... .15
87 Young Ones .... .15
88 Cable .... .15
89 Join Together .... .15
90 Checklist .... .15

Spider-Man II, 30th Anniversary © Marvel Entertainment Group, Inc.

SPIDER-MAN II 30th Anniversary

Comic Images (1992)

These cards have full bleed comic book close-up art on the fronts. The backs contain the card number, title and text plus a line drawing, all in blue, inside a red border. The text covers the first 30 years of Spider-Man's career, including his origin, key battles, and love life. The prism cards are numbered as a continuation of the Spider-Man, Todd McFarlane Era set described above. The "prizm" promo card is on a different surface than the prism bonus cards. It is marked "Not for sale" in red on the back.

Set: 90 Cards 14.00

Prizm promo card (MBa) 5.00
Promo card (MBa) 3.50

Prism cards:

P7 Assistant Needed 12.00
P8 Stan, the Man (MBa/JR) 12.00
P9 Promoted 12.00
P10 Creating 12.00
P11 Insectman? 12.00
P12 Moving On 12.00
Pack: 10 cards 1.75

CARD CHECKLIST

1 September, 1962 (SD/JK) ...... .15
2 6 Years Old .... .15
3 The Exhibition .... .15
4 Human Spider .... .15
5 Reflexes .... .15
6 Wall Climber .... .15
7 Spider-Sense .... .15
8 Web-Shooters .... .15
9 Web Fluid .... .15
10 Equipment .... .15
11 Wrestling .... .15
12 Irony .... .15
13 A Hero is Born .... .15
14 Amazing Spider-Man .... .15
15 The Chameleon .... .15
16 J.J. Jameson .... .15
17 Bad Press .... .15
18 John Jameson .... .15
19 Fantastic Four .... .15
20 Shutter-Bug .... .15
21 Duel To The Death .... .15
22 The Vulture .... .15
23 The Tinkerer .... .15
24 Doctor Octopus .... .15
25 First Defeat .... .15
26 Sandman .... .15
27 Doctor Doom .... .15
28 The Lizard .... .15
29 Four Eyes .... .15
30 Electro .... .15
31 Betty Brant .... .15
32 The Enforcers .... .15
33 Mysterio .... .15
34 Green Goblin .... .15
35 Break-Up .... .15
36 Big Shoes .... .15
37 The Hulk .... .15
38 Kraven .... .15
39 The Ringmaster .... .15
40 Daredevil .... .15
41 Sinister Six .... .15
42 The Scorpion .... .15
43 Spider-Slayer .... .15
44 Molten Man .... .15
45 The Rhino .... .15
46 The Test .... .15
47 The X-Men .... .15
48 The Shocker .... .15
49 Captain Stacy .... .15
50 The Prowler .... .15
51 Drug Abuse .... .15
52 Morbius .... .15
53 Man-Wolf .... .15

54 Gwen Stacy 15
55 Gwen's Death 15
56 Green Goblin's Death 15
57 The Jackal 15
58 The Punisher 15
59 Vigilante 15
60 Seeing Green 15
61 Black Cat 15
62 The Burglar 15
63 Hydro-Man 15
64 Hobgoblin 15
65 Kingpin 15
66 Secret Wars 15
67 The Suit 15
68 Bad Luck 15
69 The Rose 15
70 The Symbiote 15
71 The Avengers 15
72 Venom 15
73 Unmasked 15
74 Marriage 15
75 Buried Alive 15
76 Vermin 15
77 Universal Powers 15
78 Captured 15
79 Issue #300 15
80 Silver Sable 15
81 Arrogance 15
82 Spider-Man #1 15
83 Heroes 15
84 Spawn .15
85 New Rose 15
86 New Warriors 15
87 Soul of the Hunter 15
88 Parents 15
89 Spider-Man 2099 15
90 Checklist 15

Amazing Spider-Man 30th © Marvel Entertainment Group, Inc.

AMAZING SPIDER-MAN 30th

SkyBox (1992, Comics)

This is a promo card set commemorating Spider-Man's 30th anniversary in comics. It's highly collectible.

Set: 5 cards 5.00

SM-1 Spider-Man (MBa/LMa) 1.00
SM-2 Mary Jane (JR) 1.00
SM-3 Black Costume (MBa/LMa) . . . 1.00
SM-4 Origin (RF/AM) 1.00
SM-5 Enemies (AS/JSt) 1.00

AMAZING SPIDER-MAN

Marvel/Fleer cards (1994)

*This is the second set of cards of Marvel characters by Marvel's subsidiary Fleer. The first set was the Fleer (Ultra) X-Men and the Fleer name was prominently used. You can hardly find it on these cards and they are billed as "1st Edition Marvel Cards" presented by Marvel Comics and distributed by Fleer. Who cares? They're great! The Suspended Animation cards are printed on clear celluloid with a spider-web border and portrait in the center. Two previous card sets have bonus cards printed on celluloid (**Deathwatch 2000** and **The Simpsons**) but this is by far the most attractive use of this material we have seen. The Polaroid holograms are also nicely done and have proved to be very popular with collectors. They have excellent hologram images on the front and plain white backs. They somewhat resemble the special "H" bonus cards of X-Men II and Marvel Universe IV but they are much easier to collect since they come two per box. As with the Fleer Ultra X-Men set, there are different types of bonus cards in different packs. The jumbo packs have six Gold Web bonus cards which actually use the same images as the first six Suspended Animation cel cards, but with a gold background and a black border, both containing a spider web design. The Wal-Mart blue packs also have six Gold Web bonus cards; they are taken from the second six Suspended Animation cel cards. Each case comes with one Marvel Masterprints nine card panel from the series. The art is somewhat smaller than the cards and has a plain white back. The Large Web promo sheet consists of a large spider-web design. Several of the other promo sheets use various portions of the Enemies super-panel #5 card art. The nine card sheets use the whole super-panel, with a colorful promo back, but the images are only 95% of actual card size. The scarcer **Triton** magazine version is from issue #3 and has the Triton logo overprinted on the upper left corner of the back. The four card sheets have prototype backs, without card numbers. The three card strips also have unnumbered prototype backs and came in Marvel Comics on a sheet with an advertisement for Marvel Masterprints. All of the art for the series is by Mark Bagley.*

Set: 150 cards (all MBa) 25.00

Polaroid Holograms (1:18) All versions
1 of 4 Carnage 12.00
2 of 4 Spider-Man 12.00
3 of 4 Venom 12.00
4 of 4 Spider-Man 12.00

Suspended Animation (1:4) Regular packs
one Spider-Man 4.00
two Mary Jane 4.00
three Chameleon 4.00
four Venom 4.00
five Carnage 4.00
six Hobgoblin 4.00
seven Spider-Man 4.00
eight Vulture 4.00
nine Doctor Octopus 4.00
ten Spider-Man 4.00
eleven Black Cat 4.00
twelve Lizard 4.00

Gold Web (1:7) **12? card** Jumbo Packs
one Venom 9.00
two Mary Jane 9.00
three Spider-Man (=#1) 9.00
four Chameleon 9.00
five Hobgoblin 9.00
six Carnage 9.00

Gold Web (1:7) **11 card** Blue packs
one Spider-Man (=#7) 9.00
two Lizard 9.00
three Black Cat 9.00
four Vulture 9.00
five Doctor Octopus 9.00
six Spider-Man (=#10) 9.00

Masterprints panels (1:case)
Powers 5.00
Venom 5.00
Strange Transformations 5.00
Enemies I 5.00
Enemies II 5.00
Enemies III 5.00
Enemies IV 5.00
Enemies V 5.00
Allies 5.00

Promo cards
Large Web card promo, 6½" x 9" . . . 2.00
Nine card Enemies panel promo sheet, 7-1/8" x 10¾" promo back 1.50
Nine card Enemies panel promo sheet (from *Triton*) 2.50
Nine card Enemies panel promo sheet (from *Comic Book Collector* and *Card Collector Price Guide*) 2.00

Amazing Spider-Man © Marvel Entertainment Group, Inc.

Four card sheet (Venom, Spider-Man, Lizard & Hobgoblin) (from *Tuff Stuff: Collect* or from *Advance Comics*) . 1.50
Four card sheet (Doctor Octopus, Vulture, Venom, Spider-Man) from *Spider-Man Magazine #1* 1.50
Three card strips w/Master Prints ad from various Marvel comic books:
Powers strip (art = cards #7-#9) . . 1.50
Venom strip (art = cards #16-#18) . 1.50
Enemies strip (art = cards #61-#63) 1.50
Pack: 8 cards 1.50

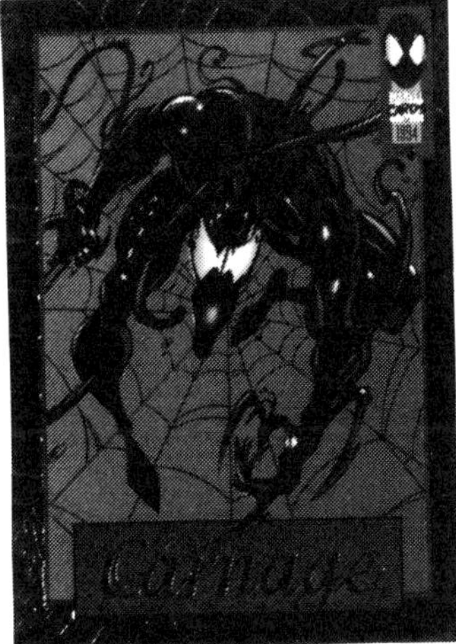

Amazing Spider-Man

CARD CHECKLIST

(Spidey's) Powers (9 card super-panel)
1 Wall-Crawling 20
2 Web-Shooting 20
3 Web-Slinging 20
4 Spider-Tracers 20
5 Spider-Agility 20
6 Spider-Signal 20
7 Spider-Strength 20
8 Spider-Leap 20
9 Spider-Sense 20
Venom
10 Vulnerable to Sonics 20
11 Web-Shooting 20
12 Spider-Agility 20
13 Living Costume 20
14 Disguise 20
15 Fearsome 20
16 Vulnerable to Fire 20
17 Immune to Spider-Sense 20
18 Super Strength 20
(Spidey's) Strange Transformations
19 Black Costume 20
20 Captain Universe 20
21 Spider-Lizard 20
22 Man-Spider 20
23 Extra Arms 20
24 Spider-Clone 20
25 Spider-Hulk 20
26 Doppelganger 20
27 Shrinking Spidey 20
Enemies I
28 Tarantula 20
29 Spider-Slayers 20
30 Jackal 20
31 Puma 20
32 Spider-Man: Avengers Files 20
33 Cardiac .20
34 Chance .20
35 Styx and Stone 20
36 Tombstone 20
Enemies II
37 Sandstorm 20
38 Demogoblin 20

Amazing Spider-Man

39 Silvermane 20
40 Hammerhead 20
41 Spider-Man: Fantastic Four Files .20
42 Man-Wolf 20
43 Warrant .20
44 Blood Rose 20
45 Calypso .20
Enemies III
46 Green Goblin 20
47 Spider-Man: Goblin's Journal 20
48 The Jury 20
49 Carrion .20
50 Vermin .20
51 Shocker .20
52 Kingpin .20
53 Sin-Eater 20
54 Rhino 20
Enemies IV
55 Beetle 20
56 Solo 20
57 Boomerang 20
58 Hydro-Man 20
59 Scorpion 20
60 Speed Demon 20
61 Kraven 20
62 Spider-Man: Jameson Editorial . . .20
63 Chameleon 20
Enemies V
64 Doctor Octopus 20
65 Vulture .20
66 Carnage 20
67 Venom .20
68 Spider-Man: N.Y.P.D. Files 20
69 Electro .20
70 Lizard 20
71 Hobgoblin 20
72 Mysterio 20
(Spidey's) Allies (Super-Panel)
73 Black Cat 20
74 Nightwatch 20
75 Spider-Man: Peter's Notebook . . .20
76 Sandman 20
77 Molten Man 20
78 Cloak and Dagger 20
79 Silver Sable 20
80 Prowler .20
81 Annex 20
Spidey's Greatest Team-Ups
82 Spider-Man & Wolverine 20
83 Spider-Man & Daredevil 20
84 Spider-Man & Punisher 20
85 Spider-Man & Avengers 20
86 Spider-Man & Green Goblin 20
87 Spider-Man & Ghost Rider 20
88 Spider-Man & The X-Men 20
89 Spider-Man & Venom 20
90 Spider-Man & Captain America . . .20
91 Spider-Man & Doctor Strange 20
92 Spider-Man & Silver Sable 20
93 Spider-Man & Human Torch 20
94 Spider-Man & Nova 20
95 Spider-Man & New Warriors 20
96 Spider-Man & Darkhawk 20
Spidey's Greatest Battles
97 Spider-Man vs. Venom 20
98 Spider-Man vs. Carnage 20
99 Spider-Man vs. Hobgoblin 20
100 Spider-Man vs. Green Goblin . . .20
101 Spider-Man vs. Doctor Octopus .20
102 Spider-Man vs. Lizard 20
103 Spider-Man vs. Firelord 20
104 Spider-Man vs. Silver Surfer 20
105 Spider-Man vs. Tombstone 20
106 Spider-Man vs. Rhino 20
107 Spider-Man vs. Hulk 20
108 Spider-Man vs. Electro 20
109 Spider-Man vs. Kraven 20
110 Spider-Man vs. Mysterio 20
111 Spider-Man vs. Kingpin 20
112 Spider-Man vs. Vulture 20
113 Spider-Man vs. Doctor Doom . . .20
114 Spider-Man vs. Puma 20
115 Spider-Man vs. Black Cat 20
116 Spider-Man vs. Juggernaut 20
117 Spider-Man vs. Vermin 20
118 Spider-Man vs. Scorpion 20
119 Spider-Man vs. Red Skull 20
120 Spider-Man vs. Sabretooth 20
121 Spider-Man vs. Morbius 20
(Spidey's) Friends
122 Mary Jane 20
123 Flash Thompson 20
124 J. Jonah Jameson 20
125 Aunt May 20
126 Joe "Robbie" Robertson 20
127 Peter Parker 20
The Origin of Spider-Man
128 The Spider's Bite! 20
129 Powers For Profit! 20
130 Not My Job! 20
131 To Catch a Thief! 20
132 A Graveside Vow! 20
Events
133 Maximum Carnage 20
134 Round Robin 20
135 Return of the Sinister Six 20
136 Revenge of the Sinister Six 20
137 The Child Within 20
138 Spirits of Venom 20
139 Fearful Symmetry 20
140 Assassin Nation Plot 20
141 The Death of Gwen Stacy 20
142 The Wedding of Peter and Mary Jane 20
143 Invasion of the Spider-Slayers . .20
144 The Osborn Legacy 20
145 The Return of Peter Parker's Parents 20
146 The Black Costume Saga 20
147 Return of the Burglar 20
148 Funeral Arrangements 20
149 Eye of the Puma 20
150 Checklist 20

Spider-Man Team-Up © Marvel Entertainment Group, Inc.

SPIDER-MAN TEAM-UP

Comic Images (1990)

The card fronts are action pictures of Spider-Man and the named friend or enemy inside a white border and stylized frame. The front also contains the card number and title under the frame. The card backs form a 5 x 9 black and white drawing of The Uncanny X-Men & Spider-Man by Todd McFarlane. The cards came in clear cello packs, with a header card to identify the series.

Set: 45 cards + header card 12.00
Box: 48 packs
Pack: 5 puzzle back cards + header 1.50

CARD CHECKLIST

Header card 15
1 Dazzler 25
2 Doc Samson 25
3 Nighthawk 25
4 Wolverine 25
5 Fantastic Four 25
6 Classic X-Men 25
7 Hulk 25
8 Ms. Marvel 25
9 Iron Man 25
10 Captain Britain 25
11 Strangle hold! (Punisher) 25
12 Nightcrawler 25
13 Havok .25
14 Angel 25
15 Crashing in! (Punisher) 25
16 Iron Fist 25
17 Ya' missed! (Wolverine) 25
18 Dr. Strange 25

19 Paladin .25
20 Man-Thing .25
21 Power Man .25
22 Together (Wolverine) .25
23 Santa .25
24 Blackcat .25
25 Captain America .25
26 Human Torch .25
27 Prowler .25
28 Silver Sable .25
29 The Beast .25
30 Against the wall (Punisher) .25
31 Sandman .25
32 Tigra .25
33 Iceman .25
34 Johnny Storm .25
35 Falcon .25
36 Frankenstein .25
37 Rematch (Gray Hulk) .25
38 Targeted (Punisher) .25
39 Thor .25
40 Hercules .25
41 Busting in! (Hulk) .25
42 Man-Wolf .25
43 Iron Man .25
44 Sub-Mariner .25
45 Checklist .25

Splatter Bowl I Preview © TRG & EEP, L.P.

SPLATTER BOWL I PREVIEW

The River Group (1993)

(Dave Lapham, Mike Witherby & Janet Jackson)

This is a preview set for the Splatter Bowl card series (which has been postponed indefinitely).

Set: 30 cards, plus foil card in tin box (48,000 made) . . . 10.00

Xcess, foil card 4.00
Two card promo sheet 1.50
Two card promo sheet for Splatter Bowl I card set 2.00

CARD CHECKLIST

1 Official Game Program .20
2 The Great Grimmax .20
3 Cutthroat .20
4 Slayer .20
5 Druber .20
6 Thrasher .20
7 Eyepike .20
8 Grater .20
9 Pincer .20
10 Bludjon .20
11 Ripglide .20
12 Zoms, Goal-renders .20
13 Zoms, Defense Zoms .20
14 Zoms, Combatrons .20
15 Skullrenders, Team Analysis .20
16 Soothslayers, Team Analysis .20
17 Whipper .20
18 Thrash .20
19 Support Troops .20
20 Support Troops .20
21 The Splatterball .20
22 The Splatterbowl .20
23 Daggerhorn .20
24 Cheerleaders, Skullrenders .20
25 Cheerleaders, Soothslayers .20
26 Splatterball History .20
27 NSL Semi-final Games .20
28 ASL Semi-final Games .20
29 NSL Championship Game .20
30 ASL Championship Game .20

SPOOF COMICS PRESENTS:

Spoof Comics (1992)

These are boxed sets of comic book hero spoofs. They're humorous, but haven't really caught on with superhero collectors as much as with non-sport card collectors. They are hard to find, but not too expensive when you do find them.

Batbabe
Set: 37 cards 12.00
0 Logo/Checklist .30
1 "Say, 'Cheesecake!'" .30
2 "You go after the Peeper" .30
3 "Loosen Up" .30
4 "Hey, **Nice** stalactites" .30
5 "At one celebrity" .30

Spider-Femme & Batbabe © Personality Comics Inc.

6 "Boss, she's getting away!" .30
7 "**No!**" .30
8 "I'm in for it now!" .30
9 "...Pepper!" .30
10 "I want **Nude pictures**" .30
11 "You may call me...**Catgut!!**" .30
12 "**But remember,** if you" .30
13 "**Alright, already!**" .30
14 "**What a mess!**" .30
15 "**Suddenly,** as if from" .30
16 "Do? Why, you created me!" .30
17 "That's right Bat-Babe!" .30
18 "I don't believe it!" .30
19 "Watch out **world!**" .30
20 "Well, I'm **certainly not**" .30
21 "Happy and contented" .30
22 "...How's about a" .30
23 "Sure, just because I'm" .30
24 "I've allowed your **perverse**" .30
25 "What the **heck** is wrong" .30
26 "The...**Peeper!!**" .30
27 "It's time for you to die!" .30
28 "It's **Bat-Babe**!!" .30
29 "Every good hero needs" .30
30 "Aaaaarrroooooooga!" .30
31 "And who the **heck**" .30
32 "Now I will have my revenge" .30
33 "Babe-pedo away!" .30
34 "Now to...find...some" .30
35 "I'm **Bat-Babe**." .30
36 "Run into that building!" .30

Bogus Heroes
Set: 37 cards 12.00
0 Logo/Checklist .30
1 Bare Devil .30
2 Smellverine .30
3 Fatman .30
4 Ghost Rooster .30
5 Splatterman .30
6 The Polisher .30
7 Green Lentil .30
8 Spoon Knight .30
9 Iron-On Man .30
10 Judge Fredd .30
11 Nick Filthy .30
12 Sump Thing .30
13 OX-Force .30
14 Spleen .30
15 Night Cruller .30
16 Kibble .30
17 Green Marrow .30
18 Dr. Sponge .30
19 The Silver Sofa .30
20 The Human Porch .30
21 Alfalfa Flight .30
22 The Sub Manager .30
23 Simperman .30
24 The Mighty Bore .30
25 Limbo .30
26 Blunder Woman .30
27 The Flush .30
28 Wild C.O.O.T.S. .30
29 Savage Deacon .30
30 Scarlet Bitch .30
31 Caulkman .30
32 Marble Girl .30
33 Mr. Fantastik .30
34 The Sex-Men .30
35 Liceman .30
36 Lycraman .30

Spider-Femme
Set: 37 cards 12.00
0 Title Card/Checklist .30
1 "No Problem,..." .30
2 "Wow, **75 Bucks**..." .30
3 "**Aaaah!** My **body**" .30
4 "Come **back** here,.." .30
5 "I'm **Spider-Femme,**" .30
6 "Just **try** to..." .30
7 "**Oooh,** my **Spider-Hips**..." .30
8 "You've **got** me?..." .30
9 "Oh my!" .30
10 "**Shew**!" .30
11 "**Hey, what's**.." .30
12 "**Say,** you" .30
13 "Geez, Penny," .30
14 "Nothing Can Stop.." .30
15 "**Fresh!**" .30
16 "Time for some new clothes!" .30
17 "?" .30
18 "BOINNG!" .30
19 "Death Duel..." .30
20 "Wow! **Quick**..." .30
21 "A Mugging..." .30
22 "**Yes.** Those men.." .30
23 "Whoa! Whatever..." .30
24 "I **love** my..." .30
25 "Ha! Ha! Ha!" .30
26 "They can if" .30
27 "Wh-what are you doing?" .30
28 "**Oh no!!** Not **that!**" .30
29 "**Sheesh**!" .30
30 "**Blast** that..." .30
31 "**Hold it**, you doofus!" .30
32 "I know..." .30
33 "...flum da **Bulgar!**" .30
34 "Oh, knock it off!" .30
35 "Yeah, **yeah**!..." .30
36 Spider-Femme! .30

Spoof Comics Month
Set: 37 cards 9.00
0 Title card/Checklist .20
1 Cuisinart! .20
2 Strike 'Er! .20

Spoof Comics Month
© Personality Comics Inc

3 "Ballaster and Simpact! 20
4 "That's right. ..." 20
5 "Don't worry! I'll just..." 20
6 "I am Chive,..." 20
7 "Resist foreshortening!" 20
8 Spudrock! 20
9 "Me? Why I'm cue-ball!" 20
10 "Let's get'em, Cyberfemmes!" 20
11 "Wow! A perfectly cooked..." 20
12 "That place is a real..." 20
13 "I'm one hulking colossus..." 20
14 "What's happening..." 20
15 "We've come to put a stop..." 20
16 "I wanted every real..." 20
17 "I Must avoid making..." 20
18 "My shorts are riding up!!" 20
19 SNS News 20
20 "I hungered." 20
21 "Why?" .20
22 "How could McFarout..." 20
23 "I remember now!..." 20
24 "Death didn't like my soup." 20
25 "If you think this pose..." 20
26 "You're Chim Nee!" 20
27 "Why, she looks like an angel!" . . .20
28 "What's that shadow?..." 20
29 "Yeh, Mom, get her!" 20
30 "Watch your **Mouth!**..." 20
31 "Uh-oh There go my radar boobs.." .20
32 "Look! Look what's happening..." . .20
33 "At the sound of the bell,..." 20
34 "By using Mon's..." 20
35 "But just who is this..." 20
36 "I'll sign...for Pat!" 20

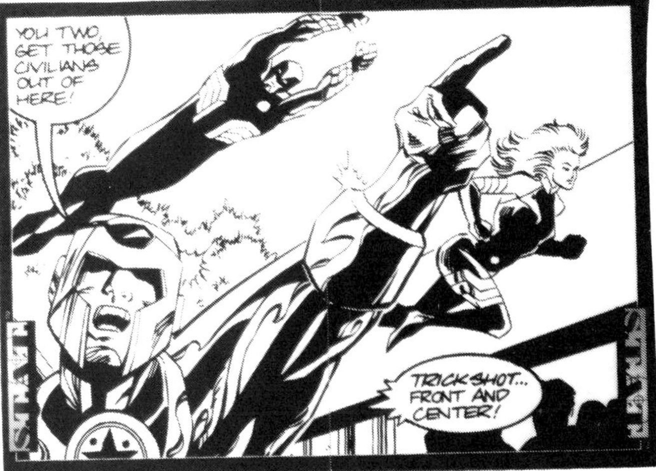

S.T.A.T. #0 © Majestic Entertainment Inc.

S.T.A.T. #0

Majestic Entertainment (1994)

These promo cards form a black and white comic book page. The backs are grey with a black border and all contain the same promotional text. Unfortunately, the actual set has been put on indefinite hold. If the set ever appears, color versions of these cards will be one of the nine card panels. The promos are untitled.

Set: 9 cards, A-1 thru A-9, B&W 10.00

STORMWATCH

Image Comics (1993)

The StormWatch #0 promo was bagged with the comic of the same name.

Jim Lee's StormWatch #0 comic promo (Scott Clark/Trevor Scott) 1.00
00 Jackson King-Battalion (JLe) . . . 5.00

SUPERGIRL

Topps (1983)

This set contains photo story cards with sticker backs from the 1984 movie. The first 33 cards tell the story and last 11 cards form a 10-card puzzle (plus completed puzzle card). The fronts have a

Supergirl © DC Comics, Inc.

blue border with yellow frame and contain the card number. Captions are taken from the yellow bordered sticker side.

Set: 44 Story cards (sticker backs) 10.00
Pack: 6 card/stickers 1.50

CARD CHECKLIST

1 Supergirl Logo Card 30
2 World's Fastest Student 30
3 A nice place to visit--? 30
4 Skyhigh 30
5 Go For It! 30
6 Wicked, Wicked Witch 30
7 (no title: Selena) 30
8 Trapped in the Phantom Zone 30
9 (no title: monster) 30
10 Supergirl (hands on hips) 30
11 Let your imagination Explode 30
12 Battle of the Century: Selena vs. Supergirl! 30
13 (no title: Supergirl on ground) 30
14 Round 1: Now I'm Really Angry! . .30
15 Visit Argo City 30
16 Hopelessly Devoted to You 30
17 Zaltar: Master of the Matterwand .30
18 Inspiration... 30
19 (no title: 3 faces) 30
20 Danger: Phantom Zone 30
21 Teen Angel 30
22 You're a real Knockout 30
23 Round 2: Supergirl Captive! 30
24 Prisoner of Love 30
25 Boo! 30
26 Supergirl (flying) 30
27 Supergirl (hands on hips) 30
28 Breakflying: What a Feeling! 30
29 Let's Beat the Odds and Win! 30
30 (no title: faces in hearts) 30
31 Supergirl (seated on rock) 30
32 (no title: Supergirl standing) 30
33 Earth, where flowers grow 30

Poster fronts

34 Supergirl (hands on shoulders) . . .30
35 Greetings from Argo City 30
36 Friendship: It's Hard to Beat 30
37 Even Supergirl Gets the Blues . . .30
38 Kara: Daughter of Alura 30
39 We're Worlds Apart 30
40 Round 3: The Best Girl Wins! 30
41 Supergirl (flying) 30
42 Supergirl (standing) 30
43 Do Not Disturb... Relationship in Progress... 30
44 Supergirl/Puzzle Preview 30

SUPER HERO STICKERS

Philadelphia Gum (1967)

The backs of these stickers are plain brown paper and the stock is so thin that the back peel separation line usually shows through to the front as a crease. Many of the stickers are miscut and look crooked. Most of the stickers in the series have the picture on a white background, but a few have color. The sticker front has the character name, the number and a humorous comment which the character is making. Cards #6 and #51 have no character name. The pack has a picture of The Hulk and names the set as above, while the box calls the set "Marvel Super Hero Stickers," but neither name is on the stickers! They only say ©1967 Marvel Comics Group ©P.C.G.C. Printed in U.S.A."

Set: 55 stickers 350.00

1 The Human Torch: "I Must Get That Roof Fixed!" 7.50
2 The Human Torch: "How Do You Like Your Hamburgers?" 7.50
3 Daredevil: "It Might Have Been Easier to Take the Elevator" 7.50
4 Thor: "That's Right, This Big! But It Got Away!" 7.50
5 The Hulk: "My Father Can Lick Your Father!" 7.50
6 (Reed & Sue Richards): "But–I Thought You Took the Garbage Out!" 7.50
7 The Thing: "It's Clobberin' Time" . . 7.50
8 The Thing: "No Fair Using Water-Guns" 7.50
9 The Human Torch: "I Wish I'd Used That Sun Tan Lotion!" 7.50
10 Iron Man: "What If I Am a High School Drop-Out?" 7.50
11 Daredevil: "Taxi!" 7.50

Super Hero Stickers © Marvel Entertainment Group, Inc.

12 Spider-Man: "Some Web Shooter! I Can't Shut It Off!" 7.50
13 Thor: "You Sent For a Carpenter?" 7.50
14 Submariner: "I'm the Only Wash-and-Wear Hero in Town!" 7.50
15 Submariner: "Yipe! That Water's Cold!" 7.50
16 The Human Torch: "Butter-Fingers!" 7.50
17 The Thing: "Stop Talking! While I'm Interrupting" 7.50
18 Daredevil: "Now–Where Did I Leave My Clothes?" 7.50
19 Thor: "Why, Yes, I Do Set My Hair Myself!" 7.50
20 The Thing: "I'm Not Fat! I'm Just Short for my Width!" 7.50
21 Spider-Man: "Aren't We a Little Too Old to Play Leapfrog, Herman?" . . 7.50
22 The Hulk: "Which Hand has the Chocolate Candy?" 7.50
23 Daredevil: "Who Moved the Trapeze?" 7.50
24 Dr. Strange: "All I Get Is Nag, Nag, Nag!" 7.50
25 The Thing: "That Dry Skin Cream is Just No Good!" 7.50
26 Submariner: "Who Stole My Pants?" 7.50
27 Daredevil: "Darn! Missed the Bus Again" 7.50
28 Iron Man: "Well, There Goes My Last Roll of Caps!" 7.50
29 Spider-Man: "But Mother, I'm Too Old for Dancing Lessons!" . . . 7.50
30 The Hulk: What Do You Mean You Don't Have My Shoe Size?" 7.50
31 The Hulk: "Who Used Up the Hot Water?" 7.50
32 The Thing: "Clyde! How You've Changed" 7.50
33 Iron Man: "Outh! Bwang!" 7.50
34 Dr. Strange: "If You Can't Beat 'Em–Call Them Names" 7.50
35 Captain America: "No, Lady, This Isn't Your Trash Can Lid!" 7.50
36 The Thing: "I May Not be Brave, But I'm Handsome!" 7.50
37 Iron Man: "Let's See Now–What's Good for Rust?" 7.50
38 The Hulk: "This is the Last Time I'll Babysit!" 7.50
39 Spider-Man: "I Must Have Made a Wrong Turn" 7.50
40 Iron Man: "My Work Is So Secret, Even I Don't Know What I'm Doing!" . . . 7.50
41 Thor: "Turn That Air Conditioner Off!" 7.50
42 Spider-Man: "Smile! Later Today You Won't Feel Like It" 7.50
43 Spider-Man: "May I Leave the Room?" 7.50
44 Iron Man: "They Just Don't Make Chains the Way they Used To!" . . 7.50
45 The Hulk: "Rah! Rah! Team!" . . . 7.50
46 Submariner: "Which Way is the Men's Locker Room?" 7.50
47 The Hulk: "The Dance is Tonight! Why Isn't My Suit Ready?" 7.50
48 The Hulk: "One, Two Cha Cha Cha!" 7.50
49 Spider-Man: "Hey Lady–You Dropped Your Package! 7.50
50 Captain America: "Regular Aspirin Just Isn't Strong Enough!" 7.50
51 "We're That New Singing Group: Him, Her and It" 7.50
52 Thor: "One More Word Out of You, Charlie, and You Get It!" 7.50
53 Captain America: "Jay Walker! Wok!" 7.50
54 Captain America: "May I Take Two Giant Steps?" 7.50
55 The Human Torch: "Don't You Call Me a Slob!" 7.50

SUPERMAN

SUPERMAN

Gum Inc. (1940) (R145)

This is it– this set is the Honus Wagner of the non-sports card field. If you've got these cards you are truly a big-time collector, but the odds are that most of us will never see a complete set of these hard-to-find gems. These cards are 2½" x 3-1/8" which is slightly shorter than today's standard card size. The pictures are in color and show Superman performing various feats of strength and battling vintage weapons and evil-doers. The backs are numbered and captioned and contain a short story related to the picture, plus an invitation to join the Supermen of America club. This is an expensive set, and if it's beyond your bankroll, see below.

Set: 72 cards 3,500.00

1 Superman 50.00
2 The Spy Trail 30.00
3 From the Jaws of Death 30.00
4 Peril in the Jungle 30.00
5 The Girl Reporter's Danger 30.00
6 Superman vs. Bank Robbers . . . 30.00
7 The Averted Train Wreck 30.00
8 Rescue at the Bank 30.00
9 Superman at the Circus 30.00
10 Fury of the Sea 30.00
11 Capture of the Kidnapers 30.00
12 Superman's Arch Enemy 30.00
13 Teeth of Steel 30.00
14 Maniac at Large 30.00
15 Panic in the Subway 30.00
16 Mountain Tragedy 30.00
17 Death on the Speedway 30.00
18 Prison Break 30.00
19 Wings of Mercy 30.00
20 Peril at Sea 30.00
21 The Runaway Horse 30.00
22 Wolves at Bay 30.00
23 Hurtling to Destruction 30.00
24 Attacked by Sharks 30.00
25 Trapped in the Air 30.00
26 Log Jam Peril 30.00
27 Rescue From a Rocky Reef . . . 30.00
28 The Flames of Doom 30.00
29 Death Dive 30.00
30 Trapped in the Glacier 30.00
31 Rescue Beneath the Sea 30.00
32 Danger on High 30.00
33 The Avalanche 30.00
34 Peril in the Oil Fields 30.00
35 Hurricane Horror 30.00
36 Facing the Firing Squad 30.00
37 Distress at Sea 30.00
38 Marooned in the Clouds 30.00
39 Disaster at the Mine 30.00
40 Racing the Shells 30.00
41 Roller Coaster Rescue 30.00
42 Danger in the Jungle 30.00
43 Fight in Mid-Air 30.00
44 Disaster at the Circus 30.00
45 The Runaway Ship 30.00
46 To the Rescue 30.00
47 Horror Beneath the Sea 30.00
48 Death in the Air 30.00
49 Danger at the Carnival 75.00
50 At the Bottom of the Sea 75.00
51 Superman vs. the Spies 75.00
52 Saving the Destroyer 75.00
53 The Girl Reporter 75.00
54 Rescue From the Flames 75.00
55 Superman Wins Again 75.00
56 Superman and the Killer-Whale 75.00
57 Battling the Hurricane 75.00
58 A Near-Tragedy 75.00
59 The Dive of Death 75.00
60 Menace in the Mine 75.00
61 Through the Mine Field 75.00
62 Peril in the Presses 75.00
63 Terror in the Tower 75.00
64 Adventure on an Iceberg 75.00
65 The Runaway Trolley Car 75.00
66 Danger at the Dam 75.00
67 Explosion in an Oil Field 75.00
68 Saved by Superman 75.00
69 Saved From Burial Alive 75.00
70 Danger in the North Woods . . . 75.00
71 Trapped in Quicksand 75.00
72 Superman vs.Torpedo 120.00

SUPERMAN

Gum Inc. (1984 reprint)

This set is a faithful reprint of the original. The only difference is the words "Limited Edition–1984 Reprint" on the back. We used

Superman (Gum Inc. reprint) © DC Comics, Inc.

two of the reprint cards for the previous photos. Even if we had one of the original cards we wouldn't have wanted to risk losing it just so you could look at its photo. Anyway, the fronts are the same.

Set: 72 cards 17.00

SUPERMAN

Topps (1966)

These cards feature black and white photos from the TV series starring George Reeves and Noel Neill which ran from 1953 to 1957. All but the first season was filmed in color. The card backs are orange with a picture of Superman on the right side and story line text in a white box. These backs resemble the backs of the Batman cards from this same year. There are two varieties of these orange back cards: 1) with copyright beneath text; 2) with 1965 copyright on the side and "Watch Superman on T.V." on the bottom. It's not clear which television show the cards refer to. The 1960s cartoon series was running when the cards came out, but the series depicted on the cards was showing occasionally in syndication (and is still being shown on Nickelodeon). The higher number cards have puzzle backs. There is also a very scarce white back version of the cards. Overall, the photos used on these cards are excellent and the set is highly regarded by collectors.

Set: 66 cards 180.00

Wrapper: 15.00
1 "Krypton is Doomed" 5.00
2 Destination: Earth 3.50
3 Superman's Parents 3.50
4 Ace Reporter 3.50
5 Superman 3.50
6 A Job for Superman 3.50
7 The Man of Steel 3.50
8 Superman's Strength 3.50
9 Metropolis' Hero 3.50
10 The Threat 3.50
11 Plotting Lois' Death 3.50
12 Lois in Trouble 3.50
13 Lois is Kidnapped 3.50
14 Jimmy and Clark 3.50
15 "He's Been Shot" 3.50
16 Clark Gets A Lead 3.50
17 "No False Moves, Kent" 3.50
18 "You're Finished, Kent" 3.50
19 Superman in Action 3.50
20 Futile Fight 3.50
21 Superman's Warning 3.50
22 The Backfire 3.50
23 Crushing Blow 3.50
24 Seeing with X-ray Eyes 3.50
25 Saved by Superman 3.50
26 Safe at Last 3.50
27 Superman's Peril 3.50
28 Jimmy, Superman & Perry 3.50
29 Great Caesar's Ghost 3.50
30 Bullets Bounce Off Him 3.50
31 In the Nick of Time 3.50
32 Superman & the Savages 3.50
33 Superman Leaps In 3.50
34 Superman to the Rescue 3.50
35 Superman's Problem 3.50
36 The Challenge 3.50
37 The Pirates' Decision 3.50
38 It's Superman! 3.50
39 Helping Hand 3.50
40 Superman & the Caveman 3.50
41 Facing the Death Ray 3.50
42 Superman's "Wedding" 3.50
43 Happy Ending 3.50
44 Reporter Clark Kent 3.50
45 Super Safecracker 3.50
46 Interviewing the Chief 3.50
47 Superman's Pet 3.50
48 At the Police Station 3.50
49 Capturing the Crooks 3.50
50 The Alien Arrives 3.50
51 Superman Gets His Man 3.50
52 Jor-El on Krypton 3.50
53 Jimmy Behind Bars 3.50
54 "Help Me, Superman" 3.50
55 Lois Threatened 3.50
56 Superman's Search 3.50
57 Pa Kent Finds Superboy 3.50
58 Held as a Hostage 3.50
59 Rocket from Krypton 3.50
60 Flight over Metropolis 3.50
61 The Kryptonite Ray 3.50
62 Superman as a Baby 3.50
63 Ruler of Krypton 3.50
64 Superman's Father 3.50
65 Visitor from Space 3.50
66 Harmless Blow 5.00

SUPERMAN IN THE JUNGLE

Topps (1968)

These cards are an extremely rare and highly desirable test set. They were issued in both the US and England (under Topps' A and BC card company). The set was a test issue in the US, and the cards came packed in an all white wrapper with a sticker of Superman attached to it. The 66 cards featured color illustrated fronts with story description backs. Of extreme interest are the die-cut punch out puzzle pieces alluded to by the wrappers, display boxes and store sales posters for the US test issue, but never actually released in the USA. They are found, however, in the English version of the series, but in very limited quantity. The English series is easier to collect than the US version, but it's still difficult to locate. It's made up of the same 66 cards, but in slightly smaller size. The wrapper is a green color, probably denoting the fact that the story takes place in the jungle! If you own this set or the original Superman Gum, Inc. set, you are already a serious comic card collector and you are exempt from this book's requirement that you own the ten most important recent sets. Besides, you probably can't afford to buy any more comics cards anyway (not that this will stop you from doing so anyway).

Set: 66 cards (test set) 2,700.00

Pack: cards + jigsaw puzzle piece 600.00

CARD CHECKLIST

1 Assignment–Africa 40.00
2 Luthor Escapes 40.00
3 A Job for Superman 40.00
4 A Jungle Inferno 40.00
5 Superman to the Rescue 40.00
6 Snuffing Out the Flames 40.00
7 Steel on Steel 40.00
8 A Grateful People 40.00
9 A Leopard Lurks 40.00
10 The Leopard Leaps 40.00
11 Luthor's Laboratory 40.00
12 The Ghastly Gorilla 40.00
13 Jimmy in Jeopardy 40.00
14 Rocking the Rhino 40.00
15 The Perilous Panther 40.00
16 Fangs of Death 40.00
17 Escape by X-Ray 40.00
18 Crisis on the Congo 40.00
19 In the Nick of Time 40.00
20 Jungle Ambush 40.00
21 Blasting the Python 40.00
22 The Evil Luthor Lurks 40.00
23 The Lost City 40.00
24 Kidnapping Congo Style 40.00
25 Into the Lost City 40.00
26 Jimmy on the Spot 40.00
27 Before Mighty Kryptonia 40.00
28 A Blade in the Back 40.00
29 Head-on Collision 40.00
30 The Sinister Plotters 40.00
31 Surprise! Surprise! 40.00
32 Useless Attack 40.00
33 Demolishing the Sun 40.00
34 Zoruk the Terrible 40.00
35 Round One to Superman 40.00
36 Kryptonite Kayo 40.00
37 The Unconscious Superman 40.00
38 Luthor Triumphant 40.00
39 Powerless Before Kryptonia 40.00
40 Superman Nears Death 40.00
41 Miraculous Madness 40.00
42 Superman Unchained 40.00
43 Lois Poses a Puzzle 40.00
44 One Down–One to Go 40.00
45 Luthor's Last Trick 40.00
46 The Awesome Android 40.00
47 Stunned Superman 40.00
48 Prehistoric Peril 40.00
49 Out of Harm's Way 40.00
50 A Trap is Sprung 40.00
51 An Awesome Apparition 40.00
52 The Dragon Disappears 40.00
53 Duel of Titans 40.00
54 Superman Strikes 40.00
55 The Arms of Death 40.00
56 Clouted by Kryptonius 40.00
57 The Chilling Climax 40.00
58 And Now...Attack 40.00
59 Snatched from the Sky 40.00
60 The Secret is Spilled 40.00
61 Victory at Last 40.00
62 Verdict for a Villain 40.00
63 A Final Vow 40.00
64 Taking Precautions 40.00
65 A Puzzling Mystery 40.00
66 The Astonishing Answer 40.00

Superman the Movie © DC Comics, Inc.

SUPERMAN THE MOVIE

Topps (1978, Movie)

"You will believe a man can fly!" was the advertising slogan for this first of the modern Superman movies, starring Christopher Reeve, Margot Kidder and Gene Hackman. It was a huge movie and merchandising event and naturally spawned a card series. The cards have color movie photos with a white border and red frame. 44 of the cards have puzzle backs which form a 4 x 11 card picture of Superman which is quite similar to card #63, but the picture is not very attractive because of the grey cardboard card stock. Thirty cards have movie facts and three are story summary cards. There are two types of stickers: six regular stickers with blue borders and six with foil borders.

Set: 77 cards/12 stickers 25.00

Pack: 10 cards, 1 sticker 2.50

CARD CHECKLIST

1 Christoper Reeve as
The Man of Steel 25
2 Christopher Reeve as Clark Kent . .25
3 Margot Kidder as Lois Lane 25
4 Zooming Across The Sky 25
5 Valerie Perrine as Eve 25
6 Ned Beatty as Otis 25
7 Jackie Cooper as Perry White 25
8 Editor and Staff
of the Daily Planet 25
9 Susannah York as Lara 25
10 Marc McClure as Jimmy Olsen . . .25
11 Glenn Ford as Jonathan Kent 25
12 The Majestic Planet Krypton 25
13 Incredible Laboratory of Jor-El . . .25
14 Lois Lane In a Jam! 25
15 A Study in Villainy 25
16 Arch Criminals on Trial 25
17 Briefing Military Police of Krypton .25
18 A World Torn Asunder..! 25
19 The Spaceship Blasts Off! 25
20 Protector of the Peace 25
21 The Might of Superman 25
22 A Final Farewell from Lara! 25
23 The Death Throes
of Planet Krypton! 25
24 Clark Kent, Ace Reporter! 25
25 Destruction of a World in Space! . .25
26 Aerial Adventure! 25
27 Escape from Destruction 25
28 Journey Across
the Gulf of Space! 25
29 Superbaby arrives on Earth! 25
30 Observing Landing
of a Spaceship 25
31 Adopting a Space Child 25
32 Young Clark Kent (Jeff East)
and his Foster Dad 25
33 The Passing of Jonathan Kent . . .25
34 The Youthful Lois Lane
and her Parents 25
35 Superman Makes the Headlines! .25
36 Paying a Call on Lois Lane 25
37 Night Flight 25
38 Flight Over Metropolis 25
39 Perils of The Big City! 25
40 The Man of Steel In Flight 25
41 Panic In the Sky! 25
42 Amazing Strength of
the Star Child 25
43 Sole Survivor of Krypton 25
44 Preparing to Leap Skyward 25
45 Facing Incredible Odds! 25
46 Trial By Fire! 25
47 On the Trail of Lex Luthor 25
48 The Icy Peril 25
49 Ready for Action! 25
50 Heroic Stranger from the Stars . . .25
51 The Amazing Man of Steel 25
52 Interview with Superman 25
53 The Incredible Scoop
of Lois Lane 25
54 Superman Leaps Into Action! 25
55 Superman To The Rescue! 25
56 A Daring Rescue! 25
57 Lois Lane thanks Superman 25
58 Rescued by the Man of Steel! 25
59 Superman (Christopher Reeve) . . .25
60 Confronting the
Arch-Criminal Lex Luthor 25
61 Portrait of a Hero 25
62 Protector of Truth and Justice 25
63 All-American Hero! 25
64 First Appearance
in the Comics (1938) 25
65 Soaring Above The City 25
66 Landing of the Spaceship 25
67 Nefarious Plan of Lex Luthor 25
68 The Scheme to Destroy Superman .25
69 Marlon Brando as Jor-El 25
70 Jor-El and Lara..
Their FInal Moments! 25
71 The Projection of Jor-El 25
72 Doomsday On Krypton! 25
73 Life-Saving Spaceship of Jor-El . .25
74 The Infant Son of Jor-El 25
75 Lex Luthor and Eve...
Companions in Villainy! 25
76 Gene Hackman as Lex Luthor . . .25
77 Conversing With The Elders 25

Blue-bordered Stickers

(1) Superman Insignia 40
(2) The Amazing Man of Steel 40
(3) The Might of Superman 40
(4) Night Flight 40
(5) Protector of Truth and Justice . . .40
(6) Zooming Across the Sky 40

Foil Stickers

(7) The Man of Steel 50
(8) Portrait of Clark Kent 50
(9) Portrait of Jimmy Olsen 50
(10) Portrait of Lois Lane 50
(11) Portrait of Lara 50
(12) Portrait of Superman 50

Superman the Movie © DC Comics, Inc.

SUPERMAN THE MOVIE, SERIES 2:

Here are 88 more photo cards from the movie, just like series 1, except with a blue frame and red border. These are numbered to follow. Half of the cards have puzzle backs and half have movie facts. There are 10 foil stickers and 6 regular ones with red borders. The packs and box say, "All New Series" and have the same artwork as the first series cards.

Set: 88 cards/16 stickers 25.00

Pack: 10 cards, 1 sticker 2.50

CARD CHECKLIST

78 Rushing to the Rescue! 25
79 Phyllis Thaxter Plays Martha Kent .25
80 Sunset in Smallville 25
81 Fabulous Lair of Lex Luthor 25
82 The Villains Discuss Their Plan . . .25
83 Christopher Reeve
Plays Superman 25
84 A Razzled Lois Lane! 25
85 Inside the Fortress of Solitude . . .25
86 A Low Moment for Clark Kent! . . .25
87 Ace Bumbler Otis! 25
88 The Dynamic Duo of Villainy 25
89 Lovely Lois Lane (Margot Kidder) .25
90 Clinging to Life! 25
91 Clark Kent as a Young
Man (Jeff East) 25
92 The Family of Jor-El on Krypton . .25
93 Superman in a Pensive Mood 25
94 Sarah Douglas Plays Ursa 25
95 Eve's Part in the Lex Luthor Plan .25
96 Clark Kent of the Daily Planet 25
97 Director Richard Donner 25
98 Christopher Reeve
Plays Clark Kent 25
99 Accident on the Road 25
100 Ned Beatty Plays Otis 25
101 Saved by the Man of Steel! 25
102 Marc McClure Plays
Jimmy Olsen 25
103 Face of Anger 25
104 Farewell to Smallville 25
105 Glenn Ford Plays
Jonathan Kent 25
106 "And Who, Disguised
as Clark Kent..." 25
107 Superman Visits the
Fortress of Solitude 25
108 Maria Schell Plays Vond-Ah 25
109 Incredible Display of Strength! . .25
110 Jack O'Halloran Plays Non 25
111 Spotting the Man of Steel 25
112 Destruction of the Dam! 25
113 The Chamber of the
Council of Elders 25
114 Fleeing the Destruction
of Krypton! 25
115 Superman in Metropolis 25
116 The One-And-Only Lois Lane! . . .25
117 Jonathan Kent in Smallville 25
118 Repairing the
Twisted Train Rails! 25
119 Terence Stamp Plays
General Zod 25
120 Mysterious Hunt for Lex Luthor . .25
121 The World's Most
Diabolical Villain 25
122 Lex Luthor Wants You 25
123 Time for a Quick Change! 25
124 200 Feet Below Grand
Central Station! 25
125 Club Reporter Jimmy Olsen 25
126 Flight Around Metropolis 25
127 Condemned to the Phantom Zone.25
128 Eve Teschmacher: Dizzy,

All card prices listed are for *Near Mint* condition.

Devious and Delightful! .25
129 Our Hero in Civilian Clothes .25
130 Clark Kent Transforms into Superman! .25
131 Jor-El in the Trial Chamber .25
132 Jackie Cooper Plays Perry White .25
133 The Incredible Scheme Begins .25
134 Eve and Her Mentor, Lex Luthor .25
135 John Barry, Master of Illusion .25
136 Amazing Hearing Powers of Superman .25
137 Ursa–Villainess Supreme .25
138 Might of the Man of Steel .25
139 Valerie Perrine Plays Eve .25
140 Lovers from Different Worlds .25
141 Susannah York Plays Lara .25
142 Gene Hackman Plays Lex Luthor .25
143 Vond-Ah and Jor-El .25
144 Valerie Perrine, Featured as Eve .25
145 The Farm of Jonathan Kent in Smallville .25
146 The Stupendous Man of Steel .25
147 Young Clark Kent and the Mysterious Crystal .25
148 Superman Spots a Crime .25
149 Can This Be the End of Lois Lane? .25
150 Night Heist .25
151 Flying Over the Dam .25
152 The Movie Set for Krypton .25
153 A Cowardly Blow from Behind! .25
154 Mission for a Bumbler .25
155 Visitor from Another Planet .25
156 Lex Luthor: Madman or Brilliant Scientist .25
157 Deceiving His Military Foes .25
158 Soaring to New Heights .25
159 'Copter Atop the Daily Planet .25
160 Death of an Exotic World .25
161 "How Did You Know the Exact Contents of My Purse?" .25
162 Threatened by a Mugger! .25
163 On His Way to the Lair of Lex Luthor .25
164 The Objective of Lex Luthor .25
165 Saving a Power Plant! .25

Foil Stickers

(13) Christopher Reeve Plays Superman .50
(14) Superman in a Pensive Mood .50
(15) Christopher Reeve Plays Clark Kent .50
(16) Superman Visits the Fortress of Solitude .50
(17) Incredible Display of Strength! .50
(18) Mysterious Hunt for Lex Luthor .50
(19) Might of the Man of Steel .50
(20) Soaring to New Heights .50
(21) On His Way to the Lair of Lex Luthor .50
(22) Superman Insignia .50

Red-bordered Stickers

(23) Villainess Ursa .40
(24) Evil Criminal Non .40
(25) Young Clark Kent .40
(26) Lovely Lois Lane .40
(27) General Zod .40
(28 The Man of Steel .40

SUPERMAN

Drakes Cakes (1979)

Set: 24 cards 75.00

Superman II (movie) © DC Comics, Inc.

SUPERMAN II

Topps (1981, Movie)

These are photo cards from the second Chris Reeves movie. The cards have a red border and yellow frame on the usual Topps cardboard stock. Cards are numbered and captioned on the front. The backs form six 3 x 3 puzzle pictures. Other card backs have character profiles, movie facts, movie star quotes, and 15 story summaries.

Set: 88 cards/22 stickers 17.00

Pack: 11 cards, 1 sticker 1.50

CARD CHECKLIST

1 Superman II – Title Card .15

Kryptonian Crystal Bank Archives

2 *The Man of Steel* .15
3 *Clark Kent* Reporter .15
4 Newswoman *Lois Lane* .15
5 *General Zod* .15
6 The Monstrous *Non* .15
7 Beautiful but Deadly *Ursa* .15
8 *Lara*, Mother of *Superman* .15
9 Bumbling Crook *Otis* .15
10 Editor *Perry White* .15
11 Young *Jimmy Olsen* .15

(Regular cards)

12 Superman to the Rescue! .15
13 Zooming into the Sky! .15
14 Trapped by Terrorists! .15
15 Phantom Zone Villains–Released! .15
16 Clark Kent Smells a Scoop! .15
17 They Don't Make Taxi Cabs Like They Used to! .15
18 Terror on the Moon .15
19 Hulking Villain from Krypton .15
20 The Fortress of Solitude .15
21 The Niagara Falls Affair .15
22 Undercover Assignment! .15
23 A Child in Danger! .15
24 Saved from Certain Death! .15
25 Reporters On The Job! .15
26 Rescued by..Clark Kent? .15
27 His Secret Revealed .15
28 Flying to Superman's Pad .15
29 Sky Trek .15
30 Inside the Fortress of Solitude .15
31 A Very Special Mission .15
32 The Fastest Boyfriend On Earth! .15
33 Dinner For Two! .15
34 Villains Arrive On Earth .15
35 Snake Trouble! .15
36 Ursa's Deadly Heat Rays .15
37 Non Tests his Powers .15
38 Welcome to our Country! .15
39 Bullets Have No Effect! .15
40 Superman's Great Sacrifice .15
41 A Message from Beyond .15
42 Inside the Mysterious Chamber .15
43 The Strength-Removing Process Begins .15
44 Superman...Now a Mere Mortal! .15
45 A New Beginning...or End? .15
46 Villains Wreak Havoc! .15
47 The Unstoppable Non! .15
48 Changing the Face of the World .15
49 Belted by a Bully! .15
50 A Desperate Appeal! .15
51 The Crystal Survives! .15
52 Back in Action! .15
53 Master of the World? .15
54 Raiding the Daily Planet! .15
55 The Destructors .15
56 Perry White Hits the Ceiling!! .15
57 The Bringers of Hate .15
58 Holding Lois Lane Hostage .15
59 The Man of Steel Returns! .15
60 The Destructive Heat Rays! .15
61 The Coolest Man in Town! .15
62 Panic in Metropolis .15
63 Battle of the Kryptonians .15
64 Superman Cages Non! .15
65 A City in Shambles! .15
66 One Way to Catch a Bus! .15
67 Ursa Hurls a Deadly Lid .15
68 Has Superman Been Defeated? .15
69 Destructive Winds .15
70 Destroying Metropolis .15
71 Reflecting the Villains' Powers .15
72 A Fight to the Finish! .15
73 Spectacular Battle! .15
74 Ring-Side Seats! .15
75 Speeding Across the World .15
76 Invading Superman's Home .15
77 Showdown at the Fortress of Solitude .15
78 The VIllains' Trump Card .15
79 The Final Stand .15
80 Lois Lane....Hostage! .15
81 A Clever Trick! .15
82 Getting A Boot Out of Ursa! .15
83 The Tables are Turned! .15
84 Kiss of Forgetfulness .15
85 Getting Even, Superman style! .15
86 Defender of Liberty .15
87 Until Next Time...! .15
88 Checklist Card .15

Sticker

1 Superman .35
2 Clark Kent .35
3 Lois Lane .35
4 Non .35
5 General Zod .35
6 Jimmy Olsen .35
7 Ursa .35
8 Perry White .35
9 Otis .35
10 Man of Steel .35
11 Phantom Zone Villains .35
12 Battle of the Kryptonians .35
13 Inside the Fortress of Solitude .35
14 Superman's Great Sacrifice .35
15 Superman Vs. the Villains .35
16 The Tables Are Turned! .35
17 Defender of Liberty .35
18 Superman in Flight .35
19 Superman Emblem .35
20 Superman II Logo .35
21 Double Emblem .35
22 The Staff of the Daily Planet .35

SUPERMAN III

Topps (1983, Movie)

Superman III *was the movie with Richard Pryor as a computer programmer. The cards have movie photos inside a black border and yellow line frame. The backs are yellow with a red border and color pictures of Superman and Pryor along with some text. The stickers are blue on a red and white striped background and the backs form a puzzle.*

Set: 99 cards/22 stickers 17.00

Pack: 10 cards, 1 sticker 1.50

CARD CHECKLIST

1 Title Card .15
2 A Comic Catastrophe! .15
3 Has Superman Been Snagged? .15
4 Soaring Through The City! .15
5 The Crime-Fighter From Krypton .15
6 A New Kind Of 'Car Pool'! .15
7 Clark To The Rescue! .15
8 A Nimble Feat–Almost .15
9 A Gloomy Gus Gorman .15
10 Computer Whiz! .15
11 In Perry White's Office .15
12 Lois Lane And Jimmy Olsen .15
13 Smallville's Finest .15
14 Off On Vacation .15
15 On The Road To Smallville .15
16 The Chemical Plant Disaster .15
17 A Job For Superman .15
18 Courageous Photographer .15
19 The Resourceful Superman .15
20 Slide To Safety .15
21 Jimmy Olsen–Injured! .15
22 Into The Fray .15

Superman III (movie) © DC Comics, Inc.

23 Rescuing Jimmy Olsen 15
24 In The Nick of Time! 15
25 Astounding Ice-Breath 15
26 The Enormous Ice Platter! 15
27 A Dapper Clark Kent! 15
28 The Smallville High Reunion 15
29 Greeting Lana Lang 15
30 Gus Has A Plan 15
31 Millionaire Ross Webster 15
32 Gus And Lorelei Ambrosia 15
33 Clark Kent 'Bumps' Into Gus 15
34 The Picnic 15
35 Ricky In The Wheat Fields 15
36 Terror Of The Thresher 15
37 Saving Ricky's Life 15
38 A New Found Friend 15
39 At The Bowling Alley 15
40 Creepy Brad Wilson 15
41 Gus Gorman's Ploy 15
42 The Way To Brad's Heart 15
43 The Ski Resort Penthouse 15
44 Gus Describes The Hurricane Affair 15
45 Lorelei Ambrosia 15
46 Skiing In Metropolis? 15
47 Smallville Honors Superman 15
48 The Esteemed Speaker 15
49 General Gus Gorman! 15
50 The Deadly Gift 15
51 Friends...Or Foes? 15
52 De-Leaning The Pisa Tower 15
53 The Villains Exercise Their Options 15
54 Goodness At The Crossroads 15
55 The 'Ultimate Computer' Scheme .15
56 Awaiting Superman's Arrival 15
57 A Disgraceful Superman 15
58 Spotting Superman 15
59 An Evil Superman? 15
60 Challenged By Clark Kent 15
61 The Man of Steel Vs. Himself 15
62 Dastardly Nemesis 15
63 Clark Kent–Defeated? 15
64 Car Crusher Terror 15
65 Clark Kent's Fight For Life! 15
66 Goodness Triumphant! 15
67 A Hero Once Again 15
68 Back In Action! 15
69 Righting Wrongs With Heat-Vision .15
70 In Search Of Ross Webster 15
71 Balloon Escape 15
72 The Only Way To Travel! 15
73 The Fantastic Computer 15
74 Confronting His Foes 15
75 The Computer Attacks! 15
76 Controlling The Computer 15
77 Trapped! 15
78 Strength Of The Man of Steel 15
79 The Kryptonite Ray 15
80 Enveloped By The Ray! 15
81 Gus Gorman Turns On His Creation! 15
82 Is Superman Doomed? 15
83 Vera's Monstrous Fate! 15
84 Robotized! 15
85 Attacking Lorelei Ambrosia! 15
86 Robot On The Rampage 15
87 Gus Gorman Is Zapped! 15
88 Allies At Last! 15
89 The Plan of Superman 15
90 Acid Indigestion Death! 15
91 Destruction Of The Ultimate Computer 15
92 Giving Gus Gorman A Lift! 15
93 Stopping Off At The Coal Mine . . .15
94 Transforming Coal Into A Diamond 15
95 The Friends Depart 15
96 A Gift From Superman 15
97 Lana Lang At The Daily Planet . . .15
98 Superman Flies Again! 15
99 Checklist 15

Sticker

1 The Man of Steel 25
2 Lana Lang 25
3 Ross Webster 25
4 Gus Gorman 25
5 Lorelei Ambrosia 25
6 Vera Webster 25
7 Jimmy Olsen 25
8 Lois Lane 25
9 Clark Kent 25
10 'General' Gus Gorman 25
11 (Superman Flying Right) 25
12 (Superman Flying Left) 25
13 Smallville's Finest 25
14 The Resourceful Superman 25
15 Astounding Ice-Breath! 25
16 The Picnic 25
17 Friends...or Foes? 25
18 Righting Wrongs with Heat-Vision .25
19 The Computer Attacks! 25
20 Strength of the Man of Steel 25
21 Enveloped by the Ray! 25
22 Robotized! 25

Sweet Lucy Technophelia © Scott Harrison

SWEET LUCY TECHNOPHELIA Set #0

Brainstorm Comics (1993)

(Scott Harrison)

These cards are from Interzone *#1*, Sweet Lucy *#1*, Interzone *#2 and* Technophilia *#1. Half have a red border with a red and white back and half have a blue border with a black and white back.*

Set: 20 cards + header slip 8.00

From Interzone #1
Linnea Steele 40
Christian "Whitey" Black 40
Fully Modified Police Dredge 40
Kailen Goetz 40
From Sweet Lucy #1
Richmond Dolinar 40
Ibo 40
Lucy Lee .40
William "Skids" Lee 40
From Interzone #2
The Matrix Plane 40
Labor Clone 40
Gorman Benway 40
Zen Phillips 40
From Technophilia #1
Myrddin the Wise 40
Daedalus Animus 40
Judgement Day 40
Technophilia 40
Duplicate cards in set
Daedalus Animus 40
Kailen Goetz 40
Judgement Day 40
Technophilia 40

T

Tales From The Crypt © Tales From the Crypt Holdings

TALES FROM THE CRYPT

Cardz (1993, TV & Comic)

Know ye, faithful readers, that long ago when evil influences were busily trying to corrupt the minds of virtuous youth with music like Rock and Roll, there sprang from the warped mind of Bill Gaines a comic book called The Crypt of Terror, *which mutated into an equally warped comic book called* Tales from the Crypt. *A casualty of the "Comics Code," it only lasted 5 years (30 issues). However, in that short time, it succeeded in addicting a generation of impressionable young minds. (Bill Gaines went on to corrupt even more youngsters with* Mad Magazine.*) Those poor souls wandered aimlessly through the '60s and were on the verge of being cured when Stephen King arrived. Some of these renewed addicts produced a TV show of the same name, in order more easily to corrupt the youth of the '90s! In these cards you get all sorts of full-bleed pictures of the animatronic puppet version of the Cryptkeeper, complete with graveyard humor word balloons. The backs are black with green slime and information on particular episodes. You also get pictures of all 30 of the comic book covers by Jack Davis or Al Feldsetin, with the table of contents on the back. The rest of the cards have more of this same humor and finally a picture of Bill Gaines, who is now dead (which is too bad) but seems to fit the theme of the cards. There are three holograms which are not captioned and a Tekchrome card of the Crypt Keeper. The four promo cards all have green backs, with text, and say "Prototype" at the top.*

Set: 110 cards 12.50

Holograms
H1 . . . . 7.00
H2 . . . . 7.00
H3 . . . . 7.00
Tekchrome
T1 (Crypt Keeper) 12.00
Prototype, i.e. promos
1 This will cost you... . . . . 1.50
2 Fourth and ghoul... . . . . 1.50
3 We're working with a... . . . . 1.50
4 Issue #24 cover 1.50
Pack: 8 cards 1.00

CARD CHECKLIST

Fright Gags/Episode quiz cards
1 This blood's for you! 10
2 The Crypt's a beach! 10
3 Bone Appetite! 10
4 Maggot P.I. 10
5 Straighten up and die right 10
6 Sergeant Pepper's Open Heart Club Band 10
7 The **King** is in the Crypt 10
8 The Ghoulish Gourmet 10
9 How about a delicious brain muffin? .10
10 These guys are all **choked up** . . .10
11 Trimming fat off healthcare 10
12 Heads will rock 'n roll 10
13 This speeder missed the bridge by a foot 10
14 Dances with Werewolves 10
15 I have a green thumb for horror culture 10
16 Bedtime gory telling 10
17 **This one** has me stumped 10
18 The man of your screams 10
19 The line just went dead 10
20 It's a **skull**...dummy 10
21 Planting a-head for the future 10
22 Fourth and ghoul to go 10
23 We're working with a **skeleton** crew 10
24 Bartender...give me another shot .10
25 Can't take my eyes off of you 10
26 I **sure** get a charge out of this! . . .10
27 T.V. or not T.V. 10
28 I've just swept a double header . .10
29 Business is **dead** 10
30 This will cost you an arm and a leg .10
31 For a **minute** there, he lost his head 10
32 This place is starting to **bug** me . .10
33 **Warning**...Stay out of the Crypt–tonight! 10
34 I've got a **bone** to pick with you . .10
35 Take another little piece of my heart 10
36 Cannibal Soup...**Mmm, Mmm, Good!** 10
37 Three heads are better than one . .10
38 You've got the right thumb, baby...uh huh 10
39 Party 'til you puke...it's **Murder Gras!** 10
40 I only read it for the articles 10
41 Another swinging single 10
42 Sometimes this job really **sucks!** .10
43 L.L. Crypt with a Def Grip 10
44 You look m-a-a-velous! 10
45 You're booked for Club Dead... Bone Voyage! 10
46 **Please** take my money...but dont kill me **again!** 10
47 Let's look **Black** To the Future . . .10
48 The coroner will see you now 10
49 Fake left and drive for the casket .10
50 His handicap is simple...**he's dead** .10
51 Open wide and scream..**aaah!** . . .10
52 This joker's **wild!** 10
53 I'm having a wonderful slime! 10
54 I've got you under my skin! 10
55 My left hook is deadly accurate . . .10
56 **So**, what makes you think people don't like you? 10
57 Loony Tunes for Dead Heads 10
58 There seems to be a hair in my "head drop" soup! 10
59 The prime cuts are specially tagged 10
60 Hey Baby...did anyone ever tell you you're drop dead beautiful? . . .10
Killer Komic Kovers & Kredits
61 #17 Werewolf Strikes Again 50
62 #18 Living Corpse 50
63 #19 Voodoo Drums 50
64 #20 Day of Death 50
65 #21 Copper Dies in the Electric Chair 50
66 #22 Down in the Grave 50
67 #23 Locked in a Mausoleum 50
68 #24 Danger...Quicksand 50
69 #25 Mataud Waxworks 50
70 #26 Sacred Graveyard 50
71 #27 Axe 50
72 #28 Buried Alive 50
73 #29 Coffin Burier 50
74 #30 Underwater Death 50
75 #31 Hand Chopper 50
76 #32 Woman Crushed by Elephant .50
77 #33 Lower Berth 50
78 #34 Jack the Ripper 50
79 #35 Werewolf 50
80 #36 Taxi Driver 50
81 #37 Skeleton Burial 50
82 #38 Axe Man 50
83 #39 Children in the Graveyard . . .50
84 #40 Underwater Monster 50
85 #41 Knife Thrower 50
86 #42 Stake in the Heart 50
87 #43 Falling From a Plane 50
88 #44 Guillotine 50
89 #45 Rat Takes Over His Life 50
90 #46 Werewolf Man Being Hunted .50
Gatekeeper Favorites
91 Top Ten Tunes 10
92 T.V. From the Crypt 10
93 Favorite Last Meals 10
94 Maddest Musicians 10
95 Stars From The Crypt 10
96 The Four Basic Food Groups 10
97 Favorite Past Times 10
98 Cliches From the Crypt 10
99 Hang-Outs or Haunts 10
100 Favorite Flicks 10
Behind the Screams: TV show credits
101 The Puppeteers Who Give "The Big Guy" Life 10
102 The Mad (But Nice) Scientist: Kevin Yagher 10
103 Clothes Make the Man(iac) 10
104 The Crypt Crew in Action 10
105 Makeup! 10
106 Show Biz Rag Sez Crypt a Keeper 10
107 "Are You Def?" It's the Crypt Jam!" 10
108 Moguls of Mayhem 10
109 John Kassir – A Voice That Can Raise the Dead 10
110 The Original Genius of the Crypt: Bill Gaines 10

Teenage Mutant Ninja Turtles Cartoon © Mirage Studios, USA

TEENAGE MUTANT NINJA TURTLES CARTOON

Topps (1989)

This first TMNT card set features comic book style art. Our favorite heroes on a half-shell spend most of their time rescuing April O'Neil, buxom TV reporter, from Shredder and his evil gang. A second story starts on card #66 and features Rocksteady and Bebop as well as Shredder and Krang. (If you don't know who these characters are already, you probably won't be interested in collecting these cards.) These cards are on standard Topps card stock for this period. The fronts have a cartoon style picture inside a lime green border, with black lines. The caption is at the bottom in a red stripe and the number is in (what else?) a green turtle shell. The backs repeat the title and number and have the story line text. The stickers are yellow with a puzzle picture back and show the four heroes together on a motorcycle. Boxes for these cards were sold at close-out prices, which keeps the price of the cards down.

Set: 88 cards/11 stickers 15.00

Pack: 5 cards, 1 sticker 50
Four different wrappers, with 25 cent price.
Cello Pack: 11 cards, 1 sticker 60
The cello packs had two different wrappers, each with a 59 cent price, and came in a 24 count box issued in 1990.

CARD CHECKLIST

1 The Epic Begins 15
2 Crime City! 15
3 The Art of Crime 15
4 "Get April O'Neil!" 15
5 Mysterious Rescuer! 15
6 Monitoring the Turtles 15
7 A Special Wake-Up Call 15
8 The Perfect Host 15
9 Pizza for Breakfast! 15
10 The Slice That Satisfies! 15
11 Splinter's Crew 15
12 It Began in Japan... 15
13 Ninjas in Training 15
14 Framed by a Foe! 15
15 The Fateful Stumble 15

16 A Man and His Turtles 15
17 Metamorphosis 15
18 Humanoid Turtles! 15
19 Man-Into-Ratman! 15
20 Splinter's Skill 15
21 Donatello! 15
22 Raphael! 15
23 Leonardo! 15
24 Michaelangelo! 15
25 The Shredder 15
26 The Master's Plan 15
27 Ready for Action! 15
28 Underground Heroes 15
29 The Ninjas Emerge 15
30 "Turtles? No Way!!" 15
31 "Here's Looking at You, Kid!" 15
32 Our Kinda Town! 15
33 Ninja Pizza Coming Up! 15
34 April...Kidnapped! 15
35 The Shredder's Evil Gang 15
36 Let's Rock 'N' Roll! 15
37 High Flyin' Hero! 15
38 Time to Fight, Dudes! 15
39 Clobbered! 15
40 Turtle Threat 15
41 Power of the Enemy 15
42 Zapped! 15
43 A Narrow Escape! 15
44 Tumble That Wall! 15
45 The Rescue of April 15
46 Trapped by Their Foe! 15
47 Making A Splash! 15
48 "Water? No Prob!" 15
49 Unsinkable April 15
50 Sword of Justice 15
51 Death-Defying Escape! 15
52 Turtles Triumphant 15
53 The Fearless Foursome 15
54 Rockabye Turtle! 15
55 Another Day, Another Battle! 15
56 Action Packed Workout! 15
57 Hero in a Half-Shell 15
58 A Tasty Treat! 15
59 "Err..Ahh...No Thanks!" 15
60 Technodrome Terror 15
61 In Cahoots With Krang 15
62 Diabolical Duo! 15
63 "What About My Story?!" 15
64 Jive Turtles! 15
65 "Sorry About That, April!" 15
66 Madness at the Zoo! 15
67 New Mutant Henchmen 15
68 Up From The Depths 15
69 Rocksteady's Revenge 15
70 When Mutants Collide! 15
71 The Long Journey 15
72 Courage of the Master 15
73 Snagged by the Shredder! 15
74 Turtles to the Rescue! 15
75 "Looks Like Another Trap!" 15
76 Surrounded! 15
77 Danger on All Sides! 15
78 Mechanical Monsters 15
79 Turtle Power! 15
80 Roused and Riled! 15
81 His Best Foot Forward 15
82 Smashed to Smithereens! 15
83 The Assault Continues 15
84 A Mean Green Machine! 15
85 The Rage of Krang 15
86 "Next Time, Turtles...!" 15
87 "Cowabunga! It's Meal Time!" 15
88 Savoring Their Reward 15

Sticker (Poster Back)

1 Raphael 25
2 Michaelangelo 25
3 Donatello 25
4 Leonardo 25
5 The Shredder 25
6 Splinter .25

Teenage Mutant Ninja Turtles Cartoon © Mirage Studios, USA

7 Cowabunga! 25
8 Turtle Power! 25
9 (Skateboarding) 25
10 (The Four Turtles) 25
11 Four Turtles on motorcycle 25

Super Glossy set in collector's box, with 22 bonus cards 25.00

The bonus cards are comic book cover paintings from Mirage Studios. The card stock is glossy and much better quality than the standard Topps issue of that time.

Bonus cover art cards:

A "Yarghil" 25
B "Battle for the Sewers" 25
C "Ambushed by the Shredder" 25
D "Trashing the Transmat" 25
E "Ninja Sunset" 25
F "Battle Above the Streets" 25
G "Mouser Attack" 25
H "Alien Encounter" 25
I "Possessed" 25
J "The Unmentionables" 25
K "Stone Sleep" 25
L "Leap Into Battle" 25
M "Leatherhead" 25
N "Day of the Dragon" 25
O "Dream Flight" 25
P "Battle in the Arena" 25
Q "Barroom Brawl" 25
R "Walk on the Wild Side" 25
S "Galactic Conflict" 25
T "Warrior Woman from Beyond the Stars" 25
U "Brothers Under the Spell" 25
V "Night of the White Ninja" 25

Deluxe Set (Topps Ireland 1990)

This set tells the same stories as the one above, but in 66 cards. The cards are on glossy stock. They were available in the U.S. in some locations.

Set: 66 cards (no stickers) in collector hanging box 8.00
Set: 66 cards, 11 stickers 10.00

1 The Epic Begins 15
2 Crime City! 15
3 "Get April O'Neil!" 15
4 Mysterious Rescuer! 15
5 Monitoring the Turtles 15
6 A Special Wake-Up Call! 15
7 The Perfect Host 15
8 Pizza for Breakfast! 15
9 Framed by a Foe! 15
10 The Fateful Stumble 15
11 A Man and His Turtles 15
12 Metamorphosis 15
13 Humanoid Turtles! 15
14 Man-Into-Ratman! 15
15 Splinter's Skill 15
16 Donatello! 15
17 Raphael! 15
18 Leonardo! 15
19 The Shredder 15
20 The Master's Plan 15
21 Underground Heroes! 15
22 The Heroes Emerge 15
23 "Here's Looking at You, Kid!" 15
24 Hero Pizza Coming Up! 15
25 April...Kidnapped! 15
26 The Shredder's Evil Gang 15
27 Time to Fight, Dudes! 15
28 Turtle Threat 15
29 Power of the Enemy 15
30 Zapped! 15
31 The Rescue of April 15
32 Trapped by Their Foe! 15
33 "Water? No Prob!" 15
34 Unsinkable April 15
35 Sword of Justice 15
36 Death-Defying Escape! 15
37 Turtles Triumphant 15
38 The Fearless Foursome 15
39 Rockabye Turtle! 15
40 Another Day, Another Battle! 15
41 A Tasty Treat! 15
42 "Err..Ahh...No Thanks!" 15
43 Technodrome Terror 15
44 In Cahoots With Krang 15
45 Diabolical Duo! 15
46 "What About My Story?!" 15
47 Jive Turtles! 15
48 "Sorry About That, April!" 15
49 New Mutant Henchmen 15
50 Up From The Depths 15
51 Rocksteady's Revenge 15
52 When Mutants Collide! 15
53 The Long Journey 15
54 Courage of the Master 15
55 Snagged by the Shredder! 15
56 "Looks Like Another Trap!" 15
57 Surrounded! 15
58 Danger on All Sides! 15
59 Mechanical Monsters 15
60 Roused and Riled! 15
61 His Best Foot Forward 15
62 The Assault Continues 15
63 A Mean Green Machine! 15
64 "Next Time, Turtles...!" 15
65 "Cowabunga! It's Meal Time!" 15
66 Savoring Their Reward 15

Teenage Mutant Ninja Turtles Cartoon II © Mirage Studios, USA

TEENAGE MUTANT NINJA TURTLES CARTOON

SERIES II Topps (1990)

More of the above! The border is black with lime green lines (the reverse of series I). The cards are numbered beginning with #89 (where Series I left off). They tell two separate stories: the first features Usagi Yojimbo, Stan Sakai's ninja rabbit from another dimension; the second, beginning on card #118, features Baxter Stockman and Krang. The stickers are blue, with a puzzle back which shows the four turtles watching TV and eating pizza with Splinter. They have no titles so we have listed the pictured character instead.

Set: 88 cards/11 stickers 10.00

Holograms, set of 4 . . . . 10.00
Pack, 5 cards, 1 sticker 50

The packs say "2nd Series" and are printed with a 25 cent price.

Pack, 11 cards, 1 sticker 75

The 11 card pack comes in two different cello wrappers, one yellow, one red.

CARD CHECKLIST

89 Our Story Opens 10
90 Pulling the Switch 10
91 Usagi Yojimbo 10
92 Unbelievable! 10
93 The Tortoise and the Hare 10
94 Defeated by Donatello 10
95 A New Caper 10
96 Turtles Undercover 10
97 Hare Today, Gone Today 10
98 Rabbit About Town 10
99 Rabbit Transit 10
100 Welcome to the Hutch 10
101 Rabbit Rampage 10
102 Turtles to the Rescue 10
103 Studying the Screen 10
104 The Plot Heats Up! 10
105 Quakes and Shakes 10
106 Enter the Dragon 10

107 Flaming Fangs .10
108 The Dragon Master .10
109 A Possible Solution .10
110 A Magic Candle .10
111 An Old Flame .10
112 Defeating the Dragon .10
113 Usagi Triumphs .10

Teenage Mutant Ninja Turtles Cartoon II
© Mirage Studios, USA

114 Praise From Shredder .10
115 A Monster Egg .10
116 Obento's Thanks .10
117 A Hare Out of Place .10
118 A New Problem .10
119 Turtle-Robics .10
120 No Pain, No Fame .10
121 TV Time .10
122 Dig This .10
123 Worried Turtles .10
124 Return of the Fly .10
125 Buzzing Baxter .10
126 Fly Trap .10
127 Angry Krang .10
128 A Gift From a Fly .10
129 Follow the Fly .10
130 Heading For Their Hide-Out? .10
131 Back to the Sewer! .10
132 Gearing Up .10
133 Sewer Surfing .10
134 Without A Paddle .10
135 Sinister Surfers .10
136 Goons and Harpoons .10
137 Down Goes Donatello! .10
138 Taking the Plunge .10
139 The Last of the Turtles? .10
140 Donatello's Discovery .10
141 Paddling Pals .10
142 A Shortcut! .10
143 A Piece of the Rock .10
144 A Familiar Place .10
145 Home of the Fly .10
146 Man Into Fly .10
147 Fly vs. Turtles .10
148 Blam! .10
149 Ninja Gerbil! .10
150 A Reluctant Rodent .10
151 A Buzzing Boss .10
152 Saving Michaelangelo .10
153 Dancin' Bebop .10
154 Will the Fly Flee? .10
155 Turtle and Gerbil .10
156 Getting Bugged .10
157 No Time To Lose! .10
158 Conquering the Computer .10
159 Not So Fast, Fly! .10
160 Who's in the Suits? .10
161 Insect Aside .10
162 Down the Tube! .10
163 Chefs of the Future .10
164 Too Many Cooks .10
165 The Kitchen of Doom! .10
166 Chop Chop! .10
167 A Turtle Once More! .10
168 Speeding Turtles .10
169 A Shaky Situation .10
170 A Finale for the Fly? .10
171 The Missing Piece .10
172 Not Quite Shipshape .10
173 Bye Bye Fly! .10
174 Pretty Please .10
175 Back Home Again .10
176 Saved by Science! .10

Sticker (Posterbacks)

1 (Krang) .20
2 (Raph) .20
3 (Mike) .20
4 (Leo) .20
5 (Don) .20
6 (Three turtles) .20
7 (Splinter) .20
8 (Bebop & Rocksteady) .20
9 (Don, with video cam) .20
10 (Baxter Stockman/Poster preview) .20
11 (April & Professor) .20

TEENAGE MUTANT NINJA TURTLES MOVIE I

Topps (1990)

These are photo cards taken from the first turtles movie. If you have any interest in these cards at all, you have probably already seen the movie, which primarily features your "Heroes in a Half-shell" rescuing April O'Neil from various dangers and battling Shredder. The cards are on white stock and have a white border along with a yellow bottom "film strip" which contains the card title and the card number, in a blue movie camera design. The backs repeat the card title in white letters and include text in a light purple box. The series name is in lime green on the left. The stickers are oval inset photos inside a red border. The backs contain just the series name (rather than the usual puzzle).

Set: 132 cards/11 stickers 12.50
Pack: 9 cards, 1 sticker .75

CARD CHECKLIST

1 The Turtles Have Arrived! .10
2 Leonardo .10
3 Michaelangelo .10
4 Donatello .10
5 Raphael .10
6 Master Splinter .10
7 Reporter April O'Neil .10
8 Crimefighter Casey Jones .10

Teenage Mutant Ninja Turtles Movie I © Mirage Studios USA, North Shore Investments & New Line Cinema

9 Danny Pennington .10
10 The Shredder .10
11 Tatsu .10
12 Chief Sterns .10
13 Crime-Crazed City! .10
14 Phantom Rescuers .10
15 "Underground" Heroes! .10
16 A Respectful Bow .10
17 Master of the Sewer Den .10
18 "And Remember...No Anchovies!" .10
19 Turtle-About-Town! .10
20 Hungry Mike .10
21 Just Hangin'! .10
22 Turtle Soul Food! .10
23 Raphael Under Cover! .10
24 The Masked Vigilante .10
25 Casey in Action! .10
26 "Who's the Champ, Pal?" .10
27 "Tough Rocks, Raphael!" .10
28 April's Boss in a Snit .10
29 Watching From Below .10
30 Fencing With O'Neil .10
31 April in a Jam! .10
32 Courage of April .10
33 Subway Assault! .10
34 Decked by the "Foot"! .10
35 Raphael to the Rescue! .10
36 One Dangerous Dude! .10
37 Airborne Hero! .10
38 Stepping on the "Foot"! .10
39 April Gets Carried Away .10
40 Pursued by the Enemy .10
41 Back From Oblivion .10
42 Furry Friend or Foe? .10
43 Startled by Splinter .10
44 Pow-Wow in the Sewer! .10
45 Splinter's Story .10
46 Mutant Turtle Baby! .10
47 Through a Sewer Darkly .10
48 Up, Up and Away! .10
49 Coming Up in the World .10
50 April's Pad .10
51 Unusual Houseguest .10
52 Distant Cousins? .10
53 A Frozen Pizza Party! .10
54 Their First Human Friend .10
55 The Sewer Den...Trashed! .10
56 "Where's Master Splinter?!" .10
57 The Rat Man Manacled! .10
58 Tatsu and His Evil "Foot" .10
59 Approach of the Evil One .10
60 Master of Plunder! .10
61 Danny is Nabbed! .10
62 Dejected Heroes .10
63 April on the Air .10
64 Watch Out Behind You...! .10
65 Spotted by Casey! .10
66 Against the "Foot" Army! .10
67 Utterly Outnumbered! .10
68 Check Out the Tube! .10
69 Raphael Holds His Own! .10
70 Fine Place For a Nap! .10
71 April's Guided Tour .10
72 The O'Neil Junk Store .10
73 Topsy-Turvey Turtle! .10
74 Special Delivery! .10
75 Creeps From on High! .10
76 Crashing April's Party .10
77 Protecting Raphael .10
78 Fighting for Their Lives! .10
79 The Battle Rages On! .10
80 The Apartment–Invaded! .10
81 "Let's Split!" .10
82 Escape From New York .10
83 Tatsu's Failure .10
84 An Evil Reprimand .10
85 Reaching Out to Danny .10
86 "I Will *Listen*, My Son!" .10
87 Bathtub Vigil .10
88 Casey–Mr. Fix-It! .10
89 "It'll Never Work!" .10
90 Whoops! .10
91 Raphael Revives! .10
92 Raph's Gonna Be Okay! .10
93 Brotherly Love, Turtle-Style! .10
94 What To Do Next...? .10
95 In Tune With the Infinite .10
96 Message From Beyond .10
97 The New Fighting Method! .10
98 Tuning Up! .10
99 Ready for a Rematch! .10
100 "It's Time to Go Back!" .10
101 Danny...Ally or Spy? .10
102 "Kill Splinter!" .10
103 Surprise for the "Foot"! .10
104 The Soprano Maker Strikes! .10
105 "Shelling" It Out! .10
106 The Battle With Tatsu .10
107 "Fore!" .10
108 Armed and Anxious! .10
109 A Foot for the "Foot"! .10
110 Turtle Power! .10
111 Rooftop Assault! .10
112 The Shredder Pours It On! .10
113 "We Got A Problem Here!" .10
114 The Face of Oroku .10
115 Saki on the Rampage! .10
116 Outwitted by Splinter! .10
117 The Final Confrontation .10
118 The Shredder's Great Fall .10
119 Dying...Without Honor! .10
120 The Victor .10
121 "Thank You, My Children!" .10
122 Father and Son Reunited .10

Teenage Mutant Ninja Turtles Movie I © Mirage Studios, USA, North Shore Investments & New Line Cinema

123 The Birth of Cowabunga 10
124 April O'Neil...Signing Off! 10
125 He *Loves* Being a Turtle! 10
126 Until Next Crime...! 10

Behind the Scenes

127 Clowning with Leonardo 10
128 The Comics Come to Life! 10
129 Preparing for "Battle" 10
130 Shooting Splinter 10
131 Last Minute Costume Check 10
132 The Gang's All Here! 10

Stickers

1 Splinter .15
2 Shredder 15
3 April 15
4 Raphael 15
5 Leonardo 15
6 April 15
7 Raphael 15
8 Tatsu 15
9 Michaelangelo 15
10 Donatello 15
11 Casey Jones 15

Deluxe Set: 132 glossy cards, boxed but **no** stickers or bonus cards . . 15.00
Pack A set of 66 deluxe cards 6.00
Pack B set of 66 deluxe cards 6.00

TMNT The Secret of the Ooze © Mirage Studios, Inc. Northshore Investments, Ltd. & New Line Cinema Corporation

TEENAGE MUTANT NINJA TURTLES MOVIE II THE SECRET OF THE OOZE

Topps (1991, Movie)

These cards were made using photos from the second TMNT movie. Shredder's new henchmen, Tokka and Rahzar appear and April gets in even more trouble! The cards have a red border with some green ooze on the left side dripping from a canister tube at the top which contains the card title. The stickers have a lime green border with color pictures, but they are not captioned. The backs form a puzzle of the movie poster.

Set: 99 cards/11 stickers (red border, green ooze) 10.00
Pack: 8 cards, 1 sticker 75

CARD CHECKLIST

1 Exactly One Year Later... 10
2 Raph 10
3 Don 10
4 Mikey 10
5 Leo 10
6 Splinter .10
7 April O'Neil 10
8 The Shredder 10
9 Rahzar .10
10 Tokka .10
11 Special Pizza Delivery! 10
12 Clobbered by Keno! 10
13 Turtles to the Rescue! 10
14 "Take Cover, Kid!" 10
15 Brawl in the Mall! 10
16 "Let's Improvise, Guys!" 10
17 Deli Dilemma! 10
18 At April's Apartment 10
19 A Turtle's Life 10
20 The Evil One Returns 10
21 Interviewing the Professor 10
22 Junk Food Fanatic! 10
23 The Clean-up Brigade! 10
24 Kitchen Catastrophe! 10
25 Rooftop Meeting 10
26 "Seek Your Answers!" 10
27 The Original Canister 10
28 Mysterious Green Ooze 10
29 Their Latest Mission 10
30 In the T.G.R.I. Lab 10
31 Startling Discovery! 10
32 The Pizza Boy is Back! 10
33 A Lesson from Splinter 10
34 April Showers! 10
35 A Bogie-like Farewell! 10
36 On the Track of a New Home . . .10
37 Prof. Perry–Kidnapped 10
38 Questionable Creations 10
39 Masters of Darkness 10
40 "They're...Babies!!" 10
41 Nabbed by the Baddies 10
42 Shredder's Captive 10
43 "We've Gotta Save Raph!" 10
44 The Rescue Party 10
45 "A Trap! I Knew It!!" 10
46 Netting Our Heroes 10
47 Triumphant Villain 10
48 Splinter's Steady Arrow 10
49 Ready For Action! 10
50 The Mutants Appear! 10
51 Weird Henchcreature 10
52 Tokka the Terrible 10
53 "They're Not So Tough!" 10
54 Beastial Bellow 10
55 No Match for Rahzar 10
56 No Stopping the Monster! 10
57 A Hasty Retreat 10
58 Man in the Manhole! 10
59 "Four...*Turtles!*" 10
60 Underground Escape! 10
61 Home Sweet Home?! 10
62 Secret of their Origin 10
63 Mutant Attack! 10
64 Rahzar on the Rampage! 10
65 April Held Hostage! 10
66 A Message from Shredder 10
67 Lab Assistants! 10
68 The Anti-Mutagen 10
69 Pizza Break! 10
70 A Dough-nutty Idea 10
71 "Let the Games Begin!" 10
72 Traditional Pre-Fight Doughnut! . .10
73 "This Better Work!" 10
74 "MMMMMMMM...!" 10
75 Invading a Rap Club! 10
76 Taking on the Terror 10
77 One Tossed Turtle! 10
78 The Monster Mash 10
79 Crashing the Party 10
80 Makeshift Experiment! 10
81 Seltzer Bottle Attack! 10
82 The Mutants – Neutralized! 10
83 Tackling the Foot Soldiers 10
84 Tatsu is Flattened! 10
85 The Birth of "Ninja Rap"! 10
86 Rockin' and Rappin' Heroes! 10
87 The Showdown 10
88 "Cool It, Keno!" 10
89 Blasting the Shredder 10
90 All's Well that Ends... Well? 10
91 Turtles on the Edge 10
92 Their Final Obstacle 10
93 Mutated Supershredder 10
94 Supershredder Terror! 10
95 Outmatched?! 10
96 Tackling the Monster 10
97 Turtles Triumphant! 10
98 The Morning After 10
99 "Can You Believe It?!" 10

Stickers (Poster Backs) (no captions)
1 thru 11, each 15

Teenage Mutant Ninja Turtles Movie III © Mirage Studios, USA & Clearwater Holdings

TEENAGE MUTANT NINJA TURTLES MOVIE III

Topps (1993, Movie)

These are photo cards from the third movie, which takes place in Japan. The story cards have a white border with a bamboo frame; the card title is at the bottom in a red bar with a turtle design on the left. The backs also have a white border and contain the series name and card number. The title is repeated in a purple box, which also contains the text and pictures of the four heroes at the bottom. There are 12 gallery cards which contain paintings of the turtles by various notable comics artists. The gallery cards have drawings inside a red pinstripe frame and the backs contain text and art credits inside a bamboo frame. The stickers are puzzle backed and uncaptioned and most contain a picture printed over a bamboo lattice work and red background. They are not captioned, so no list is provided, but the last five are the four turtles and April, all in their Japanese movie costumes. ***Please note*** *that while there is only one puzzle picture, there are two different puzzle layouts, one where sticker #7 contains the puzzle preview and the other where sticker #1 contains the preview! If you don't sort them out, you will end up with 11 stickers that don't complete the puzzle. There's no way to tell them apart without completing the puzzle. In addition, the one box we broke down had a lot more low number cards than high number cards.*

Set: 88 cards, 11 stickers 9.00

Story cards
1 The Sacred Scroll of Death 10
2 Michaelangelo! 10
3 Raphael! .10
4 Leonardo! 10
5 Donatello! 10
6 Radical Reporter April O'Neil 10
7 Teacher of the Turtles 10
8 Warlord From the Past 10
9 A Ruthless Englishman 10
10 The Rebel Leader 10
11 A Traitor to the Cause 10
12 Brought Before the Warlord! 10
13 A Disgrace to the Daimyo 10
14 Let's Make a Deal 10
15 Turtle Time! 10
16 Whoops! 10
17 Why Do We Bother? 10
18 Gifts for the Guys 10
19 An Antique Japanese Egg Timer? .10
20 A Weird Light... 10
21 Where Did April Go? 10
22 Is April a Witch? 10
23 The Old Time Switch Trick 10
24 Walker is Suspicious 10
25 Casey Jones, Baby Sitter 10
26 Behind Bars! 10
27 Let's Hit It, Dudes! 10
28 The Mysterious Scepter 10
29 Those are No Priests 10
30 In the Midst of Battle 10
31 Bad Horsey! 10
32 What Happened to Mikey? 10
33 Attacked by the Rebels! 10
34 The Art of Ninja 10
35 The Scepter is Missing! 10
36 Into the Castle 10
37 A Dirty Rescue 10
38 Don't Let Them Roast Me! 10
39 Ambushed! 10
40 The Turtle Meets the Rebels 10
41 Kappa! .10
42 What are Those Turtles, Anyway? .10
43 Village on Fire! 10
44 Find the Scepter! 10
45 Peekaboo! 10
46 Face to Face with Walker 10
47 Yoshi is Trapped! 10
48 Can Yoshi be Saved? 10
49 This is the Life 10
50 No Luck! 10
51 Donatello's Plan 10
52 Samurai Hockey Players 10
53 Mikey Makes a Snack 10
54 A Lesson From Raphael 10
55 Take Me to New York 10
56 The Substitute Scepter 10
57 A Yo-Yo for Yoshi 10
58 The Scepter is Back 10
59 Give Me the Scepter 10
60 An Audience with the Daimyo 10
61 Death to the Daimyo! 10
62 Walker and Whit, Partners! 10
63 The Demons Can be Hurt! 10
64 Clashing Swords! 10
65 The Daimyo Defeated! 10
66 He's Got April! 10
67 The Turtles are Ready! 10
68 Shoot Them! 10
69 I'll Shoot Them Myself! 10
70 Ding Dong–Cannonball Calling! . .10
71 Walker Tries to Escape 10
72 Time to Go, Guys! 10
73 No Time For Arguments! 10
74 Yo, Dudes! 10
75 Home, Sweet Home 10
76 New York! We Love It! 20

Gallery
77 Leonardo on Horseback (BHa) . . .20
78 Leonardo in Mist (Scott Hampton) 20
79 Raphael and Mountain (BSz) 20
80 Mikey with Nunchucks (JMu) 20
81 Raphael and Shrine (Mark Nelson) .20
82 Turtles and Girl (BSf) 20
83 Leonardo and Samurai (KG) 20
84 Kicking Donatello (DvD) 20
85 Raphael at Night (DIB) 20
86 Mikey vs. The Daimyo (with April) (Larson & Fastner) 20
87 Donatello with Arrows (John Van Fleet) 20
88 Donatello on Bridge (Andrew Pratt) 20

Stickers *(Two different puzzle layouts)*
1 thru 11, each 25

TEENAGE MUTANT NINJA TURTLES TOY CARDS

Playmates (1994)

In the spring of 1994 Playmates started putting cards in the blisterpacks for their TMNT toys. The exact number in this set is still to be determined, but many of their regular figures like April O'Neil and Shredder are now carded along with the "Shogun" versions of the four turtles.

TEENAGENTS

Topps (1993)

These cards came poly-bagged with TeenAgents *comics. Cards 1 and 2 were also bagged in issue #4.*

TMNT Toy cards © Mirage Studios, USA

Teenagents © Jack Kirby

0 Aurik (AH)(from Secret City Saga #4) 50

from Teenagents #1
1 Seera (RHo/JSt) 50
2 Monitor (WS) 50
3 Kaza (Kaz) 50

from Teenagents #2
4 Duit (Neil Yokes) 50
5 Kordala (Lea Hernandez) 50
6 Ornk of the Blood Legion (MZ) 50

from Teenagents #3
7 The Kreech (Neil Yokes) 50
8 Lord Ghast (Neil Yokes & Bob Wiacek) 50
9 Phtheris (Neil Yokes) 50

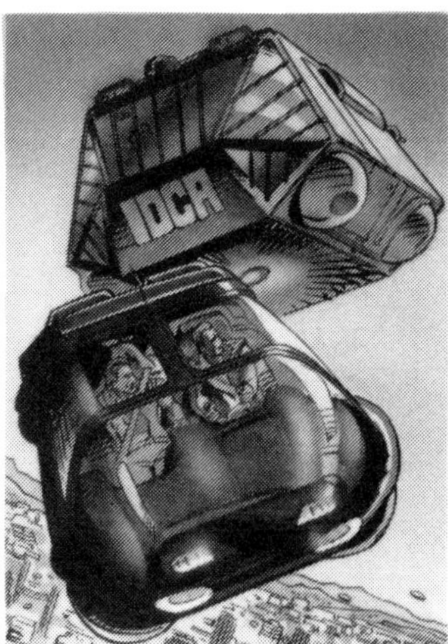

Tek World © Willian Shatner/Tek World

TEK WORLD

Cardz (1993)

(Lee Sullivan art, Ron Goulart words)

Tek World was created by ***William Shatner*** *of Star Trek fame. It has grown from a series of books into a series of comics and made-for-TV movies. The cards feature the same characters in a new story, scripted by Ron Goulart (who helped out on the novels and comics as well), with art by Lee Sullivan. Tek World is in a bleak future where cities are war zones, humans battle cyborgs and virtual reality is the drug of choice. The story stars Jake Cardigan, who works for the Cosmos Detective Agency battling an underground network of dealers in the addictive computer chips. The cards feature full bleed comic book close-up art on the front. The backs have the series logo and picture on the left with a close-up from the front overprinted with text on the right. The first 15 captions are from the cards, while the rest are from the checklist and are not on the cards, although they do describe the action. All the cards are numbered on the back. TekChrome card T1 is the same art as card #1, but with different text. The other three TekChrome cards are unique. The prototype cards are the same as cards 16 to 18, but are clearly marked as prototypes on the back.*

Set: 100 cards 15.00

TekChrome cards (LS) (1:12?)
T1 Jake Cardigan 10.00
T2 Sid Gomez 10.00
T3 Dr. Gunsmith 10.00
T4 Beth Kittridge & Jake Cardigan . 10.00
Prototypes, 3 diff. (LS), each 1.00
Four card promo sheet
(Comicfest '93) 2.50
Pack: 8 cards 1.50

CARD CHECKLIST

Character cards
1 Jake Cardigan 20
2 Sid Gomez 20
3 Beth Kittridge 20
4 Walt Bascom 20
5 Byran McMillion 20
6 Dr. Gunsmith 20
7 Hurricane Hannah 20
8 Kurt Winterguild 20
TEKnical jargon cards
9 TEK 15
10 Skycars 15
11 Weapons 15
12 The Freezer 15
13 Greater Los Angeles 15
14 Moonbase I 15
15 Miami Slum 15
Story cards
16 Forced to land 15
17 Gomez holds Jake back 15
18 Walt Bascom's tower office 15
19 Skycar crash 15
20 The vidphone message 15
21 The thugs 15
22 Android McMillion 15
23 An angry Janet 15
24 Heading for the lab 15
25 Message from Bascom 15
26 The Lab 15
27 A fallen Guardbot 15
28 The empty cabinet 15
29 A deadly blast 15
30 McMillion's missing ashes 15
31 Beth takes aim 15
32 Heading for Miami Slum 15
33 Skyvan attack 15
34 Dogfight 15
35 Disabler beam 15
36 Miami Beach Safezone 15
37 Entering Miami Slum Zone 15
38 JIJI's Beach Boutique 15
39 The Explosion 15
40 Jake comforts JIJI 15
41 Gomez at Hospital 15
42 JiJi hurriedly packs 15
43 JiJi gets into Skycar 15
44 The informant 15
45 Lets find Hannah! 15
46 Janet gets a call 15
47 Heading for Tampa Enclave 15
48 At the Ritz 15
49 Gomez arrives at Hannah's 15
50 Fanny spots Gomez 15
51 A surprise at Fanny's 15
52 Jake blasts thugs 15
53 Fanny offers info 15
54 SportsBots, Ltd. 15
55 Distracting the guard 15
56 Searching the warehouse 15
57 The crate 15
58 The body in the crate 15
59 He's alive 15
60 Attacked by androids 15
61 Backoff 15
62 Androids out cold 15
63 On the trail again 15
64 No sign of the andy 15
65 Exploding Skycar 15
66 Morning at Fishsan Sammy's 15
67 Renting a Skycar 15
68 Saying Goodbye to Fanny 15
69 Hannah's Hideaway 15
70 IDCA Raid 15
71 Surrender or else 15
72 A stunned Hannah 15
73 Jake confronts Winterguild 15
74 A mysterious crate 15
75 Shuttle lot 15
76 Heading for the moon 15
77 Docking at Moonbase I 15
78 Moonbase Inn 15
79 Visiting Newsboy Nevins 15
80 Sneaking into the Casino 15
81 Casino Control Center 15
82 McMillion 15
83 Office 20C 15
84 Enter Dr. Gunsmith 15
85 Jake and Gunsmith 15
86 Jake and the Android 15
87 Losing the Stungun 15
88 A stunned Gunsmith 15
89 A door bursts open 15
90 Enter Winterguild 15
91 IDCA escorts 15
92 Leaving Moonbase 15
93 A little bit of McMillion 15
94 Back at Bascom's 15
95 Jake and Beth 15
96 Checklist/Comic cover 15
97 Checklist/Comic cover 15
98 Checklist/Comic cover 15
99 Marvel Comic Series 15
100 William Shatner photo 25

THRILLING FICTION MYSTERIES

Karl Art (1993)

This promo card has full bleed art on a foil surface and was given away at a New York comics show as well as at the 1994 trade shows. It came with other promos from the same company.

Comic promo (John Ridgway) 2.00

TICK TEST SET

NEC Press (1992)

Ben Edlund art

The color cards have a blue border and text in blue on the back. They are not numbered; the letters below are from the checklist card. The rest of the cards are all numbered and have a white border and a white back with black text. Card 11 incorrectly duplicates the back of card 6 in the set we have.

Tick Test Set © Ben Edlund

Set: 32 cards + 4 full color (4,000 numbered sets made) . 12.00

Four color cards
A The Tick/Checklist 1.00
B The Mighty Agrippa 1.00
C Thrakkorzog 1.00
D Right's Might! 1.00
Two color cards
1 The Tick 10
2 Piano Pianissimo! 10
3 Oedipus 10
4 Arthur 10
5 Moon Marathon! 10
6 Microbe Adventure! 10
7 Spoon! 10
8 Paul the Samurai 10
9 Ninjas 10
10 Clown Colossus! 10
11 Sharpe Conflict! (back on some or all says #6 Microbe Adventure!) 10
12 Prophecy of Peril! 10
13 The Red Scare 10
14 The Man-Eating Cow 10
15 Miniscule Menace! 10
16 Sagin 10
Three color cards
17 Spellbound! 10
18 Clark Oppenheimer 10
19 Itch In Istanbul! 10
20 Incredible Invention! 10
21 Undisguised! 10
22 Sinister Spillage! 10
23 In Borneo Reborn! 10
24 Chainsaw Vigilante 10
25 Stonehenged! 10
26 Chairface Chippendale 10
27 Voodoo Vixen! 10
28 Touchdown Tick! 10
29 Running Guy 10
30 Dire Darkness! 10
31 Food's Fear! 10
32 Angus MacGuire 10

Tiny Toon Adventures © Warner Bros., Inc.

TINY TOON ADVENTURES

Topps (1991)

Tiny Toons are younger, cuter versions of the adult Looney Tunes species. The first 18 cards have character pictures and the rest have action scenes inside a blue border. The backs are red and yellow, with some text and the card number. Cards 19 to 77 tell a story. Buy the set to see how it came out! The stickers have an attractive design and poster backs. However, there are two different puzzle layouts, so unless you check, you may get 11 stickers which do not complete the puzzle.

Set: 77 cards, 11 stickers 7.50

Pack: 5 cards, 1 sticker 35

Wrappers, 4 different

CARD CHECKLIST

1 Tiny Toons Logo Card 10
2 Buster Bunny 10
3 Babs Bunny 10
4 Plucky Duck 10
5 Hamton 10
6 Dizzy Devil 10
7 Montana Max 10
8 Fifi 10
9 Elmyra 10
10 Sweetie .10
11 Furr Ball 10
12 Gogo Dodo 10
13 Calamity Coyote 10
14 Little Beeper 10
15 Shirley the Loon 10
16 Sneezer 10
17 Concord Condor 10
18 Bookworm 10
19 School's Out! 10
20 Wackyland or Bust! 10
21 Surf's Up! 10
22 A Multi-Flavored Romance! 10
23 Hit the Ice! 10
24 Duck A-Muck! 10
25 Dancin' in the Rain! 10
26 TV or not TV! 10
27 Hamton Meets his Match! 10
28 A "Tiny Toon Adventures" Classic! 10
29 "Citizen Max" 10
30 The Last Word: "Acme!" 10
31 News on the March! 10
32 Montana Max–Expelled!! 10
33 Empire of Montana Max 10
34 "We Need An Angle.." 10
35 Investigating Montana Max 10
36 "I Remember Montana Max..." . . .10
37 A Pair of Poor Pals 10
38 A Surprise 10
39 Unstoppable Montana Max 10
40 Food For Thought 10
41 "Acme? Never Heard of It!" 10
42 A Looney Education 10
43 The Plucky Interview 10
44 Plucky Duck For Hire! 10
45 Buster Wows 'Em! 10
46 Campaign Con Job! 10
47 Plucky Streak! 10
48 Moneybags Montana Max! 10
49 Media Blitz! 10
50 No Escape From Montana Max! . .10
51 The Great Debate 10
52 Lunch Scheme! 10
53 A Dizzy Delight! 10
54 Master Mudslinger! 10
55 Tracking the Race 10
56 Ahead in the Polls! 10
57 Buster Bunny...Framed! 10
58 Buster's Fall From Grace 10
59 "Now It's Personal!" 10
60 Elmyra's Story 10
61 Plucky to the Rescue! 10
62 Exposing the Creep! 10
63 Freezing the Frame-up! 10
64 Montana's Big Day 10
65 Babs in Disguise 10
66 Something's Fishy! 10
67 A Blast From Babs Bunny 10
68 Triumph...Or Travesty? 10
69 The Truth Hurts! 10
70 The Hero is a Heel! 10
71 Tomato Salesman Plucky! 10
72 Monty is Clobbered! 10
73 The Acme Mystery Solved! 10
74 What Montana Max Really Lost... .10
75 "Not Acme...Acne!!" 10
76 "Now He Tells Me!" 10
77 With Apologies to Orson 10

Tiny Toons Adventures
© Warner Bros., Inc.

Stickers, Puzzle Back

1 Tiny Toons Adventure Picture 15
2 Buster Bunny 15
3 Babs Bunny 15
4 Plucky Duck 15
5 Hamton .15
6 Dizzy Devil 15
7 Montana Max 15
8 Fifi 15
9 Elmyra .15
10 Sweetie 15
11 Calamity Coyote, Little Beeper . . .15

TINY TOON ADVENTURES

Cardz (1994)

This set is from the cartoon series and features full bleed art with excellent reproduction of the original cels. The backs have an additional picture inside a TV set screen together with the caption and card number. The activity cards have a yellow back with dotted lines which encourage the owner to (Gasp! Horrors!) cut out the character picture. The character cards are titled as listed, but the adventure cards are only titled with the name of the episode, so the card title below is from the checklist.

Set: 60 cards 7.50

TekChrome cards

T1 Tiny Toon Tidbits 7.00
T2 Tiny Toon Tidbits 7.00
T3 Tiny Toon Tidbits 7.00

Promo Cards

P1 Plucky Duck 1.00
P2 Babs Bunny 1.00
P3 Dizzy Devil 1.00
Pack: 8 cards 90

Tiny Toon Adventures © Warner Bros, Inc.

CARD CHECKLIST

Character Cards

1 Buster Bunny 10
2 Babs Bunny 10
3 Sweetie .10
4 Montana Max 10
5 Shirley The Loon 10
6 Fifi 10
7 Dizzy Devil 10
8 Furrball .10
9 Elmyra .10
10 Hamton 10
11 Plucky Duck 10
12 Bookworm 10
13 Gogo Dodo 10
14 Little Beeper 10
15 Calamity Coyote 10
16 Concord Condor 10
17 Sneezer 10

Adventure Cards

Animaniacs

18 Animation Class 10
19 Animation Emergency 10
20 Cel Painting 10
21 Dizzy Draws 10
22 Pen and Ink 10
23 Plucky Panics 10

Hollywood Plucky

24 The Winner 10
25 Hollywood Bound 10
26 Plucky in Cement 10
27 Hamton the Valet 10
28 Plucky in Disguise 10
29 The Plucky Ducky Story 10

Fields of Honey

30 Babs Wonders 10
31 Where is Honey? 10
32 The Search 10
33 TV Blitz 10
34 Honey is Funny 10
35 Honey and Bosco 10

Wheel 'O Comedy

36 Wheel 'O Comedy 10
37 Elmyra's Puppy 10
38 Dizzy Dizzy 10
39 Furrball in 3-D 10
40 Cheating Monty 10
41 Kerpluie 10

Her Wacky Highness

42 Cartoon Snooze 10
43 Caught in the Act 10
44 Wackyland Commercial 10
45 Looking for Babs 10
46 Queen of Wackyland 10
47 Escape 10
48 Checklist 10
49 Checklist 10
50 Checklist 10

Cut-Out & Stand-up Activity Cards

51 Babs Bunny 10
52 Buster Bunny 10
53 Dizzy Devil 10
54 Elmyra 10
55 Fifi 10
56 Furrball 10
57 Gogo Dodo 10
58 Hamton 10
59 Montana Max 10
60 Plucky Duck 10

TOM & JERRY

Cardz (1994, Animation)

All these cards have full bleed animation art on the fronts. The first 20 cards follow the plot of the movie. They have a purple back with a picture of Tom, Jerry and Robyn plus some text, the title and card number, and a movie logo. The next 20 cards are taken from their classic cartoons and have a green and red back. The ten historical highlights cards have an orange and green back and the game cards have yellow backs with games or trivia questions.

Set: 60 cards 8.00

Tekchromes

T1 Tom 7.50
T2 Jerry 7.50
T3 Hanna and Barbera 7.50

Promos

P1 The Fab Four promo 3.00
P2 Quiet Please promo 3.00
P3 1944 promo 3.00

Two different wrappers, one picturing Tom and the other picturing Jerry.

Pack: 8 cards 1.00

CARD CHECKLIST

Tom and Jerry–The Movie

1 Knock, Knock... It's a Wrecking Ball 10
2 The Fab Four 10

Tom & Jerry © Turner Entertainment Co.

3 A Robyn In Flight .... .10
4 Pictures in Robyn's Heart .... .10
5 A Figg That's Rotten To The Core .10
6 Robyn's (Reluctant) Return ..... .10
7 Fat Ferdy's Food Fight .... .10
8 Punished For Making A Mess .... .10
9 Stampede! .... .10

Tom & Jerry © Turner Entertainment Co.

10 Tom & Jerry... Just Hanging Around .... .10
11 Three Friends Floating Along ... .10
12 Have You Seen This Child? .... .10
13 Daddy Starling To The Rescue! . .10
14 Sailing With Captain Kiddie .... .10
15 It's Robyn's Locket .... .10
16 A Race To Robyn .... .10
17 Keep Your Eyes On The Highway .10
18 Robyn's Nest .... .10
19 Fire! .... .10
20 Two Friends In Home Sweet Home .... .10

Tom & Jerry Classics

21 Mouse In Manhattan .... .10
22 Cueball Cat .... .10
23 Kitty Foiled .... .10
24 Mouse Trouble .... .10
25 The Cat Concerto .... .10
26 Johann Mouse .... .10
27 The Two Mouseketeers .... .10
28 Quiet Please .... .10
29 Saturday Evening Puss .... .10
30 In The Hollywood Bowl .... .10
31 The Great Mousini .... .10
32 Smitten Kitten .... .10
33 Little Orphan .... .10
34 A Mouse In The House .... .10
35 Life With Tom .... .10
36 Hatch Up Your Troubles .... .10
37 Mouse Into Space .... .10
38 Fit To Be Tied .... .10
39 Snow Brawl .... .10
40 The Milky Waif .... .10

Tom & Jerry Historical Highlights

41 1940-1942 .... .10
42 1943-1944 .... .10
43 1945-1946 .... .10
44 1947-1948 .... .10
45 1949-1950 .... .10
46 1951-1952 .... .10
47 1953 .... .10
48 1954-1955 .... .10
49 1956-1963 .... .10
50 1964-1993 .... .10

Cat and Mouse Games

51 The Purrfect Find I .... .10
52 A Movie Mix-Up .... .10
53 'Toon Titles .... .10
54 Cat Got Your Tongue? I .... .10
55 The Purrfect Find II .... .10
56 A Twisted Tail .... .10
57 Cat Got Your Tongue? II ...... .10
58 The Amazing Mousetrap ...... .10
59 Checklist 1 .... .10
60 Checklist 2 .... .10

TOXIC CRUSADERS

Topps 1991

Melvin Junko (mop boy and hopeless nerd) fell into a barrel of toxic waste and became Toxie, the Toxic Crusader. Now he and his band of deformed stalwarts must save the earth from the evil plans of Dr. Killemoff and his heinous henchmen. "It's Cleanup Time!" These cards have neon yellow and orange backgrounds with more of the same on the back with the text and number. The card stock is better than standard Topps cardboard, but not as good as they used later. You can't miss 'em (or the pack either). There was also a toy line of the same characters. Each pack has a hologram, so it's a lot easier to assemble a set of them than it is to list them. They have blank white backs and no titles, but they are numbered in the holographic image.

Toxic Crusaders © Troma, Inc.

Set, 88 cards, 8 holograms 12.50
Pack, 8 cards, 1 hologram sticker .. .75

CARD CHECKLIST

1 Logo card .... .10
2 Toxie .... .10
3 Nozone .... .10
4 Major Disaster .... .10
5 Headbanger .... .10
6 Junkyard .... .10
7 Dr. Killemoff .... .10
8 Psycho .... .10
9 Bonehead .... .10
10 Radiation Rangers .... .10
11 Killemoff's Scheme .... .10
12 Destination: Tromaville .... .10
13 Junko the Nerd .... .10
14 A Present for Melvin .... .10
15 The Horrible Accident .... .10
16 Goodbye, Melvin Junko .... .10
17 Hello, Toxie! .... .10
18 Advice From Toxie's Mom ..... .10
19 Toxie's Little Buddy .... .10
20 Crusader on the Job .... .10
21 An Unscheduled Flight .... .10
22 Acid Rain on Bonehead's Parade .10
23 Toxie Gets Tough! .... .10
24 That Strange Sensation .... .10
25 Clobbering a Creep .... .10
26 Ranger Attack! .... .10
27 No Chance Against Toxie ...... .10
28 Hurray For You Know Who! .... .10
29 An American Hero .... .10
30 Bonehead's Revenge .... .10
31 Cycling Sicko .... .10
32 That Run-Down Feeling .... .10
33 One Good Turn... .... .10
34 Confronting Killemoff .... .10
35 Meet the Bug-Man .... .10
36 Toxie's Crusade .... .10
37 The New Recruits .... .10
38 Disaster's Awesome Power .... .10
39 Branching Out! .... .10
40 Polluto Strikes! .... .10
41 Sneeze Power! .... .10
42 K'O'ed by Kitty Litter! .... .10
43 Toxie Triumphant! .... .10
44 Yvonne's Latest Ditty .... .10
45 Job-Hungry Heroes .... .10
46 Greedy Mayor Grody .... .10
47 Demented Genius .... .10
48 Dim-Witted Messenger .... .10
49 Trapped in the Atom Smasher! .. .10
50 Fender-Bender! .... .10
51 Toxie the Ice Cream Man? ..... .10
52 Bender's Foul Brew .... .10
53 The Contaminators .... .10
54 This Spud's For You! .... .10
55 Nozone the Magician .... .10
56 Killemoff Takes Over! .... .10
57 Captured Crusader .... .10
58 Nozone in a Jam .... .10
59 Emergency Plan 'B' .... .10
60 Grand Gobbler .... .10
61 "Thanks a lot, Mop!" .... .10
62 Headbanger Goes Straight ..... .10
63 Aerial Assualt! .... .10
64 Battlefield: New Jersey .... .10
65 The Big Sneeze .... .10
66 Nozone Blows 'Em Away ...... .10
67 Killemoff's Cruel Plot .... .10
68 Psychic Psycho .... .10
69 Hot-Headed Headbanger ...... .10
70 Binin' Bonehead .... .10
71 The Crusaders Heed the Call! .. .10
72 Psycho Blasts Off! .... .10
73 Getting a Lift From Toxie ...... .10
74 A Strange Reward .... .10
75 Ride the Toxic Surf .... .10
76 Bonehead at the Controls ...... .10
77 A Stranger Swims Ashore ..... .10
78 Short-Circuiting Bonehead! ..... .10
79 Lending a Helping Paw .... .10
80 The Hobo and the Hound ...... .10
81 Birth of a Hero .... .10
82 Mutated Mutt .... .10
83 Junkyard Joins the Fray! ...... .10
84 Polutto Strikes Again .... .10
85 A Taste of Bad Medicine ...... .10
86 Turning the Toxic Tide .... .10
87 Junkyard's Oath .... .10
88 Canine Crusaders .... .10

Holograms

1 (Toxie with mop, sideways) ..... .25
2 (Nozone?) .... .25
3 (Killemoff) .... .25
4 (?) .... .25
5 (?) .... .25
6 .... .25
7 (Headbanger) .... .25
8 (Toxie with mop, upright) .... .25

Hulk and Spider-Man © Marvel Entertainment Group, Inc.

TRADING CARD TREATS

National Safe Kids Campaign

Impel (1991)

These cards were designed to be Halloween treats (instead of candy). They came in clear cello packs of 3 cards, with two different packs making up the 6 card set. The packs came in bags of 24, by set. The Marvel superheroes are by far the most important, as they are very similar to the Marvel Universe cards produced by Impel the same year. They have portrait art of the character inside a blue border on the front, along with the title and a small box which says "National Safe Kids Campaign." The backs contain text about the character, plus a small inset photo (Except for Spider-Man, who has a Traffic Safety message on the back). You could find the leftover bags in a few stores before Halloween 1992. The other five sets are also worth collecting. The Universal monsters have a red border, but the art work is undistinguished. The Archie cards have a yellow border, and look a lot like the Archie cards issued one year later by SkyBox (Impel's new name). The Widget, Inspector Gadget, and Nintendo cards have excellent art work, with green, orange, and black borders respectively. However, many of these bags were available again in 1993, at one-half off, so the cards have not appreciated.

Set: All 36 cards 6.00

Inspector Gadget © DIK Animation City, Inc.

Mummy © Universal City Studios, Inc.

Marvel Super Heroes, set of 6 . . . . 4.00
Captain America 75
Ghost Rider (JLe/SW) 1.00
Hulk 75
She-Hulk (JSt inks) 75
Spider-Man (JR2) 75
Wolverine 75
Archie, set of 6 50
Free-Wheelin' Archie 10
Archie and his Pals 10
Jughead's Bliss 10
Three on a Soda 10
Rah Rah Ronnie! 10
Archie and Betty make beautiful Music Together 10
Universal Monsters, set of 6 50
All Six monsters 10
The Mummy 10
The Creature 10
Dracula 10
Bride of Frankenstein 10
The Wolfman 10
Widget, set of 6 50
Mega-Slank 10
Ratchet 10
Interstellar Cop 10
Half Pint 10
Mega-Brain 10
Widget 10
Inspector Gadget, set of 6 50
Inspector Gadget 10
Gadget on Skis 10
Gadget & Pilot 10
Gadget & Bull 10
Gadget & Car 10
Gadget, Dog & Girl 10
Nintendo, set of 6 50
Link with Shield & Sword 10
Link attacked by monsters 10
Mario on castle steps 10
Mario rescues Princess 10
Raccoon Mario Flies 10
Raccoon Mario & Koopas boat 10

Widget © Zodiac Entertainment, Inc.

Trencher © Blackball

TRENCHER

Arena Magazine (1993)

Full bleed front on white background; white back with black text.

Promo card (KG) 1.00

See also: Blackball

TRIBE: THE INTRO

Press Pass (1993)

Todd Johnson writer, Larry Stroman art

These cards are designed to be put in an album to form comic book pages and have no captions. The backs form 9 pages of 3 x 3 card super-panels, with scenes inked by Larry Stroman and other noted comic book artists. We have listed a breakdown of this below. The 90 cards have an exclusive story line which is a prequel to the story in the Tribe *comic books. The five prism cards have full bleed Larry Stroman art on the front and a brick background on the backs along with number, name and text. The thermofoil cards have purple backs with white lettering. The Tribe comic cover #1 card has no art; it's all black with raised gold lettering. It's the best looking card in the set, as well as the most valuable. The back is white with black text. The four promo cards have the Tribe logo with a small white number just to the left, and no border. Otherwise, they look like cards from the set (until you read the word balloons).*

Set: 90 cards 12.50

Prism cards (1:12) (LSn)
P1 Blindspot 7.00
P2 Rosalyn 7.00
P3 Hannibal Rosalyn and the Manji . 7.00
P4 Aloof 7.00
P5 Fly Girl 7.00
Thermofoil cards (1:36) (LSn)
T1 Ditto 11.00
T2 Lord Deus Deivirile 11.00
T3 Front 11.00
T4 Steel Pulse 11.00
T5 (Contest, you name him) 11.00
Tribe Comic #1 cover (5,000) 40.00
Promo Cards, 1-4, set forms

Tribe (promos) © Todd Johnson & Larry Stroman

panel (LSn) 5.00
P.P.1 Hannibal, Rosalyn, Lord Deus Deivirile promo card (Wizard) 1.00
Unnamed comic card (Arena #9) . . . 1.00
Hannibal comic card (Arena #10) . . . 1.00
Pack: 8 cards 1.00
Four different wrappers.

CARD CHECKLIST

Backs: superpanel (Mark Texiera)
1 thru 9, each 10
Backs: superpanel (Jae Lee)
10 thru 18, each 10
Backs: superpanel (Nelson)
19 thru 27, each 10
Backs: superpanel (Larry Stroman)
28 thru 36, each 10
Backs: superpanel (Jill Thompson)
37 thru 45, each 10
Backs: superpanel (Mark Allen)
46 thru 54, each 10
Backs: superpanel (Larry Stroman)
55 thru 63, each 10
Backs: superpanel (Dwayne Turner)
64 thru 72, each 10
Backs form comic book page.
73 thru 81, each 10
Backs: superpanel (Sam Keith)
82 thru 90, each 10

The Spirit © Will Eisner

Gen 13 © Wildstorm

TRITON MAGAZINE

Attic Books (1993)

Triton: Comics Cards & Collectibles *was the first magazine devoted to comics cards, rather than non-sport cards. Thus it listed cards that came bagged with comic books, promo cards given away at shows and every hologram, chromium card, spectra card, etc. that you collect. Issue one came bagged with three exclusive Daredevil cards and the other issues had neat cards as well. The Daredevil cards were also issued as "dealer" cards with a "tritonium" foil stamped border. Tritonium is a rare metal that has a slightly reddish copper color (unless it mutates into another color on later cards). Only 2,000 of each of the dealer cards were made, so they are pretty scarce.*

Daredevil © Marvel Entertainment Group, Inc.

Daredevil cards (Issue 1)
1 of 3 (JR) 1.00
1 Tritonium Dealer card 8.00
2 of 3 (JR2/AW) 1.00
2 Tritonium card (Capital show) 8.00
3 of 3 (SMc/Hector Collazo) 1.00
3 Tritonium card (Diamond show) . . 8.00
Issue #2 cards
5 Gen 13 promo card (JLe) 1.00
5 The Spirit (WE) 1.00
Yes, we admit that one of them should have been number 4–what can we say?
Issue #3 cards
None in this series of cards
Issue #4 cards
6 Hellshock (JaL) 1.00
Issue #5 cards
Issue #5 came with one of 36 different Valiant Era II cards. See the listing for that card set for a checklist

TUROK

Valiant (1993)

Turok #1 chromium cover repro (BS/Randy Elliot) 20.00

Turok © Voyager Communications, Inc. Ultraman © Tsuburaya Productions Co., Ltd.

U

ULTRAMAN

Ultracomics (1993)

The cards have a black border with white spots plus a frame line with the series title at the top. The back is grey (with spots) and has printing in black and red. They came with Ultraman comic books, and there may be more of them.

1 Ultraman 1.00
2 Gerukadon 1.00
3 Majaba 1.00
4 . . . . 1.00
5 Bogun 1.00
6 Kilazee 1.00
7 . . . . 1.00
8 Rebirth (#2 of 3) (KSy) 1.00

ULTRAVERSE

Break-Thru comic checklist promo (Advance Comics) 1.00

ULTRAVERSE: RUNE

SkyBox (1993, Comic)

These two cards have full bleed Barry Windsor-Smith art with "Rune" at the top and "Ultraverse" at the bottom. The backs are purple and promote the three page chapters of Rune which appeared in 11 different Ultraverse titles in October 1993.

0 Promo card (BWS) (*Hero*) 2.00
00 promo card (BWS) (*Hero*) 2.00

Rune & Ultraverse © Malibu Comics Entertainment, Inc.

ULTRAVERSE

SkyBox (1993)

Despite a bewildering array of bonus cards, this series proved highly popular. The cards depict various characters from Malibu's Ultraverse *inside a grey outer border and an inner border which varies with the type of character (Heroes=blue; Villains=orange-red; Origins=green; Titles=pink; and Culture=purple). The card title is on the front and also on the back, which contains the card number and text. The bonus rookie cards depict various characters inside a gold border. Backs are similar to the regular cards. The ultimate rookie cards are similar, except the card title is in gold foil. The two ultra rookie cards are on a foil stock with a reflective surface which seems to radiate out from behind the character.*

The various promo cards resemble the regular series cards, except 01 Prime which looks like an ultimate rookie card. The promos use pictures from the series, except for 00 Boneyard, which is unique because the promo was replaced by a Barry Windsor-Smith version of Boneyard in the regular card series. Promos C1 through C5 came poly-bagged with Ultraverse comic books. The regular P0 promo card has an Ultraverse "U" logo on the back. The Heroes World and Capital City versions were given away to comic store owners who attended the 1993 trade shows sponsered by these distributors. They are rather scarce as only 1,000 were made for the Heroes World show and only 2,000 for the Capital City show.

Set: 100 Cards 12.50

Bonus Ultraverse Ultra Cards (1:36)
U1 Prime (NBy) 12.00
U2 Hardcase (DGb) 12.00
Bonus Rookie Cards (7:36)
R1 Prime (Hector) 4.00
R2 Exiles (Hector) 3.00
R3 Hardcase (JJu) 4.00
R4 Warstrike (JJu) 3.00
R5 Slayer (JJu) 3.00
R6 Freex (Kipper) 3.50
R7 Prototype (JJu) 4.00
R8 Zip-Zap (JJu) 3.00
R9 Mantra (JJu) 3.50
Bonus Ultimate Rookie Cards (1:18)
S1 The Night Man (SR) 6.00
S2 Sludge (BWS) 7.00
S3 Bash Bros. (Simpson) 6.00
S4 Solution (Calleros) 6.00
Promos in Comic Books
C1 Prime promo card (NBy) gold foil stamped name (in Prime #2) 2.50
C2 Hardcase promo card, gold foil stamped name (in Hardcase #2) .. 2.50
C3 Strangers promo card, gold foil stamped name (in Strangers #2) .. 2.50
C4 Freex promo card (in Freex #1 comic) 2.50
C5 Mantra promo card (in Mantra #1 comic) 2.50
Promo cards
0 The Night Man (*Comic Book Collector #8*) 3.00
00 Boneyard promo (*Hero #1*) 4.00
01 Prime promo card, gold foil stamped name (*American Entertainment*) .. 3.00
02 Mantra promo card, gold foil stamped name (*American Entertainment*) .. 3.00
P0 Warstrike promo card (U logo) .. 1.50
P0 Warstrike (*Heroes World*) 4.00
P0 Warstrike (*Capital City*) 3.00
P1 Prototype promo card 2.00
Four Card promo sheet, blank back, 5-3/8" x 10½" 4.00
Six Card promo sheet (National Sports Collectors Con. 7,500 made) 5.00
Pack: 8 cards 1.10

CARD CHECKLIST

Ultrahuman Heroes
1 Anything (WS) .... .10
2 Archimage (TyD) .... .10
3 Atom Bob (RHo) .... .10
4 Bash Brothers (Don Simpson) ... .10
5 En Flame (HC) .... .10
6 Boom Boy (WS) .... .10
7 Catapault (HC) .... .10
8 Choice (JiC) .... .10
9 Deadeye (BHr) .... .10
10 Twilight (CR) .... .10
11 Dropkick (HNg) .... .10
12 ElectroCute (DaR) .... .10
13 Firearm (HC) .... .10
14 Requiem (JBi) .... .10
15 Grenade (RHo) .... .10
16 Hardcase (JiC) .... .10
17 Lady Killer (DaR) .... .10
18 Lava (JeM) .... .10
19 Mantra (TyD) .... .10
20 Mustang (Fred) .... .10
21 The Night Man (DaR) .... .10
22 Outrage (KJa) .... .10
23 Plug (WS) .... .10
24 Pressure (WS) .... .10
25 Prime (NBy) .... .10
26 Prototype (DvA) .... .10
27 Veil (DvA) .... .10
28 Ranger (DvA) .... .10
29 Teknight (RHo) .... .10
30 Quixote (MB) .... .10
31 Shadowmage (HNg) .... .10

Ultraverse © Malibu Comics Entertainment, Inc.

32 Slayer (DdW) .... .10
33 Sludge (AaL) .... .10
34 Solitaire (JJ) .... .10
35 Spectral (RHo) .... .10
36 Squad (JiC) .... .10
37 Sweet Face (WS) .... .10
38 Tech (HNg) .... .10
39 Tinsel (JeM) .... .10

Ultraverse © Malibu Comics Entertainment, Inc.

40 Trax (Fred) .... .10
41 Vurk (KJo) .... .10
42 Warstrike (HNg) .... .10
43 Wrath (DvA) .... .10
44 Yrial (KJo) .... .10
45 Zip-Zap (DaR) .... .10
Ultrahuman Villains
46 Aeon (CR) .... .10
47 Backstabber (HC) .... .10
48 Bloodbath (Fred) .... .10
49 Bloodshed (Chris Wozniak) .... .10
50 Boneyard (BWS) .... .10
51 Book (Chris Wozniak) .... .10
52 Bruut (Fred) .... .10
53 Cutback (HC) .... .10
54 Death Dance (Chris Wozniak) ... .10
55 Death Mask (DaR) .... .10
56 Death Wish (RHo) .... .10
57 Doc Virtual (MB) .... .10
58 Gate (Chris Wozniak) .... .10
59 Gaunt (KJo) .... .10
60 Headknocker (JiC) .... .10
61 Hijack (KJa) .... .10
62 Firefall (Fred) .... .10
63 J.D. Hunt (RHo) .... .10
64 Lord Pumpkin (KJo) .... .10
65 Mangle (DaR) .... .10

66 Meathook (Chris Wozniak) .10
67 NM-E (JiC) .10
68 Notch (TyD) .10
69 Glare (DvA) .10
70 Quattro (Chris Wozniak) .10
71 Mercy Killer (DaR) .10
72 Stoneheart (MB) .10

Origins

73 Prototype (SR) .10
74 Warstrike (TyD) .10
75 Prime (NBy) .10
76 Hardcase (JiC) .10
77 The Night Man (SR) .10
78 Solitaire (SR) .10
79 Firearm (HC) .10
80 Sludge (AaL) .10
81 Slayer (JeM) .10

Titles

82 Exiles (BHr) .10
83 Firearm (HC) .10
84 Freex (WS) .10
85 Mantra (AH) .10
86 Prime (JOy) .10
87 Solitaire (JJ) .10
88 Warstrike (JeM) .10
89 The Solution (HNg) .10
90 The Strangers (RHo) .10

Culture (Tim Eldred)

91 Choice Corp. .10
92 Aladdin .10
93 The Lodge .10
94 Entity .10
95 Aerwa .10
96 Darkur .10
97 Nuware .10
98 Ultratech .10
99 Mother Ship .10
100 Checklist .10

Ultraverse II: Origins © Malibu Comics Entertainment, Inc.

ULTRAVERSE II: ORIGINS

SkyBox (1994)

Only 3,975 numbered 10 box cases were produced, which makes these cards scarce. This number was chosen because Rune, the voracious vampire villain in this universe, is 3,975 years old. The card images are set in a rectangular inner frame which is angled slightly away from the vertical, although some of the characters reach outside this frame. There is a white border with grey speckles which contains the card title. The card backs have text in this same color, with a grey stripe and a small color picture. The Rune subset forms a nine card super-panel and has almost full bleed art by Barry Windsor-Smith. There are not nearly as many bonus cards as in set I, which is has helped maintain their value. All the bonus cards have full bleed art with the card name in foil along the left front edge. The backs are a light orange with series name, card number and name and text plus a comic book cover picture. The autographed cards are regular cards from the series which are signed (naturally) and have a pressure embossed seal.

Set: 90 cards 17.50

Box: 36 packs (39,750 made)

Painted Bonus Cards (1:10)

B1 The Operator (JuB) 9.00
B2 ElectroCute (JBo) 8.00
B3 Lady Killer (JBo) 8.00
B4 Choice (Lurene Haines) 8.00
B5 Pressure (DvD) 8.00
B6 Sweet Face (DvD) 8.00
B7 Tech (DvD) 8.00

Ultraverse Ultra (1:36)

UB1 Mantra (JBo) 15.00
UB2 Yrial (JuB) 17.50

Autographed Cards (1:1,300)
Comic Art Exchange-Cards (1:47,000)

Promo cards

Four card promo sheet, 8¼" x 10¾" (*Previews*, December 1993) 2.00
Four card promo sheet, 7½" x 10" 2.00
P0 Mantra promo card 1.00
P00 Sludge promo card (*NY Comic Book Show, 10,000 made*) 1.00
P1 Prime promo card (*Comic Book Collector #14*) 1.00
P2 Rune promo card (BWS)(*Wizard*) 1.00

Pack: 8 cards 1.25

CARD CHECKLIST

Origins

1 Anything (BHr) .15
2 Atom Bob (WS) .15
3 Boom Boy (JeM) .15
4 Choice (BB) .15
5 Dropkick (DaR) .15

Ultraverse II: Origins
© Malibu Comics Entertainment, Inc.

6 ElectroCute (KM) .15
7 Firearm (HC) .15
8 Grenade (RHo) .15
9 Hardcase (MZ) .15
10 Lady Killer (Keith Conroy) .15
11 Mantra (JeM) .15
12 The Night Man (GeH) .15
13 Outrage/Vurk (DaR) .15
14 Plug (BHr) .15
15 Pressure (KM) .15
16 Prime (NBy) .15
17 Prototype (WS) .15
18 Shadowmage (DaR) .15
19 Slayer (JeM) .15
20 Sludge (SR) .15
21 Solitaire (JJ) .15
22 Spectral (SR) .15
23 Sweet-Face (BHr) .15
24 Tech (DaR) .15
25 Teknight (RHo) .15
26 Veil (KM) .15
27 Warstrike (HNg) .15
28 Wrath (DvA) .15
29 Yrial (WS) .15
30 Zip-Zap (RHo) .15
31 Lord Pumpkin (WS) .15
32 Boneyard (WS) .15
33 Death Dance (WS) .15
34 Mangle (SR) .15
35 Scourge (JeM) .15
36 Blind Faith (Keith Conroy) .15
37 Darkwave (Rick Parker) .15
38 Dirt Devil (Low) .15
39 Mosley (MK) .15
40 DeathWish .15
41 Arena (Tim Elred) .15
42 Heater (Mike Wieringo) .15
43 Rhiannon (Kyle Hotz) .15
44 Bloodstorm (AaL) .15
45 Pierce (Calleros/Lanphear) .15
46 Kismet Deadly (BB) .15
47 Vestige (Glenn Brown) .15
48 Hellion (DvA/JmP) .15
49 The Radicals (DvA/JmP) .15
50 Ranger (Diver/Mason) .15
51 Meathook (RCa) .15
52 Foxfire (Woj) .15
53 Mastodon (Woj) .15
54 Rivermen (Craig Gilmour) .15

Aladdin Ultrahuman Assessments

55 Prime (NBy) .15
56 Mantra (TyD/Kesel) .15
57 The Solution (DaR) .15
58 The Strangers (RHo) .15
59 Sludge (AaL) .15
60 Warstrike (JeM) .15
61 Firearm (CHm) .15
62 Hardcase (ScB) .15
63 The Night Man (JQ) .15

Battles

64 The Squad versus NM-E (ScB) .15
65 Prototype versus Prime (JeM) .15
66 Hardcase versus Aladdin (ScB) .15
67 The Strangers versus Aladdin (RHo) .15
68 Prime versus Hardcase (Rob Haynes) .15
69 Warstrike versus Wrath (HNg) .15
70 The Night Man versus Freex (Mike Miller) .15
71 Mantra versus Boneyard (TyD) .15
72 Prime versus Darkwave (AaL) .15

Rune (BWS) forms 3x3 super-panel

73 Rune .25
74 Rune .25
75 Rune .25
76 Rune .25
77 Rune .25
78 Rune .25
79 Rune .25
80 Rune .25
81 Rune .25

Rookies

82 Rush (KM) .15
83 Masque (JeM) .15
84 Flood (AaL) .15
85 Pistol (AaL) .15
86 Ripfire (DaR) .15
87 Smoke (JeM) .15
88 Rubble (JeM) .15
89 Tyrannosaur (RHo) .15
90 Checklist .15

ULTRAVERSE DEBUT CARDS

Malibu Comics/SkyBox (1994)

In this comic promotion you collected from 3 to 12 Malibu comics and photo-copied the back covers (which were numbered) and sent the copies in to receive the debut cards. The cards come in Foil Enhanced and Un-Enhanced versions and which ones you got depended on how many of the cover copies you sent in. The cards aren't out yet so we don't have a checklist or prices.

Un-Enhanced Cards

1.
2.
3.
4. (BWS)

Gold Foil Enhanced Cards

1.
2.
3.
4. (BWS)

Ultraverse SkyBox Master Series © Malibu Comics Entertainment, Inc.

ULTRAVERSE MASTER SERIES

SkyBox (1994)

These are promos for the SkyBox Master Series: Ultraverse Edition card set which will have all Dave Dorman painted art and should be out in the fall of 1994, but wasn't available at press time. (We tried to get everyone to stop producing card sets so we could include everything in this book, but, fortunately, they told us what we could do with that idea.) The promos have foil stamped titles and look great! Different ones will be given away at forthcoming comic and distributor shows, so the list below is not complete.

P0 Tyrannosaur 1.00
P01 Book promo 1.00
P02 Heater promo 1.00
P03 Solitaire promo (DvD) 1.00

Unity © Voyager Communications, Inc.

UNITY
"TIME IS NOT ABSOLUTE"

Comic Images (1992)

These cards have full bleed comic book close-up art from the 18 part Unity storyline which cuts across the entire Valiant comics universe. The cards follow the chapters by reproducing a comic cover and one to five cards which summarize the story line. All the text is on the back along with the card number and title inside a blue border and dark blue frame. The chromium bonus cards of Valiant rookies are eagerly sought by collectors and always expensive. They make this one of the ten sets you ***must own*** *to be a legitimate comics cards collector. The promo card is the cover art for the Unity #1 comic book, while the actual cover is card #71.*

Set: 90 cards 18.00
Promo Card (BWS) 6.00
Chromium Cards, Valiant Rookies
Bloodshot (DP/Wiacek) 17.00
Hotshot (DL/BL) 16.00
Rai (Guichet/Bolinger) 16.00
Turok (BWS) 19.00
Rai and the Future Force (MLe/TRy) 14.00
Screen (DL) 14.00
Pack: 10 cards 1.75

CARD CHECKLIST

1 Unity #0 (BWS) 50
2 ...From the Black Hole 20
3 Discovering the Body 20
4 The Lost Land 20
5 Solar Lends a Hand 20
6 The Heroes Gather 20
7 The Mothergod 20
8 Eternal Warrior #1 20
9 Gilad Enters the Battle 20
10 Archer & Armstrong #1 20
11 The Heroes Scatter 20
12 Archer's Future 20
13 Armstrong Takes A Hit 20
14 The Speakeasy 20
15 Magnus Robot Fighter #15 20
16 Mothergod's Tower 20
17 X-O Manowar #7 20
18 Pterodactyl Peril 20
19 X-O Frees the Slaves 20
20 Shadowman #4 20
21 Shadowman's Arrival 20
22 Erica is Forewarned 20
23 Solar Attacks 20
24 Shadowman Burns 20
25 Solar is Contained! 20
26 Rai #6 .20
27 Japan Falls 20
28 Harbinger #8 20
29 The War Goes Badly 20
30 Sting is Enraged 20
31 Erica Reacts 20
32 Solar, Man of the Atom #12 20
33 Eternal Warrior #2 20
34 The Two Gilads 20
35 Too Late 20
36 Archer & Armstrong #2 20
37 ...For Every Mother's Child 20
38 Mothergod Awakes! 20
39 ...Now Come Turok! 20
40 A Hot Shot! 20
41 A Change of Heart 20
42 Magnus Robot Fighter #16 20
43 The Baby is Born 20
44 X-O Manowar #8 20
45 Close to Finish 20
46 The Peace Treaty 20
47 Erica's Treachery 20
48 Jaws of Death 20
49 The Good Skin Returns 20
50 X-O Fights Back 20
51 Shadowman #5 20
52 Regeneration 20
53 Thwar the Mission 20
54 The Truth Revealed 20
55 Serve the Demon...Pay the Price! .20
56 Rai #7 .20
57 Last of His Kind 20
58 The Plan is Finalized 20
59 Entering the Complex 20
60 The Last Stand 20
61 Mothergod Attacks! 20
62 First Fatality 20
63 A Hero Falls 20
64 Albert's Revenge 20
65 Harbinger #9 20
66 The Containment Center 20
67 The Wormhole 20
68 Solar's Remains 20
69 Escape! 20
70 The Beginning of the End 20
71 The Hand of Destiny 20
72 Solar, Man of the Atom #13 20
73 Albert Takes His Shot 20
74 Solar Returns 20
75 The Final Battle 20
76 Triumphant! 20
77 Unity #1 (BWS) 50
78 Judgment 20
79 Trapped For Eternity 20
80 Self-Destruct! 20
81 Looking For Elya 20
82 Magnus Fights On 20
83 Just Desserts 20
84 X-O the Conqueror 20
85 From Little Acorns... 20
86 Suddenly...a Black Hole 20
87 Solar Saves the Day 20
88 The Lost Land Destroyed 20
89 ...3975 A.D. 20
90 Checklist 20

V

VALIANT ERA, THE

Upper Deck/Pyramid (1993)

The pack describes this as a "trading card history of the Valiant Universe through 1992." These are full bleed cards with U-V coating front and back. The fronts are reproductions of the cover art (not the covers) of the listed Valiant comic book. The backs provide a plot synopsis, along with the title and a small picture from the comic. The Turok and X-O Manowar promo card has the same art as card #73. The ComicCon promo cards have a white back with black text. There are quite a few bonus insert cards. The Unseen art cards use normal card stock, with "Unseen Art" foil stamped in gold on the front. The backs have a night sky background with text in white. The First Appearances cards have a reflective foil surface and the backs have a daytime sky background with text printed over a starburst. The Joe Quesada card has a reflective foil surface, like the first appearances card.

Set: 120 cards 15.00
Upper Deck logo card, scarce . . . 20.00
SP1 The Art of Joe Quesada 35.00
First Appearances
FA1 Shadowman (BH) 9.00

The Valiant Era © Voyager Communications, Inc.

FA2 H.A.R.D. Corps (BWS/RL) . . . 10.00
FA3 Tohru Nakadai 42nd Rai (BL/TRy) . . . 9.00
FA4 Tekla (BL/TRy) . . . 9.00
FA5 Toyo Harada (BWS) . . . 10.00
FA6 Ivar, The Timewalker (BL) . . . 9.00
FA7 Turok . . . 10.00
FA8 Master Darque (BH) . . . 9.00
FA9 Bloodshot (DP/RL) . . . 9.00

Unseen Art

U1 (BL) . . . 7.00
U2 (Tom Artis & Ralph Reese) . . . 6.00
U3 (BWS) . . . 10.00
U4 (DL/BL) . . . 6.00
U5 (RgM) . . . 6.00
U6 (BWS) . . . 10.00
U7 (Turok vs. T-Rex, uncredited) . . . 7.00
U8 (ANi & ViC) . . . 6.00
U9 (RL/BL) . . . 6.00
Turok & X-O Manowar promo card (Advance Comics #53)(BS/RL) . . . 9.00

Promo cards for ComicCon 1993:

Same art as #1 (PCu/BL) . . . 1.50
Same art as #5 (ANi/BL) . . . 1.50
Same art as #6 . . . 1.50
Same art as #17 . . . 1.50
Same art as #31 . . . 1.50
Same black card as #33 . . . 1.50
Same art as #36 . . . 1.50
Same art as #39 . . . 1.50
Same art as #43 . . . 1.50
Same art as #44 . . . 1.50
Same art as #46 . . . 1.50
Same art as #48 . . . 1.50
Same art as #49 . . . 1.50
Same art as #50 . . . 1.50
Same art as #53 . . . 1.50
Same art as #63 . . . 1.50
Same art as #67 (WS) . . . 1.50
Same art as #73 (BS/RL) . . . 1.50
Same art as #81 . . . 1.50
Same art as #82 . . . 1.50
Same art as #87 . . . 1.50
Same art as #98 . . . 1.50
Same art as #99 . . . 1.50
Same art as #100 (BWS) . . . 2.00
Same art as #102 (BWS/RL) . . . 2.00
Same art as #106 . . . 1.50
Same art as #110 (BWS) . . . 2.00
Same art as #118 . . . 1.50
Same checklist as #119 . . . 1.50
Same checklist as #120 . . . 1.50
Pack: 8 cards . . . 1.50

CARD CHECKLIST

1 Magnus #0 10
2 Magnus #1 10
3 Magnus #2 10
4 Magnus #3 10
5 Magnus #4 10
6 Magnus #5 10
7 Magnus #6 10
8 Magnus #7 10
9 Magnus #8 10
10 Magnus #9 10
11 Magnus #10 10
12 Magnus #11 10
13 Magnus #12 10
14 Magnus #13 10
15 Magnus #14 10
16 Magnus #15 10
17 Magnus #16 10
18 Magnus #17 10
19 Magnus #18 10
20 Magnus #19 10
21 Magnus #20 10
22 Magnus #21 10
23 Magnus #22 10
24 Solar #1 10
25 Solar #2 10
26 Solar #3 (BWS) 20
27 Solar #4 10
28 Solar #5 (BWS) 20
29 Solar #6 10
30 Solar #7 (BWS) 20
31 Solar #8 10
32 Solar #9 (BWS) 10
33 Solar #10 (all black) 10
34 Solar #11 10
35 Solar #12 10
36 Solar #13 10
37 Solar #14 10
38 Solar #15 10
39 Solar #16 10
40 Solar #17 10
41 Solar #18 10
42 Solar #19 10
43 Harbinger TPB 10
44 Harbinger #0 10
45 Harbinger #1 10
46 Harbinger #2 10
47 Harbinger #3 10
48 Harbinger #4 10
49 Harbinger #5 10
50 Harbinger #6 10
51 Harbinger #7 10
52 Harbinger #8 10
53 Harbinger #9 10
54 Harbinger #10 10
55 Harbinger #11 10
56 Harbinger #12 10
57 Harbinger #13 10
58 Harbinger #14 10
59 Harbinger #15 10
60 X-O Manowar #1 10
61 X-O Manowar #2 10
62 X-O Manowar #3 10
63 X-O Manowar #4 10
64 X-O Manowar #5 (BWS) 20
65 X-O Manowar #6 10
66 X-O Manowar #7 10
67 X-O Manowar #8 10
68 X-O Manowar #9 10
69 X-O Manowar #10 10
70 X-O Manowar #11 10
71 X-O Manowar #12 10
72 X-O Manowar #13 10
73 X-O Manowar #14 10
74 Rai #0 10
75 Rai #1 10
76 Rai #2 10
77 Rai #3 10
78 Rai #4 10
79 Rai #5 10
80 Rai #6 10
81 Rai #7 10
82 Rai #8 10
83 Shadowman #1 10
84 Shadowman #2 10
85 Shadowman #3 10
86 Shadowman #4 10
87 Shadowman #5 10
88 Shadowman #6 10
89 Shadowman #7 10
90 Shadowman #8 10
91 Shadowman #9 10
92 Shadowman #10 10
93 Shadowman #11 10
94 Unity #0 (BWS) 20
95 Unity #1 (BWS) 20
96 Archer & Armstrong #0 (BWS) 20
97 Archer & Armstrong #1 10
98 Archer & Armstrong #2 10
99 Archer & Armstrong #3 10
100 Archer & Armstrong #4 (BWS) 20
101 Archer & Armstrong #5 (BWS) 20

The Valiant Era
© Voyager Communications, Inc.

102 Archer & Armstrong #6 (BWS) 20
103 Archer & Armstrong #7 (BWS) 20
104 Archer & Armstrong #8 (BWS) 20
105 Eternal Warrior #1 10
106 Eternal Warrior #2 10
107 Eternal Warrior #3 10
108 Eternal Warrior #4 10
109 Eternal Warrior #5 10
110 Eternal Warrior #6 (BWS) 20
111 Eternal Warrior #7 (BWS) 20
112 Eternal Warrior #8 10
113 H.A.R.D.Corps #1 10
114 H.A.R.D.Corps #2 10
115 H.A.R.D.Corps #3 10
116 H.A.R.D.Corps #4 10
117 Bloodshot #1 10
118 Bloodshot #2 10
119 Checklist 10
120 Checklist 10

The Valiant Era II © Voyager Communications, Inc.

VALIANT ERA II

Upper Deck (1994)

This set continues the history of the Valiant universe through 1993. The cards are similar to the first series and again feature the cover art (not the covers) from the listed Valiant comic books. The 3-D HoloView card has a small strip of non-holographic art at the top and the title and logos are stamped on the surface so a collector will be able to identify the card at a show a lot more easily than most holograms. There are a lot of other bonus insert cards which holds prices down, but makes it more expensive to collect them all. The Promotional Art bonus cards have a full bleed image, but the border portion of the image is in blue while the inner portion is full color. The First Appearance cards are just like the ones from series I and they are accordingly numbered FA10 to FA18. Each box contains one of eight oversized card reproductions, which makes this an interesting set to collect. If that isn't enough, 36 different promo cards were issued. These were bagged with issue #5 of Triton (one per copy) and were available from other sources as well. The backs say "THANK YOU Comic Card Collector..." and have a large Pyramid logo on the right, partially cut off by the card edge.

Set: 140 cards 20.00

Box: 36 packs

HoloView 3-D (1:108)

LE1 X-O Manowar 30.00

First Appearances (1:10)

FA10 Ninjak 5.00
FA11 Dr. Eclipse 5.00
FA12 Dr. Mirage & Carmen 5.00
FA13 Solar the Destroyer 5.00
FA14 Stronghold & Livewire 5.00
FA15 New Harbingers 5.00
FA16 Armorines 5.00
FA17 Shadowman 1890 . . . . 5.00
FA18 Perp & Wipeout 5.00

The Valiant Era II
© Voyager Communications, Inc.

Promotional Art (1:10)

PA1 Ninjak & X-O (MMo) 4.00
PA2 Hard Corps (MLe/Autio) 4.00
PA3 Magnus & I-A 4.00
PA4 Shadowman 4.00
PA5 Rai & Future Force 4.00
PA6 X-O Manowar (BL) 4.00
PA7 The Musketeers (BWS) 5.00
PA8 The New Heroes (RyR) 4.00
PA9 Turok Dinosaur Hunter (RgM) . 4.00

Oversize Cards (1:Box)

OS1 Ninjak #1 (Card #248) 8.00
OS2 Dr. Mirage #1 (Card #244) 8.00
OS3 Rai #9 (Card #165) 8.00
OS4 Turok #1 Card #230) 8.00
OS5 X-O #0 (Card #249) 8.00
OS6 Bloodshot #0 (Card #250) 8.00
OS7 (Card #) 8.00
OS8 Armorines #0 (Card #251) 8.00

Promo cards

Promo card (Advance Comics #63) . 1.00
Large promo sheet (Previews January 1994) 1.00
"Thank You" promo cards (from Triton & other sources) 36 different
Same art as #165 . . . . 1.00
Same art as #166 . . . . 1.00
Same art as #167 . . . . 1.00
Same art as #168 . . . . 1.00
Same art as #169 . . . . 1.00
Same art as #170 . . . . 1.00
Same art as #171 . . . . 1.00
Same art as #172 . . . . 1.00
Same art as #173 . . . . 1.00
Same art as #174 . . . . 1.00
Same art as #175 . . . . 1.00
Same art as #176 . . . . 1.00
Same art as #177 . . . . 1.00
Same art as #178 . . . . 1.00
Same art as #179 . . . . 1.00
Same art as #180 . . . . 1.00
Same art as #181 . . . . 1.00
Same art as #182 . . . . 1.00
Same art as #183 . . . . 1.00
Same art as #184 . . . . 1.00
Same art as #185 . . . . 1.00
Same art as #197 . . . . 1.00
Same art as #198 . . . . 1.00
Same art as #199 . . . . 1.00
Same art as #200 . . . . 1.00
Same art as #201 . . . . 1.00
Same art as #202 . . . . 1.00
Same art as #203 . . . . 1.00
Same art as #204 . . . . 1.00
Same art as #205 . . . . 1.00
Same art as #206 . . . . 1.00
Same art as #207 . . . . 1.00
Same art as #240 . . . . 1.00
Same art as #241 . . . . 1.00
Same art as #242 . . . . 1.00
Same art as #243 . . . . 1.00
Pack: 8 cards 1.25

The Valiant Era II
© Voyager Communications, Inc.

CARD CHECKLIST

121 Magnus #23 15
122 Magnus #24 15
123 Magnus #25 15
124 Magnus #26 15
125 Magnus #27 15
126 Magnus #28 15
127 Magnus #29 15
128 Magnus #30 15

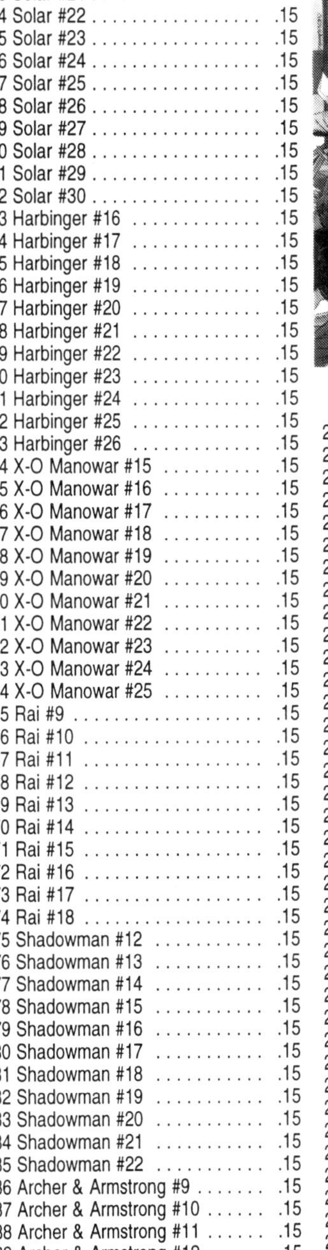

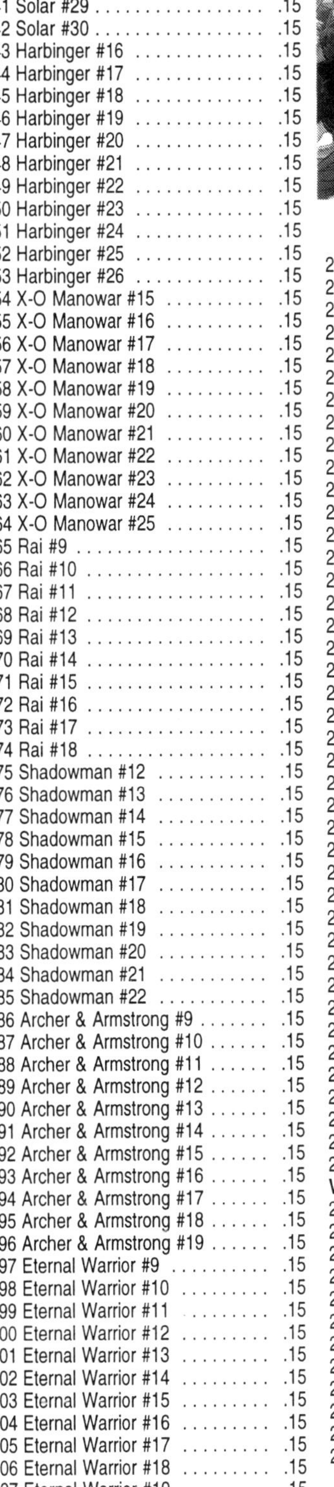

129 Magnus #31 15
130 Magnus #32 15
131 Magnus #33 15
132 Solar #20 15
133 Solar #21 15
134 Solar #22 15
135 Solar #23 15
136 Solar #24 15
137 Solar #25 15
138 Solar #26 15
139 Solar #27 15
140 Solar #28 15
141 Solar #29 15
142 Solar #30 15
143 Harbinger #16 15
144 Harbinger #17 15
145 Harbinger #18 15
146 Harbinger #19 15
147 Harbinger #20 15
148 Harbinger #21 15
149 Harbinger #22 15
150 Harbinger #23 15
151 Harbinger #24 15
152 Harbinger #25 15
153 Harbinger #26 15
154 X-O Manowar #15 15
155 X-O Manowar #16 15
156 X-O Manowar #17 15
157 X-O Manowar #18 15
158 X-O Manowar #19 15
159 X-O Manowar #20 15
160 X-O Manowar #21 15
161 X-O Manowar #22 15
162 X-O Manowar #23 15
163 X-O Manowar #24 15
164 X-O Manowar #25 15
165 Rai #9 15
166 Rai #10 15
167 Rai #11 15
168 Rai #12 15
169 Rai #13 15
170 Rai #14 15
171 Rai #15 15
172 Rai #16 15
173 Rai #17 15
174 Rai #18 15
175 Shadowman #12 15
176 Shadowman #13 15
177 Shadowman #14 15
178 Shadowman #15 15
179 Shadowman #16 15
180 Shadowman #17 15
181 Shadowman #18 15
182 Shadowman #19 15
183 Shadowman #20 15
184 Shadowman #21 15
185 Shadowman #22 15
186 Archer & Armstrong #9 15
187 Archer & Armstrong #10 15
188 Archer & Armstrong #11 15
189 Archer & Armstrong #12 15
190 Archer & Armstrong #13 15
191 Archer & Armstrong #14 15
192 Archer & Armstrong #15 15
193 Archer & Armstrong #16 15
194 Archer & Armstrong #17 15
195 Archer & Armstrong #18 15
196 Archer & Armstrong #19 15
197 Eternal Warrior #9 15
198 Eternal Warrior #10 15
199 Eternal Warrior #11 15
200 Eternal Warrior #12 15
201 Eternal Warrior #13 15
202 Eternal Warrior #14 15
203 Eternal Warrior #15 15
204 Eternal Warrior #16 15
205 Eternal Warrior #17 15
206 Eternal Warrior #18 15
207 Eternal Warrior #19 15

The Valiant Era II
© Voyager Communications, Inc.

208 Hard Corps #5 15
209 Hard Corps #6 15
210 Hard Corps #7 15
211 Hard Corps #8 15
212 Hard Corps #9 15
213 Hard Corps #10 15
214 Hard Corps #11 15
215 Hard Corps #12 15
216 Hard Corps #13 15
217 Hard Corps #14 15
218 Hard Corps #14 15
219 Bloodshot #3 15
220 Bloodshot #4 15
221 Bloodshot #5 15
222 Bloodshot #6 15
223 Bloodshot #7 15
224 Bloodshot #8 15
225 Bloodshot #9 15
226 Bloodshot #10 15
227 Bloodshot #11 15
228 Bloodshot #12 15
229 Bloodshot #13 15
230 Turok #1 15
231 Turok #2 15
232 Turok #3 15
233 Turok #4 15
234 Turok #5 15
235 Turok #6 15
236 Turok #7 15
237 Turok #8 15
238 Secret Weapons #1 15
239 Secret Weapons #2 15
240 Secret Weapons #3 15
241 Secret Weapons #4 15
242 Secret Weapons #5 15
243 Secret Weapons #6 15
244 Doctor Mirage #1 15
245 Doctor Mirage #2 15
246 Doctor Mirage #3 15
247 Doctor Mirage #4 15
248 Ninjak #1 15

Valiant Specials

249 X-O #0 15
250 Bloodshot #0 15
251 Armorines #0 15
252 X-O Trade 15
253 Rai Trade 15
254 X-O Database 15
255 Rai Companion 15
256 Eternal Warrior Yearbook 15
257 Valiant Reader 15
258 Valiant Vision 15
259 Checklist 15
260 Checklist 15

Valiant Era Comic Cards © Voyager Communications, Inc.

VALIANT ERA COMIC CARDS

Upper Deck/Valiant (1994)

These cards came in protective plastic sleeves stapled into the Valiant comics listed below. The idea was to assemble all 14 cards and then mail them in to receive the six chromium cards. You didn't get the cards back, so you had to buy two copies of each comic to get both card sets. Otherwise the cards resemble the regular cards from Series I and II with cover art from Valiant comics. These cards pick up the covers where Valiant Era II leaves off, so they can be viewed as a continuation of that series.

VP1 Magnus Robot Fighter #34 (from Secret Weapons #9) 1.00
VP2 Rai & The Future Force #19 (from X-O Manowar #28) 1.00
VP3 Archer & Armstrong #20 (from Turok, Dinosaur Hunter #11) 1.00
VP4 Shadowman #23 (from Ninjak #4) 1.00
VP5 Eternal Warrior #20 (from Bloodshot #16) 1.00
VP6 H.A.R.D. Corps #16 (from Harbinger #29) 1.00
VP7 Harbinger #27 (from H.A.R.D. Corps #18) 1.00
VP8 Ninjak #2 (from Shadowman #25) 1.00
VP9 Secret Weapons #7 (from Magnus Robot Fighter #36) . 1.00
VP10 Dr. Mirage #5 (in Solar, Man of the Atom #33) . . 1.00
VP11 Turok, Dinosaur Hunter #9 (from Archer & Armstrong #22) . . . 1.00
VP12 X-O Manowar #26 (from Rai & The Future Force #21) 1.00
VP13 Bloodshot #14 (from Eternal Warrior #22) 1.00
VP14 Solar, Man of the Atom #31 (from Dr. Mirage #7) 1.00

Chromium Cover Cards (Mail-in)
Bloodshot #1 . . . . NYD
Turok #1 . . . . NYD
X-O Manowar #0 . . . . NYD
Ninjak #1 . . . . NYD
Bloodshot #0 . . . . NYD
Shadowman #0 . . . . NYD

THE VALIANT FILES: SECRETS FROM THE HARBINGER FOUNDATION

Upper Deck (1994)

Promo cards for a set which was not available at press time.

Large promo card (Previews) 1.00
Promo card (Advance comics) 1.00

VALIANT CHECKLISTS

Three of these cards have very similar looking art, with a prominent eclipsed sun, but the pictures are different. The Wizard version has the card art and logos sideways, while the other two has them upright. The Advance version says "Advance Comics" and has the logo at the bottom. The third and fourth versions were given away at the Diamond Distribution 1994 trade show and have the logo at the top. The fourth version doesn't have an eclipsed sun in the art. Got all that? There will be a quiz tomorrow. All the backs are the same black, white and grey comics checklist.

The Chaos Effect (Wizard) 1.00
The Chaos Effect (Advance) 1.00
The Chaos Effect (Diamond) 1.00
The Chaos Effect (Diamond) 1.00

Valiant Files & Valiant Checklist © Voyager Communications, Inc.

W

WETWORKS

Card #0 has a red stripe on both top and bottom while the others have stripes on the left side and bottom. The backs are different too, but they are part of one series. #0 is from Hero *magazine and #1-#9 are from* Cards Illustrated *#2, where you had to buy three copies of the magazine (and check the bag) to get all nine cards. We did that, but didn't find card #10, which is on the checklist.*

#0 Commander Dane (Hero Mag) . . 1.00
#1 Dane 50
#2 Mother .50
#3 Claymore 50
#4 Jester. .50
#5 Dozer 50
#6 Command Unit 50
#7 Unit One 50
#8 Unit Two 50
#9 Whilce Portacio/Checklist 50
10 Team Card (not seen) 50

WildC.A.T.S. © Aegis Entertainment, Inc.

(Jim Lee's) WILDC.A.T.S

Covert-Action-Teams

Topps (1993)

This set appeared in the summer of 1993. The card fronts are full bleed pictures with a foil "W" in an oval logo on the left side. The card backs (other than #1 and #100) are in full color and are numbered, with text and a detail picture from the card front. The first 60 cards are all by Jim Lee and are uncaptioned. We have used the first few words of text for a title. The remaining 40 cards are captioned and many are by guest artists, as noted below. There is an error on the card backs as there are two cards numbered 66, with identical backs, and none numbered 68. The error card, i.e. the one that should have been #68, has a picture of Grifter on the front which does not match the back's Warblade caption and detail picture. The prism cards are on polygon reflective stock. The back repeats the front character picture in a black center stripe and contains the card number and title. The 1993 #0 promo card came bagged with WildC.A.T.S. #4 *comic and pictures Grifter and Zealot. The back contains credits in white on a black center stripe, similar to cards #1 and #100, and the prism cards. There is also a scarce red (backed?) version of the same card bagged with a lucky few of those comics. The 1992 promo card has a different back, which does not match any of the cards in the series. The promo sheet contains the same card front and states, incorrectly, that the set will appear in November 1992. It also has a picture of several Image artists posing with Topps executives. Maybe if they had skipped the picture, they would have gotten the set out on time. It's still nice.*

Set: 100 cards, (no card #68, 2 diff. card #66) 12.50

Prism cards (1:18)
1 Lord Emp 10.00
2 Grifter 10.00
3 Pike 10.00
4 Spartan 10.00
5 Warblade 10.00
6 Zealot 10.00
Promo sheet ("Coming Nov. 92") (JLe) 5.00
Promo card (1992) (JLe) 3.50
0 promo card (1993) (JLe) (from WildC.A.T.S. #4 comic) 2.50
0 Red promo card from same comic 30.00
Pack: 8 cards 1.00

CARD CHECKLIST
1 Title/Logo card 10
Untitled cards (Jim Lee)
2 "Without a home..." 10
3 "She is called Void..." 10
4 "With Void's help..." 10
5 "Void tells Marlowe..." 10
6 "In Void's recurring dream..." 10
7 "Void is lost in..." 10
8 "Certain that the battle..." 10
9 "Combat leader Spartan's..." 10
10 "Helspont, leader" 10
11 "With a mole..." 10
12 "Helspont turns to..." 10
13 "The Gnome calls..." 10
14 "A deal is struck..." 10
15 "Her name is Voodoo..." 10
16 "One of Voodoo's powers..." 10
17 "The Cabal thugs..." 10
18 "The Coda assassin..." 10
19 "Spotting the Grifter..." 10
20 "Grifter springs into action." 10
21 "Grifter moves to protect..." 10
22 "The battle in the strip..." 10
23 "Grifter's magnum saves..." 10
24 "Voodoo and Grifter..." 10
25 "Suddenly, Void..." 10
26 "With the arrival..." 10
27 "Reassured at last..." 10
28 "Turning his back..." 10
29 "She's Sister Zealot." 10
30 "With Sister Zealot's help..." 10
31 "Void saves the WildC.A.T.S..." . . .10
32 "Safely aboard..." 10
33 "A paranormal working..." 10
34 "Helspont, leader of the..." 10
35 "Sister Zealot and Grifter..." 10
36 "Black Razor, an I/O..." 10
37 "Lynch, Director of I/O..." 10
38 "Jacob Marlowe leads..." 10
39 "Spartan, Maul, and Voodoo..." . . .10
40 "The Gnome observes..." 10
41 "Inside the Cabal's..." 10
42 "Spartan and Voodoo..." 10
43 "The Youngblood press..." 10
44 "The technician McCoy..." 10
45 "When the main force..." 10
46 "Unnoticed in a..." 10
47 "Maul grows and grows." 10
48 "With the fury of the battle..." 10
49 "In the control center..." 10
50 "Zealot moves to block Pike..." . . .10
51 "Determined to win..." 10
52 "Victorious over the WildC.A.T.S..." .10
53 "With the Stargate open..." 10
54 "Having exorcised B'Lial..." 10
55 "Voodoo's assault..." 10
56 "After Spartan's interference..." . . .10
57 "The Gnome uses..." 10
58 "As the Grifter..." 10
59 "While the very walls..." 10
60 "With the Daemonite..." 10
Titled cards (Guest artists)
61 WildC.A.T.S. 10
62 Emp (CHm) 10
63 Void (BSf/SW) 10
64 Spartan (Sal Regla/JLe) 10
65 Maul (SK) 10
66 Warblade (ScC/JLe) 10
66 a) "Warblade" (actually Grifter) . . .10
67 Voodoo (JaL) 10
69 Zealot (MS) 10
70 Coda (MS) 10
71 Emp & Maul (JLe) 10
72 Zealot (BB) 10
73 Cabal (JJ/SW) 10
74 Providence (JoP) 10
75 John Lynch (MPa/Cl) 10
76 Warblade (Nick Manabat/KN) 10
77 Spartan (Vic Bridges) 10
78 Pike (JPn) 10
79 Emp (Vic Bridges) 10
80 Slag (Vic Bridges) 10
81 Spartan (JQ/SW) 10
82 The Grifter (BBh/JSc) 10
83 Voodoo (AH) 10
84 Spartan (Vic Bridges) 10
85 M'Koi (SK) 10
86 Zealot (JLe) 10
87 Maul (DK) 10
88 Spartan (Nick Manabat/KN) 10
89 Zealot (JaL) 10
90 Gifted Ones (DAb/JLe) 10
91 Voodoo (ScC/JLe) 10
92 The Gnome (MPa/Clv) 10
93 Black Razor (MPa/Alex Garner) . .10
94 Maul (JSc/JLe) 10
95 Voodoo (KN) 10
96 Attica (Vic Bridges) 10
97 Cabal (Nick Manabat/SW) 10
98 Warblade (SK) 10
99 Helspont (DK) 10
100 Credits card 10

WILDSTAR
Image (1993)

These are comic book promo cards, from two different sources.

Promo card (Arena #8)(AG/JOy) . . . 1.00
Full bleed front, with white line frame. Grey back with black text.

Promo (Zipper #1) (JOy) 1.50
Black background, red line frame. Picture on back, with black marbled border.

Wildstar © Al Gordon & Jerry Ordway; Wildstorm © Wildstorm Productions

WILDSTORM SET ONE
Wildstorm Productions (1994)

These are promo cards for a 100 card all chromium set which was not available at press time.

WildC.A.T.S. promo (JLe) 3.00
WildC.A.T.S. promo sheet (Previews) 3.00

(Wizard Cards) Santa The Barbarian © Rob Liefeld; Holly Daye © Jim Lee

WIZARD/IMAGE CARDS
Wizard Press (1992)

Wizard *began bagging special cards along with issue #11.* Wizard *has a large print run, and so practically everybody already has these cards. Indeed, many local stores have back issues of* Wizard, *with the cards, for sale for $1.00. The dealer cards were sent free to comic stores who ordered 25 copies of* Wizard. *They are sealed in a plastic holder with numbered foil seals. The numbers would indicate that about 10,000 of each dealer card were printed. Most stores and dealers have several of these cards for sale, so they are not hard to find, and still are worth collecting if the price is right.*

Series 1 (Prism cards)
1 Todd McFarlane's *Spawn* (from Wizard #11) 4.00
Dealer's gold card 20.00
2 Jim Valentino's *Shadow Hawk* (from Wizard #12) 3.00
Dealer's gold card 15.00
3 Erik Larsen's *The Savage Dragon* (from Wizard #13) 3.00
Dealer's gold card 15.00

Spawn © Todd McFarlane

4 Image Jam (Pt.1) (EL, RLd, MS & JLe) (Wizard Spec.) 3.00
Dealer's gold card 12.50
5 Image Jam (Pt.2) (TM, WPo JV) (Wizard Spec.) 2.50
Dealer's gold card 12.50
6 Marc Silvestri's *Cyber Force* (from Wizard #14) 2.00
Dealer's gold card 10.00
7 Jim Lee's *WildC.A.T.S* (from Wizard #15) 2.50
Dealer's gold card 12.50
Red foil card in WildC.A.T.S #4 . 10.00
8 Whilce Portacio's *Wetworks* (from Wizard #16) 2.50
Dealer's gold card 10.00
9 Rob Liefeld's *Santa the Barbarian* (from Wizard #17) 2.00
Dealer's gold card 10.00
9(b) Jim Lee's *Holly Daye* (from Wizard #17) 2.00
Dealer's gold card 15.00
(9c) Todd McFarlane's *Santa Todd* (from Wizard #17) 1.00
Dealer's gold card 12.50

Series 2, (Silver cards) Wizard Press (1993)

1 Dale Keown's *Pitt* (from Wizard #18) 2.00
Dealer's gold card 12.50
2 Sam Kieth's *The Maxx* (from Wizard #19) 2.00
Dealer's gold card 10.00
"Australia" variant card 8.00
3 Rob Liefeld's *Youngblood* (from Wizard #20) 2.00
Dealer's gold card 10.00
Away Team variant card 10.00
4 Jim Lee's *StormWatch* (from Wizard #21) 2.00
Dealer's gold card 10.00
5 Rob Liefeld's *Supreme* (from Wizard #22) 2.00
Dealer's gold card 10.00
6 Rob Liefeld's *Battlestone* (from Wizard #23) 2.00
Dealer's gold card 10.00
7 Mike Grell's *Shaman's Tears* (from Wizard #24) 2.00
Dealer's gold card 10.00
8 Jim Valentino's *Shadowhawk* (from Wizard #25) 2.00
Dealer's gold card 10.00
8a Unmasked variant card 2.50
9 Marc Silvestri's *Stryke Force* (from Wizard #26) 2.00
Dealer's gold card 10.00
10 Gordon & Ordway's *WildStar* (from Wizard #27) 2.00
Dealer's gold card 10.00
11 Rob Liefeld's *Brigade* (from Wizard #28) 2.00
Dealer's gold card 10.00

Special Cards (1993)

Will Eisner's *The Spirit* (from Wizard Top 100) 3.50
Dealer's gold card 13.00
Will Eisner Autographed card 75.00
Superman Tribute card (silver) 5.00
Superman Tribute card (Gold) 15.00
X-Men Turn Thirty (NKu) (from X-Men spec.) 2.00
Dealer's gold card 15.00
0 Rob Leifeld's *Youngblood* (gold) . 25.00
25th Anniv. Pog 1.00
25th Anniv. Pog (Gold) 10.00
Christmas Eve in Brooklyn chromium (JP) 1.50

Image cards, Series III (1994)

1 Violator, chromium (GCa) 1.00
Gen13 Dealer card (JLe) 12.50
2 Spawn, chromium (GCa) 1.00
3 WildC.A.T.s 1.00
4 CyberForce (MS) 1.00
5 Ripclaw (MS) 1.00
6 Union (JLe & Mike Heisler) 1.00

Wolff & Byrd © Batton Lash

WOLFF & BYRD

Topps (1993)

#0 Promo for new Topps comic series, (from Satan's Six #3) 1.00

WOLVERINE

Comic Images (1988)

The card fronts depict Wolverine and various other Marvel characters in dramatic, portrait style drawings, plus the card caption. The backs have the name of the series, the card number and a Mutantrivia question about Wolverine. This is the third set of Marvel cards from Comic Images. The first two were Marvel Universe and Colossal Conflicts. All the early card sets from Comic Images are scarce and highly collectible.

Wolverine © Marvel Entertainment Group, Inc.

Set: 50 cards + header 25.00
Pack: 4 cards + header, cello pack . 1.75

CARD CHECKLIST

1 Challenge 50
2 Masks .50
3 Confrontation 50
4 What the.... 50
5 Juggernaut 50
6 Savage Land 50
7 Trio 50
8 Attraction 50
9 Sewer Rat 50
10 Tag 50
11 Back Off 50
12 Come On 50
13 Co-Leaders 50
14 Solitude 50
15 Eye to Eye 50
16 Stalker 50
17 Re-Match 50
18 Lemme at 'Em 50
19 Whoosh 50
20 Deadly Intent 50
21 Primal Scream 50
22 Howdy .50
23 Classic Wolvie 50
24 Ready .50
25 At Odds 50
26 Surprise 50
27 Battleground 50
28 Eat Adamantium 50
29 Outta My Face 50
30 Weapon X 50
31 Slash .50
32 Dropping In 50
33 New Beginning 50
34 Reborn 50
35 Dead End 50
36 Tables Are Turned 50
37 Dream .50
38 Nightmare 50
39 Binge .50
40 Kitty 'n Me 50
41 Greetings 50
42 Blizzard 50
43 Snikt! .50
44 Saved .50
45 Pain In The Neck 50
46 Eternal Foe 50
47 Reluctant Duo 50
48 I'm Home 50
49 Teammates 50
50 Checklist 50

WOLVERINE: FROM THEN 'TIL NOW

Comic Images (1991)

The card fronts depict Wolverine and various other Marvel characters in dramatic, portrait style drawings, plus the card caption and number. The backs form a 5 x 9 black and white drawing of Wolverine by Todd McFarlane.

Set: 45 cards 12.00
Pack: 1.25

CARD CHECKLIST

1 Wolverine 25
2 Wendingo (TM) 25
3 Spider-Man (TM) 25
4 Bloodlust 25
5 Attacked 25
6 Come On 25
7 Android 25
8 The Blues 25
9 Pull Me Up 25
10 Blood .25
11 4 of Us 25
12 Brood .25
13 New Warriors 25
14 Patch .25
15 The Team 25
16 Hulk 25
17 Come ON 25
18 Ghost Rider 25
19 Cable .25
20 Logan .25
21 Meltdown 25
22 Gotcha 25
23 A-A-A-H! 25
24 The Beast 25
25 Webbed 25
26 Metamorphosis 25
27 Crucified 25
28 Buried 25
29 Deathstrike 25
30 Surrounded 25

Wolverine: From Then 'Til Now © Marvel Entertainment Group, Inc.

31 Mad as... .25
32 Werewolf (MS) .25
33 In the Dark .25
34 Trio .25
35 X-Men .25
36 Jubilee .25
37 Hodge .25
38 X-tinction .25
39 Archangel .25
40 Help Me! .25
41 Weapon X .25
42 Sedated .25
43 Rage! .25
44 Massacre .25
45 Checklist .25

Wolverine: From Then Till Now II © Marvel Entertainment Group, Inc.

WOLVERINE: FROM THEN TILL NOW II

Comic Images (1992)

The card fronts are full bleed pictures, most of which are close-ups of portions of comic book pages. The backs contain the card number and caption and text covering the career of Wolverine plus a black and white drawing.

Set: 90 cards 10.00

Prizm Promo card (JLe) 5.00

Prism Cards

P1 Archetypal 12.00
P2 Away 12.00
P3 Attitude (BWS) 12.00
P4 Healing 12.00
P5 Languages 12.00
P6 Memories 12.00

Pack: 10 cards 1.25

CARD CHECKLIST

1 Wolverine .10
2 Change .10
3 Mutation .10
4 Fox-Like .10
5 Aging .10
6 S.H.I.E.L.D. .10
7 Logan .10
8 Project X .10
9 Professor .10
10 Dr. A.B. Cornelius .10
11 Wild Beast .10
12 Helmet .10
13 I Like Him .10
14 Shiva .10
15 Triggers .10
16 Mutant Powers .10
17 Ferocious .10
18 Adamantium .10
19 Claws .10
20 Hunting .10
21 Berserk .10
22 Discipline .10
23 Wild Beast .10
24 Animalistic .10
25 Department H .10
26 First Mission .10
27 First Defeat .10
28 Weapon Alpha .10
29 In Search Of .10
30 New X-Men .10
31 Krakoa .10
32 Teammates .10
33 Just Kidding .10
34 Resentment .10
35 Magneto .10
36 Costume .10
37 Phoenix .10
38 Mariko .10
39 Alpha Flight .10
40 Hellfire Club .10
41 Slice and Dice .10
42 Old Ties .10
43 Disgrace .10
44 New Threads .10
45 The Brood .10
46 Shadowcat .10
47 Fastball Special .10
48 Vindicator .10
49 Mutant Massacre .10
50 Grey Hulk .10
51 Resurrection .10
52 Patch .10
53 Genosha .10
54 Donald Pierce .10
55 Reavers .10
56 Jubilation Lee .10
57 1941 .10
58 The X-Men .10
59 Psylocke .10
60 Gambit .10
61 Popularity .10
62 Cable .10
63 Scorpio .10
64 Appeal (DC) .10
65 Lady Deathstrike .10
66 Cylla .10
67 Punisher .10
68 Buried Alive .10
69 Deadly Imitator .10
70 Elsie Dee .10
71 Matsuo .10
72 Flashback .10
73 Maverick .10
74 Resurrected .10
75 Omega Red .10
76 Carbonadium .10
77 Honor .10
78 Sabretooth .10
79 Silver Fox .10
80 Reiko .10
81 Heavy Metal .10
82 Escape .10
83 Barbaric .10
84 Rip and Tear .10
85 Ghost Rider .10
86 Cyber .10
87 Venom .10
88 The End? .10
89 The Future? .10
90 Checklist .10

World Cup 'Toons © Warner Bros.

WORLD CUP 'TOONS

Upper Deck/Pyramid (1994)

This set was issued to commemorate the 1994 World Cup Soccer Tournament, held in the United States for the first time, and just underway as this book was completed. The set features your favorite Looney Tunes characters playing soccer (or football, as everyone but the U.S. calls it). The cards are marked with the series name and card title on two edges on the front, along with the World Cup official logo. These form a frame for the cartoon picture. Like most Americans, we don't actually know enough about the sport to be sure that 'toons don't play on most of the foreign teams, but we suspect that the accounts of the qualifying games are invented, although the scores given appear to be real. If you like this type of card, check out the four series of Comic Ball cards described earlier in this book.

Set: 120 cards 15.00

World Cup Final Qualifiers (1:2)
24 diff., each 1.00

WCT1 promo 1.00
Pack: 8 cards 1.25

CARD CHECKLIST

Qualifying Tournament

1 United States .10
2 Dominican Republic .10
3 Trinidad & Tobago .10
4 Australia .10
5 Australia .10
6 Australia .10
7 Mexico .10
8 Mexico .10
9 Mexico .10
10 Canada .10
11 Canada .10
12 Caribbean .10
13 Caribbean .10
14 Mexico .10
15 Australia .10
16 Australia .10
17 Argentina .10
18 Argentina .10
19 Argentina .10
20 Argentina vs. Columbia .10
21 Argentina vs. Columbia .10
22 Argentina vs. Columbia .10
23 Argentina vs. Columbia .10
24 Argentina vs. Columbia .10
25 Brazil .10
26 Brazil .10
27 Brazil .10
28 Brazil .10
29 Brazil .10
30 Brazil .10
31 Brazil .10
32 Africa .10
33 Africa .10
34 Africa .10
35 Africa .10
36 Africa .10
37 Italy .10
38 Italy .10
39 Switzerland .10
40 Switzerland .10
41 Switzerland .10
42 England .10
43 England .10
44 Holland .10
45 Holland .10
46 Holland .10
47 Norway .10
48 Norway .10
49 Spain .10
50 Spain .10
51 Spain .10
52 Spain .10
53 Russia .10
54 Russia .10
55 Greece .10
56 Greece .10
57 Greece .10
58 France .10
59 France .10
60 France .10
61 France .10
62 France .10
63 France .10
64 France .10
65 Greece .10
66 Russia .10
67 Spain .10
68 Spain .10
69 Africa .10
70 United States .10
71 United States .10
72 United States .10
73 Checklist .10

Greatest Players

74 Cruyff .10
75 Pele .10
76 Gullit .10
77 Zico .10
78 Charlton .10
79 Maradona .10
80 Beckenbaur .10
81 Jairzinho .10
82 Muller .10
83 Eusebio .10
84 Moore .10
85 Zoff .10
86 Platini .10

World Cup Moments

87 1930 .10
88 1934 .10
89 1938 .10
90 1950 .10
91 1954 .10
92 1958 .10
93 1962 .10
94 1966 .10
95 1970 .10
96 1974 .10
97 1978 .10
98 1982 .10
99 1986 .10
100 1990 .10
101 1994 .10

Road to the Cup puzzle cards

102 World Cup Map .10
103 World Cup Map .10
104 World Cup Map .10
105 World Cup Map .10
106 World Cup Map .10
107 World Cup Map .10
108 World Cup Map .10
109 World Cup Map .10
110 World Cup Map .10

Striker's Tips

111 Goalkeeper .10
112 Overhead Kick .10
113 Heading .10
114 Tackling .10
115 Dribbling .10
116 Passing .10
117 Control .10
118 Curving .10
119 Shooting .10
120 Practice .10

X

X-CUTIONER'S SONG

SkyBox (1992, from comics)

These are SkyBox cards, but they didn't come in packs. They only came bagged with the 12 Marvel "X" comics which formed the X-Cutioner's Song cross-over saga: Uncanny X-Men *#294-296;* X-Factor *#84-86;* X-Men *14-16 and* X-Force #16-18. *The character's picture is drawn in a big X shape frame with the name at the top and the series title at the bottom. The cards for the "Hunters" have*

X-Cutioner's Song © Marvel Entertainment Group, Inc.

a blue background with a bronze top stripe. The cards for "Prey" reverse the color pattern. All the cards have grey backs with "Stryfe's Strike File" in a red rectangle and text about the character in white letters in a black box. The cards are not numbered, and the order below is the order of appearance of the comic book.

(1) Xavier (AM/BPe) 1.00
(2) Caliban (BPe/AM) 1.00
(3) Apocalypse 1.00
(4) Cable (AM) 1.00
(5) Bishop & Wolverine (NKu) 1.50
(6) Polaris & Havoc (LSn) 1.25
(7) M.L.F. 1.00
(8) Mr. Sinister (LSn/AM) 1.00
(9) Jean Grey & Cyclops (NKu) 1.00
(10) Dark Riders (GCa) 1.00
(11) Archangel (BPe/AM) 1.25
(12) Stryfe (GCa) 1.25

X-Force © Marvel Entertainment Group, Inc.

X-FORCE

Impel (1991, from comics)
(Rob Liefeld)

One of these cards came bagged in each of the X-Force *#1 comics, so you had to buy 5 copies to get all the cards! The comics only cost $1.50 each, so the gimmick didn't turn out to be a bad investment. The cards were produced by Impel and somewhat resemble their X-Men cards. The fronts have a distinctive black border with "X-Force" in yellow and red.*

X-1 Cable 4.00
X-2 Shatter Star 2.00
X-3 Deadpool 2.00
X-4 Sunspot & Gideon 2.00
X-5 X-Force 3.00

X-FORCE

"The Beginning of the End"
Comic Images (1991)

The comic book close-up picture on the front of these cards is placed in a large "X" frame with the card title at the bottom. The

X-Force "The Beginning of the End" © Marvel Entertainment Group, Inc.

border is either green, blue or yellow. The backs have a white border and contain the card number and text inside a frame. The text follows the exploits of the X-Force in several episodes. An autographed series, in specially marked boxes, was released a few months after the regular series.

Set: 90 cards 24.00

Autographed card (1000 made) (RLd) 15.00

Pack: 10 cards 2.50

CARD CHECKLIST

1 New Mutants 25
2 The Vulture 25
3 The Plan 25
4 Escape 25
5 Nitro 25
6 Freedom Force 25
7 Rusty & Skids 25
8 Cable 25
9 The M.L.F. 25
10 Dark Valkyrie 25
11 Going Home 25
12 I'm Staying 25
13 All Aboard 25
14 Stryfe 25
15 Gunfire 25
16 Break-Out 25
17 Captured 25
18 Join Us! 25
19 X-Factor 25
20 Mystique 25
21 Fight! 25
22 Defense 25
23 New Leader 25
24 Sabretooth 25
25 Caliban 25
26 Rictor 25
27 To the Death 25
28 Snap! 25
29 Skrulls 25
30 Sunfire 25
31 Sleet 25
32 Poison 25
33 Uh, Oh 25
34 Wolverine 25
35 The Bold 25
36 Captured 25
37 Whoa! 25
38 Pals 25
39 Free 25
40 Dropping In 25
41 Get Out 25
42 A Hero Falls 25
43 Hodge 25
44 Let's Move 25
45 Stop! 25
46 Beast 25
47 Genosha 25
48 Jubilee 25
49 Archangel 25
50 Mutate 25
51 Gambit 25
52 What-to-do 25
53 Restored 25
54 Rahne 25
55 Changes 25
56 Gideon 25
57 Dad 25
58 Get Rahne 25
59 Assassin 25
60 Deadpool 25
61 Stopped 25
62 Domino 25
63 The End 25
64 Ferral 25
65 Tunnels 25
66 Proudstar 25
67 Deceit 25
68 Revenge 25
69 So? 25
70 Goodbye 25
71 Stranger 25
72 The New 25
73 Shatterstar 25
74 Found 25
75 Protectorate 25
76 Offense 25
77 Teamwork 25
78 Ferocious 25
79 Blood 25
80 Warrior 25
81 Masque 25
82 Decisions 25
83 Unmasked 25
84 X-Force 25
85 Pursuit 25
86 Wildside 25
87 Terrorist 25
88 Reaper 25
89 War 25
90 Checklist 25

X-Men © Marvel Entertainment Group, Inc.

X-MEN

Comic Images (1991)

These are full-bleed comic book close-up cards with title, number and text on the back. The back is on uncoated white stock with a black frame containing a big "X" at each corner and a large ⊗ as a watermark design. As you might expect, the text takes the extraordinary X-Men through several exclusive exploits plus some extra expeditions and extreme excursions while they encounter extraterrestrials bent on their extinction and expeditiously exterminate them. (Sorry, I couldn't help myself.)

Set: 90 cards 15.00

Pack: 10 cards 1.50

CARD CHECKLIST

1 The X-Men 15
2 The Reavers 15
3 The Mandarin 15
4 Betsy 15
5 Slaymaster 15
6 Lady Mandarin 15
7 Patch 15
8 Accommodation 15
9 The Beast 15
10 Games 15
11 My Turn 15
12 #1 Fan 15
13 Harriers 15
14 Magistrates 15
15 Lian 15
16 Storm 15
17 Gambit 15
18 Nanny 15
19 Orphanmaker 15
20 Partners 15
21 Together Again 15
22 Captain America 15
23 Friend 15
24 My Turf 15
25 Black Widow 15
26 To the Rescue 15
27 Conflict 15
28 Cyborgs 15
29 Ms. Marvel 15
30 Savage Land 15
31 Shadow King 15
32 Drained 15
33 Magneto 15
34 First Strike 15
35 Danger Room 15
36 Our Turn 15
37 Pathfinders 15
38 Strikeforce 15
39 Flight 15
40 Powerless 15
41 Warlock 15
42 Take 'Em Out 15
43 Psylocke 15
44 Cameron 15
45 Havok 15
46 Mutate #20 15
47 On Trial 15
48 Hodge 15
49 Cable 15
50 Match 15
51 Restored 15
52 Final Strike 15
53 What's Next? 15
54 Allies 15
55 Assault 15
56 Zaladane 15
57 Teleported 15
58 Deathbird 15
59 Starjammers 15
60 Imperial Fleet 15
61 Manacle 15
62 Fair Game 15
63 Lilandra 15
64 Conquered 15
65 Rejoined 15
66 Airborne 15
67 Revenge 15
68 Brainchild 15
69 Draining 15
70 Repowered 15
71 Mentor? 15
72 The Dungeons 15
73 My Wings! 15
74 Execution 15
75 We're Back 15
76 War Skrull 15
77 Aboard 15
78 In Space 15
79 Remember Us? 15
80 One-on-one 15
81 Professor X 15
82 Colossus 15
83 Testing 15
84 Old Times 15
85 Whoa! 15
86 Watch It 15
87 On the Move 15
88 Homosuperiors 15
89 Omega Red 15
90 Checklist 15

The Uncanny X-Men © Marvel Entertainment Group, Inc.

(The Uncanny) X-MEN
Impel (1992)
Jim Lee art

After the Marvel Universe I and II cards proved to be huge successes, Impel followed with another mega-hit in April 1992. These have all the quality of those previous sets and beautiful art by Jim Lee. The cards have portrait style pictures inside different colored borders which have a bunch of little ⊗'s and one big ⊗. The backs have either a light blue or light purple border, a cream colored section with card text, plus a close-up picture. The hologram bonus cards are similar to the previous sets as well. They have a full bleed image on the front, and the back has the same basic design as the regular cards, with a small color picture of the card's holographic image. The tin boxed set has one extra card, but it's just a "Power Ratings" card with no art. You do get all five holograms in a cylindrical box.

Set: 100 cards 17.50
Tin box set (7,500 made) 50.00

Holograms (JLe)
XH-1 Wolverine 10.00
XH-2 Cable 10.00
XH-3 Gambit 11.00
XH-4 Magneto 8.00
XH-5 X-Men 12.00
Magneto (promo hologram from Advance Comics #37) 6.00
Jim Lee signed card w/stamp 75.00

Promo Cards
Cable (Card #19 in set) 3.00
Magneto Card #41 in set) 3.00
Storm (Card #14 in set) 3.00
Wolverine (Card #2 in set) 3.00
X-Men (Card #71 in set) 3.00

***Note:** The promo cards are almost identical to the regular cards, but have ™ in black next to Marvel logo on back. Regular set cards have ™ in red. Other differences:*
***Cable:** Name "Unknown" vs. "Unrevealed"; different rating chart, slight picture difference*
***Magneto:** Name "Unknown"; different rating chart; back text layout differs*
***Storm:** Different rating chart; no Jim Lee signature on front, text differs*
***Wolverine:** Text layout differs; back is rotated ½ turn*
***X-Men:** Text layout differs*

Pack: 1.00
Two different wrappers with no art, one purple, one blue-green.

CARD CHECKLIST

Super Heroes *(blue borders)*
1 Beast 35
2 Wolverine 80
3 Havok 20
4 Iceman 15
5 Phoenix 15
6 Nightcrawler 20
7 Cannonball 10
8 Wolfsbane 15
9 Siryn 15
10 Lockheed 15
11 Professor X 25
12 Psylocke 30
13 Domino 20
14 Storm 30
15 Meggan 15
16 Feral 20
17 Cyclops 50
18 Gambit 75
19 Cable 75
20 Archangel 65
21 Banshee 25
22 Shadowcat 10
23 Kylun 15
24 Jean Grey 50
25 Colossus 60
26 Warpath 30
27 Polaris 20
28 Boom Boom 10
29 Jubilee 15
30 Shatterstar 30
31 Strong Guy 15
32 Captain Britain 15
33 Forge 20
34 Madrox 20
35 Quicksilver 15
36 Rogue 45
37 Widget 10
38 Bishop 75
39 Maverick 25
40 Cerise 15

Super-Villains *(purple borders)*
41 Magneto 60
42 Mr. Sinister 20
43 Deadpool 40
44 Proteus 20
45 Mojo II 10
46 Juggernaut 25
47 Sentinels 25
48 Gideon 15
49 Masque 20
50 Shiva 15
51 Apocalypse 25
52 Sabretooth 1.00
53 Mojo 25
54 Caliban 15
55 Gatecrasher 15
56 Brood 15
57 Blob 15
58 Stryfe 25
59 Warwolves 15
60 Omega Red 45
61 Black Tom 15
62 Mystique 30
63 Sauron 15
64 Saturnyne 15
65 Toad 10
66 Shadow King 25
67 White Queen 15
68 Mastermind 15
69 Deathbird 20
70 Lady Deathstrike 25

The Uncanny X-Men
© Marvel Entertainment Group, Inc.

Teams *(pink borders)*
71 X-Men "Gold" 50
72 X-Men "Blue" 50
73 X-Factor 25
74 X-Force 25
75 Excalibur 20
76 Hellfire Club 15
77 Mutant Liberation Front 20
78 Brotherhood of Evil Mutants 10
79 Upstarts 25
80 Technet 10

Ex X-Men *(green borders)*
81 Sunspot 25
82 Dark Phoenix 25
83 Longshot 35
84 Magik 15
85 Dazzler 10

The Uncanny X-Men
© Marvel Entertainment Group, Inc.

Allies *(green borders)*
86 Starjammers 20
87 Imperial Guard 10
88 Lilandra 15
89 Weird Happenings Organization . .10
90 Roma 10

Danger Room *forms 9 card super-panel*
91 Danger Room: Nightcrawler 15
92 Danger Room: Archangel 15
93 Danger Room: Storm 15
94 Danger Room: Gambit 45
95 Danger Room: Wolverine 45
96 Danger Room: Shatterstar 15
97 Danger Room: Cyclops 20
98 Danger Room: Cable 45
99 Danger Room: Colossus 15
100 Checklist/Cerebro 20
Deluxe Collector's Album 20.00
Toy Biz variants, each 1.00

The Toy Biz variant cards come one in each blister pack with Marvel X-Men action figures. They are just like the regular cards, except they have "Toy Biz" in grey inside a grey circle on the back. The card is not related to the action figure, so every card in the series has a variant (except possibly the checklist card) as far as we know. Assembling a full set would be prohibitively costly, as the action figures sell for $5.00 each, but only have collector value if kept unopened in the blister packs (with the card).

X-MEN SERIES II
SkyBox (1993)

This set features all original art (like the previous set) and the card fronts are quite similar. The little x's in the border are bigger and have a superscript "2" as does the large X, which appears in a ball, rather than a circle. The character name is bigger, so you get a little less art. The backs of the cards are completely different, with the text, name and number placed at various angles in an overall landscape (sideways) design. It's still nice looking. Several of the cards form double or triple card images, as noted below. There is also an X-Men animated subset, with the art bordered by filmstrip style sprocket holes and a different back design. One new feature was the three levels of bonus chase cards. The three

X-Men Series II © Marvel Entertainment Group, Inc.

foil cards were a departure from the usual holograms, but they do not indicate what series they are from on either the front or back (except in the background design). The nine gold foil cards resemble the regular cards, except for the gold foil stamping. The real departure was the 3-D hologram, which was very scarce and thus very valuable. It has a completely black back and can only be identified by the lettering inside the image on the front.

Set: 100 cards 17.50

Foil cards
H-1 Cable (ATi) 11.00
H-2 Magneto (ATi) 10.00
H-3 Storm (ATi) 9.00
H-X Wolverine **3-D Hologram** 70.00

All Time Greats, Gold foil: 30 Years
G-1 Cable (GCa/JP) 7.00
G-2 Cyclops (NKu/MPn) 5.00
G-3 Juggernaut (MPa/ATi) 5.00
G-4 Magneto (BPe/MFm) 6.00
G-5 Professor X (BPe/MFm) . . . 5.00
G-6 Rogue (NKu/MPn) 6.00
G-7 The Sentinels (JMd/ATi) . . . 5.00
G-8 Storm (BPe) 5.00
G-9 Wolverine (NKu/MPn) 7.00
Juggernaut prototype card 2.50
Juggernaut (Comic Book Collector) . 3.00
Pack: 6 cards 1.50

CARD CHECKLIST

Super Heroes
1 Archangel (BPe/JP) 15
2 Beast (NKu/MPn) 15
3 Bishop (BPe/JP) 15
4 Boomer (GCa/JP) 15
5 Cable (GCa/JP) 15
6 Cannonball (GCa/JP) 15
7 Captain Britain (AD/MFm) 15
8 Cerise (AD/MFm) 15
9 Colossus (BPe/JP) 15
10 Cyclops (NKu/MPn) 15
11 Domino (GCa/JP) 15
12 Gambit (NKu/MPn) 15
13 Jean Grey (BPe/JP) 15
14 Havok (JQ/JRu) 15
15 Iceman (BPe/JP) 15
16 Jubilee (NKu/MPn) 15
17 Kylun (AD/MFm) 15
18 Meggan (AD/MFm) 15
19 Multiple Man (JQ/JRu) 15
20 Nightcrawler (AD/MFm) 15
21 Phoenix (AD/MFm) 15
22 Polaris (JQ/JRu) 15
23 Professor X (AD/MFm) 15
24 Psylocke (NKu/MPn) 15
25 Quicksilver (JQ/JRu) 15
26 Rictor (GCa/JP) 15
27 Rogue (NKu/MPn) 15
28 Shadowcat (AD/MFm) 15
29 Shatterstar (GCa/JP) 15
30 Siryn (GCa/JP) 15
31 Storm (BPe/JP) 15
32 Strong Guy (JQ/JRu) 15
33 Sunspot (GCa/JP) 15
34 Warpath (GCa/JP) 15
35 Wolfsbane (JQ/JRu) 15
36 Wolverine (NKu/MPn) 15

Arch-Enemies *(*) double & (**) triple cards*
37 Archangel vs. Apocalypse* 15
38 Apocalypse* (BPe/MFm) 15
39 X-Men vs. Magneto & Acolytes** . . .15
40 Bishop (vs. Fitzroy)* 15
41 Fitzroy (BPe/AM)* 15
42 Magneto ** (BPe/MFm) 15
43 Cable vs. Stryfe* 15
44 Stryfe* (ATi) 15
45 Acolytes** (BPe/MFm) 15
46 Storm vs. Mystique* 15
47 Mystigue* (BPe/AM) 15
48 X-Factor vs. Mr. Sinister & Nasty Boys** 15
49 Wolverine vs. Omega Red* 15
50 Omega Red* (BPe/MFm) 15
51 Mr. Sinister** (JQ/JRu) 15
52 Wolverine vs. Sabretooth* 15
53 Sabretooth* (BPe/MFm) 15
54 Nasty Boys** (JQ/JRu) 15

Super-Villains
55 Arcade (ATi/JMd) 15
56 Black Queen (MPa/DPs) 15
57 Black Tom (MPa/DPs) 15
58 Blob (ATi/MPa) 15
59 Jamie Braddock (AD/MFm) 15
60 The Brood (BPe/JP) 15
61 Calisto (ATi/JMd) 15
62 Deadpool (ATi/JMd) 15
63 Deathbird (BPe/JP) 15
64 Fenris (ATi) 15
65 Gideon (ATi) 15
66 Juggernaut (ATi/MPa) 15
67 Lady Deathstrike (ATi/JMd) 15
68 Mastermind (MPa/DPs) 15
69 Mojo (ATi/JMd) 15
70 Phantazia (MPa/DPs) 15
71 Pyro (MPa/DPs) 15
72 Sat-Yr-9 (AD/MFm) 15
73 Sauron (MPa/ATi) 15
74 The Sentinels (ATi/JMd) 15
75 Shinobi (MPa/DPs) 15
76 Hazard (ATi) 15
77 Siena Blaze (MPa/DPs) 15
78 Silver Fox (MPa/DPs) 15
79 Toad (MPa/ATi) 15
80 Tolliver (ATi) 15
81 White Queen (BPe/JP) 15

Teams
82 Excalibur (AD/MFm) 15
83 X-Factor (JQ/JRu) 15
84 X-Force (GCa/JP) 15
85 X-Men: Blue Team (NKu/MPn) . . .15
86 X-Men: Gold Team (BPe/MFm) . . .15

X-Men Series II
© Marvel Entertainment Group, Inc.

87 Brotherhood of Evil Mutants (MPa/DPs) 15
88 Dark Riders (MPa/DPs) 15
89 Mutant Liberation Front (ATi) 15
90 Six Pack (ATi) 15

Animated TV Series *(artists not credited)*
91 Sabretooth Unleashed! 15
92 The Sentinel Strikes! 15
93 Persuasion, Gambit-Style 15
94 Rogue and Storm in Action! 15
95 Jubilee's Fireworks 15
96 Beast Hangs Out 15
97 The Power of Professor X 15
98 The Claws of Wolverine 15
99 The Fury of Storm 15
100 Checklist 15

X-Men Series II
© Marvel Entertainment Group, Inc.

Toy Biz Variants, each 1.00

The Toy Biz variant cards come one in each blister pack with Marvel X-Men action figures. They are just like the regular cards, except they have "Toy Biz" in grey inside a grey circle on the back. The card is not related to the action figure, so every card in the series has a variant (except possibly the checklist card) as far as we know. Both this series and the previous series were used.

Uncanny X-Men Covers © Marvel Entertainment Group, Inc.

UNCANNY X-MEN (COVERS) I

Comic Images (1990)

These are cover reprints from early 1977 to December 1983. The cover is on the front side in a white border and the credits are on the back. The header card is thin and has a black back.

Set: 90 cards + header 24.00
Box: 48 packs
Pack: 5 cards + header, cello pack . 1.50

CARD CHECKLIST
1 Giant-Size #1 25
2 Issue #94 25
3 Issue #95 25
4 Issue #96 25
5 Issue #97 25
6 Issue #98 25
7 Issue #99 25
8 Issue #100 25
9 Issue #101 25

10 Issue #102 .25
11 Issue #103 .25
12 Issue #104 .25
13 Issue #105 .25
14 Issue #106 .25
15 Issue #107 .25
16 Issue #108 .25
17 Issue #109 .25
18 Issue #110 .25
19 Issue #111 .25
20 Issue #112 .25
21 Issue #113 .25
22 Issue #114 .25
23 Issue #115 .25
24 Issue #116 .25
25 Issue #117 .25
26 Issue #118 .25
27 Issue #119 .25
28 Issue #120 .25
29 Issue #121 .25
30 Issue #122 .25
31 Issue #123 .25
32 Issue #124 .25
33 Annual #3 .25
34 Issue #125 .25
35 Issue #126 .25
36 Issue #127 .25
37 Issue #128 .25
38 Issue #129 .25
39 Issue #130 .25
40 Issue #131 .25
41 Issue #132 .25
42 Issue #133 .25
43 Issue #134 .25
44 Issue #135 .25
45 Issue #136 .25
46 Annual #4 .25
47 Issue #137 .25
48 Issue #138 .25
49 Issue #139 .25
50 Issue #140 .25
51 Issue #141 .25
52 Issue #142 .25
53 Issue #143 .25
54 Issue #144 .25
55 Issue #145 .25
56 Issue #146 .25
57 Issue #147 .25
58 Issue #148 .25
59 Annual #5 .25
60 Issue #149 .25
61 Issue #150 .25
62 Issue #151 .25
63 Issue #152 .25
64 Issue #153 .25
65 Issue #154 .25
66 Issue #155 .25
67 Issue #156 .25
68 Issue #157 .25
69 Issue #158 .25
70 Issue #159 .25
71 Issue #160 .25
72 Annual #6 .25
73 Issue #161 .25
74 Issue #162 .25
75 Issue #163 .25
76 Issue #164 .25
77 Issue #165 .25
78 Issue #166 .25
79 Issue #167 .25
80 Issue #168 .25
81 Issue #169 .25
82 Issue #170 .25
83 Issue #171 .25
84 Issue #172 .25
85 Annual #7 .25
86 Issue #173 .25
87 Issue #174 .25
88 Issue #175 .25
89 Issue #176 .25
90 Checklist .25

UNCANNY X-MEN (COVERS) II

Comic Images (1990)

These are reprints of Uncanny X-Men *covers, inside a white border, and the set is a direct continuation of the set above. The covers include comics dated between January 1984 and May 1987. The backs contain black and white comic issue credits and the card number. Covers are covers, so there are no surprises here.*

Set: 45 cards 12.00
Pack: 1.00

CARD CHECKLIST

1 Issue #177 (JR2) .25
2 Issue #178 (JR2/DGr) .25
3 Issue #179 (JR2/DGr) .25
4 Issue #180 (JR2/DGr) .25
5 Issue #181 (JR2/DGr) .25
6 Issue #182 (JR2) .25
7 Issue #183 (JR2/DGr) .25
8 Issue #184 (JR2/DGr) .25
9 Annual #8 (SL) .25
10 Issue #185 (JR2/DGr) .25
11 Issue #186 (BWS) .25
12 Issue #187 (JR2/DGr) .25
13 Issue #188 (JR2/DGr) .25
14 Issue #189 (JR2/DGr) .25
15 Issue #190 (JR2/DGr) .25
16 Issue #191 (JR2/DGr) .25
17 Issue #192 (JR2/DGr) .25
18 Issue #193 (JR2/DGr) .25
19 Issue #194 (JR2) .25
20 Issue #195 (BSz/DGr) .25
21 Issue #196 (JR2/TA) .25
22 Annual #9 (AAd/WS) .25
23 Issue #197 (JR2/DGr) .25
24 Issue #198 (BWS) .25
25 Issue #199 (JR2) .25
26 Issue #200 (JR2/DGr) .25
27 Issue #201 (RL/WPo) .25
28 Issue #202 (JR2/AW) .25
29 Issue #203 (JR2/AW) .25
30 Issue #204 (JBr/TA) .25
31 Issue #205 (BWS) .25
32 Issue #206 (JR2/DGr) .25
33 Issue #207 (JR2/DGr) .25
34 Issue #208 (JR2/DGr) .25
35 Annual #10 (AAd/TA) .25
36 Issue #209 (JR2/CR) .25
37 Issue #210 (JR2/BWi) .25
38 Issue #211 (JR2/BWi) .25
39 Issue #212 (RL/DGr) .25
40 Issue #213 (AD/PNe) .25
41 Issue #214 (BWS) .25
42 Issue #215 (AD/DGr) .25
43 Issue #216 (BWS) .25
44 Issue #217 (WS/BWi) .25
45 Checklist .25

(Fleer Ultra) X-Men © Marvel Entertainment Group, Inc.

(FLEER ULTRA) X-MEN

Fleer (1994)

This is the first set of comics cards issued by Fleer after they were 1) acquired by Marvel and 2) SkyBox's card license expired. They wasted no time, and the set appeared in mid-January. They obviously wanted to start off with a "bang" and they did! These are marvelous cards! These cards are painted, rather than drawn comic style, and so the artists' names may be more familiar to those who follow comic cover art than comic page art. Since the cards were created by a number of different artists, styles vary. We were particularly impressed by the work by Julie Bell, Joe Phillips, Bill Sienkiewicz and Brian Stelfreeze, but all of the art is quite good. The overall card quality is excellent. There's a full bleed picture on the front, with character name and series logo in gold foil at the bottom in a diagonal stripe. The backs have some of the front picture repeated, with part of the character's body replaced by contour lines, plus some text and the card number.

The card design starts to change beginning with card #97. The team cards all have a back picture of X-Men comic #1 oriented sideways. The X-over cards have a back close-up picture from the front. The team triptych cards have close-ups of the team members on the back. The "deceased" cards go back to the design of the first 96 cards and the Wolverine battle cards are oriented sideways and have a back close-up picture.

The bonus cards are numerous, with one in every 3 to 4 packs, which keeps their price fairly reasonable. The 10 card comic shop packs contain nine ***Team Portrait*** *cards which form a 3 x 3 card super panel by Greg and Tim Hildebrandt (the famous twin brother fantasy artists) and six* ***Fatal Attractions "Power Blast"*** *cards. The*

(Fleer Ultra) X-Men © Marvel Entertainment Group, Inc.

*14 card jumbo packs have **Fatal Attractions** cards and six **X-Men's Greatest Battles** cards. Wal-Mart stores have two different packs with different bonus cards. The 11 card packs contain **Team Portrait** cards and **X-Men Triptych** cards. However, the 12 card packs have one **X-Men Team Triptych** called a **red foil** card in every pack, plus **Team Portrait** cards and another set of six bonus cards: **X-Men Silver X-Overs**. This is one of the ten sets you **must own** to be a legitimate comics cards collector.*

Set: 150 cards 20.00

Team Portrait Cards (1:5) 10 card packs and 11 & 12 card Wal-Mart packs (Greg & Tim Hildebrandt) (forms 3 x 3 Super-Panel)
1 of 9 Storm 6.00
2 of 9 Psylocke & Cyclops 6.00
3 of 9 Beast & Jubilee 6.00
4 of 9 Rogue & Archangel 6.00
5 of 9 Wolverine 6.00
6 of 9 Professor X 6.00
7 of 9 Sabretooth & Iceman 6.00
8 of 9 Bishop & Gambit 6.00
9 of 9 Jean Grey 6.00

Fatal Attractions "Power Blast" (LuH)
(1:11) 10 card comic shop packs
(1:7) 14 card jumbo packs
1 of 6 Behold Avalon! 7.50
2 of 6 Cable Destroyed! 8.00
3 of 6 An X-Man No More! 7.50
4 of 6 Wolverine Crippled! 9.00
5 of 6 Magneto Defeated! 7.50
6 of 6 Exit Wolverine! 8.00

X-Men's Greatest Battles ("xxx of six")
(1:3) 14 card jumbo packs (only)
one Cyclops & Jean Grey vs. Callisto (BLr) 7.50
two Rogue vs. Avalanche & Pyro (JoP) 7.50
three Gambit vs. Mystique (JoP) . . . 7.50
four Wolverine vs. Sentinels (BLr) . . 8.50
five Professor X vs. Magneto (BSf) . 7.50
six Gambit vs. Bishop (FrS) 7.50

X-Men Silver X-Over foil cards
(1:11) Wal-Mart 12 card packs (only)
1 of 6 Mutant Massacre (JoP) 15.00
2 of 6 Fall of the Mutants (JoP) . . . 15.00
3 of 6 Inferno (Dave DeVries) 15.00
4 of 6 X-Tinction Agenda (BLr) . . . 15.00
5 of 6 X-Cutioner's Song (TP) 15.00
6 of 6 Fatal Attractions (BLr) 15.00

Red Foil/X-Men Team Triptych cards
(1:11) in 11 card Wal-Mart packs
(1:1) in 12 card Wal-Mart packs
Also found in X-Men 2099 comic books, issues #1 through #4, at Wal-Mart.

Blue Team (RyL)
1 Sabretooth & Rogue 2.00
2 Beast, Jubilee & Cyclops 2.00
3 Gambit & Psylocke 2.00

Gold Team (BLr)
4 Iceman 2.00
5 Jean Grey, Archangel, Professor X & Storm 2.00
6 Bishop 2.00

Promo cards
Nine card promo sheet, 7½" x 10½" 4.50
Nine card sheet, small 6" x 8¼" (Previews) 2.50
Four card magazine promo sheet of Cyclops, Storm, Gambit & Wolverine, with 4 football quarterbacks 2.50
Four card promo sheet (Rogue, Wolverine vs. Spider-Man, Apocalypse, Jubilee) (from Spider-Man Magazine #1) . . 1.50
Pack: 10 cards 1.75
Jumbo Pack: 14 cards ($2.59) 2.75
Wal-Mart 12 card pack 2.25
Wal-Mart packs: Metallic blue X-Men logo.
Comic shop packs: Metallic pink logo.

CARD CHECKLIST

Super Heroes
1 Cyclops (RyL) 15
2 Rogue (JoP) 15
3 Beast (DIB) 15
4 Gambit (John Estes) 15
5 Jubilee (BSf) 15
6 Wolverine (GF) 15
7 Psylocke (BSz) 15
8 Revanche (DIB) 15
9 Banshee (JuB) 15
10 Iceman (JoP) 15
11 Bishop (Ezra Tucker) 15
12 Archangel (Ezra Tucker) 15
13 Storm (JuB) 15
14 Jean Grey (BSf) 15
15 Sabretooth (DvD) 15
16 Professor X (TP) 15
17 Nightcrawler (BSf) 15
18 Phoenix (Ezra Tucker) 15
19 Shadowcat (BSf) 15
20 Domino (DIB) 15
21 Cable (BSz) 15
22 Shatterstar (FC) 15
23 Warpath (DIB) 15
24 Boomer (BSf) 15
25 Cannonball (John Estes) 15
26 Siryn (SHp) 15
27 Sunspot (VMk) 15
28 Rictor (Bill Hall) 15
29 Havok (TP) 15
30 Polaris (BSz) 15
31 Forge (JuB) 15
32 Strong Guy (BSz) 15
33 Wolfsbane (BSz) 15
34 Multiple Man (BHa) 15
35 Random (Glenn Barr) 15
36 Quicksilver (FrS) 15
37 Lilandra (JuB) 15
38 Askani (Peter Bollinger) 15
39 Tyler (VMk) 15
40 Longshot (BHa) 15
41 Feral (DIB) 15
42 Dazzler (BSf) 15
43 Weapon X (Wolverine) (KW) 15
44 Mirage (BSz) 15
45 Magma (MCo) 15
46 Sunfire (JoP) 15
47 Weapon X (DIB) 15
48 Grizzly (DIB) 15
49 G.W. Bridge (DIB) 15
50 Hammer (JVF) 15
51 Maverick (BHa) 15
52 X-Treme (CsM) 15
53 Copycat (DIB) 15

Super Villains
54 Colossus (JoP) 15
55 Magneto (BLr) 15
56 Mr. Sinister (DIB) 15
57 Deadpool (BHa) 15
58 Juggernaut (GF) 15
59 Cyber (TnS) 15
60 Apocalypse (DIB) 15
61 Omega Red (EN) 15
62 Mystique (John Estes) 15
63 Sauron (BSz) 15
64 Stryfe (EN) 15
65 White Queen (DvD) 15
66 Haven (David Braun) 15
67 Exodus (FC) 15
68 Ahab (Catherine Huerta) 15
69 X-Cutioner (CsM) 15
70 Black Tom Cassidy (TnS) 15
71 Pyro (FrS) 15
72 Arcade (Gary Ciccarelli) 15
73 Matsu'o (JVF) 15
74 Mojo (BSz) 15
75 Spiral (TnS) 15
76 Caliban (Shawn McKelvey) 15
77 Wendigo (EN) 15
78 Nimrod (Terry Britt) 15
79 Silver Samurai (Peter Bollinger) . .15
80 Sentinels (FrS) 15
81 Brood (BSz) 15
82 Gideon (JVF) 15
83 Gamesmaster (Glenn Barr) 15
84 Shinobi Shaw (BHa) 15
85 Fitzroy (JuB) 15
86 Siena Blaze (SHp) 15
87 Graydon Creed (JVF) 15
88 Slayback (Glenn Barr) 15
89 Sinsear (Peter Bollinger) 15

(Fleer Ultra) X-Men © Marvel Entertainment Group, Inc.

90 Tempo (Bill Hall) .15
91 Wildside (Peter Scanlan) .15
92 Reaper (MSo) .15
93 Forearm (KW) .15
94 Locus (JuB) .15
95 Moonstar (CsM) .15
96 Reignfire (CsM) .15

Original Team

97 Cyclops (SHp) .15
98 Iceman (BHa) .15
(98) Variation Iceman card with card number missing 2.00
99 Angel (RyL) .15
100 Beast (JR) .15
101 Marvel Girl (SHp) .15
102 Professor X (SHp) .15

X-Overs

103 Mutant Massacre (JoP) .15
104 Fall of the Mutants (JoP) .15
105 Inferno (Dave DeVries) .15
106 X-Tinction Agenda (BLr) .15
107 X-Cutioner's Song (TP) .15
108 Fatal Attractions (BLr) .15

Team Triptychs

109 to 111 X-Men Gold (TnS) .50
112 to 114 X-Men Blue (JSo) .50
115 to 117 X-Force (DIB) .50
118 to 120 X-Factor (JoP) .50
121 to 123 Excalibur (JoP) .50
124 to 126 Wedding of Cyclops & Jean Grey (BLr) .50

Deceased

127 Magik (JoP) .15
128 Warlock (BSz) .15
129 Cypher (BHa) .15
130 Goblin Queen (GF) .15
131 Sebastian Shaw (MCo) .15
132 Mesmero (FC) .15
133 Mimic (CsM) .15
134 Dark Phoenix (RyL) .15
135 Mastermind (James Sullivan) .15
136 Thunderbird (BSf) .15

Wolverine's Greatest Battles

137 Wolverine vs. Sabretooth (MSo) .15
138 Wolverine vs. Cyber (MZ & Phil Zimelman) .15
139 Wolverine vs. Omega Red (SHp) .15
140 Wolverine vs. Hulk (DLw) .15
141 Wolverine vs. The Thing (RyL) .15
142 Wolverine vs. Spider-Man (DLw) .15
143 Wolverine vs. Silver Samurai (VMK) .15
144 Wolverine vs. Hellfire Club (Peter Bollinger) .15
145 Wolverine vs. Cable (DIB) .15
146 Wolverine vs. Sauron (Dave DeVries) .15
147 Wolverine vs. Punisher (MZ & Phil Zimelman) .15
148 Wolverine vs. Lord Shingen(MSo) .15
149 Wolverine vs. Lady Deathstrike (KW) .15
150 Checklist .15

X-Men (Hanes)
© Marvel Entertainment Group, Inc.

X-Men Pocket Comics
© Marvel Entertainment Group, Inc.

X-MEN (Oversized)

Hanes (1993)

If the X-Men "knock your socks off," Hanes was willing to help you put them back on and give you a collectible card too.

Blue Team

Cyclops 2.00
Gambit 2.00
Wolverine 2.00

Triptych

Wolverine & Marvel Girl 10.00
Storm, Cyclops & Professor X 10.00
Gambit & Rogue 10.00

X-MEN POCKET COMICS

ToyBiz (1994)

X-Men pocket comics are small toy playsets with miniature figures and parts. Each comes with a trading card which reproduces the art on the front of the playset, which comes, in turn, from a comic book cover. The backs contain story line information relevant to the playset.

Asteroid 'M' 2.50
Jet Hangar 2.50
Danger Room 2.50
Spy Mission 2.50

X-MEN VIDEO

Pizza Hut (1993)

These were Pizza Hut promotional give-aways. The cards originally came with the video tape and ashcan comic, but they are also collected separately.

X-Men Team (Gold X) 3.00
With Video tape & ashcan 10.00
Professor X & Magneto (Silver X) 3.00
With Video tape & ashcan 10.00

X-Men Video & X-Men Watch cards © Marvel Entertainment Group, Inc.

X-MEN WATCH CARDS

Character Time (1993)

These are hard cards to locate. You get one when you buy an X-Men watch from Character Time. They are nice watches, but a good watch isn't cheap and not too many people will want to buy six of them just to collect the cards. The only reason we have all six of them is that they advertise in our magazines, so we made them send us the cards! The cards have full bleed pictures with the letters of the character's name in gold squares. The backs look a little primitive because the text is in a typewriter style font. The only thing identifing the card series is the watch symbol between the Marvel Comics and X-Men logos.

Cable 5.00
Cyclops (DvD) 6.00
Dark Phoenix (JSo) 7.50
Professor Xavier 5.00
Wolverine (NKu/JKu) 6.00
X-Men (KSy) 5.00

XONE FORCE

Mall Comics (1993)

Calvin Irving & Nick Tran art

The cards have full bleed art with gold foil stamping. The backs are white with black printing. We haven't seen #1 to #3, but they must be out there somewhere. These are comic book promo cards.

Promo cards

#1 of 6 .50
#2 of 6 .50
#3 of 6 .50
#4 of 6 Fang .50
#5 of 6 Xone Force Prime .50
#6 of 6 Ero versus Xone Force .50

Y

YOUNGBLOOD

Comic Images (1992)

The art for these cards is by super-star artist Rob Liefeld, creator of Youngblood. The card fronts are comic book close-ups inside a red border. The backs contain the card number, caption and text

Youngblood © Rob Liefeld

plus a small black and white drawing. The comic promo cards have a picture inside a blue border with "Youngblood" and the character's name on the front and the card number, text and a drawing on the back. #0 has a full color back and the other two are in black and white. One interesting feature of this set is that card #89 is the very first appearance of the character ShadowHawk!

Set: 90 cards 13.00

Prism Cards
P1 Sentinel 11.00
P2 Photon and Combat 11.00
P3 Diehard 11.00
P4 Shaft 11.00
P5 Cougar 11.00
P6 New Titans? 11.00
Youngblood promo (red border) 2.00

Comic Promo Cards (RLd) (blue border)
0 Youngblood (from Wizard #10) . . . 3.50
1 Shaft (bound into Youngblood #1) . 1.50
2 Bedrock (bound into Youngblood #1) 1.50
Pack: 10 cards 1.25

CARD CHECKLIST
1 Youngblood 15
2 Evolution 15
3 1985 .15
4 The Beginning 15
5 Teflon Team 15
6 Media 15
7 Super-Heroes 15
8 Employees 15
9 Nine to Five 15
10 Terms 15
11 Flip Format 15
12 Home and Away 15
13 Duel Teams 15
14 Shaft 15
15 Leader 15
16 Diversion 15
17 Shelly 15
18 Assassin 15
19 Ballpoint 15
20 Bullseye 15
21 Alert 15
22 Bedrock 15
23 Warm-Hearted 15
24 Lunch 15
25 Duty Calls 15
26 Diehard 15
27 Top Secret 15
28 Underground 15
29 Unbeatable 15
30 Chapel 15
31 Killing Time 15
32 Bearing Arms 15
33 Vogue 15
34 Unobedient 15
35 Photon 15
36 Cover-Up 15
37 Unsure 15
38 Switch Hitters 15
39 S.O.S. 15
40 Strongarm 15
41 Gage 15
42 Escape 15
43 Vandetta 15
44 Freedom 15
45 Payback 15
46 Overseas 15
47 Task Force 15
48 Air Attack 15
49 Dropping In 15
50 Sentinel 15
51 Tailored 15
52 Power 15
53 Above 15
54 Responsibilities 15
55 Warrior 15
56 Agreement 15
57 War Play 15
58 The Kill 15
59 Cat People 15
60 Taboo Love 15
61 Half-Breed 15
62 Cougar 15
63 Target Ahead 15
64 Riptide 15
65 Uneager 15
66 Oversized 15
67 Brahma 15
68 Powerhouse 15
69 Shocked 15
70 Unaffected 15
71 Psi-Fire 15
72 On Parole 15
73 Far Away 15
74 Long Distance 15
75 Little By Little 15
76 Within 15
77 For the Fun Of It! 15
78 Too Late 15
79 Let's Go 15
80 Prophet 15
81 Hand-To-Hand 15
82 Creating 15
83 The Image 15
84 Independent 15
85 Image Comics 15
86 Years Ago 15
87 Berserkers 15
88 Cross 15
89 ShadowHawk [Rookie] 1.00
90 Checklist 15

YOUNGBLOOD

The first promo card below has a black border and shows the Youngblood group looking down on Cable. Rob Liefeld's photo is on the back with some text. The second card is in gold foil with a series of Youngblood images in four strips. Its from the Heroes World 1994 trade show.

Youngblood & Cable (50,000 made) Inside Comics promo 10.00
Foil comic Promo (CBC/CCPG) (10,000 made) 1.00

Youngblood © Rob Liefeld

YOUNGBLOOD
SkyBox (1994)

These are promo cards from a set which appeared too late for inclusion in this book.

P0 Shaft promo 1.00
Badrock promo 1.00

Z

Mike Zeck Cards © Marvel Entertainment Group, Inc.

ZECK, MIKE
Comic Images (1989)

The card fronts picture various Marvel characters and contain the card caption and number. The backs form two black and white puzzle pictures. One is a 4 x 5 drawing of Punisher and the other is a signed 5 x 5 drawing of Punisher's head.

Set: 45 cards + header card 15.00
Pack: 5 cards + header, cello pack . 1.50

Mike Zeck Cards
© Marvel Entertainment Group, Inc.

CARD CHECKLIST

1 Checklist .35
2 Comin' Atcha 35
3 Coming For You 35
4 Captain America 35
5 Escape 35
6 Wolverine 35
7 Supreme Hydra 35
8 Robbie 35
9 Get Off My Back! 35
10 Hellinger 35
11 Bernie America 35
12 Deathlok 35
13 Breakfast 35
14 Scheming 35
15 Vermin 35
16 The Hunter 35
17 Constrictor 35
18 Heroes 35
19 Victory 35
20 Hi There 35
21 Stop It 35
22 Anticipation 35
23 Baron Strucker 35
24 Scarecrow 35
25 Falcon 35
26 Mad As... 35
27 Baron Zemo 35
28 Close Call 35
29 Old Friends 35
30 Spider-Woman 35
31 Confrontation 35
32 Villains .35
33 Surrounded 35
34 Fears 35
35 Baby Cap 35
36 Yeow!!! .35
37 Don't Go 35
38 Attack 35
39 Knock Knock 35
40 Partners 35
41 Preparation 35
42 Convict .35
43 I'll Be Back 35
44 Born Again 35
45 Bustin' Out 35

ZEN INTERGALACTIC NINJA

Maxx Cards (1993)

Chromium Promo cards
Zen Trading Cards promo (SK) 5.00
Zen promo "Version 2" (SK) 4.00
Zen #0 promo, blue green (JaL) . . . 3.00
Zen #0 promo, light purple (JaL) . . . 3.00
Zen #1 promo, (HNg) 3.00

Zombie War © Kevin Eastman & Tom Skulan

ZOMBIE WAR

FantaCo/Tundra (1993, comic)

This is a full bleed comic cover for Zombie War #2, *with art by Eastman and Talbot. There's also a Zombie War card set from FantaCo, which we will cover in our next book – (on science fiction and fantasy cards).*

Zombie War promo (in Zombie War #1) 1.50

ZORRO

Topps Comics (1993)

Comic promo card (BSf) 1.00

ALBUM STICKERS

Album stickers are sold in many of the same locations and collected by many of the same people as trading cards. They are generally smaller than cards (2" x 3" instead of 2½" x 3½"), so we didn't have to reduce their size as much for pictures. They are usually made of thin paper because they are designed to be stuck in albums which are conveniently provided by the sticker manufacturers, and they are generally marketed to a younger audience than trading cards. The listing below includes the ones we know about, but we have not provided comments on each set.

Aladdin
© The Walt Disney Company

ALADDIN
Panini (1993, Movie)
Set: 232 stickers + Album 14.00
Album 1.00
Pack: 6 stickers 40

Batman: The Animated Series
© DC Comics, Inc.

BATMAN: ANIMATED SERIES
Panini (1993, TV)
Set: 216 stickers + 16 holograms . . 15.00
Album, 31 pages, inc. poster 1.00
Pack: 6 stickers 40

BEAUTY & THE BEAST
Panini (1993, Movie)
Set: 232 stickers + album 14.00
Album, 32 pages 1.00
Pack: 6 stickers 40

BRAVE STAR
Panini (1987, TV Cartoon)
Set: 204 Album stickers + album . . 20.00
Pack: 1.50
Album, 32 pages 3.50

CHIP 'N DALE RESCUE RANGERS
Panini (1990)
Set: 228 Album stickers +
14 foil stickers+ album 20.00
Pack: 1.50
Album, 32 pages 2.50

CINDERELLA
Panini (1988)
Set: 225 Album Stickers + album . . 25.00
Pack: 1.50
Album 2.50

DUCK TALES
Panini (1987)
Set: 240 Album stickers + album . . 25.00
Pack: 1.50
Album 3.50
Note: 6 different wrappers

GHOSTBUSTERS
Panini USA (1987, Animated TV)
Set: 240 Album stickers +
24 plastic stickers + album 20.00
Pack: 1.50
Album 3.00

G.I. JOE
Diamond Toy (1987)
Set: 225 album stickers + album . . 20.00
Green Pack, 7 stickers 1.50
Album 2.50

HAPPY BIRTHDAY BUGS
Panini (1990)
Set: 240 Album stickers + album . . 25.00
Pack: 2.00
Album 3.00

HISTORY OF THE X-MEN
(Sticker Series II)
Comic Images (1987)
Set: 75 Album stickers + album . . . 40.00
Album, 24 pages 5.00

LION KING, THE
Panini (1994)
Set: 232 stickers + album 14.00
Album, 32 pages 1.00
Pack: 6 stickers 45

MARVEL'S MAGIC MOMENTS
Comic Images (1988)
Set: 80 Album stickers + album . . . 35.00
Album 3.50

MARVEL SUPER HEROES SECRET WARS
Leaf (1985, comic)
Set: 180 Album stickers + album . 125.00
Pack: 1.50
Album, 24 pages 5.00

MASTERS OF THE UNIVERSE
Panini (1985, animated TV)
Set: 216 Album stickers + album . . 25.00
Pack: 1.00
Album, 36 pages 2.50

MICKEY MOUSE AND HIS FRIENDS
Americana (19??)

Set: 360 Album stickers + album . . 40.00
Pack: 4 stickers 1.50
Album 2.50

MIGHTY MORPHIN POWER RANGERS
Merlin Collections (1994)

Set: 240? Album stickers + album . 25.00
Album, 24? pages 2.50

MUTANT HALL OF FAME
Comic Images (1988)

Set: 88 Album stickers + album . . . 40.00
Album, 24 pages 2.50

OFFICIAL MARVEL UNIVERSE STICKERS
Comic Images (1986-7)

Set: 77 Album stickers + album . . . 50.00
Album, 24 pages 5.00
Note: Comic Images' first sticker set.

PRINCESS COLLECTION, THE
Panini (1994)

Set: 216 stickers + 24 glitters + album 14.00
Pack: 6 stickers 40
Album, 32 pages + poster 1.00

THE PUNISHER PAPERS
Comic Images (1990)

Set: 75 Album stickers + album . . . 30.00
Pack: 5 stickers (card size) 1.50
Album, 24 pages 2.00

REAL GHOSTBUSTERS, THE
Diamond Toy (1986)

Set: 180 Album stickers + album . . 20.00
Pack: 7 stickers 1.00
Album 1.50

SHE-RA PRINCESS OF POWER
Panini (1986)

Set: 216 Album stickers + album . . 20.00
Pack: 1.50
Album 2.50

SILVERHAWKS
Diamond (1987)

Set: 240 Album stickers + album . . 25.00
Pack: 1.00
Album, 32 pages + 3-D decoder . . . 2.50

SIMPSONS, THE
Diamond Toy (1990)

Set: 126 Album stickers, 24 3-D album stickers + album & viewer 25.00
Pack 1.00
Album 2.00

THUNDERCATS
Panini (1986)

Set: 240 Album stickers + 24 foil Album stickers + album 25.00
Pack: 1.00
Album 1.50

TINY TOON ADVENTURES
Panini (1991, Cartoon)

Set: 200 Album stickers + album . . 20.00
Pack: 1.00
Album, 32 pages 1.50

TOXIC CRUSADERS
Panini (1991)

Set: 216 stickers 12.50
Pack: 6 stickers 40
Album, 32 pages 1.00

TRANSFORMERS
Diamond Toy (1987)

Set: 225 Album stickers + album . . 25.00
Album, 32 pages 1.50

VOLTRON
Panini USA (1986)

Set: 200 color stickers + 16 foil stickers + album 20.00
Album, 32 pages 2.50

Webs © Marvel Entertainment Group, Inc.

WEBS (Spider-Man)
Comic Images (1991)
(Todd McFarlane)

Set: 75 Album stickers + album . . . 25.00
Pack: 5 stickers (card size) 1.50
Album, 24 pages 3.00

WOLVERINE UNTAMED
Comic Images (1990)

Set: 75 Album stickers + album . . . 50.00
Pack: 5 stickers (card size) 2.50
Album, 24 pages 5.00

WORLD OF SPIDER-MAN
Comic Images (1988)

Set: 50 Album stickers + poster . . . 30.00
Pack: 4 stickers 1.75
Poster 7.50
Album 15.00

X-Men
© Marvel Entertainment Group, Inc.

X-MEN
Diamond Publishing (1993)

Set: 180 Album Stickers + album . . 20.00
Pack: 6 stickers 75
Album 2.00

VENDING MACHINE STICKERS

These stickers are found in vending machines in supermarkets, drugstores and other outlets. They have either a reflective silver surface or a prismatic surface called "prizm". The prizm surface usually makes lousy photos, so we have mostly pictured the others. The backs are usually blank "Kodak" paper.

We have made up all series titles and some sticker titles. They do not appear on the stickers. There are no packs; the stickers come out of the vending machines between two pieces of cardboard.

Many of these stickers are unauthorized, but some have copyright notices and have been authorized by the comic book company. No manufacturer names are evident.

ALADDIN
(1993, reflective silver surface)

Aladdin and Jasmine 1.00
Aladdin and the Genie 1.00
The Genie 1.00
The Genie, Abu and Aladdin 1.00
Iago and Jafir 1.00
Iago, Jafir and the Genie 1.00
Jafir 1.00
Jafir and Iago 1.00
Jafir and Jasmine 1.00
Jafir, Iago and The Sultan 1.00
Jafir, The Snake and Aladdin 1.00
Jasmine, Rajah and Abu 1.00

("Prizm" surface)

Abu on magic carpet (cut-out) 1.00
Abu, Rajah, Sultan, Aladdin & Jasmine (cut-outs) 1.00
Abu, Jasmine, Aladdin, Iago & Sultan (cut-outs) 1.00
"Aladdin" (& Jasmine) 1.00
Genie 1.00
Genie, Aladdin, Jasmine & Abu (cut-out) 1.00
Jafar and Iago 1.00
Jasmine & Aladdin (cut-out) 1.00
Rajah 1.00
Sultan 1.00

BATMAN
(1992 "Prizm" surface, authorized)

1. Batman, leaping 2.50
2. "Batman" 2.50
3. Batman in front of Batsignal 2.50
4. "Batman" 2.50
5. Bat symbol on yellow 2.00
6. Batman, batarang & Batsymbol . . 2.50
7. Batman, fighting Ninja 2.50

BATMAN
(1992 "Prizm" surface, Unauthorized)

Batman, in cape 4.00
Batman & Batgirl on Batcycle 4.00
Batman & Batgirl & Gargoyle 4.00
Batman in cape, running 4.00
Batman & Robin in triangle, with large checker pattern 4.00
Batman & Robin on small checker pattern (JL/DG) 5.00
Batman & Joker 5.00
Batman, cape logo 3.00
Batman, swinging on rope 4.00
Batsymbol 3.00
Penguin & Batman 4.50

BATMAN RETURNS
(1992 "prizm" numbered, authorized, with blank white back, not "Kodak")

1. "Batman Returns" 3.00
2. Catwoman, cat & moon 4.50
3. "The Penguin" 3.00
4. Batman, standing 3.00
5. "Catwoman" (JL) 4.50
6. Batmobile 3.00
7. Batman, leaping down 3.00
8. Bat symbol on blue background . . 2.00
9. Batman stands with a fist 3.00
10.Bat symbol on red background . . 2.00
11.Batman & Catwoman fighting . . . 3.50
12.Penguin 3.00
13."Batman Returns" 3.00
14."Catwoman" 4.50
15."The Penguin" with umbrella 3.00
16.Batman, Keaton face 3.00

Batman: Animated © DC Comics, Inc.

BATMAN: ANIMATED
(1993 "prizm" numbered, authorized)

1 Logo 2.00
2 Catwoman 3.50
3 Batman 2.00
4 The Riddler 2.00
5 Batman, on hang-glider 2.00
6 The Penguin 2.00
7 Batman, leaping 2.00
8 The Joker 2.50

BATMAN: ANIMATED MASK OF THE PHANTASM
(1992, i.e. 1994 "prizm" numbered, authorized, white back, not "Kodak")

1 Batman 1.50
2 Mr. Freeze 1.50
3 Poison Ivy 2.00
4 Mad Hatter 1.50
5 The Riddler 1.50
6 Bruce Wayne 1.50

Batman: Animated, Mask of the Phantasm
© DC Comics, Inc.

7 Robin 1.50
8 Two-Face 1.50
9 The Joker 1.50
10 Andrea Beaumont 2.00
11 Phantasm 2.50
12 Batman 1.50

BEAUTY AND THE BEAST
(Reflective silver surface)

Mrs. Potts, Cogsworth & Lumiere . . 2.00
Beast reclining, with Belle 2.00
Beast with torch & Belle 2.00
Belle bandaging Beast's paw 2.00
Beast & Belle feeding birds 2.00
Belle & Beast, holding hands 2.00

Beavis & Butt-Head © MTV Networks

BEAVIS & BUTT-HEAD
(Reflective silver surface)
(No copyright notice)

"It's Just Us..." 1.00
Beavis and Butt-Head 1.00
Beavis 1.00
Butt-Head 1.00
Beavis & Butt-Head with pink couch 1.00
"are just stupid cartoon people" 1.00
"Growing Old bites" 1.00
"Weiner Heads" 1.00
"That Bites" 1.00
"Rock On 1.00
"Where can we hide this crud?" 1.00
"Cool..." 1.00

SET II
(Reflective silver border)
(1993 MTV Networks copyright)

That Wuz Cool 1.00
Huh, Huh Huh 1.00
All Star Monster Truck Thrashathon . 1.00
(Giving blood) 1.00
(two ugly faces on red) 1.00
(sitting in school chairs) 1.00
(looking at self in mirror) 1.00
(at Burger World) 1.00
(on stage) 1.00
(with three guys in background) 1.00
(at home in bedroom) 1.00

DISNEY
("Prizm" surface)

Happy Birthday! (cut out) 1.50
Mickey + Mermaid on TV 2.00
Minnie, Donald, Pluto & Mickey 1.50
Mickey & Minnie & heart 1.50
Donald Duck 1.50
Minnie Mouse dancing 1.50
Minnie Mouse putting on makeup . . 1.50
Gyro Gearloose in car 1.50
Daisy Duck eating ice cream 1.50
Donald Duck on skate board 1.50
Mickey & Minnie & radio 1.50
Sorcerer Mickey & Donald 2.00
Goofy & friends on skies 1.50
Scrooge McDuck, Huey,
Duey & Looie 1.50

LITTLE MERMAID
(Reflective silver surface)
(Some from ProSet cards)

Ariel & Eric waveing (#90) 2.00
Ariel, Scuttle & Flounder 2.00
Ariel & Sebastian (#15, reversed) . . 2.00
Ariel hugs Triton 2.00
Ariel & Eric, holding hands 2.00
Ariel tickles Triton 2.00

LOONEY TUNES
(1990)
("Prizm" surface)

A-7030 Bugs Bunny 1.50
A-7031 Looney Tunes 1.50
A-7032 Tweety 1.50
A-7033 Speedy Gonzalez 1.50
A-7034 Sylvester 1.50
A-7035 Yosemite Sam 1.50
A-7036 Tasmanian Devil 2.00
A-7037 Porky Pig 1.50
A-7038 Elmer Fudd 1.50
A-7039 Daffy Duck 1.50
A-7040 Road Runner 2.00
A-7041 Wile E. Coyote 2.00
A-7042 Bugs Bunny "What's Up Doc" 1.50
A-7043 Foghorn Leghorn 1.50

MARVEL MASTERPIECE
("Prizm" surface)
(Unauthorized copies of SkyBox's cards.)

Captain America (#16) 2.00
Galactus (#30) 2.00
Hulk (#32) 2.00
Iceman (#40) 2.00
Iron Man (#38) 2.00
Silver Surfer 2.00
Thanos (#83) 2.00
Thing (#91) 2.00

MARVEL SUPERHEROES
("Prizm" surface)
(Unauthorized copies of Impel's Marvel Universe Series I cards.)

Archangel (#21) 3.50
Black Panther (#20) 4.50
Captain America (#1) 3.50
Captain America's Motorcycle (#31) . 3.50
Cyclops (#8) 3.50
Daredevil (#4) 4.50
Hulk, Grey (#17) 4.50
Hulk, Green (#3) 3.50
Human Torch (#33) 3.50
Iceman (#22) 3.50
Phoenix (#11) 3.50
Storm (#24) 3.50
Sub-Mariner (#16) 4.00
The Thing (#6) 3.50
Wolverine (#10) 4.50

MARVEL SUPERHEROES II
(Reflective silver surface)

Bishop 2.00
Cable 2.00
Gambet (sic) 2.00
Ghost Rider 2.50
The Gray Hulk 2.00
Green Hulk vs. Gray Hulk 2.00
The Punisher 2.00
Shatterstar 2.50
Silver Surfer & Wolverine 2.00
Spider-Man 3.00
Storm 2.00
Wolverine 2.00

Marvel characters
© Marvel Entertainment Group, Inc.

MARVEL SUPERHEROES III
(1992, Reflective surface, Untitled)

(Colossus) 2.00
(Hobgoblin) 2.00
(Ghost Rider) 2.00
(Green Goblin) 2.00
(Green Hulk) 2.00
(Iron Man) 2.00
(Punisher) 2.00
(Silver Surfer) 2.00
(Spider-Man, crouching) 2.00
(Spider-Man, swinging) 2.00
(Rogue) 2.00
(Wolverine) 2.00

REN & STIMPY
("Prizm" surface, untitled)

Don't You Know Cartoons... . . . . . . 1.50
(Birthday party) 1.50
Stays Crunchy Even in Milk 1.50
The Ren & Stimpy Show 1.50
Poot! 1.50
Back Off Man! 1.50
You Sick Little Monkey! 1.50
Happy, Happy! Joy, Joy! 1.50
Squeak! Squeak... . . . . 1.50
Oh Joy! We're on T.V. 1.50

SIMPSONS
("Prizm" surface, untitled)

All American Kid 1.50
Aye Carumba!! (St #16) 1.50

Ren & Stimpy © Nickelodeon

Football Rules, Man 1.50
I Will Not Belch in Class 1.50
Jingle Bells, Batman Smells 1.50
No More Television (Ca #5) 1.50
Peace, Man. (St #3) 1.50
Stay in School 1.50
Suck Suck Suck (St #20) 1.50
Teacher 1.50
There was a Little Accident(St#13) . 1.50
(Bart at Beach, with lobster) 1.50

SUPER-HEROES
("Prizm" surface)

Punisher 1.50
Spider-Man 1.50
Superman (GL/DG) 1.75
Wolverine, full body 1.50
Wolverine, face & claws 1.75

Cut-Out Images

Batman 1.50
Four Logos 1.50
Ghost Rider 1.50
Punisher 1.50
Spider-Man 1.50

Warlock
© Marvel Entertainment Group, Inc.

SUPERHERO STARS
(Silver surface, Numbers in a Star)

1 Magnus Robot Fighter 1.50
2 Diehard 1.50
3 Spawn 1.50
4 Warlock 1.50
5 The Pitt 1.50
6 Cyber 1.50
7 Wolverine vs. Sabretooth 1.50

All card prices listed are for *Near Mint* condition.

Sticker	Price
8 Shaft	1.50
9 Solar, Man of the Atom	1.50
10 Shadow Hawk	1.50
11 Venom, Carnage & Spidey	1.50
12 Shatter Star	1.50

TEENAGE MUTANT NINJA TURTLES

(1990, "prizm" surface)

Sticker	Price
A-7001 "Kick Some Shell"	1.50
A-7002 Donatello "Hero in a Half Shell"	1.50
A-7003 Leonardo, with Pizza	1.50
A-7004 TMNT at City Sewer	1.50
A-7005 "Heroes in a Half Shell"	1.00
A-7006 Michaelangelo	1.50
A-7007 The four turtles	1.50
A-7008 Leonardo	1.50
A-7008a Leonardo, larger image	1.50
A-7009 Donatello	1.50
A-7010 Raphael	1.50
A-7010a Raphael, larger image	1.50
A-7011 The four turtles, with radio	1.50
A-7012 Splinter	2.00
A-7013 Shredder	2.00
A-7013a Shredder, larger image	2.00
A-7014 Bebop	2.00
A-7015 Rocksteady	2.00

TEENAGE MUTANT NINJA TURTLES

(1992, "prizm" surface)

Sticker	Price
1 Turtles, in 4 circles	1.50
2 Turtle, characters in 4 diamonds	1.50
3 Turtle, in 4 hearts	1.50
4 TMNT in 5 rectangles	1.50
5 TMNT in 4 rectangles	1.50
6 TMNT in 2 rectangles	1.50
TMNT, surfing	1.50
TMNT, coming out of sewer	1.50
Raphael, with pizza & logo	1.50
Turtle, with pizza slices	1.50
Michaengelo, with weapons	1.50
Raphael, with weapons	1.50

X-MEN

("Prizm" surface)

(Unauthorized copies of Impel's cards.)

Sticker	Price
Beast (#1)	3.00
Bishop (#38)	3.50
Colossus (#25)	3.00
Cyclops (#17)	3.00
Excalibur (#75)	3.00
Jean Grey (#24)	3.50
Imperial Guard (#87)	3.00
Jubilee (#29)	3.50
Sabretooth (#52)	3.50
Storm (#14)	3.00
Wolverine (#2)	3.00
X-Men (#71)	3.00

X-MEN II

("Prizm" surface, names in triangle)

Sticker	Price
Bishop	2.50
Gambit	2.50
Magneto	2.50
Psylocke	2.50
Wolverine	2.50
Cut-Out Images	
Beast	2.50
Havok	2.50
Rogue	2.50
Storm	2.50
X-Men	2.50

X-MEN III

(Silver surface, X in circle logo)

Sticker	Price
Beast	1.50
Bishop	1.50
Cable	1.50

X-Men characters
© Marvel Entertainment Group, Inc.

Sticker	Price
Cyclops & Gene Grey	1.50
Iceman	1.50
Jean Grey	1.50
Magneto	1.50
Nomad	1.50
Phoenix	1.50
Quicksilver	1.50
Storm	1.50
Wolverine	1.50

NOTES

Bonus cards **(1:18)** = 1 card in 18 packs.
Price = **NYR** (Not Yet Released)
Price = **NYD** (Not Yet Determined)

Notes: The exact intended title of a card set can be difficult to determine, and may be different from its popular title. We have tried to list all cards sets alphabetically under the sets actual, or popular name.

However, series of card sets are kept together, in order of appearance, even if this is not strictly alphabetical. Thus all the "X-Men" sets are listed together, even though some sets are actually called "Uncanny X-Men." The first X-Men card sets to be issued, from Comic Images, appear first, followed by those from Impel/SkyBox and then the Fleer Ultra set.

Series of cards produced by magazines are usually listed under the name of the magazine, i.e. Triton, Wizard, Hero, Overstreet, etc., unless they are **from** a card manufacturer series.

ARTIST ABBREVIATIONS

Adams, Art	AAd
Adams, Neal	NA
Albrecht, Jeff	JAl
Ammerman, David	DvA
Aparo, Jim	JAp
Austin, Terry	TA
Bagley, Mark	MBa
Bell, Julie	JuB
Bisley, Simon	SBs
Blevins, Brett	BBl
Bogdanove, Jon	JBg
Bolland, Brian	BB
Bolton, John	JBo
Boring, Wayne	WB
Bradstreet, Tim	TBd
Brasfield, Craig	CrB
Breeding, Brett	BBr
Breyfogle, Norm	NBy
Bright, Mark	MBr
Brunner, Frank	FB
Buscema, John	JB
Buscema, Sal	SB
Byrne, John	JBy
Callahan, Jim	JiC
Campenella, Robert	RbC
Capullo, Greg	GCa
Carrasco, Dario	DoC
Chan, Ernie	ECh
Chaykin, Howard	HC
Chiodo, Joe	JCh
Chiarello, Mark	MCo
Cirocco, Frank	FC
Colan, Gene	GC
Colletta, Vince	ViC
Cooper, Dave	DvC
Davis, Alan	AD
DeLaRosa, Sam	SDR
Ditko, Steve	SD
Dorman, Dave	DvD
Duursema, Jan	JD
Eisner, Will	WE
Erwin, Steve	StE
Farmer, Mark	MFm
Fegredo, Duncan	DFg
Frenz, Ron	RF
Gammill, Kerry	KGa
Gibbons, Dave	DGb
Giffen, Keith	KG
Giordano, Dick	DG
Green, Randy	RG
Grell, Mike	MGr
Grindberger, Tom	TGb
Grummet, Tom	TG
Guice, Jackson	JG
Gulacy, Paul	PG
Hall, Bob	BH
Hampton, Scott	SHp
Harris, Tony	TyH
Harrison, Lou	LuH
Hazlewood, Doug	DHz
Henry, Flint	FH
Hester, Phil	PhH
Higgins, John	JHi
Howell, Rich	RHo
Hughes, Adam	AH
Isherwood, Geoff	GI
Janke, Dennis	DJa
Jansen, Klaus	KJ
Jarvinen, Kirk	KJa
Johnson, Jeff	JJ
Jones, Jeff	JeJ
Jurgens, Dan	DJu
Jusko, Joe	JJu
Kaluta, Mike	MK
Kane, Gil	GK
Kennedy, Cam	CK
Keown, Dale	DK
Kesel, Karl	KK
Kieth, Sam	SK
Kirby, Jack	JK
Kubert, Adam	AKu
Kubert, Andy	NKu
Kubert, Joe	JKu
Lago, Ray	RyL
Lapham, Dave	DL
Larkin, Bob	BLr
LaRocque, Greg	GrL
Larsen, Erik	EL
Lawlis, Dan	DLw
Layton, Bob	BL
Lee, Jae	JaL
Lee, Jim	JLe
Leeke, Mike	MLe
Leialoha, Steve	SL
Leonardi, Rick	RL
Liefeld, Rob	RLd
Lim, Ron	RLm
Lopez, Jose Luis Garcia	JL
Lyle, Tom	TL
Madueira, Joe	JMd
Maguire, Kevin	KM
Mahlstedt, Larry	LMa
Mandrake, Tom	TMd
Maroto, Estaben	EM
Marzan, Jose	JMz
Mayerik, Val	VMk
McFarlane, Todd	TM
McManus, Shawn	SwM
Messner-Loebs, Bill	BML
Milgrom, Al	AM
Moebius	Moe
Moeller, Chris	CsM
Morales, Rags	RgM
Morgan, Tom	TMo
Morrow, Gray	GM
Muth, Jon J.	JMu
Nguyen, Hoang	HNg
Nichols, Art	ANi
Nino, Alex	AN
Nodell, Martin	MnN
Norem, Earl	EN
Nowlan, Kevin	KN
Ordway, Jerry	JOy
Pacella, Mark	MPa
Palmiotti, Jimmy	JP
Pascoe, James	JmP
Pennington, Mark	MPn
Pensa, Shea Anton	SAP
Perez, George	GP
Perlin, Don	DP
Peterson, Brandon	BPe
Phillips, Joe	JoP
Portico, Whilce	WPo
Post, Howard	HwP
Quesada, Joe	JQ
Randall, Ron	RoR
Redondo, Nestor	NR
Reinhold, Bill	BR
Robertson, Darrick	DaR
Robbins, Trina	TrR
Rodier, Denis	DRo
Romita, John	JR
Romita, John Jr.	JR2
Rude, Steve	SR
Rubinstein, Joe	JRu
Russell, P. Craig	CR
Sanders, Jim III	JS3
Sasso, Mark	MSo
Saviuk, Alex	AS
Schane, Tristan	TnS
Sears, Bart	BS
Shanover, Eric	EiS
Sienkiewicz, Bill	BSz
Silvestri, Mark	MS
Simonson, Walt	WS
Sinnott, Joe	JSt
Smith, Barry Windsor	BWS
Starlin, Jim	JSn
Steacy, Ken	KSy
Stelfreeze, Brian	BSf
Steranko, Jim	JSo
Stiles, Steve	SvS
Stroman, Larry	LSn
Sullivan, Lee	LS
Swan, Curt	CS
Tanghal, Romeo	RT
Texiera, Mark	MT
Thibert, Art	ATi
Valentino, Jim	JV
Vallejo, Boris	BV
Vancata, Brad	BVa
Vey, Al	AV
Von Eeden, Trevor	TVE
Warner, Chris	CW
Welch, Larry	LyW
Weeks, Lee	LW
West, Kevin	KWe
Wiacek, Bob	BWi
Williams, Kent	KW
Williams, Scott	SW
Williamson, Al	AW
Wrightson, Berni	BWr
Zeck, Mike	MZ

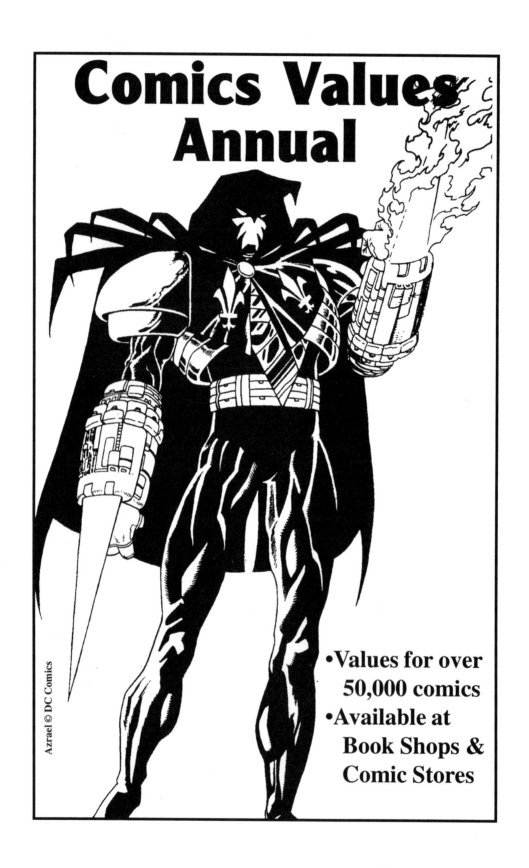